A DICTIONARY FOR ACCOUNTANTS

Fourth Edition

Eric L. Kohler

PRENTICE-HALL INC., Englewood Cliffs, New Jersey

13-209809-1
Library of Congress
Catalog card Number 69-10446
Current printing (last digit)
10 9 8 7 6 5 4 3 2 1

PRENTICE-HALL INTERNATIONAL, INC., *London*
PRENTICE-HALL OF AUSTRALIA, PTY. LTD., *Sydney*
PRENTICE-HALL OF CANADA, LTD., *Toronto*
PRENTICE-HALL OF INDIA PRIVATE LTD., *New Delhi*
PRENTICE-HALL OF JAPAN, INC., *Tokyo*

Printed in the United States of America

Preface

Although bookkeeping and a rudimentary form of accounting have existed since the beginning of civilization, the modern discipline is a twentieth-century product. Obliged to make his reports intelligible to a constantly expanding circle of readers having widely diverse backgrounds, the accountant has borrowed numerous words and phrases from the common stock of everyday language: a practice not without its perils, for it was not long before many of the borrowed terms had acquired meanings far removed from their original use. Only the technical meanings of such words are reported in these pages, except where a special meaning has been asserted but where upon examination none in fact can be discerned; in these instances the nontechnical meanings have been given. Also, many terms from fields related to accounting have taken on meanings varying, sometimes widely, from those first associated with them. Others similarly appropriated but with their meanings unchanged have never been accurately defined in their original settings, possibly because their meanings have been regarded as self-evident to practitioners in those fields.

Legislation and court decisions continue to respect and to be profoundly influenced by accounting concepts; interpretations of the accounting terms employed have often depended on observed technical applications, although precise and generally agreed-to meanings have not always been easy to find. Interest in the language of accounting has not been limited, however, to lawyers and judges. The author has had frequent occasion to discuss accounting concepts and terms with economists, engineers, business executives, students of business, investors, and government officials. He hopes that this book may in some measure prove to be helpful in explaining accounting to these and other nonaccountants; he hopes, too, that by subjecting accounting terms to the rigors of close examination, he has contributed to the clarification and delimitation of accounting concepts for accountants themselves. Because accounting has supplied a language common to the varied forms of economic activity, it has been increasingly depended on to contribute measures for judging collective human endeavor, including governmental bodies and even nations. Indeed, there is reason for believing that accounting has already become firmly established as one of the modern disciplines concerned with the organization and extension of human thought and action. By providing an intelligible yardstick, accounting serves as a major instrumentality in effectuating, administering, reviewing, appraising, and correcting man-made *policy*, whatever its source, character, scope, or application.

Of the terms appearing in this book, nearly half may be regarded as having their origins in other fields. Many of them are now associated *primarily* with accounting. Others, still in use outside the accounting domain, have had their meanings rounded out or modified as the result of their accounting applications. A not-too-precise classification by source fields, accompanied by examples and totals, yields the following:

Common English words with which narrower, technical meanings are often associated; as, *assumption, condition, consistency, event, materiality, recognize, reliability*	192
Terms that form the hard core of the accountant's method of communication; as, *allocate, amortize, audit, capitalize, deficit, expense, liability, valuation, variance*	402
Specialized terms growing out of basic concepts and having particular application; as, *base-stock method, business transaction, consolidation excess, fixed capital, revolving fund, voucher audit*	976
Terms employed in governmental accounting; as, *apportionment, appropriation, encumbrance, fund, lapse, warrant*	111
Legal terms in constant use by accountants; as, *agent, claim, corporation, fungible, merger, option, proxy, valorize*	282
Terms from the financial world; as, *acid test, arbitrage, broker, bull, debenture, hedge, round lot, syndicate*	240
Insurance terms; as, *admitted asset, common average, Dean schedule, loss ratio, proof of loss, reinsurance, valued policy*	63
Terms associated primarily with tax laws; as, *boot, bunched income, carryback, constructive receipt, progressive tax, splitup, withholding*	94
Price terms; as, *C&F price, cost-plus, escalation, free price, price leadership, target price, volume discount, zone system*	58
Commercial terms; as, *account sales, bonus, credit line, force account, machine tool, management science, past-due, staple, tare*	123
Statistical terms; as, *correlation, decile, frequency, model, normal distribution, random sampling, replication, standard error, variable*	96
Terms common to statistical quality control; as, *acceptance sampling, attribute, control chart, multiphase sampling, sample size, tolerance*	40
Mathematical terms; as, *coordinate, factorial, median, moving average, permutation, present value, rational number*	78

Terms borrowed from the economist; as, *demand, money wages, national income, quasi rent, savings, scarcity, seller's market* 49

Included in the first classification are *primitive* words and certain *linkage* terms having related meanings and uses in the fields of philosophy, logic, and other general disciplines. Their appearance here seems warranted by their continued association with accounting, and by the need of indicating the limits of their coverage as they are ordinarily employed by the accountant. They are often on his tongue, although he may be unaware that he has added to them a special nuance something less than obvious to others. Also included are several words not typical of the field but having some importance in the development of almost any system of collective endeavor. The presence of these terms may aid in clarifying the perspective and deepening the understanding of accounting by relating it at the fundamental level to other disciplines that often share its objectives.

Frequently, however, the communicative efforts of the accountant, like those of other professional people, are punctuated by well-worn words, phrases, and slogans that mean little or nothing to the layman; they may even mislead him. Upon reflection, the accountant discovers quite surprisingly that they have come to mean very little to himself. Perhaps they seem to be justified by precedent or by some legal opinion or decision, and thus to carry with them a suggestion of authority, safety, or even finality; perhaps, in some situations, as one sardonic member of the profession has noted, polysyllabic sonority has been found to confer no small measure of respectability, dignity, and conviction on the accountant's otherwise arid reports. Striking examples are found in a group of adjectives which have been employed widely in the literature and in official pronouncements, less often in oral communications. Some of them, occasionally appearing in a technical sense, warrant definition. More often, they possess the remarkable property of being freely interchangeable: one may be substituted for another without altering the intended meaning. In the Research Bulletins of the Committee on Accounting Procedure of the American Institute of (Certified Public) Accountants (1939–1957) many hundreds of examples have been noted; in Bulletin No. 2, they or their related forms appeared no less than 57 times; in Bulletin No. 29, 48 times; in a Terminology Bulletin (No. 4), 8 times; and so on. These adjectives are: *acceptable, adequate, advantageous, appropriate, desirable, material, meaningful, permissible, practicable, preferable, proper, rational, realistic, reasonable, significant, sound, systematic, useful.* When possessing the property of interchangeability, no *standard of comparison* exists; moreover, they may *symbolize* any of a number of things: a habit, often an unconscious one, of substituting authority for reason; a distaste for embarrassing, if not self-defeating, argument, as when a writer, as propagandist, is plumping for some controversial, highly dubious "principle"; an inability or unwillingness to admit motivation of any order higher than, say, a *tax advantage*; a necessity for straddling, as in a committee report that is to appear with no dissents or with as few dissents as possible; and so on. A reader encountering any of these adjectives would do well to be on his guard against special pleading; he may even be impelled to speculate a bit on the virtues of what has been avoided by their use. Fortunately the temptation to employ these terms in AICPA bulletins has been largely overcome; but their use continues in formal reports of professional accountants.

A highly specialized language is developing in connection with the rapidly growing complex of data processing and other mechanical devices associated with management services that accountants are being called upon to supply. Applications of these devices as well as the devices themselves are changing rapidly. Moreover, specialists, not primarily accountants, are being employed by accounting firms to whom this development is being entrusted. For these reasons, the issuance of a supplementary pamphlet dealing with these terms and lending itself to frequent revision and republication is under study.

As compared with the third edition of this book, 160 new terms have been added: some are items overlooked; others are explanations of terms used in existing definitions that have seemed to demand further clarification; others reflect ideas that have emerged during the past few years. In addition, many definitions have been recast, or substantially modified.

Suggestions for improvements and additions by users of the book are gratefully acknowledged.

E. L. Kohler
Chicago

A word for the reader

On compounding:

1. Of the 2,804 entries that follow, only 758 are single words. The remainder are noun-and-noun and adjective-and-noun phrases and other word combinations that in becoming a part of the vernacular have acquired meanings often sharply divergent from those of their components. In such cases the alphabetical position of the phrase or combination is determined by the first letter.
2. Conforming to the historical pattern of language development, a number of terms, originally separate words, appear as one word where their singleness and uniqueness of meaning are firmly established; as, *bookkeeping, breakeven, bylaw, byproduct, carryover, cashbook, cutoff, goodwill, markon, payroll, proforma, stockholder, withholding, writeup.*
3. Good usage requires that a prefix be united with a word, and not hyphenated; as, *antilogarithm, coinsurance, intercompany, nonoperating, overabsorption, postwar, preaudit, preemptive, semisenior, surtax, underwrite.* Exceptions occur where the combination might lead to confusion.
4. Two or more normally separate words employed as an adjectival phrase are joined by hyphens (exception: an adverb ending in -ly preceding an adjective, exemplified in the fourth and fifth words of this sentence); as, *balance-sheet comment, excess-profits tax, long-term lease, paid-in capital, profit-and-loss statement, single-entry bookkeeping, tax-benefit rule, working-capital ratio.* Experience indicates that careful observance of this rule of hyphenation adds precision to an intended meaning and makes the reading of technical papers and reports a less arduous task.

On italics:

1. Independent definitions are provided for most of the words and phrases in italics; by referring to them, the reader may gain a clearer picture of the complex of ideas for which a term stands.
2. Occasionally italics are employed for emphasis.
3. Mathematical symbols usually appear in italics.

On parts of speech:

Where a term serves as more than one part of speech, the part defined is sometimes indicated (*n.*, *v.*, or *adj.*) for the purpose of delimiting the definition; as, *arm's length, balance coordinate, credit, inventory, objective.* If a verb, its transitive or intransitive character (*v.t.* or *v.i.*) may be shown; as, *check, debit, defalcate, deobligate, pledge.* A definition having reference to the plural form of a noun is preceded by *pl.;* as, *book of account, current fund, sale.*

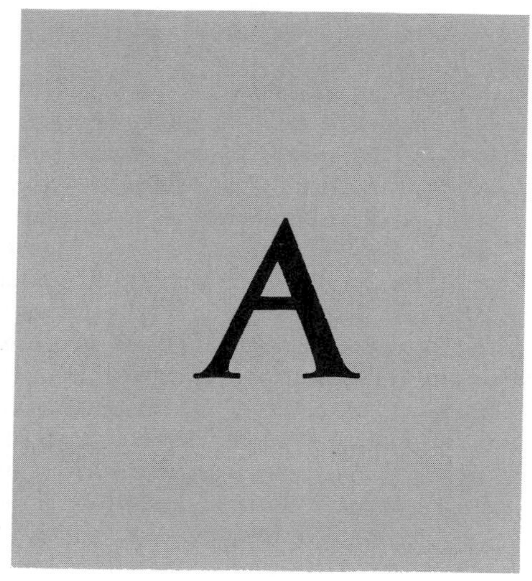

abandonment The complete retirement of a fixed asset from service, following salvage or other reclaiming of removable parts; as, the abandonment of a war plant not useful in peacetime production, an exhausted coal mine or oil well, or street-railway tracks upon the institution of bus service; see *retirement.* Under the Income-Tax Regulations (section 1.165–2), an abandonment loss deduction is allowed only on property of a capital nature (generally excluding depreciable assets employed in a business), the intention to abandon must be evident, the usefulness of the property must have been completely terminated, and there must be no possibility of any future use of the asset. Under special rules in the Regulations [section 1.167(a)–8], a retirement loss may be allowed on the abandonment of depreciable business property.

A provision in contemplation of future abandonment is a provision for *obsolescence;* such a provision or the loss recognized when the abandonment occurs is not a capital loss for income-tax purposes but may be deducted in full. See *fixed asset; depreciation.*

abatement 1. The cancellation of a part or all of a past or prospective expenditure.
2. A reduction or cancellation of an assessed tax. Under the Internal Revenue Code of 1954 (section 6404b), a claim in abatement is not permitted as to income, estate, and gift taxes.
3. Any item of incidental income accounted for as a reduction of a general cost; as, the income from minor sales to outsiders of electric power produced by a generating plant owned by a manufacturing enterprise.

aboriginal cost = *original cost(2).*

above par At a premium: applied to the market quotation or price of a security or other item of value, higher than its face amount.

above the line 1. A phrase indicating a *customary* balance-sheet or revenue-or-expense position in a financial statement; contrasts with *below the line.* Examples: customers' short-term notes shown above the line, i.e., classified in a balance sheet as a current asset; minor adjustments of past periods merged in an income statement with similar items above the line, i.e., classified as current or ordinary expense.
2. (governmental accounting) The portion of a financial showing of income and expenditure, or of a budget, financed through *appropriations* or other legislative *authorizations;* a budget *surplus* or *deficit* is yielded when projected and actual amounts are compared.

abscissa The horizontal or x axis in a *two-dimensional coordinate system* or chart. The point a in the accompanying figure has an *abscissa* of 2 and an *ordinate* of 3, as indicated by the numbers in parentheses. Where $x = 2$ and $y = 3$, the single point a identifying both is

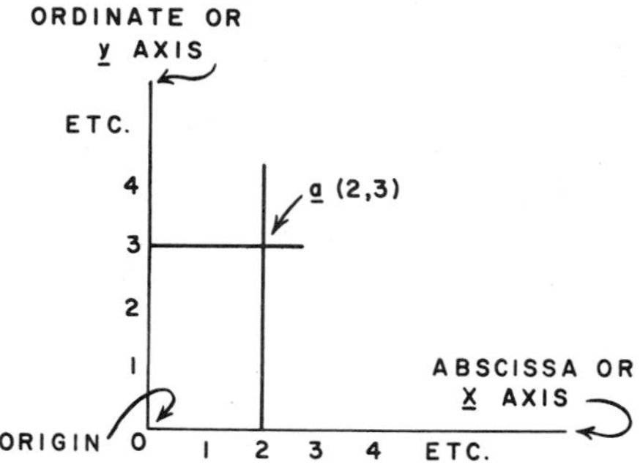

found by moving 2 units along the x axis from the origin (0) and 3 units up the ordinate, or y axis, and determining the point of intersection of perpendicular lines drawn from each of these axis values.

absorb 1. To merge by transfer all or part of an account or group of accounts with another account in such a manner as to cause the identity of the first to be lost, as by the transfer of operating expense from *basic-expenditure* accounts to work in process, or from work in process to finished stock, or from finished stock to cost of sales; or by the writeoff of a bad debt against a reserve for bad debt. 2. To include related actual costs in establishing a price or a standard cost. 3. To spread costs through *allocation* or *proration*.

absorbed cost See *cost absorption*.

absorption account A contra or adjunct account, related to and usually following another in a ledger, the items of which represent transfers to other accounts. Examples: (a) an insurance-expense account the credit entries in which reflect distributions to departments or operations benefited of premium costs appearing in a related prepaid-insurance account; (b) accumulated depreciation. In the preparation of financial statements, the balances of such related accounts may be combined (example a) or may be shown together (example b). See *contra account; cost absorption*.

absorption costing The assignment of both fixed and variable costs to goods or services produced, antonymous to *direct costing*. Compare with *cost absorption; cost finding*.

abstract *adj*. Characterizing a property or relation considered apart from local or temporary contexts, or a quality considered independently of the object or event that possesses it; pertaining to (a) that which is common to a class; (b) a meaning that can be expressed by a symbol that does not refer to anything unique; (c) features not limited to a perceived object; or (d) an expression calling attention to such features. *n*. = *trial balance*.

accelerated depreciation Depreciation at a larger than usual rate because of (a) plant operations at more than normal speed, use, or capacity; (b) a useful or economic life materially less than physical life, as (i) mine equipment the physical life of which is in excess of the estimated operating period of the mine, its cost therefore being absorbed in operating expenses over the shorter period, or (ii) assets purchased for use in connection with a contract, order, or job at the completion of which the assets will have a diminished or no foreseeable remaining utility; (c) an excessive cost of construction occasioned during a period in which materials and skilled labor are at a premium, such excessive cost being written off during what is estimated to be the high-price period; (d) the decision of the Congress to stimulate the construction of defense emergency facilities and grain-storage facilities by allowing rapid cost recovery for tax purposes, referred to as *amortization;* (e) tax advantages arising from the use of *declining-balance* and *sum-of-the-years digits methods* now permitted in the Internal Revenue Code; (f) other conditions giving rise to limited or lessened economic use. The Federal income-tax regulations give little or no recognition to items (a) and (c), except through optional methods of *depreciation*. See *emergency facilities; depreciation; depreciation method; obsolescence*.

acceptable quality level (statistical quality control) a predetermined degree of quality, generally in terms of number or percent of defective items in a lot or batch of goods, which is regarded as satisfactory in the sense that such quality will be accepted by the inspection procedure a high proportion (generally 95 percent or more) of the time; often referred to as *AQL*.

acceptance 1. A promise to pay, by the drawee of a bill of exchange, usually

evidenced by inscribing across the face of the bill "accepted," followed by the date, the place payable, and the acceptor's signature. Any words showing the intention of the drawee to accept or honor the bill are sufficient, however. The effect of the acceptance is to make the bill equivalent to a promissory note, with the acceptor as maker and the drawer as endorser. See *bank(er's) acceptance; promissory note.*
2. A *bill of exchange* accepted by the drawee.
3. A *trade acceptance.*
4. The action of one of the parties to a contract to make it valid, following the offer of the other party. The acceptance may be made orally or in writing, depending on the nature of the contract.

acceptance sampling (statistical quality control) Use of samples to determine the acceptability of submitted lots of goods. Acceptance sampling by attributes is probably the predominant practice, the inspection test involving either a classification of the sample items as good or defective or a count of the number of defects per 100 units. Acceptance sampling by variables is also possible; where feasible it possesses greater efficiency per unit inspected than does sampling by attributes. However, both methods involve assumptions concerning the distribution of quality within the lot, and these assumptions place a real restriction on the general applicability of acceptance sampling by variables. The inspection test consists of measuring some quality characteristic of each item in the sample. Judgment on the lot is then based on the data resulting from this measurement.

Acceptance sampling by *attributes* is divided into four types, according to whether single, double, multiple, or sequential (item-by-item) samples are used. Under single sampling, a *sample* consisting of a predetermined number of items is taken at *random* from a lot. On the basis of this sample evidence of product quality, the entire lot is accepted or rejected. This scheme in many cases requires a relatively large sample. Although inspection of the sample may be curtailed in various ways, this is seldom desirable. A better alternative is to seek other sampling schemes that yield corresponding (matched) protection with lower inspection costs.

Double sampling may, in many cases, and with less expense, give the same degree of quality protection as single sampling. Double sampling proceeds in two steps. A relatively small random sample of items is taken from the lot and inspected on the basis of predetermined standards. From the evidence obtained through this first sample, it may be decided to accept or reject the lot. Since the sample is relatively small, the evidence yielded by it may prove inconclusive. When such is the case, a second sample (usually larger than the first sample) is taken at random from the remainder of the lot and the results of the two samples are combined to determine whether to accept or reject the lot.

Multiple sampling constitutes a logical extension of double sampling, except that successive samples, where needed, are the same size as the first sample. For each sample, three decisions are possible: (a) accept the lot, (b) reject the lot, or (c) take another sample because the accumulated evidence through that stage is inconclusive. In multiple sampling, the "group" or "block" samples are always small relative to the single or double plans being matched and are accompanied by acceptance and rejection numbers that maintain the specified degree of quality protection and that are arranged to force a decision by at most nine (and frequently fewer) blocks.

Sequential (item-by-item) sampling resembles multiple sampling in principle, the block size being simply one item, so that the three possible decisions are available after inspection of each unit rather than at the end of the inspection of a group of units. Also, in sequential sampling, inspection could continue all the way through to complete 100 percent sorting of the entire lot, although in practice this is never done, decisions under this scheme being consistently reached after the inspection of fewer pieces on the average than under any of the other three types. Because sequential plans are easy to design, they are extremely flexible and can therefore be "custom-built" to fit special protection requirements with greater precision than is possible under any of the other three types of sampling. The major obstacles to the practicability of sequential sampling are the highly variable inspection load it imposes, with its attendant handling costs, and the necessity for careful training and supervision of the inspection personnel to be entrusted with using it.

All four types of sampling plans are based on definite protection features in terms of calculable risks; standard tables are available covering a wide range of quality protection and providing appropriate sample sizes and acceptance and rejection criteria.

Developing experience with sampling from successive lots of goods and the maintenance of a p chart (see *control chart*) in conjunction with sampling may be used as a guide for sample redesign which will result in reduced or tightened inspection.

For plans with matched protection features, techniques are available for determining how the four types of plans compare as to the average amount of inspection required to reach a decision on the lot. Multiple sampling plans will generally have a decided advantage in this respect over the corresponding single or double plans at all levels of incoming lot quality, and sequential plans will be even more frugal in this respect than multiple plans. References already cited deal with this aspect of acceptance sampling.

accommodation endorsement An endorsement by one person, without consideration, on a note or other credit instrument to which another person is a party, for the purpose of establishing or strengthening the other's credit; as, a corporation's endorsement on the bank loan of a subsidiary. See *commitment; contingent liability.*

accommodation note (or **paper**) A note signed by one person as maker, endorser, or acceptor, on behalf of another whose credit standing is weak or nonexistent. As a rule, no consideration is involved, the intent of the signer being to act as a surety or guarantor. The power of a corporation to act as such a signer is often questioned. See *contingent liability.*

account *n.* 1. A formal record of a particular type of transaction expressed in money or other unit of measurement and kept in a *ledger.*

2. = *account current.*

3. The amount owing by one person to another, often evidenced by a statement showing details. See *account stated.*

4. (governmental accounting) An *appropriation request* appearing in the annual budget of the United States.

5. As used in the expression, "for the account of": on behalf of; chargeable or creditable to.

6. *pl.* = *financial statements;* as, the annual accounts of a business enterprise. In British practice, both *books of account* and year-end financial statements may be implied.

7. *pl.* The bookkeeping records (*books of account*) of any organization, including journals, ledgers, vouchers, and other supporting papers.

v., with *for:* (a) To place in the books of account; (b) to furnish facts supported by explanations; (c) to return (tickets, coupons) as unsold or unclaimed; (d) (auditing) to obtain explanations that constitute *accounting evidence* concerning an expenditure;—with *to:* to render an *accounting(2).*

The traditional, standard form of

NAME OF ACCOUNT *Temporary Investments* NUMBER *1011*

DATE		MEMO	F	DEBIT	DATE		MEMO	F	CREDIT
19x2 Jan.	1	Balance	✓	52 461 50	19x2 Feb.	6	Sale 100 shares AST Comm.	Cr 87	4 201 32
Feb.	6	Profit on sale AST Comm.	J354	201 32					
Aug.	4	Purchase 26M CC bonds	C43	26 260 00					
	10	Purchase Treas. 2½ '63's	C46	10 150 00					
Dec.	18	Purchase Treas. 2¼ '59's	C70	18 000 00	Dec.	31	Balance		102 871 50
				107 072 82					107 072 82
19x3 Jan.	1	Balance	✓	102 871 50					

STANDARD ACCOUNT FORM

the account (sense 1) is a page divided into similar halves, as shown in the accompanying figure. The illustration reflects manual postings of transactions to a printed form, each item consisting of the date of the transaction as shown by the book of original entry or other source, a brief note identifying the nature of the transaction, the posting reference (or *folio*) indicating the page number of the book of original entry or the voucher number or other clue pointing directly to the source record of the transaction, and the money amount involved. Debit items occupy the left side of the page and credit items the right. In the illustration, all the transactions affecting the account "Temporary Investments" during a year are shown together with opening and closing balances. The "ruling off" at the year end is a common practice but is not required for an account having so few transactions in a year.

In practice, there are no mechanical standards, minimum or otherwise, for the account form. Required only are (a) the date, to identify the day or accounting period of the transaction or transaction group, (b) the source of the item, so that when an error is discovered or an internal or external audit is being made, original supporting data may be readily referred to, and (c) the money amount. Bookkeeping machines and the use of punched cards and data-processing equipment often make possible the replacement of formal journals and ledgers by a file of cards or by summaries of such original data as sales invoices. Making only total entries for each month in the general ledger is a frequent practice, and occasionally it will be found that the general ledger itself has been discarded in favor of "worksheet accounts," the latter being totals of classified transactions. In most instances a formal general ledger, often hand-posted, must be maintained, if for no other purpose, as an overall index of the transactions of a period (see illustration under *trial balance*). In all cases, however, whether the account forms be formal or of the less formal variety, a strict procedure must be followed to minimize error and maximize referability to source documentation.

Unruled ledger sheets are common where accounts are machine-posted. The following will illustrate:

Temporary Investments				*1011*
Balance from old ledger	✓	Jan. 1, '–2	52,461.50	52,461.50
Sale of 100 sh AST common	cr 87	Feb. 6, '–2	4,201.32cr	48,260.18
Profit on sale of above	j 354	Feb. 6, '–2	201.32	48,461.50
Purchase 26M cc bonds	c/ 43	Aug. 4, '–2	26,260.00	74,721.50
Purchase Treas. 2½'s	c/ 46	Aug. 10, '–2	10,150.00	84,871.50
Purchase Treas. 2¼'s	c/ 70	Dec. 18, '–2	18,000.00	102,871.50

Here the detail appears in one column, with credits marked "Cr," and the balance in another column immediately following. The many variations found in practice may be largely attributed to the desire to make the posting operation as simple and error-proof as possible, save paper, and provide a form that will fit a machine or a file.

Loose-leaf accounts are almost universally used. See *ledger; double-entry bookkeeping.*

accountability 1. The obligation of an employee, agent, or other person to supply a satisfactory report, often periodic, of action or of failure to act following delegated authority. See *responsibility; authority; accounting(2); feedback; property accountability.*
2. Hence (governmental accounting) the designation of the account or amount of a *disbursing officer's* liability.
3. The measure of responsibility or liability to another, expressed in terms of money, units of property, or other predetermined basis.
4. The obligation of evidencing good management, control, or other performance imposed by law, agreement, or regulation, as on corporation executives, trustees, public officials, and other persons controlling the financial policy of an organization or the deposit, investment, or disposition of funds. In the interest of maintaining good human relations and earning public confidence, many persons in positions of responsibility voluntarily explain their conduct of affairs to others interested and to the public generally, this practice often acquiring the force of custom. See *reporting; efficiency.*

accountability unit The unit selected as the basis of *property accountability.* See also *fixed-asset unit.*

accountable 1. Having responsibility or liability for cash or other property held in trust or under some other relationship with another. See *accountability.*
2. (government accounting) Personally liable for improper payments; said of a *certifying* or *disbursing officer.*
3. Requiring entry on the books of account: said of a transaction not yet recorded, often with reference to its timing. See *incur; recognize.*

accountable condition (or **event**) A *condition* (or *event*) giving rise to a transaction, and requiring *recognition(2).* See *transaction; accrue.*

accountable officer (governmental accounting) A *certifying* or *disbursing officer.*

accountable person One charged with *accountability.*

accountable warrant See *warrant(5).*

accountancy The theory and practice of accounting: its responsibilities, standards, conventions, and activities generally; see *accounting.*

accountant One skilled in accounting. See *public accountant; certified public accountant; private accountant.*

accountant in charge An auditor who supervises the field work of an audit engagement, allots duties to assistants, reviews their findings, and drafts reports; often limited to situations where one of several accountants assigned to an engagement is given top responsibility.

accountant's responsibility The moral obligation assumed by a public accountant, as a member of a *profession,* in subscribing to a financial statement from which information and guidance may be sought by management, creditors, and investors. A number of states, through the issue of annual licenses and the setting of minimum standards of performance, have endeavored to focus attention on such responsibility. The moral obligation of the accountant as here conceived is to be distinguished from his formal code of *ethics* or *legal liability* (*q.v.*) in that it connotes a conduct conforming to professional, community, or individual standards of propriety as opposed to those the nonobservance of which might justify or lead to legal action. In issuing a report or opinion bearing his name, the moral obligation of the public accountant, at many points corresponding to that attaching to members of other professions, has often been described in such terms as the following:

1. Since the public accountant holds himself out to the public as an expert, *public interest* requires that he should not neglect to perform his work with the same degree of skill and diligence as would be exercised under similar conditions by any conscientious member of the profession.

2. Ignorance of any usual audit standard or procedure should not be advanced as a condonation of unprofessional work. The public has the right to expect from him performance of a high order and reasonable care in all he does.

3. A mistake that might be made by any member of the profession working under similar conditions should not be interpreted as disregard of professional obligation; but the mistake must be an honest one and not an action prompted by the known attitude or expressed wish of a client or one attributable to any other unprofessional motivation.

4. Delegation to staff members of field work or other professional tasks does not relieve the accountant from responsibility for their work.

5. Essential facts should be disclosed. Professional custom rather than his own judgment should be the accountant's determinant of what "essential" means.

6. Where, during the course of his audit, the accountant suspects an irregularity, he should institute a sufficiently thorough investigation to lay bare the details of the irregularity or to satisfy himself that no irregularity in fact exists. Denial of access to records, restriction as to audit scope, or limitation of fee does not absolve the accountant from criticism under such circumstances.

7. Unequivocal language is an essential of an accountant's report, together with information helpful, rather than essential, to those who may wish to interpret the report.

8. The accountant has a broad responsibility for statements made by him in a professional capacity. His report should be prepared as though it were to be presented to unknown third persons, notwithstanding any indication that it is not to be so employed.

9. The existence and possible effect of any material limitation on the character or extent of the audit or of any important divergence from an accounting principle or canon of professional practice should be clearly set forth in the accountant's report.

See *audit; audit report; ethics; scope; opinion; legal liability; fairness.*

account current 1. Any personal account on which periodic settlements are made. 2. The formal, periodic transcript of such an account, sent by one person to another, concluding with the balance receivable or payable. Example: a consignee's periodic accounting to his consignor for sales, less agreed costs and commissions. See *account sales.*

account form The usual style followed in the presentation of a balance sheet—assets on the left and liabilities and capital, or equities, on the right, with equal totals—and less often in the case of income statements; contrasts with *report form.* See *balance sheet; income statement.*

accounting 1. The recording and reporting of *transactions* (*q.v.*).
2. Hence, by extension, the origins, *recognition*, and disposition of transactions: (a) their emergence (*timing, quantification*, often in physical-unit, as well as money terms, *classification*); (b) their *processing* (*system design, internal checks*); (c) their *recording* and grouping (*bookkeeping*); (d) their *feedback* (*internal reporting*); (e) the continuous critical *testing* of transactions (*internal auditing*); (f) the fitting of transaction groups into conventional patterns (summarization in *financial statements*);

(g) professional examinations of financial statements (*audit(4)* by *public accountants*); (h) periodic reporting to investors, government agencies, and the public generally; (i) transaction *projection* (*budgeting* and other *forward-accounting* activities); (j) external reviews of and recommendations on organizational functioning (*management services:* a natural consequence of the public accountant's familiarity with and judgments (incident to his audits) on the internal structure and needs of both successful and less successful organizations). Of these activities, (a), (b), (c), and (f) have always been traditional, though the scope of each has greatly expanded; (g) and (h) gained public recognition shortly before the turn of the century; (d) and (e) in the mid-thirties; (i) after World War II; (j)—a present-day outgrowth of the increasing involvement of accounting and accountants with organizational structure and management functioning.

Accounting and accountancy are often synonymous terms; the latter, of less frequency in the literature, may refer to the entire body of theory and practice; "accounting" is usually an all-inclusive term; but, when used adjectively, it may have a restricted area of reference: as, the field of accountancy, a school of accountancy, a journal of accountancy; but the profession of accounting, an accounting system, a course in accounting, an accounting supervisor.

An AICPA committee on terminology proposed in 1941 that accounting be defined as "the *art* of recording, classifying, and summarizing *in a significant manner* and in terms of *money*, transactions *and events* which are, in part at least, *of a financial character*, and *interpreting* the results thereof" [italics added]. Whether accounting is an art or a science or has aspects of both remains an unsettled point that does not need to—in fact, cannot—be resolved by definition. Also, what was intended by the phrase "in a significant manner" was not explained; further, the meaning of the expressions "in terms of money," "events," and "of a financial character" are conveyed by the notions inherent in *transaction*, the *recognition* and *definition* of which as a word more fundamental than "accounting" would have made unnecessary the employment of these three undefined phrases. Finally, "interpreting" is generally regarded as a function of management or of outsiders; the accountant is limited to disclosing information, thus facilitating interpretations, opinions, and conclusions by others.

In *The Basic Postulates of Accounting* (1962), Maurice Moonitz asserted that the function of accounting is fivefold: to measure the resources of entities, reflect claims against them, and measure changes in both, all with reference to periods (and points) of time, and all expressed in terms of money. But accounting has an assortment of functions other than providing the components of financial statements. Among these are its contributions to the development of modern ideas of shared management: better operating-policy formation and the improvement of controls at top levels of management; clearer delegations of management authority; operable budgets, from their inception to their administration and enforcement at all management levels; *cost consciousness* throughout an organization; the provision of cost alternatives at basic operating points; and in other ways establishing improved conduits for intraorganizational information. Without the techniques supplied by accounting in the orderly direction and coordination of the intricate affairs of today's commercial enterprises, it has often been noted that the growth and successful administration of the modern business corporation would be impossible.

3. A report of transactions by one responsible for acquiring, safeguarding, or administering assets or incurring expense, the disbursement of cash advanced,

or the carrying out of any assigned task. Examples: an accounting of an executor to a court; an accounting between parties in the settlement of a suit; an accounting for the operation of a petty-cash fund; a report by an agent to his principal, whether or not accompanied by a cash settlement for an amount owing. See *accountability*.

4. Hence, any report embracing the transactions (including all changes in *accounts*) during a designated period. The report, for example, may be in the form of or include a *budget* or a *flow statement*, accompanied by narrative explanations or footnotes essential to a full understanding by its readers.

accounting control 1. The administrative procedures employed in maintaining the accuracy and propriety of transactions and the bookkeeping record thereof. See *internal control; internal check*.

2. An accounting procedure designed to maintain continuous internal quantitative controls over business transactions: particularly, the keeping of a duplicate account or a record of totals as a basis for proving the accuracy of the aggregate of a group of accounts; the maintenance of a property ledger. See *control account; subsidiary ledger*.

3. Any of the various accounting procedures and devices having as their purpose the supplying to management of informational records and reports essential to the administration of properties, the timing of purchases, the limitation of varied types of expenditures, and the like.

accounting entity = *accounting unit*.

accounting equation See *accounting identity*.

accounting evidence (auditing) Proof, obtained by any of the various devices employed by the public accountant in the course of an audit. The process of auditing may be regarded as the collection of such accounting evidence as in the opinion of the auditor is required by standard or minimum procedures and by the peculiarities of the case in hand before he may issue his report. The evidence is derived from such varied activities of the auditor as a determination of the character and extent of the system of internal control; comparisons of current costs and cost trends with those of past periods and other organizations; detailed examinations, testchecks, or scannings of certain individual accounts or groups of accounts, securing representations from management or certifications or opinions of third persons; and personal observation or inspection. In general, accounting evidence is measured by commonly accepted auditing standards based in part on rules of law and statistics. See *audit; audit standards*.

accounting identity 1. The *identity* of the debit and credit elements of a transaction expressed in terms of double-entry bookkeeping: also known as *accounting equation*. See *double-entry bookkeeping;* see also *spread sheet* for illustration of two-way effect of representative transactions on bookkeeping records.

2. Hence, the identity of assets and equities, expressed as assets $\equiv$ equities (or $\equiv$ liabilities + capital or net worth): the consequence of the summation of a series of transactions recorded on a double-entry basis, each transaction having a debit and credit element of identical amount.

accounting manual A handbook of accounting policies, standards, and practices governing the accounts of a business enterprise or other person; it includes the *classification of accounts*.

accounting period The period of time for which an operating statement is customarily prepared. Examples: a month (the most common accounting period); four weeks; a quarter (of a year); 26 weeks; a year; 52 weeks; any irregular period of time such as that covered by an *accounting* (*2*). The accounting period of a year is the fiscal year ending on December 31 or the last day of any other month. An accounting period of more than one year may be required in the case of an estate or trust. See *fiscal year*.

accounting policy The general principles and procedures under which the accounts of an individual organization are maintained; any one such principle or procedure. An accounting policy, as distinct from a principle, is an adaptation or special application of a principle necessary to meet the peculiarities of an organization or the needs of its management. Thus, policies are required for the computation of *depreciation*, the *recognition* of capital expenditures, and the disposal of *retirements*, the general accounting principle relating to these items providing a wide latitude for individual action. See *fixed asset; depreciation*. Occasionally an accounting policy is found to conflict with accepted principles. Any major accounting policy thus in conflict, together with an estimate of its effect on the accounts, requires disclosure in financial statements. Decisions as to the range of accounting policies and their specific formulation are often left to the controller of an organization; in large organizations, management usually participates on major policies, and the board of directors may be asked to approve them. See *principle; policy; accounting procedure*.

accounting practice 1. The professional work of a public accountant; see *public accounting*.

2. Hence, the activities of public accountants generally.

3. The customs and predilections of accountants as expressed in their everyday activities; contrasts with *accounting theory*.

accounting principles The body of doctrine associated with *accounting*, serving as an explanation of current practices and as a guide in the selection of conventions and procedures. The axioms of accounting and the principles deriving from them have arisen from common experiences, historical precedent, statements by individuals and professional bodies, and regulations of governmental agencies. The validity of accounting principles rests on their simplicity, clarity, and generality in mirroring current practices and in furnishing guidance for the moral conduct of practitioners and for the further development of the profession. The endorsement by a professional body of practices (e.g., the advocacy of *lifo* methods and *accelerated depreciation*), inspired primarily by the desire to secure income-tax advantages, does not in itself qualify them as principles. See *accounting policy; system of accounts; principle; theory; convention; postulate*.

Contributions in recent years to an articulated body of accounting principles have come from two main sources. The first of these was the statement of principles underlying the preparation and presentation of financial statements, published during the period 1936–1957 by the American Accounting Association. The other is a series of pronouncements of the Accounting Principles Board (APB) and its predecessor committees of the American Institute of Certified Public Accountants commencing in 1939 and dealing with topical problems of accounting practitioners; although not constituting a coordinated body of doctrine, they have disposed of a number of troublesome factors otherwise standing as obstacles to principle formation on a broader scale. However, as yet no full-scale analysis of principles has been made, and no effort has been put forth in distinguishing fundamental *postulates, assumptions,* or *axioms* from principles and procedures derived from them.

There has been a continuous need for authoritative stands on the accounting practices reflected in published financial statements, and it was with these standards that the earliest AAA statement (1936) was concerned. Pronouncements of the succession of AICPA committees including the present APB have assumed the posture of authority. Between 1961 and 1968 twelve APB opinions were issued; these have endeavored to establish limited standards of practice acceptable to the profession, business, and governmental agencies concerned with corporate reporting. In some instances these opinions have modified previous pronouncements (1939–1961) on a variety of problems by narrowing or even widening earlier opinions. The result has *not* been an internally consistent, firmly structured, interrelated body of practices, and but few of them point to principles having any conceivably universal application. Thus, in APB 11 (1967) a figure for income-tax expense is called for that includes an accrual of future taxes that may never be *incurred* (as this term has heretofore been applied) and may never become a *liability* (again, in the ordinary meaning of this word) until an unknown (perhaps never-to-be-known) future period. Moreover, although discounted future liabilities are permitted in the APB opinion on pension funds (No. 8 [1966]) a stand is taken in APB 11 against discounting future tax accruals. The resulting further alienation of the *income statement* (already burdened by other pronouncements) from the statement of *cash flow* to which investment analysts in recent years have been turning for operating information does not augur well for the reliability and credibility of the current brand of income statement.

Perhaps the main difficulty in resolving principles applicable to financial statements lies in the belief that financial statements, fully footnoted and in their idealized form (for which the APB, for example, is now striving), will provide the information that investors and other presumed readers of such statements will find "useful." This will never be true. The information furnished by conventional financial statements will always be limited—in some cases it is of minor consequence—and it has not yet been realized that current criticisms of financial statements are in a more realistic sense criticisms of the restricted information-supply system now in effect. Although the scope of disclosures in annual reports to stockholders has been steadily increasing, publication—and comparisons with operating results—of management forecasts prior to the reporting period has been conscientiously avoided; any projection for the forthcoming period is currently rejected not for its possible exposure of management's inability to see ahead but on the ground that competitors might profit by it—the onetime argument opposing the publication of sales and costs of sales.

However, certain generalizations of accepted practices affecting financial statements which would be classified by many accountants as principles have emerged from the AAA–AICPA pronouncements; in general these are practices to which exceptions are sometimes found, although hopefully not without explanatory or reconciling notes:

1. The objective in accounting is the classification, recording, summarization, and reporting of the *transactions* of individual *entities* in terms of *revenues*, *transfers*, and *costs*, including the *conversion* of costs into cash and other *assets*, or their dissipation as *expense* or *loss*.

2. Because management has the ever-present obligation of striving for and maintaining *lowest possible cost*, much of the accounting process is constructed with the view of aiding in the attainment of that obligation.

3. The basis of asset valuation is the *price* (i.e., the amount of money or objectively established *money's worth*) paid in an exchange between independent parties. A *lump-sum purchase* of a group of assets is spread over the assets or asset classes acquired on the basis of their *appraised values* or *depreciated costs*.

4. In public utilities, and often in competitive enterprise, the excess over depreciated *original cost* of the price paid for an asset or asset group is regarded

as the purchase of excess earning power, separable from depreciated cost and amortizable over the years to which the continuance of the excess earning power has been imputed.

5. Where buyer and seller are under common control, the obligation of lowest possible cost requires that asset transfers between them be priced at the seller's depreciated cost.

6. Arm's-length cost or, for limited-life assets, depreciated cost, is the only objective basis of value; it is the consequence of actual transactions and is thus comprehensible to and is capable of serving the interests of management, investor, and consumer. It is an operable medium for applying both internal and external controls and for portraying the responsible discharge of management accountability.

7. Replacement cost, index-number valuation, or other hypothetical worth exceeding cost varies in amount with underlying assumptions and, neither having objective existence nor reflecting management accountability, is unsuited as a basis for accounting records and reports. As supplemental data in corporate reports to stockholders it may have some significance, as yet not fully developed, to management, investors, and others.

8. Similarly, discovery value, timber growth, and other forms of accretion are not recognized as income until realized through sale.

9. By convention, and in an effort to achieve both simplicity and substantial accuracy, the investment in limited-life, service-yielding assets is allocated over their useful lives on a "production" or "straight-line" basis; the amount not yet allocated is referred to as *depreciated cost* or simply *cost*.

10. A portion of the cost of an item of inventory may be expensed before the item is sold in order that the remaining cost may be not greater than (a) the probable future outlay for similar items; or, if similar items are no longer to be acquired, (b) the expected future disposal price less any estimated, identifiable increment in expense to be incurred in carrying or selling. The identification of cost with items sold has been generally regarded as dependent on the practice of putting into production or selling earliest-purchased items or any item of the same kind without regard to the time of its purchase. The *lifo* inventory valuation has generally been adopted for the purpose of gaining a tax advantage, which does not justify the violation of the cost principle cited above: an issue not yet squarely faced by the profession.

11. Discount and expense on long-term obligations is, in effect, interest not yet accrued, payable at maturity, and is an offset to the face value of the indebtedness. In practice, however, the item appears as a deferred charge on the balance sheet.

12. Unamortized discount and expense remaining from an obligation which has been refunded is an expense of the year in which the refunding takes place. Note, however, the three alternatives permitted by APBO 6 (1965).

13. Income from construction contracts involving periods greater than a year may be recognized in proportionate amounts as billings are made or collections received. On installment sales, however, the general rule is to recognize the gross profit at the time of sale except where collections may be doubtful or are spread over an extended period of time. See APBO 10 (1966).

14. A breakdown of sales and costs of sales by products or departments is a necessary addition to an income statement whenever the disclosure might influence the interpretations of readers of the statement. If the trend of any of these items is significant, comparative data are also essential. Recognition of this principle by the APB appears in a special bulletin (1967).

15. The income statement reflects revenue and expense *recognized* during

the current accounting period, notwithstanding that certain items may be associated with operations of prior years. No revenue or expense, however, may be recognized during the current accounting period in anticipation of transactions of future periods which, if they occur at all, will be dependent on future events and conditions or decisions then to be made. This principle was violated in APBO 11, as noted above.

16. A final section in the income statement may be employed for any material amounts of nonrecurring income and expense, extraordinary losses, "prior-year" charges, capital gains and losses, gain or loss from the discharge of an obligation at less or more than its recorded amount, and other *income deductions* and items worth distinguishing from more usual operations in the interest of aiding comparability. *Net* income (or loss) is what remains after all these items have been taken into account. See, however, *income deduction.* A corollary to this proposition is that no income, expense, or loss may be credited or charged directly to retained earnings. The APB has wavered here and its present position is far from clear; see APBO 9 (1966).

17. Provisions for contingencies and other possible *future* losses are not items that belong in an income statement; they are reservations of *retained earnings,* and accumulations of such provisions are classifiable under that head on a balance sheet. Related expenses and losses subsequently arising belong in the income statement of the period in which they are recognized. Reserves of this character, actually unnecessary, often confuse and may even mislead the reader of financial statements. This principle was, in substance, seconded in AICPA pronouncements; however, approval was confined to a "general" reserve for contingencies. See *reserve for contingencies.*

18. Corporate *net worth* (invested capital) consists of *paid-in capital* (stockholders' contributions) and *earned surplus* (*retained earnings*).

19. An acquisition of *treasury stock* is chargeable against paid-in capital to the extent permitted by the average amount paid in for that class of stock, any excess of acquisition cost being, in effect, a distribution of retained earnings. Resales are recorded in the same manner as original sales. See APBO 6.

20. A reduction of the par or stated value of capital stock for the purpose of absorbing a deficit is a *quasi reorganization* subject to the approval of the stockholders; thereafter, for a limited period, retained earnings is so labeled as to indicate that it dates from the time the deficit was eliminated.

accounting procedure The day-to-day operation of a particular system of accounts; the practices, or any of them, followed under such a system. See *accounting policy; accounting principles; system of accounts.*

accounting records The formal journals and ledgers, and the vouchers, invoices, correspondence, contracts, and other sources or support for such records; = *books of account.*

accounting system = *system of accounts.*

accounting transaction = *internal transaction.*

accounting unit (or **entity**) 1. A business enterprise or other economic unit, or any subdivision thereof for which a system of accounts is maintained. Whether a separate accounting system for a subdivision of a business enterprise is instituted is an administrative determination dependent on such factors as its distance from the general office, the degree of operating independence granted its management, reporting requirements, and the frequency, complexity, and points of origin of its transactions. Accounting records may be installed, usually without duplication or overall loss in efficiency, wherever management needs are best served. See *entity; establishment; economic unit.*
2. An individual account maintained

for recording the cost or other basis of *fixed assets*, usually coinciding with a *replacement unit* or *retirement unit;* but it may also embrace the several retirement units of a single structure, and be supported by a cost report or other record from which the cost of a retirement unit may be readily obtained. See *depreciation.*

accounting valuation 1. The historical money amount attaching to any asset or expense, generally representing cost: i.e., money outlay at the time of acquisition. It is with cost and its disposition that accounting is principally concerned. It is sometimes said that accounting does not involve valuation; on the contrary, it may also be said that cost is itself the main, and in most instances the only, valuation employed in the day-to-day operation of business enterprise. Decisions of management are based on cost: past, present, and future. The assignment of costs to activities or products, and particularly the division of joint and common costs between the operations served by them, may be regarded as a valuation process within the larger area of *cost absorption.* The portion of cost that is to be detached from the outlay associated with an inventory, where the rule of the lower of cost or market is being applied, likewise involves a valuation process the endproduct of which may be a partial cost which continues to attach to certain inventory items. But in all of these accounting operations, cost is the subject matter; its ultimate disposition is the central problem of cost accounting and a major problem constantly facing the general accountant. See *cost absorption.*
2. Any amount other than money outlay employed as a basis of accounting; as, a market value higher than cost in the case of an investment-company portfolio.

account payable 1. An amount owing to a creditor, generally on open account, as the result of delivered goods or completed services; distinguished from *accruals* and other *current liabilities* not arising out of everyday transactions. See *payable; trade account payable.*
2. Hence, a ledger account for such a liability.
3. *pl.* A general-ledger account controlling a group of such accounts. See *control account.*

account receivable 1. A claim against a debtor, generally on *open account,* its application usually limited to uncollected amounts of completed sales of goods and services; distinguished from deposits, accruals, and other items not arising out of everyday transactions. See *receivable; trade account receivable.*
2. Hence, a ledger account for such a claim.
3. *pl.* A general-ledger account controlling a group of such accounts. See *control account.*

account receivable discounted 1. An account receivable that has been assigned or sold with recourse; until paid by the debtor, the amount of the account is a contingent liability of the seller.
2. *pl.* The seller's contingent liability for customers' accounts receivable so assigned or sold: a balance-sheet term. See *balance sheet.*

account sales An interim or final statement rendered by a consignee or sales agent showing particulars of sales of goods consigned, expenses incurred, commissions, and the balance, if any, due the consignor; an *account current.*

account stated An *account* (*3*) the balance of which, as determined by the creditor, has been accepted as correct, sometimes implicitly, by the debtor. The term has significance in law, since it bars the debtor from attempting to disprove the accuracy of the computation, the bar being raised either by the debtor's explicit approval of the account and his promise to pay or by his failure within a reasonable time to indicate any exception to it.

In a few cases the Federal courts have recognized the principle of the account stated with respect to income taxes. Thus, if a revenue agent's report reflects a proposed refund to which the taxpayer agrees in writing, the resulting account stated may be held to give rise to a new cause of action upon which the taxpayer may recover within a new limitation period of six years.

accretion 1. An addition of principal or income to a fund as the result of a plan of accumulation; distinguished from *appreciation* and *increment*. In a pension fund, for example, an accretion may arise from payroll contributions or from revenue received on fund investments.
2. Increase in economic worth from any cause; as, the growth of timber, the aging of wines, the increase of flocks and herds.

accrual 1. The *recognition(1)* of events and conditions as they occur.
2. The partial recognition of an item of revenue or expense and its related asset or liability: the result of the lack of coincidence of the accounting period and the contractual or benefit period.
3. An amount accrued. See *accrue*.

accrual basis (of **accounting**) The method of accounting whereby revenues and expenses are identified with specific periods of time, such as a month or year, and are recorded as *incurred*, along with acquired assets, without regard to the date of receipt or payment of cash; distinguished from *cash basis*. See *accrue* (*2*); *double-entry bookkeeping; accrued-expenditures basis*.

accrual date The date through which an accrual extends.

accrue *v.i.* 1. To grow; to increase; to accumulate.
2. To *recognize* in the accounts, usually at the end of a conventional period of time, as the result of the occurrence of *accountable events* or the emergence of *accountable conditions* that are in the process of continuous change. Interest on a debt, whether receivable or payable, increases day by day. The conventions of bookkeeping permit the increase to be recorded daily, weekly, monthly, or yearly, in keeping with the frequency of financial statements prepared from the records or with the *closing* of the books. Other common accruing items are wages, taxes (on income or property), royalties, and depreciation of fixed assets. The term applies mostly to a continuing flow of services rather than to *physical assets*, and the process of accruing is employed by both the supplier and the recipient of the services. Upon recognizing an accruing item, a *transaction* in the form of an *adjusting entry* (or its equivalent) is recorded. On the books of the supplier, an asset account (e.g., interest receivable) is debited and a revenue account (e.g., interest earned) is credited; while on the books of the recipient, an expense account (e.g., interest expense) is debited and a liability account (e.g., accrued interest payable) credited. Accruals are possible because persons who supply services have become accustomed to a period of waiting after the service has been rendered before being paid: e.g., typical bond-interest coupons become due after six months' interest has accumulated; wages are paid at the conclusion of a week's, two-weeks', or month's work. *Accrue* contrasts with *prepay*. See also *accountable condition* (or *event*)*; recognize; transaction; double-entry bookkeeping*.
3. To come into existence; to become vested. Example: Rights to property accrue to a person's heirs upon his death; a right to a dividend accrues to a stockholder from the date of declaration.
v.t. To give effect to an accrual; to record revenue or expense in the accounting period to which it relates, notwithstanding that the required receipt or outlay may take place, in whole or in part, in a preceding or following period.

accrued asset The amount of interest, commission, services rendered to others, or other item of revenue neither received nor past due but *earned;* often a part of a larger whole. When past due, such an item, if still deemed collectible, is usually classified as an account receivable. See *accrue* (*2*).

accrued depreciation 1. The total depreciation suffered by an asset or asset group, based on customary or fairly determined rates or estimates of useful life, now generally referred to as *accumulated depreciation.* See *depreciation; depreciation method; fixed asset.*
2. The amount appearing in an accumulated-depreciation account.

accrued dividend The amount of unpaid and undeclared dividend on preferred stock. It differs from *dividend in arrears* by consisting of or including a provision for the period after the date on which the last dividend would ordinarily have been paid. Strictly speaking, a dividend does not accrue, since the stockholder usually has no legal claim to a dividend until it has been declared by the board of directors. See *dividend; unpaid dividend.*

accrued-expenditures basis A basis of analysis, statement preparation, or reporting characterized by the setting forth of goods received and services performed, and exemplified in a *funds-flow statement.* Such a statement contains the summary elements of an *income statement*, together with analyses of changes in assets, liabilities, and net worth, and may therefore be regarded as an *accounting(3)* of the differences between the items of successive balance sheets.

In Federal-government accounting, the term is employed in contradistinction to the *obligations basis* and the *cost basis,* the former signifying the inclusion of goods and services ordered but not received; the latter, goods and services *consumed.* The obligations basis has in the past applied primarily to *appropriations* by the Congress; at present many budgets and appropriations have been put on the accrued-expenditures basis; operating statements are said to be on a cost basis provided provisions for depreciation, if any, inventory used, and the like, replace asset acquisitions. All three bases, however, presume the *accrual method* of accounting.

accrued expense The liability covering an expense *incurred* on and before a given date, payable at some future date. Examples: accrued interest on notes payable; accrued wages. See *expense; accrue; accrued liability.*

accrued income = *accrued revenue.*

accrued liability An amount of interest, wages, or other expense *recognized* or *incurred* but not paid; *accrued expense.*

accrued revenue Revenue earned, but neither received nor past due. See *accrued asset; accrue.*

accumulated amount of 1 = *compound amount of 1.*

accumulated depreciation The *fixed-asset valuation account* offsetting depreciation *provisions;* also known as *reserve for depreciation* and *accrued depreciation.* See *depreciation; depreciation method; fixed asset.*

accumulated dividend = *dividend in arrears.*

accumulated income (or **earnings** or **profit**) Net income retained and not paid out in dividends or dissipated by subsequent losses; *earned surplus* or *retained earnings.*

accumulation 1. The periodic addition of (a) interest or other increase to the principal of a fund, (b) annual net income to *retained earnings*, or (c) amortized discount to an investment or obligation in order to raise the principal sum to the amount ultimately receivable or payable. See *bond discount; deferred charge; accumulation schedule; amortization.*
2. The act of compounding. See *compound.*
—*accumulate, v.t.*

accumulation factor The formula $(1 + r)^n$ applied to a principal amount bearing interest at r rate for the purpose of determining its total at the end of n periods. See *compound amount of 1.*

accumulation schedule A table in which computations are provided for the periodic writeup until maturity of the discount relating to an investment or obligation.

Annual charges for the elimination of the recorded discount sustained on a bond issue outstanding are actually accumulations or increments provided for raising the book value of the obligation to the amount due at maturity. Following is a form for such a schedule, in this instance a five-year noninterest-bearing loan of $20,000 by an individual to a corporation, against which at a discount of 4 percent per annum he advanced $16,438.54 (see table of present values, pp. 334–335). See *bond discount*.

Year	Discount Earned at 4%	Accumulated Amount
Initial amount		$16,438.54
1	$ 657.54	17,096.08
2	683.84	17,779.92
3	711.20	18,491.12
4	739.64	19,230.76
5	769.24	20,000.00
Total	$3,561.46	

accuracy The effectiveness of a statement, account, set of accounts, or document, such as a voucher, in portraying facts or opinions. The *degree* of accuracy is measured by the relative correspondence of a statement, account, or document to the facts. See *precision; reliability; validity; bias; replication*.

The term *accuracy* has a closely related technical meaning in accounting, statistics, the natural sciences, and engineering. As contrasted with *precision*, it means the success with which the nearness to a true value is attained. Precision relates to the tendency of tests to give the same value even though the value is inaccurate. On the other hand, *reliability* indicates the *probability* that a specified level of precision will be attained. Precision may be sacrificed for reliability, and vice versa, for a given sample size and method. Thus, high precision may be attained with low reliability, or low precision may be attained with high reliability for a given sample size and method.

In sampling procedures followed by an auditor, an increase in both precision and reliability requires either a larger sample or an improved sampling method, or both. For example, in certain circumstances both precision and reliability may be improved by dividing the sample into two parts, for a small part of which information is obtained with much care, time, and possibly cost per item sampled, and a larger part for which information is obtained on a more cursory, rapid, and less costly basis. The purpose of the larger part may to be secure greater *reliability* through a much larger sample size than would otherwise be used, whereas the purpose of the smaller part is to secure greater *precision* than would otherwise be obtained because of cost, time, and other considerations. The two sections of the sample may then be combined by various techniques to increase both precision and reliability. This procedure is often followed in an audit where a detailed examination is made of transactions covering a small portion of a period, while those belonging to the rest of the period are subjected only to a rapid scanning. See *verification; scan*.

acid test The determination of the ratio of the total of cash, trade receivables, and marketable securities of a business concern to its current liabilities. The term is used by credit analysts. If the ratio is 2 or more, a minimum risk is presumably indicated. See *current ratio; statement analysis*.

acquire To come into the ownership and possession of (property or services).

acquired surplus 1. The surplus of an enterprise existing at the date of acquisition of its control by another.

2. The excess over investment cost of dividends received by a parent or holding company from a subsidiary's earnings before consolidation; see *controlling-company accounting*.

3. The initial surplus of a successor enterprise where there has been a *pooling of interests* (i.e., no change in beneficial interests) and no full capitalization of surplus. The initial surplus may be paid-in or earned surplus (retained income) or both, depending on the nature of the surplus of the predecessor: paid-in

surplus to the extent necessary to recognize the full paid-in capital of the predecessor; earned surplus in an amount not in excess of the predecessor's earned surplus, diminished by any increase in the amount attributed to paid-in capital. Example: Corporation *A*, having outstanding par-value capital stock amounting to $100,000, paid-in surplus of $50,000, and earned surplus of $25,000, is acquired by Corporation *B*, an existing company, in exchange for a block of the latter's capital stock the stated value of which is $150,000. Before the merger, *B*'s paid-in capital was $600,000 and its earned surplus $100,000. After the merger, with the capital stock at $750,000 and combined earned surplus at $125,000, the amount of each stockholder's equity in paid-in capital and earned surplus remains unchanged. Had the relative equity altered in the process, the transaction would have been a sale rather than a pooling of interests, in which case the earned surplus would be classified as capital paid in, thereafter not available for dividends. Continuing the illustration, if Corporation *B*'s original capital stock and earned surplus had been $900,000 and $100,000, respectively, *A*'s stockholders would have retained only a $\frac{150}{1050}$ or $\frac{1}{7}$ interest (instead of a $\frac{1}{5}$ interest) in the combined surplus of $125,000. Under such circumstances, a purchase rather than a pooling of interests would have occurred, *A*'s earned surplus thus acquiring the status of paid-in surplus in *B*'s accounts. See *merger; consolidation; pooling of interests; earned surplus*.

acquisition adjustment (public-utility accounting) An account in which is recorded the difference between the cost of utility plant to the owning utility and original cost to any preceding owner who first dedicated it to public use. See *original cost* (2).

activity 1. The work, or one of several lines of work, carried on within any organizational subdivision.

2. That portion of the work of an *organizational unit* relating to a specific function or class of functions: any point where organizational and functional lines intersect. See *function; activity account; program; project*.

3. The whole of the work carried on by any organization or individual.

activity account An income or expense account containing transactions over which an activity supervisor assumes responsibility and maintains control. The transactions may include both materials and services, but not overhead or other items that are the responsibilities of other persons. To insure the following of a performance design predetermined by higher authority, limitations in the form of permissible objects and ranges of expenditure, the number and qualifications of employees, and the adherence to standards of operation and output are commonly imposed on the activity and become a part of its definition. The propriety, correctness, and "fit" of every item of operating income or cost are then the responsibilities of the activity head. Because he must be familiar with and approve such detail, he is normally supplied with a monthly or other periodic summary or copy of the activity account, and the latter must therefore contain whatever information is required by him for a critical review. There may thus be differences in the variety of detail furnished, depending on the nature of the activity and the needs of the activity head. See *activity; activity accounting*.

activity accounting A form of *management accounting:* the classification and operation of activity accounts with the object of aiding in the process of conforming organizational performance to plan; accounting by *functions*. Its principal application is to situations where forward planning, *authority, responsibility*, and *accountability* can be associated with operating units or centers each of which is identified in the organizational structure with an *organizational unit* or section of such a unit. By emphasis on transaction responsibility and accountability, activity accounting supplies substance as well as incentive to the delegation of management authority; further, it provides a series of well-defined focal points for the application and maintenance of budgetary and other operational controls. Following is a summary of definitions and principles adopted in one instance but having general application to any other operating establishment:

1. The work or tasks of a private or public enterprise, such as a corporation, consist of *projects* and *programs*, each of which is carefully defined before its commencement.

2. A *project* is a major property acquisition. Expenditures under a project are asset additions. An expenditure may involve the purchase of different kinds of assets, all contributing to a common function, or it may relate to "own" construction.

A project budget, the result of planning and programming, bears the approval of top management in advance of commitment; prospective unit costs are a feature. Examples of such units are material weights, labor hours, types of operation, and completed parts of structures.

As the project is being acquired or is building, quantity and cost records are maintained; where construction is being carried on, frequent conferences are had between engineers and accountants on emerging unit and total costs and their relation with the project budget and, ultimately, with the completed-project cost report. Total reported cost is identical with the project cost reflected in financial statements at the end of the fiscal year during which the project is completed. The report breaks down total cost by subactivities or sections; for each section the unit costs, wherever possible, are compared with their budgeted counterparts and with costs obtaining on similar projects carried on elsewhere (variances explained in detail).

Property records for the completed project are based on and initially tie in directly with the cost report. See *plant ledger*.

Proposed minor acquisitions for a fiscal year are grouped under a single project designation. Minor replacements of equipment are given a separate project designation in order to surround them with special safeguards.

3. A *program* is a major operation. Expenditures under a program are operating costs. A program is *short-term* if it is to be completed within a fiscal year and *long-term* if it extends into a future period.

4. Subprojects and subprograms are defined (e.g., geographical) breakdowns of projects and programs, fitted to expedient delegations of management controls.

5. An activity is thus a project or program, a subproject or subprogram, or any convenient division to which authority is delegated. It is the lowest practicable coincident level of function, budgeting, and accounting.

An activity is always a unit of functional and organizational control; its orderly establishment and operation are dependent equally on specific, defined delegations of authority and on clear, nontechnical assignments of objectives.

Responsibility for the conduct of an activity, strictly within prescribed limits, must always be assumed by one person (the activity head) designated by higher authority and known to associates and outsiders to have accepted such responsibility.

The activity head often takes the initial step in the preparation of a budget; subsequently he administers the portion of the budget determined by higher authority to be applicable to his activity.

The lines of authority and the flow of information between activity head and top management are as simple and direct as possible.

6. An *organizational unit,* the smallest administrative subdivision, is designated to carry on one or more activities.

An organizational unit is one of the subgroups within an administrative (as contrasted with functional) division of the enterprise.

An organizational unit may be charged with a number of activities, but an activity may not extend beyond a single organizational unit; that is, the activity is to be generally recognizable as the exclusive task, or as one of the exclusive tasks, of such a unit.

The activity head is invariably the head of the organizational unit in which the activity is carried on.

The activity is the function, and the organizational unit the manpower, assigned to carry out an enterprise task.

7. At least one account is maintained for each activity, and no item of income or cost of an economic unit can escape assignment as the direct income or direct cost of an activity for which some one person is responsible. Once carried to an activity account it remains there.

The one account may contain material, labor, and other *objective* items of cost, a distinctive symbol being given to each object class for overall recapitulation; but income always necessitates a separate account.

Several accounts may be required to facilitate the yield of component unit costs. No proration of the time of any individual or of the cost of any supply or service is subsequently made, excepting only prepayments, accruals, or deferrals.

A copy of each activity account, showing individual transactions, is given to the designated activity head periodically (e.g., monthly) and he is looked to by top management as the one responsible for the accuracy, propriety, and meaning of its content.

Explanations of transactions and other transaction data appear in such detail as may be arranged with the activity head.

8. One synthesis of activity accounts yields *financial* (functional) *statements* of projects and programs; another, capital outlay, income, and expense by organizational divisions, ordinarily required for budget comparisons.

9. The analysis of any activity account yields expenditures by *objects;* its recapitulation and comparison with quantities yield one or more unit costs.

10. Where activity accounting is carried on, a *budget* is a forward estimate of the income and cost of individual activities, with subtotals by projects and programs and by organizational divisions, or combinations of both.

11. *Accountability* may be supplied by oral or written reports to superior authority and by any of numerous other devices, such as group meetings of supervisors (e.g., factory foremen) where individual as well as interrelated problems may be discussed and solutions may be proposed and recommended.

act of bankruptcy See *bankruptcy.*

act of God (insurance) An event leading to a property loss caused by forces of nature that could not have been prevented by reasonable care or foresight; e.g., flood, lightning, earthquake, hurricane.

actual cost 1. Cost, as of acquisition or production, the former net of discounts and allowances but including transportation and storage, the latter consisting of direct material, labor, and variable overhead. See *direct cost; inventory valuation.*

2. A term suggesting a degree of accuracy in a cost computation not insured by the approximations inherent in appraised, average, estimated, or standard costs; *historical cost.* When applied to product costs, it often means directly measured material and labor cost, but since these measures frequently involve prorations, averages, and varying lot quantities, the realism intended by "actual" may be somewhat illusory. See *joint cost; standard cost; historical cost; specific cost.*

3. Cost based on completed rather than estimated transactions.

actuarial Relating to insurance mathematics and statistics.

actuarial basis A basis compatible with principles followed by actuaries: said of computations involving compound interest, retirement and mortality estimates, and the like.

actuary One skilled in insurance mathematics and statistics.

added value Any of the segments of the selling price of a commodity or service attributable to the present or a prior stage for its origin: thus the price (e.g., $10) paid by the consumer of a given product may be assumed to have its origin in the respective selling prices of (a) the *producer* of a component raw material—e.g., an ore ($2); (b) the *processor* of the raw material who disposes of his output at a price ($6) that includes his processing costs and profit; (c) the *distributor* who wholesales the product ($7); and (d) the *retailer* who in turn retails the product ($10) to the *consumer*. Hence, by omitting successive costs of constituent materials and services which have already been accounted for as sales, these four stages may be said to have contributed *added* (dollars of) *value* of 2, 4, 1, and 3, respectively.

added-value tax A percentage tax on the value added (see *added value*) of a commodity or service as each constituent state of its production and distribution is completed: essentially a sales tax divided among the *economic units* contributing to the production and availability of the commodity or service. As compared with the commoner form of sales or turnover tax, an added-value tax reaches back in time and assessment to earlier completed transactions; and by circumventing the compounding effect of a succession of taxes on gross sales it may have to be imposed at a somewhat higher rate than the ordinary form of sales tax it replaces in order to yield a comparable total.

addition (as relating to fixed assets) = *capital expenditure*. See *fixed asset*.

additional markon (retail accounting) An addition to a previously established *markon*.

adequate Fulfilling minimal requirements; satisfactory; acceptable; sufficient.

adjunct account = *absorption account*.

adjusted basis (Federal income taxes) The *basis* used in computing depreciation or gain or loss on sales of fixed or noninventory assets; it includes improvements and other additions over the period of ownership that have not been expensed, and it is decreased by depreciation and other writedowns of cost.

adjusted gross income (Federal income taxes) The *gross income* of an individual reduced by (a) business expenses [as to employees, only those specified in section 62(2) of the Internal Revenue Code], (b) any deductions allowed for income-producing property, (c) certain losses from sales or exchanges of property, (d) self-employment expenses, and (e) moving expenses. Adjusted gross income is the basis for determining the *standard deduction*, the limitation on medical costs (except for persons over 65), contributions, the child-care deduction of working wives, and the possible use of the *optional tax* table.

adjusted historical cost *Historical cost* raised to *current cost* through the medium of a *price index* or series of price indexes. See *current cost*.

adjusting (journal) entry 1. The record made of an *accounting transaction* giving effect to the correction of an error, an accrual, a writeoff, a provision for bad debts or depreciation, or the like. See *journal entry*.

2. (auditing) Any change in the accounts required by an auditor, expressed in the form of a simple or compound journal entry.

adjustment Any change in an account produced by an *adjusting entry*.

administered price The price per unit of commodity where the amount to be paid or received is directly established or substantially influenced by a controlling agent. Such a price, reflecting secular influences, is ordinarily the result of a planned control little influenced by short-term considerations of expanding sales and maximum profits. Administered price may be classified by the character of the controlling agency and the nature of the control thus:

1. A government-administered price, of which there are three general classes:

(a) Ceiling price: a maximum price directly established by government decree, often used in planned economies but also used, in emergencies, in other economies. Effective ceilings limit price as an equilibrating mechanism between supply and demand and must, therefore, be accompanied by rationing or other supplementary measures.

(b) Support price: a price substantially influenced by government control of supply through production control and of trading and credit policies in an effort to maintain minimum price levels for purposes of a redistribution of income within the economy.

(c) Fixed rate: a price directly established by government decree, such as the price for the services of a public utility, usually derived by computing a fair return on the investment, the purpose being to minimize consumer costs and insure adequate service.

2. Industry-administered price: the price usually determined under oligopolistic conditions by the dominant member of the industry or group of dominant members controlling a substantial portion of the industry's production and acting as the price leader for the industry, the purpose being to stabilize the relative position of the individual concern, the group, or the industry as a whole. This price differs from a cartel price in that it is not necessarily the result of an explicit agreement but is nonetheless adopted by all the members of the industry because they recognize that it will advance their mutual interests or because each recognizes the possibility of punitive action by other dominant members who control key resources or who may resort to local price cutting. Although an industry-administered price takes any of numerous forms, it can usually be derived by formula:

(a) Base price: the price from which all other prices are computed, usually reflecting the hypothetical or actual sale of the basic grade of the commodity from a specific geographic (basing) point to customers in a specific geographic location. It may be directly established, but it is usually influenced by manipulation of the supply function of the market by the controlling agents.

(b) Computed price: the price resulting from the application of a formula usually involving an adjustment of the base price for arbitrary or hypothetical transport costs, and differentials in the grade of the commodity. This price may be on a delivered FOB or zone basis and is the price charged in transactions.

(c) Millnet or netback price: the price realized by the producer or seller resulting from the use of the computed price; it may be more or less than the base price depending on the formula used and the location of the purchaser.

Each of the foregoing is illustrated by the price system employed in the steel industry prior to 1924. Under this system all suppliers quoted a uniform delivered price at each destination, made up of the *base price* at Pittsburgh plus standard railroad freight from Pittsburgh to destination, regardless of the mode of shipment (truck, water, or other means). The Pittsburgh price as established by the industry price leader was usually followed by all firms in the industry regardless of mill location. For example, a mill in Chicago would sell to Chicago customers at the *com-*

puted Pittsburgh *base price*—including the standard freight cost to Chicago. The Chicago *millnet* would be the price realized by the Chicago producer after deducting the actual cost of shipping from the *computed price* at which the sale took place.

3. Individual-firm price: the price established by an individual business for its own products regardless of the price charged by competitors, usually under conditions in which the firm has enough control over the market to disregard demand fluctuations and prices of competitors for appreciable periods of time. See *price.*

administration 1. That branch of management embracing the supervision and operation of any organization. One trained in the administration of business enterprise has acquired an intimate working knowledge of forms of business organization: how capital is obtained; relations with financial institutions; labor management; procurement problems; market conditions and methods of market exploitation; foreign trade; the coordination of the various parts of an enterprise so as to achieve the purposes for which the enterprise is carried on; methods of internal organization; the institution and maintenance of internal controls; methods of delegating responsibility; public and human relations; regulations of governmental bodies affecting business; how adaptations may be made to economic and social trends within the business and the industry and in the world at large; and, perhaps the most important feature of all, how any business problem may be recognized, analyzed, and solved. See *policy.*

2. The carrying on of a business or other operation, usually involving a force of employees and relations with outsiders.

3. The collection of an intestate's assets, the payment of his debts, and the distribution of any assets remaining.

4. = *management* (2).

administrative accounting That portion of the accounting process generally associated with management: for example, the functions of the controller, internal auditing, and decisions as to prorations, valuations, reserves, charge-offs, and reporting. The term is sometimes employed in contrast with *cost accounting;* in such use, it is roughly the equivalent of *financial accounting.*

administrative action Within a corporation, a decision of management (as contrasted with *corporate action*), or a decision on a matter of policy ordinarily made by the board of directors. Administrative action embraces the whole field of administration, or the everyday decisions that must be made promptly and as a matter of course, in order that operations may be carried on smoothly and efficiently. The theoretical dividing line between the two types of action is, however, no clearer than that separating the general fields of policy and administration, the one being dependent on the other. In practical situations, the dividing line is still less clear except in those cases in which careful and vigorous attention is continuously devoted to the definition of policy. See *corporate action; policy; administration.*

administrative audit (or **review**) 1. = *preaudit.*

2. = *internal audit.*

administrative budget A financial plan under which an organization carries on its day-to-day affairs under the common forms of administrative *management;* a *budget.* The term is usually employed in contradistinction to *capital* budget or *fund* budget, where the plan covers transactions of a nonoperating, usually carefully circumscribed character.

administrative expense A classification of expense incurred in the general direction of an enterprise as a whole, as contrasted with expense of a more specific function, such as manufacturing or selling, but not including *income deductions.* Items included under this head vary with the nature of the business, but usually include salaries of top officers, rent, and other general-office expense. Typical are the following:

Salaries—officers & executives
Salaries—general-office employees
Travel expense
Legal & auditing
Office-building maintenance
Depreciation—furniture & fixtures
Stationery & office supplies
Telephone & telegraph
Postage
Light & water
Taxes other than income
Insurance on lives of officers
Subscriptions & dues
Donations
Revenue stamps

administrator 1. One skilled in administration.
2. One named by a court to take charge of the assets of an intestate and to dispose of them in accordance with law or ruling of the court. See *executor*.

admissible asset 1. (Federal income taxes) An asset which under provisions and regulations of former excess-profits-tax laws had been allowed as an inclusion under invested capital.
2. (insurance accounting) = *admitted asset*.

admitted asset (insurance) Any asset, as determined under the laws of various jurisdictions, having a value in liquidation.

ad valorem Designating a property tax or import or other duty computed as a percentage (rate) of the value of the property.

advance 1. A payment of cash or the transfer of goods for which an *accounting(2)* must be rendered by the recipient at some later date.
2. A payment on a contract before its completion.
3. The payment of wages, salaries, or commissions before they have been earned.

adventure A commercial speculative undertaking: specifically, one involving goods sent abroad for sale at the best price obtainable; a security flotation by a syndicate; a *joint venture*. The term is now seldom used.

affiliate (or **affiliated company**) A corporation or other organization related to another by owning or being owned, by common management or by a long-term lease of its properties or other control device. See *control* (*3*).

affiliation Control of, by, or under common control with, another. An affiliation exists between a *holding* or *parent* company and its *subsidiary*, or between two corporations or other organizations owned or *controlled* by a third. See *control* (*3*).

affreightment A contract for transporting goods by sea: a *charter party* or an ocean bill of lading.

age The number of years or other time periods an asset or asset group has remained in service at a given date.

agency 1. The relation between principal and agent. See *agent*.
2. (governmental accounting) Any unit of government administering an appropriation, allocation, or allotment; as, a department, commission, authority, administration, or board.

agency fund A fund consisting of assets held under an agency relationship for another.

agenda 1. Work to be done; an auditor's agenda consisting of notes made in the field, inquiries, and other matters to be taken care of at a later point in the audit.
2. Any list of points for discussion or action.

agent One who represents, acts for, and accounts to another. The powers of a *general* agent are broad. He initiates transactions in the name of his principal and carries on operations within a large discretionary area. His functions often resemble those of a general manager. A *special* agent, on the other hand, is restricted to the performance of a single act or the conduct of a single transaction.

aging An analysis of the elements of

individual *accounts receivable* according to the time elapsed after the dates of billing or the due dates, usually the former; employed as an aid in determining an allowance or the propriety of an allowance for bad debts.
—age, v.t.

AJE = *adjusting journal entry.*

algorism Mathematics employing the ten Arabic digits.

algorithm 1. = algorism.
2. A rule for solving ordinary arithmetic problems such as the area of a circle.

allied company = *affiliated company.*

all-inclusive income statement An income statement containing all items of profit and loss given recognition during the period covered by the statement. Because it leaves little to the discretion of management and the public accountant, and is thus claimed to be more objective than a statement in which "nonperformance" items or prior-year adjustments are omitted, it has been favored by the Executive Committee of the American Accounting Association (Accounting Concepts and Standards Underlying Corporate Financial Statements), and by the Securities and Exchange Commission (in its 14th Annual Report (1948), p. 111). However, in SEC Regulation S-X, as revised December 20, 1950, Rule 5.03, items 16–18, the Commission adopts a "straddle." The current AICPA position also fails to resolve the issue. See *income deduction.*

allocate 1. To charge an item or group of items of revenue or cost to one or more objects, activities, processes, operations, or products, in accordance with cost responsibilities, benefits received, or other readily identifiable measure of application or consumption. Examples: to charge the amount of a voucher to an expense account; to spread fire-insurance-premium costs to departments in proportion to the insurable values of the assets located in such departments. In this sense, allocation may refer to a direct or indirect expense. See *prorate.*
2. To distribute the total cost of a *lump-sum purchase* over the items purchased or departments affected.
3. To spread a cost systematically over two or more time periods.
4. (governmental accounting) To transfer, by administrative authority, an *appropriation* or a part thereof from one agency to another.

allocation The process or result of allocating.

allotment 1. (governmental accounting) The administrative assignment by an agency of a part of an *appropriation, allocation,* or *apportionment* to a subdivision of the agency. The authority thus conferred is to incur liabilities or obligations up to a specified amount for prescribed, often broad or discretionary, purposes.
2. An assignment of pay for the benefit of dependents.
3. The division of available or anticipated revenues among specific classes of expenditures.
4. The distribution of securities in accordance with or in proportion to applications from subscribers; the assignment of shares in a syndicate or other undertaking; the number of shares or amount so assigned.
—allot, v.t.

allotment ledger (governmental accounting) A subsidiary ledger containing an account for each allotment, showing the amount allotted, expenditures, encumbrances, and unencumbered balance.

allowance 1. Permitted tolerance in measurement, quality, or quantity of goods; also normal or permitted shrinkage, breakage, spoilage, or other loss in handling, using, or holding.
2. In the settlement of a debt, a deduction granted or accepted by the creditor for damage, delay, shortage, imperfection, or other cause, excluding discounts and returns.
3. An expenditure permitted by superior administrative authority to an organizational subdivision or to an agent. Often in the form of a round sum, it

may be more or less in amount than the expense incurred, thereby obviating the need for securing proof of payment. Examples: an allowance for branch-office rent; an allowance in lieu of actual expenses, as for the maintenance and operation of an automobile owned by a salesman.

4. An account reflecting lost usefulness, or a loss or an absorption of cost (i.e., an accumulation of expired or transferred costs). See *reserve (1); provision; depreciation; expense.*

5. A provision or an accumulation of provisions for the loss or decline in worth of an asset: a *valuation account* or an addition to a valuation account offset by a charge or charges to expense; a *reserve(2)*. Example: an allowance for bad debts or for depreciation; on a balance sheet allowances appear as a reduction of the asset value to which they are related.

all-purpose financial statement A financial statement serving, as far as possible, the needs of all users. The financial statements to which professional accountants append their reports are nearly always all-purpose statements, since the accountant does not limit the use to which the statement will be put. The term is used in contrast with *condensed statement*, which has now largely fallen into disuse, and *special-purpose statement*.

alteration An improvement or modification made of a fixed asset that does not represent an addition to or increase in the quantity of the services to be yielded by the asset.

alternative cost Cost under conditions other than those currently obtaining, as from a change from producing to purchasing, a change in a production method, the use of a more efficient machine, the substitution of one raw material for another, a modification in a product specification, or an increase or decrease, whatever the cause, in one or more component costs. Where no plant alterations are involved, overhead remaining the same, the elements making up an alternative cost are direct and variable items. Although they may serve many purposes, alternative costs are most often estimated and compared with actual costs in the testing of cost-reduction proposals or in providing background for the problems of future production. See *opportunity cost; cost.*

amalgamation A combination under a single head of all or a portion of the assets and liabilities of two or more business units by *merger* or *consolidation*.

amortization 1. The gradual extinguishment of any amount over a period of time: as, the retirement of a debt by serial payments to the creditor or into a sinking fund; the periodic writedown of an insurance premium or a bond premium.

2. A reduction of the book value of a fixed asset: a generic term for the depreciation, depletion, writedown, or write-off of a limited-life asset or group of such assets, an acquired intangible asset, or a prepaid expense, either by a direct credit or through the medium of a *valuation* account; hence, the amount of such a reduction. See *depreciation.*

3. = *accelerated depreciation.*

amortization schedule 1. A table in which computations are provided for the periodic writedown until maturity of the premium paid on a bond or note.

2. Any table of prospective payments or writedowns relating to an obligation or account.

An *accumulation schedule* contrasts with an *amortization schedule* by building up the initial cost or other amount to a higher figure.

Using the example provided under *bond valuation*, an amortization schedule could be prepared similar to the one at the top of the following page.

A less exacting amortization method would be to charge each year with $\frac{1}{20}$ of the premium of \$78.12, or \$3.906—52

Year	Actual Interest	Effective Interest	Amortization	Book Value
Cost of bond				$1,108.12
1	$ 20.00	$ 16.62	$ 3.38	1,104.74
2	20.00	16.57	3.43	1,101.31
3	20.00	16.52	3.48	1,097.83
4	20.00	16.47	3.53	1,094.30
5	20.00	16.41	3.59	1,090.71
6	20.00	16.36	3.64	1,087.07
18	20.00	15.65	4.35	1,038.89
19	20.00	15.59	4.41	1,034.48
20	20.00	15.52	4.48	1,030.00
Totals	$400.00	$321.88	$78.12	

cents more than the initial item of the schedule, the same for the 11th year, and 58 cents less for the 20th year.

amortize 1. To write off a portion or all of the cost of an asset; to *depreciate* or *deplete*.
2. To retire (debt) over a period of years.
3. To subject any amount to a process of extinguishment.

amortized cost Cost less portions written off: the valuation basis of capital assets and of investments, inventories, and other assets where original cost has been reduced by depreciation or to an amount equal to market or other standard of valuation. See *cost absorption; depreciated cost.*

amount of an annuity = *compound amount of 1 per period.*

amount of 1 = *compound amount of 1.*

analytic schedule (insurance) A system of evaluating the relative fire hazards involved in such matters as protection, exposure, construction, and occupancy; used as a standard in some states for determining fire-insurance rates except for dwellings, churches, and certain other structures.

analyze 1. To determine or examine the composition of an item, account, or amount, usually by reference to its historical origin; particularly (auditing) to review and set forth in a working paper the details or classified summary of items in an account, obtained or substantiated, where necessary, by reference to sources, and accompanied by explanations of major items and by cross-references to related accounts. See *scan; verify; vouch; audit.*
—*analysis, n.*
2. To interpret or draw conclusions from a financial statement or statements.
3. To review a transaction or series of actual or proposed transactions to determine their effect on the accounts or on the principles to be followed in giving effect to them.

annual audit An *audit(4)* by a professional accountant covering a year's transactions.

annual closing The posting of *closing entries* taking place at the end of a fiscal year.

annual financial statement A balance sheet of any *accounting unit* as at the end of the last day of its fiscal year, or an income or other related statement covering the year's operations or bearing that date.

annualize (Federal income taxes) To expand to an annual basis: the procedure under the Internal Revenue Code whereby taxable income for a fractional year (e.g., in the case of a change of accounting period) is multiplied by a fraction equal to 12 divided by the number of months in the shorter period. The tax computed on the income thus expanded is then reduced by application of the same fraction reversed. This process is necessary in order to subject taxable income in the short period to the same effective tax rate as would be applicable to the proportionately larger income of a full year.

annual report 1. Any report prepared at yearly intervals.
2. A statement of the financial condition and operating results of an enterprise, prepared yearly for submission to interested parties; particularly, a report rendered each year to stockholders, and often to the employees and the public, by the board of directors or one or more of the principal officers

of a corporation, summarizing its operations for the preceding year and including a balance sheet, income statement, often a funds-flow statement, and the auditor's report, together with comments by the chairman or president of the corporation on the year's business, labor relations, research program, public service, market prospects, and the like. See *reporting; audit report.*

annuitant The recipient of an *annuity.*

annuity 1. A series, or one of a series, of equal payments at fixed intervals; the right to receive such payments. An annuity may be for a specified period, as in the case of payments into a sinking fund: contingent, as in the field of life insurance, or perpetual, as in the case of an endowment fund. See interest table indexed under *compound-interest formula.*

2. A periodic payment to a retired employee; a *pension.*

annuity agreement (or **contract**) An agreement whereby money or other property is made available to another on condition that the recipient bind himself to hold and administer the property and to pay the donor or other designated person a stipulated annuity ceasing with a specified date or event such as the annuitant's death; also called annuity bond.

annuity certain An annuity payable for a stated number of periods as distinct from one dependent for its duration upon some contingency, such as marriage or death. See *annuity due; annuity.*

annuity cost A term referring to an accrual or outlay in connection with anticipatory payments under a pension plan to retired employees. In creating the fund and maintaining it, periodic contributions by the employer will ordinarily include, in the case of employees on the payroll before the plan was instituted, an amount based on past as well as present services.

annuity due An annuity where payment is made at the beginning of each period, rather than at the end, as in an *ordinary annuity.*

annuity fund 1. The amount resulting from the accumulation of periodic payments of *annuities.*

2. The fund created as the result of an *annuity agreement.*

annuity method (of depreciation) See *depreciation method.*

antedate To affix a date preceding the date written or executed, as in an insurance policy, where the coverage often begins at a point of time earlier than the day the policy is officially issued.

anticipated cost The addition to operating costs resulting from the use of *lifo* during a period of rising prices; also known as *inventory profit.*

anticipated (or **anticipatory**) **profit** A profit recorded in advance of its realization; paper profit. Examples: profit on sales contracted for but not yet consummated; profit on installment sales represented by installments not currently due. See *realize; accrual basis.*

antilogarithm The number obtained when the base of a logarithm system is raised to the power indicated by the *logarithm;* symbolized by "antilog" for the common logarithm system. For example, to determine the 11th root of 15 (or $\sqrt[11]{15}$), let x be the value sought; then

$$\log x = \frac{\log 15}{11} = \frac{1.176091}{11} = 0.106917 + .$$

The value 176091 is taken from the illustrative logarithms on page 268. It is now necessary to determine x, the antilogarithm of 0.106917. By reference to the logarithm table, the values 106871 and 107210 are found to be the closest to 106917, the fractional interval being

$$\frac{106917 - 106871}{107210 - 106871} = \frac{46}{339},$$

or about $\frac{1}{7}$. The antilogarithms of the two values 106871 and 107210 are revealed by the tables to be 1279 and 1280. The value of x lies about $\frac{1}{7}$ of the interval between them, and, since the characteristic of x is 0, x, the antilogarithm of 0.106917, is thus 1.27914, correct to the fourth decimal. See *logarithm.*

APB The Accounting Principles Board of the American Institute of Certified Public Accountants.

a posteriori Pertaining to the process of *reasoning(2)* whereby *principles* or other *propositions* are derived from observations of *facts.*

application of funds See *statement of sources and applications of funds.*

applied cost Cost that has been allocated to a product or activity. See *cost; overhead.*

apportionment 1. The distribution of a cost over several periods of time in proportion to anticipated benefits. See *spread; overhead.*
2. (governmental accounting) The administrative assignment, subject to the approval of the Bureau of the Budget, of all or a portion of an appropriation to a part of a fiscal year or to a specific activity or object.

appraisal The act of *appraising;* the result of appraising; an appraisal report.

appraisal method (of depreciation) See *depreciation method.*

appraisal report A statement, in summary or detail, prepared by engineers or other qualified persons, of the cost or value of an asset, asset group, or all of the fixed assets of a business.

appraisal surplus The excess of estimated depreciated replacement cost, or other basis of measurement, of fixed or other assets over their cost or book value. It is given expression as a credit on books of account when appraisal values are recorded (a practice at present rare), and thus may find its way into financial statements. It is sometimes referred to as unrealized profit, and it was customary during the inflationary period of the 1920's periodically to reduce appraisal surplus by transfers to depreciation expense, to the allowance or reserve for depreciation, or to earned surplus. In recent years such credits have been disapproved, thus leaving the account intact; but the disposal of an appraisal-surplus account, particularly after the property to which it relates is no longer in existence, presents a problem that has not yet been satisfactorily resolved. Under the laws of most states, appraisal surplus is generally not available for cash or property dividends to stockholders; at the time of its creation it is essentially a valuation account rather than "surplus." See *realized appreciation.*

appraise 1. To establish cost or value by systematic procedures that include physical examination, pricing, and often engineering estimates.
2. To examine and weigh critically.

appraised value Cost or value established by appraisal; as, cost of reproduction less observed depreciation. See *appraise.*

appraiser One who appraises property: an owner, a prospective buyer, or, more commonly, a group of professionally skilled persons holding themselves out as experts on *valuation.*

appreciation Increase in value of property: the excess of the present value of property over book value. The term is applied (a) to the excess of appraisal value over book value of fixed assets (= *appraisal surplus* when given expression on books of account), and (b) to the increase in the market price of securities and commodities sold or quoted on exchanges.
—*appreciate, v.t. & i.*

appreciation surplus = *appraisal surplus.*

appropriate Suitable, desirable, reasonable, or necessary in a particular context; often used by accountants as signifying conformity with the value judgments implicit in current practices. See *significant; proper.*

appropriated surplus Earned surplus (retained earnings) earmarked on the books of account and in financial statements for some specific or general purpose. It takes the form of a separate account to which earned surplus is transferred, usually by action of the board of directors or stockholders; it remains as a subdivision of earned surplus, and is preferably so shown on the balance sheet, although sometimes appearing in a separate category preceding net worth. Its purpose is to indicate that an equivalent unearmarked amount in assets is not to be paid out as dividends but is to be retained as a safeguard against the contingency or event indicated. It is ultimately returned to earned surplus undiminished, the related expenditure, if any, being currently expensed or capitalized according to its nature. Examples: an appropriation for a plant extension or for a possible future inventory shrinkage. See *earned surplus.*

In practice, appropriated surplus was at one time the repository of charges relating to the purpose of the account which thus escaped classification as items of profit and loss. This is no longer considered good practice. See *income deduction; nonrecurring charge.* Some accountants have advocated the permanent separation of appropriated surplus from earned surplus, particularly where it offsets an equivalent investment in fixed or other noncurrent assets.

appropriation 1. An expenditure authorization with specific limitations as to amount, purpose, and time; a formal advance approval of an expenditure or class of expenditures from designated resources available or estimated to be available. An appropriation may vary in binding force from an expression of intent by the management of a business concern to a restrictive limitation by the legislature imposed on a government agency.
2. The amount of future expenditures so approved.
3. The document evidencing the act and the amount, describing the purpose, and giving essential particulars concerning the character of authorized future expenditures, as in the case of appropriations for capital assets.
4. A distribution of net income to various accounts. See *appropriation of net income.*
5. An earmarking of *retained earnings;* = *appropriated surplus.*
—*appropriate, v.t.*

appropriation account 1. (governmental accounting) The account of a government agency to which the amount of a legislative appropriation is credited; it is eventually offset by expenditure or by a cancellation, return, or lapsing of any remaining balance.
2. (British usage) The account to which the profit-and-loss balance for the year is carried and taxes and dividends are charged, the balance being transferred to *revenue reserves.*

appropriation act A law providing funds for the operation of a governmental agency over a specified period, usually a year, the activities making up the operation usually having previously been authorized by an *organic act.*

appropriation budget A document fixing specific allowances for the budget period.

appropriation ledger (governmental accounting) A subsidiary ledger containing an account with each appropriation, showing the amount appropriated, the expenditures, and often the encumbrances and the unencumbered balance of each appropriation; or, if allotments are made and a separate ledger maintained therefor, the appropriations, the allotments, and the unallotted balance of each appropriation. Appropriation ledgers have recently been replaced by records maintained on an ordinary accrual-accounting basis.

appropriation of net income The disposition of noncorporate net income by the owner or partners, or of corporate net income by resolution of the directors (or, in Britain, by stockholders), sometimes summarized at the foot of an income statement; as, the setting aside or commitment of net income for dividends, the allocation of net income to a sinking fund or other *appropriated-surplus* reserve, or the transfer of net income or the balance of net income to earned surplus (retained earnings). Among corporate enterprises there is some difference of opinion as to what items are income deductions (i.e., deductions from operating revenue before the determination of net income) and what items should be regarded as net-income appropriations; as a rule, the former are unusual expenses including losses; the latter, transactions with stockholders or an earmarking of earned surplus. In British practice, appropriations also include "direct" (i.e., income) taxes. See *income deduction; net income.*

appropriation period (governmental accounting) The year or other period of time during which an *appropriation* may be obligated or expended.

appropriation receipt (governmental accounting) A receipt of a special fund or trust fund, available for expenditure only for specified purposes.

appropriation refund (governmental accounting) The return of an advance or the recovery of an improper disbursement, regarded as a full or partial cancellation of the original expenditure and hence available for reobligation or re-expenditure.

appropriation reimbursement (governmental accounting) An addition to an appropriation arising from the sale of goods or services to another branch of the government or to an outsider.

appropriation request (governmental accounting) A petition for funds by an administrative or other agency of government to the legislature. Under current practices, the request, known as an *account(5)*, consists of suggested appropriation language, brief schedules of anticipated costs of *programs* with a narrative *justification* for each, particulars of any financing available from other sources, and an *objective statement.*

appropriation section A final division sometimes attached to an income statement showing the disposition of net income as between dividends, surplus reserves, and earned surplus (retained earnings). See *appropriation of net income.*

appropriation (transfer) warrant See *warrant(5).*

approximate Containing *error;* a quantity, or verbal characterization, which cannot validly be claimed to coincide in all respects with results which might be secured by more *precise* consideration or treatment.

approximation A procedure designed to elicit *approximate* results.

a priori 1. Pertaining to a line of *reasoning(2)*, based on specific assumptions, rather than experience; deductive.
2. Characterizing the formulation of explicit hypotheses, definitions, axioms, and rules of inference prior to undertaking an investigation or embarking on a course of action.

arbitrage Buying and selling simultaneously the same commodity in two or more markets with the expectation of profiting from temporary differences in prices.

arbitrary Determined by individual judgment for which no better explanation can be given in terms of accepted rules or standards than for an alternative judgment. Arbitrary decisions are often the basis for disposing of such problems as the allocation of overhead, the division of cost between joint products, the classification of unusual but minor costs, the making of an allowance to a customer, and the disposal of minor additions to or improvements of fixed assets. See *value judgment.*

arithmetic mean The result obtained by dividing the sum of two or more quantities by the number of items; usually denoted by a symbol such as $\bar{Y}$. It is often intended as a representative quantity or as a measure of the central tendency of a group of items. See *average; mean; geometric mean.*

Arithmetic means are of two kinds: simple and weighted. The simple arithmetic mean, or simple average, sometimes called unweighted, is the sum of a set of values divided by the number of such values. To obtain a weighted arithmetic mean, each value is multiplied by some index of importance or weight before the summation is made. The divisor is then the sum of the weights. The most widely used weights are the frequencies (such as inventory quantities) with which the values (such as inventory prices) occur. Thus, the numbers 4, 7, and 10 may occur with frequencies of 5, 3, and 2, respectively. The simple mean would be

$$\frac{4 + 7 + 10}{3} = 7,$$

while the weighted mean, using the frequencies as weights, would be

$$\frac{(5 \times 4) + (3 \times 7) + (2 \times 10)}{5 + 3 + 2} = 6.1,$$

the smaller result being attributable to the greater frequency of the smaller numbers, which have a larger influence on the calculation. In mathematical symbols, the tabular expression of the above figures may be expressed thus:

	f	Y	$f \cdot Y$
	5	4	20
	3	7	21
	2	10	20
Totals	10	21	61
	$\Sigma(f)$	$\Sigma(Y)$	$\Sigma(f \cdot Y)$

where f stands for the frequencies (the number of times the Y's occur), Y the value, and $f \cdot Y$ the weighted value. Σ means "the sum of," a symbol used to indicate that the amount following it is the sum of a series of f's, Y's, $f \cdot Y$'s, or other numbers; thus, $\Sigma(f) = 10$, the sum of the three preceding "f, s," 5, 3, and 2.

The formula expressing the relation between a weighted arithmetic mean ($\bar{Y}$) and the group of values from which it is derived may be stated thus:

$$\bar{Y} = \frac{\Sigma(f \cdot Y)}{\Sigma(f)}.$$

For the simple arithmetic mean, where the frequency f of each value Y is uniformly 1, the formula becomes

$$\bar{Y} = \frac{\Sigma(Y)}{\Sigma(f)}.$$

The arithmetic mean may be characterized as the *central tendency* of a group of values, because the sum of the differences, or weighted differences, when the mean is subtracted from each of the values, is zero. Thus, in the above examples, $(4 - 7) + (7 - 7) + (10 - 7) = 0$; and $5(4 - 6.1) + 3(7 - 6.1) + 2(10 - 6.1) = 0$. This suggests a second method of determining the arithmetic mean: by first estimating its value, and then employing the above formula to determine its exact amount. If A is the estimated arithmetic mean, then, using the first of the above equations and subtracting A from each side, the weighted arithmetic mean may be determined:

$$\bar{Y} - A = \frac{\Sigma(f \cdot Y)}{\Sigma(f)} - A = \frac{\Sigma(f \cdot Y) - \Sigma(f \cdot A)}{\Sigma(f)}$$

$$= \frac{\Sigma(f \cdot [Y - A])}{\Sigma(f)};$$

Transposing, and substituting d (representing deviations) for $Y - A$, and N (number of items) for $\Sigma\,(f)$,

$$\bar{Y} = A + \frac{\Sigma(f \cdot d)}{N}.$$

Thus, in the example, if the weighted arithmetic mean is estimated as 5,

$$\bar{Y} = 5 + \frac{5(4 - 5) + 3(7 - 5) + 2(10 - 5)}{5 + 3 + 2}$$

$$= 5 + \frac{11}{10} = \frac{61}{10} = 6.1.$$

The formula indicates that, to find the arithmetic mean, it is necessary only to add to an estimated mean the weighted average of the deviations d of the other values from the estimated mean. The same relation holds for the simple arithmetic mean as well, the simple mean being merely a special case of the weighted mean in which each frequency f is equal to 1.

When it is noted that A is arbitrary and that d may be stated in any unit, further computational simplifications become possible. A may be set equal to zero and d stated in units of one. Only at the end of the computations need A and d be adjusted. This may be illustrated by reproducing the data on sugar-refining costs given under *correlation table;* in this table the costs range from $1,160 to $1,500. By restating them in units of $10, an initial simplification can be made for purposes of computation; the original units can be restored after the calculations. With this simplification, the data are first grouped into classes, called *class intervals,* and the center of the class, or class midpoint, is chosen as representative of the items. When the frequencies are listed, the results may be expressed in tabular form (see the following table).

Y		d	f	fd
Class Intervals	Class Midpoint	Deviations	Frequencies	Frequencies Times Deviations
116–120	118.5	−2	8	−16
121–125	123.5	−1	13	−13
126–130	128.5	0	19	0
131–135	133.5	1	7	7
136–140	138.5	2	3	6
141–145	143.5	3	0	0
		3	50	−16
		$\Sigma(d)$	$\Sigma(f)$	$\Sigma(fd)$

The arbitrary origin chosen was at class midpoint 128.5 and was set equal to zero for purposes of computation, while the class intervals, which were originally stated five units apart, were reduced to units of one. Substitution of the adjusted results in the formula for the arithmetic mean gives

$$\bar{Y} = A + \frac{(\Sigma fd)(c)}{N} = 128.5 + \frac{(-16)(5)}{50}$$
$$= 126.9,$$

where c denotes the class-interval-unit adjustment. Hence, the arithmetic mean is 126.9 × $10, or $1,269.00.

The steps may now be summarized. After the data have been grouped into class intervals of equal width, such as the five units used above, and centered on the class midpoints, the following operations may be performed:

1. Assume an arbitrary origin A, which for convenience may be at one of the class midpoints.
2. Set $A = 0$.
3. Take positive and negative deviations d, in units of one, about the arbitrary origin; that is, write down the integers 1, 2, . . . , with plus signs in one direction and minus signs in the other direction.
4. Multiply the individual deviations d by their respective frequencies f, and add together the results of all such multiplications.
5. Correct the result of this last operation by adjusting to the original units; i.e., multiply Σfd by the class-interval unit c (5, in the above example).
6. Average these results to obtain $\Sigma fd \cdot c/N$, and add them to A, the arbitrary origin. The result will be the arithmetic mean, since $A + \Sigma fd \cdot c/N = \bar{Y}$.

arithmetic progression A numerical series the value of which increases from one term to the next by the same amount; as, 1, 3, 5, 7, 9, . . . ; .25, .5, .75, 1, 1.25, ... The total of such a series, where S is the total, a the first and l the last of the series, d the constant difference, and n the number of terms, is expressed as follows:

$$S = a + (a + d) + (a + 2d) + \cdots + (a + [n - 1]d);$$

and

$$S = l + (l - d) + (l - 2d) + \cdots + (l - [n - 1]d).$$

Hence,

$$2S = a + l + a + l + a + l + \cdots + a + l = n(a + l),$$

and

$$S = \frac{n}{2}(a + l).$$

If a, d, and n are known and l is unknown, then

$$S = \frac{n}{2}(2a + [n - 1]d);$$

if both a and d are 1, then

$$S = \frac{n}{2}(n + 1).$$

See *geometric progression.*

arm's-length *adj.* On a commercial basis, dealing with or as though dealing with independent, unrelated persons; competitive; straightforward; involving no favoritism or irregularity; as, an arm's-length purchase. A buyer and a seller both free to act, each seeking his own best economic interest and agreeing on a price, are said to have an arm's-length relationship. Transactions between affiliated companies are not ordinarily recorded (or regarded by outsiders) as being at arm's length even though expressed in terms of market values.
—*arm's length, n.*

arrangement 1. A proceeding under Chapter XI of the National Bankruptcy Act, designed to simplify settlements with creditors by financially embarrassed small corporations under the jurisdiction of a Federal court. See *bankruptcy.*
2. Loosely, any agreement with creditors covering the disposition of amounts owing.
3. (statistics) Any ordering of n objects. See *permutation.*

array A group of numbers or other symbols placed in order, as in increasing or decreasing sequence.
—*array, v.t.*

arrival draft See *draft.*

articles of incorporation The document prepared by the persons establishing a corporation in the United States and filed with state authorities; one copy, returned with a certificate of incorporation, becomes the corporate charter, enabling the corporation to function. The information filed with the state includes the corporate name and address, the names of the incorporators, the nature of the property to be acquired and the business to be carried on, proposed corporate powers, and the character and amount of capital stock to be authorized and issued. The older word, *charter*, at one time referred to an individual statute that through the first quarter of the 19th century was the only device employed by state legislatures for permitting the establishment of a private corporation. The corporation laws of the United States and foreign countries alike now provide for the creation and licensing of a business corporation by action of administrative authorities. See *corporation.*

articulation statement = *spread sheet.*

artificial person An organization, such as a corporation, endowed by law and custom with functions or powers resembling those of individual beings; an unincorporated association may have similar characteristics, as where it can sue and be sued in its own name. The term originated with Chief Justice Marshall in the Dartmouth College Case (4 Wheat. 626 [1819]): "A corporation is an artificial being, invisible, intangible, and existing only in contemplation of law." A more modern concept is to regard a corporation as a group of natural persons authorized to act as though they were but one person.

as at At: a phrase qualifying the date of a financial statement or an action taken, often indicating that adjustments or other decisions made after that date have been incorporated.

as is In its present condition; without warranty: a designation attaching to an item held for sale which forestalls any claim on the seller after a sale has been made.

ask(-ed, -ing) price The price at which the owner of property, particularly a security or commodity, formally offers to sell it, as on an exchange.

assessable capital stock 1. Capital stock not fully paid, and subject to calls. See *capital stock.*

2. The capital stock of banks formerly subject to "double liability": for the par value paid in plus an equal amount subject to call in case of insolvency. See *double liability.*

assessed value The value of property as appraised for taxation and other purposes. Appraised values are for the most part determined by an assessor whose jurisdiction extends over a designated primary or overlapping assessment district. Primary districts, fixed by state law, are frequently counties, which together cover the entire state. Assessors in primary districts establish values for both state and local-government levies. Cities, for various reasons, may not be satisfied with the county assessor's valuations and may ask and obtain permission from the state legislature to establish values for property located within their boundaries. Thus, city property may have one assessed value for state, county, township, and school-district purposes and another for city-tax purposes. Every state has primary districts; approximately half of the states have overlapping districts.

Properties are assessed as at a certain date. Personal property is usually appraised annually, and real property annually, biennially, or even quadrennially. If real property is not appraised annually, adjustments may be made each year for depreciation, for new construction or improvements, and for destruction or damage during the year.

Real estate is appraised by the assessor on the basis of a field examination involving the same factors as those underlying the valuation of property for sale or mortgage purposes. Separate values are usually established for land and buildings. Personal property, on the other hand, is most often self-assessed; that is, the taxpayer is required to fill out a form in which he lists various classes of property owned by him and indicates their values. These returns are subject to review and sometimes field tests by the assessor.

Properties of utilities and other concerns whose assets and business extend into two or more counties or across state borders may be assessed by a state agency which determines the valuation falling within each county. The same state agency may also fix the taxable values of the capital stock of business corporations located within the state and certify to local assessors the portions of the value located within the various assessment districts.

After properties have been appraised, their assessed values, legal descriptions, owners, addresses, and similar items are entered on an assessment roll. In the case of real estate, the assessed value may also be entered in a permanent assessment record containing a detailed description of all of the factors that went to make up the particular assessment: a photograph of the property, its dimensions, the kinds of materials used in improvements, and other details. A new assessment roll is prepared each year, while the permanent assessment record, serving for many years, presents a complete history of the assessed valuation of each item of real property.

Provision is usually made for the review of individual assessments by an administrative agency either upon appeal by the taxpayer or on the agency's own initiative. If the taxpayer is not satisfied with the decision, he may in some cases appeal to a higher administrative agency and in others directly to a court of law. His appeal to the court must usually be premised on the ground that the assessment is illegal, that the assessor or the administrative review agency has acted fraudulently or arbitrarily, or that the property has been grossly overvalued either in relation to the values of other like property or in respect to its own inherent value.

After the assessed values have been established and reviewed, the assessment rolls are turned over to another agency for the computation of the amount of tax. The first step is to determine the rate of tax by dividing the total taxes to be levied by the assessed value applicable to the property unit. For example, a county levies $1,000,000 in property taxes, the assessed valuations being $100,000,000. The tax rate will be 1 percent of the assessed value or, as it is more commonly designated, $1 (i.e., on each $100 of assessed value). The owner of an item of property located in the county and having an assessed value of $10,000 will have to pay county taxes in the amount of $100. In addition, the same property will also have to pay city, township, school, and, if the state levies property taxes, state taxes. The tax levied by each of these units would be determined and distributed in the same manner as the county tax.

After the rates have been computed, a tax roll is prepared consisting of a list showing the legal description of each item of real estate or the name of the owner in the case of personal property, the assessed value, the tax rates, and the total taxes to be paid. The same tax roll may list the taxes applicable to all governmental units with two possible exceptions: the taxes of overlapping assessment districts, and those of any governmental unit that collects its own taxes. Thus, a county may collect the taxes for all the taxing units located within it except cities.

The nature of the property tax is such as to encourage property undervaluation, despite the fact that the law may specify that property shall be assessed at its "true" or "full" value, which is ordinarily defined as the value which a buyer is willing to give for it and a seller is willing to accept under conditions where there is no pressure on either of the parties. Undervaluation is often practiced in those states that levy state property taxes; by undervaluation local governments can escape paying a larger share of the state tax levy.

To avoid undervaluation or to nullify its effects, state laws usually provide for the adjustment of assessed values by boards of equalization who may order counties or other districts to raise their assessed values. Equalization may be applied to all property in the district on a uniform basis, to certain types of property, or to particular units within a district. If a city assessment district has been established, it may be necessary to equalize the assessed values of city property with those of properties located within the primary district but outside the city.

Since the property tax is still an important source of revenue for local governments, the assessed values constituting the bases of these taxes are of prime importance. The assessor has a large responsibility in the determination of whether local governments are to have adequate revenues. Where the state law or charter provides that the rate must not exceed a certain figure, the assessor, or a board of equalization, by increasing assessed values, can make it possible for a city or other local government to increase its revenues; by reducing them, an assessor might materially subtract from the local unit's revenues.

Assessed valuations are often employed in setting the limit on the amount of indebtedness that a governmental unit may incur under the provisions of constitution, statute, or charter. For example, the constitution of the

State of Illinois provides that no governmental unit within the state shall incur indebtedness which in the aggregate will exceed 5 percent of the assessed value of its taxable property. An increase or decrease in assessed values thus not only affects the amount of property taxes which can be raised but may also limit the amount of indebtedness that can be incurred. Sometimes, too, state aid is distributed among local units on the basis of their assessed valuations.

It may be of importance to governmental units to know the assessed value of (Federal, religious, and other) property exempted from taxes so that the consequent loss in revenues may from time to time be subject to review. In some states, homesteads with an assessed value up to a certain amount (e.g., $7,500) are exempt from taxation. In those cases, as soon as a homestead property acquires an assessed value in excess of the allowed maximum, it becomes subject to property tax.

assessment 1. The process of valuing property for taxation purposes.
2. Any recurrent tax (e.g., a real-estate or personal-property tax) levied by governmental authority.
3. A tax for improvements or improvement repairs relating to such items as paving, sidewalks, sewers, or drainage constructed by municipal authority; also known as a "special assessment" or "improvement" tax.
4. Entry of a tax on an official tax roll.
5. A levy on stockholders, owners of beneficial interests, members of a club, and others, for the purpose of raising additional capital or absorbing a loss.

asset Any owned physical object (tangible) or right (intangible) having a money value; an item or source of wealth, expressed in terms of its cost, depreciated cost, or, less frequently, some other value; hence, any cost benefiting a future period.

Asset is to be distinguished from *property* in that *asset* (a) means any balance-sheet item, and (b) is usually associated with cost or the portion thereof recognized for balance-sheet purposes. *Property*, having a more restricted application, is more often applied to items transferable between persons, any right to its uses and benefits being safeguarded and governed by a body of law.

Accounting conventionally recognizes certain sources of wealth as assets but not others. Typical examples of the former are cash, investments, claims against others (receivables), materials, supplies, goods in process of manufacture or held for sale, land, buildings, machinery, tools and other plant assets, prepaid expenses, purchased goodwill, patents, and trademarks. An item of wealth may be an asset recognized in the accounts, even though not realizable in cash, as, for example, a prepaid expense relating to an expected future activity, such an expenditure being regarded as recoverable in the form of future services or benefits. The amounts at which assets are recorded do not usually indicate their current value, but rather cost or that portion of cost fairly allocable to succeeding periods.

Assets not conventionally recognized in the accounts are generally intangibles or are derived from costs not readily assignable to them. Thus an advertising campaign, managerial foresight, standing with the trade, or competence of its technical staff may constitute or create the most valuable sources of income of a business enterprise. Although such items are sometimes designated as assets in a broad sense, their costs, even where determinable, customarily appear as expense in the books of account and on financial statements.

In economics, *asset* is sometimes synonymous with *capital;* but in this sense, only useful material objects owned by natural persons are included, and property rights and claims against other individuals or organizations are excluded. The accounting meaning of *ownership* as applied to an asset is usually legal ownership, but there are exceptions: an equity in an item of property, coupled with possession and use, is considered an asset to the owner of the equity. Thus, when an automobile is purchased on the installment basis, all the obligations and benefits of ownership are present and the automobile is regarded as an asset of the purchaser, although legal title may not be transferable until a certain number of installment payments have been completed.

Perhaps the most important characteristic of an asset recognized by the accountant is its usefulness to the owner. An object or right is considered useful if it is the source of, or can be used to secure, future services economically advantageous, not to *any* person, but to its present owner. A machine, for example, is an asset if the services which the machine can perform in the future are of economic importance to the owner. If these services are not of economic importance to him, the machine in his hands has no worth beyond its trade-in or salvage value.

The monetary amount attaching to an asset, determined by the application of a number of *conventions*, is often referred to as *book value*, *unamortized cost*, or *undepreciated cost*. Assets not subject to depreciation (e.g., land and long-term investments), are customarily recorded and reported at cost to the owner. Assets subject to depreciation are similarly recorded; periodically a portion of cost is transferred to expense as the estimated economic usefulness of the asset to the owner becomes exhausted. See *fixed asset; depreciation*.

Inventories of raw materials, goods in process, finished goods, and merchandise are customarily reported at cost or, where replacement cost is lower, at something less than cost. See *inventory valuation*. Marketable securities and other assets are subject to the same general treatment; some assets are valued at what their salvage will bring. See *cost basis*.

It is customary to reflect in the balance sheet under "deferred charges" or "prepaid expenses" costs pertaining to services or benefits to be enjoyed in future periods. See *deferred charge*.

For balance-sheet purposes, assets are broadly grouped as current, fixed, or intangible, and, within such groupings, by more descriptive titles, such as receivables, inventories, investments, plant and equipment, goodwill, and patents. See *balance sheet*.

assets and equities = *balance sheet*.

assets cover Underlying security. (British usage)

assignment The transfer to another of any right or interest in real property, or of the title to and interest in an item of personal property, as a patent or a receivable.
—*assign, v.t.*

associated company 1. = *affiliated company*.
2. A corporation exactly 50 percent of whose voting capital stock is owned by another. See *subsidiary*.
3. A corporation in which another company holds a *trade investment*. (British usage)

association 1. An economic unit, not incorporated, owned by or existing for the benefit of a group of persons or other economic units, and carrying on transactions with or without a profit objective. See *corporation*.
2. (Federal income taxes) An unincorporated business may be an *association taxable as a corporation*. The Regulations (Sec. 301.7701–2) list six corporate characteristics or traits which may brand an unincorporated organization as an association: (a) the existence of associates, (b) an objective to carry on business and divide the profits, (c) continuity of life, (d) centralized management, (e) limited liability, and (f) free transferability of ownership interests. An organization lacking either of the first

two traits will never be classified as an association. As to the remaining four traits, generally speaking, an organization may be an association though lacking one of them. In 1964 the IRS issued the so-called Kintner regulations which restricted requests for corporate classification by associations. Recently many states have enacted laws permitting professional men to set up their practice in association or corporation form, in order to qualify for tax benefits as employees of their association or corporation.

3. (statistics) The tendency for two or more sets of characteristics or classifications to display interconnections or interrelations. The term may refer to either quantitative characteristics (*variables*) or qualitative ones (*attributes*), but there is a tendency to restrict its usage to qualitative relations, reserving the term *correlation* for the study of quantitative characteristics. The term includes both the tendency toward interconnection and the deviations from that tendency. Association becomes stronger as the tendency toward interconnection becomes more pronounced and the deviations from interconnection become less pronounced. As Kendall, in *The Advanced Theory of Statistics*, notes: "It is necessary to point out . . . that statistical association is different from association in the colloquial sense. In current speech we say that A and B are associated if they occur together fairly often; but in statistics they are associated only if A occurs relatively more or less frequently among the B's than among the not-B's. If 90 percent of smokers have poor digestion, we cannot say that smoking and poor digestion are associated until it is shown that less than 90 percent of nonsmokers have poor digestion." See *correlation; contingency table; coefficient of association*.

assumed liability An obligation of another for which responsibility for payment is taken, as in the acquisition of a going concern.

assumption A premise; a statement, accepted without proof, sometimes unconsciously, as a basis for a line of reasoning or course of action, either because its applicability is deemed to be self-evident, or because its implications appear to justify exploration. One method of judging an argument, exposition, or what appears to be an arbitrary procedure, is to identify the assumptions, including biases, on which it is based, and determine their acceptability by weighing the inferences of tenability that follow. See *rule; standard; axiom*.

assured A person to be indemnified by another against a risk or eventuality; any beneficiary of an insurance policy.

at par A quotation or price identical with the face or nominal amount of a security, or of a fixed transfer rate of foreign exchange. See *par; face amount* or *value*.

attest To authenticate formally, as in a report; to express, after careful investigation, an opinion of correctness or *fairness* as in the auditor's short-form *audit report*. "Attest function" refers to the extension of the public accountant's role to any situation where he may be called upon for an objective statement of fact or opinion that may assist in the making of judgments by others.

attribute 1. A quality or group of qualities reduced to quantitative form for purposes of accounting, mathematical, or statistical analysis. Quantitative data can always be reduced to attributes by a coding or classification scheme, but the reverse is not necessarily true. Thus, the attributes of a business may be determined by the results of financial and cost analyses which are combined as a basis for judging the worthwhileness or success of a venture.

2. In *statistical quality control*, the fraction or percent defective out of the total amount of a given type of goods produced or received, constituting a measure of the quality of the production

process used to manufacture the goods, or the quality of the supplier who has furnished the goods. See *association; correlation; contingency table; correlation table.*

attribute gage (statistical quality control) See *go-and-not-go gage.*

audit 1. The examination of contracts, orders, and other original documents for the purpose of substantiating individual transactions before their settlement; =*preaudit; voucher audit; administrative audit.*

2. Any systematic investigation or appraisal of procedures or operations for the purpose of determining conformity with prescribed criteria; the work performed by an internal auditor; see *internal auditing.*

3. Any inspection by a third person of accounting records, involving analyses, tests, confirmations, or proofs.

4. (auditing) An exploratory, critical review by a public accountant of the underlying internal controls and accounting records of a business enterprise or other economic unit, precedent to the expression by him of an opinion of the propriety ("fairness") of its financial statements; often accompanied by a descriptive adjective or phrase indicating scope or purpose: e.g., annual audit, balance-sheet audit, audit for credit purposes, cash audit.

In general, the term does not refer to specific procedures but connotes only whatever work an accountant undertakes in the way of substantiating or examining a transaction, the records of a series of transactions, a financial statement, or a schedule reflecting one or more transactions or accounts. In a narrower sense, the term refers to the particular procedures generally recognized by accountants as essential in acquiring sufficient information to permit the expression of an informed opinion as to a financial statement or statements. See *audit report*(*1*).

Somewhat more specific objectives of an auditor, particularly in making an annual examination of a business concern, are to satisfy himself that with respect to the financial statements and the notes or explanations accompanying them: (a) no material asset, liability, or item or net worth has been omitted; (b) no untrue item or statement appears; (c) no material fact is included or omitted that would cause the statements to be misleading; (d) the assets shown at the date of the balance sheet were owned and the liabilities were amounts actually owing (or contingently owing, in the case of contingent liabilities); (e) the nature and classification of capital stock have been set forth, and the amounts shown therefor are not in excess of the amounts of capital stock issued; (f) surplus (paid in and earned) is broken down into its principal classes, with a showing of the amount applicable to each class; and (g) the income statement reflects fairly the operating results for the period indicated in the statement heading.

Compare with *audit standards.*

audit adjustment An *adjusting journal entry* (*2*) following an examination by public accountants.

audit certificate = *audit report* (*1*).

audited voucher A voucher that has been administratively examined and approved for payment.

auditing 1. Act or process of making an audit. See *audit.*

2. That branch of accountancy dealing with audits (*4*).

audit notebook A record, used chiefly in recurring audits, containing data on work done and comments outside of the regular subject matter of working papers. It generally contains such items as the audit program, notations showing how sections of the audit are carried out during successive examinations, information needed for the auditor's office and for staff administration, personnel assignments, time requirements, and notations for use in succeeding examinations. It may be a part of the *permanent file.*

auditor 1. One who, either as a regular employee or in an outside and professional capacity, *audits* books of account and records kept by others. See *public accountant; certified public accountant; internal auditor; audit.*
2. *sing.* or *pl.* A firm of professional accountants.
3. Any person appointed by higher authority to examine and report on accounts and records.

audit period The period covered by an *audit;* e.g., a year. The audit is often performed partly within the audit period and partly in the period following.

audit program 1. The procedures undertaken or particular work done by an accountant in prosecuting an *audit.*
2. A description, memorandum, or outline of the work to be done in an audit, and often of the time allotted and personnel assignments, prepared by a principal as a definition of audit scope, or by an auditor for the guidance and control of assistants.

audit report 1. (short form) An auditor's statement, following an audit made by him, of the work he has done and his expression of belief or opinion as to the propriety of financial statements. The standard short-form audit report, addressed to stockholders or directors and entitled "Audit(ors') Report (or Certificate)," comprises "scope" and "opinion" paragraphs or sections; the common standard in recent years follows this form:

To the Board of Directors
AB Company
New York, N. Y.

We have examined the balance sheet of the *AB* Company at December 31, 19–1, and the related statements of income, retained earnings, and funds-flow for the year then ended. Our examination was made in accordance with generally accepted auditing standards, and [accordingly]* included such tests of the accounting records and such other auditing procedures as we considered necessary [in the circumstances].

In our opinion, the accompanying financial statements and appended notes present fairly the financial position of the *AB* Company at December 31, 19–1, and the results of its operations for the year then ended, in conformity with generally accepted accounting principles applied on a basis consistent in all material respects with that of the preceding year.

Hyatt, Paterson & Company
Certified Public Accountants

April 10, 19–2

A briefer version follows:

Board of Directors
ABC Company, Chicago, Ill.

In our opinion, the accompanying financial statements present fairly the position of *ABC* Company at December 31, 19–1, and the results of its operations for the year then ended, in conformity with generally accepted accounting principles applied on a basis consistent with that of the preceding year. Our opinion is based on an examination of the statements which was made in accordance with generally accepted auditing standards and included such tests of the accounting records and such other auditing procedures as we considered necessary [in the circumstances].

Hyatt, Paterson & Company
Certified Public Accountants

April 10, 19–2

A still simpler report, omitting, as self-evident, reference to both scope and accounting principles, omitting also the customary salutation, and not currently in use, is designed for incorporation on the balance sheet:

In our opinion the above balance sheet and accompanying income statement present the financial position of the *X* Company at December 31, 19–1, and the results of its operations for the year then ended.

Hyatt, Paterson & Company
Certified Public Accountants

May 6, 19–2

In practice there are numerous variations in the report form made necessary by the conditions of the audit or by factors within the business requiring qualification or disclosure. See *scope; opinion; fairness; consistency; auditing standards; accounting principles; disclo-*

*Items bracketed, redundant expressions, are included in the AICPA version of the standard short-form report.

sure; qualification; accountant's responsibility.

2. (long form) A detailed report or letter prepared by an auditor, following an audit made by him. Addressed to the management or directors, it may supplement, contain, or replace the short-form report. There is no established pattern for a long-form report, but it often contains details of the audit scope, comments on operating results and financial condition, a funds-flow statement, causes of changes as compared with preceding years, and procedural suggestions.

audit standards Standards applying to the conduct of the field work of an audit by a public accountant and the unqualified report based thereon. In September 1948 at the annual meeting of the American Institute of Accountants a resolution was adopted containing an interpretation of the phrase "generally accepted auditing standards." Nine basic standards were indicated, as follows: *General standards:* (a) The audit must be conducted by a person of adequate technical training and experience who must (b) maintain an independent mental attitude throughout, and (c) exercise due professional care during the audit and in his report. *Field-work standards:* (d) The work must be adequately planned, and assistants, if any, properly supervised; (e) internal controls must be studied and evaluated as a basis for reliance and for determination of the extent to which audit tests may be restricted; and (f) adequate evidence must be obtained through inspection, observation, inquiries, and confirmations that will supply the basis for the audit report. *Reporting standards:* The report must indicate (g) whether the financial statements conform to "generally accepted principles of accounting," (h) whether these principles have been followed consistently and conform to those of the preceding period, and (i) any exceptions to the adequacy of disclosures appearing in the financial statements (j) it also must contain an opinion, qualified where necessary, on the financial statements.

More detailed standards, particularly those applying to the examinations of various types of accounts, are the subject matter of such auditing texts as Montgomery, *Auditing* (eighth edition), chapters 8–22; Kohler, *Auditing: An Introduction* (second edition), chapters III–XV; and Grady, *Inventory of Generally Accepted Accounting Principles*, pp. 16–17.

audit trail The reference, accompanying a transaction *entry* or *posting*, to source records or documents. A "good" audit trail is one where the labor of tracing transactions to original documents has been reduced to a minimum; such trails are essential, built-in features of *systems of accounts*.

audit year The year covered in an annual or balance-sheet audit: usually the *fiscal year*.

authority 1. The right to perform certain acts or prescribe *rules* governing the conduct of others. Although often regarded as absolute in the sense of not requiring prior approval or consideration of the desires of those immediately affected, the *arbitrary* exercise of such rights often proves to be (a) impracticable or inefficient because of possible consequent resistance or misunderstandings, and (b) unnecessary because such alternatives as exemplary conduct, persuasion, education, and better means of communication between individuals can be employed. Successful *delegations of authority* require (a) a definition of scope capable of being understood by other persons as well as by those immediately affected, and (b) the institution of an environment that obviates the need for the arbitrary exercise of power. Under balanced schemes of corporate management, administrative authority represents the activation of corporate policy and is coupled with *responsibility* and *accountability*.

2. Hence, a person regarded as being

in a position to exercise such a right. 3. A person commonly regarded as possessing an extensive knowledge in any given field.

authorization (governmental accounting) A program sanction created by a legislative body under which an *agency(2)* is created and permitted to operate; general policies are established; and limitations, as of time, areas of authority, and relationships, are specified. Funds for its operation are subsequently provided by an *appropriation.*

authorized capital stock The number of shares and usually the par or stated value of the capital stock that may be issued by a corporation under its *articles of incorporation.* In some instances the stockholders or directors may determine the stated value per share. See *capital stock.*

automatic machine A machine which after commencing its *cycle* of operations requires no attention from the operator; sometimes called *fully automatic* to distinguish it from a semiautomatic machine which may require intermittent attention during its cycle of operations.

automatic reinstatement The continuance of an insurance contract, after a loss has occurred, in an amount equal to the face value of the contract.

auxiliary activities (institutional accounting) Operations of a business character carried on by an institution for the service of its employees and patrons, but often not directly related to the primary functions of the institution. Examples: university dormitories, dining halls, infirmaries; a student union; a bookstore.

auxiliary equipment An accessory, improvement, or separately acquired addition to a major item of equipment; as, a motor or a safety device.

available assets Assets, including *available cash,* free for any general use, unencumbered, and not serving as collateral.

available balance 1. (governmental accounting) An appropriation, apportionment, or allotment, less expenditures and outstanding commitments. 2. Actual receipts, plus amounts on order, less reservations: said of an inventory item.

available cash 1. Cash in bank, excluding outstanding checks, and on hand; cash that may be used for general purposes. 2. (governmental accounting) Cash in bank and on hand in a given fund that can be utilized in meeting current *obligations (2).*

available (earned) surplus = *unappropriated earned surplus or retained income.*

average 1. = *arithmetic mean.* 2. Any central tendency of a series of quantities. See *arithmetic mean; harmonic mean; median; geometric mean; mode; moving average; progressive average; weighted average.* 3. (marine insurance) Any of certain losses or expenses arising from perils at sea, and the distribution of the loss among the several persons at interest. See *general average; particular average.*

average (accounts) *v.* To ascertain the date upon which the settlement of an account consisting of several items due at different dates may be made without loss of interest to either party to the transactions.

average deviation A measure of the variation of a group of numerical data from a designated point: the arithmetic mean of the differences between each item and the arithmetic mean of the data or other selected point, where the differences are added without regard to sign. Thus the arithmetic mean of 5, 6, and 7 is $(5 + 6 + 7)/3 = 6$ and the average deviation, taken without regard to sign, is $(1 + 0 + 1)/3 = \frac{2}{3}$. The smaller the result, the more representative the data. See *standard deviation; dispersion.*

average income (Federal income taxes) A tax benefit permitted individuals whereby the excess of the current year's taxable income over four-thirds of the average taxable income for the four preceding years is spread over the five-year period (section 1.1301). *Capital gains* and certain other items may affect the computation of the tax liability.

average life The estimated useful-life expectancy of a group of assets subject to *depreciation*. The application of a rate of depreciation, presumably straight-line, based on average life, gives rise to error if relative cost is not also weighted with expected life, as may be observed from the following table.

Asset	Original Cost	Estimate of Years of Life When Purchased	Years of Active Use Since Purchase	Accumulated Depreciation	Amount Yet to be Depreciated	New Estimate of Remaining Life	Annual Depreciation Provision
A	$10,000	10	8	$8,000	$ 2,000	4	$ 500
B	3,000	12	8	2,000	1,000	1	1,000
C	6,000	15	6	2,400	3,600	3	1,200
D	8,000	5	4	6,400	1,600	2	800
E	4,000	4	2	2,000	2,000	2	1,000
F	12,000	8	2	3,000	9,000	6	1,500
Average life		9	5			3.0	
Totals					$19,200		$6,000

The six assets, heretofore individually depreciated, are now to be depreciated as a group. By giving each asset a weighting of 1, years of average remaining life are now estimated as 3.0, as contrasted to 4.0 on the basis of the original estimate; but by giving each asset a weight equal to its undepreciated cost, average (remaining) life may be obtained by determining the ratio of the remaining undepreciated cost ($19,200) to the indicated annual provision ($5,200), thus yielding 3.2 years (= 19,200/6,000). In practice, the average life of an asset group of a hundred or more items, purchased over a period of time and each year replaced in part, changes very slowly.

average outgoing quality (statistical quality control) A term applicable only to an inspection procedure that enforces good 100 percent inspection of each rejected lot to remove therefrom all defective items, which (in theory at least) are then replaced by good items. The term applies to the quality of material ultimately passed into stock by these procedures. Accepted lots leave an inspection station at virtually the same quality they had when submitted for inspection. Rejected lots, however, always have their quality improved by enforcement of the screening operation. The result of mixing improved lots with those already accepted is to dilute the overall fraction defective ultimately passed into stock and thus to establish an "average outgoing quality" (*AOQ*) for product inspected. For every sampling plan and for each level of incoming product there is a calculated *AOQ* value easily obtainable from the *OC* curve (see *operating-characteristic curve*) for the plan. Plotting these *AOQ* values over a scale of lot quality *p* gives an *AOQ* curve showing how this feature varies with lot quality.

average outgoing quality limit (statistical quality control) The maximum *AOQ* value associated with a given sampling plan when screening of each rejected lot is enforced; the maximum point on the *AOQ* curve for a plan. It represents the poorest quality level on the average that will exist in product ultimately passed into stock under *AOQ* inspection procedures.

average sample number (statistical quality control) For each sampling plan, and for each level of incoming-lot quality, the number of items, on the average, that an inspector can expect to examine from the lot before he will be able to reach a decision to accept or reject the lot; often referred to as *ASN*. An *ASN* curve for a given sampling plan is determined by plotting the *ASN* values as a function of incoming-lot quality measured in percent defective. For plans having matched *OC* (operating-characteristic) curves (i.e., possessing matched protection features), the respective *ASN* curves give a graphic comparison of the average amount of inspection required by the plans.

axiom A general statement the truth of which is not questioned; a *postulate;* a principle which is itself incapable of proof but is assumed to be true in order to proceed with or test the consistency of a line of reasoning; a statement concerning relations between *primitives* in a symbolic system, such as a branch of mathematics or logic, or an exact science. Axioms may be identified in every branch of reasoned discourse, although there may be reasoned discourse without awareness of axioms; thus, the axioms of arithmetic were not completely identified until the last century. An axiom cannot be proved true or false in terms of the discipline which uses or depends upon the axiom: thus, the axiom of contradiction of classical logic cannot be proved by means of that logic; the Euclidean axiom, "between two points there passes at most one straight line," can be proved, but not by the techniques of Euclidean geometry. Prior to the 19th century, axioms were often defined as "self-evident truths." This usage has not entirely disappeared, although it is now regarded as confusing (a) the problem of achieving consistency in formal operations with a given set of symbols and (b) the empirical problem of determining which symbols accurately represent facts.

Since by definition axioms are not directly examined or criticized for their truth-value, the critical study of axioms is directed at their (a) consistency, (b) independence, (c) completeness, and (d) fecundity. Statements accepted as axioms may prove to be inconsistent with one another, although the demonstration of such inconsistency may be difficult. A set of axioms is said to be independent if no one of them can be deduced from the others; complete, if any propositions which may be expressed in terms of the *primitives* of the system can be shown to follow from the axioms (i.e., if any proposition can be demonstrated to be true or false and no relevant proposition will merely be undecidable by reasoning from the axioms); and fecund, if many useful and important propositions can be deduced from them. There are, of course, many systems of logic and mathematics which are not known to be useful, although some of them have more important consequences than might be supposed. For example, the Boole–Shröder algebra, which has only the numbers 1 and 0 in addition to algebraic numbers, and no coefficients or exponents, has done much to systematize the testing of the reasoning present in the employment of ordinary language.

In an applied field, such as accounting, the axioms are identical with propositions which belong equally to other disciplines. Some of the axioms often employed in accounting are: (a) an economic unit has an identity apart from other economic units; (b) the life of a typical economic unit extends indefinitely into the future; (c) relations between economic units are carried on by means of identifiable, separable, and measurable transactions; (d) the transactions of an economic unit are expressed in terms of a common medium of exchange; (e) transactions, collectively, measure both economic wealth and economic activity. See *principle; assumption; rule; proposition; postulate; primitive.*

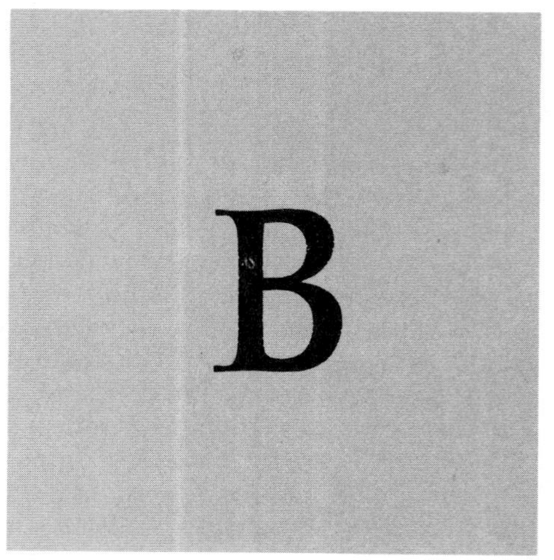

backdoor financing (Federal accounting) A Congressional sanction giving rise to spending authority without formal appropriation, as from legislation permitting the issuance of bonds to the public or borrowing from the Treasury as need may arise.

backing sheet In machine bookkeeping, a form receiving successive carbon impressions of postings to individual accounts, often serving as a *journal*.

backlog reporting The disclosure (e.g., in reports to stockholders) of unfilled orders from customers. Information on backlogs is periodically supplied by some trades, and regarded as confidential in others. The present trend in improved corporate reporting to stockholders calls for comparative data on backlogs, on projections of future volumes of production, and even on operating costs: in essence, the corporate budget for future months or years, based on prospective deliveries of goods and services to customers.

back order The portion of a customer's order undelivered for any reason, but usually because the product or merchandise will be available only at a later date.

backwardation (London Stock Exchange) The fee, including interest, paid by a speculator for the delayed delivery of stock he has sold, pending what he hopes will be a decline in its price. See *contango; short sale.*

bad debt 1. An uncollectible receivable.
2. *pl.* Specific receivables determined to be uncollectible in whole or in part, either because the debtors cannot pay or because the creditor finds it impracticable to enforce payment, and charged to profit and loss or to a *reserve* or *allowance for bad debts,* where such a reserve is maintained.
3. *pl.* The account to which is charged periodically, usually with an offsetting credit to a reserve or *allowance* for bad debts, the estimated loss from uncollectible accounts based, for example, on a percentage of (credit) sales for the period, a percentage of outstanding accounts at the end of the period, or a review of the individual accounts: in each case, any balance remaining in the reserve from past periods being taken into consideration; a *provision* for bad debts.

bailment A delivery or transfer of possession of money or personal property for a particular purpose, as on consignment or for safekeeping or repairs. A bailment constitutes a contract, express or implied, that the purpose of the delivery or transfer will be carried out. The person making the delivery is the bailor, the recipient the bailee; thus, a railroad in accepting goods for transportation becomes a bailee.

bailout (Federal income taxes) See *section 306 stock.*

balance *n.* 1. The difference between the total debits and the total credits of an *account* or the total of an account containing only debits or credits.
2. The equality of the total debit balances and the total credit balances of the accounts in a ledger, as in the expression: "The accounts are in (or out of) balance." See *trial balance.*
3. Agreement of the total of the account balances in a subsidiary ledger with its general-ledger control.
v.t. 1. To determine and enter the balance (sense 1) of an account or group of

accounts so that the sum of the debit postings will equal the sum of the credit postings.

2. To prove the equality of debits and credits in a ledger or of the total of the accounts in a subsidiary ledger with the controlling account; to prepare a trial balance the total debits of which equal the total credits.

balanced addition (national-income accounting) A complete *facility(1)* ready for operation; an addition to *capital(6)* in the form of a complete producing unit but not including inventory or prepaid expense; a facility independently capable of processing marketable raw materials into marketable endproducts. Such materials may be acquired from other departments within a single entity and the processed endproducts may be disposed of internally. The test is whether additional processing is required before the materials or endproducts can be marketed. Usually, balanced additions are estimated at the average value for an industry at the time of installation; contrasts with *unbalanced addition.*

balanced budget A *budget* in which forward *expenditures* for a given period are matched by expected *revenues* for the same period. See *accrued-expenditures basis.*

balanced economy A condition of the national economy in which imports equal exports.

balance of trade (or **payments**) 1. The difference between a country's imports and exports over a given period of time, such as a fiscal year.

2. The cumulative balance of such differences at any moment of time.

3. The portion of this amount owing to or from another country or group of countries. A persistent excess of imports, known as an unfavorable balance of trade, gives rise to "soft-currency" and other unhealthy economic conditions within a country. During the 1930's and continuing through World War II and into the 1950's, the balances of trade continuously owing to the United States by western European nations made necessary the formation of international banks of settlement, Lend-Lease contributions of equipment and supplies during the war, and the institution of the Marshall Plan (ECA, later AID), the Organization for Economic Cooperation and Development (OECD), and the European Monetary Agreement (EMA) after the war.

balance sheet A statement of financial position of any economic unit disclosing as at a given moment of time its *assets,* at cost, depreciated cost, or other indicated value; its *liabilities;* and its ownership equities. The traditional, most-followed form of the balance sheet is the *account form,* with assets on the left and liabilities and owners' equities on the right; in British and continental practice, the order of assets and liabilities is usually reversed. In recent years, experimental attempts have been made to simplify the presentation of balance-sheet information, with the result that the *report form,* with numerous variations, has been employed by some accountants for external reporting. Examples of both forms appear on pp. 50 and 51.

Standards generally observed in the structure and content of the balance sheet, aside from its form, are:

1. Current assets and liabilities are the first items shown. In the account form, they head the asset and liability sides, respectively; in the report form, current liabilities follow current assets and are subtracted in total from the current-asset total, yielding the amount of *working capital.* At one time it was common practice for fixed assets to precede current assets, as the consequence of emphasis on the ownership of property to which the investment of stockholders had been primarily devoted. Because of the growing importance of operational problems and the need of reporting first on the operating environment, the practice survives only in the utility field.

2. Items other than cash making up

current assets and items of current liabilities are generally limited to those convertible into cash or payable out of cash, respectively, within the year following the balance-sheet date; where, nevertheless, long-term installment accounts, work in process, or other items are included as current assets, they are identified and some indication of the time of their liquidation accompanies them. See *operating cycle.*

3. Current assets are listed in the order of their likely liquidity, commencing with cash; current liabilities, in their conventional groupings, have no such order but often appear in the following sequence: bank loans, other loans (including maturing portions of long-term obligations), accounts payable, deferred income, accruals.

4. The five major divisions of current assets are cash, temporary investments, receivables, inventories, and prepaid expenses. As a rule, no detail supplements their bare titles unless an exception to their customary definitions (*q.v.*) appears.

5. Current assets are regarded as cash (or as costs or other recognized amounts in the process of conversion into cash) available for general use. Where its withdrawal or uses are limited, cash is separately shown and qualified. If restricted to purchases of fixed assets, it is normally excluded from current assets altogether. Reductions, in the form of writedowns or the creation of or addition to reserves, are necessary for those current-asset items whose convertibility is doubtful. Thus, the amount of cash in a closed bank is reduced to the sum estimated to be recoverable; temporary investments having a market value substantially less than cost are reduced to that value; receivables are decreased by the estimated unrecoverable amounts they include; the portion of inventories replaceable or salable at less than cost are reduced to "market"; and prepaid expenses are marked down prorata to that portion of their cost that pertains to the future services expected from them. The basis of valuing investments and inventories is disclosed. In periods of rising prices, where the *lifo* method of valuing inventories has been followed, the outlay for inventories carried into the next period is reduced to levels sometimes materially below the more common valuation basis of "cost or market, whichever is lower," making necessary the disclosure of the amount of the understatement. See *cash; temporary investment(2); receivable(2); inventory(3); prepaid expense(2).*

6. Investments in and advances to affiliated companies may appear on unconsolidated balance sheets, and on consolidated balance sheets where the *consolidation policy* excludes certain affiliates, such as one in which less than a majority of the voted stock is owned. The usual valuation basis is cost, adjusted to underlying book values if less than such cost. In some instances, the interest in the net income of a subsidiary is taken up on the books of the controlling company, but this practice is not generally favored. See *controlling-company accounting.*

7. Fixed assets are most often valued at depreciated cost, despite the often-encountered likelihood of a much larger replacement outlay if the business were to be re-established. The principal breakdowns disclosed are buildings, machinery and equipment, and land. See *fixed assets; depreciation.*

8. Intangibles are no longer common items on balance sheets. They may arise at the outset of an enterprise or at a later date when a going concern is purchased. See *lump-sum purchase; good-will; intangible value.* Their basis of valuation is indicated. In recent years it has been customary to write off good will by a gradual process of amortization or by a direct charge to retained earnings.

9. Other types of assets are infrequently encountered. *Deferred charges*

are now limited largely to prepaid expenses, which in recent years have been restored to current assets; factory and office supplies are generally classified as inventory or as prepaid expense. A long-term receivable is given a classification following current assets, unless it is of the installment variety, which under customary trade practices is accorded a current-asset classification; but, whether or not so classified, some indication of the time of collection is generally inscribed in its title. A claim for a tax refund is given a noncurrent classification if the immediacy of its collection is not known, but is omitted from the balance sheet if a basis for settlement has not yet been agreed to by the taxing authority. A *sinking fund* in which cash and investments are being accumulated to cover a future retirement of securities is occasionally met with; where the assets it contains are no longer under the control of the debtor or cannot be used for any other purpose, the amount of the sinking fund may be deducted on the face of the balance sheet from the liability to which it relates. Funds created to meet future pension obligations (see *pension fund*) have appeared in a few balance sheets during recent years. Such funds are shown as separate asset items and the securities included therein are usually valued at cost, or at less than cost if the market value is less; with a pension fund as with a sinking fund, if the control of its assets is shared with or is in the hands of others, the amount of the fund may be deducted on the balance sheet from its related liability.

10. *Current liabilities* are generally confined to amounts shortly to be paid for goods and services already received or in settlement of recognized losses. Their leading features have already been mentioned. If any current liability is secured, the nature and amount of the security is indicated, usually parenthetically or in the form of a footnote.

11. Long-term liabilities are accompanied on the balance sheet by a description that discloses their nature, security, maturity date or dates, the rate of interest they bear, and any special features, such as convertibility. Reacquired bonds or bonds held in a sinking fund for redemption are a reduction of the bond amount, as may be the remaining items in a sinking fund that can be legally employed only in the redemption of the issue.

12. Net worth or equities of stockholders are divided between capital paid in (contributions of stockholders), subdivided by classes of stock and often as between *par* or *stated value* and *paid-in* or *capital surplus*, and *earned surplus* (*retained earnings*). Details of changes in earned surplus are shown (a) on the balance sheet, as on page 50 and above, where the changes are few; (b) at the bottom of the income statement, as on page 229; or (c) in a separate rate schedule, especially where the changes have been numerous. Changes in paid-in capital, if any, are detailed, usually in an attached schedule. The cost of reacquired capital stock (see *treasury stock*), like that of reacquired bonds, although occasionally appearing as an asset, is usually deducted from related net-worth elements or from the net-worth total.

balance-sheet account An account the amount of which alone or in combination with others appears in a *balance sheet*. Balance-sheet accounts remaining on a general ledger after revenue and expense accounts have been closed for a fiscal period constitute the items of a *post-closing trial balance*.

balance-sheet audit = *audit* (*1*). This term, along with *examination*, *special examination*, *annual audit*, and other terms designed to indicate varying responsibilities of the auditor, have now largely given way to the simpler term, *audit*.

bank(er's) acceptance 1. An instrument utilized in the financing of foreign trade, making possible the payment of cash to an exporter covering all or a part of the amount of a shipment made by him.

[ACCOUNT FORM]

UNITY STEEL WORKS, INC.
(An Illinois Corporation)
Consolidated Balance Sheet, December 31, 19-2

Assets

Current Assets:			
Cash		$ 2,465,761	
U. S. Government securities, at cost (market values, $5,828,500)		5,826,332	
Receivable from customers		5,380,826	
Inventories, at the lower of cost or market—			
Finished product	$3,264,913		
Work in process	535,568		
Materials & supplies	6,504,137	10,304,618	
Prepaid insurance and other expense		136,468	$24,114,005
Fixed Assets, at cost less depreciation:			
Buildings		$ 6,233,817	
Machinery & tools		28,958,873	
Automotive equipment		216,841	
Total		$35,409,531	
Less accumulated depreciation		18,291,234	
Book value of depreciable assets		$17,118,297	
Land		844,968	17,963,265
Total assets			$42,077,270

Liabilities

Current Liabilities:			
Payable to suppliers		$ 2,347,783	
Accrued—			
Federal income tax		4,535,412	
Other taxes		191,072	
Payrolls, etc.		1,086,696	$ 8,160,963
Stockholders' Equity:			
Paid-in capital—			
Preferred stock, $100 par value (authorized, 80,000 shares; outstanding, 50,000 shares)	$ 5,000,000		
Common stock, no-par value (authorized, 1,060,000 shares; outstanding, 1,060,000 shares, stated value $25)	26,500,000	$31,500,000	
Retained earnings—			
Balance, January 1, 19-2	$ 607,656		
Net income for year	3,093,651		
Less dividends in 19-2—			
Preferred, $4.50 per share	−225,000		
Common, $1 per share	−1,060,000	2,416,307	33,916,307
Total liabilities			$42,077,270

[REPORT FORM]

UNITY STEEL WORKS, INC.
(An Illinois Corporation)
Consolidated Statement of Financial Position
Years Ended December 31, 19-2 and 19-1

	December 31	
	19-2	19-1
Net Assets in Which Capital Is Invested		
Current assets:		
Cash	$ 2,465,761	$ 1,862,785
U. S. Government securities, at cost	5,826,332	4,247,945
Accounts & notes receivable	5,380,826	5,034,653
Inventories, at the lower of cost or market—		
Work-in-process & finished product	3,800,481	3,620,418
Raw materials	4,655,413	4,281,457
Supplies	1,848,724	946,203
Prepaid expenses	136,468	78,486
Total current assets	$24,114,005	$20,071,947
Less—current liabilities:		
Accounts payable	$ 2,347,783	$ 2,589,581
Accrued—		
Taxes	4,726,484	2,801,493
Payrolls, etc.	1,086,696	1,005,244
Total current liabilities	$ 8,160,963	$ 6,396,318
Net current assets	$15,953,042	$13,675,629
Property, at cost less depreciation—		
Buildings, machinery, & tools	$35,409,531	$34,147,377
Less portion recovered through depreciation	−18,291,234	−16,559,318
Land	844,968	843,968
Net property	$17,963,265	$18,432,027
Total net assets in which capital is invested	$33,916,307	$32,107,656
Capital Invested, and its Sources		
Preferred stock (4½% cumulative):		
Authorized—80,000 shares, $100 per value		
Outstanding—50,000 shares	$ 5,000,000	$ 5,000,000
No-par-value common stock:		
Authorized and outstanding—		
1,060,000 shares, stated value $25	26,500,000	26,500,000
Net income employed in the business	2,416,307	607,656
Total capital invested	$33,916,307	$32,107,656

Such an arrangement originates with the foreign importer, who instructs his local bank to provide for a "commercial acceptance credit" with, for example, a New York bank in favor of a named American exporter; the New York bank then issues an acceptance credit, in effect guaranteed by the foreign bank, to the exporter, under the terms of which he may draw a time bill of exchange maturing in 60 or 90 days. Supported by the required evidence of shipment, the bill of exchange is accepted by the bank, by endorsement on the face of the bill, thus signifying that it will pay the bill at maturity. The exporter may retain the bill until maturity or sell it on the so-called "discount market." See *foreign-trade financing*.

2. A similar instrument employed in domestic trade, particularly in the financing of sales of staples. The direct liability

of the bank, effective upon endorsement of the bill of exchange, gives added marketability to the paper and makes available to dealers or other investors in such paper a security having a firm, short-term due date and carrying with it virtually no risk.

bank balance The amount remaining at a given date in a checking or deposit account, differing from a bank statement of the same date because of outstanding checks, deposits in transit, and sometimes other, usually minor, items.

bank charge An amount charged to a customer by a bank for collection, protest fees, exchange, checks drawn, or other services, exclusive of interest and discount. An imputed bank charge, offset by a credit of equal amount for imputed interest on demand deposits, appears in the computation of *national income*.

bank discount The charge by a bank for discounting a note or bill of exchange; it is usually equal in amount to simple interest on the face amount of the note or bill, from the date of discounting to the due date; known also as simple discount.

bank note A promise to bearer made by a bank, issued under banking laws and intended to serve as money. Before 1935, national banks in the United States could issue bank notes; since then the issuance of bank notes has been confined to the Federal Reserve System.

bank overdraft The amount owing to a bank by a depositor as the consequence of checks drawn by him in an amount exceeding his deposits in a commercial account.

bank reconciliation A statement displaying the items of difference between the balance of an account reported by a bank and the account appearing on the books of the bank's customer. Among such items are outstanding checks and deposits in transit.

bankruptcy 1. The condition of *insolvency,* in which the assets of a debtor have been turned over to a receiver or trustee for administration.

2. The process of administering a debtor's assets and liabilities by a Federal court, following the granting by the court of a petition on the part of the person or his creditors, the purpose being to insure the full or prorata settlement of the debtor's obligations in an orderly manner or, where possible, to reorganize the debtor's affairs so that he may continue or re-enter business, and in some instances to relieve him from further liability on the unsatisfied portion of his obligations. See *arrangement; statement of realization and liquidation.*

bank statement 1. The formal periodic statement of the assets, liabilities, and net worth of a bank.

2. The statement (usually monthly) rendered by a bank to a depositor.

bar chart A statistical series, such as a *frequency distribution,* represented by means of relative or absolute heights of a group of rectangles.

bareboat charter A *charter* giving to the charterer the same rights and privileges to the use of a ship as he would have under conditions of full ownership.

barter The delivery or exchange of goods and services directly for other goods and services without the use of a medium of exchange such as money. The basis of valuation to either seller is the market or cash-equivalent value of whatever he receives: its price had he paid for it in cash, or, lacking a price, the price of a competitive product performing an identical function, or the average price, suitably weighted, of products performing higher and lower functions; if no comparables are present, then the cash price of the product given in exchange; if no such cash price is ascertainable, the *book value* of the product given in exchange may be assigned to the product received without recognition of gain or loss. Some accountants advocate the last-described procedure for all barter transactions, contending that "realization" cannot be effected unless cash is to mark the termination of the deal. See *sale; exchange.*

base period (Federal excess-profits tax) The four-year period 1946–1949 (for certain corporations with fiscal years, it may be the 48-month period ended March 31, 1950, if a lesser tax is thereby produced) the operating and financial data pertaining to which may have been employed in the computation of the *excess-profits credit.*

base-stock method (of valuing inventory) See *inventory valuation.*

basic cost Outlay measured in terms of the original purchaser-for-use of an item of property; distinguished from the outlay of a succeeding purchaser, which may contain an increment or decrement arising from a change in utility or from any of the numerous pricing factors attending a resale or transfer. Basic cost also differs from original cost in that the latter (a) is cost to the present owner or, in the case of an asset owned by a public utility (see *original cost* [*2*]), cost to the person first devoting the asset to the public service, and (b) has not necessarily been reduced by the full amount of outlay expiration taking place while the asset was in the hands of a previous owner–user. See *cost.*

basic dimension (statistical quality control) A theoretically exact size, such as the dimension of a shaft or hole for a machine part, to which a tolerance is applied for practical production and operation. Thus, a basic diameter for an axle might be $1\frac{1}{2}''$, to which a tolerance of $\frac{1}{16}''$ may be added for practical manufacture. Axles less than $1\frac{7}{16}''$ or greater than $1\frac{9}{16}''$ would then fall outside maximum and minimum tolerance limits. Usually basic sizes or dimensions lie midway between a maximum and minimum. In certain cases a basic size may be at a minimum limit with a plus tolerance, or at a maximum limit with a minus tolerance; in other cases, a basic size may be closer to one limit than another. Where a tolerance is only plus or only minus, it is known as a *unilateral tolerance;* otherwise, it is a *bilateral tolerance.* In recent years, much effort has been expended in simplifying and standardizing parts dimensions, one of the most important results of this effort being the development of the American Standard for Limits and Fits for Engineering and Manufacturing, which includes a preferred series of basic sizes and diameters. Tables of preferred tolerances and allowances and other important items, such as screw threads, have also been prepared. These tables are extensively used to reduce the total number of sizes manufactured and to standardize parts and machine manufacture. In engineering design, standard or preferred values taken from these tables are generally used, unless a good reason exists for departing from the standard. General engineering use of such a standard or preferred value reduces excess cost in both design and operation and stimulates the growth of the interchangeable-parts system of manufacture. Thus economies possible from standardization in a single plant or firm may be extended to all firms.

basic expenditure A term often used to identify a cost as it is first classified in the accounting records; thus, a raw-material cost which may ultimately be reclassified as a part of the cost of work in progress. See *absorb; primary account; terminal account.*

basic standard cost 1. A standard cost that serves as a point of reference from which to measure changes in current standard cost as well as in actual cost. It is customarily modified only when the character of the activities carried on changes. See *standard cost.*

2. A standard cost developed from engineering studies in the light of assumed objectives; it may or may not be currently attainable.

basing point A geographical location at which the quoted price of a commodity serves as the foundation for the price of the same product in another location, the difference being the transportation cost between the two locations. See *administered price.*

basing-point system (of pricing) See *price system.*

basis Cost, or a value employed as a substitute for cost; *allocated* cost; *unit cost:* a term frequently appearing in Federal income-tax law and regulations: in a property sale, "gain" is proceeds minus basis, and "basis" is the amount on which depreciation is computed. See *cost basis.*

basis of accounting The method employed in the recording and reporting of transactions. Two bases are commonly recognized: the *accrual method* and the *cash basis,* the latter, especially in small organizations, personal records, and the like, serving as a substitute for the former. The two bases are not independent, the cash basis often being characterized as an "incomplete" accrual method. Where receivables, inventories, fixed assets, and liabilities are negligible in amount as compared with operating expense, the two bases yield similar results. See also *accrued-expenditures basis.*

basket purchase The purchase, as a unit, of a group of assets, particularly capital assets, at a single negotiated price, often a round figure, that must subsequently be divided as between the various assets or asset groups only on some arbitrary basis; = *lump-sum purchase.*

batch A specific quantity of materials or parts composing a purchase of goods; a withdrawal from stock for processing; a selection for testing, a production run, and so on. The quantity may be planned as a standard or may be the actual quantity called for or furnished in a requisition or production order.

batch costing A method of cost accounting whereby costs are accumulated by batches or runs, as in the petroleum, chemical, and rubber industries. The costs attach to a particular quantity of raw material as it is charged into a refining or other process and often, in addition to the cost of the material itself, they include the whole of the operating expenses of the plant or process during the treatment period. The resultant total, less the market value of by-products, is sometimes spread over the major endproducts in proportion to their weight, volume, or market value.

batch process A method of *production (2)* in which a limited quantity of material or parts is processed during a given time interval and is identifiable with a particular output; contrasts with *continuous process.*

bear (security and commodity markets) One who believes that prices will fall, and sells in anticipation of that event. He may also speculate on *short account* through a broker, which means that he promises to deliver a stock or commodity at a certain date and price, hoping in the meantime to buy the item in the market at a lower price. A "bearish" market is one in which the prevailing trend in prices is downward; a "bearish" attitude is one that reflects the belief that prices are about to decline. See *bull.*

bearer stock Corporate capital stock evidenced by certificates not registered in any name. They are negotiable without endorsement and transferable by delivery, as are coupon bonds, and carry numbered or dated dividend coupons. In European countries, capital stock is commonly issued in the form of bearer certificates. It is unknown in the United States. See *warrant; right.*

beating the gun A trading expression indicating that offers to sell and sometimes actual commitments to deliver have been made by salesmen of security dealers to customers before a formal public offering has been made, which, in the case of securities that must be qualified with the U. S. Securities and Exchange Commission, is not earlier than the effective date of the registration statement.

below par At a discount; less than face amount.

below the line 1. An expression indicating an out-of-the-ordinary revenue or expense classification or an extraordinary and material nonrecurring item requiring a separate showing or grouping on a balance sheet or income statement. Examples: a substantial fire loss shown below the line, i.e., as an extraordinary item of expense; cash reserved for plant rehabilitation placed below the line, i.e., not classified as a current asset. Compare *above the line.*
2. (governmental accounting) The portion of a financial showing of income and expenditures, or of a budget, not financed through an appropriation or other legislative authorization; see *above the line (2).*

beneficial interest 1. An interest in property held in trust, as distinguished from legal ownership, or in the benefit arising from an insurance policy or other contract; a certificate of such interest. 2. *pl.* The proprietorship represented by the outstanding shares of stock of a corporation; the collective rights of persons having any common proprietorship interest.

benefit The service—past, present, or future—that is the object of every expenditure, and that, when yielded by a limited-life item, causes it to become an expense; an expenditure from which no service has been or will be yielded is a loss. See *service, n.*

betterment An expenditure having the effect of extending the useful life of an existing fixed asset, increasing its normal rate of output, lowering its operating cost, or otherwise adding to the worth of benefits it can yield. The cost of adapting a fixed asset to a new use is not ordinarily capitalized unless at least one of these tests is met. A betterment is distinguished from an item of *repair* or *maintenance* in that the latter has the effect merely of keeping the asset in its customary state of operating efficiency without the expectation of added future benefits. See *fixed asset; capital expenditure; repair; maintenance.*

bias 1. The propensity, often unconscious, to search for, assemble, present, or use *evidence* in such a manner as to point to a particular endproduct or conclusion. Bias does not of necessity lead to error, since it may be anticipated and allowed for: by employing adjusted weighting devices, ostensibly inaccurate results may be interpreted by allowing for the known error. By this means it is possible to extract evidence and synthesize an objective and *valid* picture even when employing biased or potentially biased sources of information. A principal objective in the process of auditing is the search for and correction of biases. An auditor determines the presence or lack of bias in a group of accounts receivable by circularizing persons against whom claims are held. Offsetting biases are regularly taken advantage of in the construction of *internal controls.* By the operation of a normally patterned system of *internal check,* valid results are deemed to follow by placing individuals with independent, opposing interests in opposition to each other and making them participants in the recording of the same transaction. The assumption underlying any such device is that the offsetting biases are of the same relative order of magnitude.
2. (statistics) Systematic, as distinct from random, error. It may be present in the method of collecting or processing data, as when nonrandom elements are introduced into the sample, or it may be present in the method of estimation. The amount of bias in an estimating method is determined by the magnitude with which the expected value departs from its universe value. See *expected value; random.*

bid An offer to buy.

bid price The price at which a prospective owner of a security, commodity, or other property formally offers to buy.

bill *n.* 1. An *invoice* of charges for goods or services.

2. = *bill of exchange.*
v.t. To prepare and dispatch an invoice covering charges for goods sold or services rendered to another.

billing machine A machine employed in the preparation of invoices or in the keeping of customers' accounts or similar records.

bill of exchange 1. An unconditional order in writing addressed by one person to another, signed by the person giving it, requiring the person to whom it is addressed to pay on demand or at a fixed or determinable future time a sum certain in money to order or to bearer (Uniform Negotiable Instruments Law); synonymous with *draft* or *acceptance* when referring to a domestic transaction.
2. Any order to pay money arising out of a foreign transaction.

bill of lading A written acknowledgment issued by a carrier as bailee constituting both a receipt for goods and a contract undertaking to deliver the goods at a specified place to a named person or to his order. Title to the goods may be passed by transfer of the bill of lading.

bill of materials A specification of the character and quantity of the materials and parts entering into a particular product. Considered along with quantities to be produced and the rate of production, it forms the basis of and justification for raw-material and parts orders, minimum and maximum on-hand quantities of raw materials and parts, cost estimates, work-in-process valuations, and production planning generally.

bill of sale A written agreement by the terms of which the title or other interest of one person in goods is transferred or assigned to another. See *sale.*

bill payable 1. A bill of exchange owing.
2. = *note payable.*

bill receivable 1. A bill of exchange receivable.
2. = *note receivable.*

B/L = *bill of lading.*

black market The buying and selling of commodities or foreign exchange (including local currency) in violation of governmental restrictions; also, the location of such an activity. Compare with *gray market.*

blanket insurance An insurance contract relating to any class of property; the number of items covered may fluctuate from time to time.

blind entry 1. An entry stating only the accounts and the amounts debited and credited, but not giving other information or explanation essential to an adequate record. See *journal entry.*
2. A posting in a ledger not supported by a journal voucher or other record.

blocked currency Money the exchange of which for the money of another country is forbidden by law. Thus, American business firms currently selling their products in Europe and receiving foreign currency in exchange have at various times found it impossible to convert such currency into dollars. In several countries, current profits may be converted but not advances of goods or capital. See *foreign exchange.*

block method (for controlling accounts) A system of subcontrol accounts maintained for ease in keeping subsidiary accounts, as with customers, where their number makes necessary the division of labor and responsibility for their accurate maintenance.

blotter 1. A memorandum record in which notations are made of business transactions as they take place, often without regard to orderly classification or form, and from which entries or entry summaries are subsequently made in formal books of original entry; a *daybook.*
2. In stock-brokerage accounting, a formal book of original entry in the nature of a cash-receipts or cash-disbursements journal, with elaborations peculiar to the business.

blue-sky law The popular term for a state law regulating issues of securities. Kansas was the first (1911) to adopt an act of this kind. In general, these laws are coordinated, often informally, with Federal acts; many of them provide for the licensing of dealers, brokers, and others

2. = *bill of exchange*.
v.t. To prepare and dispatch an invoice covering charges for goods sold or services rendered to another.

billing machine A machine employed in the preparation of invoices or in the keeping of customers' accounts or similar records.

bill of exchange 1. An unconditional order in writing addressed by one person to another, signed by the person giving it, requiring the person to whom it is addressed to pay on demand or at a fixed or determinable future time a sum certain in money to order or to bearer (Uniform Negotiable Instruments Law); synonymous with *draft* or *acceptance* when referring to a domestic transaction. 2. Any order to pay money arising out of a foreign transaction.

bill of lading A written acknowledgment issued by a carrier as bailee constituting both a receipt for goods and a contract undertaking to deliver the goods at a specified place to a named person or to his order. Title to the goods may be passed by transfer of the bill of lading.

ill of materials A specification of the character and quantity of the materials nd parts entering into a particular oduct. Considered along with quan- es to be produced and the rate of uction, it forms the basis of and cation for raw-material and parts minimum and maximum on-hand es of raw materials and parts, mates, work-in-process valua- roduction planning generally. written agreement by the h the title or other interest on in goods is transferred or another. See *sale*.

A bill of exchange owing. *ble*.

A bill of exchange re-

g and selling of exchange (in- violation of governmental restrictions; also, the location of such an activity. Compare with *gray market*.

blanket insurance An insurance contract relating to any class of property; the number of items covered may fluctuate from time to time.

blind entry 1. An entry stating only the accounts and the amounts debited and credited, but not giving other information or explanation essential to an adequate record. See *journal entry*. 2. A posting in a ledger not supported by a journal voucher or other record.

blocked currency Money the exchange of which for the money of another country is forbidden by law. Thus, American business firms currently selling their products in Europe and receiving foreign currency in exchange have at various times found it impossible to convert such currency into dollars. In several countries, current profits may be converted but not advances of goods or capital. See *foreign exchange*.

block method (for controlling accounts) A system of subcontrol accounts maintained for ease in keeping subsidiary accounts, as with customers, where their number makes necessary the division of labor and responsibility for their accurate maintenance.

blotter 1. A memorandum record in which notations are made of business transactions as they take place, often without regard to orderly classification or form, and from which entries or entry summaries are subsequently made in formal books of original entry; a *daybook*. 2. In stock-brokerage accounting, a formal book of original entry in the nature of a cash-receipts or cash-disbursements journal, with elaborations peculiar to the business.

blue-sky law The popular term for a state law regulating issues of securities. Kansas was the first (1911) to adopt an act of this kind. In general, these laws are coordinated, often informally, with Federal acts; many of them provide for the licensing of dealers, brokers, and others offering securities for sale, and of each salesman or agent; most of them require registration of new issues, the registration varying between the filing of specified information and action leading to formal approval of the issue by the state regulatory body. Prevention of the grosser forms of fraud has often been the predominant aim of these laws.

board of directors The persons elected by stockholders and charged under corporation laws with the responsibility of supervising the affairs of a corporation. Their number is dependent on the provisions of the articles of incorporation and bylaws; a minimum of three is often required, and they may or may not be stockholders. Although a chief function of a board of directors is generally held to be policy-making, as distinct from *administration*, many policies, initiated by management, are now subject only to the sufferance of or a nominal review by the board.

BOM = *beginning of month.*

bond 1. A certificate of indebtedness, in writing and often under seal. Bonds are issued in the form of coupon or bearer instruments, or are registered in the name of the owner as to principal only (registered coupon bonds) or as to both principal and interest (registered bonds). Their title usually indicates broadly the purpose for and the security upon which they are issued, also the method of payment or redemption; e.g., consolidated-mortgage bonds, equipment bonds, and first-mortgage bonds. Bonds may be classified by (a) the type of issuing body, e.g., government, state, municipal, railroad, or other utilities; (b) the nature of the project financed, e.g., farm-loan, irrigation, reclamation, or development bonds; (c) the type of currency in which they will be paid, e.g., dollar, sterling, gold, legal-tender bonds; (d) special privileges, e.g., participating or convertible bonds; (e) the type of lien, e.g., underlying, junior lien, first- or second-mortgage bonds; (f) fitness for investments, e. g., savings-bank or trustee bonds; (g) maturity, e.g., short-term or long-term bonds.

2. An obligation in writing, binding one more parties as surety for another; a surety bond. Such a bond is often required of litigants by the courts to secure costs, damages, and debts, and of receivers, administrators, executors, guardians, trustees, and others to protect the interests they represent; and by the government and other authorities and employers, of persons holding positions of public or private trust. Surety bonds may be issued by a guaranty company or by one or more individuals.

3. As used in the expression *in bond:* pertaining to goods in a bonded warehouse that cannot be released except by payment of certain duties or taxes.

bond discount (and **expense**) The excess of the face amount of a bond or class of bonds over the net amount yielded from its sale.

The cost of a bond issue, made up of identifiable costs, such as legal, accounting, appraisal, and engineering fees, costs of registration and printing, and the excess of face value over disposal price (discount) are often absorbed as an expense at the time they are incurred; or they may be combined in a single account and regarded as a deferred charge, allocable to the years during which the bonds are outstanding. The commission paid to a dealer for selling the security is usually regarded as a deduction in determining *net proceeds* and therefore does not find its way into the accounts as a cost and in a strict sense should not be regarded as an addition to the deferred-charge account: a situation arising where the dealer contracts to purchase the bonds at a fixed price (more or less than face value), his commission or profit arising from the addition made to this fixed price when the bonds are sold to the public.

By regarding the discount as a deferred charge and so classifying it on the balance sheet, it has been said that the accounting standard (stating that only costs or amortized costs should appear as assets) is violated. On the other side of the balance sheet, the face amount of the bonds outstanding appears, a figure in excess of what the bondholders in the first instance have contributed to the business and actually less than what will ultimately have to be paid back where a retirement premium attaches to the issue or a part of it. Some accountants have advocated that the net proceeds of a bond issue be shown initially as a liability, and that this figure be increased each year by charges to current expense until the maturity date and amount are reached. In reality, the bond discount is a species of premium, since it is the extra payment, in addition to regular interest, that must be paid to the investor to induce him to loan his money, and it is payable at the same time that a formal premium is payable. Thus, if a corporation receives net proceeds of $99,000 from the sale of a bond issue that has a face value of $100,000 and is repayable at 102 ten years hence, the discount of $1,000, along with the redemption premium of $2,000, is to be paid out at maturity. What was borrowed was $99,000; what is to be repaid is $102,000; and in conformity with the principles of accrual accounting, the difference of $3,000 calls for recognition in the accounts as an expense during the loan period of ten years. Following are several methods that have been advocated by various authorities for disposing of this amount:

1. Record the loan in the amount of the net proceeds received ($99,000); on a balance sheet at the time the loan is made, report as the obligation the amount received, and parenthetically state both the face value and the redemption amount; each year increase the liability by $300, at the same time charging financial expense. Thus, by a process of *accumulation*, the liability is raised to its full amount in the year of retirement. This is a preferred but seldom-followed procedure.

2. Record the loan at its face amount ($100,000). Charge cash $99,000 and unamortized bond discount $1,000; each year charge $100 to financial expense or bond discount amortized and credit unamortized bond discount; each year charge the same expense account with $200 and credit accrued bond-retirement premium. On a balance sheet include the amortized bond discount under deferred charges, show the liability for the bond issue as $100,000 and, as a separately stated addition thereto, the accumulated amount of the retirement premium. This is the procedure generally found in practice.

3. A variation of the latter procedure is occasionally found. An unamortized-bond-discount account is maintained, with periodic writedowns as described, but no provision for the accumulation of the retirement premium is made, the premium paid during the year of retirement being treated as an expense of that year.

Discount and premium on serial-bond issues may be segregated by classes or dates of maturity and the amortization or accumulation pertaining to each class may be computed separately; or the discount and expense (and premium) for all classes may be lumped together. Either method, supplying a basis for substantially similar results, is acceptable to accountants.

The usual method for spreading bond discount (and premium) over the years in which a serial obligation is in force is known as the *bonds-outstanding method*.

Considerable controversy has arisen in past years as to the disposition of unamortized discount and expense in connection with a bond issue that has been refunded. Three methods of disposition, in the order of their general preference, have been employed:

1. Charge it to expense (or retained earnings) in the year of retirement.

2. Continue to amortize it on the old basis, as though the retired issue were still outstanding.

3. Add it to any discount and expense on the new issue and thus amortize it over the life of the new issue.

Of the three methods, the first and second have often been employed; the third, but rarely, although permitted under SEC-approved practices. In support of the first it may be said that the unamortized discount and expense are deductible for income-tax purposes in the year of refunding; moreover, it is argued, when the old issue disappears, all the accounts maintained for it should be eliminated at the same time, the unamortized sum becoming a current expense (if *significant*, possibly treated as an extraordinary one) of the year of the refund. A basic objection to the second and third methods is that they result in an overstatement of subsequent interest costs, since the debt-service cost of the new issue, which is usually completely independent of the old, is increased by a part of the debt-service cost of an issue no longer in existence. Support is sometimes given to the second method provided the total of the periodic charge for interest and debt-discount amortization does not exceed that which would have resulted if the refunding operation had not taken place. See *deferred charge*.

bond dividend A *dividend* paid in the issuing company's own bonds.

bonded debt Debt evidenced by bonds outstanding. See *funded debt*.

bond fund (municipal accounting) A fund established by a municipality or other government agency for the receipt and disbursement of the proceeds of a bond issue. See *fund*.

bond premium The net amount yielded by the sale of a bond or class of bonds in excess of its face value. On the books and balance sheet of the issuer it appears as a deferred credit and is commonly amortized over the life of the bonds by the *bonds-outstanding method*, the periodic transfer to income being subtracted from or appearing with interest expense—such treatment being justified from the supposition that, if the interest rate had been smaller, a premium would not have been realized from the sale. Upon premature retirement of the bonds and in various other situations, the unamortized premium is disposed of in a manner resembling the disposition of *bond discount* (*q.v.*).

bond register 1. A record in which each outstanding bond and often the payment of each successive coupon are registered. Two types of bond registers are in common use. In one, separate sections are provided for the various series, each section being subdivided by the denominations of the bonds. Columns are provided for the consecutive symbols and numbers of the bonds and for coupon dates. Notations in these columns are made as coupons are paid. In the second type, a separate page appears for each outstanding bond; in addition to provision for the bond symbol and number, each page is divided into rectangles of the size of the coupons and bearing their consecutive numbers. Each coupon paid is pasted into its rectangle; the open spaces represent outstanding coupons.
2. A record kept by a bond registrar wherein outstanding bonds of a specified issue are registered in the name of the holder.

bonds-outstanding method (of amortizing bond discount) A term referring to the spread of *bond discount* over the life of a bond issue by periodic charges to expense, determined by a ratio equal to the fraction having as its numerator the face value of bonds outstanding during the period and as its denominator the total of such face values for all the periods during which the bonds are outstanding. The same fraction may be derived from dividing interest expense for the period by all the interest to be paid on the bonds during the life of the issue, assuming no prepayments.

Example: A 4 percent first-mortgage-bond issue was sold to the public on January 1, 19-1 through an investment dealer on the basis shown in table (1).

(1)

Block	Principal Amount	Maturity	Cost to Investors	Net Proceeds to Issuer	Redemption Price at Maturity
A	$ 400,000	12-31-19-4	$ 407,500	[The two blocks were	$ 409,000
B	600,000	12-31-19-8	608,800	sold as a unit]	611,000
Total	$1,000,000		$1,016,300	$969,560	$1,020,000

On June 30, 19-3, twenty $1,000 bonds of block *B* were repurchased by the issuer on the open market at 100¼ and immediately thereafter were canceled.

It may thus be seen that, in addition to interest at 4 percent, the financing will cost the issuer $50,440, the difference between the net proceeds at the time of sale and the price at which it has agreed to redeem the bonds at their maturity, four and eight years hence. The cost to investors, $1,016,300, is the result of transactions between them and the dealer and is not entered on the issuer's records, unless the dealer was acting merely as an agent and not as a principal in selling the issue. In this instance it may be assumed that the dealer or a dealer group purchased the bonds from the issuer, paid the expenses of the issue, and was thus acting as a principal. It will be further observed that the amount of $50,440 consists technically of discount of $30,440 and redemption premium of $20,000.

Since the $50,440 is as much of a cost to the issuer as interest itself, it will have to be absorbed over the eight years during which the bonds, or a part of them, will be outstanding. Merely to amortize one-eighth each year would not give due weight to the portion of the issue to be redeemed at the end of four years; to absorb the cost by spreading it as between the two blocks on the basis of the broker's sales to the public would not give effect to the essential character of the discount premium as an adjustment of interest to be paid. Hence, the annual amortization may be determined on the bonds-outstanding basis, as summarized in table (2).

The annual charge may be assumed to be the amortization (or *accumulation;* see *bond discount*) of the discount until the latter is absorbed; thereafter the

(2)

Block	Life of Block: Years	Life of Block: Amount	Dollar-Years: Years × Amount	Fraction	Discount	Annual Cost
A	4	$400,000	1,600,000	$\frac{1}{4}$	$12,610	$3,152.50
B	8	600,000	4,800,000	$\frac{3}{4}$	37,830	4,728.75
Totals			6,400,000		$50,440	$7,881.25

(3)

Price paid on repurchase (100¼)			$20,050.00
Less—book value of 20 block-*B* bonds—			
Par value		$20,000.00	
Less—unamortized discount now on books—			
Applicable portion of discount originally recorded—$\frac{1}{30} \times \frac{3}{4} \times 30,440$	$761.00		
Less amount written off—$\frac{1}{30} \times 4,728.75 \times 2.5$	394.06	366.94	19,633.06
Loss on repurchase			$ 416.94

(4)

Before adjustment	\$4,728.75
Less annual amount applicable to repurchased bonds ($\frac{20}{600}$)	157.63
Net annual amortization	\$4,571.12

(5)

Original sale:		
Cash	\$969,560.00	
Unamortized discount on bonds (a deferred charge)	30,440.00	
4% first-mortgage bonds		\$1,000,000.00
Sale of issue to *L*, *M*, & *N*, Inc. for lump sum.		
Discount and premium expense, first year:		
Interest and discount on bond issue (an expense)	7,881.25	
Discount on bonds		7,881.25
Proportion of discount and premium applicable to 19-1, on straight-line basis.		
Repurchase in third year:		
4% first-mortgage bonds	20,000.00	
Interest and discount on bond issue (loss from purchase)	416.94	
Unamortized discount—($\frac{20}{600}$ × 4,728.75 × 5.5)		366.94
Cash		20,050.00
Purchase and cancellation of bonds, par \$20,000 at 100¼.		
Typical amortization entry (after fourth year):		
Interest and discount on bond issue (an expense)	4,571.12	
Accrued premium on bonds (a noncurrent liability)		4,571.12
Portion of bond discount and premium applicable to block *B*.		

credit offsetting the charge would be made to an "accrued premium" account. In this instance, the changeover would occur in the fourth year.

The repurchase on June 30, 19-3, of the lot of 20 block-*B* bonds would require the recognition of a loss from the retirement and an adjustment of the amortization schedule—see table (3).

The loss may be added to the expense account (bond discount amortized or bond-interest-and-discount expense) to which the periodic amortization charge is regularly carried.

Adjustment of annual amortization after the third year, applicable to block *B*—see table (4).

The effect of these transactions on the books of account and the financial statements may be noted through examination of the journal entries in table (5).

bond table A book in which are tabulated, on the basis of the yield at each of an extensive series of interest rates, the *present value* of a bond of a specified maturity bearing interest at any customary rate. Most bond tables show values for yields that progress by 0.05 and ⅛ percent and on bonds bearing interest at rates from 1 to 8 percent per annum, the interest rates progressing by ¼ or ½ percent with coupons payable semiannually, and the bonds maturing from within one month to 50 or 100 years in monthly, semiannual, or yearly intervals. Special bond tables deal with high-yield, serial, or short-term bonds, and with bonds that are callable or payable at a premium or that pay interest quarterly or once a year. Short-term bond tables show values for maturities progressing by days.

bond valuation 1. The process followed by an investor in determining what he is willing to pay for a bond; involved is the determination of a value based upon the redemption price of the bond when held to maturity or earlier fixed date, the nominal or coupon rate of interest, and the effective rate or desired yield. 2. The value resulting from the application of the process.

Example: A $1,000 bond, paying 4 percent interest semiannually and due 10 years hence at a premium of 103 is being considered for purchase by an investor who is satisfied with a semiannual return of $1\frac{1}{2}$ percent. The maximum price he would be likely to pay is computed thus:

As to principal:

Present value of 1, at $1\frac{1}{2}\%$, due 20 periods hence, is 0.7424704 (see present-value table, page 334)	
The principal then due, $1,030, thus has a present value of 1,030 × 0.7424704, or	$764.7445

As to interest:

Present value of 1 per period for 20 periods at $1\frac{1}{2}\%$ per period is 17.1686388 (see annuity table, page 336)	
The interest actually payable is $20 per period, and is thus worth 20 × 17.1686388, or	343.3728
Maximum price the investor is willing to pay, covering both principal and interest	$1,108.12

The same result is produced by determining the premium the investor would be willing to pay and adjusting face value by that amount. The premium is equal to the present value of the excess of the nominal rate over the yield rate, plus, in this case, the present value of the redemption premium:

Present value of 1 per period for 20 periods at $1\frac{1}{2}\%$ is 17.1686388.	
The excess of interest, $20 − $15, or $5, thus has a present value of 5 × 17.1686388, or	$ 85.8432
To this total must be added the present value of the premium at maturity, 30 × 0.7424704, or	22.2741
Maximum premium, as indicated above, is	$ 108.12

Bond tables are available where direct readings of the combined present values of principal and interest may be made.

A similar computation applies to situations where the effective rate exceeds the nominal rate, the result then being a figure less than the redemption value of the bond.

Valuations of this type are employed mostly by persons who must invest funds in such a manner as to meet specific future annuities or other obligations.

bonus 1. Premium or extra allowance paid to an employee.
2. Securities issued as a premium with a purchase of bonds or stocks.
3. A lump-sum payment for a lease, particularly in extractive industries, in addition to royalties.

book *n.* = *book of account.*
v. To record a *transaction;* to make an *entry.*

book inventory 1. An inventory which is not the result of actual stocktaking but of adding the units and the cost of incoming goods to previous inventory figures and deducting the units and cost of outgoing goods. Without units of quantity of input and output the term is usually qualified to denote its tentative character.
2. The balances of materials or products on hand in quantities, dollars, or both, appearing in perpetual-inventory accounts. See *perpetual inventory.*

bookkeeper One engaged in *bookkeeping.* The term is applied to a person who does all the bookkeeping of an enterprise, or whose work is specialized, such as one who maintains the general ledger or who works on accounts receivable. A bookkeeper may also be an accountant if, in addition, he prepares or supervises the preparation of financial statements from the accounts, designs and modifies the methods employed, or supervises transaction recording.

bookkeeping The process of analyzing, classifying, and recording transactions in accordance with a preconceived plan, for the purpose of (a) providing a means by which an enterprise may be conducted in an orderly fashion, and (b) establishing a basis for recording and reporting the financial affairs of the enterprise and the results of its operation. See *double-entry bookkeeping.*

book of account 1. Any *journal, register,* or *ledger* which forms a part of a *system of accounts.*
2. *pl.* All the *books of original* and *final entry,* and the invoices, vouchers, contracts, correspondence, and the like that result from the occurrence of transactions and the operation of a *system of accounts;* often shortened to *books.*

book of final entry A record book in which the money amounts of transactions, accumulated according to a previously established classification of accounts, are transferred or *posted;* a *ledger.*

book of original entry A record book, recognized by law or custom, in which transactions are successively recorded, and which is the source of postings to ledgers; a *journal.* Books of original entry include general and special journals, such as cashbooks and registers of sales and purchases. Memorandum books, check stubs, files of duplicate sales invoices, and the like, wherein first or prior notations may already have been made, although commonly regarded as a part of the *books of account,* are also referred to as *business papers* or *supporting records* and are not referred to as books of original entry unless they are used as posting sources.

book of secondary entry = *book of final entry.*

book profit 1. Profit as shown by the books of account before verification or audit or as contrasted with "economic" profit or profit determined on some other basis.
2. *pl.* Profits based on book figures, especially in cases where book figures differ from actual cost.

books = *book of account (2).*

book surplus 1. *Surplus* before giving expression to audit corrections, or before separating *paid-in, earned,* and *writeup* elements.
2. *Surplus* as shown by the books, on a *going-concern basis,* as distinct from a figure that would result from putting the accounts on a liquidating or some noncost basis.

book value (or **cost**) 1. The net amount at which an asset or asset group appears on the books of account, as distinguished from its market value or some intrinsic value. *Gross book value* is the amount appearing in an asset account; while book value (or net book value) is the gross book value less any applicable portion of accumulated depreciation or other *valuation account.*
2. The face amount of a liability less any *unamortized discount and expense.*
3. As applied to capital stock: (a) the book value of the *net assets;* (b) in a corporation, the book value of the net assets, divided by the number of outstanding shares of capital stock; it is based on the *going values* customarily reflected in balance sheets. It may also mean the portion of the proceeds applicable to each share of stock following a no-gain, no-loss liquidation at a given balance-sheet date. Without specific provisions to the contrary in the articles of incorporation or the governing state law, the book value of a share of *preferred stock* would be its agreed value in involuntary liquidation plus cumulative dividends in arrears, if any, provided that the total is not in excess of the corporate net worth; to common stock would be assigned the balance, if any, of net assets. Book value attaches only to outstanding shares of capital stock, and not to unissued or reacquired shares.

boot Something in addition; specifically (Federal income taxes) in a property exchange that would otherwise be tax-free (e.g., certain like-kind or reorganization exchanges), money or other property passing in the exchange; in general, if the recipient of the boot realizes gain in the exchange, the boot received is taxable (Code Secs. 351(b), 356, 361(b), 371(b), and 1031(b)).

bordereau A docket; (insurance accounting) now restricted to a tabular register or report containing abstracts of insurance written.

Boston ledger A type of ledger in which the record on each account progresses horizontally in columnar sections assigned to successive accounting periods. Several accounts may be kept on a single page. This form of ledger eliminates the necessity of preparing a separate trial balance, the aggregate of balances in each section taking its place.

BOY = *beginning of year*.

boycott A refusal to perform a customary act: usually an action participated in by more than one person for a common purpose; a refusal to buy or handle goods of an organization whose employees are on strike; hence, any refusal to buy or sell.

breakdown An analysis, usually summarized in terms of transaction classes, of an account balance or other figure; e.g., the process followed in the preparation of a *spread sheet*.

breakeven chart Any of several types of charts on which the *breakeven point* is shown. As employed in accounting, it is typically an important tool of *forward accounting:* a projection of a year's operations in which costs and profits are shown under varying sales volumes. The projection may involve the business as a whole, a department, an operation, or a product.

Example: the Simplex Manufacturing Company is the manufacturer of several lines of finished parts that become the raw material of other producers. During emergency periods, its volume of business has been dependent to a great extent on the availability of raw materials. The business is competitive, and the margin of net profit is, as a rule, narrow.

On December 12, 19-0, the company's budget committee, consisting of the chairman of the Finance Committee of the Board of Directors, the president, the controller, the sales manager, and the production vice-president, approved the figures appearing in the first six columns of the schedule which follows. These were derived in part from past experiences plus the expectation of increases in the prices of raw materials. The prospect of increasing selling prices was considered dim. It was the opinion that the sales volume for 19-0, which at that time looked as though it were going to be somewhat

PROJECTIONS *(in thousands)*

Item	*Original Projection Made on Dec. 12, 19-0 for the Year 19-1*						*Reprojections Full Year after Close of Quarter*			*Actual for Full Year**
	Fixed Costs	*—Varying Sales Volume—*					*Q1*	*Q2*	*Q3*	
Sales	650	1,000	2,000	3,000	4,000	5,000	4,200	4,600	4,400	4,300
Material	0	250	500	750	1,000	1,250	1,200	1,300	1,200	1,200
Labor	0	400	600	750	800	1,000	800	850	850	850
Overhead	250	250	400	500	600	650	250	300	300	300
							450	400	300	300
Selling	50	150	300	400	450	500	100	100	100	100
							350	400	350	300
Administration	150	200	300	300	350	400	150	150	150	100
							300	200	250	250
Depreciation	100	100	100	100	100	100	100	100	100	100
Interest	100	100	100	100	100	100	100	100	100	100
Income tax	0	0	0	50	300	450	300	350	300	300
Dividend	0	0	0	0	200	250	50	250	250	250
Retained income	0	−450	−300	50	100	300	50	100	150	150

*Not yet filled in on chart.

more than \$4,000,000, might be expanded under favorable conditions during 19-1 to \$5,000,000. The primary budget goal, therefore, was set at the latter figure, but a budget goal "*B*" of \$4,000,000 was also established as a floor below which business was not likely to drop, short of exceedingly unfavorable conditions.

Immediately the controller converted the figures into the first section of the chart appearing on page 66.

The supplemental bar charts, *Q*1–*Q*4, were prepared within a period of two weeks following the end of each quarter of 19-1, the first column in each case representing last year's sales (column "*LY*" on the chart) broken down by actual costs of the principal factors of production. Both the second and third columns reflect the sum of actual sales for the first three months plus re-estimated sales for the balance of the year, broken down by the originally projected factor costs extended over from the main section ("*P*" on the chart), and by factor costs for the first three months plus a re-estimate of costs for the balance of the year ("*R*" on the chart), it being borne in mind that, as each quarter ends, a better vantage point is gained from which the estimates of December 19-0 may be critically recast. In the seventh, eighth, and ninth columns of the schedule there are the reestimates of the year's volume and costs, prepared, as indicated, after the close of each of the first three quarters. The final column of the schedule reflects the actual volume and the actual costs for the year, prepared in January 19-2; these remain to be entered on the chart. Estimates of total sales were increased at the end of the second quarter because of an expected volume of new business that only partially developed. Material costs continued to increase throughout the year and there was also some fluctuation in the estimate of fixed overhead, based upon anticipated increases in the cost of fuel, which proved to be minor.

Each quarter the chart, with newly added quarterly fill-ins, is Xeroxed and distributed to top executives and board members at their quarterly meetings, accompanied by explanations of principal variations and by financial statements showing detailed quarterly comparisons of operating results. By supplying these persons with the latest re-estimate of probable operating results and an over-all comparison with last year's actual business and last year's estimate of this year's business, the chart serves to transmit one type of operating information in capsule form and at the same time provides a check on forecasting skills. It is primarily informational in character.

breakeven point 1. The volume point at which revenues and costs are equal: a combination of sales and costs that will yield a no-profit, no-loss operation. The following formula may be employed:

$$s_1 = \frac{f}{1 - v/s}, \qquad (1)$$

where f is the total of fixed costs, v the total of present costs varying directly with sales, s the present sales volume, and s_1 the sales volume required to cover costs. Thus, if $f = \$90{,}000$, $v = \$50{,}000$, and $s = \$125{,}000$,

$$s_1 = \frac{90{,}000}{1 - 50{,}000/125{,}000} = \$150{,}000.$$

This means that, to cover expenses, total sales must be not less than \$150,000.

The breakeven point may also be expressed in terms of a percentage of total plant capacity. This may be obtained in the above example by altering the formula to

$$r = \frac{f}{(1 - v/s)c}, \qquad (2)$$

where c is the plant capacity in terms of maximum sales volume and r is the ratio sought; if c is \$200,000, the breakeven point is 150,000/200,000, or 75 percent. Or, if plant capacity is stated in terms of present operations, the

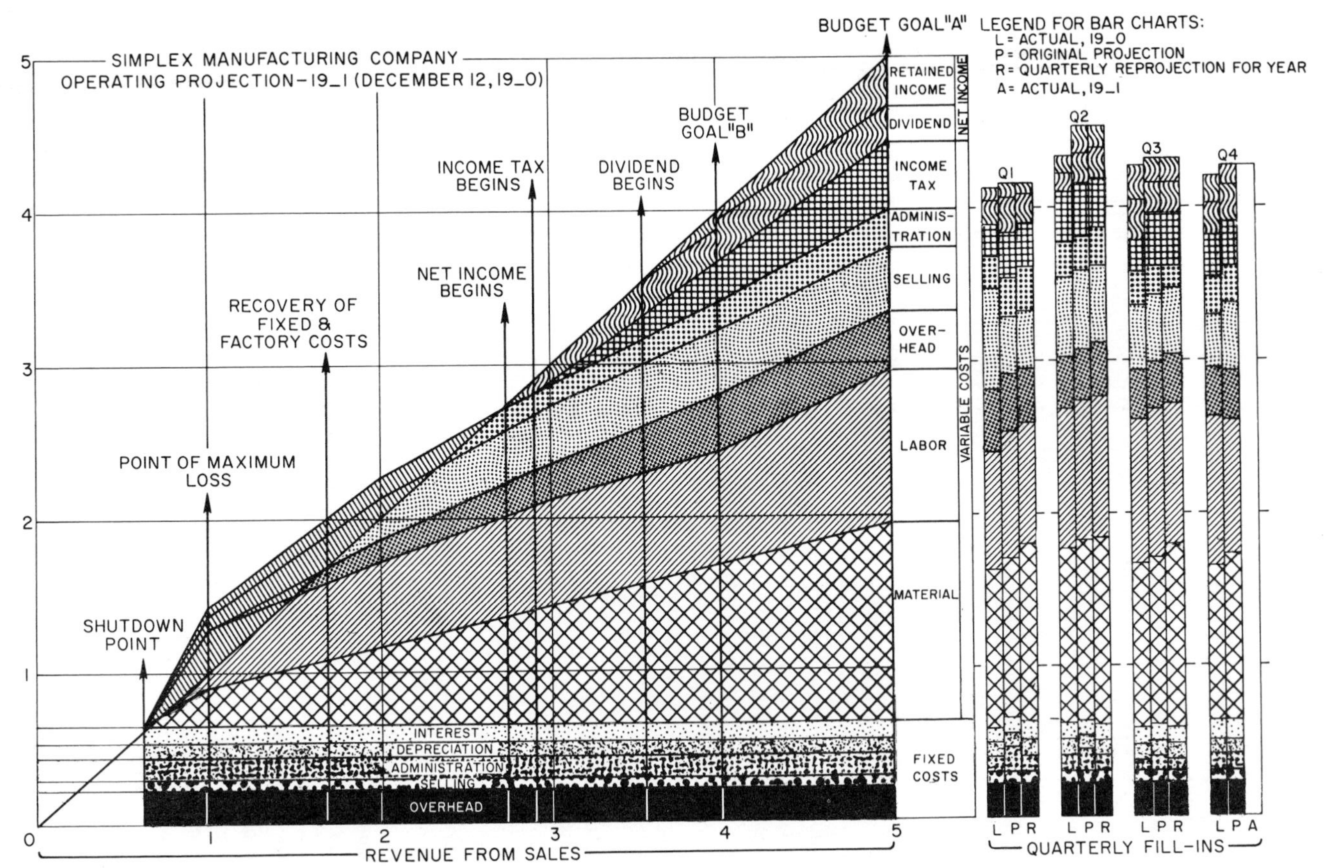

BREAKEVEN CHART, AFTER THIRD QUARTER.

formula becomes

$$r = \frac{fc_1}{s - v}, \qquad (3)$$

where c_1 is the ratio of present plant utilization to total plant capacity; if c_1 is $62\frac{1}{2}$ percent, then

$$r = \frac{90{,}000 \times 0.625}{125{,}000 - 50{,}000} = .75 = 75\%.$$

2. That point in the cost of a variable factor of production at which one or more alternatives are equally economical.

break-up value The amount which can be obtained for assets at forced sales, upon discontinuance of their use in a business; salvage value.

bring forward To inscribe the balance or the total debits and credits of an account, worksheet, or any tabular statement upon a new page or sheet or upon a cleared section of an old sheet.

broker Any special type of agent acting as intermediary between the buyer and seller of real or personal property or service; he does not take title to property in the typical transaction but receives a fee from either or both parties, thereby identifying himself as agent to one or both. The term is often loosely applied to *dealers*, especially in securities.

brokerage commission 1. The fee charged by a broker on the purchase or sale of a *commodity* or *service*.
2. The commission or fee of a member of the New York Stock Exchange, based on the money amount of a transaction:

broker's loan A borrowing from a bank by a broker or investment dealer for the purpose of purchasing or carrying securities or for carrying customers' margin accounts.

budget 1. Any financial plan serving as an estimate of and a control over future operations.
2. Hence, any estimate of future costs.
3. Any systematic plan for the utilization of manpower, material, or other resources.

Budgets assume varying forms, depending on the operating methods, scope, and complexity of an enterprise. They may, however, be divided into two main classes: capital budgets, directed toward proposed expenditures for *project* activities and often requiring special financing; and operating budgets, directed toward planning and controlling *program* activities. Operating budgets may be subdivided further into sales, advertising and marketing, production and labor, inventory and purchases, maintenance, and overhead budgets, as well as special-purpose short-term budgets, such as those constructed for job-order or batch production.

Financial budgets such as the cash budget, for planning and controlling cash receipts and disbursements, and budgets constructed for longer-range financing can be keyed directly into *proforma* balance sheets at the end of the budget period, and into projected statements of income and expense.

Operating and capital budgets may

Round Lots			Odd Lots		
Per-Share Cost	Commission Percentage of Cost per Share	Plus	Price of Lot	Commission Percentage of Lot Price	Plus
\$ 1– 4	200	\$ 3	\$ 100– 400	2	\$ 1
4–24	100	7	400–2,400	1	5
25–50	50	19	2,401–5,000	$\frac{1}{2}$	17
Over 50	10	39	Over 5,000	$\frac{1}{10}$	37

Minimum commission, \$6; maximum, \$75; an additional odd-lot-fee maximum, \$1.50 per share.

also be classified by type into appropriation, forecast, and flexible budgets. Appropriation-type budgets, involving usually a lump-sum-expenditure ceiling with such supporting detail as may be necessary or possible, are used in governmental bodies, or for controlling capital expenditures or programs, such as advertising, where it may be difficult, because of the absence of past experience or developed standards, to relate performance to expenditure in detail. Forecast-type budgets may be used for either projects or programs. They are distinguished from flexible budgets in that budgetary estimates and controls are designed for only one level of activity. Should any wide deviation from that level of activity occur, the forecast budget loses much of its relevance. Flexible budgets, on the other hand, provide estimates as a basis for control at varying rates of activity. A flexible budget requires careful segregation of costs into fixed, semifixed, and variable; it also requires well-developed standards for relating costs to production or other enterprise activities. See *breakeven chart.*

Many business concerns employ a combination of appropriation, forecast, and flexible budgets for purposes varying from mere forecasting to the establishment of current operating controls and standards of performance. Moreover, complete budgets covering all phases of an enterprise, as well as incomplete budgets covering only certain phases, are also met with in practice.

In the Federal government, extensive use has been made of the principle of the operating budget which is called a *program* or performance budget. The aim has been to establish a form of budget which serves not only (a) as an aid to the Congress in determining the expenditure ceiling for each governmental agency but also as the basis for (b) management controls over operations and (c) performance review by both insiders and outsiders. Because of these objectives the classification of budget detail has followed the pattern of the accounts and financial statements, and the agency's controller has played a leading role in budgetary preparation and execution—with ultimate responsibility resting on the agency's administrator.

budgetary accounts (governmental accounting) Accounts reflecting budgetary operations and conditions such as those maintained for estimated revenues and appropriations. They are distinguished from *proprietary accounts* which show actual financial condition and operations and are exemplified by such accounts as cash, taxes receivable, vouchers payable, and bonds payable. Examples of budgetary accounts are estimated revenues, appropriations, encumbrances, reserves for encumbrances, reserves for authorized expenditures, required contributions, and anticipated earnings.

There has been a tendency, particularly in Federal-government accounting, to omit budgetary accounts from the formal bookkeeping records, on the ground that the information and controls they were once thought to furnish can be better supplied by other devices. See *activity accounting.*

budgetary control The control of revenue and expense, and of changes in assets and liabilities, through the use of budgetary methods.

budget document (governmental accounting) The instrument used in presenting a comprehensive financial program to the appropriating or authorizing body. The budget document ordinarily includes a balanced statement of the revenues and expenditures and other exhibits reporting the current financial condition or estimated condition of the several funds (a) at the end of the last completed year, (b) at the end of the fiscal year in progress, and (c) at the close of the ensuing fiscal period.

budget period The period of time covered by a budget: a year, a quarter, sometimes a month, occasionally two or more years.

building-and-loan association See *savings-and-loan association.*

bulk cargo Unpackaged cargo.

bull (security and commodity markets) One who believes that prices will rise and who invests his money in securities or other property or advises others to do so, thus creating a *long* position. A "bullish" market is one in which the prevailing trend in prices is upward; a "bullish" influence is one that inflates or tends to inflate prices. See *bear.*

bullion Uncoined but refined gold or silver; generally in the form of bars or ingots.

bunched cost See *lump-sum purchase.*

bunched income (Federal income taxes) Income from personal services, from a literary, musical, or artistic work, from an invention, or from back pay of an employee—where largely received in one year for work for the most part performed over a longer period. Such income was taxed as if it had been received during the years of performance. Comparable relief from income bunching is available for damages collected for patent infringement, breach of contract, and antitrust injuries. The concept of bunched income has been replaced by *average income,* q.v.

burden Costs of manufacture or production not directly identifiable with specific products; factory overhead or service cost; indirect costs; apportionable costs; See *overhead.*

bureau A major organizational and functional subdivision of a department of the Federal government. Examples: the Bureau of Accounts in the Department of the Treasury; the Bureau of the Budget, before 1939 a Treasury subdivision and now nominally a part of the Executive Office of the President, reporting directly to the President.

burning ratio (insurance) The ratio of an actual loss by fire to the total value of burnable property.

business 1. The carrying on of trade or commerce, involving the use of capital and having, as a major objective, income derived from sales of goods or services; industrial and commercial activity generally.
2. The exchange of goods or services for cash, promises to pay, or other goods or services, whether or not involving gain.
3. Any establishment for the conduct of trade or commerce; a business enterprise.

business combination The bringing together of two or more business entities, usually corporations, accomplished by transferring the net assets of one or more of the entities to another of them (a *merger*) or to a new one created for that purpose (a *consolidation*). Either action may, in effect, be a purchase, with one or more groups of stockholders retiring, or a *pooling of interests* may occur in which the stockholders of all the participants share.

business corporation A corporation engaged in ordinary business pursuits, such as manufacturing or trading, as distinguished from other types, such as financial corporations (banks and insurance companies), railroads, public-service companies, schools and other nonprofit corporations, and cooperative enterprises.

business enterprise (or **entity** or **unit**) 1. A proprietorship, partnership, joint adventure, trust, or corporation; a group of persons having common interests of any kind, carrying on any economic activity, and constituting a unit commonly recognized as having a separate and distinct existence in the community; see *legal entity; entity; economic unit.*
2. Business collectively.

business income The net income of a corporation or of corporations generally. See *net income.*

business-interruption insurance Insurance against continuing expense, sometimes including payroll, and loss of business net income following the partial or full interruption of business activity caused by fire or other insured peril.

businessman's investment Bonds or stock of a business firm whose profits vary markedly with business trends: an investment suitable for a businessman who is in a position to watch market conditions closely.

business transaction 1. Any *transaction* with a business enterprise; also, a transaction governed by well-established, generally recognized commercial standards.

2. = *external transaction.*

business trust A form of organization for carrying on a joint venture or business operation; its assets are held by a trustee, and the owners or contributors of capital (*cestuis que trustent,* or shareholders) possess evidences of ownership known as certificates of beneficial interest. Like a partnership, the owners may be personally liable to creditors unless the latter are on notice that they may look only to the trust assets for the settlement of their claims. Depending on the nature of the trust declaration and the laws of the state, a trust of this character may enjoy the status of a corporation, with limited liability to creditors. A business trust is generally subject to the Federal income tax applicable to corporations. It is also known as a Massachusetts or common-law trust. If, however, the *cestuis que trustent* exercise a large degree of control over daily operations, the result may be a partnership and the partners may have an unlimited liability to creditors.

business-type *adj.* (governmental accounting) Employing the accrual basis of accounting; = *cost-type.* The term, characterizing the budget, system of accounting, and financial exhibits of government agencies, was first employed in the Government Corporation Control Act (1945; 59 Stat. 597).

but-for income That portion of the income attributable to a process or product in which a certain factor of production has been included as a cost in excess of what the cost would have been if the factor had been omitted or another factor had been substituted. The elements to be considered in determining the excess include costs associated with the factor and the effect on sales arising from any change in the characteristics of the product to which the factor may have contributed.

buyers' market A favorable condition for buyers within an industry characterized by an excess of supply over demand; contrasts with *sellers' market.* Under competitive conditions among sellers, a buyers' market results in lower market prices.

bylaws In a corporation, the rules adopted by the stockholders setting forth the general method by which the corporate functions are to be carried on: the time, place, and nature of meetings of the stockholders and directors; how directors are chosen; the appointment of officers and their duties; the issue and transfer of capital stock; the fiscal year; the appointment of auditors; how bylaw amendments are to be made; and so on. The bylaws must not, of course, be in conflict with the articles of incorporation or the laws of the state of incorporation or domicile.

byproduct A secondary product obtained during the course of manufacture, having a relatively small importance as compared with that of the chief product or products. The cost of a byproduct is commonly regarded as indeterminable; the revenue, if any, from its sale is typically credited to the operation concerned. See *joint product.*

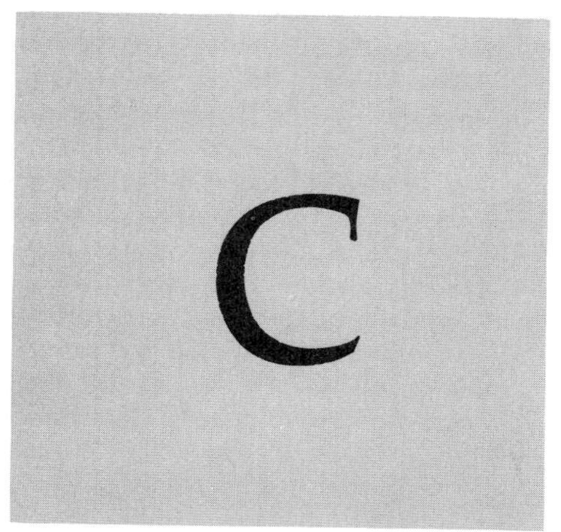

call 1. A demand on a subscriber to capital stock for all or a portion of the unpaid amount of his subscription.
2. A transferable option to buy a specified number of shares of stock at a stated price (usually somewhat above current market) at any time during a stated period. Such an option is purchased by a speculator anticipating a price rise above the delivery price. Should that event occur, he will order the delivery of the shares to him and sell them on the market, thus earning a profit on an investment of only the cost of the option. If the price declines, he will allow the option to expire, thus sustaining a loss equal to its cost. See *put*.

callable bond A type of bond permitting the issuer to pay the obligation before maturity by giving notice of redemption in a manner specified in the indenture. See *call premium*.

call loan A loan terminable at will by either party. The term is confined mostly to loans made by banks to stockbrokers.

call premium The excess above par payable by the issuer of a bond if redeemed before maturity, as provided by the bond indenture. The amount of the premium may vary, usually decreasing as maturity nears.

call price The price at which a callable bond is redeemable.

canceled check A check paid by the drawee bank and returned to the depositor; it serves as support for the bank's charge against the depositor's account and as the depositor's receipt from the payee.

cancellation 1. (of an insurance policy) The termination of an insurance contract or bond before the end of the policy period: designated as *flat* where the termination occurs on or before the effective date of the policy; prorata where the amount of the premium as adjusted is in the same proportion as the time the policy was in force compared with the original policy life; and short-rate where the insured cancels, the net premium cost being somewhat higher than prorata.
2. (of documents generally) Voiding by defacement, perforation, or other means whereby restoration is made impossible, so that any person subsequently inspecting or coming into possession of the instrument is put on notice of the voiding.

C&F Cost and freight: a term indicating that the quoted price of an object of sale includes charges for handling and freight up to delivery to a foreign port, the purchaser assuming costs of insurance and unloading, transportation, and other costs at or from the foreign port. Title passes to the buyer upon delivery to the ocean carrier. See *CIF*.

C&F price *FAS price*, plus freight to destination but excluding marine insurance. Title and responsibility are usually regarded as transferring to the buyer upon delivery to the ocean carrier. Freight is arranged by the seller for the account of the buyer.

capacity Ability to perform under stipulated conditions. See *capacity ratio*.

capacity cost Cost when operating at full capacity: said of a plant, process, department, overhead, or unit of product. Capacity cost, although generally more than partial-capacity operating cost, is not likely to vary proportionately with the rate of production, since numerous constituent items are of a fixed or semifixed character. See *fixed cost.*

capacity ratio The ratio of actual to maximum possible output. As used in national-income accounting, it is defined as the ratio of maximum possible output to current employment in a plant, industry, or other grouping. An approximate measure of maximum potential capacity is obtained by multiplying this ratio by current output. An approximate measure of maximum practical capacity is obtained by introducing adjustments for absenteeism, labor turnover, machine down time, and other like interruptions deemed to be unavoidable. Collections of capacity ratios for plants in a single industry are sometimes divided by the lowest ratio in the group to provide an *index number* of expansibility. This is a measure of relative expansion which assumes that the least efficient plant (the one with the lowest capital ratio) is operating at 100 percent maximum practical capacity. Such indexes may be derived on a one-, two-, or three-shift basis. Further adjustments may be introduced for various refinements of this measure. The following assumptions are, however, almost invariably required:

1. Constant *marginal productivity* of labor.
2. Constant product mix.
3. An adequate supply of labor and materials.
4. *Factors of production* are not substituted one for another because of changes in their relative prices.
5. Plant facilities and equipment are not subjected to more than minor alterations.

capital 1. Goods produced and intended for further production.
2. The amount invested in an enterprise—proprietorship, partnership, or corporation—by its owners; *paid-in capital.*
3. *Legal capital:* that portion of stockholders' contributions allocated to capital-stock account by the board of directors, bylaws, articles of incorporation, or agreement with stockholders; *stated capital.*
4. The amount so invested plus retained income (or earned surplus); *net worth; net assets; stockholders' equity.*
5. Net worth plus long-term liabilities; also, the equity of securityholders.
6. (economics) (a) One of the factors of production: goods produced by man and used in further production; wealth (of an individual) devoted to obtaining money income; any wealth employed with productive intent; e.g., consumers' capital; *producers' capital.* See *capital asset.* (b) Hence, net worth plus all liabilities; the total of *assets.* See *assets(2).*

Because of these varied meanings, all of which have wide currency, a better understanding results where the intended meaning is made clear.

capital account 1. Fixed assets as a class. In this sense, the term is used in such expressions as "additions during the year to capital account."
2. Any permanent proprietorship account.

capital asset 1. An asset intended for continued use or possession, common subclassifications being (a) land, buildings and equipment, leaseholds, mineral deposits, timber preserves (fixed assets); (b) goodwill, patents, trademarks, franchises (intangibles); (c) investments in affiliated companies.

In economics, the term is synonymous with *fixed capital,* and has essentially the same meaning as in the preceding paragraph: assets used in production that are exhausted gradually, in contrast with "circulating capital," which disappears or changes form in productive operations. An item of fixed capital is expected to yield to the owner, by aiding production, both an income and, during its economic life, a sum not less than his investment in the item.

In accounting terminology, the term may be synonymous with *fixed asset,* usually indicating any tangible asset, such as plant and equipment, and sometimes an intangible, such as a patent.

Capital assets are ordinarily those purchased for use in production over relatively long periods of time rather than for resale or for conversion in a single operation or within a short time period. See *fixed asset.*

2. (Federal income taxes) Any asset, *except* inventory, stock in trade, property used in the taxpayer's trade or business, and a copyright or artistic production owned by the creator of the work. See *capital gain.*

capital bonus = *stock dividend;* a British term.

capital budget 1. The portion of a budget, or a separate budget, devoted to proposed additions to capital assets and their financing.

2. (municipal accounting) A plan of municipal improvements instituted usually for a period of 5 years or more, including the method of financing them. The plan covers all proposed improvements of the municipality during the period, including self-supported enterprises such as municipal utilities. Also taken into account are improvements contemplated by overlapping or adjacent units of government, since both the need for a particular improvement and the means of financing it might be affected.

Factors taken into account in developing a capital budget include population trends, economic forecasts, and maintenance-cost estimates. Thus, the presumption of an increase in child population calls for the building of additional schools, the expansion of the municipal water plant, and increased park and playground facilities. Economic conditions may indicate a need to provide work for the unemployed or may point to the possibility of obtaining labor and materials at more or less than current rates. It may be difficult to raise taxes or other revenues and even more difficult to sell bonds during depression times. It is generally held that a municipality should, other things being equal, plan its construction program during periods of depression. Finally, in considering whether or not to proceed with a certain project or whether to construct one project instead of another, subsequent operating and maintenance estimates must be taken into account.

Methods of financing are a most important factor. It is recognized as desirable to finance construction from current revenues and thereby avoid interest expenses, but such a course of action may be impracticable because of tax-rate limits, particularly where the tax rates are already high. The alternative is to issue bonds and spread the cost over future years—often those most benefited. A part of the problem is to spread the maturities of the bonds so as to have approximately equal annual debt-service costs after taking into consideration other outstanding bonds and their maturities. If the project is to benefit a particular group, it may be financed from special assessments payable in one lump sum or installments. If the assessments are payable in installments, it will usually be necessary to issue bonds with maturities arranged in such a way that, as assessment installments are collected, they can be used immediately to retire a like amount of bonds. If the project is a utility or other self-supporting enterprise, bonds will of necessity have to be issued to finance it, since such a project cannot begin to earn revenue until it is put into operation. In that case, the question arises as to whether the bonds are to be backed by the "full faith and credit" of the municipality or whether revenue bonds are to be issued. The usual advantage inherent in full-faith-and-credit bonds is that they command a lower interest rate than revenue bonds. The disadvantage is that the municipality will be required to make good any deficiencies in bonds or interest payments if the revenues of the enterprise are not at a level sufficient to meet the related debt-service charges.

The capital budget is preferably revised each year so as to take into account new developments and plans. The data shown for the earliest year in the capital budget should be transferred, with such modifications as may be necessary, to the capital-expenditures section of that year's budget. In turn, an additional year's expenditures and means of financing may be added to the current year's capital budget.

capital coefficient (national-income accounting) Average cost of acquiring an additional unit of annual productive capacity. Capital coefficients are usually obtained by the *least-squares method*, using a straight-line *regression equation*, $Y = a + bX$, where X and Y are *time series* of expenditures and *capacity* increases, respectively. The value obtained for b provides an estimate of the capital coefficient. Further refinements, such as trend analysis and adjustments for variation in dollar cost are sometimes introduced to obtain "real" (or "physical") capital coefficients.

capital dividend A dividend charged to and hence deemed to be paid from paid-in capital.

capital expenditure 1. An expenditure intended to benefit future periods, in contrast to a *revenue expenditure*, which benefits a current period; an addition to a capital asset. The term is generally restricted to expenditures that add fixed-asset units or that have the effect of increasing the capacity, efficiency, life span, or economy of operation of an existing *fixed asset*.

2. Hence, any expenditure benefiting a future period.

capital gain The excess of proceeds realized from the sale or exchange of a noninventory asset (or capital asset as defined under section 1221 of the Federal Internal Revenue Code) over its book value or, sometimes in the determination of taxable income, other basis for gain. It is accounted for as is any other gain or profit: carried into the income statement (separately shown if material in amount) and thence to earned surplus or other proprietorship account. Some economists have urged that capital gains should not be combined with gains from other sources, the supposition being that capital gains are immediately reinvested. For many years this point of view has prevailed, in varying degrees, in the Federal income-tax law; under the Internal Revenue Code, long-term capital gains of individuals and corporations are taxed at rates less than those applicable to ordinary income. Also, in the computation of national income, both in the United States and abroad, capital gains are excluded. The general attitude of accountants is that this omission has the effect of seriously understating national income, since securities and other sources of capital gains are commodities differing in no essential way from other commodities, and that in times of inflation as well as depression, many capital gains find their way into the income stream.

Short-term capital gains are currently defined in the Federal income-tax law as those arising out of sales or exchanges of capital assets held for six months or less; long-term capital gains are those flowing from sales or exchanges of capital assets held for more than six months.

Although property used in the trade or business of a taxpayer (and held for more than six months) is excluded from the tax definition of "capital asset," a net gain on sales or exchanges of such property is treated as long-term capital gain under section 1231 of the Code.

capital goods 1. (economics) A term commonly used for fixed assets, sometimes including items or forces contributing to production for which no business outlay is required; synonymous with *producers' capital* or *goods*, i.e., capital used to further production. These terms may also refer to the material forms of producers' goods, such as machines, equipment, etc., in contrast with *capital values*, the monetary measures of such goods.

2. = *fixed assets*.

capitalization unit An expenditure for a fixed asset or addition thereto that has the effect of enlarging physical dimensions, increasing productivity, lengthening future life, or lowering future costs. In borderline cases, the cost, if it is to be capitalized, is often required to be well under the capitalized value of either (a) the resultant added service to be yielded, or (b) future costs saved. See *retirement unit; fixed asset; depreciation.*

capitalize 1. To record and carry forward into one or more future periods any expenditure the benefits or proceeds from which will then be *realized.* See *capital expenditure.*
2. To add to a fixed-asset account the cost of plant additions, improvements, and expenditures having the effect of increasing the efficiency or yield of a capital asset or making possible future savings in cost from its use.
3. To transfer surplus to a capital-stock account, as the result of the issue of a stock dividend, a recapitalization, or, under the laws of some states, resolution of the board of directors. See *stock dividend; capitalized surplus; splitup.*
4. To *discount* or calculate the *present worth* of the projected future earnings of an asset or business. See *capital value; capitalized value.*

capitalized expense An item of cost usually charged to profit and loss but, because related to a period of construction, added to a capital-asset account. Examples: taxes on property under construction; interest and other expenses incurred on new construction before its operating period commences. The generally preferred practice is not to capitalize in excess of the expense that would have been incurred had the construction activity not been in progress. See *fixed asset;* compare with *carrying charge.*

capitalized surplus Surplus (paid in or earned) of a corporation that has been transferred to capital stock, through the issue of a stock dividend, by increasing the par or stated value of capital stock without an issue of additional shares, or by a simple resolution of the board of directors. These actions, when authorized under articles of incorporation or amendments thereof, usually require ratification by stockholders. See *capitalize(3).*

capitalized value 1. The present worth of a future service, often determined on the basis of an assumed periodic yield and unit cost.
2. = *present value.*

capital leverage See *leverage.*

capital liability 1. = *long-term liability.*
2. = *net worth.*

capital outlay = *capital expenditure.*

capital paid in = *paid-in capital.*

capital-reconciliation statement = *statement of sources and applications of funds:* a British term.

capital reserves (British usage) That portion, or any detail thereof, of the *net worth* or *total equity* of an enterprise consisting of such items as premium on capital stock, revaluation surplus, reserve for the retirement of capital stock, and sometimes capital gains and other items, all of which is regarded as unavailable for withdrawal by proprietors; contrasts with *revenue reserve.*

capital stock 1. The ownership shares of a corporation authorized by its articles of incorporation.
2. The money value assigned to a corporation's issued shares, constituting generally the legal capital of the corporation. The capital stock of a corporation may be divided into several classes of shares having various rights, preferences, and priorities. It may have a par value within limits set by law, or it may have no par value. The latter is given a declared or stated value. See *stated value; legal capital.*
3. The account maintained for such par or stated value. See *authorized capital stock; issued capital stock.*

capital sum The original amount or principal of an estate, fund, mortgage, bond, note, or other form of financial investment, together with accretions not yet recognized as income.

capital surplus That part of the paid-in capital of a business not assigned to capital stock; i.e., contributions by stockholders in excess of par or stated value of shares; = *paid-in surplus.* This term is falling into disuse. It is being replaced by "paid-in surplus" or, more descriptively, "capital paid in in excess of par or stated value," or some variation thereof.

capital value (economics) 1. The investment in capital goods (fixed assets), measured in terms of cost or other value.
2. The total, on a discounted basis, of the estimated income stream from capital goods.

cardinal number A symbol expressing a quantity of units: 1, 2, 3, etc.; any *digit* or combination of digits; an *integer.*

card of accounts = *chart of accounts.*

carried interest (petroleum industry) The fraction of a *working interest* that advances no portion of the outlay necessary to pay for current costs, as of drilling, such costs being borne by the "carrying interest" making up the balance of the working interest. The agreement between the parties commonly provides for the recoupment of these costs out of the first proceeds from production.

carry (to) To *enter* or *post.*

carryback (Federal income taxes) 1. The amount of the net (operating) loss for a given year of an individual, corporation, or other taxpayer carrying on a business, subject to certain adjustments, that may be deducted from the net income of three preceding years; if not thus fully absorbed, the balance may be treated as a *carryover.*
2. The unused portion, if any, of the excess-profits credit that was added to the excess-profits credit of the preceding year under one-time tax laws; any amount not thus absorbed was treated as a *carryover.*

carry down To transfer the balance of a two-column account that has been ruled off, usually at the close of an accounting period, to a line immediately below the ruling, the purpose being to reopen the account as a single net figure at the beginning of the next accounting period. See *account.*

carry forward *v.* 1. To defer the classification of an item of revenue or expense as *nominal* until such time as the revenue is earned, or the benefit is received from the expenditure; during the interval, it appears on a balance sheet as deferred revenue or prepaid expense. A loss, i.e., an expenditure from which no commensurate benefit is being or will be received, is occasionally carried forward for absorption in some later period, although the accepted standard is to recognize its nominal character at the time the flow of benefits ceases.
2. To transfer the balance of an account from one ledger to another, from a temporary account to a permanent account, or from one period to the period immediately succeeding.
3. To transfer the total of a column of figures to another column or to another page, especially where a column or a page has been filled with entries or postings.
n. 1. The amount so deferred or transferred.
2. = *carryover.*

carry-forward working papers *Working papers,* often a part of a *permanent file,* containing running analyses or summaries of fixed assets, reserves, net worth, and other accounts the future understanding and interpretation of which are at least in part dependent on the auditor's accumulation of information concerning them.

carrying charge 1. A recurring cost incident to the possession or ownership of property, usually regarded as a current expense but occasionally added to the cost of an asset held for ultimate disposition where the market or likely disposal proceeds are judged to be sufficient to absorb the cost thus enhanced. Examples: taxes and mortgage interest on real estate; storage and insurance on merchandise; interest charged by brokers on margin accounts.
2. The addition to or *loading* of the price of merchandise sold on the installment plan.

carrying value 1. The amount at which

a property is recorded on the books, net of depreciation, if any; *book value.* 2. A value of market or less fixed by a lending bank on a security pledged as collateral.

carryover (Federal taxes) *a.* The amount of the net (operating) loss for a given year, of an individual, corporation, or other taxpayer carrying on a business, subject to certain adjustments, that to the extent not absorbed as a *carryback* may be deducted from the taxable income of succeeding years. The effect in the accounts and on financial statements, as discussed in APBO 11 (1967), is termed *carryforward. b.* The portion, if any, of the excess-profits credit of the preceding year that to the extent not absorbed as a carryback may be added to the excess-profits credit of the current year (section 432 [c] of the Federal Internal Revenue Code of 1939). *c.* The net capital loss of an individual, corporation, or other taxpayer that may be applied in reduction of capital gains (and, in the case of individuals, up to $1,000 of other income) during the succeeding five-year period.

carryover file = *permanent file.*

cartel A group of separate business organizations that has agreed to institute measures to control competition.

Such agreements, which may be open or secret and with or without government approval, are directed toward price, production, or marketing controls. Market quotas, or the division of territories, constitute a common form of agreement. Another device is the use of a single sales outlet for like products of member firms. Since no other method of disposal exists, the sales outlet can distribute the entire demand among member firms in agreed proportions, even when violent fluctuations in demand occur. Another arrangement allowing more flexibility to individual members of the cartel consists of a scale of fines and bonuses. Members that exceed agreed production rates are penalized and the funds are paid into a common pool. From this pool, bonuses are paid to those firms that have been unable to produce their full quotas.

Cartels have many forms. As common control increases in degree and duration, the cartel may pass through the voting-trust form into *monopoly.* Monopoly consists of a single legal entity exercising control of the entire production and sale of a commodity; *monopsony* takes the form of a single firm purchasing the entire production of a commodity. Monopoly and monopsony have found their more enduring and effective form in the *holding company.*

Cartels, generally not as effective as monopolies, have difficulty in maintaining themselves without recourse to governmental aid. Thus, through political or other maneuverings, they often attempt to move toward monopolistic devices. Lack of success may, on the other hand, drive cartels toward the economic condition of *oligopoly,* which differs from the cartel in that each of the individual firms is left to its own devices. No explicit agreement or form of control exists. Oligopoly (or oligopsony, the counterpart on the purchasing side) often proves even more rigid and less effective than the cartel. Each firm is so large that it is afraid to adjust to changing situations because any adjustment will immediately affect the other firms and result in retaliation—or, even in the absence of retaliation, the other firms will at least have to adjust to the new situation. Since the kind and degree of adjustment of other firms is for each an unknown magnitude, the tendency is for every firm to cling to its traditional practices. The existence of such a condition is known as oligopolistic (or oligopsonistic) uncertainty.

Oligopoly, oligopsony, and like conditions are classed as phenomena of imperfect competition. Firms operating under imperfectly competitive conditions share with monopoly the characteristic that each firm is so large and furnishes so significant a proportion of the product that changes in the firm's policies will affect market prices. But such firms share with pure competition the characteristic that firms may leave or enter the industry freely, as prospects of profit seem to dictate. Only when (a) each firm is so small that it has no significant influence on market prices, and (b) free access is available to all firms that seek to leave or enter the industry, can pure competition be said to prevail.

Cartesian coordinate system A *coordinate system,* with uniformly scaled axes at right angles to each other, devised by René Descartes, French philosopher of the 17th century, as a means of solving algebraic and geometric problems. See *coordinate system.*

cash *n.* Money, negotiable money orders and checks, and balances on deposit with banks after deducting outstanding checks. As an unqualified balance-sheet caption under *current assets,* cash may be assumed to be available for any ordinary use within the enterprise; hence it does not include the proceeds of security issues or other amounts that may be applied only to the acquisition of fixed or other noncurrent assets, or to the liquidation of funded debt or other noncurrent liabilities. Cash having such limited uses, bearing a descriptive title, is given a separate balance-sheet position. See *balance sheet; current asset.*

v. To exchange a check or other document for money.

cash asset Cash and any asset which may be converted immediately into cash without upsetting day-to-day operations; *marketable securities* are excluded. Examples: cash on hand; cash deposited in banks; cash in transit; demand certificates of deposit; trade acceptances. Cash in the hands of a trustee for the liquidation of debt is not regarded as a cash asset. The term should not be confused with *liquid assets* or *quick assets.* See *balance sheet.*

cash audit An audit limited to the examination of cash transactions for a stated period, its purpose being to determine whether or not all cash received and receivable has been recorded, disbursements are supported by authorized vouchers, the cash balance is represented by cash actually on hand or in bank, and the cash records and internal controls surrounding cash are in good order.

cash basis A basis of keeping accounts, in contrast to the *accrual basis,* whereby revenue and expense are recorded on the books of account when received and paid, respectively, without regard to the period to which they apply. The cash basis is a frequently unsatisfactory variation of the accrual basis, but in instances where transactions are limited to cash revenue and outgo, the two methods may virtually coincide.

cashbook A book of original entry for cash receipts, disbursements, or both.

cash budget An estimate of cash receipts and disbursements for a future period, cash requirements at various points within the period, and cash on hand at the end of the period.

cash-disbursement journal A *journal* in which are entered individual disbursements or blocks of disbursements as they occur. There are many varieties: some with a single money column, with entries made by hand; others with distribution columns that are machine-entered. See *check record.*

In a single business enterprise there may be several cash journals; e.g., a cash-receipts journal at each location receiving cash, one for each cashier or each depositary. Convenience, speed in recording, the competence and bonding of receiving and disbursing clerks, the nature of protective crosschecks, recording machinery available, and methods of internal control including the depth and frequency of internal audits, are among the factors determining the size, rulings if any, details preceding and accompanying entry, and disposition of cash records. Basic requirements call for accuracy, adequate supervision, and "built-in" good (internal and external) *audit trails.*

cash discount An amount allowed for the prompt settlement of a debt arising out of a sale. Cash discounts taken or allowed are usually shown in an income statement as reductions of sales or purchases; or, now less frequently, as financial expense or income on the theory that the prompt settlement of a receivable or payable is a prepayment, the "normal" payment being at the end of a credit period. In either case, the receivables and payables are first stated in the accounts at their gross amounts and the discounts are recorded in separate accounts as they are taken. A third method is to record in the first instance payables (or less commonly, receivables) at their net amounts, and to record the discounts *missed*, those arising from customers' accounts being an item of income and those from creditors' accounts an item of expense. The last-named method presumes the "normal" payment date to be the invoice date. In recent years there has been a slight trend toward the adoption of the third method for payables, although the first method has gained considerable popularity. A discount of more than 2 percent, even though allowed for prompt payment, has long been conventionally classified as a *trade discount*. See *discount*.

cash dividend A dividend paid in cash, as distinguished from one paid in corporate stock, bonds, or other obligations or in property other than cash. See *dividend*.

cash-flow statement A statement of cash income and outgo, its components often identified with items appearing in *balance sheets* and intervenient *income statements*. Accountants have followed a variety of ways in determining, classifying, and tabulating source-and-application amounts of sales, receivables, inventories, and payables, and occasionally other items; by means of a continuous segmentation through split balance-sheet and income accounts these variant practices can be noted. Thus, in the illustrations shown on page 80, if the item "materials and parts" is to appear in a cash-flow statement, some accountants would choose $4,807,400 (cash paid to materials suppliers regardless of the year of purchase); others would bring out different figures: $4,509,000 (this year's purchases); $4,393,000 (this year's purchases paid for); $4,505,800 (transfers of materials to work in progress—a transfer to a more liquid form of asset); $4,516,400 (materials in completed finished products—a still more liquid form of asset); or $4,472, 100 (the materials component of sales of finished products—materials now in the form of receivables or cash.) The first of these six amounts reflects the year's disbursements of cash identifiable with purchased materials (some received last year, some this year) and is the one used in the first of the two accompanying statements illustrating cash flows. Should the third or the fifth of these items be required at regular intervals, additional split accounts would be created (for finished-goods inventory and for the principal classes of transactions cleared through accounts payable). Each of the six amounts represents a completed cash flow or one about to take place. The time at which the payment is given recognition for statement purposes varies from some point in a preceding period to some point in the current period or some following period.

Split accounts, which include running analyses of cash receipts and disbursements, simplify the selection and determination of the amounts desired for a cash-flow statement. The practical justification for the simplest procedures (some procedures may involve a number of anticipated rather than past cash transactions) is found in the usual absence of significant differences between the possible alternatives appearing above: differences diminishing in significance still further in comparative presentations provided they have been consistently derived.

Cash-flow statements are often regarded by security and credit analysts

[1ST VERSION]

BELFORD MANUFACTURING COMPANY

Cash-flow Statement
Calendar Year 19-7

(thousands of dollars)

Cash was received from			
Operations			
Collections from customers		$9 351 8	
Dividends from investments		32 7	$ 9 384 5
Sale of retired equipment			40 0
Financial transactions—			
Added bank loan		$1 200 0	
Sale of investments		312 0	1 512 0
Total cash received			$10 936 5
Cash was paid out for			
Goods			
Raw materials		$4 807 4	
Supplies			
Factory	$ 240 7		
Office	112 4	353 1	
Factory equipment		483 0	$ 5 643 5
Services			
Direct labor	$1 255 8		
Other factory labor	113 2		
Administrative & selling	882 6	$2 251 6	
Utilities & other outside services			
Factory	$1 205 3		
Office	498 6	1 703 9	3 955 5
Income taxes, 19-6 and 19-7; in part 1968			865 4
Temporary investments			296 5
Quarterly dividends to stockholders			180 0
Total disbursements			$10 940 9
Decrease in cash			4 4

Note: Capital stock having a paid-in value of $170,000 was issued to the company's president, in lieu of cash, as compensation for services.

[2ND VERSION]

BELFORD MANUFACTURING COMPANY

Cash-flow Statement
Calendar Year 19-7

(thousands of dollars)

Cash was derived from		
Operations		
Collections from customers	$9 351 8	
Dividends from investments	32 7	$ 9 384 5
Sale of retired equipment		40 0
Financial transactions		
Increase in bank loan	$1 200 0	
Sale of investments, net	15 5	
Decrease in cash	4 4	1 219 9
Total cash derived		$10 644 4
Cash was disbursed for		
Operating costs		
Raw materials & supplies	$5 160 5	
Wages & salaries	2 251 6	
Outside services	1 703 9	$ 9 116 0
Income taxes		865 4
Factory equipment		483 0
Dividends to stockholders		180 0
Total cash disbursed		$10 644 4

as providing a better basis for judgments concerning profits, financial condition, and financial management than the basis supplied by traditional but now often compromised income statements. One common derivative from cash-flow statements often cited by analysts has been growth trends.

A projected cash-flow statement, based on past actual experience as modified by expected price changes and other factors provides a useful basis for both planning and budgeting. See *flow statement; funds-flow statement; cash basis; budget.*

cash fund 1. A deposit or investment of cash for any purpose, readily reconvertible into cash: a *cash asset.*
2. *pl.* = *temporary investments*, as in the phrase "cash and cash funds."

cashier One responsible for the handling and initial recording of cash receipts and disbursements, and of cash on hand, or of a limited class of cash transactions.

cash in bank The balance of money on deposit with a bank, subject to withdrawal, after deducting outstanding checks and adjusting for bank charges and credits; often included is a minimum amount on deposit required under a service or short-term loan agreement.

cash in transit Cash (currency and checks) in movement to or from an organization at a specific moment of time and thus not appearing on the organization's books. If the sender or receiver of the cash is a subsidiary, home office, or branch, the in-transit item, not appearing as such on the books of either, is the subject of a reclassification entry whenever combined or consolidated financial statements are prepared.

cash items Receipted bills, checks, and other vouchers for disbursements from imprest or other cash funds, held for collection or for reimbursement from general cash; checks, drafts, and other paper credited to a depositor's account, to be collected by the bank.

cash journal A cashbook; a columnar journal or equivalent in which all transactions are entered, whether or not cash is involved. See *cashbook; ledger journal; cash disbursements journal.*

cash on hand Cash in immediate possession, represented by coin, paper money, and negotiable checks and other paper commonly accepted for immediate credit by a bank in a deposit of cash.

cash price The price charged when payment is effected within a specified interval of time, either immediately or within a limited credit period such as 30 days. It is usually the same as *COD* price. See *price.*

cash-receipts journal A journal in which cash receipts are entered chronologically. Some forms provide for a single entry per day for cash sales and other types of receipts over which separate controls are maintained. See comments under *cash-disbursements journal.*

cash records The records and evidences of the receipt, disbursement, deposit, and withdrawal of cash. Cash records include cash-receipt, cash-disbursement, and petty-cash books; registers of receipts and disbursements; checkbooks, stubs, or registers; canceled checks; copies of deposit slips; and receipt and disbursement vouchers and subvouchers and their attachments. See *book of account; system of accounts.*

cash requirements See *estimate of cash requirements.*

cash resource = *cash asset.*

cash sale 1. The delivery of goods or the performance of service accompanied by a concurrent receipt of *cash.*
2. *pl.* A classification of sales made up of such transactions. See *sale.*

cash statement A statement rendered periodically, often daily, to the management, usually showing the opening and closing balances of cash on hand and in each bank, a summary of the receipts and disbursements of the period or day, and particulars of deposits and withdrawals. The statement may be cumulative and may also contain an estimate of the resources and requirements of the immediate future. See *cash-flow statement.*

cash surrender value See *surrender value.*

casting out nines See *check figure(1)*.

ceiling Any limit in physical amounts or dollars, imposed by legal or administrative authority. Examples: a ceiling price; a personnel ceiling limiting the number of employees or their compensation. See *price*.

ceiling price See *price; administered price*.

central tendency The pattern displayed by a collection of interrelated data when plotted as *coordinates*. See *arithmetic mean*.

cents percent See *insurance premium*.

certificate See *audit report (1)*.

certificate of deposit 1. A formal instrument, frequently negotiable or transferable, issued by a bank as evidence of indebtedness and arising from a deposit of cash subject to withdrawal under the specific terms of the instrument: (a) demand certificates, payable upon presentation, seldom bearing interest; (b) time certificates, payable at a fixed or determinable future date, usually bearing interest at a specified rate.
2. A formal certificate, usually printed or engraved, ordinarily negotiable or transferable, and issued by a depository or agent against the deposit of bonds or stock of a corporation under the terms of a reorganization plan or other agreement.

certificate of incorporation A document issued by the secretary of state or other state official, establishing a corporation. See *articles of incorporation*.

certificate of indebtedness 1. One of a series of bearer obligations, usually of comparatively short term, interest-bearing, unsecured, issued by a corporation in conjunction with temporary financing, or by the Treasury of the United States, for current requirements of the government, in anticipation of taxes or the sale of long-term bonds.
2. A general term applied to a bond or other security evidencing debts owed, as distinct from a certificate of stock, which represents a share in the equity.

certificate of necessity (Federal income taxes) An authorization by a defense agency (section 168 of the Internal Revenue Code) permitting the *amortization* or *accelerated depreciation* on a 60-month basis of the cost of all or a portion of *emergency facilities*, the purpose being to induce taxpayers to build or acquire items of plant or equipment essential to production during a period of national emergency.

certified check A depositor's check on which a bank guarantees payment by endorsement, usually across the face of the check, an action accompanied by a debit against the customer's account and a credit to certified checks payable. Verbal guarantees, sometimes given by banks, may have the same effect.

certified financial statement A balance sheet or other financial statement accompanied by and related to a report of a public accountant. See *audit report*.

certified public accountant An accountant who, having met the statutory requirements of a state or other political subdivision of the United States of America as to age, education, residence, moral character, and experience, has been registered or licensed to practice public accounting and is permitted to call himself "certified public accountant" and use the initials "CPA" after his name.

certifying officer (governmental accounting) A bonded employee authorized to approve vouchers for payment.

cestui que trust (cestuis que trustent, *pl.*) "He who trusts"; a person entitled to the beneficial or equitable interest in property held in trust, the legal title being held by a trustee; the beneficiary of a *trust*.

chain discount A series of trade-discount percentages or their total; thus, if a list (catalog) price is subject to a 40-15-15 discount to dealers, the total chain discount is 56.65 percent (i.e., $40 + .15 \times 60 + .15\,[.85 \times 60]$). See *trade discount*.

change fund Cash committed to cashiers or placed in change machines for the purpose of supplying change to customers and others, for cashing payroll checks, and sometimes for making advances to employees. It may be maintained on an *imprest-fund* basis.

channel discount A discount comparable to a distributor's discount but differing by being applied against sales to institutional buyers, including state and Federal agencies, and to purchasers who further process the product or assemble it in a larger unit. Because such purchasers distribute a different product, larger or smaller discounts than distributor discounts may be justified on the ground that a different class of customer is being served.

characteristic (of a logarithm) The integer to which the *mantissa* of a base-10 logarithm table must be attached in order to obtain a logarithm.

For the logarithm of 10 or any greater number, the characteristic is equal to the total number of digits the whole number contains, less 1; for the logarithms of the numbers 1 to 10, the characteristic is 0; for positive decimal fractions of 1, the characteristic, expressed as a minus number, is equal to the number of zeros immediately following the decimal point, plus 1. Thus the value shown in the illustrative logarithms, page 268, for 4353 is 638789, but this value is the mantissa only and must be written .638789; the characteristic is 4 — 1, or 3. For 4.353, the characteristic would be 0; for .4353, the characteristic would be —1; and for .04353, the characteristic would be —2. The logarithms of these numbers may then be expressed as follows:

Number	Logarithm		
4353	3.638789		
4.353	0.638789		
.4353	−1.638789	or	9.638789 − 10
.04353	−2.638789	or	8.638789 − 10

See *logarithm; mantissa.*

charge *n.* A *debit.*

v.t. To debit.

charge-and-discharge statement A tabular summary prepared for an executor, administrator, trustee, or other fiduciary, accounting for the principal and income for which he has been responsible and constituting a part of either an interim or final report on his activities. The statement may be in two parts: the first accounting for principal, the second for income, but only where such a division is required, as by law or court order. The "charges" commence with the inventory at the time the fiduciary takes over; if the fiduciary is under the jurisdiction of a court (as he generally is), he seeks court approval for both the inclusiveness of the inventory items and their value. He may also call upon a public accountant for necessary accounting records, methods of recording various types of transactions, forms of periodic reports, and, from time to time, audits of transactions and statements. Other "charges" appearing in the charge-and-discharge statement will consist of assets discovered after the inventory has been taken and approved; gains (over inventory valuations) from the disposal of assets; and income from the assets or operations over which the fiduciary has jurisdiction. "Discharges" are composed of expenses, losses, and distributions chargeable to "principal"; expenses and distributions applicable to income; and, if the statement is an interim one, the inventory of assets remaining at the end of the last day covered by the statement.

One form of a charge-and-discharge statement is shown on page 84; here an executor is reporting to a court on his handling of the affairs of a deceased person. The period of the executor's administration is not yet ended, since the last item on the statement is an inventory; a final statement would show distributions of the assets and no inventory. A charge-and-discharge statement is usually in brief form, with supporting schedules for individual items where they are numerous or require lengthy explanations.

charge off *v.* To treat as a loss; to write off; to designate as an expense or loss an amount originally recorded as an asset.

RALPH J. DOLSON, EXECUTOR

Estate of William M. Kinder, Deceased

Interim Statement of Charge and Discharge
February 14, 19-1 (date of death) to December 31, 19-1

I have charged myself with—		
A. Inventory filed with Court February 25, 19-1:		
Cash on hand	$ 14.60	
Cash in First National Bank	21,482.95	
Account receivable—Edward Hart	2,500.00	
1,220 shares of common stock of Erg Supply Company at market value of $31.50 per share on February 14, 19-1	38,430.00	
Household furniture, at nominal value	1,000.00	$63,427.55
B. Gain on sale of 600 shares of stock at $35 per share		2,100.00
C. Cash dividends on stock—		
$3 on 1,220 shares	3,660.00	
$1 on 620 shares	620.00	4,280.00
Total		$69,807.55
I have credited myself with—		
A. Expenses—		
Funeral	$ 1,150.00	
Household bills	40.00	
Court fees	250.00	
Executor's bond	15.00	
State inheritance tax (preliminary)	2,610.00	$ 4,065.00
B. Loss on sale of household furniture		125.50
C. Allowance to widow of $300 per month		3,150.00
D. Assets on hand December 31, 19-1:		
Cash in First National Bank, including undistributed income of $1,130.00	$12,937.05	
620 shares of common stock of Erg Supply Company at original inventory value of $31.50 per share	19,530.00	
U. S. Savings Bonds—Series F, purchased June 1, 19-1	30,000.00	62,467.05
Total		$69,807.55

Notes: 1. Remaining taxes to be paid, as now computed, will be approximately $3,200.00.
2. Other unpaid expenses, including compensation of executor, are estimated at $275.00.

chargeoff *n.* The elimination by a transfer to expense of a portion or all of the balance of an account in recognition of the expiration of any continuing value. Most chargeoffs are of such a nature as to require authorizations or approvals at top-management levels.

charm price A price the cents portion of which is somewhat less than a dollar or terminates with a 9 or other "eye-catcher," and which is regarded as having "customer appeal"; e.g., $4.95, $3.98, $1.79: a term employed in retail stores and mail-order houses.

charter 1. See *articles of incorporation.*
2. See *charter party.*

charter party The contract between a shipowner and the person hiring the ship. It specifies the price; the cargo to be carried; the ports of loading and destination; the period of time, including allowable *lay days;* the rate of demurrage, where the number of agreed lay days is exceeded; special facilities to be provided; and other conditions. The contract may be in the nature of an outright lease to the hirer or it may merely provide that transportation services be furnished by the owner.

chart for attributes (statistics) A type of statistical chart used to analyze the quality of a production or inspection process or a source of supply. See *statistical quality control.*

chart of accounts A systematically arranged list of accounts applicable to a specific concern, giving account names and numbers, if any. A chart of accounts, accompanied by descriptions of their use and of the general operation of the *books of account,* becomes a *classification* or *manual of accounts:* a leading feature of a *system of accounts.*

chattel Any item of personal property or of any interest in land other than full ownership; as, a *good, a commodity,* a growing crop, a *lease.*

chattel mortgage A mortgage on personal property.

check *n.* A bill of exchange drawn on a bank, payable on demand. The British spelling of the word, "cheque," is now obsolete in the United States.

v.t. To compare for accuracy; to test or sample; to testcheck; to verify; to gain a knowledge of. As a verb, the word has no exact meaning and its employment without a descriptive qualification is usually avoided.

check figure A whole number, derived from and representing another, sometimes employed in verifying arithmetic operations. There are two systems, both occasionally found in bookkeeping practice and elsewhere, particularly in the absence of adding or computing machines. Both involve the determination of the check figure from the individual digits of the number represented, and its use in a "proof" operation.

1. In the 9-check-figure system, known also as "casting out the 9's," the representative (or check) figure is determined by subtracting from the sum of the individual digits of the number to be represented the highest included multiple of nine; thus, for the number 24,107, the check figure is $(2 + 4 + 1 + 0 + 7$, or $14) - 9 = 5$; the check figure of 999 is $(9 + 9 + 9$, or $27) - 27 = 0$; the check figure of 10 is 1. Adding these three original numbers by ordinary arithmetic gives 25,116, the check figure of which is $15 - 9$, or 6; the sum of the check figures of the three numbers is $5 + 0 + 1 = 6$; and the addition is said to be correct. Again, $348 - 95 = 253$; and the check figures for the three numbers $6 - 5 = 10 - 9$ again indicate the correctness of the arithmetic operation. Also, $348 \times 95 = 33{,}060$, and $(6 \times 5) - 27 = 12 - 9$; $1{,}493 \div 124 = 12\frac{5}{124}$, and $\frac{8}{7} = [(3 \times 7) + 5 - 18]/7$.

2. Under the 11-check-figure system, the check figure is obtained by subtracting the alternate digits, commencing with the second from the right, from the sum of the remaining digits, employing 11 or a multiple of 11 in such a manner as to secure a positive result of less than 11. For the three numbers illustrated above, the check figures are: $-(0 + 4) + (7 + 1 + 2) = 6$, $-(9) + (9 + 9) = 9$, and $-(1) + (0) + 11 = 10$. The total of the numbers, 25,116, has a check figure of $-(1 + 5) + (6 + 1 + 2) = 3$; the sum of the individual check figures is $(6 + 9 + 10) - 22 = 3$. The check figures of the two multiplied numbers and their product are 7, 7, and 5, respectively, and $(7 \times 7) - 44 = 5$. Finally, applying the test to the division, $\frac{8}{3} = [(1 \times 3) + 5]/3$.

check register A journal in which checks issued are recorded. Where supported by a *voucher register* or its equivalent, it often takes the form of a single-column journal, containing only check numbers and amounts; see *voucher system.*

chunk (statistics) A sample selected other than on a *probability* basis. See *probability sample.*

CIF Cost, Insurance, and Freight: a term indicating that the quoted price of an object of sale *includes* charges for handling, insurance, and freight up to delivery to a foreign port, beyond which the purchaser must assume any further handling, insurance, and transportation charges. See *C&F.* The seller may also undertake to provide insurance and transportation *for the account of* the buyer. Title passes to the buyer upon delivery to the ocean carrier unless otherwise agreed to by the parties.

CIF price Same as *C&F price*, except that the seller includes the cost of marine insurance. Title passes to the buyer upon delivery by the seller to the ocean carrier unless otherwise agreed to by the parties. Freight and insurance are arranged by the seller for the account of the buyer.

circularization = *confirmation* (*2*).

circulating asset = *current asset;* a British term.

circulating capital That part of a business investment that is being constantly consumed and renewed in operations, such as raw materials, labor costs, and other outlays contributing to a production process, contrasting with *fixed capital; current assets.* See *turnover; capital* (*6*).

circulating decimal = *repetend.*

circulation of costs The method employed or the amount involved in the distribution of *variances* to the products or activities believed to be responsible for them.

claim 1. A demand for payment, reimbursement, or compensation for injury or damage, under law or contract.
2. (insurance) The demand for the payment of a loss under an insurance contract or bond; the estimated amount to be paid or the amount actually paid.
3. = *equity.*

class Any group of things, characteristics of things, or events having features in common.

classification The grouping of transactions, entries, or acccounts under a common head or heads; a list of such groupings. See *classification of accounts; system of accounts.*

classification of accounts A list of accounts, systematically grouped (= *chart of accounts*), suitable for a particular organization, with descriptions setting forth the meaning, function, and content of each account and the relation of one to another; frequently accompanied by designs and descriptions of the records to be kept, the forms to be used in recording transactions, instructions covering their use and disposition, and the maintenance of controls. See *accounting manual; system of accounts.*

classified trial balance A *trial balance* having its component items arranged in groups, each group with its subtotal, and each subtotal constituting an item of a financial statement. The purpose of such a trial balance is to *routinize* financial-statement preparation; see *illustrative trial balance* on pp. 396–397.

class interval The number or range making up a class in a frequency distribution; thus, in the *correlation table* on page 122, two groups of class intervals are shown, the first in each series being 116–120 and 36–40. The interval in both series is 5, and it may be assumed in the former, for example, that the interval commences with 115.5 and ends with 120.5, its midpoint being exactly 118. Or it may be assumed that the interval commences with 116.0 and ends with 120.9, in which case the midpoint would be 118.5.

class rate 1. (insurance) The cost, in terms of cents per $100 of risk, of insuring against various perils, a different rate applying to different classifications of persons, properties, and hazards.
2. A rate fixed by a common carrier, usually with governmental approval, for the transportation of commodities of a given type.

Clayton Act A Federal law (38 Stat. 730), passed in 1914, directed against "unfair competition" and any act that would tend to lessen competition or create a monopoly, such as price discriminations, secret rebates, pressures on dealers not to sell competitive products, and acquisitions of competing enterprises.

clearance (statistical quality control) See *tolerance.*

clearing account A *primary* account containing costs that are to be transferred to other accounts; an intermediate account to which is transferred a group of costs or revenues or a group of accounts containing costs or revenues and from which a distribution of the total is made to other accounts. Examples: a construction account to which materials, payrolls, and other costs relating to the construction are carried and which is eliminated upon completion of the construction by a distribution to one or more *capital-asset* accounts; a *profit-and-loss* account set up as at the close of a fiscal period, containing income and expense account balances and closed out by a transfer to retained earnings.

clearing house A voluntary association or corporation acting as a medium for the daily settlement of transactions between its members or stockholders. It makes possible multilateral exchanges of checks, drafts, and notes as between banks of a given area, thus eliminating unilateral settlements between individual banks; and, in the case of stock and commodity brokers, it provides a means of disposing of mutual transactions promptly, safely, and uniformly, with a minimum of paper work.

clearing-house statement 1. A statement, submitted by a broker to the clearing house of a security or commodity exchange, on which are shown his trades on the exchange and the quantities and amounts by which his purchases in each security or commodity exceed his sales or vice versa. On the basis of a reconciliation of the statements of the clearing-house members, the net amount due to or by each broker is paid by or to the clearing house, and the net quantity of each security or commodity deliverable or receivable by each broker is delivered to or by the clearing house, thus involving a minimum number of transfers of cash, securities, and other evidences of ownership.
2. The formal statement issued by a clearing house to show the results of its activities and its financial position.

clerical error As applied to books of account, any incorrect entry or posting, especially when involving *routine* transactions; typical causes are a mistake in coding, a faulty computation—as in an extension or footing, a failure to enter or post, a posting to a wrong account or to the wrong side of an account.

close (the books) 1. To transfer the balances of revenue and expense accounts at the end of an accounting period directly, or through a profit-and-loss (or *clearing*) account, to *retained earnings* or to another proprietorship account or accounts, so that only balance-sheet (asset, liability, and net-worth; = *real*) accounts remain open on the general ledger. The transfer is made by means of one or more *closing entries.*
2. Hence, to give effect to adjusting entries and otherwise put the books of account in order at the end of a month, quarter, or other less-than-a-year period so that a trial balance can be extracted and financial statements prepared.

close corporation A corporation with a comparatively small number of stockholders, all of whom often are active in the conduct of its affairs. Frequently the stockholders are also directors, a voting trust or proxies have been executed to insure continuity of management, and the articles of incorporation or bylaws restrict stock transfers. See *corporation.*

closed account An account with equal debits and credits.

closed-end company A company maintaining an investment service for a limited group of stockholders, often specializing in a particular type of security. With no redemption privileges, its shares may be listed on a stock exchange.

closed mortgage (or **bonds**) A mortgage (or issue of bonds) against which no amount may be borrowed in addition to the total already reached.

closing The process of preparing, entering, and posting *closing entries.*

closing agreement (Federal income taxes) A written agreement between the taxpayer and the Commissioner of Internal Revenue, subject to approval by higher authority, as to the settlement of a specific item or of a tax relating to a specified period of time. The agreement is regarded as final in the absence of fraud, malfeasance, or misrepresentation of a material fact.

closing date The date as of which the accounting records of an organization are made ready for a trial balance and the preparation of financial statements: conventionally, the last day of a month, year, or other accounting period; but there may be "special" closings on other dates. In some organizations, the term is also applied to certain dates preceding the end of the period which mark cutoffs on certain classes of transactions; that is, dates after which transactions will be included in a subsequent period. Thus, the closing date for sales in a 31-day month may be established as the 28th, because the lag in recording sales for the final three days might delay the preparation of financial statements; with the growth of improved bookkeeping devices, this practice, at one time very common, has been largely eliminated.

closing entry 1. A periodic entry or one of a series of periodic entries by means of which the balances in revenue and expense accounts and the nominal elements of mixed accounts are adjusted for the purpose of preparing financial statements. At the end of the fiscal year, a final closing entry eliminates the year's revenue and expense (nominal) accounts, their net total being carried to *retained earnings* (earned surplus) or other proprietorship accounts.

2. An entry, usually annual, uniting separately maintained nominal elements of a *split ledger account*.

3. An entry having the effect of balancing an account, a set of accounts, or a ledger.

closing trial balance = *postclosing trial balance*.

CMS Rating Committee The Combined Marine Surcharges Committee of the Institute of London Underwriters. Its purpose is to study and establish marine-insurance rates.

COD 1. Cash (or Collect) On Delivery. An instruction attaching to a lot of goods requiring the payment of a specified amount of cash by the buyer as the goods are turned over to him or as services are rendered.

2. A classification of sales made up of such transactions, contrasting with *cash sale*, *credit sale*, and *barter*. See *sale*.

code *v.* 1. To affix a distinguishing reference number or other symbol.

2. To designate on a voucher or other medium the account affected, a description of the transaction, and other data, as a condition precedent to an entry or posting.

n. The symbolization, transaction description, and other information required under a given system of accounts to be affixed to vouchers and transaction records generally for the purpose of identification and disposal; *codification*.

codicil A written change in a will.

codification (or **coding**) A number or distinctive symbol attached to an account, entry, invoice, voucher, or other record or document serving as a device for distinguishing the members of a class of items from each other and as an index. Examples: the symbolization accompanying the classification of accounts; the numbering of recurring monthly journal entries so as to indicate the month and nature of the entry; the numbering of invoices or vouchers so that the number reveals the date or period of entry.

coding clerk A clerk who designates the accounts affected and the *legend*, if any, accompanying the *entry* or *posting* of completed transactions.

coefficient 1. Any one or more numbers or symbols placed before another number or symbol and serving as its multiplier; in the expressions $6a$, $3ab$, $abcd$, the respective coefficients of a, b, and d are 6, $3a$, and abc.

2. (statistics) A conventional measure of the relation or lack of relation between magnitudes, of which the following are the principal types:

(a) *Coefficient of alienation:* A measure

of the lack of relation between two or more variables; the value secured when the correlation coefficient is subtracted from unity. It is usually written $k = \sqrt{1 - r^2}$, where k is the coefficient of alienation and r the *coefficient of correlation*.

(b) *Coefficient of association:* Any measure designed to show the degree of association between two or more sets of characteristics. Generally, the measure is chosen so that it is equal to +1 when there is complete positive association, −1 when there is complete negative association, and 0 when there is no association between the attributes. For the type of phenomenon lending itself to the 2 × 2 table appearing under *contingency table*, it may be developed as follows:

When the attributes are independent—that is, lack either positive or negative association—then

$$\frac{a}{a+c} = \frac{a+b}{N} = \frac{b}{b+d},$$

where a & c and b & d are two sets of characteristics and N is $a + b + c + d$; from the first two of these ratios, the following is derived:

$$a = \frac{(a+b)(a+c)}{N}. \qquad (1)$$

Positive association is said to exist when

$$a > \frac{(a+b)(a+c)}{N} \qquad (2)$$

and

$$a - \frac{(a+b)(a+c)}{N} > 0. \qquad (3)$$

Negative association is said to exist where the inequality sign is reversed. In either case, expression (3) will always result in a number, positive or negative, that may be represented by the symbol D; upon simplifying (3),

$$D = \frac{ad - bc}{N}, \qquad (4)$$

and the association is positive, independent, or negative, depending on whether $D \gtreqless 0$.

Because (4) may yield a magnitude greater than 1 or less than −1, the following ratio is often employed:

$$Q = \frac{ad - bc}{ad + bc}. \qquad (5)$$

In the case of independence, or lack of association, $ad = bc$ and $Q = 0$. Perfect positive association yields $bc = 0$ and $Q = 1$. Perfect negative association yields $ad = 0$ and $Q = -1$. All other cases will fall between these extremes. If the association is positive, $ad > bc$ and $Q > 0$; if the association is negative, $ad < bc$ and $Q < 0$.

For the case displayed in the contingency table (page 106), the value of Q becomes

$$Q = \frac{ad - bc}{ad + bc} = \frac{(276)(66) - (473)(3)}{(276)(66) + (473)(3)} = 0.86,$$

showing a strong positive association between inoculation and absence of attack by cholera. As the values in the table are reduced in proportion to the total, Q tends toward 0.

It should be remembered that the coefficient of association Q applies only to 2 × 2 contingency tables. Measures for analysis of more complex cases may be found in statistics texts.

(c) *Coefficient of correlation:* A measure of strength of the linear relationship between two statistical series, ranging between 0, or no relation, and +1, perfect correspondence, or −1, perfect inverse correspondence. It is the square root of the excess of 1 over a fraction the numerator of which is the square of the standard error of estimate and denominator is the square of the standard deviation. See *least-squares method; standard deviation; correlation table.*

(d) *Coefficient of determination:* (i) The square of the correlation coefficient; usually written r^2. It assesses the proportion of the total *variance* in the *dependent variable* that is explained or accounted for by its linear relation to the *independent variable*. (ii) Gain in efficiency as measured by least-squares equations.

(e) *Coefficient of multiple correlation:* A measure of the degree of relation between several variables; usually written as R with subscripts attached to denote the variables of relation.

(f) *Coefficient of nondetermination:* A measure of the lack of relation between two or more variables; the square of the correlation coefficient subtracted from unity; usually written $k^2 = 1 - r^2$.

(g) *Coefficient of partial correlation:* A measure of the degree of relation existing between two variables when the effect of other variables is taken into account.

For example, $r_{12.34}$ is intended to show the degree of relation existing between X_1 and X_2 when the effects of X_3 and X_4 have been allowed for. The coefficient $r_{12.34}$ is sometimes referred to as the *second-order* correlation coefficient, where the order is determined by the number of subscripts to the right of the decimal point. The order thus specifies the number of other variables whose effect has been allowed for. Thus, $r_{12.3}$ would be a *first-order* coefficient, measuring the degree of relation between X_1 and X_2 when possible effects of X_3 are allowed for. The ordinary coefficient of correlation r_{12}, between X_1 and X_2, is known as a *zero-order* correlation coefficient and may be regarded as a special type of partial-correlation coefficient which does not take explicitly into account the possible effects of other variables such as X_3 and X_4 on either X_1 or X_2.

(h) *Coefficient of variation:* The standard deviation divided by the arithmetic mean of a group of figures. Combining the two in this fashion provides a relative measure of dispersion independent of units of measure and thus allows comparisons which would not be possible if either the mean or standard deviation were used alone. When the *standard error* of a statistic is expressed in this form, a measure of relative *precision* or *accuracy* is secured which is referred to as the percent standard error. If $\sigma_{\bar{x}}$ represents the standard error of the mean and σ the universe standard deviation, and N and n represent the universe and sample size, respectively, then

$$\frac{\sigma_{\bar{x}}}{\mu} = \sqrt{\frac{N-n}{N-1} \times \frac{\sigma^2}{n\mu^2}} = \text{\% standard error of the mean } \mu.$$

Such a measure also implicitly defines the degree of *reliability;* hence, the measure provides a convenient device in sample design. For a specified design, it may be used to determine the sample size necessary to obtain desired levels of precision and reliability. The equation $10\% = \sigma_{\bar{x}}/\mu$ implies that samples of size n will lie within 10 percent of the universe mean approximately two-thirds of the time in samples drawn from a normal universe with a *variance* σ^2. If $10\% = 1.96\,\sigma_{\bar{x}}/\mu$, this will be true about 95 percent of the time (see *normal table*). Applied in reverse, this formula may be used to determine sample size n necessary to achieve prescribed levels of precision and reliability. Suppose, for example, that this 10 percent precision and 2/3 probability (or reliability) is desired for samples drawn from a universe of size $N = 1{,}000$, $\mu = 10$, $\sigma = 10$, and $\sigma_{\bar{x}}/\mu = 10\%$. Substituting these values,

$$\frac{10}{100} = \sqrt{\frac{1{,}000 - n}{1{,}000 - 1} \times \frac{100}{n \times 100}}$$

and $n = 91$ will be a sample of sufficient size to guarantee this result. If it is desired to increase the reliability to 0.95, the above result must be multiplied by $(1.96)^2$, or approximately 4, yielding $n = 364$. The same result would be secured if the measure of reliability were left at 0.67, had it been desired to increase the precision from 10 percent to 5.

coinsurance clause A provision in an insurance contract, such as one covering loss by fire, limiting the liability of the insurer to a proportion of any loss no greater than the ratio of the amount of insurance carried to an amount equal to 80 percent or some other stated percentage of the "cash value of the property" at the time of the loss. Thus, if a loss of $60,000 is incurred on property having a cash value of $150,000 on which insurance of $100,000 is carried—the policy containing an 80 percent coinsurance clause—the insurer will pay not in excess of 100/120 of $60,000, or $50,000. Had the insurance been $120,000 or more, the full loss, up to the amount of the insurance, would have been covered.

collapsible corporation (Federal income taxes) Under the Federal income-tax law (section 341), a corporation formed or availed of principally to manufacture, construct, or produce property, or to purchase inventory, or to hold stock in such a corporation in order that the stockholders may realize capital gain by disposing of the stock before the corporation has realized income from the property. Commencing with 1950, such gains may be taxed as ordinary income.

collateral Real or personal property pledged as part or full security on a debt.

collateralize To secure a debt in part or in full by a *pledge*. A note is said to be collateralized if the debtor has deposited property with his creditor as part or full security for the payment of principal or interest or both.

collateral-trust bonds Bonds secured by other bonds or by stock.

collectible Capable of being converted into cash, now (*due*) or ultimately (not yet due).

collusion A secret understanding between two or more persons to take advantage of another with the object of depriving him of a right or property.

—*collusive, adj.* Said of bidding which occurs whenever suppliers agree among themselves to submit identical or nearly identical bids to a prospective purchaser.

columnar system A system of bookkeeping whereby use is made of columnar records for continuous analysis and grouping of items, thus reducing the labor of posting. The use of columns may not be confined to books of original entry but may extend to ledgers as well.

combination 1. An agreement between two more or business organizations, often constituting a trade group, for purposes of mutual benefit, such as a price or other trade-practice agreement; sometimes prohibited by law.

2. = *business combination.*

3. *pl.* The *arrangements* or *permutations* of a collection of n objects into two mutually exclusive classes of r and $n - r$ items, where r is the number selected for sampling or other purpose; commonly represented by the symbols C_r^n or ${}_nC_r$; see formula 4 under *permutation.*

combined depreciation-and-upkeep method (of depreciation) See *depreciation method.*

combined financial statement A financial statement in which the assets and liabilities or revenue and expense of a group of related companies or other *entities* have been added together so as to disclose their financial position or operating results as though they were a single business unit: a *consolidated* or *group financial statement.*

combining financial statement A *group financial statement* showing constituent units, usually prepared in the style of a worksheet.

commercial expense A general expense of operating a business, as contrasted with a cost of manufacturing or marketing. Commercial expense generally includes administrative, selling, and general expense and other general overhead, such as advertising and research. As employed in contracts, the term requires detailed specification.

commercial law That branch of law relating to business enterprise and commercial transactions generally: contracts, partnerships, negotiable instruments, estates and trusts, sales, debtor and creditor, corporations, real estate, and securities.

commercial paper 1. A type of loan, now seldom found, taking the form of simple discount notes usually in five- and ten-thousand-dollar denominations, sold to financial houses and by them distributed to banks or investors. Issuers are mostly larger manufacturers or distributors with top credit ratings and substantial working-capital ratios.
2. Any form of *negotiable* instrument, such as a check or draft; = *bill of exchange (1)*.

commission Remuneration of an employee or agent relating to services performed in connection with sales, purchases, collections, or other types of business transactions, and usually based upon a percentage of the amounts involved.

commitment 1. An anticipated expenditure, evidenced by a contract or purchase order given to an outsider. Commitments are not given expression on accounting records, except sometimes on those of government agencies, since the signing of a contract or issuance of a purchase order does not give rise to a transaction. Disclosure of the amount and nature of a commitment in a balance sheet or balance-sheet footnote is, however, generally regarded as required where substantial additions to capital assets are involved or where the amount of prospective goods or services contracted for is substantially in excess of a 60- or 90-day supply or of whatever is regarded as normal to the business, or where the market price has declined or is likely to decline before delivery substantially below the contract price, thus giving rise to the likelihood of a loss. But disclosure is ordinarily not required where a commitment is covered by a firm-price contract or purchase order from customers. See *liability; contingent liability; obligation; deal.*
2. = *encumbrance (1).*

commodity = *good;* often used as a singular for (economic) *goods.*

common average 1. = *simple average.*
2. = *particular average.*

common carrier Any *person* who undertakes and is authorized to transport persons or goods as a regular business. Under common law, such a person must provide facilities for all that apply, at fair and nondiscriminatory rates; and he is held liable for any accident or damage in transit except those attributable to an act of God, a foreign enemy, or carelessness by the person transported or by the shipper of the goods. The liability of a common carrier for any loss or injury to property received by it for transportation is in effect that of an insurer. With respect to passengers, however, the common carrier is liable only for want of proper care.

common cost The cost of facilities or services employed in the output of two or more operations, commodities, or services. Thus, the premium paid for a fire-insurance contract covering unrelated lots of merchandise in a warehouse is a common cost. The resulting benefits extend to each lot. The assignment, if any, of a portion of the premium cost to any one lot is primarily an arbitrary process; insurance and other common costs applicable to a number of unrelated items are more often treated as a period cost. Common costs of related outputs are known also as *joint costs.*

common-law corporation See *joint-stock association.*

common-law trust = *business trust.*

common logarithm See *logarithm.*

commonsense A *judgment* or set of judgments taken to be obvious or inevitable in a given social group and reflecting some definite or partially formulated general approach to problems deemed related. The *principles* of commonsense cannot be rigorously formulated, but their applications are accepted because they have been found to work with relative success through the operation of habit or custom. From the point of view of precise logical analysis, commonsense approaches to problems and their solutions often exhibit mutually contradictory elements.

common stock The class of capital stock

of a corporation which, after considering the rights attaching to preferred classes, if any, is neither limited nor preferred in its participation in distributions of the surplus earnings of a corporation or in the ultimate distribution of its assets; the class of stock representing the residual ownership of all the assets of a corporation after the liabilities and other proprietary claims have been satisfied.

communication Any process of passing information from one person to another, as by instructing or reporting; also, the initiation of a mutual interaction, human or mechanical, or both, such as that resulting from the operation of any *control(1)* or *feedback* device. Varying degrees of communication (to readers) may be achieved by financial statements as a whole or by an item or footnote in such statements.

community of interest The coordination of the policies or operations of two or more separately owned organizations by any of various devices short of actual control. See *control(3)*. Ownership of capital stock in common with others, interlocking directorates, a common source of supply (as in the case of certain chain filling stations, drug stores, and groceries), the existence of but one or a few customers, are examples; the effects are often the same as those brought about by formal controls. See *trade association*.

community property Property owned by husband and wife "in community," each sharing equally in the income derived from it. Community-property laws are in force in eight states—Arizona, California, Idaho, Louisiana, Nevada, New Mexico, Texas, and Washington. Since the Federal Revenue Act of 1948, income-splitting between husband and wife has been permitted, giving a comparable income-tax benefit to married couples in all states.

company 1. A *corporation*.

2. Loosely, any organization consummating transactions in its own name.

comparability The quality attributable to two or more items or groups of items whereby the presence of a comparable or disparate condition or trend may be discerned. In the preparation of comparative financial statements, the accounting objective is not only a sequential arrangement of similar elements, but also the furnishing of information that will be helpful to their joint consideration. Comparability does not connote similarity but often striking differences.

comparative balance sheet Two or more balance sheets of the same organization with different dates, or of two or more organizations with the same date, customarily displayed in parallel columns to facilitate the observation of variances; supplementary columns are sometimes added to show differences. See *balance sheet*.

comparative cost A cost so computed as to be comparable with another, and obtainable by like methods of compilation, adjustment for differences in price or volume, elimination of divergent elements, and the like. See *cost*.

comparative statement A statement of assets and liabilities, operations, or other data, giving figures in comparative form for more than one date or period or organization.

compare (auditing) To establish the correspondence or similarity of differently located items.

compensation 1. Payment to an individual for services performed.

2. Reimbursement or other payment for losses or damages sustained.

compensatory balance A minimum balance in a commercial checking account equal to a voluntary or agreed percentage (e.g., 20 percent) of a *credit line* or of an outstanding loan from a bank. In effect, the result is to supply the bank with semipermanent capital, in return for which the depositor may gain unlimited checking privileges, a liberal credit line, or a favorable rate of interest when a loan is required.

compensatory time Time off allowed an

employee for overtime, usually on an informal basis and at the discretion of his supervisor, thus obviating an overtime accrual.

competitive price 1. The price established in a market by the bargaining of a considerable number of buyers and sellers, each acting independently of the other, no one of them having power enough to dominate the market. See *price.*
2. (economics) The price per unit of a commodity sold under conditions of perfect competition. Under such hypothetical conditions, in the short run a competitive price will tend to cover a seller's marginal cost—i.e., cost added by producing an additional unit. This may be above or below its average total unit cost (average variable cost plus average fixed cost) but not below average variable (out-of-pocket) cost. In the long run, a competitive price tends to equal a seller's average total unit cost as well as his marginal cost, including a normal or average return on his investment.

complete audit An audit of all transactions, often made for limited periods, for special transactions, or for small concerns. See *detailed audit.*

complete transaction A transaction that will not normally be followed by another transaction dealing with the same subject matter: contrasts with *incomplete transaction.*

complex number A combination of two real numbers (x,y) with the *imaginary number* i, typically written $x + iy$, i being the mathematical entity whose square (i^2) is -1.

complex trust (Federal income taxes) In general, a trust that may accumulate income or make a charitable contribution. See *simple trust.*

composite-life method (of depreciation) Depreciation computed on the *depreciation base* of a fixed-asset group considered as a whole. See *depreciation method.*

composition = *arrangement (1).*

compound To add interest to principal at periodic intervals for the purpose of establishing a new basis for subsequent interest computations.

compound amount of 1 The total produced by compounding the principal of 1 at a given percentage over a given period of time.

Thus, $1, compounded at 2 percent per period for 20 periods, amounts to $1.49; for 50 periods, $2.69. A formula for the amount of 1 may be derived from the following reasoning: At the end of the first period, at 2 percent compound interest per period, a principal of $1 will amount to $1.02; at this point, simple interest and compound interest are the same. At the end of the second period, 2 percent of $1.02 establishes the amount of interest for the second period at $0.0204, the 4/10 mill being "interest on interest" or simple interest on the amount of $0.02. The new principal at the end of the second period is $1.02 + $0.0204, or $1.0404. At the end of the third period, the new principal is $1.0404 + $0.020808, or $1.061208. These figures may be formulated as follows:

$$1.00 + .02(1.00) = (1 + .02)(1.00) = 1.02,$$
$$1.02 + .02(1.02) = (1 + .02)(1.02) = 1.02^2,$$

and

$$1.02^2 + .02(1.02^2) = (1 + .02)(1.02^2) = 1.02^3.$$

The compounding operation thus yields a result that is a power of the total at the end of the first period. In terms of rate of interest per period i and number of periods n, the formula becomes $(1 + i)^n$.

A table of illustrative values for this formula appears on pp. 96–97.

compound amount of 1 per period The amount, at a future date, of periodic deposits drawing compound interest.

Periodic deposits drawing compound interest are in reality a series of *compound amounts of 1.* Thus, if an individual is able to save $1,000 out of his earnings each six months and invest it at the end of each six months' period at 3 percent per annum, compounded semiannually, he will have accumulated at the end of three years the amount shown in the following schedule:

Number of Deposit	Interest Periods	Formula ($i = .015$)	Accumulated Amount
1	5	$(1 + i)^5$	$1,077.28
2	4	$(1 + i)^4$	1,061.36
3	3	$(1 + i)^3$	1,045.68
4	2	$(1 + i)^2$	1,030.23
5	1	$(1 + i)$	1,015.00
6	0	(1)	1,000.00
Total			$6,229.55

A formula for such computations may be derived by first restating the six items in terms of the customary symbols, t being the accumulated total amount resulting from the periodic deposits of 1, i the rate of interest per period, and n the number of periods:

$$t = (1 + i)^{n-1} + (1 + i)^{n-2} + (1 + i)^{n-3} + (1 + i)^{n-4} + (1 + i)^{n-5} + 1. \quad (1)$$

Multiplying each side of the equation by $(1 + i)$,

$$t(1 + i) = (1 + i)^n + (1 + i)^{n-1} + (1 + i)^{n-2} + (1 + i)^{n-3} + (1 + i)^{n-4} + (1 + i)^{n-5}. \quad (2)$$

Subtracting (1) from (2),

$$t(1 + i) - t = (1 + i)^n - 1. \quad (3)$$

Simplifying the left half of the equation and dividing both sides by i,

$$t = \frac{(1 + i)^n - 1}{i}, \quad (4)$$

which is the compound interest for n periods divided by the rate of interest. See *geometric progression.*

Illustrative values for the formula appear in the table on pp. 98–99.

compound discount The excess of a payment or a series of payments to be made in the future over their present value. See *present value of 1.* Its mathematical expression is $1 - 1/(1 + i)^n$.

compound (journal) entry A *journal entry* having three or more elements and often representing several transactions; contrasts with *simple journal entry,* which contains single debit and credit elements. The compound-journal-entry form is often employed to indicate compactly the accounting effect of a series of related transactions.

compound interest Interest resulting from the periodic addition of simple interest to principal, the new base thus established being the principal for the computation of interest for the next following period. To obtain the amount of compound interest on an amount of 1 remaining on deposit over any number of periods, the formula for the *compound amount of 1* can be utilized by subtracting 1 from the result:

$$(1 + i)^n - 1,$$

where i is the rate of interest per period, and n the number of periods. The table of values for $(1 + i)^n$, pp. 96–97, supplies the basis for the more common computations; or logarithmic tables may be used. Thus, to obtain the compound interest on $450 at $2\frac{1}{2}$ percent for 15 periods, the amount of 1, at the same rate and over the same period of time, is shown by the table to be 1.4482982: this figure, less 1, multiplied by 450, gives the required answer, or $201.73. See *compound amount of 1.*

compound-interest formula A formula involving the use of compound interest. The common formulas in the accounting and financial fields are given in the table on page 100. This table gives the derivation and use of these formulas, together with the names of the abbreviated tables illustrating their application to usual situations. A number of books of tables currently available on the market give values for many more rates and periods. *Interpolation* will supply approximations of values not shown in these tables.

n	½%	1%	1½%	2%	2½%	3%
1	1.0050 000	1.0100 000	1.0150 000	1.0200 000	1.0250 000	1.0300 000
2	1.0100 250	1.0201 000	1.0302 250	1.0404 000	1.0506 250	1.0609 000
3	1.0150 751	1.0303 010	1.0456 784	1.0612 080	1.0768 906	1.0927 270
4	1.0201 505	1.0406 040	1.0613 636	1.0824 322	1.1038 129	1.1255 088
5	1.0252 513	1.0510 101	1.0772 840	1.1040 808	1.1314 082	1.1592 741
6	1.0303 775	1.0615 202	1.0934 433	1.1261 624	1.1596 934	1.1940 523
7	1.0355 294	1.0721 354	1.1098 449	1.1486 857	1.1886 858	1.2298 739
8	1.0407 070	1.0828 567	1.1264 926	1.1716 594	1.2184 029	1.2667 701
9	1.0459 106	1.0936 853	1.1433 900	1.1950 926	1.2488 630	1.3047 732
10	1.0511 401	1.1046 221	1.1605 408	1.2189 944	1.2800 845	1.3439 164
11	1.0563 958	1.1156 683	1.1779 489	1.2433 743	1.3120 867	1.3842 339
12	1.0616 778	1.1268 250	1.1956 182	1.2682 418	1.3448 888	1.4257 609
13	1.0669 862	1.1380 933	1.2135 524	1.2936 066	1.3785 110	1.4685 337
14	1.0723 211	1.1494 742	1.2317 557	1.3194 788	1.4129 738	1.5125 897
15	1.0776 827	1.1609 690	1.2502 321	1.3458 683	1.4482 982	1.5579 674
16	1.0830 712	1.1725 786	1.2689 855	1.3727 857	1.4845 056	1.6047 064
17	1.0884 865	1.1843 044	1.2880 203	1.4002 414	1.5216 183	1.6528 476
18	1.0939 289	1.1961 475	1.3073 406	1.4282 462	1.5596 587	1.7024 331
19	1.0993 986	1.2081 090	1.3269 507	1.4568 112	1.5986 502	1.7535 061
20	1.1048 956	1.2201 900	1.3468 550	1.4859 474	1.6386 164	1.8061 112
21	1.1104 201	1.2323 919	1.3670 578	1.5156 663	1.6795 819	1.8602 946
22	1.1159 722	1.2447 159	1.3875 637	1.5459 797	1.7215 714	1.9161 034
23	1.1215 520	1.2571 630	1.4083 772	1.5768 993	1.7646 107	1.9735 865
24	1.1271 598	1.2697 346	1.4295 028	1.6084 372	1.8087 259	2.0327 941
25	1.1327 956	1.2824 320	1.4509 454	1.6406 060	1.8539 441	2.0937 779
26	1.1384 596	1.2952 563	1.4727 095	1.6734 181	1.9002 927	2.1565 913
27	1.1441 519	1.3082 089	1.4948 002	1.7068 865	1.9478 000	2.2212 890
28	1.1498 726	1.3212 910	1.5172 222	1.7410 242	1.9964 950	2.2879 277
29	1.1556 220	1.3345 039	1.5399 805	1.7758 447	2.0464 074	2.3565 655
30	1.1614 001	1.3478 489	1.5630 802	1.8113 616	2.0975 676	2.4272 625
35	1.1907 269	1.4166 028	1.6838 813	1.9998 896	2.2732 052	2.8138 625
40	1.2207 942	1.4888 637	1.8140 184	2.2080 397	2.6850 638	3.2620 378
45	1.2516 208	1.5648 107	1.9542 130	2.4378 542	3.0379 033	3.7815 958
50	1.2832 258	1.6446 318	2.1052 424	2.6915 880	3.4371 087	4.3839 060
55	1.3156 289	1.7285 246	2.2679 440	2.9717 307	3.8887 730	5.0821 486
60	1.3488 502	1.8166 967	2.4432 198	3.2810 308	4.3997 897	5.8916 031
65	1.3829 103	1.9093 665	2.6320 416	3.6225 231	4.9779 583	6.8299 827
70	1.4178 305	2.0067 634	2.8354 563	3.9995 582	5.6321 029	7.9178 219
75	1.4536 325	2.1091 285	3.0545 917	4.4158 355	6.3722 074	9.1789 257
80	1.4903 386	2.2167 152	3.2906 628	4.8754 392	7.2095 678	10.6408 906
85	1.5279 715	2.3297 900	3.5449 784	5.3828 788	8.1569 642	12.3357 085
90	1.5665 547	2.4486 327	3.8189 485	5.9431 331	9.2288 563	14.3004 671
95	1.6061 121	2.5735 376	4.1140 921	6.5616 992	10.4416 038	16.5781 608
100	1.6466 685	2.7048 138	4.4320 456	7.2446 461	11.8137 164	19.2186 320

OF COMPOUND AMOUNT OF 1

$3\frac{1}{2}\%$	4%	$4\frac{1}{2}\%$	5%	$5\frac{1}{2}\%$	6%
1.0350 000	1.0400 000	1.0450 000	1.0500 000	1.0550 000	1.0600 000
1.0712 250	1.0816 000	1.0920 250	1.1025 000	1.1130 250	1.1236 000
1.1087 179	1.1248 640	1.1411 661	1.1576 250	1.1742 414	1.1910 160
1.1475 230	1.1698 586	1.1925 186	1.2155 063	1.2388 247	1.2624 770
1.1876 863	1.2166 529	1.2461 819	1.2762 816	1.3069 600	1.3382 256
1.2292 553	1.2653 190	1.3022 601	1.3400 956	1.3788 428	1.4185 191
1.2722 793	1.3159 318	1.3608 618	1.4071 004	1.4546 792	1.5036 303
1.3168 090	1.3685 691	1.4221 006	1.4774 554	1.5346 865	1.5938 481
1.3628 974	1.4233 118	1.4860 951	1.5513 282	1.6190 943	1.6894 790
1.4105 988	1.4802 443	1.5529 694	1.6288 946	1.7081 445	1.7908 477
1.4599 697	1.5394 541	1.6228 530	1.7103 394	1.8020 924	1.8982 986
1.5110 687	1.6010 322	1.6958 814	1.7958 563	1.9012 075	2.0121 965
1.5639 561	1.6650 735	1.7721 961	1.8856 491	2.0057 739	2.1329 283
1.6186 945	1.7316 764	1.8519 449	1.9799 316	2.1160 915	2.2609 040
1.6753 488	1.8009 435	1.9352 824	2.0789 282	2.2324 765	2.3965 582
1.7339 860	1.8729 812	2.0223 702	2.1828 746	2.3552 627	2.5403 517
1.7946 756	1.9479 005	2.1133 768	2.2920 183	2.4848 021	2.6927 728
1.8574 892	2.0258 165	2.2084 788	2.4066 192	2.6214 663	2.8543 392
1.9225 013	2.1068 492	2.3078 603	2.5269 502	2.7656 469	3.0255 995
1.9897 889	2.1911 231	2.4117 140	2.6532 977	2.9177 575	3.2071 355
2.0594 315	2.2787 681	2.5202 412	2.7859 626	3.0782 342	3.3995 636
2.1315 116	2.3699 188	2.6336 520	2.9252 607	3.2475 370	3.6035 374
2.2061 145	2.4647 155	2.7521 663	3.0715 238	3.4261 516	3.8197 497
2.2833 285	2.5633 042	2.8760 138	3.2250 999	3.6145 899	4.0489 346
2.3632 450	2.6658 363	3.0054 345	3.3863 549	3.8133 923	4.2918 707
2.4459 586	2.7724 698	3.1406 790	3.5556 727	4.0231 289	4.5493 830
2.5315 671	2.8833 686	3.2820 096	3.7334 563	4.2444 010	4.8223 459
2.6201 720	2.9987 033	3.4297 000	3.9201 291	4.4778 431	5.1116 867
2.7118 780	3.1186 515	3.5840 365	4.1161 356	4.7241 244	5.4183 879
2.8067 937	3.2433 975	3.7453 181	4.3219 424	4.9839 513	5.7434 912
3.3335 904	3.9460 890	4.6673 478	5.5160 154	6.5138 250	7.6860 868
3.9592 597	4.8010 206	5.8163 645	7.0399 887	8.5133 088	10.2857 179
4.7023 586	5.8411 757	7.2482 484	8.9850 078	11.1265 541	13.7646 108
5.5849 269	7.1066 833	9.0326 363	11.4673 998	14.5419 612	18.4201 543
6.6331 411	8.6463 669	11.2563 082	14.6356 309	19.0057 617	24.6503 216
7.8780 909	10.5196 274	14.0274 079	18.6791 859	24.8397 704	32.9876 909
9.3567 007	12.7987 352	17.4807 024	23.8399 006	32.4645 865	44.1449 716
11.1128 253	15.5716 184	21.7841 356	30.4264 255	42.4299 162	59.0759 302
13.1985 504	18.9452 547	27.1469 963	38.8326 859	55.4542 036	79.0569 208
15.6757 375	23.0497 991	33.8300 964	49.5614 411	72.4764 263	105.7959 935
18.6178 588	28.0436 049	42.1584 551	63.2543 534	94.7237 906	141.5789 045
22.1121 759	34.1193 333	52.5371 053	80.7303 650	123.8002 059	189.4645 112
26.2623 286	41.5113 859	65.4707 917	103.0346 764	161.8019 179	253.5462 550
31.1914 080	50.5049 482	81.5885 180	131.5012 578	211.4686 357	339.3020 835

n	$\frac{1}{2}\%$	1%	$1\frac{1}{2}\%$	2%	$2\frac{1}{2}\%$	3%
1	1.0000 000	1.0000 000	1.0000 000	1.0000 000	1.0000 000	1.0000 000
2	2.0050 000	2.0100 000	2.0150 000	2.0200 000	2.0250 000	2.0300 000
3	3.0150 250	3.0301 000	3.0452 250	3.0604 000	3.0756 250	3.0909 000
4	4.0301 001	4.0604 010	4.0909 034	4.1216 080	4.1525 156	4.1836 270
5	5.0502 506	5.1010 050	5.1522 669	5.2040 402	5.2563 285	5.3091 358
6	6.0755 019	6.1520 151	6.2295 509	6.3081 210	6.3877 367	6.4684 099
7	7.1058 794	7.2135 352	7.3229 942	7.4342 834	7.5474 301	7.6624 622
8	8.1414 088	8.2856 706	8.4328 391	8.5829 691	8.7361 159	8.8923 360
9	9.1821 158	9.3685 273	9.5593 317	9.7546 284	9.9545 188	10.1591 061
10	10.2280 264	10.4622 125	10.7027 217	10.9497 210	11.2033 818	11.4638 793
11	11.2791 665	11.5668 347	11.8632 625	12.1687 154	12.4834 663	12.8077 957
12	12.3355 624	12.6825 030	13.0412 114	13.4120 897	13.7955 530	14.1920 296
13	13.3972 402	13.8093 280	14.2368 296	14.6803 315	15.1404 418	15.6177 904
14	14.4642 264	14.9474 213	15.4503 820	15.9739 382	16.5189 528	17.0863 242
15	15.5365 475	16.0968 955	16.6821 378	17.2934 169	17.9319 267	18.5989 139
16	16.6142 303	17.2578 645	17.9323 698	18.6392 853	19.3802 248	20.1568 813
17	17.6973 014	18.4304 431	19.2013 554	20.0120 710	20.8647 304	21.7615 877
18	18.7857 879	19.6147 476	20.4893 757	21.4123 124	22.3863 487	23.4144 354
19	19.8797 169	20.8108 950	21.7967 164	22.8405 586	23.9460 074	25.1168 684
20	20.9791 154	22.0190 040	23.1236 671	24.2973 698	25.5446 576	26.8703 745
21	22.0840 110	23.2391 940	24.4705 221	25.7833 172	27.1832 741	28.6764 857
22	23.1944 311	24.4715 860	25.8375 799	27.2989 835	28.8628 559	30.5367 803
23	24.3104 032	25.7163 018	27.2251 436	28.8449 632	30.5844 273	32.4528 837
24	25.4319 552	26.9734 649	28.6335 208	30.4218 625	32.3490 380	34.4264 702
25	26.5591 150	28.2431 995	30.0630 236	32.0302 997	34.1577 639	36.4592 643
26	27.6919 106	29.5256 315	31.5139 690	33.6709 057	36.0117 080	38.5530 423
27	28.8303 701	30.8208 878	32.9866 785	35.3443 238	37.9120 007	40.7096 335
28	29.9745 220	32.1290 967	34.4814 787	37.0512 103	39.8598 008	42.9309 225
29	31.1243 946	33.4503 877	35.9987 009	38.7922 345	41.8562 958	45.2188 502
30	32.2800 166	34.7848 915	37.5386 814	40.5680 792	43.9027 032	47.5754 157
35	38.1453 781	41.6602 756	45.5920 879	49.9944 776	54.9282 074	60.4620 818
40	44.1588 473	48.8863 734	54.2678 939	60.4019 832	67.4025 535	75.4012 597
45	50.3241 642	56.4810 747	63.6142 010	71.8927 103	81.5161 312	92.7198 614
50	56.6451 630	64.4631 822	73.6828 280	84.5794 015	97.4843 488	112.7968 673
55	63.1257 750	72.8524 573	84.5295 989	98.5865 337	115.5509 214	136.0716 197
60	69.7700 305	81.6696 699	96.2146 517	114.0515 394	135.9915 900	163.0534 368
65	76.5820 618	90.9366 488	108.8027 722	131.1261 554	159.1183 303	194.3327 578
70	83.5661 055	100.6763 368	122.3637 529	149.9779 111	185.2841 142	230.5940 637
75	90.7265 050	110.9128 468	136.9727 806	170.7917 728	214.8882 970	272.6308 556
80	98.0677 136	121.6715 217	152.7108 525	193.7719 578	248.3827 126	321.3630 185
85	105.5942 969	132.9789 971	169.6652 255	219.1439 390	286.2785 695	377.8569 517
90	113.3109 358	144.8632 675	187.9299 004	247.1566 563	329.1542 533	443.3489 037
95	121.2224 295	157.3537 550	207.6061 425	278.0849 598	377.6641 540	519.2720 257
100	129.3336 984	170.4813 829	228.8030 433	312.2323 059	432.5486 540	607.2877 327

COMPOUND AMOUNT OF 1 PER PERIOD

3½%	4%	4½%	5%	5½%	6%
1.0000 000	1.0000 000	1.0000 000	1.0000 000	1.0000 000	1.0000 000
2.0350 000	2.0400 000	2.0450 000	2.0500 000	2.0550 000	2.0600 000
3.1062 250	3.1216 000	3.1370 250	3.1525 000	3.1680 250	3.1836 000
4.2149 429	4.2464 640	4.2781 911	4.3101 250	4.3422 664	4.3746 160
5.3624 659	5.4163 226	5.4707 097	5.5256 313	5.5810 910	5.6370 930
6.5501 522	6.6329 755	6.7168 917	6.8019 128	6.8880 510	6.9753 185
7.7794 075	7.8982 945	8.0191 518	8.1420 085	8.2668 938	8.3938 376
9.0516 868	9.2142 263	9.3800 136	9.5491 089	9.7215 730	9.8974 679
10.3684 958	10.5827 953	10.8021 142	11.0265 643	11.2562 595	11.4913 160
11.7313 932	12.0061 071	12.2882 094	12.5778 925	12.8753 538	13.1807 949
13.1419 919	13.4863 514	13.8411 788	14.2067 872	14.5834 982	14.9716 426
14.6019 616	15.0258 055	15.4640 318	15.9171 265	16.3855 907	16.8699 412
16.1130 303	16.6268 377	17.1599 133	17.7129 828	18.2867 981	18.8821 377
17.6769 864	18.2919 112	18.9321 094	19.5986 320	20.2925 720	21.0150 659
19.2956 809	20.0235 876	20.7840 543	21.5785 636	22.4086 635	23.2759 699
20.9710 297	21.8245 311	22.7193 367	23.6574 918	24.6411 400	25.6725 281
22.7050 157	23.6975 124	24.7417 069	25.8403 664	26.9964 027	28.2128 798
24.4996 913	25.6454 129	26.8550 837	28.1323 847	29.4812 048	30.9056 525
26.3571 805	27.6712 294	29.0635 625	30.5390 039	32.1026 711	33.7599 917
28.2796 818	29.7780 786	31.3714 228	33.0659 541	34.8683 180	36.7855 912
30.2694 707	31.9692 017	33.7831 368	35.7192 518	37.7860 755	39.9927 267
32.3289 022	34.2479 698	36.3033 780	38.5052 144	40.8643 097	43.3922 903
34.4604 137	36.6178 886	38.9370 300	41.4304 751	44.1118 467	46.9958 277
36.6665 282	39.0826 041	41.6891 963	44.5019 989	47.5379 983	50.8155 774
38.9498 567	41.6459 083	44.5652 101	47.7270 988	51.1525 882	54.8645 120
41.3131 017	44.3117 446	47.5706 446	51.1134 538	54.9659 805	59.1563 827
43.7590 602	47.0842 144	50.7113 236	54.6691 264	58.9891 094	63.7057 657
46.2906 273	49.9675 830	53.9933 332	58.4025 828	63.2335 105	68.5281 116
48.9107 993	52.9662 863	57.4230 332	62.3227 119	67.7113 535	73.6397 983
51.6226 773	56.0849 378	61.0070 697	66.4388 475	72.4354 780	79.0581 862
66.6740 127	73.6522 249	81.4966 180	90.3203 074	100.2513 638	111.4347 799
84.5502 777	95.0255 157	107.0303 231	120.7997 742	136.6056 141	154.7619 656
105.7816 7	121.0293 9	138.8499 7	159.7001 6	184.1191 7	212.7435 1
130.9979 1	152.6670 8	178.5030 3	209.3480 0	246.2174 8	290.3359 0
160.9468 9	191.1591 7	227.9179 6	272.7126 2	327.3774 9	394.1720 3
196.5168 8	237.9906 9	289.4979 5	353.5837 2	433.4503 7	533.1281 8
238.7628 8	294.9683 8	366.2378 3	456.7980 1	572.0833 9	719.0828 6
288.9378 6	364.2904 6	461.8696 8	588.5285 1	753.2712 0	967.9321 7
348.5300 1	448.6313 7	581.0443 6	756.6537 2	990.0764 3	1300.9486 8
419.3067 9	551.2449 8	729.5577 0	971.2288 2	1299.5713 9	1746.5998 9
503.3673 9	676.0901 2	914.6323 4	1245.0870 7	1704.0689 2	2342.9817 4
603.2050 3	827.9833 3	1145.2690 1	1594.6073 0	2232.7310 2	3141.0751 9
721.7808 2	1012.7846 5	1432.6842 6	2040.6935 3	2923.6712 3	4209.1042 5
862.6116 6	1237.6237 0	1790.8559 6	2610.0251 6	3826.7024 7	5638.3680 6

Name of Formula	Other Names	Deposits or Payments	Given Element	Element to be Ascertained	Mathematical Expression
Compound amount of 1	Compound-interest table	A single deposit	Present deposit	Future amount	$(1 + i)^n$
Present value of 1	Compound-discount table	A single deposit	Future amount	Present deposit	$\frac{i}{(1 + i)^n}$
Compound amount of 1 per period	Amount of ordinary annuity		Periodic deposit	Future amount	$\frac{(1 + i)^n - 1}{i}$
Present value of 1 per period	Present value of ordinary annuity	A series of equal payments made at the end of each of n periods	Periodic payment	Present deposit	$\frac{(1 + i)^n - 1}{i(1 + i)^n}$
Periodic payment accumulating to 1	Sinking-fund table, or rent of ordinary annuity		Future amount	Periodic payment	$\frac{i}{(1 + i)^n - 1}$
Periodic payment with present value of 1	Installment table		Present deposit	Periodic payment	$\frac{i(1 + i)^n}{(1 + i)^n - 1}$

compound-interest method (of depreciation) See *depreciation method.*

comptroller 1. = *controller:* a misspelling of *controller,* which is derived from the French *contrôleur,* from *contre* (Latin *contra*), against; *rôle* (Latin *rotulus,* a little wheel, records at one time having been in rolled form), list, roll; and *-eur* denoting an actor, agent; the whole originally meant a person who checks or compares one list or source of information with another. *Comptroller* has no French counterpart, but is an anglicized concoction of the French *compte* (Latin *computum,* account, *computare,* to count), account; *rôle;* and *-eur:* the combination thus arising from the confusion of *compte* with *contre.*
2. = *Comptroller General.*

Comptroller General The head of the General Accounting Office, an arm of the Legislative branch of the Federal government, reporting directly to the Congress on financial position, operating results, and accounting systems of government agencies, and providing critiques of agency organization and management.

computed price See *administered price.*

concept Any abstract idea serving a systematizing function.

concern Any economic unit.

conclusion The end result of a reasoning process, as distinguished from the data or the premises; in a formal system, a theorem.

condensed balance sheet A balance sheet in which less essential detail has been combined, the purpose being to provide a quickly comprehensible picture of the main factors of financial position. See *balance sheet; all-purpose financial statement.*

condition 1. A proposition that establishes or aids in establishing and delimiting the scope, applicability, or truth of another; a condition precedent, as in a contract; see *sufficient condition; necessary condition.*
2. Any part or accompaniment of a *process* that is operating continuously and thus is a function of time; as, the depreciation occurring as the result of the ownership of a fixed asset. See *events and conditions.*

confirmation 1. Generally, the substantiation of a fact or condition by one having direct knowledge of it; the establishing of the truth of a statement; proof of existence, character, or amount.
2. (auditing) Substantiation of the

existence and sometimes the condition and value of a claim against another or of an asset in the possession or control of another, or of the existence and amount of a liability. A confirmation usually takes the form of a written request and acknowledgment, but it may also be obtained orally, or through observation, as by the inspection of a passbook containing entries for deposits, or of records reflecting a certain transaction. See *representation.* Either of two types of confirmation is commonly employed: a positive confirmation requesting a reply in any event, or a negative confirmation requesting a reply only in the event of a discrepancy.

conflict of interest Any relationship whereby an individual may benefit (by way of a present or prospective gift, gratuity, commission, discount, preference, future employment, or the like) from a transaction of his employer where he is identified with or has influenced in any way its initiation, specifications, terms, conditions, completion, or acceptance. A conflict of interest may be asserted, even where no material benefit is involved, no added cost or loss of profit is in prospect for the employer, or the relationship is known to stockholders or owners; the mere possibility of a benefit accruing to the individual at some indefinite future time is enough to justify the assertion.

conglomerate financial statement A *balance sheet* in which materially different financial positions of two or more business entities have been combined or consolidated; or a single *income statement* in which differing lines of products or activities, or legally separable lines of products or activities, have been merged. Current standards of disclosure require their separate presentation as well, in reports to stockholders and outsiders. See APB statement of conditions requiring disclosure (APB Special Bulletin, September, 1967).

consent dividend (Federal income taxes) A portion or all of the retained earnings of a *personal holding company,* credited to paid-in surplus rather than paid out to stockholders. The amount is reported on the stockholders' income-tax returns as an ordinary dividend, and at the same time the investment cost of the stock to which the dividend pertains is increased in like amount.

consequential loss (insurance) The indirect loss arising out of fire or other insured peril; e.g., food spoilage caused by disablement of refrigeration equipment.

consideration The benefit to a contracting party that has induced him to enter into the contract, taking the form of a promise, the performance of an act for which the performer would not otherwise be obligated, the refraining from doing something that the refrainer would otherwise be free to do, or, as is most common in commercial contracts, payment in money or transfer of property.

consignment Goods shipped for future sale or other purpose, title remaining with the shipper (consignor), for which the receiver (consignee), upon his acceptance, is accountable. Consigned goods are a part of the consignor's inventory until sold. The consignee may be the eventual purchaser, may act as the agent through whom the sale is effected, or may otherwise dispose of the goods in accordance with his agreement with the consignor.

consistency 1. (auditing) Continued uniformity, during a period or from one period to another, in methods of accounting, mainly in valuation bases and methods of accrual, as reflected in the financial statements of a business enterprise or other accounting or economic unit. There are three generally recognized types: vertical consistency, within an interrelated group of financial statements bearing the same date; horizontal consistency, as between financial statements from period to period; and a kind of third-dimensional consistency, at a single date, as compared with organizations of the same type or organizations generally. A lack of vertical consistency has occasionally been noted where fixed assets have appeared on a balance sheet at appraised values while in the related income statement depreciation on the same assets has been based on cost. The reverse situation has sometimes occurred: assets valued at cost, and depreciation provisions based on estimated replacement costs. Both practices are now obsolete.

Any material change in valuation and accrual methods from one year to another demands a disclosure accompanying the financial statements of the year of change and setting forth the nature of the difference in method, the reason for the change, and the effect in dollars as compared with the result that would have been produced had the previous year's method been continued. The same sort of disclosure is required where the accounting methods of an organization are at variance with those of the industry of which it is a part, or with methods universally employed, regardless of the nature of the organization.

It has been said that the omission of inventories altogether from financial statements would have no effect on net profit, provided, and only provided, that the dollar amount thereof remained constant over the years. The same is true of accounts payable for purchases and of expense accruals. But the proviso is all-important. The quantities and valuations of successive inventories of every business enterprise *do* fluctuate, often substantially, and so do the dollar amounts of payables and accrued expense. Further, without these items, the current solvency—revealed by the balance sheet—would not be disclosed. On the other hand, the failure to record small items or to allocate them between accounting periods will not affect conclusions as to operating results or financial position, and a strict application of conventional rules to such items is occasionally relaxed. The justification for relaxation, however, can rest only on the smallness of the possible fluctuation over the years and on the smallness of any one item and of the total of all other excepted items in relation to financial position at any one time. Regardless of the size of the amount involved, the observance of correct practices is greatly to be preferred, lest the infection of laxity spread to other, more material, accounts.

2. The property of a set of simultaneously assumed propositions, such that no contradictions are deductible from them under prescribed rules of inference.

consolidated balance sheet A balance sheet in which the assets and liabilities of a *controlling company* are combined with the corresponding items of the organizations it owns or controls in such a manner as to disclose the financial position of the related companies as though they were a single economic unit. Minority interests in subsidiary companies customarily appear as a separate item, often expressed as a liability rather than as a part of *net worth*. *Ownership* of a subsidiary is considered to exist when a majority of the voting stock is owned by the holding company or by the same interests; *control*, a question of fact in each case, may exist with a much smaller percentage of stock ownership or even with no stock ownership. See *consolidated financial statement; control; controlling company; affiliated company; consolidating financial statement.*

consolidated financial statement A statement showing financial condition or operating results of two or more associated enterprises as they would appear if they were one organization. The preparation of a consolidated statement involves eliminations of intercompany accounts, investments, advances, sales, and other items. See *consolidation policy; group financial statement; combined financial statement; intercompany elimination;*

eliminations ledger; minority interest; controlling-company accounting; subsidiary-company accounting.

consolidated goodwill = *consolidation excess.*

consolidated group Affiliated corporations whose financial statements meet the tests for consolidation.

consolidated income statement A statement combining the income statements of two or more associated enterprises as a single economic unit. See *consolidating financial statement.*

consolidated surplus (or **retained earnings**) The combined surplus accounts of all companies whose accounts are consolidated, after deducting minority stockholders' interests therein, the interest acquired by the parent company in the subsidiary companies' surpluses existing at the date of their acquisition, and intercompany eliminations.

consolidated working fund (governmental accounting) A fund established by an agency for the purpose of accounting for the collective advances from two or more other agencies for particular construction services to be performed, or for goods to be delivered, usually within a single year.

consolidating financial statement A financial statement in worksheet form displaying the details that go into the making of consolidated financial statements. In its conventional form, the trial balances of controlling company and subsidiaries appear in parallel columns with one or two "eliminations" columns and "total" columns following. In lieu of the eliminations columns there may be the trial balance of an *eliminations ledger*. See *intercompany elimination.* Such a worksheet ties together book figures with published financial statements; it is occasionally furnished along with the more formal consolidated balance sheet and income statement in order to supply information as to the sources of various consolidated items, particularly where some unique financial or operating feature attaches to one of the constituent companies, the significance of which could not as readily be communicated by other means. It may be useful also where some diversity exists between individual subsidiaries but not enough to warrant independent statements, or where material intercompany eliminations are not readily determinable from other data in a report. See *grouping financial statement; conglomerate statement.*

An example of a consolidating financial statement or worksheet is shown in the table on the following page.

consolidation 1. The combination of two or more enterprises, accomplished by the transfer of their net assets to a new corporation organized for the purpose; distinguished from *merger.*

2. The preparation of a consolidated balance sheet or other consolidated financial statement from those of related enterprises.

3. The group of enterprises (in either of the preceding senses) considered as a unit.

consolidation excess That portion of the amount paid by a *parent* or *holding company* for its investment in a *subsidiary* company attributable to unusual earning power or other intangible value not recorded on the subsidiary's books; sometimes called *consolidated goodwill.* It is measured by the amount of the parent or holding company's investment in stocks and other equity securities less the book value reflected in the subsidiary's accounts at the time of purchase. It is common practice to reduce at once investments in subsidiaries by the amount of the consolidation excess, in keeping with the current movement to eliminate intangible items from the balance sheet. The writeoff becomes an *income deduction.* Equally common is the practice of amortizing the excess over the first few (i.e., five) years of ownership. An example will be found in eliminations *a* and *b* in the example

DEMAND PRODUCTS COMPANY

Consolidating Financial Statements
December 31, 19-8

Balance Sheet	*Demand Products Company*	*Supply Material Company*	*Adjustments* Debit	*Adjustments* Credit	*Consolidated*
Cash	35 800	23 500			59 300
Receivables	113 700	150 700			264 400
Inventory-finished goods	54 000	520 100		b 400	573 700
-work in process	62 300				62 300
-raw material	89 000				89 000
Advances to Supply	106 000			c 106 000	
Investment in Supply stock	235 200			a 235 200	
Investment in Demand bonds		14 400		d 14 400	
Fixed assets	568 800	47 200		e 4 000	612 000
Depreciation reserve	−347 500	−21 600	e 640		−368 460
Unamortized discount	1 400			d 600	800
Current liabilities	−187 200	−292 300			−479 500
Advances from Demand		−106 000	c 106 000		
5% mortgage bonds	−120 000		d 15 000		−105 000
Capital stock-Demand	−300 000				−300 000
-Supply		−200 000	a 140 000		−60 000M
Retained earnings-Demand	−228 300		b 500		
			e 3 520		−224 280
-Supply		−124 000	a 86 800		−37 200M
Dividends paid-Demand	20 000				20 000
-Supply		18 000		a 12 600	5 400M
Net income-19-8	−103 200	−30 000	20 740		−103 460
					−9 000M
Income Statement					
Sales	−828 900	−148 000	b 14 700		−962 200
Interest received		−750	d 750		
Bond discount accrued		−300	d 300		
Earnings of subsidiary	−21 000		a 21 000		
Cost of sales	518 500	96 800	b 400	b 15 200	600 500
Depreciation expense	20 200	1 900		e 160	21 940
Bond discount amortized	700			d 300	400
Interest paid	6 000			d 750	5 250
Other expense	201 300	20 350			221 650
Net income-19-8	103 200	30 000		20 740	112 460
Totals	0	0	410 350	410 350	0

Explanations of adjustments

The adjustments appearing in the consolidating worksheet shown above and described below may be newly formulated each time consolidated statements are prepared or they may be the elements of a trial balance of an *eliminations ledger*, q.v.

(a) On March 8, 19-1, Demand purchased 70% of Supply's outstanding capital stock from its then stockholders at a cost of $220,000. At that time the book value of Supply's net worth (paid-in capital plus retained earnings) totaled $282,000 of which 70% was $197,400. Demand's cost in excess of this equity in Supply's book value, $22,600, was immediately charged to Demand's retained-earnings account—a common practice in many of today's takeovers; thereafter, its investment account had been annually adjusted to 70% of the book value of Supply's net worth. The eliminations required at December 31, 19-8, for consolidation purposes were 70% of Supply's paid-in capital ($140,000), accumulated earnings at the beginning of the year ($86,800), dividends paid ($12,600), and the recorded share of Demand's interest in Supply's net income ($21,000). It will be noted that the second and fourth of these eliminations have not been modified by consolidating adjustments since those affecting consolidated net income have been wholly assumed by the majority interest; see (f) below.

(b) Supply's inventory at the beginning of the year contained items purchased from Demand on which the latter's gross profit had been $500; for consolidation purposes it was necessary to reduce by that amount 19-8's cost of sales to which the overstated opening inventory had been charged; required also was a corresponding reduction of the opening balance of consolidated retained earnings in order to reflect its consolidating downward adjustment by the same amount at the close of the preceding year. A similar type of over-statement, $400, required a reduction of the year-end consolidated inventory and a corresponding addition to 19-8's consolidated cost of sales in order to offset the excess therein arising from an overstated closing-inventory credit. Sales of goods by Demand to Supply during the year were also eliminated by reducing consolidated sales and cost of sales by $14,700.

(c) Demand's advances of $106,000 to Supply were offset against the subsidiary's liabilities of equal amount.

(d) Supply's ownership of one-eighth of Demand's outstanding 5% mortgage bonds had been acquired in a prior year at a discount which was being amortized (upward) at the rate of $300 a year. When combined with the discount expense of $700 amortized on Demand's records, a consolidated net discount expense of $400 was the result. This amount is consistent with the consolidated book value at the year end of the net unamortized discount of $800 (= 1,400 − 600) which was to be accounted for over the remaining two years of the indicated life of the bonds. Interest of $750 received by Supply on its holding was a partial offset to Demand's interest expense of $6,000.

(e) A building sold in 19-4 by Demand to Supply at a profit of $4,000 was being depreciated at a rate of 4% per annum; the resulting overstatement of 19-8 consolidated depreciation expense, $160, required a correction for the current year in that amount, similar corrections totaling $480 for the three preceding years, a reduction ($4,000) of Supply's recorded cost of the building, and a deduction of $3,520 (= 4,000 − 3 × 160) from consolidated retained earnings at the beginning of the year.

(f) The four elements of the minority interest (M) in Supply's net worth have been separately set forth on the consolidated worksheet. These included equities of 30% in both retained earnings and the year's net income neither of which, from the viewpoint of the minority group, were subject to any of the consolidating adjustments described above. As indicated in (a), the portion of retained earnings and net income ascribed to the majority interest thus bore the full amount of the consolidating adjustments.

under *consolidating financial statement.* See *consolidation policy; goodwill (3).*

consolidation ledger = *eliminations ledger.*

consolidation policy The policy of a controlling (parent or holding) company whereby affiliated organizations are included or excluded from consolidated financial statements. The most widely accepted policy is that consolidated statements can be justified only where the subsidiaries and the controlling company are integral parts of a single business enterprise, and where the display of the financial or operating characteristics of any one subsidiary is not material to an understanding of the group as a whole. The strongest case for consolidated statements is the situation in which a controlling company and its wholly owned subsidiaries are engaged in similar operations or together constitute an integrated line of economic endeavor under the same management.

Since the purpose of consolidated statements is primarily to give information beyond that appearing in the statements of the controlling company, their general effect is carefully weighed before publication. Included in the consolidated group are all subsidiaries regardless of the percentage of stock ownership, excepting only, where material, those that for some reason are regarded as not fitting into the integrated whole, as, (a) a subsidiary whose operations are unrelated to those of its controlling company and any other subsidiary (see *conglomerate* operations); (b) a subsidiary about to be disposed of; (c) an uncontrolled company, even though its capital stock may be owned (see *control*); (d) a subsidiary where control is being exercised only temporarily; (e) a subsidiary the financial statements of which bear a date differing from that of the controlling company's statements; (f) a foreign subsidiary, especially where the rate of exchange has been fluctuating widely, restrictions exist on the withdrawal of funds, unfavorable legislation is in force, or the foreign government is in the process of change; (g) a subsidiary the control of which has been acquired at a figure substantially and unaccountably in excess of or less than the corresponding fraction of the recorded or appraised amount of its net assets at the date of consolidation.

Consistency in consolidation is much to be desired in order that maximum value may be obtained from comparisons of statements of successive years. New additions and omissions, if any, of consolidating units are noted on published statements, and their general effect on the total indicated. When subsidiaries are not included in the consolidated group, their separate financial statements, wherever they reflect material amounts, should accompany the consolidated statements, individually or in group form; see *combined statement.*

Separately published financial statements of unconsolidated subsidiaries, included in, or supplementary to, consolidated statements, reveal in their headings the name of the controlling company and the equity owned by it.

For policies concerning items of individual statements included or omitted, see *intercompany elimination.*

consolidation surplus = *surplus from consolidation.*

constant A quantity that enters as a fixed element in the structure of an equation or other mathematical expression. Constants may be general, and may be denoted symbolically by the first letters of the alphabet ($a, b, c, \ldots$), or they may by expressed as particular values, such as 1, $\frac{1}{2}$, -10, and so on. See *variable.*

constant cost = *fixed cost.*

constituent company A company which is one of a group of affiliated, merged, or consolidated corporations.

constructive receipt (of income) (Federal income taxes) a. The legal fiction whereby an item is considered to be the income of an individual on the cash basis, even though not actually received by him, because unconditionally available to him; as, matured but unclipped bond coupons; salary due a corporate official and credited to his account on the books of the corporation. b. Income of one person not received by him but paid to another; as, an exchange of items of property between persons recorded or reported at less than their fair market value; the payment of rent by a lessee to a person other than the lessor.

consular invoice An invoice covering goods shipped from one country to another, made up in prescribed form to give the information required by the country to which the goods are sent, sworn to before a consular officer stationed in the exporting country, and bearing his visa.

consumed cost 1. Any cost the benefits from which have expired or have been lost or destroyed; as the cost of goods sold, or of raw materials that make up a part of manufactured products sold, or of that portion of the cost of a *fixed asset* represented in a periodic provision for depreciation. Generally, a consumed cost is any cost that has been recognized as an item to be reported in an *income statement;* i.e., *all* costs appearing in an income statement are consumed costs and all consumed costs must be so reported.

2. Any cost transferred to a *secondary* or *terminal account.*

consumer(s') goods (economics) Goods satisfying human wants; contrasted with *producers' goods,* which are used to facilitate the production of other goods.

consumer's risk (statistical quality control) A calculated *probability,* under a given sampling plan, that a lot of any given quality will be accepted by the plan. It is generally stated only for lots at the *lot-tolerance-percent-defective* level.

consumption The removal from the *accounts* (7) of a part or all of the cost of an *asset* (either directly or over a period of time through the medium of a *valuation account*) because of use, disposal, or loss. Examples: cleaning supplies used; a worn-out tool discarded; the portion of the total utility of a machine reflected in a *provision for depreciation* which has been added to an account for *accumulated depreciation; merchandise* or *finished goods* sold.—*consume, v.t.*

contango (London Stock Exchange) The interest and other charges paid by a speculator for the delayed acquisition of and payment for stock he has purchased, pending what he hopes will be a rise in its price. See *backwardation.*

context The circumstances, environment, or disclosure out of which a statement emanates and on which a part of its meaning may depend; also, the environment or accompanying circumstances of an action.

contingency A possible future event or condition arising from causes unknown or at present undeterminable. See *contingent liability; reserve for contingencies.*

contingency table (statistics) A table constructed for the purpose of analyzing or discovering associations between qualitative characteristics (*attributes*). It is distinguished from a *correlation table* by the fact that use of the latter is restricted to the study of quantitative characteristics (*variables*).

The 2×2 contingency table shown below was used to study the association between inoculation against cholera and exemption from attack (data from Greenwood and Yule).

	Not Attacked	Attacked	Total
Inoculated	276	3	279
	(a)	(b)	$(a+b)$
Not inoculated	473	66	539
	(c)	(d)	$(c+d)$
Total	749	69	818
	$(a+c)$	$(b+d)$	$(a+b+c+d=N)$

If the attributes were independent —i.e., if inoculation had no effect on cholera incidence—the totals in each cell would depend only on the proportions in which inoculated and not-inoculated persons were present in the total. In cell *a*, there would appear $279/818 \times 749 = 255$ cases; in cell *b*, there would appear 24 cases; in cell *c*, there would appear 494 cases; and in cell *d*, there would appear 45 cases. This would result in zero association; the presence of persons attacked by cholera would depend only on the total number of persons examined and the numbers attacked and not attacked. There would be no relation to inoculation or its absence.

If perfect positive association were present, all persons inoculated would not be attacked by cholera, and all persons not inoculated would be attacked. The association would be +1. Cell *a* would contain 279 cases; cell *b*, 0 cases; cell *c*, 0 cases; and cell *d*, 539 cases. Perfect negative association would display the opposite result: cell *a* would contain 0 cases; cell *b*, 279 cases; cell *c*, 539 cases; and cell *d*, 0 cases; and the coefficient of association would be −1.

Most contingency tables will display associations which lie between these extremes. See *coefficient of association.*

contingent annuity A periodic payment dependent on some contingency, such as the death of a person.

contingent asset An asset the existence, value, and ownership of which depend upon the occurrence or nonoccurrence of a specified event or upon the performance or nonperformance of a specified act; contrasts with *contingent liability*, often growing out of such a liability.

contingent charge (or **cost** or **expense**) An outlay the incurring of which is dependent on some event or condition; as, interest on income bonds the accrual of which is to be made only if the gross or net earnings of the business are equal to or exceed an agreed amount.

contingent fund 1. Assets set apart for use in contingencies, usually of a specified character.

2. (municipal and institutional accounting) A portion of available resources reserved for emergency expenditures or authorized transfers upon proper authority to other appropriations.

contingent liability An obligation, relating to a past transaction or other event or condition, that may arise in consequence of a future event now deemed possible but not probable. If probable, the obligation is not contingent but real (ordinarily, a current liability), and *recognition* in the accounts is required, notwithstanding that its amount must be estimated in whole or in part. The possibility of a future loss, as from a fire, not linked with a past event, does not give rise to a contingent liability. Following are common sources of contingent liabilities:

1. A lawsuit growing out of a breach of contract, patent infringement, damages for personal injury or to property, an antitrust-law violation.

2. A commitment for a purchase in a fluctuating market that may have to be settled without delivery of goods, or a purchase contracted for, now known to be in excess of needs.

3. A guaranty by endorsement or otherwise of securities or other obligations, or of transactions of a subsidiary, supplier, or customer, including installment accounts sold and notes receivable discounted.

4. New-product guaranties, where experience cannot be applied to the computation of a reasonable allowance therefor.

5. Possible, but not agreed-to, additional income tax for a past period.

6. A subscription to capital stock, subject to assessment or indefinite call.

7. An obligation passed on to a buyer of real estate where the vendor has not secured a release from the mortgage or a guaranty against loss from a responsible third person.

8. Possible additional compensation for a past period arising out of a labor dispute.

Not regarded as contingent liabilities

are the following:

1. Any of the above items that are likely or probable future liabilities; thus, the propriety of a proposed additional assessment of income taxes disclosed in a revenue agent's report might be admitted in part, thereby causing the amount so admitted to be classed as a current liability; the balance, believed by counsel to be improper, would be classed as a contingent liability.

2. Minor items, such as those amounting to a figure equal to much less than a fraction of 1 percent of total assets, although in the case of balance sheets on which a given type of contingency has been revealed year after year, the practice may continue, regardless of size.

3. Preferred-stock dividends in arrears, because no liability to "outsiders" is involved, and because they merely constitute a first claim in liquidation against net worth.

4. Possible assessments under mutual-insurance policies, for the reason that the chance of such assessments is too remote.

Although contingent liabilities are not entered on books of account, standard practice requires their disclosure on balance sheets. They sometimes appear between liabilities and net worth, but more often in appended footnotes. The disclosure is sometimes qualitative only, because of the wholly indeterminate character of the item or because of the lack of experience in the making of a reasonable estimate.

contingent profit Profit the realization of which is dependent on an uncertain future event or condition.

contingent reserve *Retained income* appropriated in anticipation of possible future losses or expenses; a *reserve for contingencies*.

contingent transaction A *contingent asset* or *liability*.

continuing account Any *asset* or *liability(2)* account carried over from one fiscal period to another.

continuing appropriation (governmental accounting) An appropriation the balance of which, at the end of a fiscal year, does not *lapse(2)* but is carried over and is available for expenditure thereafter.

continuity concept (of accounting) The assumption that in all ordinary situations an *economic unit(1)* persists indefinitely: an assumption basic to the preparation of *financial statements*.

continuous audit Any audit the detail work of which is performed continuously or at intervals during the fiscal period, the purpose being to uncover and correct undesirable practices and errors before the end of the year as well as to relieve the auditor's work-load thereafter.

continuous budget A *moving projection* of financial operations for a series of weeks, months, or quarters immediately ahead; at the end of each such period the portion of the projection then lapsed is removed and a new projection for a period of similar length is added to the series, but no intervening-interval estimates are changed if critical judgment on projection ability is a feature of the process.

continuous inventory A process of testing inventories and of maintaining an equality between inventory-item quantities physically determined by count, weight, or measure and those appearing at the same time on perpetual-inventory records. Where the number of items is large, the full time of one or more persons (sometimes an inventory "crew") may be required to make the count, usually at times of low stocks; compare the amount with the book record maintained by the stock- or store-keeper; search for, and correct, where practicable, any observed discrepancy; suggest steps to be taken for the avoidance of future errors; and report the results. The frequency of the count will vary with the relative value per item, strictness of controls over issues, rate of turnover, possibility of alternative over-all measures of consumption, as of raw materials such as steel or of purchased parts, by working back from reported factory activity or output, and other factors peculiar to individual plants. A common standard of testing frequency is once yearly. See *perpetual inventory*.

continuous process A method of *production(2)* permitting an uninterrupted flow of material and parts into a processing operation and of completed endproducts out of the operation.

contra account One or two or more accounts which partially or wholly offset another or other accounts; on financial statements, they may either be merged or appear together. Examples: an account receivable from and an account payable to a single individual; stock subscriptions, a receivable, and capital stock subscribed, a *net-worth* account; a *reserve for depreciation*, and plant and equipment. Contra accounts include *absorption accounts*.

contract authorization (governmental accounting) Permission given in an appropriation act to a governmental agency to enter into contracts or commitments involving expenditures up to a specified amount to be made in periods succeeding that covered by the current appropriation, and to be appropriated for at a subsequent date. The purpose is to avoid showing as appropriated for the current year amounts to be expended in and to benefit subsequent years. In the procurement of heavy electrical equipment, for example, delivery may follow the date of contract by two or more years, thus making necessary advance authority to purchase.

contract price The price or price formula stipulated in a contract of purchase or sale, such as—

1. Firm price: a fixed price not expected to be open to negotiation or adjustment after agreement.

2. Target price: a basis price, subject to adjustment under specified terms, generally restricted to incentive contracts under which it is adjusted by bonus and penalty provisions depending on such factors as the quality and quantity of work performed or the promptness of delivery.

3. Escalation price: the amount to which the contract price may be adjusted as specified contingencies, such as increased labor costs, occur.

4. Cost price: price based on cost, usually including a fixed fee or percentage of cost as a profit element.

5. Futures price: the price at which commodities are currently traded on an organized commodity exchange for future delivery; the price quoted on the exchange relates to a basic grade, and the agreement to purchase or deliver follows a standard form familiar to the trade. Such prices are largely determined by the relationship between the cash price for immediate delivery and the purchaser's and seller's estimates of market conditions at the time of future delivery.

See *price*.

contra entry An item on one side of an account which offsets fully or in part one or more items on the opposite side of the same account.

contributed capital The payments in cash or property made to a corporation by its stockholders (a) in exchange for capital stock, (b) in response to an assessment on the capital stock, or (c) as a gift; *paid-in capital;* often, though not necessarily, equal to capital stock and paid-in surplus. In British usage, the term is applied to the par value of the capital stock outstanding, thus including discounts and excluding premiums; see *capital reserve*.

contributed surplus = *paid-in surplus*.

contribution 1. (Federal income taxes) A gift to a charitable, religious, educational, or other institution as defined in the Internal Revenue Code, currently deductible (a) by individuals, up to 20 percent of adjusted gross income with an additional 10 percent where the donee is a church, an educational institution, a hospital, or a medical research organization, any excess being

subject to *carryover* privileges; and (b) by corporations, up to 5 percent of taxable income. Corporations, but not individuals, have a two-year carryover to the extent that contributions are less than the 5 percent maximum.
2. The payment by a person of his portion of a loss shared with others; specifically (insurance) an insurer's prorata share of a loss where the insured has contracted against the same risk with two or more insurers.
3. Any payment by a person to a corporation representing the purchase of capital stock, a gift, or an *assessment*(5).
4 = *benefit*.
5. See *contribution theory*.

contribution margin = *marginal income*.

contribution theory The theory that sales of commodities or services supply a source of funds, often varying, from which overhead and other costs are paid. Under systems of direct costing, *marginal income*—the excess of selling price over direct costs—is the measure of such contribution. Also involved is the notion that the determination of the amount by which the selling price is to exceed direct costs is a responsibility of top management, some products often being required to provide a greater *marginal income* in proportion to selling price than others. The practical effect of this concept is the elimination of any formal distribution of *indirect costs* and the recognition of the bulk of factory overhead as a joint cost, as is administrative overhead.

control 1. The process by which the *activities* of an *organization* are conformed to a desired plan of action and the plan is conformed to the organization's activities. The *concept* of control embraces the following elements:

a) The basic wish, need, directive, or statute, and the *authority* and capacity for its exercise;
b) A common understanding of the purpose and consequence of the ends sought;
c) A plan of organization and action;
d) *Organizational units*, each with *delegated*, delimited authority;
e) Evidence of the assumption of *responsibility* for the exercise of such authority;
f) Identification of the activities to be carried on within each organizational unit;
g) *Policies* governing *operation*, *internal control*, including *internal audit*, and *reporting;*
h) Operable *standards of performance* and related *standards of comparison;*
i) Provision for continuing views by superior authority of the flow of *performance* through *internal reports* (*feedbacks*) and direct observations, followed by *judgments* leading to action on proposed changes in purpose, scope, and procedures; and
j) Periodic professional surveys (*external audits* and external *management reviews*) of the objectives of the organization, the accomplishments reflected in its activities, *appraisals* of the worth and acceptance of its *endproducts*, and the relevance of the current operating plan and performance, along with suggestions for their improvement, modification, curtailment, or possible elimination.

2. (statistical quality control) The state of equilibrium reached when deviations from a given norm (such as the process average) are only random in character and without assignable cause.
3. The relation whereby one or more corporations or other persons possess the power to choose at least a majority of the members of the board of directors of another corporation. The power is usually a direct one, evidenced by the ownership of a majority of the other's outstanding shares of voting capital stock, but an equally effective control may be of an indirect type: the possession of less than half of the voting stock

may be sufficient to insure the domination of meetings of stockholders, provided there exists, to the necessary degree, any one or more of the following conditions: (a) continued ability to obtain proxies from other stockholders; (b) ownership of voting stock by subsidiaries, officers, employees, nominees, or other persons having subordinated interests; (c) inactivity of minority stockholders who do not attend stockholders' meetings and do not give proxies; and (d) possession of a lease or other contract which carries with it the virtual ownership of assets without any formal ownership of capital stock. Occasionally instances are found where, although a majority ownership of capital stock exists, there is no domination of the other company's policies and hence no effective control, as where ownership is temporary, where a strong, self-sufficient management is in the saddle, or where the other company is an obligor under a lease or contract of the type mentioned in the preceding sentence. Under Regulation S-X of the U. S. Securities and Exchange Commission, control "means the possession, direct or indirect, of the power to direct or cause the direction of the management and policies of a person whether through the ownership of voting securities, by contract, or otherwise." See *community of interest*. 4. = *internal control.*

control (or **controlling**) **account** An account containing primarily totals of one or more types of transactions the detail of which appears in a subsidiary ledger or its equivalent. Its balance equals the sum of the balances of the detail accounts.

control chart (statistical quality control) A diagram based on systematic inspection data and used to discriminate between random and nonrandom (assignable) causes of product or process variation as a means of analyzing performance and controlling quality: a *scatter diagram*, usually in the form of a *time series*, containing average and control lines for judging process performance and determining when corrective action should be taken. The importance of the methodologies followed in long-established practices of maintaining quality in production lies in the possibility of applying these practices to management controls generally.

Control charts may be constructed for data in the form of either *attributes* or *variables.* Attribute data arise from an inspection procedure that merely classifies or counts occurrences of some observable characteristic, such as the number (or percent) of defectives in a group of items or the number of defects on a unit of product; variables data arise from an inspection procedure that actually *measures* some characteristic of the product, such as a dimension. The most widely used control charts for variables are: (a) a chart for averages, known as an $\bar{X}$ (X-bar) chart, and (b) a chart for dispersion, known as an R (range) or σ (sigma) chart, depending on whether the *range* or *standard deviation* is used to measure dispersion.

A table giving factors for computing control limits for variables data, originally prepared by the American Society for Testing Materials, is widely available in full or in part in many textbooks and other technical publications concerned with statistical quality control. The table of factors which follows, page 112, has been adapted from Table B2 in the *ASTM Manual on Quality Control of Materials.*

Use of this table in the construction of control charts for variables may be illustrated by the following case study reported by Mason Wescott in *Conference Papers*, First Annual Convention of the American Society for Quality Control and Second Midwest Quality Control Conference. The problem involved controlling the length of a valve stem which was designed with a *basic dimension* of 4.800″ and *tolerances* of ±0.005″. The stem was processed on a screw machine, and, although the operation

CONTROL-CHART FACTORS FOR COMPUTING 3-SIGMA CONTROL LIMITS FOR $\bar{X}$ AND R CHARTS

(For Samples of n Greater than 15, see ASTM Manual on Quality Control of Materials)

No. of Observations in Sample n	Factor for $\bar{X}$ Chart A_2	Factors for R Chart: Lower Control Limit D_3	Upper Control Limit D_4	Factor for Estimating σ' from $\bar{R}$ d_2
2	1.880	0	3.267	1.128
3	1.023	0	2.575	1.693
4	0.729	0	2.282	2.059
5	0.577	0	2.115	2.326
6	0.483	0	2.004	2.534
7	0.419	0.076	1.924	2.704
8	0.373	0.136	1.864	2.847
9	0.337	0.184	1.816	2.970
10	0.308	0.223	1.777	3.078
11	0.285	0.256	1.744	3.173
12	0.266	0.284	1.716	3.258
13	0.249	0.308	1.692	3.336
14	0.235	0.329	1.671	3.407
15	0.223	0.348	1.652	3.472

was entirely mechanical, except that the tool slide was moved by hand, considerable difficulty had been experienced in production.

The information contained in the table of factors was secured from *random samples*, each consisting of five completed pieces drawn from a tote pan during production at intervals of 20 minutes, more or less.

It is important in control-chart work to maintain a record of the time sequence of production and samples, because often the most helpful clue to locating sources of nonrandom behavior—i.e., *assignable* causes of variation worth investigation—is the time at which the nonrandom deviation occurred. The varying time periods between samples may help in the avoidance of *bias*.

The table opposite shows the results of gauging the length of each of the five pieces (X_1, X_2, X_3, X_4, X_5) in each sample. To simplify computations, all measurements are recorded with $4.800'' = 0$, the basic dimension, in units of $0.001''$. The last two columns contain the calculated sample mean $\bar{X}$ as well as the range R from the lowest to the highest dimension for ech sample of five pieces. These values are computed for each of the 20 samples and the results totaled and divided by the number of samples, 20, to yield the over-all mean, $\bar{\bar{X}}$ ($= 4.03$), and the average range, $\bar{R}$ ($= 4.55$). $\bar{\bar{X}}$ is a tentative estimate of the average dimension to which the process is working; $\bar{R}$ is a tentative estimate of the average spread or variability to be expected in samples of five pieces from the process. If the charts show that the process is operating in statistical control, then $\bar{\bar{X}}$ may be regarded as the best available estimate of the *universe* (or process) mean, and $\bar{R}$ may be used to make a valid estimate of universe (or process) dispersion.

Inspection of the data shows that positive deviations above the basic dimension have been more frequent than negative deviations. Since this represents nonrandom behavior about the basic size, an investigation was

DATA FOR ONE DAY'S PRODUCTION MACHINING TIP OF VALVE STEM ON MACHINE XX BY OPERATOR XXX

(Unit of Measurement .001")

Sample No.	Time	X_1	X_2	X_3	X_4	X_5	$\bar{X}$	R
		Sample Pieces						
1	8:00 A.M.	3	6	2	5	4	4.0	4
2	8:20	2	1	4	3	2	2.4	3
3	8:45	3	4	2	4	5	3.6	3
4	9:15	0	1	6	0	2	1.8	6
5	9:30	9	9	9	7	9	8.6	2
6	9:50	15	8	9	7	6	9.0	9
7	10:20	4	0	4	4	4	3.2	4
8	10:45	5	6	4	8	4	5.4	4
9	11:10	8	1	6	9	7	6.2	8
10	11:30	7	0	3	0	8	3.6	8
11	12:05 P.M.	7	6	9	8	9	7.8	3
12	1:30	4	0	−3	0	2	0.6	7
13	1:50	2	−1	0	3	0	0.8	4
14	2:15	3	5	0	4	3	3.0	5
15	2:40	7	5	7	6	7	6.4	2
16	3:00	3	1	0	3	3	2.0	3
17	3:30	8	6	8	6	8	7.2	2
18	3:45	0	1	1	−1	0	0.2	2
19	4:10	3	3	−2	3	3	2.0	5
20	4:40	4	−2	5	3	4	2.8	7
Totals							80.6	91
Averages ($\bar{\bar{X}}$ and $\bar{R}$)							4.03	4.55

undertaken which showed that, because of the incentive system used, the machine operator preferred to err on the upward side; such errors resulted in rework when caught by inspection, whereas errors on the downward side resulted in scrap.

To determine whether the process is in control even at the level where the operator is actually functioning—as distinct from the tolerance levels of design—control charts are plotted consisting of scatter diagrams with superimposed central and control limit lines. In the following charts, values for the central lines ($\bar{X} = 4.03$ and $\bar{R} = 4.55$) have already been obtained. Control

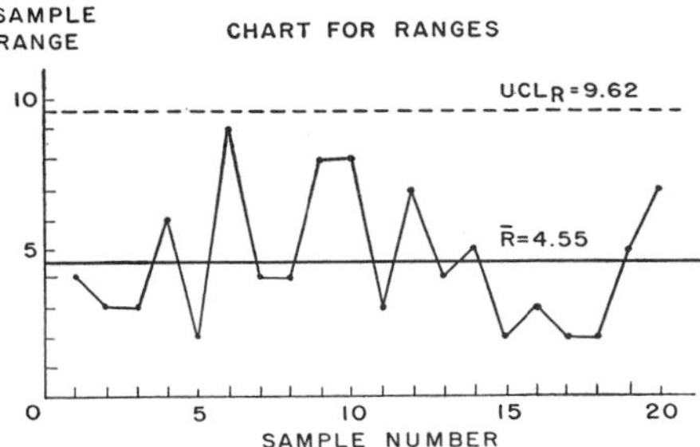

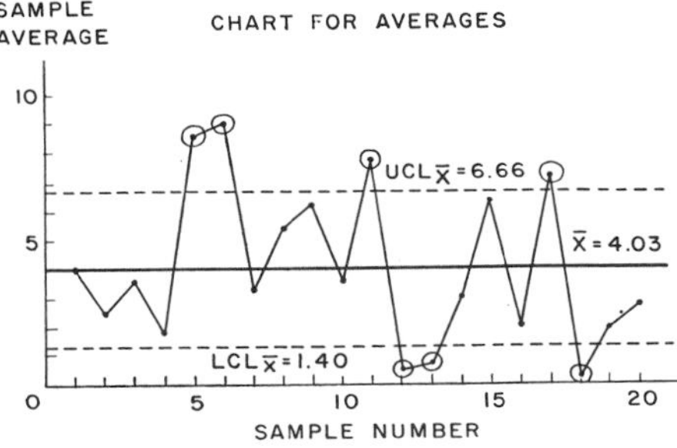

limits on these charts depend on (a) the value of $\bar{\bar{X}}$, (b) the value of $\bar{R}$, and (c) the sample size n. For these data, $n = 5$, the table of control-chart factors is entered at the row $n = 5$ and read horizontally to locate factors for the respective control limits. In the A_2 column we find the entry 0.577. Using $UCL_{\bar{x}}$ for "upper control limit on averages" and $LCL_{\bar{x}}$ for "lower control limit on averages," the formulas for these limits are

$$UCL_{\bar{x}} = \bar{\bar{X}} + A_2\bar{R},$$

and

$$LCL_{\bar{x}} = \bar{\bar{X}} - A_2\bar{R}.$$

Substitution in these formulas gives

$$UCL_{\bar{x}} = 4.03 + (0.577 \times 4.55) = 6.66,$$

and

$$LCL_{\bar{x}} = 4.03 - (0.577 \times 4.55) = 1.40.$$

These values constitute upper and lower control limits plotted about the over-all mean $\bar{\bar{X}}$ on the chart for averages ($\bar{X}$ chart). Calculation of control limits for the chart for ranges ($\bar{R}$ chart) is made by using the formulas

$$UCL_R = D_4\bar{R},$$

and

$$LCL_R = D_3\bar{R}.$$

The necessary values D_4 (= 2.115) and D_3 (= 0) are taken from the table of control-chart factors to obtain

$$UCL_R = 2.115 \times 4.55 = 9.62,$$

and

$$LCL_R = 0 \times 4.55 = 0.$$

Only the upper control-limit value need be plotted on the chart for ranges when the lower limit value is zero.

Inspection of the chart for ranges shows that all points are within the control limits. At the initial or installation stage of statistical quality control, a chart for ranges or other measure of dispersion is used, sometimes dispensed with later. Ranges falling outside control limits constitute a signal not only of the presence of assignable causes of excessive dispersion but also of samples that may be coming from different *universes*, thus resulting in data that are not homogeneous. Sample averages, under these circumstances, lose meaning as measures of central tendency; the over-all mean $\bar{\bar{X}}$ represents not an estimate of a single universe mean, but an average of means drawn from different universes.

Since the chart for ranges does not show lack of control, the $\bar{X}$'s may be treated as meaningful. Turning to the $\bar{X}$ chart, or chart for averages, the out-of-control points are indicated by ⊙. The pattern of the out-of-control points, falling first on one side and then on the other, plus the wide control limits for $\bar{R}$ and $\bar{X}$, indicate that the operator is "hunting": rejects arising from lengths exceeding tolerances result in over-compensated machine resettings, thus causing points to fall out of control on the lower side. The wide control limits also indicate an excessive number of machine resettings, which is probably reducing quantity as well as quality of product processed.

When these defects, as well as other defects discovered by successive applications of control-chart technique, were corrected, it was finally found possible to bring the operation into control at $\bar{\bar{X}} = 0.53$ and $\bar{R} = 3.00$, a process average much closer to the basic dimension 4.800″, accompanied by much less dispersion—i.e., a more homogeneous product. Both quantity and quality of product were substantially increased.

With the process in a state of *statistical control*—i.e., with all variations resulting from only random or nonassignable causes—it was possible to effect other economies as well. The bilateral *tolerance* ranged from an upper specification limit (USL) of 4.800″ = 0.005″ to a lower specification limit (LSL) of 4.800″ − 0.005″, or a total of ten units about the basic dimension. Comparing these limits with control-chart data, it was possible to determine whether reduced inspection was safely possible.

Inspection applies to individual parts, whereas the $\bar{X}$ control chart is designed to apply to averages. Use of averages makes it possible to draw on known laws of statistical behavior. See *expected value*. The control charts used here employ 3σ (3-sigma) limits. These limits or "error bands" are standard in this work. Experience has shown that, in the majority of applications, 3σ control limits strike an economic balance between two costly types of error: (a) the error of looking for trouble in a process when actually nothing is wrong with it, and (b) the error of failing to look for and correct undesirable process performance when something really *is* wrong. The constants A_2, D_3, and D_4 in the table on page 112 are designed to give 3σ control limits on average and range charts. Employment of other than 3σ limits may, of course, be desirable in some cases; they may be calculated by simple modifications of the control-limit formulas based on the use of the constants in the table.

Three-sigma limits yield, approximately, a probability of error of three times per 1,000 observations: when the process is in a state of control there are roughly only three chances in 1,000 that a variation will appear to be the result of an assignable cause—i.e., a sample average will fall outside the control limits—when, in fact, the variation is only random in character. But these limits are set by means of the *standard error* of sample averages rather than by the *standard deviation* of individual stem lengths. To determine modified control limits or convert to tolerance limits, it is necessary to use the standard deviation, because interest is shifted to individual lengths rather than statistical averages. From the data for $\bar{R}$ (= 3.00) and use of the factor d_2 (= 2.326), found in the table of control-chart factors opposite the sample size n (= 5), it is possible to estimate σ' (the standard deviation) by means of the formula which follows:

$$\sigma' = \frac{\bar{R}}{d_2},$$

where σ' = *universe* standard deviation. For $\bar{R} = 3.00$ and $d_2 = 2.326$,

$$\sigma' = \frac{3.00}{2.326} = 1.29.$$

This is the appropriate measure to use in setting the 3σ limits on individual stem lengths in order to determine whether the state of control—or the tightness of control limits for averages—is sufficient to insure that the individual stem lengths will fall within specification limits. For an upper limit measured from $\bar{\bar{X}}$ (= 0.53), the data show that

$$\bar{\bar{X}} + 3\sigma' = 0.53 + (3 \times 1.29) = 4.40,$$

which is less than the upper specification limit *USL* (= 5.00). On the lower side,

$$\bar{\bar{X}} - 3\sigma' = 0.53 - (3 \times 1.29) = -3.34,$$

which is not as low as *LSL* (= −5.00). Since the process is operating in statistical control, these results are important. They indicate that the process has a *natural tolerance* of about 7.74 (= 3.34 + 4.40) on individual stem lengths as compared with a total print spread of 10.00. Reduced inspection may, therefore, be used with assurance. Almost all product will be produced within the specification limits as long as this state of control is maintained. In other words, inspection need be undertaken only on the number of items necessary to supply data for statistical work; it may be abandoned as far as insuring conformance with design specifications is concerned.

Other types of control charts are available in addition to the charts for variables. In some cases it may not be possible or desirable to measure product quality directly, but instead merely to classify the items by means of a *go-and-not-go gauge;* in other cases defects, and hence rejections, may arise from so many sources that it becomes awkward and expensive to keep track of each. In such situations, use may be made of control charts for attributes, the most extensively used being the p chart, or chart for fraction defective.

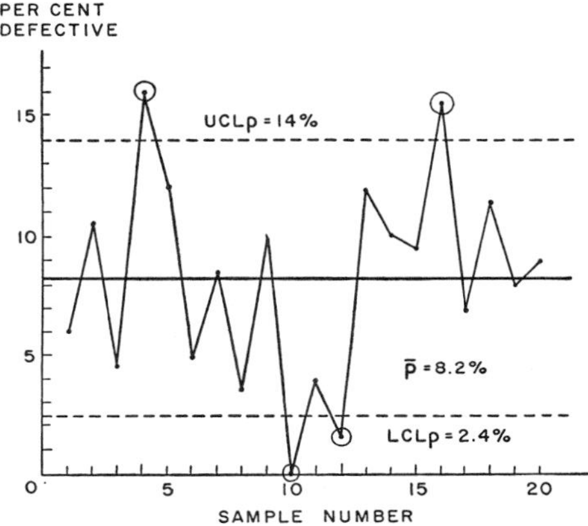

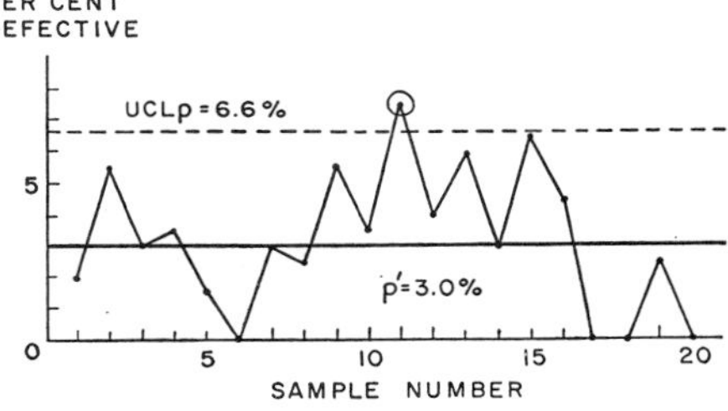

Construction of a p chart may be illustrated by means of data given by Mason Wescott in a study of an enameling process in which all items were subject to visual inspection, and in which defective product could arise from any of six major sources (e.g., the applied enamel might be chipped, scratched, too thin, too thick, etc.). The table on page 116 shows the results of three days' inspection, in which lots of 200 were inspected at one time. Using the symbol p to denote percent defective, the average percent defective $\bar{p}$ over 20 lots of 200 items each is found to be as follows:

$$\bar{p} = \frac{328}{4000} \times 100 = 8.2\%.$$

The standard deviation for such a chart, necessary to determine the 3σ limits, may be found from the formula

$$\sigma = \sqrt{\frac{\bar{p}(100 - p)}{n}} = \sqrt{\frac{8.2(91.8)}{200}} = 1.94\%.$$

Control limits are then

$$UCL_p = \bar{p} + 3\sigma = 8.2 + (3 \times 1.94) = 14\%$$

and

$$LCL_p = \bar{p} - 3\sigma = 8.2 - (3 \times 1.94) = 2.4\%.$$

Observations are plotted on a scatter diagram for comparison with the control limits, as shown in the control chart on page 112.

The analysis of charts for attributes as a means of securing and maintaining control proceeds in much the same way as in charts for variables, with one important distinction: *standard values* are not set on variables charts for maintaining control of future production until a process has been brought into a satisfactory state of control relative to design specifications. Attribute charts, however, are not working against a set of blueprint specifications, but rather against an ultimate goal which places the central line on the chart as close to zero as will represent a profitable balance between the cost of better quality and the value of quality refinement. Also, attribute charts have a strong psychological appeal to plant personnel. It is desirable to capitalize on this inherent asset by settting up tentative standards, or "target values," as soon as it becomes apparent that operating personnel can be expected to meet or beat these standards. Thus, the second of the two charts shows performance against tentative standards of $p' = 3.0$ percent and $UCL = 6.6$ percent. This chart was set up as a blank chart with only the p' and UCL lines on it about six weeks after the first of the two charts on page 112. During this time, the process had been gradually improved from its initial state of nonrandomness about a level of $\bar{p} = 8.2$ percent to a point where a p' standard of 3 percent seemed attainable. Note the run of points above the center line, with one point out of control. The process has not yet attained stability at a 3 percent level, but this is clearly a fair target to strive for and may very well represent the best that can be done without spending more for quality than it is worth.

It is not always possible to secure samples or lots of constant size, such as the n used in the above example. Since n appears in the denominator of the standard deviation formula, this will affect the control limits. Problems involving variable sample size (n) may, however, be handled by a variety of devices. For example, an average sample or lot size n may be calculated

PERCENT DEFECTIVE IN AN ENAMELING PROCESS

Sample Size (or n)=200

Sample No.	No. of Defectives np	Percent Defective $p = (np/n)$
1	12	6.0
2	21	10.5
3	9	4.5
4	32	16.0
5	24	12.0
6	10	5.0
7	17	8.5
8	7	3.5
9	20	10.0
10	0	0.0
11	8	4.0
12	3	1.5
13	24	12.0
14	20	10.0
15	19	9.5
16	31	15.5
17	14	7.0
18	23	11.5
19	16	8.0
20	18	9.0
Total	328	

and used for determining control limits. Against these control limits the fraction or percent defective in each lot or sample may be judged; for particular cases which seem to warrant further investigation, control limits may be recalculated for individual sample or lot sizes.

As noted under *statistical quality control,* these techniques have proved to have wide areas of application, including such areas as cost, credit, and inventory control. Problems in sales and budgetary controls have recently been successfully approached with these techniques and while no cases seem to have been reported, standard- and estimating-cost controls offer promising opportunities.

control concept (of accounting) The recognition of accounting information as an essential tool in the exercise of management functions.

controllable cost 1. Cost that varies with volume, efficiency, choice of alternatives, and management determinations generally; *variable cost.*

2. Any cost that an organizational unit has the authority to incur.

controlled company A company that is under the active control of a holding or parent company; a subsidiary. See *control.*

controller An accountant in charge whose technical skills and professional interests are confined to a single organization or organizational group, and who has been given that title by the management or directors of the organizations. The title is commonly in use in corporate enterprise, whether privately or publicly owned, and in governmental and other noncorporate organizations.

Other names sometimes given to persons exercising the functions of a controller are *auditor, chief accountant,* or simply *accountant.*

The New York Stock Exchange Committee on Stock List at one time recommended that, in the interest of objective accounting, the controller be appointed by and report to the board of directors. This shortening of the line of administrative authority over the top executive of the corporation has often been objected to by management authorities as being a source of confusion and friction within the organization. In practice, a controller so appointed has usually resolved the potential difficulty by conforming the administrative practices in his own office to those of the remainder of the organization, by agreeing with the top executive as to jurisdictional lines in considerable detail, by furnishing analyses and other periodic information in the form and content desired, and by cooperating fully with management in its effort to institute and enforce internal controls.

The controller's responsibilities may include internal audit, but this function has frequently been delegated by the board of directors (occasionally the chairman of the board) or top executive to an officer so designated who reports directly to the delegating authority. See *internal auditor.* Some controllers welcome this separation of function, particularly in a widespread organization where much of the work of the internal auditor is concerned with management and operating problems; others regard the separation as an unfortunate split of closely allied and often inseparable functions, especially where the internal auditor is depended on to supplement the controller's staff during load periods, as at the month- or year-end.

Among the responsibilities commonly assigned to the controller by the authority creating the office are the following:

1. Institution, enforcement, and operation of a system of accounts and external financial reports, including those of subsidiary companies.

2. Furnishing routine and special reports and information to the board, the top executive, activity heads, and other persons within the organization.

3. Explanation to others of financial statements and other reports from his office.

4. Study of the uses of internal reporting, to the end that they may be eliminated, continued, or modified to meet the needs of users.

5. Institution of system of periodic and special reports to the controller's office, from officials and other employees of the organization, on controls, commitments, collections, expenditures, or other financial matters under their jurisdiction.

6. Preparation and filing of income-tax returns and other regular and special reports to governmental agencies; representation of organization before such agencies.

7. Administrative audit and approval before payment of vouchers and payrolls.

8. Countersigning of checks.

9. Preparation of budget for approval of board.

10. Aiding in budget enforcement within the organization following its approval.

11. Maintenance of files for leases, contracts, open purchase orders, and other corporate documents.

12. Furnishing of advice on corporate problems when requested by board or management.

Not infrequently the controller is also charged with the supervision of the functions of the treasurer, purchasing agent, and office manager.

controlling account See *control account.*

controlling company A corporation owning or controlling one or more other corporations; it may be either a *holding company* or a *parent company*. See *control(3)*.

controlling-company accounting The method followed by a holding or parent company in recording its investment in and transactions with a subsidiary. It is usual to find an investment account in which are maintained the cost of the owned shares of the subsidiary, a current account for various types of everyday intercompany transactions, and occasionally an asset account for "profits accrued."

In general, no practical benefits are derived from accruing profit and loss from subsidiaries on the books of the controlling company; reserves for losses on investments in subsidiaries are preferably based on estimates of ultimate realization rather than on amounts of operating losses. However, accountants differ on this question. Some prefer to follow the conservative practice of adjusting for operating losses but not for profits, or for operating losses in excess of operating profits since the date of acquisition, the adjustment taking the form of a valuation reserve against the investment. This practice is unobjectionable if the addition to the reserve is a reasonable increase in the expected loss from realization. There is also support for the practice, occasionally encountered, of adjusting the investment account of the controlling company so that it will always be in agreement with its equity in the subsidiary's net worth.

A cash or stock dividend of a subsidiary effected through a credit to an account with the controlling company on the subsidiary's books and reflected as income in the amount on the books of the controlling company and as a debit to a corresponding account with the subsidiary is a financial device usually preferred over the practice of taking up the subsidiary's profit merely as an accrual. An accrual reflects only a potential right to the profit; as a dividend, the same amount becomes a creditor's equity in the subsidiary's assets.

If paid from earnings prior to the date of acquisition, dividends of subsidiaries are treated as liquidation dividends and credited to the investment account or to a valuation account applicable to the investment; should such dividends exceed the investment cost, the excess may be credited to an "acquired surplus" account in order to distinguish it from other sources of accumulated earnings.

Sales by a controlling company of subsidiary shares are best treated in the ordinary manner: their cost is average cost; the profit or loss is the difference between selling price and the average cost. On consolidated statements the effect is a reduction of a portion of the consolidated excess or surplus, if any, and a gain or loss differing from the controlling company's by the amount of the applicable undistributed profit or accumulated loss since the date of acquisition. See *consolidation policy*.

convention A statement or rule of practice which, by common consent, express or implied, is employed in the solution of a given class of problems or guides behavior in a certain kind of situation. A convention, as distinct from an *axiom*, may be said to exist when it is known that an alternative, equally logical rule or procedure is available but is not used because of considerations of habit, cost, time, or convenience. Thus, the convention of omitting the characteristic in the construction of *logarithm* tables increases their convenience and saves time and cost in their compilation and publication. Placing debits on the left and credits on the right of an account supplies another example. The adoption of a particular convention may even be a historical accident, but once adopted, a convention acquires value as a means of communication and cooperation. Thus, many other signs were employed for arithmetic operations when "+" and "−" were introduced by Widman in 1489; the latter were not commonly accepted until the 17th century, but they became a part of the mathematician's stock in trade because they conveyed meaning without elaborate explanations or translations. An axiom and a convention may be indistinguishable; thus, the use of straight-line depreciation in many cases, long regarded as a convention, has tended to take on the character of an axiom as it becomes increasingly clear that alternative methods are neither more logical, rigorous, nor accurate, and as its propriety and utility are less often challenged.

Ultimately, the choice of axioms must be regarded as conventional. A particular set of axioms may be regarded as a set of conventions in that alternative systems can be devised in which what are now theorems are used as the starting point, and what are now axioms become *theorems*. Conventionality does not, however, impair the analytical usefulness of axioms; it merely implies that, if an unconventional system is demonstrated to possess greater analytical power, fecundity, or simplicity, the only obstacle to its adoption is the accumulated habits of the professional community.

Convention dictates many of the activities and observances of the public accountant in such diverse matters as his measures of *materiality*, the style and content of *financial statements*, the features he builds into his *audit reports*, and, in general, the forms of communication he follows with his staff, his clients, and the world at large. Modified conventions emerge in the world of accounting from time to time; they are generally ascribable to the growth of the *public interest* in the improvement of financial reporting.

conversion The replacement of a holding of one class of corporate *security* with that of another class; e.g., the surrender, at the option of the owner, of one or more face-value units of long-term indebtedness or par-value units of preferred stock in exchange for a fixed number of shares of common stock: a feature often accompanying the financing of an expanding enterprise, designed to provide for the investor present security and a prospect of future gain through sharing in profits at a rate in excess of the interest return, or through an increase in the market price of the common stock beyond the agreed level of exchange. To the corporation, advantages lie in the possibility of relief from accumulating funds for repayment of the obligation and in the reduction of fixed costs; a full conversion would also lift the operating and financial restrictions that are often attached by underwriters to loan agreements; see *restricted surplus*.

convert 1. To substitute one form of property for another, as by sale or exchange. Examples: the sale of goods for a promise to pay; the liquidation of such a promise by the payment of cash; the exchange of a bond of an original issue for one of a related refunding issue.
2. = *compound*.
3. To misappropriate, as the funds of others for one's own use.
4. To process raw material, thereby giving it a new form or utility.
—*conversion, n.*

convertible bond A bond that under the terms of the bond indenture may be exchanged, at the option of the holder, and subject to specified limitations of time, rate of exchange, and other conditions, for common stock or another security of the issuer; the exchange may involve a contribution of an additional amount of cash by the investor. See *bond*.

cooling period = *waiting period*.

cooperative A form of organization, permitted under state laws, its purpose being to gain for producers or consumers the profits or savings which would otherwise accrue to middlemen. Its capital is contributed by its stockholders or members, who appoint a general manager; where its net income is periodically distributed to them in proportion to individual purchases or other transactions rather than in proportion to their investments, the cooperative is not subject to Federal income tax. Buyers' and sellers' cooperatives, particularly in farm communities, have been in existence for many years; there are also cooperatives that distribute power; others refine and sell at retail petroleum products; still others can and market fruits and vegetables; and so on. The "Rochdale principles" under most or all of which a cooperative operates are: (a) membership open to any individual paying in a nominal amount for a single share; (b) one vote per member present at a meeting, no proxies being allowed; (c) a cash basis for sales to members and others; (d) a moderate interest return per share; (e) net income returned to members as above mentioned; (f) neutrality on religious and political issues; (g) education of members in cooperative principles and benefits.

cooperative bank See *savings-and-loan association*.

coordinate 1. *v.t.* To bring together or fashion to common purposes; to synchronize.
2. *adj.* Of equal rank, importance, or authority.
3. *n.* (mathematics) Any of two or more magnitudes that determine the location of a point. See *abscissa; variable.*

coordinate system Any method of locating or designating points in space by reference to scaled axes. The axes start at a common point called the *origin*, and are so oriented and scaled that points can be related to them. The number of axes necessary to locate a single point uniquely is called the *dimension* of the system. Two axes are required to locate each point, as in the illustration on page 121. Three axes would be required to locate every point between the covers of this book. The axes may be at right angles, with the same scale on each, as in the illustration accompanying *abscissa*, thus conforming to a *Cartesian coordinate system.* Other coordinate systems may employ obliquely tilted axes and scales of different orders. Thus, in the diagram which follows, the angle between the two axes is 60 degrees. The horizontal axis, known as the *abscissa* or x axis, is scaled in *integer* units—the "natural-number" scale: 0, 1, 2, ... The other axis, called the *ordinate* or y axis, is in this instance measured in *logarithms.* Commencing (at the origin) with 1, the logarithm of 0, and continuing as 1, 2, 3, . . . , the scale intervals are the logarithms of these numbers. Any point is located uniquely by drawing lines parallel to the axes. Thus, *P*, at (2, 3), has the natural number 2 as its abscissa and the logarithm of 3 as its ordinate. If the angle between the axes in the diagram is increased to 90 degrees, it becomes a *semilogarithmic chart.*

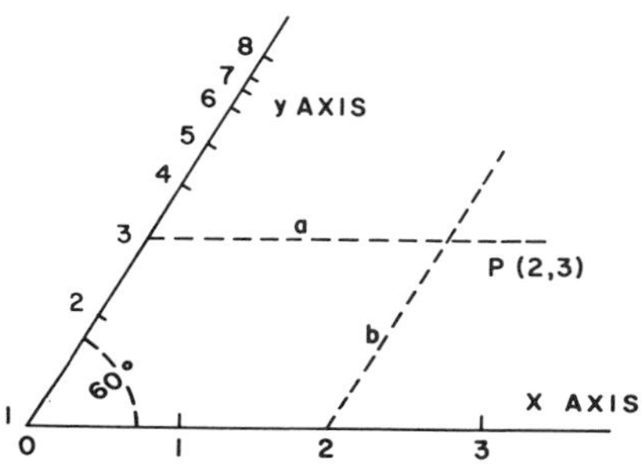

co-partner = *partner.*

copyright The exclusive right conveyed by Federal statute to reproduce and sell a book, pamphlet, drawing, design, formula, musical composition, map, photograph, or other creation, and to forbid the publication of excerpts, digests, or other imitations thereof. An account for copyrights seldom appears, since the cost of procuring a U. S. or international copyright is nominal and is usually absorbed at once as an operating expense. An exception lies where a copyright, already established, is purchased, as by one publisher from another; here the cost is customarily spread over a relatively short period of time, such as two or three years, or is expensed at once, in accordance with estimates of revenue-producing life. A copyright extends over a 28-year period, with a renewal privilege thereafter for a similar period. See *intangible asset; balance sheet.*

corporate action A policy decision made by or receiving the approval of the stockholders or the board of directors of a corporation, as contrasted with *administrative action,* or decision of management; the distinction between the two fields of action is dependent on the requirements of corporate law, the provisions of bylaws of the corporation, and local or general custom. Thus, a recapitalization, including a *quasi-reorganization,* requires the approval of stockholders under the laws of most states; the appointment of a controller can be a prerogative of the board of directors imposed on it by the bylaws; a proposal to alter a product line, or to sell a major item of equipment, might be referred, by custom within the corporation, to the board of directors for decision. The term may also be applied to decisions of management, where management has assumed, or has been given by the board of directors, sometimes tacitly, broad powers of policy-making. The professional accountant is frequently in the position of advising with his clients on matters requiring, in his opinion, corporate action on either of these levels. See *administrative action; policy; administration.*

corporation A legal entity operating under a grant of authority from a state or other political autonomy in the form of articles of incorporation or a charter. In the United States, each of the states, territories, and possessions has its own general- or business-corporation act. The basic attributes of the corporation are: (a) an exclusive name, in which it can hold property, contract, and sue or be sued; (b) continued existence within the limits established by its articles of incorporation, independent of that of any of its stockholders or members; (c) paid-in capital represented by transferable shares; (d) limited liability, in that its stockholders or members, except in special cases, are not liable for its debts and obligations beyond the amount of full-paid capital stock; and (e) over-all control vested in the directors, whose authority is subject to restrictions imposed by law, the articles of incorporation, the bylaws, and the stockholders or members who appoint them.

A corporation with a single shareholder is possible. Under federal revenue acts, the term includes associations, joint-stock companies, and certain types of limited partnerships.

corpus The principal or capital of an estate, fund, or trust, as distinguished from the income or proceeds. See *trust; estate accounting*.

correlation table A frequency table designed to assist in the determination of the relations, if any, between variables. It differs from a *contingency table* in that the latter is concerned with *attributes*, while the correlation table is concerned with variables or quantitative classifications. In a correlation table, the order of rows and columns is determined by the values of the variables, whereas in a contingency table, the order of the rows and columns is arbitrary.

In the correlation table which follows, the variables X (total output per week) and Y (total cost of production per week) are plotted on the horizontal and vertical axes, respectively. Data for output and costs are grouped into class intervals ranging from 36–40 · · · 91–95 for X, and 116–120 · · · 146–150 for Y. The data for X are stated in units of one ton and the data for Y are stated in units of $10. Reading from the intersection of column 1 and row 1: only for one week did production fall between 36 and 40 tons with a cost ranging from $1,160 to $1,200.

The frequencies f are given in the text of the table. Thus, outputs ranging from 61 to 65, column 6, occurred

TOTAL OUTPUT PER WEEK (X)

TOTAL COST OF PRODUCTION PER WEEK (Y)

ITEM NUMBER →				1	2	3	4	5	6	7	8	9	10	11	12	13	14	15	16
	CLASS INTERVAL →			36 40	41 45	46 50	51 55	56 60	61 65	66 70	71 75	76 80	81 85	86 90	91 95				
		MID-POINT →		38	43	48	53	58	63	68	73	78	83	88	93	f	fd_x	fd_x^2	fd_xd_y
↓	↓	↓	d	−7	−6	−5	−4	−3	−2	−1	0	1	2	3	4				
1	116 120	118	−2	1	1		2	1	2	1						8	−29	135	58
2	121 125	123	−1			2		1	1	4	4	1				13	−18	68	18
3	126 130	128	0							1	4	8	2	4		19	23	53	0
4	131 135	133	1									2	3	2		7	14	32	14
5	136 140	138	2										1	1	1	3	9	29	18
6	141 145	143	3																
7	146 150	148	4																
8	f			1	1	2	2	2	3	6	8	11	6	7	1	50	−1	317	108
9	fdy			−2	−2	−2	−4	−3	−5	−6	−4	1	5	4	2	−16			
10	fdy^2			4	4	2	8	5	9	8	4	3	7	6	4	64			
11	fdydx			14	12	10	16	9	10	6	0	1	10	12	8	108			

Correlation Table Showing Cost-Output Relations in Sugar-Refining Operations. (Adapted from Lyle, *Regression Analysis of Production Costs and Factory Operations.*)

twice with costs ranging from 116 to 120, row 1, and once with costs ranging from 121 to 125, row 2. For purposes of computation, these ranges may be eliminated and the data treated as though all observations occur at the center of the class, or class midpoint. Thus it would be said that an output of 63 tons occurred twice at a cost of \$118 × 10 and once at a cost of \$123 × 10.

The correlation table may also be viewed as a type of *scatter diagram* for purposes of obtaining a picture of relations between X and Y. For this purpose, it may be helpful to picture the table as being turned about its X axis through an angle of 180° in order to align it with the system used on ordinary graph paper. It can be seen, by inspection, that the main tendency disclosed by the data is along a curve which increases at a gradually increasing rate; i.e., as output increases, costs rise—at first slowly, and then more rapidly as 63 tons is passed. About the curve, there is, however, some tendency to scatter or disperse.

Under *arithmetic mean*, a shortcut method of calculation for grouped data is described. This same method is applied to both X and Y for convenient calculation of the correlation coefficient. For X, an arbitrary origin is assumed at 73, and for Y, an arbitrary origin is assumed at 128. In other words, 73 and 128 are each set equal to 0. About these origin points, deviations d, both positive and negative, may then be taken in units of one, or class-interval units. The distinction between the X and Y deviations d may be preserved by the following notational device: Let d_x represent the X deviations, and d_y the Y deviations.

The correlation coefficient r, in terms of deviations about an arbitrary origin, is defined as

$$r = \frac{p}{\sigma_x \sigma_y},$$

where

$$p = \left[\frac{\Sigma f d_x d_y}{N} - \left(\frac{\Sigma f d_x}{N}\right)\left(\frac{\Sigma f d_y}{N}\right)\right] \times c^2,$$

$$\sigma_x = \left[\sqrt{\frac{\Sigma f d_x^2}{N} - \left(\frac{\Sigma f d_x}{N}\right)^2}\right] \times c,$$

and

$$\sigma_y = \left[\sqrt{\frac{\Sigma f d_y^2}{N} - \left(\frac{\Sigma f d_y}{N}\right)^2}\right] \times c,$$

where c represents the class intervals, 5, of the X and Y scales, which were compressed into d_x and d_y.

The values to be substituted in these formulas may be extracted from the table. The total frequencies of the X's are given in column 13, and the total frequencies of the Y's are given in row 8. Thus, the frequency f of X for d_y at -2 is given by summing directly across row 1. The total is 8. This represents the number of X's that were paired with the same value of Y. A similar addition is performed for all of the X's at each value of Y, and the results listed in column 13. The process is repeated for the Y's at each value of X. The results of these additions down each column are listed in row 8. Since every X is associated with a Y, the total frequencies of the X's must be equal to the total frequencies of the Y's. This total, 50, given at the intersection of row 8 and column 13, provides a check on the accuracy of addition as well as showing the total number of cases, $N = 50$, on which observations were taken.

The next figures needed, by reference to the formulas for r, are Σfd_x and Σfd_y. The data for each fd_x (frequency of occurrence times d_x) are given in column 14. Thus, the first figure, -29, represents the multiplication of each d_x by its frequency of occurrence, with $d_y = -2$: $[1 \times (-7)] + [1 \times (-6)] + [0 \times (-5)] + [2 \times (-4)] + [1 \times (-3)] + [2 \times (-2)] + [1 \times (-1)] + (0 \times 0) + (0 \times 1) + (0 \times 2) + (0 \times 3) + (0 \times 4) = -29$. This process is repeated for d_x at each value of d_y. The sum Σfd_x

$= -1$ is given at the intersection of column 14 and row 8. The same method, moving down the columns, produces $\Sigma fd_y = -16$ at the end of row 9.

To obtain fd_x^2, the process described above is repeated, but each d_x is squared before multiplying by its corresponding frequency f. Moving across each row, for a given d_y the fd_x^2 listed in column 15 is obtained. Thus, $[1 \times (-7)^2] + [1 \times (-6)^2] + [0 \times (-5)^2] + [2 \times (-4)^2] + [1 \times (-3)^2] + [2 \times (-2)^2] + [1 \times (-1)^2] + (0 \times 0^2) + (0 \times 1^2) + (0 \times 2^2) + (0 \times 3^2) + (0 \times 4^2) = 135$, the figure appearing at row 1, column 15. The sum $\Sigma fd_x^2 = 317$ is given in column 15, row 8. The same method, moving down each column, is applied to secure $\Sigma fd_y^2 = 64$, shown in row 10, column 13.

Finally, the cross-products fd_xd_y are obtained. Since fd_x and fd_y have already been calculated, as shown in column 14 and row 9, respectively, it is only necessary to multiply the fd_x already obtained by its corresponding d_y to obtain fd_xd_y. Thus, d_y at -2 multiplied by fd_x of -29 yields 58, the first item in column 16, and so on. The sum $\Sigma fd_xd_y = 108$ is given in column 16, row 8. Similarly, fd_yd_x may be obtained by multiplying the fd_y in row 9 by the d_x in the same column. Since $\Sigma fd_yd_x = \Sigma fd_xd_y$, the sum of row 11 should equal the sum of column 16.

Recapitulation: 1. Sum, horizontally and vertically, the frequencies appearing in the body of the table. This yields $\Sigma f = N = 50$ (column 13, row 8).

2. To obtain fd_x, multiply every d_x by its corresponding frequency for each d_y (column 14). Sum the resulting column to obtain $\Sigma fd_x = -1$ (column 14, row 8).

3. To obtain fd_y, multiply every d_y by its corresponding frequency for each d_x (row 9). Sum the resulting row to obtain $\Sigma fd_y = -16$ (column 13, row 9).

4. To obtain fd_x^2, square each d_x before multiplying by its frequency (column 15). Sum the resulting column to obtain $\Sigma fd_x^2 = 317$ (column 15, row 8).

5. To obtain fd_y^2, square each d_y before multiplying by its corresponding frequency and sum down the column (row 10). Sum the resulting row to obtain $\Sigma fd_y^2 = 64$ (column 13, row 10).

6. To obtain fd_xd_y, multiply each fd_x already obtained (column 14) by its corresponding d_y (column 16). Sum the resulting column to obtain $\Sigma fd_xd_y = 108$ (column 16, row 8).

7. Step 6 should be checked by performing the same operation on fd_y (row 9), multiplying this value by d_x to obtain fd_yd_x (row 11). Σfd_yd_x should equal Σfd_xd_y, previously obtained.

8. Substitute the values so obtained in the formulas which appear at the bottom of this page.

9. Recall (a) that r is a linear coefficient of correlation, and (b) that the

$$p = \left[\frac{\Sigma fd_xd_y}{N} - \left(\frac{\Sigma fd_x}{N}\right)\left(\frac{\Sigma fd_y}{N}\right)\right] \times c^2 = \left[\frac{108}{50} - \left(\frac{-1}{50}\right)\left(\frac{-16}{50}\right)\right] \times 25 = 53.84,$$

$$\sigma_x = \left[\sqrt{\frac{\Sigma fd_x^2}{N} - \left(\frac{\Sigma fd_x}{N}\right)^2}\right] \times c = \left[\sqrt{\frac{317}{50} - \left(\frac{-1}{50}\right)^2}\right] \times 5 = 12.59,$$

$$\sigma_y = \left[\sqrt{\frac{\Sigma fd_y^2}{N} - \left(\frac{\Sigma fd_y}{N}\right)^2}\right] \times c = \left[\sqrt{\frac{64}{50} - \left(\frac{-16}{50}\right)^2}\right] \times 5 = 5.43,$$

and

$$r = \frac{p}{\sigma_x\sigma_y} = \frac{53.84}{12.59 \times 5.43} = \frac{53.84}{68.3637} = 0.79.$$

particular straight line assumed is the one calculated by the *least-squares method*. As a matter of fact, inspection of the above data plus economic and accounting analysis point toward the use of a nonlinear function, such as $Y = a + bX + cX^2$. Correlation coefficients may, of course, be calculated for these higher-order functions. See *index of correlation*.

The other values necessary to linear regression and correlation analysis may also be calculated directly from the table by means of the following formulas:

1. By definition, $r^2 = 1 - S_y^2/\sigma_y^2$, where S_y is the *standard error of estimate* of Y, and σ_y is the standard deviation of Y. This definition shows that r^2 represents a measure of the gain in efficiency (reduction of error) resulting from the use of the regression line rather than the *mean*. From this definition, it follows that

$$S_y = \sigma_y\sqrt{1 - r^2} = 5.43\sqrt{1 - (0.79)^2} = 3.31.$$

2. The least-squares regression equation becomes

$$y = r\frac{\sigma_y}{\sigma_x}x,$$

in which σ_x represents the standard deviation of X, just as σ_y represents the standard deviation of Y. Substituting $y = Y - \bar{Y}$ and $x = X - \bar{X}$ in this last relation, where $\bar{Y}$ and $\bar{X}$ are the arithmetic means of Y and X, respectively, the equation becomes

$$Y = \bar{Y} + r\frac{\sigma_y}{\sigma_x}(X - \bar{X})$$

$$= \left(\bar{Y} - r\frac{\sigma_y}{\sigma_x}\bar{X}\right) + r\frac{\sigma_y}{\sigma_x}X.$$

All that remains is to calculate and substitute the values

$$\bar{Y} = A_y + \left(\frac{\Sigma fd_y}{N}\right) \times c = 128 - \frac{18 \times 5}{50}$$

$$= 126.2,$$

and

$$\bar{X} = A_x + \left(\frac{\Sigma fd_x}{N}\right) \times c = 73 + \frac{1 \times 5}{50} = 73.1.$$

The least-squares regression equation then becomes

$$Y = \left[126.2 - 0.79\left(\frac{5.43}{12.59}\right) \times 73.1\right] + 0.79\left(\frac{5.43}{12.59}\right)X;$$

or, simplifying,

$$Y = 101.3 + 0.34X.$$

This equation states a linear relation between costs and rate of output. In other words, over the range of production rates studied, fixed costs constituted \$1,103 of the total, while variable costs increased at the rate of \$3.40, on the average, for every ton increase in the rate of output per week.

This equation might be used to estimate probable future costs. Suppose, for example, that it is desired to estimate probable costs for production scheduled at a rate of 85 tons per week. Substituting $X = 85$ tons in the equation, the single best straight-line estimate becomes

$$10 \times Y = (101.3 + 0.34 \times 85) \times 10 = \$1{,}302.$$

(Multiplication by the factor 10 is necessary because, it will be recalled, Y is expressed in units of \$10.)

The implied *precision* in estimation given by the single figure \$1,302 is, of course, illusory. For most purposes, a range of costs at the specified level of production would be more satisfactory. Subtraction and addition of \$3.31, the value obtained for S_y, from or to the single estimate \$1,302 provides a range within which approximately $\frac{2}{3}$ of the observations lie—if the data are distributed reasonably close to normal about the regression line. Addition and subtraction of this standard error of estimate S_y at 85 tons results in an estimate of potential production costs ranging from $1,269 to $1,335. These results may be compared with estimates obtained by use of the mean, $Y = \$1,262$, and standard deviation, $\sigma_y = \$54$. Application of these latter measures yields a range of from $1,208 to $1,316, a much wider range of estimates with about the same degree of *reliability*.

A measure of the gain in efficiency secured by use of the regression line as compared to the mean is given by the *coefficient of determination*, $r^2 = 0.62$. Stated somewhat differently, the relative gain in *precision* for the same degree of reliability is approximately 38 percent. Better estimates and a higher *coefficient of determination* may be obtained by use of a higher-order equation, such as $Y = a + bX + cX^2$. See *least-squares method*. It should also be noted that, while in the linear equation *marginal cost* and *average variable cost* are identical, this is not true for higher-order equations. See *equation; function*.

cost 1. An *expenditure* or outlay of cash, other property, capital stock, or services, or the incurring of a liability therefor, identified with goods or services purchased or with any loss incurred, and measured by the amount of cash paid or payable or the market value of other property, capital stock, or services given in exchange. Implicit in the concept of cost is the *accrual basis* of accounting. See *cost basis; accounting valuation; barter*.

2. Hence, the object of any such expenditure or outlay; e.g., direct-labor in the expression "direct-labor cost."

3. = *residual cost;* thus, an inventory, or inventory item, priced at the lower of cost or market, is said to be valued at cost, the inference being that, where market price is the basis, a portion of cost equal in amount to the market price is retained in the inventory account, the balance of cost being absorbed as an expense in the year the price fell.

4. (economics) Payments or commitments for factors of production, and to suppliers of commodities or services, the conditions of which, if modified, alter the quantity or rate at which the supplies of factors, products, or services are forthcoming. Costs, as distinct from *profits*, are known, with certainty, in advance; as distinct from rents, they represent payments, for a given time and place, necessary to obtain the benefit of productive services at a specified rate or volume.

Expenditures are classified in accounting records and reported for management use by functions (e.g., manufacturing, selling, and financing); by units or departments of a business; by product lines; or by location of operations; or in other ways suited to the operations of the particular enterprise.

When used in valuation and rate problems of public utilities, the term "cost" has a restricted meaning as the result of court decisions and rulings of regulatory commissions of the several states and the Federal government. See *original cost* (*2*); *objective cost; cost absorption* (*2*); *allocated cost*.

cost absorption 1. The expensing of an added cost, such as freight, not passed on to a customer.

2. The recognition of an expenditure as an operating cost or expense, either at the time incurred and first given expression to in the accounts, or at a subsequent point of time; at the end of the period in which it is designated as an expense it is transferred with other like items to a *profit-and-loss* or other *clearing* account, and thence to *retained earnings* (earned surplus). An income statement may be regarded as reflecting the costs absorbed during the period to which it relates. The cost-absorption process involves the recognition of expense under the following conditions:

(a) Correspondence with physical movement. The bulk of transactions in most business enterprises falls into this category, as where merchandise is bought and sold within the same year. A sale is made, and the cost of the merchandise sold is transferred from an asset status to one of expense; the whole of the expense thus recognized in an accounting period is the summation of the costs customarily associated with individual units sold. In a merchandising concern, the unit cost is invoice cost plus minor items, such as freight, sometimes added to invoice cost; in a manufacturing enterprise, material, labor, and overhead would in most instances be involved. But in both cases, the unit cost attaches equally in amount to each item sold and on hand, out of the same lot, or produced in the same batch. See, however, (c) below.

(b) Service or benefit yielded. Fixed assets supply a stream of services the costs of which are measured by provisions for depreciation: that is, the cost of fixed assets is divided into two parts—one representing services yielded or otherwise lost to the business; the other, services expected to be yielded to the business in the future—the accounting aim in both cases being to attach an aliquot portion of cost to each unit of service yielded or lost and remaining to be yielded. Again, the annual benefit from a long-term loan is measured by a year's interest expense the amount of which, on an accrual basis, bears a constant relationship with the principal outstanding. Operating expenses generally come under this head. Accounting seeks here to reach the same objective as in (a), above: that is, to spread costs ratably over units of acquired goods and services and to expense the unit costs thus assigned as the units are consumed.

(c) Most recent costs. *Lifo* methods of *inventory valuation* have the effect of transferring the latest costs of merchandise or raw materials to the physical units of inventory sold or put into production, regardless of when the units were acquired, or whether sales prices have increased or remain unchanged. In times of rising prices, the inventory remaining is valued at a cost disproportionately low as compared with the cost of its replacement and lower than its actual cost, since in the physical movement of goods, the older items are as a rule disposed of first. Many accountants disavow the use of latest costs as a substitute for actual costs, contending that, when prices are rising, the main effect is to conceal profit, lower income taxes, and give a false impression of "economic" cost, since cost of sales is priced within the limits of goods actually purchased toward the end of the accounting period rather than under the conditions of the market actually existing at the time of purchase. On a falling market, some lifo advocates have been inclined to revert to fifo methods. See *inventory valuation*.

(d) Market declines. By following the basis of the lower of cost or market for inventories, investments, and sometimes other current assets, a portion of their cost may be recognized as an expense before they have been disposed of, in order that the future may bear as an expense an amount no greater than it would have been if the inventory carried forward had been purchased or manufactured in its entirety on the final date of the accounting period. An exception is generally noted for items purchased and applied to sales contracts in which prices remain unchanged by subsequent market declines. As in (c), objections are often raised to the recognition of cost as an expense before the item to which it attaches has been disposed of; proponents of such recognition, however, regard the writedown to market as being in the nature of a loss attributable to the hazards of purchasing. See *inventory valuation*.

(e) Period charge. A property tax is a typical item here; it is usually accrued as an expense on the books of account over the year preceding the date it falls due. A "benefit-yielded" basis would be difficult—in most cases, impossible—to apply, since the services received are of an indirect character and are not measurable in their effect on operations. Depreciation and interest may also be regarded as period charges, but the primary effort in accounting for both items is to put them on a service basis. The periodic regularity of their accrual simply denotes a coincidence of the two bases. Another type of period charge is illustrated by selling expenses: in the clothing industry, for example, the selling effort for a succeeding season is usually completed before the end of the fiscal year. At one time, in an effort to follow a service-yield basis, the selling expense relating to this effort was temporarily capitalized; today the prevailing practice is to regard next season's selling expenses already incurred as a period charge, the change being attributable to the conviction that the bulk of selling cost relates as much, perhaps more, to the maintenance of continuous relations with customers and hence is logically a current expense. In recent years some attention has been given to the notion of factory overhead as a period charge, thus giving primary recognition to its components as organizational rather than product costs. Because overhead can be attached to product only by arbitrary methods of allocation, and such attachment can so often be justified only by severely straining the service-yield basis of expense recognition, the movement has gained ground, and doubtless will continue to do so.

(f) Losses. Losses are a type of expense that often stands in a class by itself. Arising in various forms in every business enterprise, losses are unrelated to the preceding classes and become an expense the moment they occur, although in certain types of enterprise, such as public utilities, there was at one time a tendency to carry forward any major loss for gradual amortization over succeeding periods, thereby softening its impact against income from ratepayers. Distinction is sometimes drawn between ordinary and extraordinary losses, current expense and adjustments of past periods, and recurring and nonrecurring costs, some accountants regarding the one as expense that should appear in the current income statement, the other as a surplus charge. An alternative practice is to make such a distinction only for purposes of classification within an income statement, the more important items in any of the indicated categories appearing under *income deductions* (*q.v.*).

(g) Minor asset purchases. New equipment or replacements the cost of which does not exceed a stated limit may be classified as an expense when given expression on the records. In some business concerns, the limit is $50 or $100; in larger companies, it may be $1,000 or even more. Similarly treated are various types of improvements, office supplies, and bookkeeping forms, a single purchase often yielding benefits extending beyond the current year. Nevertheless, in the interests of simplicity and savings in inventorying and recordkeeping, minor items may be expensed immediately; accountants generally approve such policies provided that the cumulative effect at any one moment of time has no important relation to total assets, and provided that the same policy is followed over the years. The quantitative effect on net income is, of course, much less than the effect on assets, since it must be measured by the difference between this year's total and last year's total of such items.

cost accountant One skilled in cost accounting.

cost accounting That branch of accounting dealing with the classification, recording, allocation, summarization, and reporting of current and prospective costs. Included in the field of cost accounting are the design and operation of cost systems and procedures; the determination of costs by departments, functions, responsibilities, activities, products, territories, periods, and other units, and of forecasted future costs and standard or desired costs, as well as historical costs; the comparison of costs of different periods, of actual with estimated, budgeted, or standard costs, and of alternative costs; the presentation and interpretation of cost data as an aid to management in controlling current and future operations. See *standard cost*.

cost accounts A group of accounts constituting the record of production and, often, distribution activities.

cost allocation The transfer of the cost of a good or service or the total of a group of such costs from a *primary* account to one or more *secondary* accounts, the purpose being to identify the cost with the product to which the goods or services have contributed.

cost basis (of accounting) The valuation basis followed in recording and reporting expenditures. It rests on the assumption that cost or depreciated cost is a valid and workable quantitative measure of economic activity, both for decisions of management and for the conclusions and opinions of those who rely on reports prepared from accounting records. It embraces the following conventions:

1. (a) Cost is net cash outlay; (b) where assets or services are acquired with capital stock, it is the market value of the stock; (c) if there is no such market value, it is the fair market value of the asset or service acquired; and (d) if the asset or service has no fair market value, then it is the depreciated cost of the acquired asset or the best estimate thereof in the hands of the seller. See *unit cost; stock dividend.*

2. Depreciated cost is cost less accumulated (accrued) depreciation or less any other related valuation account representing an absorption of cost: a residual amount, carried forward to the succeeding period and believed to be the source (a) of exchange value or (b) of services at least equal to such value. Besides accumulations of (reserves for) depreciation, valuation accounts may include reserves for bad debts, and reserves having the effect of marking down cost to an amount not in excess of market value, as in the case of reserves covering temporary investments and merchandise inventories. See *inventory reserve*.

3. Depreciated original cost is a standard valuation basis for assets acquired by a public utility whether from affiliated or nonaffiliated predecessor owners. See *original cost* (*2*).

4. Intangibles, once common on the balance sheets of American corporations, have virtually disappeared through writeoffs or gradual writedowns. Because of the difficulty or impossibility of determining their continuing value, and even where there is no evidence of limited usefulness, accountants have welcomed their amortization and the growing universality of balance sheets containing only assets of tangible benefit to future operations. See *goodwill.*

The term is sometimes employed to indicate the *consumption* elements of the *accrual method* of accounting. See *accrued-expenditures basis*.

cost center An organizational division, department, or subdivision; a group of machines, men, or both; a single machine and its operating force: any unit of activity into which a manufacturing plant or other operating organization is divided for purposes of cost assignment and allocation (= *activity*). For each such center, accounts are maintained containing direct costs for which the center's head is accountable.

cost conscious Evidencing awareness of the need for keeping costs under a specified ceiling or at the lowest possible level consistent with the performance of a specified task; endeavoring to incur a minimum of cost.

cost control The employment of management devices in the performance of any necessary operation so that pre-established objectives of quality, quantity, and time may be attained at the lowest possible outlay for goods and services. Such devices include a carefully prepared and reviewed bill of materials; instructions; standards of performance; competent supervision; cost limits on items and operations; and studies, interim reports, and decisions based on these reports.

cost distribution = *cost allocation; overhead.*

cost finding Determination of the cost of an operation or product by allocation of direct costs and proration of indirect costs; *absorption costing.* Cost finding often involves assumptions as to methods of parceling out common costs that vary materially as between the individuals who make them. The questioning of such assumptions has not infrequently led to the adoption of direct-costing methods.

cost flow The concept of an item of cost or a group of costs passing through two or more stages within an economic unit; as, the movement of raw-material costs from requisition to purchase, receipt, stores, production, sales, and collection. Charts and tables of cost flows may be devised to serve such diverse purposes as a procedural directive, an analysis of interrelations within a group of cost accounts, an illustration of operational steps, a representation of financial management, a demonstration of working-capital requirements, and so on.

cost-flow concept (of accounting) The association of costs with functions, productive processes, endproducts, and other operational objectives, by direct identification of constituent materials and services, or, in the case of *overheads,* by any of a variety of *allocation* methods based on value judgments, administrative fiat, or established convention: essentially a *cycling* concept beginning, for example, with *planning* and ending with cash; see *cost flow; cash-flow statement.*

cost fraction 1. The cost identified with a unit of operation or production, as by dividing total direct costs by the number of units of operation or production.

2. Any portion of the outlay for an asset or expense; as, the cost fraction of an asset represented by accumulated depreciation, or of an expense that has been prorated to one of several accounts.

costing The process of ascertaining the cost of activities, processes, products, or services; *cost accounting.*

costing unit = *cost unit.*

cost ledger A subsidiary ledger containing accounts used in computing or summarizing the cost of goods manufactured or of services produced.

cost of goods purchased The purchase price of goods bought, plus the cost of storage, transportation, and delivery to the point where they are to be used, and other costs pertaining to their procurement and receipt.

cost of production Expense incurred in and allocated to a manufacturing operation: the cost of materials, labor, and often overhead charged to work in process.

cost of reproduction The estimated present cost of replacing existing property as it was when new.

cost of sales 1. (retail) (a) The total cost of goods sold during a given accounting period, determined by ascertaining for each item of sale the invoice and such other costs pertaining to the item as may have been included in the *cost of goods purchased.* (b) The cost of goods purchased adjusted by the *inventory variation.*

2. (manufacturing) The *cost of production* of finished goods sold. In some instances overhead, especially fixed items of overhead, is excluded; rarely, certain selling and administrative expenses are included.

cost-or-less principle The principle, basic in accounting, that the cost of a good or service destined eventually to be expensed may under certain well-recognized conditions be written down or eliminated in part, but that under no circumstances may cost be appreciated, or may partly amortized cost be restored, notwithstanding its enhancement in price or increased value in use. Writedowns of current-asset costs are customary when market or anticipated selling prices have declined; fixed assets are regularly amortized through periodic provisions for *depreciation*. See *accounting principles*.

cost or market, whichever is lower The lower of cost price or market value: a basis of valuation applied to the individual items or groups of like items within an inventory, less frequently to the constituent parts of a manufactured unit. See *inventory valuation; cost; market price* (or *value*).

cost-plus A term indicating a method of determining the selling price of goods produced or services performed under a contract whereby the cost of the goods or service is increased in the amount of a profit equal to an agreed increment to such cost. Usually the factors entering into the determination of cost (including overhead) under a cost-plus contract are strictly defined and subject to verification by the recipient of the goods or service. The method is often used when these factors cannot be estimated in advance without undue risks to the contracting parties. See *price*.

cost-plus pricing The practice of determining selling price by adding a profit factor to costs. When employed as an internal-control device, as in the heavy-capital-goods industries, the resulting price is in the nature of a *target*, which is subject to reduction in the negotiation of sales. See *contract price*. Cost-plus pricing is often employed in arriving at a contract sales price where the supplier wishes to avoid the risks of cost prediction. It is likely to be used in experimental or developmental contracts for the production of new units or in purchase contracts for large machinery units requiring an extended period of production.

Cost-plus pricing may be either of the cost-plus-a-fixed-fee or cost-plus-a-percentage-of-cost-fee variety. The latter type of cost-plus pricing in contracts let by Federal agencies is prohibited by law.

cost price 1. = *cost*.

2. = See *contract price*.

cost rate = *overhead rate:* a term sometimes employed to indicate the inclusion of fixed as well as variable overhead costs.

cost records Ledgers, supporting and supported by records, schedules, reports, invoices, vouchers, and other documents evidencing the cost of a project, job, production center, process, operation, product, or service.

cost recovery The recapture of cost through expense recognition; *cost absorption*.

cost-recovery basis A method of accounting for the sale or other disposal of an asset whereby credits are made against the cost of the asset as proceeds of the sale or liquidation are received or realized; the method is sometimes employed where the total amount to be received is in doubt, the proceeds are wholly or partly in the form of an asset having no immediately determinable market value, or the ability of an installment purchaser to pay the full amount of the sale is uncertain. It is commonly regarded not as an everyday method of accounting but as one available for exceptional transactions arising occasionally from the liquidation of noncurrent assets. Example: The management of a manufacturing concern, disposing of an old building that had housed one of its plants, had cost $100,000, and had been depreciated to $9,000, decides to segregate the asset from the buildings account and transfers its cost and accumulated depreciation to a new account pending liquidation. In journal-entry form, the action is expressed as shown at the top of the next page.

Accumulated depreciation—buildings	$91,000.00	
Plant *M*, in liquidation	9,000.00	
Buildings		$100,000.00
Transfer of cost and accumulated depreciation pertaining to Plant *M* to a liquidation account.		

Demolition costs of $5,200 are incurred:

Plant *M*, in liquidation	5,200.00	
Accounts payable		5,200.00
Contract cost of demolition.		

Sales of scrap take place:

Cash (or accounts receivable)	8,000.00	
Plant *M*, in liquidation		8,000.00
Proceeds of scrap sales of Plant *M* materials.		

Other scrap sales are made:

Cash (or accounts receivable)	7,000.00	
Plant *M*, in liquidation		7,000.00
Further sales of Plant *M* scrap.		

The total of sales of scrap, $15,000.00, now exceeds the residual cost of the building plus the demolition expense. A profit must therefore be recorded:

Plant *M*, in liquidation	$800.00	
Profit from Plant *M*, in liquidation		$800.00
Excess (15,000.00 − 14,200.00) of sales of Plant *M* scrap over residual cost and demolition outlay.		

The profit account is reported as miscellaneous income in the company's statement of operations; any further sales of Plant *M* items will be credited in full to the same profit account (or to a similar account if the liquidation extends into a succeeding period).

cost-reduction programs The employment of management devices in the performance of any necessary operation so that a maximum decrease in cost as compared with past cost or standard cost may be attained. Such devices include the search for cheaper materials, improved methods of production and inspection, and improved standards of quality and timing.

cost saving A reduction of cost brought about by some special act, such as the taking of a cash discount on a purchase, the elimination of a specification involving an unnecessarily narrow tolerance in an article of manufacture, or the adoption of a more efficient method of production or distribution.

cost sheet A statement showing a summation of the elements entering into the cost of a product. Collectively, cost sheets may serve as a subsidiary ledger supporting a goods-in-process or finished-goods control.

cost standard The projected cost of an activity, operation, process, or item of product, established as a basis for control and reporting.

cost system A system of accounts, often subsidiary to the general ledger, by means of which the cost of products, processes, or services is determined. Cost systems are usually regarded as falling into two broad classes: *job-order* and *process-cost* systems; *estimated* or *standard costs* may be a feature of either. See *cost accounting*.

cost-type *adj.* (governmental accounting) Employing the accrual basis of accounting; said of a budget, an accounting system, or a financial or statistical schedule. Inherent in the concept is the recognition of *expense* as contrasted with *expenditure*, the former signifying a good or service consumed and associated with output, the latter a good or service acquired for future use or consumption. The application of the term is often limited to the affairs of noncorporate government organizations. See *business-type*.

cost unit The quantity or amount selected

as a standard for the measurement of the cost of a given product or operation. Examples: a square yard of pavement; a barrel of flour; a thousand pounds of steel; machine output per hour. The determination of cost per unit facilitates comparison with a standard cost, a past cost, or the cost of a similar unit in another organization. See *unit cost*.

cost value *Cost:* a term used to indicate that cost is a value; contrasts with *market value* or *scrap value*.

cost-volume-profit relationship The area of interest, within an organization, of management and accountants in observing and controlling the relations between prospective and actual manufacturing costs (both fixed and variable), rates of production, and gross profits. *Breakeven charts* epitomize these relationships at planning and forecasting stages, and various types of comparative cost statements provide information and the basis for action at operating, review, and reporting levels.

coverage 1. The extent or range of subject matter; scope; as, audit coverage; see *scope*.

2. (insurance) The amount of insurance carried against any risk.

3. (statistics) The portion of the universe included in a survey.

covering entry 1. The record made in a journal or journals of all the elements of any transaction; the journalization accompanying a transaction.

2. The concealment of a transaction by giving expression to an entry for a fictitious transaction of equal amount.

covering warrant (governmental accounting) A document, issued by the Secretary of the Treasury and countersigned by the Comptroller General, accompanying a deposit of cash receipts within the Federal government.

cover into (governmental accounting) To transfer to: said of receipts and appropriation and fund balances deposited in or relinquished to the U. S. Treasury.

cpm See *critical-path accounting*.

credit *n.* 1. The ability to buy or borrow in consideration of a promise to pay within a period, sometimes loosely specified, following delivery.

2. The source of a transaction.

3. A bookkeeping entry recording the reduction or elimination of an asset or an expense, or the creation of or addition to a liability or item of net worth or revenue; an entry on the right side of an account; the amount so recorded. Compare with *debit*.

4. The balance of a liability, net-worth, revenue, or valuation account.

v.t. To record a credit by a bookkeeping entry.

credit line An agreement by a bank, usually informal and of indefinite span, to make a loan, not to exceed a specified amount, when needed by a customer. Continuance of the line is usually dependent on the customer's maintaining in a commercial account at all times a *compensatory balance* equal to a substantial fraction of the prospective loan and keeping the bank informed of financial condition, operating results, and major operating developments.

credit memorandum A notice to a purchaser that the seller has decreased an amount owing to him; the effect is usually the reduction of an invoice previously rendered.

creditor One to whom a debt is owed.

creditors' equity The collective amount of *liabilities* (*2*) or amounts owing to outsiders other than stockholders.

creditors ledger A ledger containing accounts with creditors. The total of the accounts which contain mostly credit balances is usually supported by the credit balance of a control account in the general ledger.

credit sale 1. The delivery of goods, or the performance of a service, accompanied by the receipt of a *promise to pay*. See *sale*.

2. *pl.* A classification of sales made up of such transactions.

credit system A feature of any form of economic organization of society which permits future payments of cash by consumers and other persons in exchange for the present receipt of *goods* or *services*.

credit union A type of cooperative having as its purposes the promotion of thrift and the making of small loans to members. Many are Federally incorporated, coming under the jurisdiction of and audit by the Federal Deposit Insurance Corporation.

cremation certificate A sworn statement by a trustee or other appointed agent that reacquired and retired securities have been destroyed.

critical path The most time-consuming of any of a series of operative stages contributing to a given endproduct; or any stage in which a possible obstruction in performance would delay the programmed time or add to the cost of completing the endproduct.

critical-path accounting A procedure for collecting and dispensing information essential to the management of a project or program where the "critical-control method" (cpm) has been instituted; involved are detailed projections of material, labor, and overhead costs by activities and stages, time schedules for beginning and completing each activity, prompt reporting, and close study of results, including the ascertainment of causes of variances. The objectives include the determination of the timing and amounts of financing requirements, tight controls over costs and completion dates, the timely discovery of possible bottlenecks, and the accumulation of experience of value in similar future operations.

crop insurance Insurance against failure of or damage to a crop, the value of the crop being usually predetermined; the risk most frequently insured is loss from hail.

crosscheck 1. To add horizontally as well as vertically in order to assure the accuracy of totals.

2. To perform one operation, as in auditing, which will have the effect of aiding in determining the accuracy, propriety, or other characteristic of another operation.

cross-section study Study of the properties of component segments of a complex entity or of the structural relations between the segments of the entity, for some definite time period—e.g., study of the income, expenditure, and savings characteristics of two-person families in the continental United States for some designated annual period; or an analysis of a set of accounts for selected months in order to determine the probable structure of relevant transactions in other periods.

cum dividend A term indicating that the quoted price of shares of capital stock on which a dividend has been declared includes the right to receive the dividend. The term attaches from the date of declaration to the date appearing in the resolution on which the holders are said to be of record; cf. *ex dividend*.

cumulative dividend A dividend on *cumulative preferred stock* payable under the terms of the issue at stated intervals and before any distribution is made to the holders of common stock. Unpaid cumulative dividends are a part of the obligation to preferred stockholders in the event of liquidation. See *dividends in arrears*.

cumulative preferred stock Capital stock on which unpaid dividends accumulate as a claim upon past and future earnings and generally, in the event of liquidation, to the extent of available earned surplus, before any distribution can be made to the common stockholders. The right to cumulative dividends is generally expressly provided or is inferred from a guaranty of the dividends. Where there is no indication of intent, some courts have held preferred stock cumulative.

cumulative voting A method of voting for the election of the board of directors of a corporation whereby a minority stockholder or minority group of stockholders may, by concentrating its votes, endeavor to elect one or more members of the board. The owner of any one share is allowed as many votes for one or more candidates as there are directors to be elected.

In noncorporate bodies, or corporate bodies having no capital stock, the common-law rule of voting is that each member is entitled to one vote, regardless of the size of his investment, if any; in corporate bodies, a stockholder is entitled to as many votes as he has shares. To permit representation from minorities, a number of state corporation laws require that when directors of stock corporations are elected, a stockholder is permitted to distribute his individual votes for directors in whatever way he pleases. In other states, cumulative voting is permitted if provided for in the articles of incorporation. Thus, if there are two stockholders or two stockholder groups in a corporation, one owning 600 shares and the other 400 shares, and 5 directors are to be elected, the votes may be cast thus:

Voters	Shares Owned	Number of Directors Voted for 1	2	3	4	5
A (majority)	600	3,000	1,500	1,000	750	600
B (minority)	400	2,000	1,000	667	500	400

It will be observed that if B votes for candidates differing from those nominated by A, he can elect 2 directors, and even 3 (667 each), thus winning control, if A scatters his votes equally for each of 5 candidates (600 each). A is more likely, however, to divide his votes as between three candidates (1,000 each) or four candidates (750 each), thus permitting B to have but two representatives on the board.

The number of shares necessary to elect a desired number of directors can be obtained from the following formula:

$$n = \frac{dN}{D+1} + 1,$$

where n is the number of shares necessary, d the desired number of directors to be elected, N the total number of voting shares, and D the total number of directors to be elected. Thus, if 7 directors are to be elected, a majority group of stockholders wishes to elect not less than 5, and the total shares to be voted are 1,000, the minimum number of shares required will be

$$n = \frac{5 \cdot 1,000}{7+1} + 1 = 626.$$

Again applying the formula, if the majority group wishes to elect all seven directors, 876 shares out of the thousand will be required; if a minority group wishes to elect 1 director, it will have to cast a vote of 126 shares. If the division happened to be exactly 875 and 125, and the majority casts equal votes for each of 7 candidates and the minority its entire vote for one candidate, a deadlock would result; but there is no record that any comparable situation has ever developed in practice. In terms of percentages of the total number of voting shares, the minimum required to elect one director is given in the following table:

Directors To Be Elected	One Share More Than
3	25 %
5	$16\frac{2}{3}$
7	$12\frac{1}{2}$
9	10
11	$8\frac{1}{3}$
13	$7\frac{1}{7}$
15	$6\frac{1}{4}$

currency Paper money and coin; see *cash*.

current 1. Existing in the present but having a transitory or shifting character. Examples: current assets; current funds. 2. Relating to the present, in contrast to the past or future. Examples: the current year; the current budget.

current account 1. A running account, usually between two related companies, reflecting the movement of cash, merchandise, and other items in either or both directions; a periodic settlement is not usually required; it may differ from an *account current*.

2. An account with a partner reflecting salary withdrawals, and other transactions. The balance of the account may be transferred periodically, as at the end of the fiscal year, to the partner's capital account.

current asset Unrestricted cash, or other asset held for conversion within a relatively short period into cash or other similar asset, or useful goods or services. Usually the period is one year or less, but for some items, e.g., installment receivables, the period may be much longer. In some enterprises the period may be extended to the length of the *operating cycle*, which may be more than a year. The five customary subdivisions of current assets are cash, temporary investments, receivables, inventory, and prepaid expenses. See *balance sheet*.

current-asset cycle The period of time required for sales to equal current assets. See *cycle(2); ratio*.

current budget The projection of income and expense at anticipated levels of activity rather than in terms of ideal goals.

current cost Cost at present-day price levels of some or all of the items making up a balance sheet or income statement, obtained by applying to *historical cost* one or more *index numbers* (= *adjusted historical cost*) or by substituting for historical prices prevailing prices of equivalent goods and services (= *replacement cost*). See *fixed asset; inventory valuation*.

current expenditure An expenditure covering an operating cost or an addition to plant during a given period.

current expense 1. An expense of a given period.

2. A normal operating expense, as compared, e.g., with a *nonrecurring charge*.

current fund 1. = *general fund*.

2. *pl.* Cash and other assets convertible into cash within a short time; included are temporary investments, short-term notes, and accounts receivable, current funds thus differing from *current assets; quick asssets*.

current income 1. Income of a given accounting period.

2. (institutional accounting) Receipts and accruals of the present fiscal period expendable for general operations, or for designated specific activities, exclusive of receipts for plant additions or receipts designed to increase the principal of a fund.

current investment An expenditure for readily marketable securities having as its purpose the profitable use of cash temporarily in excess of immediate requirements; *temporary investment*.

current liability A short-term debt, regardless of its source, including any liability accrued and deferred and unearned revenue that is to be paid out of current assets or is to be transferred to income within a relatively short period, usually one year or less, or a period greater than a year but within the business cycle of an enterprise. The currently maturing portion of a bond issue is thus classified unless it is to be paid from a sinking fund or other noncurrent asset source. See *liability*.

Current liabilities, assuming a business cycle of one year, may thus consist of:

Trade accounts and notes (i.e., arising from transactions with suppliers of goods and services common to the business).

Bank loans (repayable within a year).

Current maturities (i.e., of long-term debt, payable within a year).

Loans from other financial institutions.

Deposits and advances from customers, including deposits on containers.

Dividends declared but unpaid (including unclaimed dividend checks from prior declarations).

Accruals (both due and not due) of interest, income and property taxes, payrolls, payroll and social-security taxes, commissions, royalties, vacation pay, bonuses, realized profits shared, and the like. Accruals are often *rounded off*, without affecting *significant amounts*, especially where minor portions of the accrual may be contingent on future events and conditions.

Purchased tax-anticipation notes are the only class of assets that may offset taxes payable, but even there the notes must be of the type that cannot legally be used for any other purpose.

current maturity The portion of a long-term obligation to be retired during the ensuing 12 months, usually classified as a *current liability*.

current operating performance The term used in AICPA publications to characterize *operating-performance income statements* (*q.v.*).

current-outlay cost A cost requiring a current cash expenditure; a present out-of-pocket cost; contrasts with *sunk cost*.

current price The price of record at the time of sale. See *price*.

current ratio The ratio of current assets to current liabilities. See *statement analysis*.

current return A percentage based on the ratio of annual per-share dividends paid during the 12 months immediately preceding and the market price per share at the end of the period. Employing the average price during the period, sometimes advocated, is generally regarded as misleading.

current standard cost A *standard cost* based on anticipated outlays for materials and services and the best performance efficiency reasonably attainable under existing conditions of production.

current taxes Taxes from the date the assessment rolls are approved by the taxing or tax-review authority to the date on which a penalty for nonpayment is attached.

curve The *graph* of a mathematical expression, usually drawn to scales provided by a *coordinate system*.

curve fitting The process of associating curves or mathematical functions with quantitative empirical information on the basis of a criterion or *hypothesis*. Frequently, the data are put in graphic form before fitting. Curve fitting based on rigorous mathematical methods yields unique functions or curves; this is not a general characteristic of casual methods.

The process of fitting may be either (a) exact (as when a straight line is fitted to two points), in which case all points for which observations are obtained lie directly on the curve, or (b) statistical, in which case few, if any, points lie directly on the curve. In statistical fitting, the data are viewed as being subject to various "errors" which mask or conceal the underlying relation. In either exact or statistical fitting, the process may proceed "empirically" or by known laws or theories from which the behavior of the data is deduced. Either casual methods, such as visual inspection, freehand drawing, or use of threads, or rigorous methods, such as *least-squares regressions*, may be used. See *scatter diagram*.

customary form Said of financial statements and meaning the *account form* of balance sheet and the *report form* of income statement.

customers ledger A ledger containing accounts with customers. The total of the accounts, which mostly have debit balances, is usually supported by a debit balance of equal amount in a general-ledger control account.

cutoff An interruption of the continuity of recording transactions for the purpose of comparing book records with totals available from external sources. The interruption may relate to the flow of transactions in books of account or to the intermingling of physical goods. See *cutoff date*.

cutoff date 1. The date selected for stopping the flow of cash, goods, or transactions generally, for closing or audit purposes. Thus, when a physical inventory is taken, a cutoff date for both purchases and sales is customarily selected. This may involve a brief closing of receiving and shipping rooms, permitting a count of goods on hand, or the special labeling of items so that the transactions of one period may be kept apart from those of the succeeding period. The idea of a cutoff date carries with it the likelihood of the omission from the current year's transactions of items properly belonging there but relegated to the succeeding period—a situation tolerated even under rigorous methods of accounting—where the effect on the balance sheet is minor and the effect on the income statement is virtually nil because of the existence of a similar situation at the close of the preceding period. See *physical inventory.*

2. (auditing) The date selected by an auditor, such as one ten days after the close of a period under audit, for a supplementary verification of a cash balance. The procedure may involve obtaining from his client's bank a *cutoff statement* (with canceled checks) covering the brief period, preparing a schedule reconciling the transactions reported by the bank with those appearing on the books, tracing through deposits in transit at the end of the period, examining returned checks outstanding at the end of that period, and making other inquiries, comparisons, and reviews. The object of the supplementary examination is to strengthen the auditor's conclusions as to the propriety of the cash balance at the end of the period under audit. Comparable cutoff dates may be established for inventory additions and other transaction groupings.

cutoff statement An interim statement of transactions between two persons, prepared by one at the request of the other, usually for audit purposes. See *cutoff date*(*2*).

cybernetics A term (from the Greek kybernētēs, meaning "steersman" or "governor") currently embracing the presumably related concepts of *control* (*1*) underlying recently developed fields of *automation*, *computers*, *communication*, *probability* applications, game theory, and the like.

cycle 1. Any of a series of operational sequences having similar endproducts of goods or services: applied to a machine, process, or plant, or to business operations generally. The elapsed time from start to finish is the cycle time.

2. Hence, the time required for such a sequence. Thus, a clock cycle is 12 hours; a lunar cycle, 28 days; a business cycle, a year or the period beginning with an "upswing" and lasting through a depression. See *cyclical movement.*

cycle count A count completed within a given period of time, such as a month or a year, the reference being to a method of more or less continuous verification of inventory quantities where each inventory subdivision or location is physically inspected at least once during the period.

cyclical movement The movement from economic prosperity through inflation, recession, depression, recovery, and finally back again to prosperity.

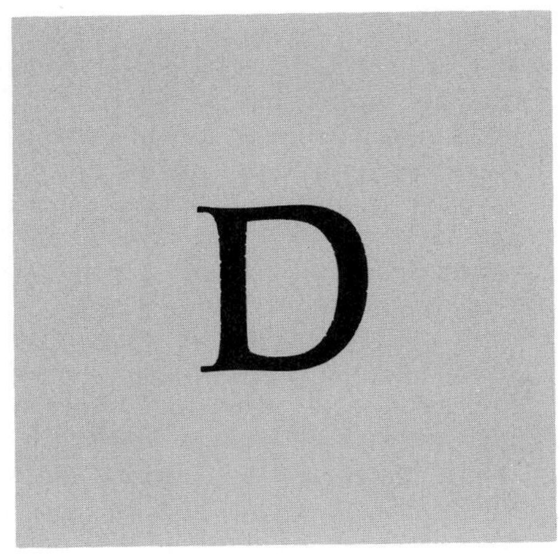

data (*sing.* datum) = *facts.*

dated earned surplus Earned surplus (*retained earnings*) of a corporation accumulated from the date of a *reorganization* or *quasi-reorganization.* On a balance sheet or statement of surplus, the date appears as an integral part of the title, as "Retained earnings from July 1, 19-1, $ . . . ," and this title is repeated over a period of years. Under the regulations of the U. S. Securities and Exchange Commission (Rule 5.02.35[c] of Regulation S-X), the *amount* of the absorbed deficit must be disclosed in the earned-surplus description for a period of at least three years.

date of acquisition 1. The effective purchase date of an asset. From the date of acquisition, the asset must appear in the accounts and in financial statements, and its gradual decline in usefulness (*depreciation*), if any, must be offset against it. Usually, this is the date title is acquired or the burdens of ownership are assumed and the asset is in possession. 2. The date on which the control of a subsidiary was obtained as the result of a stock purchase or otherwise by a parent or holding company. See *control.*

daybook A chronological record of business *transactions;* a *blotter;* a business diary. Transactions recorded in a daybook are subsequently translated into bookkeeping terms to show the accounts affected, and in this revised form they are entered in a journal and posted to a ledger. A daybook is now rarely used; the *journal,* in varied forms, is the *book of original entry.* Original invoices and other supporting documents have largely replaced the descriptive detail formerly inscribed in daybooks. See *journal.*

deadweight The weight of a vessel or other means of transportation, without cargo.

deal An agreement, such as a *purchase order,* between buyer and seller, which, if fulfilled, will give rise to one or more *transactions,* but which in the unfulfilled state does not give rise to an entry in the formal books of account. See *commitment; transaction.* A purchase on credit, paid for on a later date, constitutes one deal but two transactions.

dealer (in securities) A person who buys securities and holds them until sold, as distinguished from a *broker,* who characteristically buys or sells only upon a customer's order and does not take title. Over-the-counter transactions are generally handled by dealers; transactions on exchanges, by brokers. The title "dealer" is often used in referring to either type of person, since brokers, under certain conditions, may acquire and sell securities in their own name.

Dean schedule (insurance) = *analytic schedule.*

death benefits (Federal income taxes) Receipts from the proceeds of life insurance, and receipts by an employee's estate or beneficiaries from or on behalf of an employer because of the employee's death; under the current Internal Revenue Code, the former are tax-exempt and the latter exempt in an amount not exceeding $5,000.

debenture (bond) A security ranking ahead of preferred stock and not protected by collateral or a lien on tangible assets but only by the general credit of the issuer; the underlying indenture may require such protective measures as the maintenance of a specified working-capital ratio, the immediate maturity of the issue in case of default in the payment of interest, the placing of a prior lien on the assets of the issuer in favor of debenture holders when a subsequent issue of bonds is made, limitations on the amount of any additional funded debt, restrictions on dividends to stockholders, and protection of debenture holders in various forms) in case corporate assets are sold or transferred. Interest on debentures is a prior lien on the net income, is payable before dividends are distributed, and may be cumulative. See *income bond*.

debenture capital Proceeds derived from the sale of debentures.

debenture stock = *debenture;* a British term.

debit *n.* 1. The goods or benefit received from a *transaction;* a bookkeeping *entry* or *posting* recording the creation of or addition to an *asset* or an *expense*, or the reduction or elimination of a liability, credit *valuation account*, or item of *net worth* or *revenue;* an entry on the left side of an *account;* the amount so recorded. Compare *credit*.
2. The balance of an asset, expense, or debit *valuation account*.
v.t. To *enter* or *post* a debit.

debit memorandum A document, other than an invoice, showing the reason and authority for creating a *debit;* issued, *e.g.* by a bank, having the effect of reducing a depositor's or customer's account, or by a customer to his supplier for goods returned to the latter; contrasts with *credit memorandum*.

debt Money, goods, or services owing to another by virtue of an agreement, express or implied, giving rise to a legal duty to pay. See *incur*.

debt discount The excess of face value over the net proceeds of a loan. See *bond discount*. When the discount relates to a loan (e.g., a bank loan) standing as a current liability, it is treated as a *prepaid expense*, or, less frequently but more accurately, as a debit *valuation account*, deductible on the balance sheet from the face value of the loan. See *bond discount*.

debt limit (municipal accounting) The maximum amount of indebtedness that a governmental unit may legally incur. Fixed by the provisions of a state constitution, statute, charter, or combination of any or all three of these, the limitation is usually expressed as a percentage of total assessed values, a common rate being 5 percent. *Assessed value* is used as a basis because debt limitations were first imposed in the 19th century, when the property tax was almost the sole source of municipal revenue and the assessed value indicated the municipality's potential taxing power. Even today assessed values are considered by investors a good index of a municipality's financial strength.

If several governmental units overlap, each has its own assessed value for debt-limit purposes, although all of them may be levying taxes on the same property. This fact has been partly responsible for the establishment of *ad-hoc* authorities. For example, if a city is unable to incur further indebtedness for park purposes because it has reached or is close to the debt limit, it may persuade the legislature to establish a park district. Although the boundaries of such a district may be coterminous with those of the city, the district may be given an assessed valuation equal to that of the city itself and will be able to levy the same amount of taxes and incur as much indebtedness as the city itself, unless the legislature imposes a particular restriction on it.

Debt limits are provided for in numerous state constitutions, and where there is no stated limit, statutes fill the gap. Sometimes, however, both constitution and statutes may impose debt limits. In such cases, the statutes restrict further the limitation imposed by the constitution. For example, a state constitution may impose a debt limit of 5 percent; a statute may restrict the debt limit further to, say, 3 percent.

The restriction may apply to both long-term indebtedness such as bonds and short-term debt such as notes payable or vouchers payable. It does not ordinarily cover revenue bonds. The limit usually refers to the net and not the gross debt; that is, the governmental unit may thus offset outstanding indebtedness by the amount of sinking funds or any other cash or securities legally available for debt retirement.

The difference between the maximum amount of debt which the municipality is legally permitted to incur and the amount of outstanding debt applicable to the debt limit is designated as the *legal debt margin.* See *assessed value; overlapping debt.*

debtor 1. One who owes a debt and has a legal duty to pay it; contrasts with *creditor.*

2. *pl.* = *receivables.*

debt service The payment of matured interest and principal; the outlay needed, supplied, or accrued for meeting such payments during any given accounting period; a budget or operating-statement heading for such items.

decentralize 1. To delegate *authority* to subordinate levels within an administrative hierarchy, and to fix areas of *responsibility* for the propriety of actions taken thereunder.

2. To increase the authority and responsibility of field units geographically removed from a central office or headquarters.

3. Loosely, to establish an operating entity to which delegations are made beyond the purview of previous norms or experience.

decile Any of the values that divide a frequency distribution into ten parts; there are nine deciles, four preceding the median, the median, and four following the median. See *quantile.*

decision 1. A choice, followed by a related action, taken in preference to an alternative; the coupling of action with intent.

2. An act or preference that terminates a discussion, controversy, or period of reflection or hesitation.

3. A collection of acts, statements, and intentions, explicit or implicit, which, from the point of view of a particular *model,* and apart from the randomness defined by or implied in that model, displays a systematic pattern or sequence of patterns.

declaration 1. The formal action of a board of directors by which the liability for the payment of a dividend is created; see *dividend.*

2. *pl.* (insurance) That part of an insurance contract containing the insured's statement of underwriting information pertinent to the risk covered.

declared capital = *stated capital.*

declared dividend A dividend, formally authorized by a corporation's board of directors, for payment on a specified date; see *dividend.*

declared value 1. = *stated value.*

2. The value given by a corporation to its capital stock for any of various taxation purposes.

declassified cost The cost, as of a manufactured product, restated in terms of material, labor, and other basic objects of expenditure.

decline in economic usefulness See *depreciation.*

decrement A decrease in value from one point of time to another. See *increment.*

deduction 1. (logic) Reasoning for which there is a necessary conclusion, i.e., a conclusion completely implied by the premises. Strictly, necessary conclusions are possible only within sets of symbols. Whether they are true, and thus applicable to an existing condition, must be determined empirically.

2. Any cost or expense set off against revenue.

deductions from gross income 1. A classification prescribed by the Interstate Commerce Commission in its uniform system of accounts for carriers and other utilities, consisting of deductions from gross operation and nonoperating income in the determination of net income. The classification includes such items as rents, taxes, interest, and amortization of debt.

2. In general, any item deducted before arriving at *operating income.*

deductions from income = *income deductions.*

deductions from net income A classification prescribed by the Interstate Commerce Commission in its uniform system of accounts for carriers and other utilities, consisting of deductions from and the disposition of net income; included are such items as appropriations for reserves and dividends.

deed A written instrument under seal, conveying an interest in real property.

deed of trust A conveyance of property to a trustee, subject to release or disposal under prescribed terms; usually equivalent to a mortgage; = *trust deed.*

de facto In fact, actually; a corporation *de facto* is a group of persons or an organization that is conducting its affairs as a corporation but has no lawful authority to do so because of delay in filing incorporation papers, failure to comply with state law, lapse of charter, or other cause. See *de jure.*

defalcation *n.* The embezzlement of money. See *embezzlement.—defalcate, v.i.*

default Failure to pay debt interest or principal when due, or to perform any other obligation required by contract.

deferral (or **deferment**) The accounting treatment accorded the receipt or accrual of revenue before it is earned, or the incurrence of an expenditure before the benefits therefrom are received. Such items are balance-sheet liabilities or assets and are carried forward to the income account of succeeding periods as the revenue is earned or as the benefits are received from the expenditure. *—defer, v.t.; deferrable, adj.*

deferred asset = *deferred charge; prepaid expense.*

deferred charge An expenditure not recognized as a cost of operations of the period in which incurred but carried forward to be written off in one or more future periods. There are four main types: outlays the benefits from which will be enjoyed over an indefinite number of succeeding periods; outlays in the nature of long-term prepaid expenses for research and development (R&D) that are presumed to be of benefit over a fairly well defined number of future periods; *prepaid expenses* or *costs*—the only type of deferred charge that is classified as a current asset; and expenditures or losses that benefit no past, present, or future period.

1. General future benefits. When a corporation is established, various sorts of legal, accounting, engineering, stock-issue, and other organization costs may be incurred. Normally these costs are small in amount and are absorbed during the period of their incurrence; or, they may be amortized over a period as short as three or five years. Theoretically they confer benefits throughout the life of the corporation, or over a long term of years; practically, having no tangible or realizable value, they are diffcult to explain to stockholders, are regarded by many as an eyesore on the balance sheet, and hence are conventionally written off as quickly as earnings permit. In rare cases they have been permanently capitalized.

The expense of selling an issue of stock may be that of the broker or the corporation, depending on the method of marketing. If the issue is sold *en bloc* and under contract to an investment dealer, the commission and selling expenses will in most cases be borne by the dealer, so that the contract price is a net figure,—i.e., selling price to the public less selling costs and selling profit. If the broker has acted as the corporation's selling agent, or the corporation has sold the stock to the public, the selling costs are those of the corporation and are so recorded. Where organization costs are found on the balance sheet, it may be assumed that they consist of the costs of marketing equity securities.

Reorganization costs are treated in much the same fashion as costs of organization.

2. Long-term benefits. Some expenditures, occasionally classified as deferred charges and designed to benefit operations of a number of succeeding years, are better regarded as "capital expenditures," i.e., additions to fixed assets; illustrations are mine-stripping costs, well-drilling costs, the cost of building access roads, the outlay for temporary structures accompanying a limited-period operation, and other property-development costs. Such expenditures can readily be identified with and justified as relating to physical assets that will contribute services to future operations and hence are best treated as capital assets subject to depreciation or depletion.

Research-and-development costs relating to product design, improvement, packaging, and marketing, processing changes to increase output or efficiency, and the testing of new outlets are examples of less tangible expenditures from which long-term benefits may well be derived. They are conventionally regarded as deferred charges, to be written off over the years during which benefits from them have been anticipated. If, however, research-and-development operations of a similar character are constantly in progress, it is common to find each year's expenditures treated as current expense, the reason being that they resemble maintenance costs in that their purpose is to keep up without break a continuously high level of operating effectiveness.

Bond discount is another type of deferred charge (better regarded, however, as a debit valuation account) having an application to a limited period of years.

3. Prepaid expenses. Insurance premiums, rent, and licenses are examples of operating costs which by custom are often paid in advance. The benefits from them are ordinarily receivable within the period of a year or at most a few years, thus justifying their inclusion as current assets and distinguishing them from longer-term items such as bond discount. If nominal in amount they are often expensed as incurred. See *prepaid expenses.*

4. Losses. Occasionally losses are classified as deferred charges, although the practice has generally met with the strong disapproval of accountants. The purpose of the classification is to spread the burden of the loss over several years rather than one. Public-utility regulatory bodies have often approved this classification for fire and flood losses.

Except for prepaid expenses, as noted above, the usual position of deferred charges is at the end of the asset section of the "account-form" balance sheet.

In recent years there has been a marked tendency to reduce the number of, or to eliminate from American balance sheets, repetitive deferred charges other than a material item of prepaid expenses.

deferred credit = *deferred revenue.*

deferred debit = *deferred charge; prepaid expense.*

deferred dividend A dividend declared and recorded as a liability but not payable until a specified time has elapsed beyond the usual date of payment or until a specified event has occurred.

deferred expense = *deferred charge; prepaid expense.*

deferred liability 1. A debt the payment of which is deferred beyond a legal or customary date; e.g. a *deferred tax.* 2. Any long-term liability.
3. = *deferred revenue.*

deferred maintenance Delayed repairs, or upkeep, measured by the outlay required to restore a plant or individual asset to full operating characteristics. Through planned maintenance, depreciation, although not stopped, can usually be kept within normal limits. Deferred maintenance arises from such causes as (a) the inability to close a plant or remove a machine for repair without interfering with a production schedule; (b) the scheduling of periodic repair periods during which accumulated repairs and overhauls are made; (c) the relatively high cost of pulling out a single item for an overhaul as compared with the collective overhaul of a group of such items following an operating period; (d) the lack of need for future efficiency, as in the case of an item about to be sold; (e) the lack of funds to make needed repairs. In every operating plant and machine, there is always some element of deferred maintenance, and a combination of engineering and management skills is necessary if undue wear, plant breakdowns, or other undesirable results of less-than-maximum efficiencies are to be avoided. The decision of when to repair is usually based on whatever action (or inaction) as to maintenance will produce the minimum effect on cost, or the maximum effect on profit. See *maintenance; depreciation.*

During a fiscal year, a reserve for (deferred) maintenance is often employed to equalize as far as possible the year's maintenance cost. This is a particularly useful device where reliance is had on monthly financial statements. Under a typical procedure, total maintenance costs are first estimated for the year and monthly accruals equal to one-twelfth of the estimate are made by debiting maintenance expense and crediting the reserve; then, as actual maintenance costs are incurred, they are charged against the reserve, and at the year-end the debit or credit balance of the reserve is spread prorata over the maintenance-expense accounts. Occasionally, where the maintenance cycle is believed to extend beyond a single 12-month period, the balance of such a reserve is carried forward into the following year; or a reserve for maintenance and replacements may have been established to which asset-replacement costs as well as maintenance costs would be charged. Both of these practices have largely disappeared: the first, because estimates of maintenance costs beyond a short period of time are so often grossly inaccurate and because fluctuations in maintenance costs as between years have come to be regarded as normal and to better reflect management policies; the second, because of the improvement in methods of providing depreciation.

Deferred maintenance plays an important part in the determination of the selling price of any asset, whether it be a whole plant or a single machine. In the sale of utility properties, an estimate of the outlay required to offset deferred maintenance is frequently deducted from the selling price based upon the original or replacement cost less accrued depreciation, and the amount appears on the books of the purchaser as a valuation account; on a balance sheet it is deductible, like accumulated depreciation, from the asset to which it relates. Thereafter, as repairs and other deferred-maintenance costs are incurred, the other valuation account is decreased until it has been exhausted.

deferred-payment sale 1. An *installment sale.*

2. Any sale the settlement of which is extended beyond a customary credit period.

deferred repairs = *deferred maintenance.*

deferred revenue (or **income**) 1. Revenue or income received or recorded before it is earned: i.e., before the consideration is given, in whole or in part, for which the revenue is or is to be received; also known as *deferred credit, unearned income,* and *unrealized revenue.* Examples: rent received in advance, transportation sold in advance, unearned subscriptions. Like deferred charges, their classification as a current liability (and, hence, as working capital) depends upon the period of time to which they relate. Advance ticket sales are in effect temporary deposits and hence a current liability. Prepaid rent covering an immediately following period, even though not refundable except in the event of the destruction of the property, similarly constitutes a current liability in that it, too, has the characteristic of a deposit out of which maintenance and other expenses are to be paid, leaving a balance, if any, that is to be regarded as income. On the other hand, rental received for the last year of a lease running for ten more years is in the nature of a long-term debt and may be shown as a special item below current liabilities. As indicated, rent is a mixture of future income and of liability for the expenses of maintaining the property during the same period, and, if the amount involved is material, it may be divided between prospective cost, to be included as a current liability, and the remainder, constituting estimated income that may be excluded from that category. Thus, if rental of $10,000 is received for a year in advance and it is known that the only costs are insurance and taxes totaling $3,000, that amount may be shown as a current liability and the balance of $7,000 as deferred income *below the line*.

2. Income subject to adjustment or held in suspense until offsetting charges have been determined and deducted, until a period of time has been completed, or until it has been fully identified.

deferred tax A tax liability accrued on income reported for current accounting purposes but not to be subject to income tax until a later period. APBO 11 provides an outline of conditions and methods. Income on which taxes are thus deferred include long-term contracts, installment sales, and subsidiary earnings. A deferred tax, whether treated as a *deferred credit* or *long-term liability*, is a form of *equalization reserve* (*2*): an income-leveling device having the effect of taking the "bumps" out of corporate annual earnings and per-share analyses, and thus widening the differences between net income and income derived from statements of cash (and fund) flows.

deficiency 1. The amount by which the *liabilities* (*1*) of an enterprise exceed its assets. See *deficit; insolvency*.

2. (Federal income taxes) The excess of a tax as computed by the Commissioner over the amount shown on the taxpayer's return plus any amount previously assessed or collected.

deficiency account (or **statement**) A statement accounting for an estimated or actual loss to creditors and owners, usually prepared by creditors of a financially embarrassed debtor in connection with a statement of affairs in the course of bankruptcy proceedings or at the close of an investigation. See *statement of affairs* and the illustration on page 409.

deficiency appropriation (governmental accounting) A legislative grant of spending power to meet obligations incurred in excess of a previously enacted *appropriation*. Like a *supplemental appropriation*, it is added to and identified with the original appropriation.

deficiency letter 1. An informal notice by the U. S. Securities and Exchange Commission questioning one or more items in a formal filing.

2. (Federal income taxes) A notice from the IRS permitting an appeal by a taxpayer to the Tax Court within a 90-day period concerning a proposed additional tax (Section 301.6213-1).

deficit 1. The amount by which the paid-in capital of a business is impaired; the amount by which the total assets of a business fall short of the sum of its *liabilities* (*1*) and paid-in capital or proprietary investment: sometimes referred to as "negative" earned surplus, or earned-surplus deficit.

2. The ledger account or balance-sheet heading for such an amount.

deficit account A ledger account for a deficit; an earned-surplus account with a debit balance.

definition A statement that sets forth and delimits the meaning of a word, phrase, or other symbolic expression, as used in a given discourse or context. Definitions serve to instruct persons who are ignorant or uncertain of a usage, to determine the consistency of usage and of reasoning in which a term or symbol is used, and

to help systematize a body of knowledge. Depending upon the purpose, one or another of the following types of definition may be employed:
1. Ostensive: a mere pointing to the object or series of objects intended.
2. Synonymous: an alternative term or symbol, presumably better known by the person to whom the definition is presented.
3. Extensive or denotative: an enumeration of all of the objects covered by the defined term.
4. Operational: a specification of the procedures which lead unequivocally to the item defined, the definition of *arithmetic mean* being an example: given any set of numbers, if the operations of addition and division are performed on them in a prescribed manner, the result will be the arithmetic mean of the numbers.
5. Intensional or connotative: identification of the essential characteristics of the defined object or event; the traditional method of intensional definition is to treat the *definiendum* (that which is to be defined) as a class (species) included in a larger class (genus), from whose other members the species is distinguished by some characteristic attribute or quality (called the *differentia*): thus, man (species) is an animal (genus) that is rational (differentia); an insurance claim (species) is a demand for payment of a debt (genus) which is said to be incurred under a contract to protect the claimant against a loss (differentia); paid-in surplus (species) is proprietorship (genus) which represents the excess of invested funds over the investment required by law, agreement, or resolution (differentia).
6. Recursive: the application of a primitive form to synthesize a more complete, complex, or precise expression; the primitive notions of "zero" and "successor of" in Peano's *axiom* system have been used to define the system of positive integers and the operations of addition and multiplication.

When the purpose of definition is to systematize a body of knowledge, great care is exercised in relating one definition to another. Among ancient scientists and philosophers, such systematic definitions (usually of the intensional type) were believed to identify the "essence" of the thing defined, and some infallible connection between the definition and the thing defined was supposed to constitute scientific knowledge. Such an interpretation of definition is now regarded as (a) based upon a misconception of language, (b) contributing to the delusion that knowledge of fact can be increased by the activity of defining without reference to factual evidence, and (c) conducive to the treatment of differences in word preferences as if they were disagreements regarding facts. These abuses of definition are avoided by using the form, "By X I mean Y" instead of the classical form of definition, "X is Y."

de jure By right; under authority of law: a corporation *de jure* is an organization that has complied fully with state law in establishing and maintaining itself as a corporation. Compare with *de facto*.

del credere Of or pertaining to the obligation to make good a loss arising from failure of a purchaser to pay, undertaken by (a) a sales agent with respect to his principal, or (b) any assignor with respect to one who buys or advances cash against the assignor's accounts receivable. Under (b), when the goods are sold or shipped, the accounts may be formally assigned and made payable to a financial institution or a commission house, which immediately advances an agreed portion of their amount, less commission and discount based on the net amount collectible from the customer; the balance of the account is paid to the assignor upon collection of the account. In some instances, the assignee may assume the credit risk and may purchase the accounts outright. Commission houses often add to their function of selling agent those of financing the sales of their principals and of guaranteeing their accounts.

del credere agent An agent who agrees to protect his principal against loss resulting from the extension of credit to third parties by the agent on behalf of his principal. In the absence of an agreement, an agent has no responsibility to a principal for default on the part of third parties.

delegation of authority The authorization by a superior to a subordinate to reach *decisions* within a defined area, subject only to postaudit or review.

deliberation The process of thinking preceding and leading to a *decision*. Deliberation involves the review of alternative decisions in such a way as to minimize at a later date the possibility of surprise over failure to reckon with overlooked purposes or interests, or with other consequences; it requires an investigation of fact, and consideration of established policies, standards, and interests that serve as guides or warnings in determining the relevance of facts.

delinquent tax A tax remaining unpaid on or after the date on which a penalty for nonpayment attaches. Even though the penalty may be subsequently waived and a portion of the taxes may be abated or canceled, the unpaid balance of the tax continues to be delinquent until abated or canceled.

delivered price A quoted or invoice *price* that includes delivery costs to the *FOB* (free-on-board) point, the latter being a freight terminal, a warehouse, or another location commonly accepted in the particular trade or specifically agreed to between buyer and seller; to eliminate misunderstanding, a price quotation is often followed by a parenthetical notation of the *FOB* point.

delivery The passage or transfer of possession of goods or services from one person to another, as in a *sale*.

demand 1. The desire by any person for an economic good or service.
2. The sum total of such desires by all persons, contrasting with supply: in economics, a series of levels each representing a price and the quantity of the commodity or service that buyers are ready to take when the price stands at that level or lower.
3. The action of a creditor causing the maturity of a debt, as of a note payable on demand.

demand deposit A deposit in a financial institution, such as a bank, that may be withdrawn without notice and is usually subject to check.

demurrage A charge by a carrier for loading or unloading time in excess of agreed or customary limits. See *laydays*.

deobligation *n.* (governmental accounting) The cancellation of an encumbrance (e.g., a purchase order for supplies), thereby releasing, to an unencumbered balance, funds previously reserved.—*deobligate, v.t.* or *i.*

department A cost center, operating unit, or area; a *function;* an *activity*.

departmental burden = *departmental overhead*.

departmental charge A charge additional to the direct cost of a particular production or operation, directly or indirectly applicable to a department, such as departmental overhead or a portion of general overhead. See *overhead*.

departmentalization The subdivision of an accounting process by departments or centers of activity, for the purpose of allocating operating costs.

departmental overhead The overhead directly and indirectly charged to a department, often including a portion of the general overhead as well as direct costs. See *overhead*.

departmental profit 1. The profit on the sales or operations of a department derived from dealings with customers, after deducting direct departmental costs and expenses and sometimes a proportion of general-overhead charges.
2. The profit attributable to a sector of an integral business enterprise when charged with operating costs and credited

with the amount at which its product could immediately have been sold to outsiders. Thus, in an integrated oil enterprise, crude oil produced may be credited to the production division at the current market price and charged to the refining division at that figure, thus making possible the obtaining of a current "profit" on the output of the production division regardless of the timing of the sale of finished product to the public. See *interdepartmental profit.*

dependent (Federal income taxes) A relative or nonrelative, as defined in the Internal Revenue Code, receiving more than half of his support from the taxpayer (either alone or with certain others under a multiple-support agreement); under current provisions, an exemption of $600 is permitted for each dependent whose gross income is less than $600 or who is a child under 19 years of age or a student (regardless of how much income such child may have) over half of whose support is furnished by the parent.

dependent variable A variable the value of which is determined by other elements (variables or constants) in the structure of an equation or other mathematical expression. See *variable; function.*

depletable Subject to *depletion;* wasting; said of a natural resource such as a mineral deposit or timber tract.

depleted cost *Residual cost* after deducting accrued depletion. The term is applied to mineral, coal, oil, natural-gas, and timber properties.

depletion 1. The exhaustion of a natural resource: applied to an oil or mineral deposit, standing timber, and the like.
2. The amount of prorated cost or other indicated value assigned to the extracted or otherwise removed portion of a natural resource owned or under lease.
3. The periodic assignment of cost made in the accounts for the exhaustion of a natural resource.
4. = *percentage depletion.*
5. The process of measuring and recording the exhaustion of a mineral resource.
Depletion differs from *depreciation* in that the former implies removal of a natural resource (i.e., a physical shrinkage or lessening of an estimated available quantity), while the latter implies a reduction in the service capacity of an asset through use, obsolescence, or inadequacy. See formula (1) under *depreciation.*

deposit 1. Currency, checks, or coupons presented to a bank by or for a customer for credit to his account. The deposit may be credited to a "commercial" account, from which unrestricted withdrawals are made by means of checks, or it may be credited to a special account, established for some specific purpose, and subject to withdrawal in accordance with the terms of the deposit arrangement.
2. Money, securities, or other valuables temporarily lodged with others.

depositary A bank or other institution accepting cash deposits from customers; also, an individual or organization that receives and safeguards property in any form. "Depositary" and "depository" are interchangeable; originally, the former referred to a *person* and the latter to a place.

depreciable Subject to *depreciation;* wasting: said of buildings, machinery, equipment, and other limited-life fixed assets.

depreciable cost That part of the cost of a fixed asset that is to be spread over useful life; i.e., cost less the estimated recovery from resale or salvage. See *service cost; depreciation base.*

depreciate 1. To diminish in service capacity or utility.
2. To reduce a fixed-asset cost by entering in the accounts a provision for *depreciation.*

depreciated cost 1. *Cost* less accumulated *depreciation,* if any, and less any other related valuation account having the effect of reducing original outlay to a recoverable cost; the *book value* of a fixed asset. The net amount remaining, although equal to a fraction of original cost or to market value, is *unrecovered cost:* that portion of cost judged to be fairly assignable against likely recoveries or against operations of future years. Compare with *depreciable cost.*

2. Cost that has been expensed; depreciation expense.

depreciated original cost *Original cost* less *accumulated depreciation:* the basis of valuation in public-utility corporations where property has been transferred from one owner to another, whether or not affiliation exists between transferor and transferee.

depreciated value 1. *depreciated cost.*

2. In public-utility accounting, *depreciated original cost,* unless otherwise defined by local law or regulation with reference to specific applications.

depreciation 1. Lost usefulness; expired utility; the diminution of service yield from a *fixed asset* or fixed-asset group that cannot or will not be restored by repairs or by replacement of parts, caused by numerous factors, as recounted below. See *depreciation method; depletion; amortization.*

2. The cost of lost usefulness: (a) = *depreciation expense;* (b) = *accumulated depreciation.*

3. Loosely, any wasting away of a physical asset and hence its cost, especially where not accompanied by a change in outward appearance, as in a slow-moving inventory of styled goods; functional loss of value.

4. The process of estimating and recording lost usefulness.

Depreciation basically is that part of the bundle of services believed at an earlier date to have been obtainable from a limited-life asset or, more commonly, a group of limited-life assets, and now found (a) consumed as originally estimated; (b) consumed, at a greater or less rate, from anticipated causes; (c) physically dissipated by accident or other unanticipated cause; (d) uneconomical when compared with the same or similar services available from other sources; or (e), following changes in product, product demand, or operating methods, unsuited to the future needs of the owner. In these senses, the term does not involve dollar costs but simply has reference to the physical functioning—past, present, and future—of the limited-life asset to which it is applied. A machine in use for some time is said to be partly depreciated; a machine worn out or for any other reason incapable of profitable use by its owner is said to be fully depreciated with respect to that owner, and hence ready for resale to a new owner who have some residual use for it; or, perhaps, ready for the junk heap.

Depreciation, as of a machine, may thus be regarded as a function of

1. Use: A machine wears when operated from day to day, and it is usually expected to wear out at least twice as fast when used 16 hours a day. This loss of serviceability is commonly regarded as the primary cause of depreciation, often being referred to as "ordinary wear and tear."

2. Disuse: A machine standing continuously idle becomes potentially less and less useful as time goes on; in fact, certain machines, like farm implements standing in the open, may age even more speedily from disuse than from use.

3. Maintenance: A high standard of maintenance prolongs the life of an asset; from lack of maintenance, or for want of skilled maintenance or operation, a machine may deteriorate rapidly.

4. Change in production: If the manufacturing process in which the machine is used is altered—for example, in the interest of increased overall efficiency or because of a change in a product line—the machine may not be adaptable to the change, and its future productivity *to its owner* may be greatly lessened.

5. Restriction of production: When the source of supply of a raw material on which a machine operates becomes less or ceases altogether (as from a natural cause or governmental order), the machine may have fewer employable service units to yield in succeeding periods.

6. Decrease in demand: The falling off in consumer use of products to which the machine contributes or the emergence of increased competition may also curtail its future employability.

7. Progress of the arts: When new devices are perfected and another machine has become available that will perform the same operation more simply, more quickly, or more cheaply, a machine's future usefulness to any owner may be seriously limited or cease altogether.

Obsolescence is loss of usefulness occasioned by improved production methods or by such other external causes as changes in demand, and in legislation or regulation leading to the reduction of future production (items 5, 6, and 7 above). *Inadequacy* is loss of usefulness brought about by business change; a building or machine may have to be replaced because it cannot be adjusted to an alteration in the character or rate of output (item 4 above). Since obsolescence and inadequacy relate to conditions common to all business, they are normally allowed for in periodic estimates of future usefulness. Where the advent of any of these factors is sudden and cannot reasonably be anticipated, the obsolescence or inadequacy is referred to as "extraordinary" and may be of such material amount as to require special treatment in the accounts and separate disclosure in the income statement.

Because these numerous factors affect in varying degrees the carry-forward costs of machines, buildings, and other limited-life fixed assets of every enterprise, and because they are interrelated and often inseparable, the reckoning of expired services normally proceeds, as described below, on an averaging basis, as though they were a function only of time. Furthermore, depreciation factors may be measured compositely more accurately than individually, not only because of their interrelated character, but also because the collective experience from which future estimates of usefulness necessarily derive has a more accurate application to a group than to an individual item.

In everyday business-and-accounting usage, the term *depreciation* is applied to the estimated *cost* of expired usefulness and to making or accumulating book entries based on the application of depreciation rates in recognition of the cost of the services which a limited-life asset or asset group will no longer yield, regardless of whether such services have actually been yielded, or, if yielded, whether they have benefited production. *Rates* of depreciation are percentages the application of which to cost yields an annual amount of depreciation expense. It is always best, therefore, to couple the word with another in order to make the meaning clear—for example, "depreciation rate," "depreciation expense," "reserve [or allowance] for [accumulated] depreciation."

Depreciation-expense computations are thus based on the assumption that every fixed asset, with the exception of land, can yield a limited quantity of useful services and has a limited life. The cost of the asset, less whatever can be anticipated in the way of resale or scrap yield, is a prepaid expense that by some method must be spread over its operating life while in the hands of its present owner. If the quantity of service units is measurable, the first method that suggests itself is reflected in the following formula for periodic depreciation expense:

$$d = \frac{q}{Q}(c - s), \tag{1}$$

where d is the periodic expense; q, the actual quantity of service units given off during the period; Q, the estimated quantity of utilizable service units that will be yielded during the whole life of the asset; c, the original cost of the asset; and s, the portion of original cost estimated to be recoverable from salvage, i.e., resale or scrap. The application of the formula, however, is usually impracticable, since only in the rarest instances can the quantity of service units of ordinary fixed assets or fixed-asset groups found in a manufacturing enterprise be measured. For most fixed assets, there is no recognized unit of service.

Formula (1) is, nevertheless, basic for such wasting assets as coal, timber, and other natural products, in which d becomes *depletion* expense; q, the quantity of such units currently extracted; and Q, the estimate of tons, square feet, or barrels extractable (including q). But since Q changes as new "proven" areas are developed under or on the land or lease of which c is the cost, the rate q/Q may have to be re-established from time to time; and the formula becomes

$$d = \frac{q}{Q_1}(c - s - r), \qquad (2)$$

Q_1 being the estimate of quantities removed and to be removed in the current year and future years, and r the balance of the reserve for depletion accumulated in and carried over from prior years. When rates (the fractions shown above) change because of re-estimates of remaining available serviceability, it is customary (a) to include all of the year of the change in the new computation, and (b) not to alter accumulations of previous years, a procedure also applicable to depreciation recomputations.

In ordinary depreciation accounting, the simplest and most prevalent practice in determining annual depreciation expense is to apply a percentage rate to the cost of an asset group like "machinery," the formula being

$$d = \frac{1}{y}c, \qquad (3)$$

where y is the estimated average number of years during which the group of assets is expected to be in use. The ratio $1/y$, expressed as a percentage, is a composite rate—one that may have application to many items of the same class and even to many enterprises. Thus, one of the commonest depreciation rates that may be found in all sorts of businesses is the furniture-and-fixture rate of 10 percent. As a composite rate, it has evolved from general experience with large groups of fixed assets; applied to a particular enterprise or to a small asset group, it may prove more conventional than accurate. It is not uncommon to find the cost of an asset group such as furniture and fixtures completely offset by accumulated provisions, notwithstanding that the assets are still in use. Similarly, conventional rates may be applied to other classes of assets; these, too, may be found to be inaccurate when utilized in individual enterprises, even though they may represent a reasonable average for an industry.

The above three formulas are so-called "straight-line" formulas, as are also the following two variants

$$d = \frac{1}{y}(c - s) \qquad (4)$$

and

$$d = \frac{1}{y_1}(c - s - r), \qquad (5)$$

where y is the number of years of useful life estimated from the time a new asset or asset group is acquired, y_1 the estimated number of years of remaining life including the current year, and r the depreciation accumulated in and brought forward from prior years. Each of these variants has its advocates, but in most instances they yield substantially the same results, notwithstanding theoretical distinctions. Of the five depreciation formulas, (5) is probably the most accurate, provided that its application is accompanied by periodic remaining-life studies leading to the frequent correction of y_1.

A further variant arises from the use of a *lapsing schedule*, a practice commonly followed by Federal internal-revenue agents where no running inventory of a fixed-asset group is maintained; it is essentially the separate application of formula (3) to each year's acquisitions, a separate schedule being prepared for each principal class of fixed assets.

Occasionally depreciation is accrued on individual assets. The back of a card maintained for each item may be used for recording provisions for depreciation and the total thus far provided, as illustrated on page 327; the sum of the accumulated provisions on all cards may be made to agree with a general-ledger depreciation-reserve account. Some accountants believe this to be a desirable refinement of the methods previously described, provided formula (5) is applied to each item; statistically, it offers no advantage over the results produced by the periodic application of formula (5) to an entire asset group.

Depreciation is often computed for fractional years on both additions and retirements, an average of $\frac{1}{2}$ year being assumed; or it may be computed down to the month or half-month. No objection can be raised to this procedure, but no greater statistical accuracy is added by fractional-year depreciation adjustments for any one period unless there have been major one-sided changes in fixed-asset accounts during the period; even then, the effect on the balance sheet and income statement may be negligible.

Where accumulated depreciation has been built up by the application of composite rates to asset groups, retirements are best charged in full against the reserve, exceptions being made only in the case of individual major assets that have been in use substantially less than the average life of that class, as reflected in the depreciation rate. A "major" asset might be regarded for this purpose as one whose cost is greater than 20 percent of the depreciation reserve applicable to that class of assets; a "substantially less" life might be one that does not exceed half of the average for that class. These are not to be interpreted as general standards but as types of tests that an auditor, for example, might employ in discussing with his client the effects of varying procedures. A more common but statistically less desirable practice is to regard as current expense or income every variation between the original cost of an asset retired, less scrap value, and the proportional depreciation accrued during the years an asset has been in use. Thus, a machine acquired at a cost of $1,000 and scrapped seven years later belongs to a group of 100 machines against which an annual composite depreciation rate of 10 percent has been applied. If a half-year basis is followed for additions and retirements, or if the balance at the beginning of each calendar year is the basis for applying the depreciation rate, seven years' depreciation will have been accumulated. With a scrap-value allowance in each year's computation equal to 5 percent of cost and with, say, a presently expected realization of $100 from the sale of the machine, the problem of classifying the "unrecovered" cost of $235 remains. Is this (a) a charge against the accumulated depreciation on machinery, (b) additional depreciation for the year, or (c) a loss on the disposal of fixed assets? Preference is given to the first alternative because a composite rate of depreciation will often result in apparent overprovision in the case of assets in use for periods longer than the average, and the remaining cost of $235 will ordinarily be absorbed where such averages are in use. The second method can be justified statistically if it can be demonstrated that the average rate of 10 percent is too low for the class of assets as a whole, but usually such a demonstration is impossible unless numerous "premature" retirements have been experienced. The effect of the second method is to modify the annual provision for depreciation above or below the average indicated by the rate, by the amount of the net excess of the "underprovision" or "overprovision," respectively. The second and third methods, although often found in practice, should be confined to situations where a sale is made of an asset that, if not sold, would continue to yield useful services to its owner. Classification in the third category often arises because of the failure to recognize the principle of averages involved in depreciation rates and reserves.

On the whole, the preferable standard of depreciation practice is to use a composite rate for each of the main fixed-asset groups; to charge to the reserve the full cost, less recoveries, of each asset retired, except under conditions described above; and to test the *adequacy* of accumulations periodically and revise the composite rate where the tests reveal an accumulation of material over- or under-provisions.

To test the propriety of an annual provision for depreciation, an engineering survey may be made by examining each asset covered by the reserve and estimating its remaining years of useful life. A "book value" for each asset, consisting of original cost less accumulated depreciation at rates in force since its acquisition, is then determined and divided by the estimated years of remaining useful life. The sum of the quotients thus obtained, divided by the total original cost of the same asset group, indicates the theoretical percentage of accumulations that should have been recorded. The same basic data will also serve in a test for accumulation adequacy. Sampling methods applied to asset groupings containing large numbers of components of the same class yield equally satisfactory results.

Many accountants accept the practice of removing from the accounts the costs of fixed assets shown by lapsing schedules to be wholly depreciated. This practice may be modified in instances where larger retirements are individually recorded, but the practice is recognized as a much less desirable alternative to the full reporting and recording of each retired asset. A lapsing schedule is never a good substitute for a plant ledger.

Management attention to depreciation is weakened by the not uncommon assertion that the annual provision for depreciation is at best a crude and arbitrary estimate—an estimate that has wide flexibility. See *appropriation method* under *depreciation method.* This attitude leads occasionally to the manipulation of depreciation provisions in the interest of "making a showing"—decreasing provisions in years of poor profit margins and increasing them in good years. Attempts to modify the depreciation charge to correspond with units produced are not often successful, as has already been noted. Nevertheless, where such an attempt is made, the worth of the result produced depends on the care with which the altered rates have been arrived at after a careful study of relevant engineering reports and such factors as the actual use of the assets, rates for normal years, the ability of normal and abnormal rates to absorb cost during useful life, and the effect of possibly mounting obsolescence and inadequacy on such rates. The latter factors are almost invariably present and operate inexorably to shorten economic life, notwithstanding non-use.

During a war period, several causes contribute to greatly accelerated accumulations of depreciation in corporate enterprise. High prices, established by government procurement agencies because of their presumed effect in stimulating the production of materials of war, lead to substantial profits and the incentive to show increased costs as the justification therefor. Accelerated depreciation, called *amortization* in both world wars, was permitted under the Federal income-tax laws—likewise as a stimulant to war production. The future utility of new plants, or of old plants adapted to war production, is always problematical. At the end of World War II, a review of the balance sheets of 100 leading industrial corporations indicated that the ratio of depreciation accumulations to fixed assets varied between 28 and 86 percent, with an average somewhat in excess of 50 percent. These ratios decreased as war plants were sold or abandoned. Suggestions that these ratios be revised downward by the transfer of "excess" depreciation to retained earnings were, however, hardly attuned to corporate responsibility to the public. A better plan was to follow the preferred standard practice, already referred to in a preceding paragraph, for revising future depreciation charges. It may be restated thus:

> Where studies indicate that the recorded accumulation of depreciation of an asset or asset group is over- or understated, the current rate of depreciation should be so adjusted as to spread equitably any excess of provisions or any unrecovered cost over remaining useful life.

An exception might be made where, because of a management decision or other anticipated cause, obsolescence must be recognized in a substantial amount; in that event, the resultant sudden increase in the depreciation incurred, or the writedown of remaining cost, may be important enough to be shown as a separate item in the income statement of the current period. Accountants have always taken a firm stand against the restoration of depreciated costs. Costs, once recovered, should be forgotten. To seek to recover the same cost twice would not only be dubbed poor accounting, but where the excessive depreciation was accumulated during the war period, it would conflict squarely with the public policy that gave rise to the higher prices or lower taxes that the owner of the assets enjoyed.

The management policy on depreciation is best kept on an objective level, with periodic engineering studies and internal reviews of depreciation rates and reserve adequacy as a major feature of information and control.

In the income statement, the amount of depreciation expense is shown on the face of the statement or in a footnote. The amount of any amortization provided under permissive tax laws or of any other form of extraordinary depreciation or obsolescence should also appear as a separate item.

Where depreciation expense for income-tax purposes differs from that appearing in the income statement by an amount greater than, say, 10 percent of the latter or 5 percent of the net income for the period, a footnote to the income statement would preferably be employed to reveal the amount and the reason therefor. Depreciation for tax purposes, as such, is never an acceptable basis for accounting and reporting purposes.

Depreciation accumulations (often termed "reserves") on the balance sheet are now as a general rule subtracted from the assets to which they relate. The principal exception may be found in public utilities, a few of which are still not on a full "depreciation basis"—that is, their reserves cover only fairly immediate replacements and have sometimes been classed with other "reserves" on the liability side of the statement; but the better practice, reflected in the requirements of regulatory bodies, is to subtract the accumulations (reserves) from the assets even though they may not have reached their proper level, since they are still valuation accounts, notwithstanding their insufficiency.

Summary details of annual changes in fixed assets and depreciation accumulations in schedule form accompany some published financial statements. The practice is an excellent one and deserves a larger following. See *fixed-asset schedule*.

depreciation accounting The systematic, periodic writedown or allocation, most frequently on a *straight-line* basis, of the cost of a limited-life asset or asset group, in conformity with the best available estimate of usefulness lost to date, remaining usefulness, and recovery values; contrasts with *replacement* or *retirement* methods of accounting, as described under *depreciation method*.

depreciation adequacy The sufficiency of *accumulated depreciation*, with due regard for the fairness of prospective allocations of cost to future operations; see *depreciation*.

depreciation base The recorded cost or other basis of a fixed asset or fixed-asset group that is to be recovered through depreciation, excluding estimated recovery from resale or salvage; *depreciable cost.*

depreciation expense That portion of the cost or other basis of a fixed asset or fixed-asset group charged against the operations of an accounting period; for a single year, the *depreciation base* times the *depreciation rate;* any provision for depreciation. See *depreciation.*

depreciation fund Money or marketable securities set aside for the purpose of replacing or providing assistance in replacing depreciating fixed assets.

depreciation method The arithmetic procedure followed in determining a provision for depreciation (an *expense*) and maintaining the accumulated balance (a *valuation account*). The principal methods advocated at different times by various authorities have been:

Age-life method: The unrecovered portion of the cost of an asset or asset group is determined periodically by applying to cost at the end of a period a ratio equal to estimated remaining life (averaged, if an asset group) divided by total expected (average) life. The depreciation expense for the period is, then, the excess of the *cost fraction* at the beginning of the period over that at the end of the period. This method, a *straight-line* variant, is a technically correct one, and the term may be applied to any situation where *depreciation rates* are periodically redetermined for future periods in the light of the most recent judgments as to remaining life expectancy. Compare with *composite-life method,* below.

Annuity method: The annual provision for depreciation of an asset or asset group is a constant amount equal to the sum of (a) a periodic provision, accumulating over useful life at a specified rate of interest deemed necessary to recover such cost; (b) interest on previous accumulations of periodic payments; and (c) interest, often illustrated as being at a higher rate, on the declining investment in the asset. Items (a) and (b) are those composing the sinking-fund method described below; item (c) does not appear in any other method. If the rate of interest under (c) is the same as in (b), the credit to the reserve will be the same for each period; if the rate is greater, the annual credit to the reserve will be on an ascending scale, as illustrated in the following example:

A machine having an initial cost of \$10,000, no determinable salvage, and an estimated life of five years, is expected to "earn" 6 percent annually on its unrecovered investment, while theoretical interest is figured at 3 percent annually on the gradually accumulating reserve for depreciation. The applicable formula is thus

$$d = (c - s)(i_1 + p),$$

where d is the fixed annual amount of depreciation, c the initial cost of the asset, s the salvage value, i_1 the rate of return expected from the asset, and p the periodic payment into the reserve, at the rate i, that will amount to 1 when the asset has become fully depreciated. Values for p may be found in the sinking-fund table on pp. 318–319. Applying the figures in the example,

$$d = 10{,}000(0.06 + 0.1883546) = 2{,}483.55,$$

and the annual addition to the reserve is the excess of this constant amount of \$2,483.55 over interest provisions, as may be seen in the table on page 156, top.

It will be observed that depreciation expense has been charged with \$12,417.75 during the five-year period, interest income has been credited with \$2,417.75, and the depreciation reserve has been credited with increasing amounts totaling \$10,000.00. Because the interest income has been created by a charge to depreciation expense, and because hypothetical interest is rejected by accountants, this method, also known as the *compound-interest method,* is not found in practice.

Year	Interest at 6% on Asset Balance	Interest at 3% on Reserve	Balance: Provision for Depreciation	Balance Invested in Asset
Cost	$ —	$ —	$ —	$10,000.00
1	600.00	—	1,883.55	8,116.45
2	486.99	56.51	1,940.05	6,176.40
3	370.58	114.71	1,998.26	4,178.14
4	250.69	174.66	2,058.20	2,119.94
5	127.20	236.41	2,119.94	—
Totals	$1,835.46	$582.29	$10,000.00	

Appraisal method: The annual depreciation expense is the difference between the appraisal value of the fixed assets at the beginning and end of the period. This method has disappeared from practice. See *appraisal.*

Appropriation method: Depreciation expense is a fraction of sales or other income amount, or is otherwise arrived at without regard to the concept of lost usefulness: a method occasionally followed in the belief that the determination of the annual amount of depreciation is a matter of financial policy—an amount that might well depend on and vary with available profits. In some instances, amounts provided have been roughly proportional to asset use, particularly where the amount of profit has more or less reflected business activity. Although universally criticized by accountants, the method is still occasionally followed in practice.

Combined-depreciation-and-upkeep method: The usual *depreciation base* is increased by estimated total maintenance cost over the useful life of the asset, maintenance costs incurred being charged directly to the reserve. The purpose is to equalize maintenance charges, which often occur irregularly, over the years the asset is in use, but the method is no longer in use, since in most situations maintenance costs do not vary greatly.

Composite-life method: The application of a single rate to a large group of assets, usually of the same general class, such as buildings, machinery, or trucks; details of this method appear under *depreciation;* see also *age-life method,* above. Essentially an application of straight-line depreciation, it is deemed by many accountants to yield more dependable results than other methods. Under Federal income-tax regulations, the composite-life method may be applied not only to individual classes of assets but to all classes combined. Such an extension of the method would find practical application, however, only in cases where the whole asset group remained relatively stable over a long period of time and where frequent tests are made of average remaining life. See page 196 for illustration of depreciation schedule where the composite-life method has been applied.

Declining-balance or *diminishing-provision methods:* The annual charge for depreciation is the amount obtained (a) by applying a fixed percentage to the diminishing balance of the asset account, that is, the balance after deducting preceding depreciation provisions; or (b) by applying a diminishing rate to the original cost of the asset. An illustration of (a) may be observed in the following example, where a constant rate of 10 percent has been applied:

Year	Annual Depreciation	Balance of Asset Cost
Cost	—	$1,000.00
1	$100.00	900.00
2	90.00	810.00
3	81.00	729.00
4	72.90	656.10
5	65.61	590.49
6	59.05	531.44
7	53.14	478.30
8	47.83	430.47
9	43.05	387.42
10	38.74	348.68

At the end of the tenth year, more

than one-third of the cost remains; the process goes on until the balance is arbitrarily absorbed in a single year.

If the constant rate had been 20 percent, the result would have been as follows:

Year	Annual Depreciation	Balance of Asset Cost
Cost	—	$1,000.00
1	$200.00	800.00
2	160.00	640.00
3	128.00	512.00
4	102.40	409.60
5	81.92	327.68
6	65.54	262.14
7	52.43	209.71
8	41.94	167.77
9	33.55	134.22
10	26.84	107.38

In both of these examples, the *cost fraction* remaining at the end of n years is thus seen to be the equal of the *present value* of the cost to be depreciated, or

$$c_1 = c\frac{r}{(1 + r)^n},$$

where c_1 is the *cost fraction*, c the cost to be depreciated, and r the rate of depreciation. A discount table such as that on pp. 334–335 cannot, however, be utilized because of the large value of r.

A formula sometimes suggested for this method is

$$r = 1 - \sqrt[n]{\frac{s}{c}},$$

where r is the annual rate of depreciation, n the number of years of expected life, s the salvage value, and c the asset cost. Thus, the rate applicable to the declining value of an asset purchased for $1,000, having an expected life of 10 years and salvage of $100, would be

$$r = 1 - \sqrt[10]{\frac{100}{1{,}000}},$$

$$= 1 - \text{antilog}\,\frac{2 - 3}{10},$$

$$= 1 - \text{antilog}\,(.9 - 1),$$

$$= 1 - .794328 \text{ [from page 268]}$$

$$= .205672.$$

The balance at the end of each year of the ten-year period would then be—

Year	Annual Depreciation at 20.5672%	Balance Remaining
Cost	—	$1,000.00
1	$205.67	794.33
2	163.58	630.75
3	129.73	501.02
4	103.04	397.98
5	81.84	316.14
6	65.02	251.12
7	51.64	199.48
8	41.02	158.46
9	32.59	125.87
10	25.87	100.00

A diminishing-rate variant known as the *sum-of-the-years-digits* method involves the determination of an annual depreciation provision by the application to the asset cost of a fraction the numerator of which is the number of years remaining (including the current year) in the estimated life of the asset, and the denominator, the sum of all such numbers. Thus, the successive fractions applicable to the cost of a delivery truck having a life expectancy of five years would be 5 divided by $5 + 4 + 3 + 2 + 1$, or, roughly, 33, 27, 20, 13, and 7 percent, respectively. Where the life expectancy is ten years, the initial fraction would be $\frac{10}{55}$, or 18 percent, and the final fraction $\frac{1}{55}$, or 2 percent.

At one time in common use in this country and in England, particularly when depreciation provisions were being credited directly to the asset accounts on which they were based, this method had until recently nearly disappeared from American practice. The spread of cost by this method was generally judged to be wholly capricious, notwithstanding the argument, once advanced, that the earlier years in the life of an asset should bear a larger proportion of cost, while the later years, burdened with a constantly heavier maintenance cost, should bear a smaller amount. Experience has shown, however, that maintenance costs generally vary but little; in those cases where maintenance has been neglected, there is good reason for bringing out the variation in such costs as operating charges in the year in which they are actually incurred, but no logical support for a change in depreciation method.

In recent years, interest in diminishing-provision methods has been revived. There have been several reasons: (a) buildings and equipment may have been acquired at inflationary prices, and management may desire to amortize such costs—or the inflationary portions of them—as quickly as possible in order that future periods will not be burdened with costs ascribable to the present; (b) the current revenues of the owner of the assets may be regarded as reflecting an economic condition that cannot continue—hence, cost inflations in some degree match and ought to offset revenue inflations; (c) a greater amount of depreciation, made possible by declining-balance methods, has been regarded by some business managements and their accountants as an acceptable substitute for straight-line depreciation on replacement costs—the expression of the last-named in financial statements, other than in footnotes, having met with professional disapproval; (d) large amounts of depreciation should be provided in years when income-tax rates are high, thus in some measure equalizing the tax burden over the years; (e) as the depreciation base becomes exhausted, the pressure on the Congress to permit depreciation on current replacement costs in income-tax returns will become virtually irresistible; and (f) the Federal income-tax law and regulations now permit any of numerous declining-balance variants.

The argument against any declining-balance method is that, regardless of the formula adopted, there is no more than a chance relationship between it and the condition to be corrected, whatever that condition may be. Moreover, the advantage of a larger depreciation amount on new assets in the years immediately following the adoption of a declining-balance method will be offset by lower depreciation quantities on older assets, thus eventually bringing about in the case of a stable business the equivalent of straight-line depreciation. Immediate income-tax reductions have supplied the principal incentive for its use (e.g., AICPA Research Bulletin No. 44); too frequently the effect on future financial policy is overlooked.

Equal-annual-payment method: = *annuity method* or *sinking-fund method*.

Production-basis method; Production-unit-basis method; Service-output method; Unit-of-product method: The provision for depreciation is computed as a fixed rate per unit of product, based on an estimate of the total number of units the property will produce during its service life. See *depreciation*.

Policy method: A method dictated by financial or social *policy* rather than service yields. In some instances, as in public-works projects, the costs of improvements having service lives extending indefinitely into the future are *allocated(3)* against the income derived from the projects over a period known to be less than their useful lives. The policy leading to this foreshortening of the period of depreciation originates with the governing body. Thus, the cost of projects financed with serial bonds (for example, those of the St. Lawrence Seaway Development Corporation) may be deprecatied in amounts equal to the repayment installments as they fall due, although the project may live on and yield services for many years thereafter. The costs of projects financed by government appropriations (out of income or property taxes) which as a matter of tacit public policy rather than law or agreement are to be repaid from earnings (for example, the costs of the concrete structures of the dams of the Tennessee Valley Authority at present being depreciated at the rate of 1 percent per annum) may also be disposed of through depreciation provisions substantially in excess of those based on useful life.

Replacement method: (a) An estimate

is made of the cost of replacing the limited-life assets actually in use; the amount of current depreciation expense, usually on a straight-line cost basis, is increased by a percentage derived from a comparison of the anticipated replacement cost with recorded cost. (b) Another practice given this designation is occasionally found where the cost of major replacements is disposed of in the same manner as that accorded minor replacements under approved methods of depreciation: the cost of replacements is charged to expense, the asset account remaining unchanged except for additions; no depreciation, as such, is provided.

Retirement method: Provision is made only for the value of property units shortly to be retired. This method, at one time in vogue among public utilities, has now been generally abandoned.

Service-capacity method: = *declining-balance method.*

Sinking-fund method: This method consists of setting aside periodically equal amounts which, with compound interest, will produce a sum equal to original cost or expected replacement cost of the property at the end of its service life. See *periodic payment accumulating to 1; sinking fund.*

Straight-line method: The annual depreciation expense is one of a series of equal amounts the total of which, at the end of service life, will equal the property cost otherwise unrecoverable; for features of this method and its varied forms, see *depreciation; lapsing schedule.* The straight-line method has now almost entirely displaced other methods. The *age-life method* (see above) is essentially *straight-line.*

Sum-of-the-years-digits method: A *declining-balance method.*

Unit method: Composite depreciation is calculated, as on a straight-line basis, for each item rather than the group.

Unit-summation method: Under this method, the depreciation rate is calculated anew each year for application to the book cost of the units in a property group. The rate is calculated in such a manner as to produce a total charge equal to the sum of the accruals which would be obtained if individual rates had been applied to each item in the group: a variant of the *straight-line method.*

Working-hours method: The computation is based on a fixed rate per hour of use, determined by estimating the total number of hours the property will be in use during its service life. Except in rare cases this method is inapplicable because total operating hours cannot be estimated with any degree of accuracy.

depreciation rate A percentage which when applied to the *depreciation base* will yield *depreciation expense* for a year.

depreciation reserve = *accumulated depreciation:* a term still in popular use by accountants but now increasingly avoided in published balance sheets.

depreciation unit The asset or asset group against the cost of which the depreciation rate is to be applied. It may be an individual asset or asset part, such as a machine or the walls of a building, in which case the depreciation method is referred to as *unit depreciation,* or it may be a number of similar assets, where a single rate can be applied to their collective cost (*group* or *composite depreciation*). See *depreciation; fixed asset.*

descent The disposition of the real property of an intestate.

descriptive financial statement A form of financial statement, now seldom employed, in which a brief explanation follows each item in the statement, the purpose being to assist the reader in grasping the meaning of the item. It was found, however, that brief explanations of certain items might, without some knowledge of accounting and business practices, lead to incorrect inferences; with such knowledge, most of the explanations were superfluous.

descriptive statistics That branch of statistical studies devoted to the summarization of the group characteristics of particular sets of observed data. See *statistical inference.*

detail account One of a group of accounts that constitute a *subsidiary ledger*.

detailed audit An examination of the books of account, or a portion thereof, whereby all or substantially all entries and transactions are reviewed and verified, as contrasted with the more usual examination by means of tests or samples. See *audit; sample; testcheck*.

determine To conclude; particularly (auditing), to reach an opinion consequent to the observation of the fit of sample data within the limit, range, or area associated with substantial conformance, accuracy, or other predetermined standard. The process of auditing may be regarded as a series of lesser determinations contributing to a major determination of overall propriety.

development expense 1. An expenditure made in opening up and developing mineral properties, oil wells, timber lands, and the like. Development expense may be capitalized and written off at a fixed rate per unit of product or over a limited initial period of operations; or it may be written off as incurred.

2. = *promotion expense*.

devise The disposition of real estate by will.—*devise, v.*

differential cost 1. = *marginal cost*. See *incremental cost*.

2. That portion of the cost of a *function* attributable to and identifiable with an added feature: cost including the added feature less cost without the added feature. If the addition becomes permanent, the added cost tends to merge with other costs and lose its identity.

digit Any single symbol expressing quantity: in the decimal system, any one of the symbols 0, 1, 2, 3, 4, 5, 6, 7, 8, or 9.

dilution Relative loss or weakening of equity position.

diminishing-provision method (of depreciation) See *depreciation method*.

direct cost 1. The cost of any good or service that contributes to and is readily ascribable to product or service output, any other cost incurred being regarded as a *fixed* or *period* cost (= *actual cost*).

Commonly recognized direct costs of manufactured product are outlays for labor, material, and overhead that vary with the volume of production. Under recent trends in concepts of management controls, every cost is a direct cost, and is identifiable with or contributes to an endproduct or intermediate service. As a basis for standard costs or inventory valuation, direct costs have gained a considerable degree of acceptance.

2. = *variable cost*.

direct costing 1. The process of assigning costs as they are incurred to products and services.

2. The doctrine that *direct cost* is the basis of valuing output. Direct costing in a business enterprise requires a classification of accounts in which recognition is given (a) to the separability and assignment to output of *direct* or *variable* costs, the amounts of which fluctuate with output volume; and (b) to unallocated *fixed* or *period* costs which reflect the maintenance of a readiness to manufacture and to sell, and which remain relatively unaffected by volume changes. Often included in the concept is the valuation of inventories. Sales less the direct cost of sales is known as *marginal income*. In *absorption costing*, which contrasts with direct costing, no distinction between fixed and variable costs is made in the accounts, and supplementary statistical analyses are required to bring out relationships between costs, volume, and profit. Direct costing is not a complete costing plan in itself, but it is a feature that may be introduced into either *process-cost* or *job-order-cost* systems, and *standard costs* may or may not be employed. Direct costing is sometimes regarded as a return to primitive cost accounting, under which only the prime cost of products was determined.

Instability of product unit costs under conditions of fluctuating volume of sales and production was recognized as a serious problem in the early development of cost accounting. Accountants met the problem with the concept of normal or standard volume and often determined product costs on the assumption that a factory would operate at standard volume. Such unit costs are essentially long-run average manufacturing costs implicitly assumed to be proportionately variable with volume and so controllable. With each product unit bearing its proportionate share of the fixed manufacturing costs, this plan has been the essence of *absorption costing.*

The standard-volume concept ceases to be useful when the objective is to measure changes in short-run costs and profits resulting from changes in volume. Under absorption costing, volume changes are reflected in variances which measure the overall effect of deviating from standard production volume, but volume variances are not readily associated with individual managerial decisions. Moreover, the effect which sales-volume changes have on periodic profits is obscured unless inventories remain constant. Techniques such as flexible budgets, marginal analyses, and break-even charts were evolved for measuring functional relationships between cost, volume, and profits. These techniques are often integrated with the accounting records.

Early applications of direct costing were made independently by a number of organizations. An NAA (NACA) research report (*Direct Costing,* Research Series No. 23) states that the earliest published description of direct costing was contained in an article written by Jonathan N. Harris and published in an NAA Bulletin of January 15, 1936. The term "direct costing" appears to have been originated by the author of that article, and since then direct costing has expanded rapidly. In Great Britain, the equivalent term is *marginal costing.*

Under direct costing, separate accounts are provided for the accumulation of fixed and variable costs. Direct material and direct labor are ordinarily variable with production volume, and no change is usually made in methods of accounting for them. Manufacturing overhead, however, contains both variable and fixed components. Consequently, new accounts are provided to differentiate between these two elements.

Income statements prepared for individual product classifications commonly show separately fixed costs directly traceable to a product group and fixed costs of a general nature associated with products only by allocation.

Direct costing has three principal areas of usefulness corresponding to the following purposes for which cost data are used:

1. Controlling current costs.
2. Period or project profit planning.
3. Determining periodic income and financial condition.

In complete applications, direct costing is used for all three purposes, but partial applications are common. Moreover, accounting statements for internal use are often prepared on a direct-costing basis while reports to outsiders are prepared on an *absorption-costing* basis.

Where control over current costs is the objective, experience shows that control is more effective if costs associated with current volume are separated from those that are independent of current volume. Techniques of *flexible budgeting* developed for this purpose rest upon classifications of costs according to variability with volume in both budgets and departmental cost ledgers.

In predicting profit consequences of decisions to approve or reject a sales-promotion idea, an order at a special price, a proposal to make rather than to buy, or other proposals causing changes in volume, the ready availability of relevant cost data simplifies and speeds decision making. It may also improve the quality of decisions. Key figures for this purpose are rates of change in variable cost and marginal income per unit of volume and the periodic amount of fixed cost. For some purposes, marginal income is expressed in units of the factor which limits production—for example, material, machine capacity, and so forth. Incorporating these figures on product cost cards and in product, territorial, and summary income statements, both budgeted and historical, puts profit-planning data into the hands of management and lessens the need for special analyses. Users of direct costing commonly state that the major benefits therefrom lie in this application to profit planning.

Under direct costing, periodic net profit varies directly with sales volume, provided that factors other than sales volume remain constant. In contrast, under absorption costing, changes in the fixed-cost component of inventories tend to obscure relationships between sales volume and profits. For any given period, the difference in profits shown by the two methods is equal to the amount of fixed cost taken out of inventory or added to inventory through inventory reduction or buildup. Profit differences tend to be greater for short periods than for long periods, because production and sales tend to be more nearly in balance over long periods. The literature on direct costing has presented considerable evidence to show that those who use income statements often fail to understand the influence exerted on profits by changes in inventory.

Direct costing, like other managerial tools, must be applied with skill and understanding. Its principal limitations are generally held to be these:

1. It is a technique emphasizing short-run decisions in which fixed costs tend to remain constant in amount and hence do not affect comparisons between periods or alternatives. To use the same data as the basis for long-range decisions may be misleading. Thus, when unutilized capacity is available, it may be advantageous to take an isolated order at a price which returns something less than a full share of fixed overhead, but serious losses will result if the company's entire production is so priced over an extended period. An overall pricing policy is required that specifies levels at which manufacturing-margin limits are set forth. Statistical allocation of fixed manufacturing costs has merit in determining product cost and profit figures for pricing and sales emphasis, although repetitive allocations are eliminated from the bookkeeping process where direct costing is employed.

2. It rests upon the distinction between fixed and variable costs. In application, this distinction requires certain assumptions and perhaps arbitrary classifications of borderline items. Resulting figures must be used with due appreciation of the degree of precision with which they are measured, and revisions are required when underlying assumptions no longer hold. For example, fixed cost determined with the expectation that the present salaried supervisory force will be maintained regardless of volume changes must be redetermined if management decides to increase or decrease the number of supervisors.

3. Difficulties arise in switching from absorption costing to direct costing. For example, tax authorities have usually been unwilling to approve the change in accounting method for determining taxable income when a substantial writeoff of fixed costs in inventory has been proposed in the year of change. Where this obstacle exists, some users have adopted direct costing for internal purposes only. In these cases, fixed operating costs are allocated in lump sums to inventory and cost of goods sold when financial reports for external circulation are prepared.

4. Direct costing reduces the working-capital ratio and the dollar amount of working capital displayed in the balance sheet. Generally, the effect on inventory depends upon the pricing methods employed before instituting direct costing. However, where such depreciation and

property taxes have never been included in production costs inventory value may be little affected by the introduction of direct costing; other techniques, such as *lifo*, may affect inventory costs more significantly than direct costing.

direct expense = *direct cost.*

direction of effort Ultimate purpose: a characterization of any expense distribution based on benefits conferred.

direct labor Labor applied directly to a product; the cost of such labor. Compare with *indirect labor.*

direct liability An obligation of a debtor arising from money, goods, or services received by him from another person; excluded would be assumed or contingent liabilities.

direct material Material entering into and becoming a constituent element of a product; the cost of such material.

direct overhead Factory, selling, or other expense attributed solely to a certain product, and thus constituting a *direct cost.*

direct shipment = *drop shipment.*

disallowance (governmental accounting) See *exception (2).*

disbursement Payment in currency or by check. The term is not synonymous with *expenditure (q.v.).*

disbursing officer (governmental accounting) A bonded employee authorized to pay out cash or issue checks in settlement of vouchers to the propriety of which a *certifying officer* has attested.

disclaimer A statement in an *audit report* indicating the inability of the auditor to express an opinion of the *fairness* of one or more of the financial statements referred to in the report. Thus, on a first audit a disclaimer may attach to the income statement because the correctness of the inventory and possibly other items at the beginning of the period cannot be established.

disclosure A clear showing of a fact or condition on a balance sheet or other financial statement, in sideheads, in footnotes, or in the text of an audit report. See *qualification.*

discount 1. The difference between the estimated worth of a future benefit and its present value; a compensation for waiting.

2. An allowance given for the settlement of a debt before it is due. See *cash discount; trade discount.*

3. The excess of the par or face value of a security over the amount paid or received for it. See *debt discount; bond discount; stock discount.*

4. Commission deducted by a banker or broker for selling an issue of securities.

5. A promissory note acquired by a bank at a discount and rediscounted with another bank or held as an asset under a title that distinguishes it from other classes of loans.

discount earned 1. A reduction in the purchase price of a good or service because of early payment. See *cash discount.* Today it is usually deducted in arriving at invoice cost regardless of the time of payment; under such circumstances, it does not appear as a separate item in an income statement. If the deduction is taken only when payment is made, it is customary to regard it as miscellaneous income.

2. *pl.* (retail accounting) Cash discounts applicable to merchandise sold: the equivalent of cash discounts taken, adjusted for opening and closing discount allowances applicable to unsold merchandise.

discount lost 1. A cash discount on a purchase, not taken advantage of because of failure to pay before the expiration of the discount period.

2. *pl.* Hence, an expense account maintained for the purpose of recording such discounts. Where this practice is followed, the purchase is recorded at the net amount—i.e., less the cash discount. Should it be necessary to pay the gross amount, or should the amount of the discount be paid to the creditor at a later date, the additional charge, representing the discount lost, is carried to an account bearing that name.

discovery period (insurance) The period

of time allowed the insured after the termination of an insurance contract or bond in which to discover losses occurring during the time the coverage was in force and coming under the terms of the contract.

discrepancy Any observed difference between opinions or facts, often with the implication of an error or other impropriety in one or more of them.

dishonor To refuse *acceptance(1)* or payment: said of the drawee of *checks* and other *commercial paper(2)*.

dispatch earning A saving in shipping costs arising from a prompt unloading at destination.

dispersion A measure of the variation of a group of numerical data from a central tendency, such as an arithmetic mean, by determining the *range* of such data or their *average deviation* or *standard deviation (q.v.)*.

disposable income (social accounting) *Personal income(2)* less income and other taxes paid by the individual, the balance being available for consumption expenditures or savings. See *social accounting.*

disposition of net income (or **net profit** or **net earnings**) A financial statement sometimes appearing in auditors' reports and annual reports to stockholders or owners showing dividends declared or profits withdrawn, provisions for and returns from appropriated surplus, and other items, together with the balance added to *retained earnings* or *proprietorship.* See *income statement.*

distort *v.* To create a false impression; specifically, to overstate or understate a conclusion, amount, or other representation of opinion or fact to a degree that may lead to faulty conclusions or decisions by others; to *mislead.*—*n., distortion.*

distraint (Federal income taxes) The procedure under which the property of a taxpayer may be seized after he has neglected or refused to make payment within ten days after notice and demand.

distress merchandise Merchandise marked down in order to make possible its rapid disposal: a situation brought about by a financial stringency or other emergency demanding a quick *turnover (1)*. The term may also relate to a job lot of merchandise acquired by one dealer from another.

distribution 1. Any payment to stockholders or owners of cash, property, or shares, including any of the various forms of dividend; in noncorporate enterprise, a *withdrawal.*

2. A spread of revenue or expenditure or of capital additions to various accounts; an *allocation.*

3. Disposal of a product by sale.

4. The function of promoting sales and making deliveries.

5. = *statistical distribution.*

6. The apportionment and disposition, by authority of a court, of the balance of an intestate's personal property after payment of debts and costs.

distribution column A money column, often one of several, in a worksheet, journal, or ledger, providing some desired analysis or breakdown of each entry or posting.

distribution expense (or **cost**) *Selling expense,* including advertising and delivery costs.

distributor discount An allowance usually determined as a fixed percentage of the list or retail price; *trade discount.* By the use of discounts, sellers may limit publication to a single price—in most cases, the retail price—which the consuming public identifies with the product. Discount schedules are released only to the distributor trade and do not become general public information. The amount of discount is the gross margin to compensate distributors for selling and servicing the product. Frequently, distributors share the gross margin by rediscounting to subdistributors and retailers. The practice is generally employed in the sale of nationally advertised branded products under fair-trade laws. The manufacturer in such cases places considerable emphasis on identifying the product with a fixed or "suggested" price to consumers.

diurnal *n.* An old name for *journal* or *daybook.*

divided account See *nominal account(2).*

dividend 1. Cash or other assets, evidences of corporate indebtedness, or shares of the issuer's capital stock constituting a *distribution* to a class of stockholders of a corporation, the amount ordinarily being charged to *retained earnings* (*earned surplus*). A liability for a dividend is expressed in corporate accounts only after formal action (*declaration*) has been taken by the board of directors. This action is authorized by a resolution by the board setting forth (a) the medium of payment, (b) the account to be charged, (c) the rate (in dollars per share or percentage), (d) the date of declaration, (e) the date the stock records are to be closed for the purpose of determining the particular stockholdings against which the dividend is applicable, and (f) the date of payment. A dividend occasionally consists of assets other than cash. A dividend of cash or property charged to an account other than *retained earnings* (*earned suplus*), such as paid-in surplus, revaluation surplus, or a depletion or depreciation reserve is termed a *liquidating dividend(2)* and *(3).*

2. A payment made to creditors during or following involuntary liquidation; see *liquidating dividend(1).*

dividend-equalization reserve An appropriation, now obsolete, of *retained earnings* for the payment of future dividends in periods when current profits may not be adequate for the purpose.

dividend in kind = *property dividend.*

dividend payable 1. The unliquidated liability for a cash or property dividend created by the declaration of the dividend, ranking in case of liquidation with liabilities to general creditors. See *dividend.*

2. The balance-sheet heading for cash or property dividends declared but unliquidated either because the due date is subsequent to the balance-sheet date or because of inability to make delivery to stockholders.

dividends in arrears The amount of undeclared dividends accumulated on *cumulative preferred* stock, expressed as dollars per outstanding share or as a total amount.

domestic corporation A corporation created under the laws of a given state or country. In the Federal Internal Revenue Code (section 7701 [4]), the term refers to a corporation established under the laws of the United States or of any of the states or territories; in a state corporation law, the term relates to a corporation created under a law of that state. See *association; corporation; foreign corporation.*

donated (capital) stock Issued shares of capital stock donated to the issuing corporation, usually for resale at an amount not subject to legal restriction: a practice now obsolete. Where the stock was originally issued in exchange for fixed assets or an intangible, the proceeds of its resale were credited against the recorded amount of the property so acquired; if the property originally acquired was cash or some asset subsequently sold, or if if the recorded value of tangible assets acquired was independently and fairly determined, the proceeds of resale were credited to the recorded amount of any intangible assets acquired, or, in the absence of such assets, to a donated or paid-in surplus account. See *paid-in surplus.*

donated surplus Surplus arising from contributions without consideration, by stockholders and others, of cash, property, or the company's own capital stock. Donated surplus is a form of *paid-in surplus.*

donation 1. A return of capital stock to an issuing corporation at no cost to the corporation; see *donated stock.*

2. Any gift, particularly to an incorporated charity or other institution serving the public on a nonprofit basis.

double-account-form balance sheet A balance-sheet form, based upon the double-account system sometimes used in Great Britain, having two sections: capital or financing, and operating or general. The capital section is on a cash basis and reflects the capital receipts and expenditures as shown by the capital-account ledger. On the one side are shown the proceeds from the shares of stock and debentures, including any premiums, and on the other side the various fixed assets on which the proceeds have been expended, including legal charges in the procurement of land and, at an earlier date, parliamentary expenses in promoting special Acts of Parliament. The balance of the capital account is carried down to the second section or "general balance sheet." The general balance sheet consists of current assets and liabilities, reserve fund, retained "profit and loss," and all other items. The fixed assets are never depreciated in the capital account, but depreciation may be provided by charging operations and crediting a reserve account that appears in the general balance sheet, such accounts having been compulsory in some classes of companies. See *balance sheet.*

double-account system A system of accounting, prescribed in Great Britain for companies formed to undertake public works, such as railroads and gas companies, under sanction of special Acts of Parliament. Its distinctive feature is the separation of the fixed from the current assets and liabilities of the undertaking so as to show clearly that the capital, whether contributed by shareholders or otherwise obtained, has been provided for the special purpose of acquiring or constructing the fixed property. See *double-account-form balance sheet.*

double distribution The *re*distribution or *proration* of any expense, expense group, or other cost whereby, from an initial classification, as by *object,* the cost is transferred to another account or spread over several accounts.

double-entry bookkeeping The method usually followed for recording *transactions.* Formal bookkeeping records consist of *journals, ledgers,* or their equivalent, and supporting documents and files. These records are necessary for the purpose of giving expression promptly, systematically, and conventionally to the thousands of transactions that even a relatively small organization enters into. The ultimate repository of the amounts of individual transactions or groups of similar transactions is the "account"—one of the classified pages of a ledger on which appear dates, monetary amounts, and often other essential transaction data.

Thus, in a retail establishment one would expect to find in a ledger a "sales" account in which the money amounts of daily, weekly, or monthly sales (or other income) would appear, with totals, probably, for the year to date; a "purchases" account listing the money amounts of individual merchandise purchases or groups of purchases; a series of "expense" accounts containing money amounts of individual expenses or expense totals. These three types of accounts are often called "nominal" accounts because at the end of the year or other period the account pages are removed and the total money amounts reflected on them are transferred to a single "net-result" account.

In addition to the nominal accounts, there is a group of "real" accounts, the hardy perennials among accounts that outlast the annuals or nominal accounts because they are maintained through the years, some of them changing, like cash, each day, week, or month, some decreasing, some increasing, others remaining the same; the real accounts reflect separately such items as cash balances, amounts owing from customers, the cost of merchandise left over at the end of a period, the cost of store fixtures and of other property to which the establishment lays claim, all these being "assets," or things *owned;* a second class of real accounts reflects the liabilities or the amounts *owing to* creditors for purchases or services received from them but not yet paid for, and to the owners of the business for their original investment and for the retained profits that swell their investment.

There are thus income and expense, or nominal, accounts; and asset and liability, or real accounts; each account will be found occupying one or more pages in a ledger—a book containing only accounts. The accounts are arranged alphabetically according to the formal names given them, or in four main sections following the fundamental groupings just recounted.

A journal is a means of giving first expression to transactions; it exists in various forms, shapes, and numbers but is always essentially a chronological record containing lists of individual transactions added to as they occur. It keeps on growing during the day, week, month, or year of its active existence; and its details, or more often its totals, reflecting transactions of various types, are periodically transferred to whatever accounts in the ledger are affected. A journal is thus a chronological transaction-recording device and a medium for obtaining transaction details or totals that, often in classified form, go into the ledger. No amount gets into a ledger without also appearing in a journal, and every money figure appearing in a journal that represents the amount of a transaction also appears in some account in a ledger.

The recording of the amount of a transaction in a journal is called an *entry;* its transfer in detail or total to an account in a ledger, a *posting*. For every transaction or group of similar transactions, there must be an entry; for every entry or group of similar entries, there must be a posting. Traditionally the transaction is first recorded in a journal, thence posted to a ledger; under many modern machine bookkeeping systems, the journal entry may take place at the same time as the ledger posting. In some instances, the journal itself has virtually disappeared, its main function being to "prepare" a transaction for a ledger posting; and, since the ledger has significance only to the extent that it yields financial statements and other reports, various abbreviated and time-saving forms to replace the ledger are sometimes adopted.

In double-entry bookkeeping, each transaction involves a two-way, and hence self-balancing, entry and a two-way, self-balancing posting. This identity of transaction elements arises from the nature of the transaction itself, of which there are two basic kinds: the business (or external) transaction, and the accounting (or internal) transaction. In a retail establishment owned by an individual, the following principal types of business transactions or transactions with outsiders will be found:

Cash and property coming in from owner (original and subsequent investments)

Cash going out to owner (salary; profits)

Purchases of merchandise (cash or credit)

Payments of credit purchases

Sales to customers (cash or credit)

Receipts from credit sales (cash or goods returned)

Salaries of clerks, rent, and other expenses (cash or credit)

A business transaction nearly always involves the ultimate outgo or income of cash; if not immediately, it is followed by a cash settlement at a subsequent date. Where credit is received or extended, and the eventual recording of two transactions is necessary, the two transactions together may be referred to as a "deal." Each business deal, upon analysis, is thus found, with infrequent exceptions, to affect in the end the size of the cash balance in the business and at the same time to effect a corresponding but opposite change in some other account.

The two-way characteristic each transaction possesses in common with every other transaction may be expressed in the form of the simplest of identities, $a \equiv b$.

That is, in double-entry bookkeeping, two identical money elements are given expression following the *recognition* of each transaction. Since the two elements are to be recorded in the same records and the notion of equality is to be preserved throughout, the identity takes the derived form $a - b = 0$; one element is thus positive, the other negative. The positive element is called a *debit;* the negative element, a *credit.* Including amounts owing to owners as liabilities, a debit may be

An asset increase.	Cash received from a customer; merchandise received from a supplier
A liability decrease.	An obligation paid off
An expense increase.	A salary paid
An income decrease.	A sale, previously recorded, canceled,

while a credit may be

An asset decrease.	Merchandise sold; cash paid out for any purpose
A liability increase.	A promise to pay in exchange for merchandise purchased from a supplier
An expense decrease.	An expense reduced upon refund of an overpayment
An income increase.	A sale.

Both journals and ledgers have separate money columns for debits and credits; in a ledger, individual accounts are "balanced" periodically, an excess of debit postings over credit postings within an individual account being termed a *debit balance,* and an excess of credit postings over debit postings a *credit balance.*

Because the amount of every transaction is twice expressed in the accounts (once as a debit and again as a credit), it follows that the sum of all account balances should be zero: that is, the total of debit balances is equal to the total of credit balances. A listing and totaling of accounts is called a *trial balance.* Three types of trial balances taken from the ledger accounts of the *M* Company are shown at the bottom of this page.

The nature of the transactions making up this trial balance, determined by analysis of the accounts, appears under *spread sheet.*

See also *debit; credit; journal; ledger; transaction; trial balance.*

double liability The personal liability formerly attached to shareholders in national banks and, in some states, attaching to the stockholders of other types of corporations, for additional contributions equal to the amounts originally paid in or subscribed. It is a contingent obligation of stockholders only if the corporation is unable to pay its obligations in full.

double sampling (statistical quality con-

M COMPANY

Trial Balance December 31, 19-1

Account	Type 1 Total Debits and Total Credits: Debit	Type 1 Total Debits and Total Credits: Credit	Type 2 Debits and Credit Balances: Debit	Type 2 Debits and Credit Balances: Credit	Type 3 List of Account Balances
Cash	$ 42,774.52	$ 33,870.08	$ 8,904.44	$	$ 8,904.44
Investments	5,100.00	1,000.00	4,100.00		4,100.00
Receivables	32,395.08	22,500.67	9,894.41		9,894.41
Inventory	5,633.51		5,633.51		5,633.51
Payables	28,792.96	35,014.59		6,221.63	−6,221.63
Capital stock		20,000.00		20,000.00	−20,000.00
Sales	784.12	32,395.08		31,610.96	−31,610.96
Purchases	28,679.40	5,633.51	23,045.89		23,045.89
Expenses	6,525.23	270.89	6,254.34		6,254.34
	$150,684.82	$150,684.82	$57,832.59	$57,832.59	$ 0.00

trol) A plan for dividing a sampling operation into two stages. After inspecting the first sample, the lot may be either accepted, rejected, or held pending inspection of a second sample. After inspection of the second sample, an acceptance or rejection decision is forced by the plan.

downstairs merger (Federal income taxes) A merger of a parent corporation into a subsidiary.

down time The time required for *setup*, overhaul, or maintenance; or lost time attributable to idleness.

draft A written order drawn by one party (drawer) ordering a second party (drawee) to pay a specified amount of money to a third party (payee). See *bill of exchange; check; arrival draft; sight draft; time draft.* The draft of commercial practice is an "arrival" draft: a means of completing a transaction, without the necessity of handling currency, between a seller and a buyer, following an understanding between them as to the method of settlement. The initiative is taken by the seller, who prepares the instrument and deposits it at his bank accompanied by an invoice and a shipping receipt. These papers, forwarded by the bank to a designated bank at the destination point, are surrendered to the buyer upon acceptance or payment of the draft by him.

drop shipment A shipment from a manufacturer or supplier direct to the customer of a distributor or other supplier without passing through the hands of the latter.

dualism The basic twofold characteristic of various concepts, as the debit-and-credit dualism of double-entry bookkeeping.

dualism concept (of accounting) The recognition of source and disposition (or *credit* and *debit*) as the two basic elements of *transactions*, both *external* and *internal;* the unvarying equality of these elements facilitates their immediate separation and regrouping, and leads to the recording and reporting of the cost-and-yield flows dominating the operation of *economic units.*

due *adj.* 1. Matured, and payable (owing *to* others) or receivable (owing *by* others) now or in the immediate future.

2. Maturing; in this sense, the word is accompanied by some reference to a particular date.

due from other funds (governmental and institutional accounting) A receivable for money loaned, stores issued, work performed, or services rendered to or for the benefit of another fund.

due to other funds (governmental and institutional accounting) A payable for money borrowed, stores received, work performed, or services from another fund.

dumping The practice by a vendor, particularly in international trade, of selling goods at or below generally recognized market prices while maintaining higher prices in areas where government protection or other preferred treatment can be secured. Such vendors often allocate their fixed and overhead expenses to goods sold in protected areas and, because of the risks involved, regard returns on dumped goods less direct costs as net profit.

duty = *tariff.*

duty drawback A *tariff* concession allowing a rebate of all or part of the *duty* on goods imported for processing prior to their reexport.

e The base of natural (Naperian) logarithms: 2.718281828459+. See *logarithm.*

E&OE Errors & Omissions Excepted: an abbreviation sometimes placed at the foot of an invoice or statement for the purpose of reserving to the maker of the statement the right to amend the document should it subsequently prove to be incorrect in any particular.

earmark 1. To give expression to a restriction imposed by law, by contractual agreement, or by corporate or administrative action, on the use of an account or of an equivalent amount of assets represented by an account, as where, following the purchase of treasury stock, earned surplus becomes unavailable for dividends. Other illustrations are found in separate accounts maintained for the proceeds from the sale of security issues, available only for specified purposes; cash segregated for investment in some noncurrent asset; sinking-fund cash and reserves; a reserve for working capital.
2. To transfer temporarily a portion of one account to another, as in the creation of a sinking-fund reserve out of earned surplus.

earn To become entitled to income as the result of services performed for another; also often applied to revenue from the sale of goods, or to interest from investments based on the passage of time. See *income.*

earned Realized or accrued as revenue through sales of goods, services performed, or the lapse of time.

earned income 1. Income derived from personal services rendered as distinct from other kinds of income.
2. = *realized revenue; earnings.*

earned surplus = *retained earnings:* a term still actively employed by accountants and frequently appearing in this book and in AICPA publications, but less often on published balance sheets.

earning-capacity value = *earning power.*

earning power Present value equal to the assumed worth of estimated *earnings* (*2*). The term may be used in the valuation of an enterprise as a whole or in the valuation of a class of securities.

earnings 1. A general term embracing *revenue, profit,* or *income.*
2. *Net income;* both *earnings* and *net earnings* are used in this sense by financial writers and in the term *retained earnings.*
3. *Revenues* commonly associated with a natural person, as wages, interest, rent; = *income*(*3b*).
4. = *earned income*(*1*).

earnings per share Net income divided by the average number of shares of common stock outstanding during the year (APBO 9 [1966]) or, perhaps more correctly, where the character and volume of the business has not changed during the year as the result of common shares issued or retired, the number of shares outstanding at the year-end. A second "earnings per share" may be appended in which shares outstanding would be increased by the shares that may be issued under convertible securities, options, and warrants (APBO 12 [1967]).

earnings statement 1. = *income statement.*
2. Any analysis or presentation of earnings in statement form.

easement The right of a land owner to erect or make use of a road, power line, water, or other benefit on adjacent land.

economic 1. Pertaining to *economics;* contributing to production or other business activity.
2. Lowest-cost; economical.

economic activity 1. The *production* and *distribution* of *goods and services.*
2. The contribution of one or more persons to the production of useful goods or services: applied to work performed by a person or other economic unit; see *activity.*

economic cost = *current cost.* See also *alternative cost.*

economic entity = *entity* (*2*); used in contradistinction to *legal entity.*

economic good A commodity or service having exchange value and the capacity to satisfy or aid in satisfying human wants. See *good.*

economic interest The ownership of all or part of a business enterprise; also, the ownership of an obligation of a business enterprise.

economic life The period during which a fixed asset is capable of yielding services *useful to its owner;* contrasts with *physical life,* a period often longer, during the whole of which it can continue to function notwithstanding its acquired obsolescence or inadequacy. See *service life; depreciation; accelerated depreciation.*

economic lot size The number of units to be ordered in a single purchase, or to be produced in a single run before machines are reset for another item, such that minimum costs are incurred or maximum benefits are secured. Formulas for the calculation of economic lot sizes may be found in Rautenstrauch and Villers, *The Economics of Industrial Management,* and Thuesen, *Engineering Economy.*

economics The discipline whose major focus of study is the allocation of scarce resources in the satisfaction of human wants, the description of the functioning of past and present social schemes for effecting the allocation, the establishing of criteria of efficiency and stability necessary for judging such schemes, and the development of methods for their improvement.

economic unit 1. Any *person* or group of persons having a name, common purpose, and transactions with outsiders; examples: a natural person, a family, a profit or nonprofit enterprise, a governmental organization; see *business enterprise.*
2. A group of business enterprises operating under a common control, especially where there are numerous transactions between members of the group. A parent company and its subsidiaries furnish a common example; their involvement in intercompany transactions and other relationships lead to the preparation of consolidated financial statements. See *entity; controlling company.*

economy The business activities of a region or country.

education (for accounting) The education of an accountant may be regarded as technical, professional, and general. Some courses of study contribute to all three types. Technical education or training includes learning the vocabulary and skilled operations required in accountancy as distinguished from other occupations. Professional education is the acquisition of those attitudes and understandings which enable the accountant to work without detailed supervision, to adjust his performance to the needs and conditions of other occupations, and to solve intelligently novel and nonroutine problems. General education comprises all other learning from preschool conditioning to advanced studies in the liberal arts and sciences that assists the accountant in developing intellectual interests along varied lines, finding solutions for his personal problems, and participating in community life.

effective pay rate The rate of pay (e.g., weekly) after adding back deductions from basic pay (e.g., withholding and Social-Security taxes) and including insurance and other fringe benefits not deducted from basic pay.

effective rate The ratio of periodic *income* (interest, and service charges if any), to the market value of an investment or to a sum invested or borrowed, as distinguished from *nominal rate* or the ratio of a quoted interest rate to *par* or *face value*.

efficiency 1. Any conventional measure of performance in terms of a predetermined standard or objective; applied to a machine, operation, individual, or organization.
2. As physical or engineering efficiency: the ratio of output to input, such as the number of BTU's of heat produced for each ton of fuel consumed.
3. (economics) The relative ability to produce at a given rate with lower costs; or, with the same cost, to produce at a higher rate.
4. In its popular sense, rate of profitability. Such a measure may, however, suggest misleading conclusions; a high rate of profit may be wholly transitory and may arise as the result of monopoly, government contracts, or other abnormal situations that over a period of time may have the effect of deteriorating the organization or altering the conditions out of which its substantial profits have grown. However, in various sectors of an enterprise, a profitable efficiency may be directly measured. Thus, the efficiency of a purchasing activity may be readily determined by testing prices, quality, delivery service, and other features with the same elements found elsewhere. Comparisons between the units within an organization or with the results of past periods illustrate other efficiency measures commonly employed.
5. As applied to a business organization generally, any or (seldom) all of the following qualities: balanced operating achievement featured by exemplary labor relations, a higher-than-average productivity per employee and per machine, minimum executive salaries consistent with high performance and other uniformly low management and operating costs, profit restricted to a moderate return on the investment, top quality in output, a product price at the bottom of the industry's range of prices, a high degree of adaptability to needs of customers and the public generally, strict observance of law and of governmental regulations, continuous contributions to educational activities, participation in community affairs, and other accomplishments arising from the adoption of sometimes diverse and often conflicting standards imposed by responsibilities to persons immediately affected, and by a constantly growing accountability to the local environment as well as the world at large. Concepts of what these standards should be and how they should be applied have differed greatly; in recent years they have been basically modified and extended. The 20th-century trend has been and continues to be in the direction of their increase in number and complexity, consistent with a high sense of social responsibility.

efficiency variance A *variance* resulting from causes other than a change in the price of direct costs of materials or labor.

elimination See *intercompany elimination*.

eliminations ledger A ledger maintained by a controlling company as an aid in providing an orderly, consistent record of *intercompany eliminations* when *combined financial statements* are prepared. The accounts in such a ledger increase or decrease balance-sheet and income-statement items and are built up historically, following the classification appearing in the combined statements; they are modified from time to time for sales or purchases of subsidiary securities, and, on statement dates, for intercompany profits and other items. Aside from providing the connecting links between financial statements of individual companies and the combined statements—the information appearing in the "eliminations" column of a *consolidating financial statement* (e.g., see page 104)—the eliminations ledger makes it possible to say that the consolidated statements have been compiled from recorded data appearing in their entirety on books of account. See *intercompany elimination*.

embezzlement The fraudulent appropriation of property lawfully in one's custody, as of cash or securities by a cashier or trustee (a *defalcation*) or of stores by a stock clerk. It may be accomplished by such devices as pocketing receipts from cash sales or from customers *on account;* shipping merchandise to nonexistent customers; and preparing false disbursement vouchers. Fraudulent attempts are often made to cover up such transactions by *kiting*, lapping, not appropriating items in excess of some broadly established tolerance limit for breakage, spoilage, shrinkage, weighing, or counting. Although professional auditors are careful to follow many procedures designed to uncover such frauds, the detection of frauds is no longer a major or even minor objective of an audit. Guards against frauds are rather one of the principal features of modern systems of internal control, and therefore a prime management responsibility.—*embezzle, v.t.* or *i.*

emblements Growing crops constituting personal property or chattels of a tenant farmer or other person who has devoted labor to their production.

emergency amortization = *accelerated depreciation(c)*.

emergency facilities Plant and equipment, sometimes land, purchased or constructed during a specified period for use in fulfilling national-defense contracts and amortizable under section 168 of the Internal Revenue Code over a period of five years. To be accorded the privilege of such accelerated depreciation, a *certificate of necessity* must be obtained from the Director of the Office of Defense Mobilization. See *accelerated depreciation*.

emolument Compensation (1) for personal services: a salary, wage, fee, commission, award, noncontractual expense reimbursement, price concession, illegal fees, or other personal benefit received or accrued.

empirical Derived from experience; sometimes contrasted with *rational* (i.e., derived from some plan or principle).

employee As distinguished from an independent contractor, a person subject to the will and control of an employer with respect to what the employee does and how he does it. Under Federal income-tax and Social-Security-tax procedure, if the "how" is absent, the individual is regarded as an independent contractor.

encumbrance 1. (governmental accounting) An anticipated expenditure, evidenced by a contract or purchase order, or determined by administrative action.

2. = *commitment*.

3. Any lien or other liability attaching to real property.

endowment fund A *fund*, usually of a nonprofit institution, arising from a bequest or gift the income of which is devoted to a specified purpose.

endproduct 1. The result consequent on the application of a method of reasoning or action.

2. The output—goods or services—of any organization.

enter 1. To record a *transaction* in a *journal;* to make an *entry;* to *journalize;* with *in* or *on*.

2. = *post*.

enterprise 1. Any business undertaking; a *business enterprise;* without qualification, the term refers to an entire organization rather than a subdivision thereof; see *entity*.

2. Collectively, all business organizations.

3. That quality of business management characterized by energy, initiative, resourcefulness, and adaptability.

enterprise accounting Accounting for a whole enterprise, as contrasted with accounting for the several entities, branches, or departments of which the enterprise may be composed.

enterprise cost Cost to present owners of an asset, as distinguished from its cost to prior to subsequent owners. See *original cost*.

enterprise value = *going-concern value*.

entity 1. A division of the activities of a natural person, partnership, corporation, or other organization, separate and complete in form, usually distinguished from a larger identity such as a head office, controlling corporation, or other more inclusive economic unit; an *establishment*. An entity is often an *accounting unit*. See *economic unit; business enterprise*.
2. Two or more corporations or other organizations operating under a common *control*, their individual financial positions and operating results often being susceptible of consolidation into *combined financial statements*. See *consolidation policy*.

entity accounting Accounting for an entity, independent of that of a predecessor or controlling organization.

entity concept (of accounting) The recognition of the accounting process as the molder, identifier, and retainer of *economic units* within any field of *economic activity*.

entrepreneur An undertaker of enterprise: a conceptual person who assumes on his own initiative, because of his desire for private gain, the responsibility for bringing together the various factors of production or distribution or both necessary for the establishment and operation of a business enterprise, takes the risk of its success or failure, plans the production and distribution of goods and services, and directs operations; he is regarded as hiring both labor and capital for employment in the enterprise rather than being hired by either. His identity and functions in real life are distributed among those of promoters, investment houses, investors, boards of directors, and management. The term, having the same roots, was borrowed from the French because of the connotations of the word "undertaker."

entry 1. The record of a *transaction* in a *journal*.
2. A *posting*.

EOM = *end of month*.

EOY = *end of year*.

equal-annual-payment method (of depreciation) See *depreciation method*.

equalization point = *basing point*.

equalization reserve 1. An absorption account credited at regular intervals by amounts offsetting charges to operations of sufficient proportions to cover expenditures made more or less irregularly during an accounting period, the object being to spread the expense as uniformly as possible over each subperiod's operations or product. At the end of the fiscal year, any balance in the reserve is transferred to the operations or product to which the reserve relates. See *deferred maintenance*.
2. A similar reserve persisting during two or more accounting periods; example, a *tax reserve* (*q.v.*). Reserves of this type have been criticized because of the creation of a provision of an income-tax expense that may never be paid.
3. = *mixed reserve*.

equalizing dividend A dividend paid to correct inequities caused by changes in established regular dividend dates. Example: When a company advances its dividend date or when companies having different dividend dates are consolidated into one company, an equalizing dividend may be paid. See *dividend-equalization reserve*.

equation A relation between two mathematical functions, as *variables* or *constants*, specifying that one function assumes the same values as the other for some restricted set of values out of the entire mathematical domain under consideration. See *inequation; identity*.

equipment Fixed-asset units, usually movable, accessory or supplemental to such larger items as buildings and structures; examples: lighting fixtures, lockers, communication devices, air conditioners. Machinery and fixtures are not generally classified as equipment, although they fall under the definition. The term is frequently used in conjunction with some word that limits its application; as, "factory equipment," "delivery equipment," "office equipment," and the like. See *fixed asset.*

equipment-trust certificate An interest-bearing document evidencing part ownership of a trust created for the purpose of purchasing equipment and selling or leasing it to a user. An equipment trust serves as a device for avoiding direct ownership by the user, particularly in the case of railroads where such ownership would bring the newly acquired asset under existing mortgages and thus make it impossible to have it serve at the same time as security under a conditional-sales or installment-purchase contract.

equity 1. Any right or claim to assets; a *liability* (*2*). An equity holder may be a creditor, part owner, or proprietor.

2. An interest in property or in a business, subject to prior creditors; *equity ownership. Total equity* is an equivalent British term.

3. Hence, *common stock.*

equity financing The sale of *capital stock* by a corporation.

equity method The periodic adjustment of a parent company's investment in a subsidiary, consolidated or unconsolidated, to the book value reflected in the subsidiary's records, adjusted for the eliminations common to consolidated financial statements. See, however, APBO 10 (1966).

equity ownership 1. The interest of an owner in property or in a business or other organization, subject, in case of liquidation, to the prior claim of creditors.

2. The interest (*paid-in capital* and *earned surplus*) of a stockholder or of stockholders collectively in a corporation; *proprietorship.*

equity receiver A person appointed by a court of equity at the request of the owner, or of creditors, to take over the property of an enterprise and to reorganize it, continue its operation until it can be returned to the owner, or wind up its affairs and distribute any assets remaining.

equity security 1. A transferable certificate of ownership: a term sometimes applied to capital stock, less frequently to bonds or other evidences of indebtedness.

2. A controlling company's holding of stocks, bonds, notes, and other formal evidences of ownership or indebtedness of a subsidiary.

equity transaction Any transaction having the effect of increasing or decreasing *net worth* or involving transfers between the accounts making up net worth.

ergonomics The matching of men and machines in such a manner as to increase *efficiency* (*5*), as by expanding *productivity,* raising *output* quality or quantity, reducing training periods, promoting better working conditions, and improving labor–management relationships.

error A discrepancy, as between definitions, axioms, and rules of inference employed in a logical argument, or as illustrated in such clerical lapses as a *transposition* or *slide* (see *trial balance*).

2. Deviation, inaccuracy, or incompleteness in the measurement or representation of a *fact.* Errors known to be present are sometimes measured and the range of possible errors controlled. The *random* devices of statistics are often employed for this purpose.

Most business decisions are unaffected by small degrees of error, and costs required to increase accuracy may not be warranted. *Value judgments* are required to balance costs of detecting, reducing, or controlling error against benefits that might possibly derive therefrom. Errors arising from carelessness or inadvertence which could have been eliminated by employing usual methods of detection or control are generally held to be not excusable. Accountants are expected to be on the alert for possible sources of errors, to be informed and ready to employ available means for their control or detection, and to assess the possible net benefit to be gained by instituting additional safeguards.

escalation price See *contract price*.

escalator clause A clause inserted in a purchase contract which permits, under specified conditions, adjustments of price or profit, or of allowances for variations in cost.

escapable cost Cost that may be dispensed with upon the contraction of business activity; such cost is conceived as a *net* figure: the savings in cost by curtailing or dropping an activity, less the added cost to other operating units, assuming that any part of the activity must be continued; contrasts with *unavoidable cost*.

escape clause 1. A provision allowing one or more of the parties to a contract, under stipulated conditions, to withdraw or to modify promised performance. 2. A clause inserted in tariff agreements under the Trade Agreements Act which allows the U. S. Tariff Commission to recommend that the President withdraw a previously granted concession on the ground that it threatens serious injury to American suppliers.

establishment 1. A plant or group of plants under a single management, located in one geographical area, and engaging in a set of related processes or in the production of a group of related end items. An establishment may be one of several formally recognized entities within a larger administrative organization such as a corporation. An establishment usually has its own receiving and shipping points for rail, truck, or ship transportation, and a separate mailing address. It is ordinarily an *accounting unit*. The plant or plant group constituting an establishment may consist of several factory buildings and such adjuncts as a powerhouse, warehouse, factory, and directly related administrative offices, the latter often housing procurement and sales as well as supervisory activities. See *economic unit; business enterprise*.

2. *The Establishment*. Loosely, those in power in business and government and the system under which such power is exercised, maintained, and extended.

estate 1. Any right, title, or other interest in real or personal property.

2. The property of a person, often a decedent's property in the process of *administration*.

estate accounting The preparation and keeping of accounts for property in the hands of executors, administrators, or trustees acting under the jurisdiction of a probate court or other legal authority.

estate income The revenue or income of an estate as determined under the provisions of a will or deed, or of Federal or state laws and regulations.

estate tax A Federal graduated tax on estates of deceased persons in excess of $60,000; current rates are as high as 77% on valuations exceeding $10,000,000. See *inheritance tax*.

estimated cost 1. The expected cost of manufacture or acquisition, often in terms of a unit of product, computed on the basis of information available in advance of actual production or purchase. Broadly, estimated costs include *standard costs;* both relate to future operations, and their amounts may coincide. However, in everyday usage, the terms may differ in both amount and purpose, the former indicating a projection of anticipated actual costs and the latter a basis with which actual costs may be controlled and ultimately compared. See *standard cost*.

2. Allocated cost of a unit of product or of one of several departments or product lines. See *cost accounting*.

estimate of cash requirements A forward schedule of cash needed for current operations or capital expenditure, at required points or periods of time:

a required element in budgeting estimates, often the product of a *cash-flow statement*.

estimating-cost system A method of accounting whereby estimated costs are the basis for credits to work-in-process accounts, thus serving in lieu of actual costs which are accounted for only in total. See *standard cost*.

ethics A system of moral principles and their application to particular problems of conduct; specifically, the *rules* (*1*) of conduct of a profession imposed by a professional body governing the behavior of its members. In the accounting profession, rules of professional conduct applying to members of the American Institute of Certified Public Accountants may be summarized thus:

1. A member (or member firm) may express an opinion in an *audit report* (*1*) or certificate only if he (and each of his partners, if any) is independent of his client. Lack of independence exists where any such member has a present or prospective investment in the client's business or is employed by or holds any position with the client.

2. A member must not commit any unprofessional act.

3. There must be no violation of the confidential relationship between a member and his client.

4. Contingent fees are permitted in tax cases and fees fixed by courts or other public authorities in other cases, but are forbidden elsewhere.

5. A member's signature on an audit is prohibited where the audit has not been made by the member, an employee, or a licensed accountant.

6. In or attached to financial statements audited by a member, there must be a disclosure of every material fact which if omitted might mislead the reader, of any material misstatement, or of a material departure from any generally accepted, applicable accounting principle or audit procedure; the opinion of a member as to financial statements may not be given on the basis of inadequate information or where exceptions may have the effect of making his opinion meaningless. See *fairness*.

7. The audit report or certificate must contain an unqualified opinion, a qualified opinion, or a disclaimer of opinion with reasons; where no audit report is furnished, each page of the financial statements must prominently display a note that no audit has been made.

8. A member may not subscribe to the accuracy of an estimate of future earnings or permit any inference to that effect.

9. Advertising is prohibited, and professional announcements (of personnel of firms, or of changes of address) are restricted in size and content; a paid directory listing may not appear in display type or be otherwise distinctive.

10. A competitive bid is not in the *public interest* and is therefore unprofessional.

11. A member must not accept a fee or commission on work for another person upon the member's recommendation, or pay a fee or commission to another upon obtaining professional work.

12. Members or member firms may employ the phrase "Member(s) of the American Institute of Certified Public Accountants" in their reports.

13. A member may not permit another person not a partner or employee to practice in his name.

14. Employees of members are not to be permitted to perform services for clients which members themselves are not permitted to perform.

15. A member engaged in public accounting may not carry on a collateral activity "incompatible or inconsistent" with professional activities.

16. A member performing services similar to those rendered by public accountants is expected to observe the Institute's rules of conduct.

17. Members are not permitted to be connected with a corporation engaged in public-accounting practice.

18. The practice of another public accountant is not to be encroached on.

19. Services rendered as the result of referrals by another member are not to go beyond the work referred unless the member is consulted.

20. Employment may not be offered to any employee of another public accountant without first informing the employer, unless the employee seeks a change on his own initiative or in response to an advertisement.

even lot = *round lot.*

event 1. A *process* or a part of a process having a particular moment and place of occurrence. A typical event is a *transaction* with an outsider. See *process; condition.*

2. (statistics) A categorical term referring to phenomena observed or recorded at a given time and place by an investigator: a term taken as a *primitive* notion in the theory of *probability,* and interpreted as a class of logically possible observations.

events and conditions A term covering all the phenomena of economic change recognized in the accounting process and constituting the subject matter of *transactions. Events* are the usual cause of external transactions, while *conditions* are characteristic of internal transactions.

evidence A collection of *facts,* admittedly or allegedly accurate, relevant, and sufficient, offered in verification of a *proposition.* Its recognition and admissibility are established under rules laid down by courts, learned professions, and other institutions. Evidence should be distinguished from belief, which may not be supported by acceptable evidence. An auditor may believe that a given corporate management is competent and able to extricate itself from an important current weakness in financial position, but this belief should have no effect on the accountant's construction and presentation of the evidence of such weakness, as it would ordinarily be disclosed, in a balance sheet or operating statement.

ex 1. Without, as in *ex-dividend; ex-rights.*

2. (followed by a named location) A term indicating that the price quoted to or paid by a purchaser does not include any transportation or handling costs and that the seller assumes neither cost nor risk beyond the named location (or beyond the moment of time specified in the sales contract) at which the buyer takes delivery.

exact duplicate A copy conforming in every detail with an original and often so attested.

exact interest Simple interest for a fractional year based on a year of 365 days, contrasting with *ordinary interest,* which has a base year of 360 days. The ratio of exact interest to simple interest is $0.\dot{9}863013\dot{6}$, and of simple interest to exact interest, $1.013\dot{8}$.

examination 1. = *audit(1).*

2. A *limited audit(1);* when thus employed, the term is accompanied by words or phrases indicating the character of the limitation.

examine (auditing) To probe records, or inspect securities or other documents, review procedures, and question persons, all for the purpose of arriving at an opinion of accuracy, propriety, sufficiency, and the like.

exception 1. A qualification by an auditor in his report, indicating a limitation as to the scope of his audit or disagreement with or doubt concerning an item of a financial statement to which he certifies. See *audit report.*

2. (governmental accounting) A written notification by the Comptroller General to an accountable officer or employee questioning an expenditure; failure to supply a satisfactory explanation may lead to a *disallowance,* following which the officer or employee may be required to recover the amount from the payee, personally reimburse the government, or obtain *relief.*

3. The difference between a *standard cost* and *actual cost*. See *management by exception*.

excess-profits credit (Federal income taxes) The dollar yardstick (provided by sections 435–437 and 458 of the Revenue Code of 1939) marking the division of corporate income between so-called "normal" and "excess" profits, based on 83 percent of the excess-profits net income of the three best years in the *base period* or, if larger, the amount obtained by applying a percentage to *invested capital* determined under either the "asset" or "historical" method, with adjustments for capital additions and reductions and for *inadmissible assets*.

excess-profits tax (Federal income taxes) The tax levied on the excess of a corporation's net income, after certain adjustments, over the *excess-profits credit*. Excess-profits taxes were in effect during the periods 1917–1921, 1940–1945, and 1950–1953.

exchange 1. The transfer of money, property, or services in return for money, property, or services; or for promises to deliver money, property, or services, or any combination of these items; a barter.

2. = *foreign exchange:* the exchange of legal tender or other currencies in ratios authorized by sovereign powers or as transacted in a money market. See *rate of exchange*.

3. A market for a commodity, such as a stock or produce exchange.

exchange check A check given in return for cash or for another check.

excise tax A privilege tax falling on the manufacture, sale, or consumption of a commodity; also a tax or license paid by persons following certain occupations or conducting certain types of business activities.

exclusion (insurance) A provision in an insurance contract or bond limiting the scope of the insurance agreement.

ex-dividend A term indicating that the price of shares of capital stock excludes a dividend payable on a certain future date to stockholders of record on a specified preceding date. See *dividend*.

executor A person or one of two or more persons named in a will as the fiduciary who is to take charge of the deceased's estate and administer or dispose of it as directed in the will.

executory lease An obligation calling for the payment of rentals of real or personal property over a period of years. If the commitment is a substantial one, the annual payments and the terms, if any, covering the ultimate return or disposal of the property are summarized in notes accompanying the financial statements of the lessee.

exemption (Federal income taxes) A deduction from gross income allowed an individual, in the nature of a minimal or token amount, for his own support and that of his family. Under current law, a deduction of $600 is permitted for each such person (see *dependent*), and added deductions of the same amount for old age (65 or over) and for blindness.

exhibit A financial or other statement of a formal character prepared for the information of others, as in an auditor's report.

expectancy = *expected value*.

expected life *Expected value* of length of life or years of service of an asset or asset group at a particular moment of time.

expected value (statistics) The average or mean of a *statistical distribution;* represented in formulas by E.

The term is often used interchangeably with "mathematical expectation," the latter term having at one time been associated with efforts to analyze games of chance. The notion of mathematical expectation still underlies the analysis of such games, as well as other fields such as insurance. Suppose, for example, that under the rules of a certain game a player receives a sum $\$a$ when he wins, with probability p, and pays a sum $\$b$ when he loses, with probability

q, where $p + q = 1$. Over a long series of plays, he will tend to win or lose an amount $p \cdot a + q \cdot (-b)$, if (a) he either wins or loses, but not both, on each play, and (b) the probability of winning or losing at each play does not depend on the outcome of previous plays. This sum $pa - qb$ is defined as the mathematical expectation and yields, on the average, the amount which will be won or lost in the game. If the sum $pa - qb = 0$, the game is said to be fair or unbiased; if the sum is positive, the game is biased in favor of the player; if negative, it is biased in favor of his opponent. The amount by which the result differs from zero represents the amount of *bias;* this can be eliminated and the game made fair by requiring the person whom the game favors to pay to his opponent a sum equal to his expected gain as a fee for playing.

Expected value is the average of all possible values from samples of a given size. Thus, the expected value of the *arithmetic mean* is the average of the sample means. The difference, if any, between the expected value and the *universe parameter* is the amount of *bias* in the method of estimation. What is involved may be illustrated by means of a simple example.

Five balls, on each of which the number 2, 4, 6, 8, or 10 is stamped, are placed in an urn, from which *random samples* of two balls at a time are to be drawn. Plotted on a graph, the frequency distribution of this universe would appear rectangular in character. It would have an *arithmetic mean* $\bar{X}$ of 6, and a *variance* σ^2 of 8, as calculated in the following table:

Frequency	Value	Deviations from Arbitrary Origin		
f	X	d	fd	fd^2
1	2	−2	−2	4
1	4	−1	−1	1
1	6	0	0	0
1	8	1	1	1
1	10	2	2	4
5	—	0	0	10

Hence,

$$\bar{X} = \frac{\Sigma fX}{N} = A + \frac{\Sigma fd}{N} = 6 + 0 = 6,$$

where f is the frequency, X the values, and d the deviations from the arbitrarily chosen origin (A) of 6. See *arithmetic mean; variance; standard deviation.* The variance is arrived at thus:

$$\sigma^2 = \frac{\Sigma f(X - \bar{X})^2}{N} = \left[\frac{\Sigma fd^2}{N} - \left(\frac{\Sigma fd}{N}\right)^2\right]c^2$$

$$= \left(\frac{10}{5} - 0\right) \times 2^2 = 8,$$

where c $(= 2)$ is the class-interval unit of d, the deviations about the arbitrary origin A $(= 6)$.

All the combinations of the two balls that might be drawn under random sampling appear in the table below. There are ten possible samples. From these, the sample means $\bar{x}$ and sample variance s^2 may be calculated. Moreover, the behavior of the dispersion of sample means $\bar{x}$ about the universe mean $\bar{X}$ may also be studied by analyzing the behavior of sample averages in relation to the universe average; the following symbol will be used to denote this relation: $\sigma^2_{\bar{x}} = E(\bar{x} - \bar{X})^2$—i.e., the average or expected value of the variance of sample means about the universe mean.

Sample Values	Sample Means	Sample Variances	Contributions to Variance of Sample Means
(x_1, x_2)	$\bar{x} = \frac{x_1 + x_2}{2}$	$s^2 = \frac{\Sigma(x - \bar{x})^2}{2}$	$(\bar{x} - \bar{X})^2$
(2,4)	3	1	9
(2,6)	4	4	4
(2,8)	5	9	1
(2,10)	6	16	0
(4,6)	5	1	1
(4,8)	6	4	0
(4,10)	7	9	1
(6,8)	7	1	1
(6,10)	8	4	4
(8,10)	9	1	9
Totals	60	50	30

Since there are exactly ten samples,

the expected value, E, of the sample means is given by $E(x) = \frac{60}{10} = 6$. This is exactly the value of the universe mean. Since $E(\bar{x}) = \bar{X}$, no bias is involved under random sampling if sample means are used, without adjustment, to estimate the universe mean.

This is not the case for sample variances, for $E(s^2) = \frac{50}{10} = 5$, whereas the universe value was calculated to be $\sigma^2 = 8$. In other words, the use of sample variances without adjustment, even when random samples are used, results in an underestimate of the universe variance. This bias is generally present and is not restricted to the example under study. The relation can be shown to be

$$E(s^2) = \frac{N(n-1)}{n(N-1)} \times \sigma^2,$$

where N = the number of items in the population and n = the number of items in the sample. $N/(N-1)$ is called the *finite population correction* and $\frac{n-1}{n}$ is called the *sample correction factor*—corrections which may be ignored when N is very large relative to n. If N is very large, but n small, the relation is sometimes written as

$$E(s^2) = \frac{n-1}{n} \sigma^2.$$

Simple algebra results in the following rearrangement:

$$\frac{n(N-1)}{N(n-1)} \times E(s^2) = \sigma^2.$$

In other words, sample values adjusted by the product of the reciprocal of the finite population and sample correction factors will yield unbiased estimates of the universe variance for samples of any size.

Application to the present example gives

$$\frac{2 \times 4}{5 \times 1} \times 5 = 8,$$

which is an unbiased estimate of σ^2.

The first two columns in the following table constitute a recapitulation in the form of a frequency distribution of the sample means $\bar{x}$.

f	$\bar{x}$	d	fd	fd^2
1	3	−3	−3	9
1	4	−2	−2	4
2	5	−1	−2	2
2	6	0	0	0
2	7	1	2	2
1	8	2	2	4
1	9	3	3	9
10	—	0	0	30

Since this frequency distribution displays the behavior of sample means, it is called a *sampling distribution*, or, more exactly, a sampling distribution of arithmetic means. Such sampling distributions may be devised for other statistics, such as the variance; they may also be calculated for samples of varying size. It will be noted that the remarkable property of *arithmetic means* to distribute themselves in the form of a *normal distribution*, for random samples drawn from any *universe*, is already beginning to be displayed, despite the rather adverse conditions of relatively small samples used in drawings from a rectangular universe. As can be seen from the frequency column f, the sample means are distributed symmetrically about the universe mean, $\bar{x} = 6$. No such tendency is manifested in the distribution of the sample variances, which may be demonstrated by forming a frequency distribution of the sample values.

Sampling distributions of any statistic have their own *standard deviation*, which is called the *standard error*. Thus, the square of the standard error, or *variance*, of sample means calculated from the table is $\frac{30}{10} = 3$. Upon inspection of the table, this value will be found equal to the expected value of the variances of the sample means, since $\Sigma s_{\bar{x}}^2 = 3$. That is, denoting this value by $\sigma_{\bar{x}}^2$, $E(s_{\bar{x}}^2) = \sigma_{\bar{x}}^2$. Moreover, there is a relation between the universe variance σ^2 and $\sigma_{\bar{x}}^2$.

This relation is given by the formula

$$E(s_{\bar{x}}^2) = \sigma_{\bar{x}}^2 = \frac{N-n}{N-1} \times \frac{\sigma^2}{n},$$

where N is the number of items in the universe and n the number of items in the sample. Substitution of these values in the present problem yields

$$\frac{5-2}{5-1} \times \frac{8}{2} = 3,$$

which is equal to the value of $\sigma_{\bar{x}}^2$ already calculated.

The existence of relations such as these makes it possible not only to estimate *parameters* from *statistics*, but also to determine the probability that a given statistic might have been drawn from a universe characterized by a specified *parameter*. It is the latter procedure which underlies that part of *statistical inference* known as the "testing of hypotheses."

expendable fund A *fund* the assets of which may be applied by administrative action to specific or general purposes.

expended appropriation (governmental accounting) That portion of an *appropriation* equal to the *accrued expenditures* incurred thereunder; the balance of the appropriation may be *obligated* or *unobligated*.

expenditure 1. The incurring of a liability, the payment of cash, or the transfer of property for the purpose of acquiring an asset or service or settling a loss. When unqualified, the *accrual basis* of accounting is assumed.
2. The amount of cash or property paid or to be paid for a service rendered, or an asset purchased.
3. Any cost the benefits of which may extend beyond the current accounting period.
—*expend, v.t.*

expenditure rate An administratively imposed ceiling on the expenditures, usually on an accrual basis, of any organization, organizational subdivision, function, or activity, within any forward period of time.

expense *n.* 1. An *expired cost:* any item or class of cost of (or loss from) carrying on an activity; a present or past expenditure defraying a present operating cost or representing an irrecoverable cost or *loss;* an item of capital expenditures *written down* or *off:* a term often used with some qualifying word or expression denoting function, organization, or time; as, a selling expense, factory expense, or monthly expense.
2. A class term for expenditures *recognized* as operating costs of a current or past period.
3. Hence, any expenditure the benefits from which do not extend beyond the present.
v. To designate a past or current expenditure as a present operating cost or loss; to *write down* or *off*.

expense account 1. Any *account* (*1*) maintained for a particular expense.
2. A general term for the total cost of goods sold, expired services, or irrecoverable losses.
3. A general term for *accounts*(*1*) periodically cleared through *profit and loss*(*1*).
4. A statement of an individual's outlays, usually covering a limited time and purpose.

expense budget The planned cost of the volume at which it is expected that an activity will be undertaken. See *current budget*.

expense center Any location within an organization at which the coincidence of organization and function has been recognized; an *activity*. An expense center may be a machine, a department, a service shop with which operating costs are identified, its supervisor deriving his authority from and being accountable to a higher level of management. Fixing discretionary responsibilities on supervisors, establishing expenditure limitations, measuring the quantity and quality of work output, and comparing incurred unit costs with predetermined standards and with costs of similar activities elsewhere are features of expense-center accounting.

expense control Any method designed to keep future costs within a predetermined rate or amount. Included are such devices as holding supervisors responsible for restricted functional-cost areas, confining expenditures to certain classes, limiting the amount that may be incurred within a relatively short period of time, and projecting a standard unit cost to which actual cost is expected to conform. See *control*.

expense distribution The identification of an expense with the purpose—for example, a process or product—for which it was incurred. An expense readily identifiable with a particular purpose is a *direct expense;* a joint or common cost that contributes to two or more purposes and is allocable to any one purpose only by some method of averaging is an *indirect expense* or overhead. Where it has been decided that a joint or common cost is to be distributed according to some measure of benefit received, the methods of distribution most often employed are direct-labor cost, direct-labor hours, machine hours, and space occupied (square feet or cubic feet). See *overhead; direct cost.*

experience rating (insurance) The establishment of a non*manual rate* for a specific risk based on a comparison of the cost of such risk with the average cost of all risks within the class; the adjusted rate may be higher or lower.

experiment 1. A controlled or partially controlled operation, undertaken for the purpose of determining the nature, frequency, or other characteristics of events occurring under stated conditions. An experimental observation may contribute to or test a generalization. 2. Loosely, anything tried.

expired cost An *expenditure* from which no further benefit is anticipated; an expense; a cost *absorbed* over the period during which benefits were enjoyed or a loss incurred.

expired utility 1. That portion of the anticipated *usefulness* or service yield of a fixed asset no longer to be availed of by or available to its owner, whatever the cause; = *depreciation.*
2. *Accumulated depreciation.*

exposure (insurance) The extent of a risk, measured in terms of payroll, receipts, area, nature of surrounding properties, or other risk factors.

express trust A trust created by specific provision in a deed or other written instrument. See *trust.*

ex-rights A term used in connection with the price of a share of capital stock indicating that a right to subscribe to new shares, formerly attaching to the stock, no longer attaches, the rights being retained by the seller or having expired. See *right.*

extended coverage An addition or endorsement to a fire-insurance policy that includes such risks as those arising from windstorms, hail, earthquakes, riots, and other possible causes of property damage.

external audit An audit by a person not an employee; an independent audit. See *audit* (*4*).

external auditor = *public accountant;* contrasts with *internal auditor.*

external transaction A *transaction* with an *outsider;* known also as a "business" transaction; contrasts with *internal transaction.* Sales and purchases of goods and services, collections and deposits of cash, and payments of liabilities constitute the bulk of the external transactions of a business enterprise.

extra dividend A dividend paid in excess of a previously maintained annual rate, without assurance that the additional payment is to continue; also called *special dividend.*

extraordinary depreciation Depreciation caused by unusual wear and tear, unexpected disintegration, obsolescence, or inadequacy beyond that attributable to ordinary loss of physical or service life. A provision for depreciation will normally cover both ordinary and extraordinary depreciation. See *depreciation*. Extraordinary depreciation is not usually regarded as a type of *accelerated depreciation*.

extraordinary expense An expense so unusual in type or amount as to be accorded special treatment in the accounts or separate disclosure in financial statements. See *loss; income deduction*.

extraordinary repairs Repairs making good deterioration attributable to hard use, neglect, or other cause of deferment of normal maintenance or repair; an overhaul correcting both major and minor defects, and often requiring replacements of parts. Certain types of extraordinary repairs, at one time regarded as offsetting depreciation and therefore chargeable against accumulated depreciation, are now treated as an expense; in anticipation of this expense, during the period of delayed repair, an accrual for extraordinary repairs may be provided. See, however, *deferred maintenance*.

extrapolation (statistics) An extension or projection lying outside the data available; as, an estimate of the country's population two years hence; the probable position of wholesale prices next week. —*extrapolate, v.t.* or *i*. See *interpolation*.

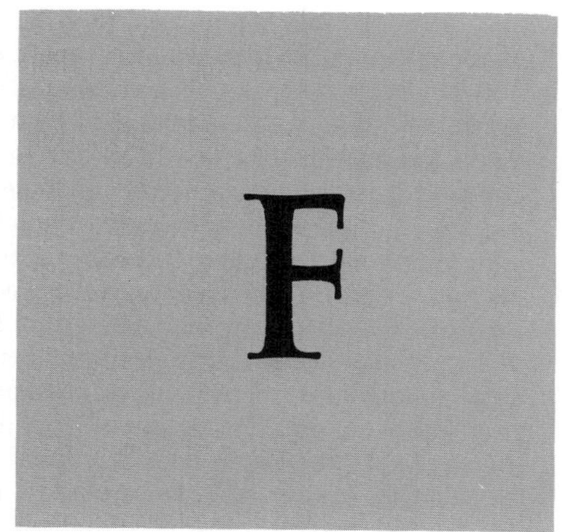

F = *folio reference.*

face amount (or **value**) The nominal amount of a bond, note, mortgage, or other security as stated in the instrument itself, exclusive of interest or dividend accumulations. This may or may not coincide with the price at which the instrument was first sold, its present market value, or its redemption price. The nominal amount of each share represented by a stock certificate is usually referred to as *par* or *stated value.*

face-amount certificate A form of contract between certain investment companies and investors whereby the latter agree to make required installment payments to the company until the total called for by the contract has been paid in. During the payment period, the certificate has a cash surrender value; at the "maturity" date, the surrender value is the *face amount,* which, because of accruing interest in excess of the loading cost applicable to the certificate, often exceeds the amount paid in by the investor.

facility 1. A coordinated group of *fixed assets*—land, buildings, machinery, and equipment—constituting a *plant;* sometimes called a "complete" facility.
2. Any item of physical equipment that contributes to production: a building, machine, or shop; a *factor of production* in the form of any item of plant.

fact 1. A statement embodying evidence or findings based on explicitly or partially formulated *rules* of observation not wholly derivable from a structure of logical relations to other propositions. Hence, a fact is at best only probable and not certain; what appears to be fact depends upon the context, state of knowledge, and point of view of the observer.
2. Loosely, any proposition held to be true. This usage fails to distinguish between a simple event or observable characteristic and an inference or systematic statement (such as a *principle, theory,* or other generalization) about a mass of related observations or observable facts.

factor 1. One who buys trade receivables with or without recourse, his profit coming from a commission, usually a fraction of 1 percent, and from interest on advances. Factoring predominates in the textile industry, is found to a lesser degree elsewhere. Factors were formerly selling agents for merchandise of various kinds, differing from brokers in that they handled the merchandise themselves.
2. (mathematics) Any of the numbers or symbols that, when multiplied together, form a product.
3. Hence, any component; e.g., any influence that contributes to, modifies, or otherwise affects an endproduct.

factorial The product of a specified number and all the positive whole integers preceding it. The factorial symbol is the exclamation point; thus $4! = 4 \times 3 \times 2 \times 1$, or 24; $n! = n(n-1)(n-2)\ldots \times 2 \times 1$. Factorials are large numbers (e.g., $10! = 3{,}628{,}800$), and logarithm tables have been prepared to facilitate their use. See *permutation.*Both 0! and 1! are treated as "1" in factorial formulas.

factor of production Any of the various agents (natural resources, labor, processes, capital, and the entrepreneur) contributing to the production or supply of a good or service; the combined cost of these factors equals the supply price.

factory cost = *manufacturing cost.*

factory expense An item of manufacturing cost other than raw material and direct labor; *manufacturing expense; indirect expense; overhead.*

factory ledger A subsidiary ledger containing such operating costs of a manufacturing establishment as materials, labor, and factory overhead. The total of its accounts may be the cost of *goods in process;* or included in the ledger may be inventory accounts for raw materials, supplies, and finished goods, as well as *work in process.*

fair market value 1. Value determined by bona-fide bargaining between well-informed buyers and sellers, usually over a period of time. See *market value.* 2. An estimate of such value, in the absence of sales or quotations.

fairness The ability of *financial statements* to convey unambiguous, adequate information, particularly when accompanied by the *representation* (in a short-form *audit report*) of a public accountant, to "present fairly" the detail required by *convention* for depicting *financial position* and *operating results.* This representation —as distinguished from the financial statements themselves—is commonly understood to mean that, without clearly stated exceptions or qualifications, no less than the following conditions have been complied with by the accountant:

1. *As to his examination,* (a) his independence, [observed in the conduct of his examination,] is affirmed by the character of his report; (b) no limitation, natural or imposed by his client, has reduced the scope of his examination below the level he considers minimal; (c) records and other supporting evidence required by him have been available to and utilized by him; (d) he has tested receivables by correspondence, and has substantiated by observation opening and closing inventories that have been valued not in excess of current market; or he has satisfied himself with respect to these items by other, not less rigorous means of his choice; (e) he has accepted responsibility for the report, if any, of another accountant (e.g., on a branch or subsidiary), which has been combined or consolidated in the financial statements, or he has submitted the other's report collaterally with his own; (f) contingencies and other uncertainties that might affect present or future interpretations of the financial statements have been *appraised(2)* by him and reported as he has judged necessary; (g) his short-form-report language follows the professional standard (on occasion modified by him to express a qualified, adverse, or disclaimer of opinion), or he has prepared no report and has disassociated himself from the financial statements; and (h) he has exercised professional care and professional judgment throughout his examination.

2. *As to his client's internal controls and accounting methods during the period reviewed,* (i) internal controls have been adequate; (j) the client's applied accounting principles, policies, and procedures have been acceptable; (k) accounting policies have been consistent during the current and preceding periods; and (l) the books of account have been brought into agreement with the financial statements.

3. *As to the financial statements, including appended notes,* (m) terminology common to financial statements has been employed or notes defining uncommon terms are attached; (n) the arrangement of financial-statement items follows the conventional pattern; (o) the financial statements are comparable in form and item with those of similar organizations; (p) unamortized acquisition cost which in his judgment may be carried forward to the succeeding period is the best basis for asset valuation; any other basis is described along with the amount by which it differs from acquisition cost less recorded allowances for accumulated depreciation or for loss from expected realization; (q) depreciation methods for both accounting and tax purposes, and current provisions and accumulations, are

revealed; (r) more-than-minor (e.g., 5%) differences between net income and taxable income are explained; (s) an unusual large-scale transaction, an important change in activities, or other major post-balance-sheet event or condition is footnoted; (t) annual rentals and other provisions of general interest in long-term leases, pension plans, compensation agreements, and stock-option and bonus plans are set forth; (u) no known misstatement or misrepresentation is reflected in the financial statements; (v) facts and conditions are included without which the financial statements might be interpreted as misleading; (w) information that may contribute to the reader's better understanding is provided, even though without it the statements cannot technically be regarded as misleading; and (x) financial statements and their attachments are management's, although at times prepared by the accountant for management or added to or modified at his instance; hence, any item omitted from them and judged by him to be of importance appears in his report.

4. *As to any departure, deemed by the public accountant to be material in character or amount, from any of the preceding conditions,* (y) his report identifies the item with the financial statements and provides information designed to aid an outsider's appraisal of its significance.

fair-trade price The resale price of a branded product fixed or "suggested" by the manufacturer for the purpose of eliminating or minimizing price competition between wholesalers and between retailers. See *fixed resale price; price maintenance.*

fair value Reasonable or equitable value; the legal concept of value on which an investor is entitled to a "fair return." The term is often used by public utilities to indicate the basis of valuation employed in the establishment of service rates.

family partnership A partnership whose members are confined principally or wholly to a single family. For Federal income tax purposes, such a partnership is not recognized as to any partner who is not considered to be the real owner of his partnership interest. Recognition is not denied, however, merely because the capital of one partner is derived by gift from another family partner, nor because tax-saving is a motive, provided that capital is a material income-producing factor in the business.

fanout The breakdown of an account into two or more basic accounts.

farm-price method The valuation of the inventory of a farmer, employing market price less any known or estimated direct cost of marketing or other disposition, and sanctioned by income-tax Regulations, Sec. 1.471–6(d). See *unit-livestock-price method.*

FAS Free Alongside Ship: a symbol indicating that the export price of a given lot of goods includes the obligation of the seller to deliver it to the ship that is to transport it abroad without additional cost to the buyer.

FAS price The price, when used without further specification, charged a foreign buyer, including inland transportation, warehousing, trucking, lighterage, insurance, and the like, to a point within reach of the loading tackle of the vessel, the seller retaining risks of ownership to this point.

favorable difference (or **variance**) A term characterizing an excess of projected cost over actual cost, or of actual revenue over projected revenue, the reverse condition being referred to as an *unfavorable difference.* Both terms, sometimes unexpectedly, can be highly inaccurate designations, particularly in reports intended for management review and action, and are best avoided. A "favorable" difference may actually signalize a situation needing immediate attention and correction, while an "unfavorable" difference, the cause of which is already known, may require no attention at all. Also, where equality exists, an inefficiency of a past period may be indicated.

Where the term *management by exception* is actively employed, differences thus labeled may lead to serious oversights.

Federal Trade Commission A quasi-judicial administrative agency of the Federal government charged with the general responsibility of maintaining the freedom of business enterprise, curbing monopoly and unfair business practices, and keeping competition "both free and fair." Its basic legal authorities are the Federal Trade Commission Act of 1914 (38 Stat. 717), the *Clayton Act*, passed in the same year, the *Robinson–Patman Act* of 1936, and subsequent amendments. The first of these acts enumerates a number of commercial practices deemed unfair, such as misbranding, misleading advertising, false pricing, threats of lawsuits, filching trade secrets, and various other acts intended to affect competitors adversely. A general intent is to enforce the spirit of fair competition by preventive action or by voluntary settlements, without recourse to the courts unless other measures have failed.

Among FTC activities of interest to accountants is its Bureau of Economics, which, aided by the Securities and Exchange Commission, issues quarterly reports summarizing the financial position and operating results of American manufacturing corporations.

feedback Any system involving the periodic supplying of information on operating performance, the comparison of such information with a standard of performance, and the taking of corrective action based on the comparison; in accounting, = *accountability*, an essential feature of which is the *reporting* to higher authority. See *activity*.

feeder organization An organization whose income, inuring to an exempt corporation, is subject to income tax under sections 502 and 511 of the Internal Revenue Code; before 1951, such income in certain instances was held to be exempt from taxation.

fellow subsidiary One of two or more subsidiaries of a controlling company.

fidelity bond Insurance against losses arising from dishonest acts of employees and involving specified money, merchandise, or other property; persons or positions may be covered.

fiduciary Any person responsible for the custody or administration, or both, of property belonging to another; as, a trustee.

fiduciary accounting 1. The preparation and keeping of accounts for property in the hands of a trustee, executor, or administrator, whether under the direct jurisdiction of a court or acting by virtue of a private deed of trust or other instrument of appointment.
2. *Estate accounting*.

field auditor An internal auditor whose function is to audit the accounts of plants or branches located away from the principal office; a traveling auditor.

fifo = *first in, first out*. See *inventory valuation*.

final dividend 1. = *year-end dividend*.
2. The last of a series of *liquidating dividends*.

finance *v.t.* & *i.* To supply with funds, through the sale of stocks or bonds, floating loans, extending credit on open account, or transferring or appropriating money from internal sources.
n. The theory and practice underlying dealings, including speculation, in money and its investment: the operating field of commercial and investment banks, and of security and commodity markets, brokers, and dealers.

financial accounting The accounting for revenues, expenses, assets, and liabilities that is commonly carried on in the general offices of a business: a term often contrasted with *cost accounting;* see also *administrative accounting*.

financial accounts *Balance sheets* and *income statements;* = *financial statements*.

financial expense A cost incident to the financing of an enterprise, as distinguished from one directly applicable to operations. Examples: interest on indebtedness; *bond discount* amortized.

financial position (or **condition**) The *assets*

and *liabilities* of an organization as displayed on a balance sheet, following customary practices in its preparation. The term is sometimes applied to a *balance sheet*.

financial ratio See *ratio*.

financial report A report on *operating results* and *financial position:* an *income statement* and a *balance sheet*, with interpretive annotations.

financial statement A *balance sheet, income statement, funds statement*, or any supporting statement or other presentation of financial data derived from *accounting records*.

finder On who for a fee brings together a buyer and seller; e.g., in the security field, one who brings together a corporation proposing to issue securities and a firm of investment bankers, his fee being a flat sum or a percentage of the underwriting profits. He may be an *underwriter* under the Federal Securities Act if his promotional effort extends to the formation of a selling syndicate.

finished goods (or **stock**) 1. Manufactured product, ready for sale or other disposition; to be distinguished from finished parts which will enter production or assembly, and *merchandise*, a term covering articles of commerce bought for resale.

2. An account in which appear (a) completed products, e.g., transferred from a work-in-process account; and (b) transfers of such products to completed product sold (*sales*), the balance representing completed product on hand: an inventory asset commonly valued at cost or less. See *inventory; inventory valuation*.

firm *n.* A partnership; loosely, a term often used in economics to denote any business organization: a proprietorship, partnership, or corporation.

adj. Binding; as, a *firm contract*.

firm contract Any contract such as one which obligates a seller to deliver and a buyer to accept at a specified time goods described as to quantity, quality, and price; or one that requires an underwriter to deliver cash from the sale of securities within a specified period of time.

firm policy 1. A *policy* formally adopted and effectively enforced.

2. Hence, a *policy* followed by any individual or organization.

firm price See *contract price*.

first cost 1. = *object cost*. Costs to be found in *primary accounts* are first or object costs.

2. = *original cost*(*2*).

first in, first out (fifo) A method of inventory identification and valuation. See *inventory valuation*.

fiscal period 1. = *accounting period*.

2. The partial *fiscal year* resulting from the formation or dissolution of an enterprise or change in fiscal year.

fiscal year 1. Any accounting period of 12 successive calendar months, 52 weeks, or 13 four-week periods. When the fiscal year is divided into 50 two-week or 13 four-week periods, additional days may be added to the last week or period to make it coincide with the end of the calendar year or month. Under full adherence to weekly periods of seven days, the fiscal year may from time to time consist of 53 weeks, or include one five-week period, to avoid having its termination too far removed from the close of the calendar year or month.

2. A 12-month period ending with the last day of any month other than December: a usage defined in section 441(e) of the Federal Internal Revenue Code.

fit 1. (statistics) See *curve fitting; trend analysis*.

2. The relation of the period benefited by a *transaction* and the period during which it is incurred and recorded.

fixed asset 1. A *tangible asset* held for the services it yields in the production of goods and services; any item of *plant*.

2. Hence, any *capital asset* or noncurrent *asset*.

3. *pl.* A *balance-sheet* classification denoting *capital assets* other than *intangibles* and *investments*(*6*) in affiliated companies

or other long-term investments. In British usage the term may include *intangibles(2)*.

Included in the usual fixed-asset categories are land (from which the flow of services is seemingly permanent), buildings, building equipment, fixtures, machinery, tools (large and small), furniture, office devices, patterns, drawings, dies, and often containers; generally excluded are goodwill, patents, and other intangibles. The characteristic fixed asset has a limited life (land is the one important exception), and, in organizations where expenses are accounted for, its cost, less estimated salvage at the end of its useful life, is distributed over the periods it benefits by means of provisions for depreciation. See *depreciation; depreciation method.*

Valuation. The traditional basis for fixed assets is cost—cash, or money's worth having objective substantiation in a purchase or exchange with third persons. This basis is adhered to in a great majority of commercial transactions and is firmly established as an accounting principle. Questions occasionally arise that involve the measure of "money's worth," "true economic value," and the definition of "third persons," but the principle is universally supported. In the 1920's, appraisal values were often substituted for cost in the belief that the financial appearance and borrowing power of the business would be improved, but the continuance of depreciation based on cost as an operating expense was general. In the end, the demand for consistency and, in the early 1930's, the general fall of prices and profits led to a reversion of appraisal values to cost. The main objections to the raising of fixed-asset costs to values in excess of cost are generally held to be these:

1. Since a leading objective of a business enterprise is to produce profits for stockholders, accounting procedures are premised on that basic notion. Thus, the income statement ends with the net profit to stockholders that is added to retained earnings, a stockholder's account. Cost to the stockholder is what he (or his predecessor as a stockholder) originally contributed to the enterprise, and an appraisal surplus that is neither contributed nor earned is to him simply one of a series of factors that may or may not lead to larger earnings in the future. He realizes the improvidence of accounting for such earnings before they have been reduced to cash or a promise to pay cash.

2. Borrowing power is rarely influenced by increased value, resulting from appraisals. Established earning ability, its relation to money that has been put into the business, and the prospect of its continuance, together with conservative financial management, are the major factors that attract investors.

3. The appraiser who determines amounts greater than cost labors under two fatal handicaps: he may be under pressure to produce enhanced values in order to justify his employment; and, to support his computations, he must make assumptions that are thoroughly unrealistic and, as a rule, buried in a welter of figures and descriptions. These assumptions, if disclosed in a published financial statement, would prove to be wholly unconvincing. However, an appraiser who verifies cost or develops an estimate of original cost where acquisition data are unavailable is quite another matter. In the installation of a plant ledger, the appraiser can also serve a most useful function. See *cost basis; cost absorption.*

4. The term "true economic cost" as the justification for introducing current values of fixed assets into the accounts is founded on the legend that somehow the word "economic" relates either to the costs that would be encountered by a currently beginning enterprise (*marginal* cost) or, from a quite different point of view, to the cost of expected fixed-asset replacements to an enterprise long

established. A newcomer in a manufacturing field where depreciation is a material element of product cost would hardly be regarded as an "economic man" if he failed to weigh the risk of competing with established producers whose product costs include depreciation based on older, lower-cost fixed assets; and his prospective competitors would most certainly not think of raising their depreciation costs to current or future replacement-cost levels if they expect to compete with the newcomer or even with each other. Much of the notion of "current value" has been inherited from the NRA days of the 1930's where one of NRA's announced (but quickly-to-be-discovered *illegal*) objectives was the elimination of price competition, a dubious prospect for free enterprise, which was cut short by NRA's downfall. Unavoidably higher costs of a marginal producer are neither those to which competive costs automatically gravitate nor those to which previously established producers aspire. Moreover, because of constantly improving technologies, costs of replacements in kind may involve less dollars than former outlays; by the time they become necessary, replacements may differ in both character and price, neither of which may be possible to estimate. An "economic man" would not likely confuse future costs with present costs: traditionally, he faces the future and its risks when he approaches them.

Writedowns may be as objectionable as writeups. In the mid-depression 1930's, reductions in fixed assets became very common; they were inspired by the desire to rid the books of assets or values that had doubtful or no remaining worth. Often the reduction could be attributed not only to price declines but also to plant or equipment disuse brought about by the depression; in some cases, book reductions followed appraisals aimed at carrying forward only conceivably useful costs. In other instances, writedowns of a class of assets were arbitrary and could not be allocated to specific assets, the aim often being to ease depreciation provisions for future years and thus achieve some degree of competitive advantage over business rivals. During the war, many plants were completely amortized as war facilities, despite the likelihood of their continued use after the war, because large profits were available and because the operating hazards in their postwar use loomed large. In many medium-sized enterprises, the lack of stable fixed-asset-valuation policies has occasioned not a little misinterpretation of their financial statements.

To meet the tests of good management and accounting, the board of directors of a manufacturing enterprise has adopted the following writedown policy:

> No loss of cost other than through the application of normal, well-established depreciation rates is to be expressed on the books except under the following conditions: (a) the complete abandonment of a specific plant or other major fixed asset, evidenced by a plan for its disposition and by the consideration and approval of the plan by the board of directors; (b) the abandonment of a specific minor fixed asset, after a review of alternatives by a management committee reporting to the board; (c) the recognition of a partial loss of value of specific fixed assets, arising from construction premiums, excessive prices paid for materials or labor, the excess costs of a type of construction or capacity or other feature—that is, the extra outlay that can be justified for a particular emergency such as the recent war—provided the determination of the amount follows engineering or other objective, fact-finding studies and provided all such actions are reported to the board, leaving to the board the final determination of the writedown of any major asset or of any large number of minor assets.

Any material disturbance in the customary recording, depreciation, or disposal of fixed assets is a financial matter of first rank to be decided on, not merely as the result of factual research but from the point of view of top business policy. The consequent discipline that this imposes on management adds measurably to internal controls, to the confidence with which the outside accountant can accept such decisions, and to the protection of investors from arbitrary and ill-considered decisions.

Where the standard of original cost has not been maintained and a writeup has been put on the books or a writedown has been effected, standard practice requires a full disclosure in financial statements of the basis followed; the dollar amount of the effect of such basis on accrued depreciation and depreciation expense for the fiscal period is footnoted.

Capitalizable Costs. A basic problem is the cost that may be permitted in fixed-asset accounts. Much depends on the definition of a unit of capital-asset expenditure and the permissible costs that may attach to each such unit (a) when it is acquired, and (b) thereafter, during its useful life. Some accounting textbooks have referred to the problem as one that involves the drawing of lines between "capital and revenue" expenditures—that is, the types of expenditure that should be capitalized (carried as an asset) as contrasted with those types that should be charged at once against operations.

For individual assets purchased, the standard of valuation practice is invoice cost plus freight and installation, less all discounts. For assets constructed, the standard is the cost, less discounts, of material and parts, plus direct labor, plus, in some instances, overhead. Perhaps the best practice on overhead is to include only the demonstrable overhead differential—that is, only the increments in the amount of specific overhead activities that can be positively identified with construction. Salaries and other expenses of an engineering staff that has devoted its time exclusively to construction would be an addition to construction costs either as a direct cost or as overhead. But a similar treatment of even a part of the expenses of a maintenance-supervisor's office that, in a brief interruption of its maintenance operations, has designed a new structure or a new machine, is always questionable. The preferred practice is not to include in construction costs any such overhead except where obvious additional costs have been incurred because of the design or construction—and then only in an amount not exceeding such additional costs.

The acquisition of a fixed asset from an affiliated company, or design or construction work performed by one affiliated company for another, raises the question of the inclusion of both overhead and profit as a "cost"; "affiliated company" here means a subsidiary or a company controlled by the same interests, as these terms are commonly employed in commercial practice and by regulatory bodies, including situations where minority stockholders' interests exist in either or both of the two companies involved. In commercial and utility enterprises alike, a leading reason for the formation and continuance of affiliated interests is to gain the economic advantages enjoyed by a single business organization. Deals between affiliates are never actually at arm's length; if they are made so artificially, the very large economic advantage of low cost may be denied to the ultimate user of the asset and the service that the asset supplies. In the case of public utilities, it has often been asserted that the public has the right to demand an accounting on a strict cost basis to the whole economic unit when rates are established. In competitive establishments, the advantage inherent in lower costs should lead to the exclusion of intercompany profit. The rule, based on such premises, may be stated thus: exclude profit on the sale of fixed assets to an affiliate; include overhead only on the basis approved for a single enterprise. The presence of a minority stockholder's interest will ordinarily not affect the general application of the rule; such an interest is rarely on the "selling" side of fixed-asset sales to affiliates, but if it is, and the loss of profit is material in amount, other financial devices are available whereby the minority stockholders may be compensated.

In practice, the rule is frequently not observed. The notion of the economic unit is obscured by the problems of separate managements and the often-recognized need for a strong semblance of competition and arm's-length relationships between them. In any event, it is usually held that in the published financial statements of single affiliates or the economic unit, the basis of valuation must be clearly stated. Where any element of intercompany profit remains in the gross amount of the fixed assets, its nature and amount are disclosed.

The amount of any lump-sum purchase of fixed assets that has not been separated into its elements may lead to difficulties of interpretation. Not only does the item often contain an intangible that should be excluded from the fixed-asset category, but the provision for and accumulation of depreciation based on the gross amount may be most inaccurate.

Reference to additions and improvements raises the question of fixed-asset "units." A "unit" refers to a carefully defined size or type of fixed asset or expenditure relating to a fixed asset. Below the dollar cost of the unit, no adjustment of a fixed-asset account occurs; above it, an adjustment is required. There may be units of capitalization, replacement, retirement, and accounting. A purchased building or a machine is a unit of capitalization; that is, either one is universally recognized as a fixed asset. A machine may be a unit for accounting purposes, or machinery collectively may be the unit when there is no plant ledger. A building may be an accounting unit and its cost may be carried in the books without diminution until it is torn down or sold, or the cost of the building may be broken down into several replacement and depreciation units, such as foundation, wall, and roof. Depreciation at varying rates may be provided for these elements, or a composite rate may be applied to the building's total cost for depreciation-accounting purposes. The cost of replacing a roof would be an expense if the retirement unit is the building, or it would be an addition to the fixed asset provided the roof is a retirement unit. In the latter case, the cost of the old roof would be a charge against the reserve-for-roof depreciation, or against the composite reserve for the building as a whole.

The adoption of minimum-dollar units eliminates minor charges to fixed assets; charging small amounts to expense avoids "double handling" (i.e., capitalization and depreciation). Such a unit is commonly set for new assets as well as for additions, replacements, alterations, and improvements. Every hand tool and small machine may be capitalized, or only those above a certain dollar cost. In practice, these limitations vary widely—perhaps $10 in a small enterprise, and as much as $500 or $1,000 in larger concerns. Whatever the practice adopted, it should be followed consistently.

It is difficult in any business to frame rules that will cover precisely all future work that may be performed on existing fixed assets. The general test for an addition or betterment to a fixed asset is that it must increase dimensions (e.g., a new wing on an old building) or productivity, or lower future operating costs (e.g., a fitting that will speed up the normal productivity of an old machine or lengthen its useful life). Occasionally, certain types of expenditure, including exceptional maintenance costs such as overhauls, are charged against the reserve for depreciation, but the better practice today is to charge against depreciation reserves only the cost of units replaced or retired, and to clear costs affecting fixed assets through asset and expense accounts.

Because of these variations in the

disposition of both old and new costs and the need for consistency from year to year, the establishment and maintenance of a well-defined capitalization-and-retirement policy accompanied by unit definitions is a most desirable addition to internal controls.

Internal Controls. Internal controls over fixed assets are inadequate in many business enterprises. One reason is that the accounting profession has not interested itself sufficiently in the subject, accounting literature dealing with fixed-asset controls being meager and incomplete. Another reason is that business management has likewise taken little interest; not infrequently, there is a general feeling that fixed assets, unlike current assets, cannot easily disappear, and that depreciation provisions and accumulations are at best good guesses which are not made more accurate by elaborate records. The external auditor is often prevented from making an adequate examination by reason of the lack of supporting records and competent studies by the management of depreciation-expense-and-reserve requirements.

The several elements of fixed-asset internal controls are generally held to be the following:

1. *Plant ledger.* A plant ledger is of value to any enterprise, regardless of size. It may be difficult to install after years have passed by without one, but the trouble experienced in getting it started and the small expense of maintaining it thereafter are repaid many times in more accurate costs, wiser planning, and improved internal controls. The most practicable plant-ledger standard involves the use for each accounting unit of a card or sheet on which appear such data as location, identification, date of purchase, invoice and other costs, reports of condition, and, after retirement, the cause thereof and the amount realized from sale or scrap. When, for example, this information is written or punched on cards, the cards may serve as a detail ledger; after assets have been disposed of, the cards become the basis of retirement studies invaluable in the setting of depreciation rates. See *plant ledger*.

2. *Unit definitions.* When units have been carefully defined, a more accurate and consistent treatment of fixed-asset charges is possible. See *fixed-asset unit*. Following are sample definitions that may be applied to average situations:

(a) Capitalization unit: an expenditure in excess of, say, $100 for a single fixed asset or for an addition thereto that clearly has the effect of increasing physical dimensions or productivity, lengthening future life, or lowering future costs. In doubtful situations, the amount of an expenditure, if it is to be capitalized, must be well under either (i) the capitalized value of the resultant added service to be yielded, or (ii) future costs saved.

(b) Accounting, retirement, or replacement unit: a capitalization unit or the sum of two or more such units when they constitute a single physical item; or any replaceable part of a capitalization unit where the cost of the part exceeds, say, $100. An accounting unit usually coincides with a retirement or replacement unit, but it may also consist of several retirement units when it is a single structure; in that event, it should be supported by a cost report from which the cost of each such retirement unit may be readily obtained.

(c) Depreciation unit: buildings, factory machinery, small tools, patterns and dies, furniture and fixtures, automotive equipment.

In many cases, it may be desirable to vary the definitions for each class of assets, particularly with respect to the test for capitalization.

3. *Periodic reviews.* An annual or other periodic checkup of fixed assets is a useful means of determining depreciation-reserve adequacy. The review may serve also to verify the existence and condition of each asset; comments on condition and estimates of remaining

useful life may thus be compiled. A plan for the periodic verification of the existence and condition of each class of fixed assets is an essential element of every well-conceived plan of internal control.

4. *Acquisition controls.* In organizations whose financial operations are controlled through budgets, additions to fixed assets are usually planned far in advance of their purchase. These may take such forms as lump-sum provisions for various departments, established at the beginning of each year, or detailed breakdowns with a description of each asset to be purchased. Regardless of the breakdown or even of the existence of a budget, it is common practice to have major specific fixed-asset purchases (e.g., above $1,000) authorized by some management group, such as an equipment committee, which reports to the board of directors or the chief executive officer. Whatever the basic authority, the elements of control are: a review of the need for new equipment; the choice of a contractor or manufacturer by calling for bids or otherwise; a decision as to price, installation, other costs, and the method of financing; an authorization for the disposal, physically and in accounts, of superseded equipment, together with the costs, past and prospective, that will be involved; and a review of the construction or purchase, including costs, after its completion. Decisions to contract or purchase are usually accompanied by some form of authorization, such as a work order, and in the event of larger acquisitions or constructions, a cost report is desirable as an aid to the equipment committee's review of the project; such a report should bring out the division of costs among the accounting units to be recognized, with reasons for variations of detail or totals from original estimates. Dispositions of major fixed assets not accompanied by new acquisitions are often considered by the same or a similar group: its records should reflect such details as reasons for the removal, the consideration of alternative methods of disposal, the selection of the highest bidder, the book cost and accumulated depreciation, and the treatment of remaining balances.

5. *Tools and dies; patterns and drawings.* Tools, dies, patterns, and drawings in nearly every manufacturing establishment are numerous and almost always offer accounting difficulties. They may be kept on an "inventory" basis, with periodic physical counts at cost, or, where necessary, at estimated cost, to which the books are adjusted. Accrued depreciation may be estimated at the time the physical inventory is taken, and the book amount of accumulated depreciation modified accordingly. Or, a lapsing schedule may be set up on the basis of a composite average life of, say, five years, with annual reductions of the asset account for items depreciated throughout that period. A third variety of accounting may be to fix the asset account at a "basic" figure and to charge all additions thereafter to expense. Only in rare cases is this class of asset accounted for by perpetual-inventory methods. Occasionally, the auditor finds a resemblance to such methods in subaccounts, corresponding to models, that are eliminated when the models become obsolete. The most satisfactory form of internal control is a periodic inventory-and-depreciation study, and, between such studies, the capitalization of items exceeding in amount an established sum and the accumulation of depreciation based, at least in part, on past experience. The book figure of cost-less-depreciation for a period of years should be reasonably related to model life, changes in production, and volume of product manufactured; and the management should follow a consistent practice in the application of accounting controls.

6. *Maintenance and repairs.* The relation of maintenance and repairs to fixed assets and to internal controls is always of importance; the details of accounts

reflecting their costs should be consistent with the policy of capitalizing items which meet the tests of adding productivity, lessening cost, or extending useful life. The details of the account should also compare with similar types of expense in previous years. Fluctuations as between years may be material, for the account is a variable with wide limits, and it may reflect in one year fixed assets worked to capacity, and in another, idle time or a shutdown that has made major overhauls possible. The management of every enterprise knows the meaning of *deferred maintenance*—the putting off of repairs until a chance opportunity arises.

The same care that surrounds equipment purchases should be exercised over maintenance-and-repair operations. The equipment committee frequently supervises them and issues blanket work orders for ordinary repairs and special work orders for extraordinary or emergency repairs. In some instances a separate department is established, the head of which is a maintenance engineer who reports to the top executive of the organization; in others, the responsibility resides in the plant superintendent, occasionally with no upper limit on expenditures. Obviously, these are widely varying practices. But present in all cases should be an agreed-upon delegation of maintenance-and-repair authority to some individual or organizational unit: work orders or their equivalent; preliminary estimates of costs, followed by studies of variations with actual costs; and an active interest, within the management, in maintaining low-cost levels already established or seeking cost levels lower than the present ones.

Maintenance reserves that have as their purpose the equalization of maintenance-and-repair expense as between years are sometimes encountered. Combined *depreciation-and-maintenance reserves* also exist. They are subject to the same objection as other equalization reserves; where such a reserve is found, its amount is almost invariably an arbitrary figure that is not the endproduct of studies of maintenance deferred. A blast-furnace relining reserve, often present in the accounts of steel producers, is usually interpreted as an accumulation of depreciation rather than a maintenance reserve, and is preferably so treated on the balance sheet.

fixed-asset schedule A summary, by classes, of fixed assets, such as that sometimes appearing in annual reports to

M COMPANY

Statement of Changes in Fixed-Asset Costs & Accumulations of Depreciation
Year ended December 31, 19-2 (thousands of dollars)

Assets	*Jan 1 19-2*	*Retirements*	*Additions*	*Dec 31 19-2*
Land	15 2	–	2 6	17 8
Buildings	396 1	32 6	53 8	417 3
Machinery	584 5	87 0	116 2	613 7
Office equipment	78 3	3 9	9 4	83 8
Totals	1 074 1	123 5	182 0	1 132 6

Accumulated depreciation	*Jan 1 19-2*	*Retirements*	*Disposal income*	*Year's expense*	*Dec 31 19-2*
Buildings	134 5	32 6	3 8	8 2	113 9
Machinery	264 1	87 0	25 1	47 9	250 1
Office equipment	22 0	3 9	0 4	8 1	26 6
Totals	420 6	123 5	29 3	64 2	390 6

Method of depreciation: composite basis

stockholders. Following is such a schedule showing balances at the beginning of the reporting period, additions, retirements, and balances at the end of the period. A corresponding schedule of changes (retirements, recoveries, and added provisions) in related *accumulations* of (*reserves* for) depreciation, also shown, supplies further details of general interest to both stockholders and investment analysts.

These schedules comply with the demand for more information on fixed assets and accumulated depreciation called for in APBO 12 (1967).

fixed-asset unit An item or group of items recognized in the accounting processes governing the fixed assets of an individual enterprise. Five types of units are commonly found, not always clearly defined in particular instances; these types and their usual specifications are:

1. The *capitalization unit:* the character of new items that may be added to fixed assets, the minimum expenditure that may be recognized, and the tests to be applied to determine the propriety of the amount capitalized.

2. The *accounting unit:* (a) the control accounts to be carried in the general ledger, and (b) the detail accounts to be carried in plant ledgers.

3. The *retirement unit:* the character and minimum amount of what are to be regarded as items removable from the accounts when taken out of service.

4. The *replacement unit:* the character and minimum amount of what are to be regarded as capitalizable items taking the place of items retired—usually the same as a retirement unit.

5. The *depreciation unit:* the basis—item or group of items—to which periodic depreciation rates are to be applied. See *fixed asset.*

To these is sometimes added the *accountability unit:* the unit described to —and made the basis of observation and reporting by—a person charged with *property accountability;* this unit is the same as (1), (2b), (3), or (4).

fixed budget A budget providing firm allowances for individual activities or allowances that do not vary with the volume of production or other overall measure of work done. See *budget.*

fixed capital The investment in *capital assets.*

fixed charges Unavoidable overhead, particularly interest costs, depreciation, amortization of discount on funded debt and of intangibles, and rent of leased property. Occasionally the term is extended to elements of factory overhead remaining more or less constant under varying rates of production; see *fixed cost.*

fixed cost (or **expense**) An operating expense, or operating expense as a class, that does not vary with business volume. Examples: interest on bonds; rent; property tax; depreciation (sometimes in part); minimal amounts of selling, and general overhead. A cost designated as fixed is often a function of capacity, and thus, although fixed with respect to volume, varies with the size of the plant. Or, one department of a plant may bear a monthly service charge originating in another department; to the former, the charge is looked upon as a fixed cost beyond its immediate control; to the latter, the charge may in a large measure derive from variable costs over which it has primary control. Fixed costs are not fixed in the sense that they do not fluctuate or vary; they vary, but from causes independent of volume. Although usually defined with respect to volume, the term *fixed cost* may also be applied when some other factor is the independent variable, and *cost* the dependent variable. See *semivariable cost; variable cost; overhead; period cost; direct cost.*

fixed liability = *long-term liability.*

fixed resale price The minimum price that a manufacturer or fabricator requires distributors and retailers under contract with him to charge on sales of goods purchased from him. "Fair-trade" laws, some declared unconstitutional but others still effective in several states, legalize this type of price-fixing by manufacturers of their branded products, but the courts have refused to enforce such laws with respect to resellers not under contract. Many manufacturers now provide a "suggested" retail price, the nonobservance of which may be subject to sanctions imposed by the manufacturer or supplier. See *price; price maintenance.*

fixed trust An organization for the joint investment of funds; it is created by a trust indenture between an incorporated manager, a trustee, and the investors whereby a block of specified units of investments is deposited with the trustee against which one or more certificates of interest are sold to the investor at a price equal to his proportionate interest in the current market value of the block plus a loading percentage to cover the expenses and profit of the manager.

fixture Anything attached to a building which cannot be removed without damage to the real estate, usually having utility only in that location (an immovable fixture), or which by custom or under the terms of a lease or other instrument can be detached (a movable fixture). A fixture is classified as a *fixed asset.*

flash report A report covering the elements of financial condition or all or a portion of the operations of an accounting period, prepared before all transactions are known or recorded, or before the books have been closed; it is often followed at a later date by a more formal, complete, and possibly more accurate report. Its purpose is to supply information needed by management for immediate review and decision. The characteristics of and standards for such reports vary greatly, being dependent on the manner in which management conducts its affairs.

flat Without the addition of interest: said of the price of a bond in default, a non-interest-bearing loan, or a bond quoted or sold at a price that does not include accrued interest.

flexible budget 1. A *budget* containing alternative provisions based on varying rates of production or other measures of activity.
2. A budget subject to change as operations proceed. See *budget; overhead.*

flexible standard A *standard cost* determined for a particular class of expenditure, expressed as a formula that provides a stated number of dollars for a fixed or minimum allowance for such an expenditure plus a rate per unit of volume for the variable portion of the expenditure.

float Uncollected deposits that have been credited conditionally by a bank to its customers' accounts. Checks may not be drawn against such deposits until the paper constituting the deposits has cleared; three days or less are normally required for domestic paper. Where the bank's experience with a customer or with certain types of paper has been satisfactory, no such restriction may be imposed.

floating asset = *current asset.*

floating capital That portion of the capital of an enterprise not invested in fixed or other capital assets, but in current and working assets; *working capital.*

floating debt Current or short-term obligations; *current liabilities.*

floating liability = *current liability; floating debt.*

flow chart A graphic presentation of operational sequences in the handling of materials or documents, or in the progressive accumulation of costs.

flow statement A schedule depicting a projection of transaction transfers between accounts: a generic term. See *cost-flow statement; cash-flow statement; funds-flow statement; statement of sources and applications of funds; split-ledger account.* The trial balance pictured on pages 396–397 provides the data for the analyses accompanying each of the four types of statements referenced above. A simple instance of cost flow is provided by following the cost transfers reflected in accounts 31, 32, 16, 17, 62; of cash flow, in accounts 3, 16, 41, 31, 32, 16, 17, 62, 60, 10, 9, 2. See *input–output statement.*

FOB (followed by a named location) Free On Board: a symbol indicating that the invoice cost to a purchaser includes the cost of delivery, at seller's risk, at an agreed point, beyond which all transportation and delivery costs and risks must be borne by the purchaser. On domestic shipments, the chances of misunderstanding between buyer and seller are not great: FOB Chicago means delivery by the seller to a freight terminal in that city; freight, handling, or trucking charges thereafter must be paid by the buyer, the seller usually providing a bill of lading or other receipt from the shipping agency. Foreign shipments often give rise to misunderstandings because of unfamiliarity of the foreign purchaser with American commercial practices; in such cases, the original contract between buyer and seller should be specific as to trucking charges, port and customs fees, and loading costs, as well as to the arrangement for special packaging, shipping directions, and other matters peculiar to international trade.

FOB price The price, when used without further qualification, charged at a designated location—i.e., farm, factory, wellhead, mine mouth, mill, or warehouse—where the goods were produced, extracted, fabricated, or stored. Although generally restricted to the price charged at the point of shipment, the term may be qualified by specific reference to intermediate points—e.g., FOB port, or even destination—thus making it the equivalent of *delivered* price. Under *FOB pricing,* the seller retains title and the risks of ownership until delivery is made at the FOB point, as evidenced by a carrier bill of lading or other receipt releasing him of possession; at that point the purchaser takes title and bears the risks of ownership.

FOB pricing The practice of selling for delivery at the seller's plant, buyers paying the freight from plant to destination. See *FOB.* The advantage of this practice over delivered pricing is that a uniform *millnet* or *netback price* can be achieved, thus avoiding pricing complications under fair-trade and antitrust acts. It is an economically feasible method during a sellers' market, when the seller is not required to meet price competition in markets located nearer competitors' mills. Under these market conditions, buyers are willing to incur higher delivered costs from more distant mills in order to get necessary supplies. Its disadvantages are apparent in a buyers' market rather than in periods of short supply, where the seller, wishing to compete for distant customers located nearer other mills, must reduce his quoted FOB price because, not supplying the freight, a part of the freight cannot be absorbed. This results in varying FOB prices and, thus, price discrimination, which is more clearly evident than varying netbacks or millnet prices resulting from freight absorption.

folio reference A page number or voucher or other number in a book or document of original or final entry, which refers to the disposition or source of an entry or posting; abbreviated, *F.* For illustration, see "*F*" column under *account.*

force account A term employed by engineers to denote that a construction project is undertaken by the owner acting as his own contractor; thus, a city may extend its water system by force account, meaning that its own engineers design the work and hire and supervise the labor force required for construction and installation.

forced-sale value The price obtainable from an immediate sale, where the seller is under either legal or voluntary compulsion to sell; *liquidation value.*

foreign corporation In state corporation laws, a "foreign" corporation means one created under the laws of another state or country. In the Federal income-tax law, the term refers to a corporation established under the laws of another country. See *corporation; domestic corporation*.

foreign exchange 1. The method by which settlement is made for international transactions in lieu of an actual shipment of gold. See *exchange*.
2. A generic term applied to bills of exchange and to monetary and credit instruments, such as gold, silver, banker's drafts, letters of credit, and traveler's checks, used in payment of foreign debts, and expressed in the foreign currency.

foreign-trade financing Any of the methods available for the settlement of transactions between persons in different countries. Most of the difficulties of settlement arise out of the use of unlike currencies, necessitating a balancing off against transactions flowing in the opposite direction, barters between individuals, settlements in gold, the piling up of international debt, or international subsidies, the latter being the method followed by the United States in the operation of the Marshall Plan, beginning in 1948. Many international sales are on an open-credit or consignment basis at the time of shipment; or the shipper may demand settlement when the goods are delivered to the port of exit: an arrangement facilitated through a letter of credit or other device instituted by the domestic or foreign bank serving the exporter or importer. Certain countries maintain dollar deposits in U. S. banks arising from investment earnings in the U. S. of their nationals (who receive the local currency of their country rather than dollars) and other sources; from these deposits the foreign country's more urgent dollar purchases may be paid. See *bank acceptance; letter of credit*.

forgery Any false writing with intent to defraud.

formal Referring to or derived from the pattern, structure, or rules of organization, rather than from the content of discourse, experience, or social processes.

forward accounting The areas of interest in the preparation of *standard costs*, *budgeted* costs and revenues, *estimates of cash requirements*, *breakeven charts*, and *projected financial statements*—and the various studies required for their estimation; also the *internal controls* regulating and safeguarding future operations. Although often based on *historical costs*, forward costs are expected to reflect realistic situations to be encountered and thus modifications of existing patterns of operation and costs. The techniques of forward accounting differ from those accompanying historical accounting in that only transaction groups are dealt with, no bookkeeping records are kept, and the major items reflect what are essentially management decisions and projections of directives.

forward financial statement An estimate of condition (*balance sheet*) or operating results (*income statement*): an endproduct in the preparation of a *budget* for an ensuing period (e.g., a year). See *cash-flow statement*.

founders' shares A portion of a corporation's capital stock with special privileges or stipulations, issued to its founders or promoters for services rendered. Founders' shares (also called "managers' shares" and "deferred shares") are issued commonly in Great Britain, rarely in the United States. Their combined voting power is usually equal to the voting power of the common stock, and they generally have a special claim on earnings, either before or after the payment of dividends to other stockholders. Their participation in the assets of the corporation in the event of dissolution is usually limited to the remaining assets after other stockholders have received the amounts to which they are entitled according to the provisions of the respective issues.

frame (statistics) A system of records or other assembled collections of data from which samplings are to be taken.

Ideally, the identification of the frame should define the scope of the survey as well as other primary categories of the material to be covered; the date, source, and definitions underlying the frame are of central importance. In actual survey design and execution, frames that are initially indicated frequently require amplification and adjustment, e.g., in *multistage sampling*.

franchise 1. A privilege, granted by governmental authority, sanctioning a monopoly or permitting the use of public property, usually subject to regulation.

2. The privilege, often exclusive, conferred on a dealer by a manufacturer, to sell the manufacturer's products within a specified territory.

3. A certificate of incorporation.

4. (insurance) The percentage or portion of a risk establishing the top limit of loss to be borne by the insured; if the loss is greater, the entire amount is borne by the insurer. Franchise insurance contrasts with "deductible" insurance, where a specified portion of the loss must be borne by the insured, regardless of the amount of loss. See *coinsurance clause*.

fraud The successful practice of deception or artifice with the intention of cheating or injuring another. Ordinarily fraud involves willful misrepresentation, the deliberate concealment of a material fact for the purpose of inducing another person to do or to refrain from doing something to his detriment, or the failure to disclose a material fact; thus a person may be fraudulently misled into giving up a claim to property, waiving legal rights, or entering into a disadvantageous contract. See *negligence*.

free currency Money that may be exchanged for the money of another country without restriction. See *blocked currency*.

free price The price of a commodity unit sold or purchased under conditions in which each participant is relatively free to effect necessary economic adjustments, including price changes, in response to its own individual assessment of the demand-and-supply relation which confronts it, while attempting to obtain maximum profits. Such price may be a free competitive price or a free (noncollusive) oligopoly price, depending upon the structure of the industry in which the commodity is being bought or sold. See *price*.

free surplus 1. That portion of *earned surplus* (*retained earnings*) available for common-stock dividends—i.e., after deducting any amounts legally restricted by reason of such items as preferred-stock dividends in arrears, the repurchase price of treasury stock, or loan agreements calling for a minimum cash balance or a minimum asset-liability ratio.

2. That portion of earned surplus not in excess of cash assets over and above *working-capital* or other immediate requirements.

freight 1. A charge by a carrier for the transportation of goods.

2. Physical cargo.

freight absorption The practice of a seller of not charging the customer with freight out.

freight inward Freight paid on incoming shipments, treated as an element of cost of goods or materials received, or refunded by the seller or deducted on his invoice, according to custom or the terms of sale.

freight outward Freight paid or allowed by the seller on outgoing shipments to customers. In the accounts it may appear as a selling expense or, if included in the selling price, as a deduction from sales.

frequency Relative or absolute number of occurrences of a class of events.

frequency chart A *bar chart* of a *frequency distribution*.

frequency curve A smooth curve formed by *extrapolation* and *interpolation* of values in a frequency chart, and intended to portray an ideal or underlying statistical distribution.

frequency distribution A statistical series consisting of a number of quantities arranged in the order of their class and number, or frequency of occurrence, within each class. See *statistical distribution.*

frequency polygon A geometric picture of a *frequency distribution* formed by connecting the midpoints of the rectangles in a *frequency chart.*

fringe benefit A pension provision, retirement allowance, insurance premium, or other cost representing a present or future return to an employee, which is neither deducted on a payroll nor paid for by the employee. It may be distributed with other labor costs or maintained as a separate item on an operating statement.

full-faith-and-credit debt (municipal accounting) Debt of a municipality or municipal enterprise the repayment of which is a direct obligation of the municipality; = *general-obligation bond.* See *revenue bond.*

full liability A liability not shared with others.

full-paid capital stock A share or shares of capital stock on which the whole amount of the par or stated value or the subscription price has been paid. Such stock is nonassessable unless, by law, double or other special liability attaches to it.

function 1. Relative utility or usefulness.

2. The general end or purpose sought to be accomplished by a department or organizational unit. Examples: administration; selling; instruction; research; operation of a power plant; tax collection.

3. A group of related *activities.*

4. A magnitude related to another and varying with it; a relation between variables. Thus, depreciation is a function of plant capacity, since the greater the capacity, the larger the period provision for depreciation will have to be. But depreciation is also said to be a *fixed cost* and not a function of volume, since a change in the rate of production may take place without any modification in the depreciation cost. Again, interest cost is a function of borrowed money outstanding and is not a function of business volume, since the amount of interest expense is not influenced by the obligor's sales of merchandise.

5. (governmental accounting) Any responsibility charged to an agency by legislative or administrative authority; an authorized activity or group of activities having related purposes. In the governmental field, the classification of expenditures by functions and activities has made possible the use of expenditure data in the preparation of performance budgets in which the main emphasis is on activities rather than organizational units and objects. Furthermore, because functions and activities may disregard organizational lines, these classifications have made possible the compilation of national financial statistics on a uniform basis. The National Committee on Governmental Accounting has developed a functional classification of expenditures for municipalities and the State and Local Governments Division of the U. S. Bureau of the Census has put the classification (with some modifications) into nationwide use by compiling and publishing financial statistics of state and local governments based on the classification. See *activity.*

Following is a list of the functional classification of expenditures recommended by the National Committee on Governmental Accounting for municipalities, together with the activities pertaining to the function of "general government":

- Legislative—
  - Municipal council or commission
  - Legislative committees and special bodies
  - Ordinances and proceedings
  - Clerk of council
- Executive—
  - Mayor
  - Manager
  - Boards and commissions

Judicial—
  Criminal courts
  Grand jury
  Public defender
  Civil courts
  Domestic relations courts
  Law library
  Medical and social service
Elections—
  Supervision
  Registration
  Primary elections
  General elections
  Special elections
Finance—
  Supervision
  Accounting and internal auditing
  Independent accounting and auditing
  Budgeting
  Assessment and levy of taxes
  Collection, custody, and disbursement of funds
  Licensing
  Purchasing and custody of supplies
  Debt administration
  Administration of special funds and investments
Law—
  Counsel and legal advice
  Criminal prosecution
  Special civil counsel
  Special criminal prosecution
Recording and reporting—
  Municipal clerk
  Recording deeds and mortgages
  General public reports
Administrative offices and boards
Planning and zoning—
  Planning
  Zoning
Personnel administration—
  Personnel selection and supervision
  Pension administration
Research and investigation—
  Research bureaus and reference libraries
  Special research projects
  Public officers' associations
General government buildings—
  Supervision
  Office buildings
  Rental of offices and buildings
Community promotion—
  Advertising
  Expositions
  Entertainment of visitors
Public safety
Highways
Sanitation and waste removal
Conservation of health
Hospitals
Charities
Correction
Schools
Libraries
Recreation
Public-service enterprises

In addition, the National Committee has recommended that interest on bonds, the redemption of serial bonds, and contributions to sinking funds, because they represent fixed charges and because some of them cannot be readily allocated among the foregoing functions, should each be set up in a separate group in an expenditure statement. The National Committee also provides for showing any other expenditures which cannot be allocated among the foregoing functions in a "miscellaneous" group. Examples of these expenditures may be found in judgments rendered by a court against the municipality, and state and other taxes levied on the municipality by another government.

Because the Federal government carries on many activities not performed by municipalities, the functional expenditure classification appearing in its budget is somewhat different, as may be observed from the following list of functions; by way of example, the four-activity subdivision of the "labor" function is shown:

Military services
International security and foreign relations
Finance, commerce, and industry
Labor:
  Employment service and unemployment compensation administration
  Labor training and standards
  Mediation and regulation of labor relations
  Labor information, statistics, and general administration
Transportation and communication
Natural resources
Agriculture and agricultural resources
Housing and community development
Education and general research
Social security, welfare, and health
Veterans' benefits and services
General government
Interest

6. (mathematics) A statement of the form of the relation to be assumed by two or more *variables* over a defined

range of values; generally indicated symbolically by the letters f, F, ϕ, followed by parentheses in which the variables are placed; as, $f(x, y)$; $F(x,y,z)$; $\phi(x, y, z)$. Standard forms for expressing functional relations between two variables are: $f(x, y) = 0$ and $y = F(x)$. The former is referred to as the *implicit* and the latter as the *explicit* form. No distinction is drawn, in the first case, between x and y as *dependent* or *independent variables;* the value of either variable may be chosen within the range for which the function is defined, and values of the other variable are then determined by equating the result to zero. In the second case, y is explicitly stated in terms of x as the independent variable. Thus, the expression $f(x, y) = ax + by = 0$ defines implicitly a straight-line (or linear) relation between x and y, while $y = F(x) = a' + b'x$ states an explicit relation in which y is the *dependent variable* linearly related to the *independent variable* x through the *constants* a' and b'. Functional relations are not restricted to (a) the linear forms used for illustration, or (b) only two variables. The notion of function includes any number of variables, finite or infinite. Functional *symbolization* is compact and simple and of wide generality; as such, it has proved of great importance in extending the fields of mathematical and related inquiries, such as physics, statistics, and economics. See *production function; statistical distribution; least squares; variable.*

functional *adj.* Adapted to and capable of performance.

n. A *function* or service performed by one *organizational unit* for another.

functional accounting Accounting by *functions* and *activities;* = *activity accounting.*

functional statement A statement of costs subdivided by *functions*(*5*) or subfunctions.

fund *n.* 1. An asset or group of assets within any organization, separated physically or in the accounts or both from other assets and limited to specific uses. Examples: a *petty-cash* or *working fund;* a replacement-and-renewal fund; an accident fund; a contingent fund; a pension fund.

2. Cash, securities, or other assets placed in the hands of a trustee, principal or income or both being expended in accordance with the terms of a formal agreement. Examples: a trust fund created by a will; an endowment fund; a sinking fund.

3. (government accounting) A self-balancing group of accounts—asset, liability, revenue, and expense—relating to specified sources and uses of capital and revenue. See *fund accounting.*

4. *pl.* Current assets less current liabilities (on an *accrual basis*): *working capital;* a term used in flow statements.

5. *pl.* = *cash.*

v.t. 1. To convert currently maturing liabilities into a long-term loan.

2. To provide for the ultimate payment of a liability by the systematic accumulation of cash or other assets in a separate account or trust.

Fund accounting. In governmental and institutional accounting, a fund is a sum of money and often other assets constituting a separate *accounting entity*, created and maintained for a particular purpose and having transactions subject to legal or administrative restrictions. Its double-entry accounts are self-balancing, and from them a balance sheet and operating statement may be prepared. A separate budget is provided for each fund.

Funds common to municipal accounting are usually required by law. Statutes may provide that the use of each fund be limited to specified purposes. Or the law may not name the individual funds, but the limitations it attaches to the application of revenues from certain sources may necessitate the creation of one or more funds. Thus, if the law provides that a tax is to be levied for park purposes, the establishment of a park fund provides a control over the proceeds from the levy. Similarly, if the law authorizes the issuance of bonds, a bond fund is established so that the proceeds of their sale may be limited to indicated purposes.

Funds may also be established where not required by law. For example, from management's point of view it may be both desirable and necessary to account for utility transactions in a separate fund. Again, assets held by the municipality in the capacity of trustee or agent for others are controlled through one or more special funds.

The creation of multiple funds may lead to inflexibility in operating authority. Every fund should serve some managerial need. The National Committee on Governmental Accounting advocates that a municipality employ as a maximum the following ten funds:

General fund
Special-revenue fund
Bond fund
Sinking fund
Special-assessment fund
Trust-and-agency funds
Working-capital fund
Utility fund
General fixed-assets fund
General bonded-debt fund

The *general fund* accounts for the revenues and activities not required by law or administrative decision to be accounted for in a special fund. Ordinarily, the general fund has a great variety of revenues and is used to finance many more activities than any other fund.

Purchases of fixed assets which are made through the general fund are transferred to the general fixed-assets fund, described below, where they are regarded as a contribution from the general fund; the assets of the general fund are confined to those ultimately to be converted into cash or otherwise available to support current operations. Again, unmatured municipal bonds do not appear in the general fund until their maturity approaches and even then only if they are to be repurchased out of general funds; until then they remain as liabilities of the bond fund.

A *special-revenue fund* is created for taxes and other revenues levied or set aside for specified purposes. For example, if a separate tax is authorized for schools, a special-revenue fund is set up to account for its disposition. The accounting principles, procedures, and financial statements of a special-revenue fund resemble those of the general fund.

A *bond fund* has as its purpose the receipt and disposal of the proceeds from the sale of funded debt. It is not concerned with their retirement, which is transacted through the general fund, a special-revenue fund, or a sinking fund, depending on the required method of retirement. Bonded debt is, therefore, not shown in the bond-fund balance sheet; instead, it is set up in the general bonded-debt fund described below. If bonds are issued for the purpose of financing the construction or purchase of fixed assets, the resulting assets appear in the general fixed-assets fund.

A *sinking fund* may be created for the retirement of bonds all or a major portion of which mature at one time; it is created and added to by periodic transfers, usually from the general fund, and is operated in a manner similar to that established to retire the bonds of a commercial enterprise. Maturing serial bonds to be paid for out of the general tax levy appear as a liability of the general fund at the time the tax is accounted for.

Special-assessment funds are employed in the financing of permanent improvements (e.g., the construction of streets, sidewalks, sewers) or services (e.g., street oiling) where they are to be paid for wholly or in part from levies against benefited properties. Although assessments are the main source of revenue, the cost is often shared with the general fund. Property owners may be given the privilege of paying assessments in installments, the project then being financed in the first instance through a bond issue or bank loan. Interest is paid and the obligation is retired as the installments mature and are collected. Interest on unpaid installments is usually applied to pay interest on the bonds.

Where special-assessment bonds are issued, the special-assessment fund may account for the proceeds; it then serves as a bond fund because it is used to account for the proceeds received from the sale of the special-assessment bonds. It is a special-revenue fund because it receives interest on assessments and uses it to pay bond interest. It acts also as a special-revenue fund in collecting special assessments and using them to retire bonds. The fund thus contains three self-balancing groups of accounts relating, respectively, to construction, bond retirement, and interest payments.

Two additional points should be noted. No fixed assets are shown; instead, the improvements are carried in the general fixed-assets-fund balance sheet. Again, bonds are shown as a liability of the fund because they are ultimately to be retired from collections of special assessments.

Trust-and-agency funds account for those transactions in the handling of which the municipality acts as agent or trustee for others.

One or more *working-capital funds* may be instituted to finance and account for services rendered by one activity for a number of others, such as an auto-repair shop; a central garage; an asphalt plant; a central-stores department. These activities are distinguished from regular services rendered by the municipality to the public, whether or not for compensation, such as police, fire, and health protection and the procurement and sale of electric light and water, the latter being accounted for in separate utility funds.

Capital for and additions to a working-capital fund may be provided by the funds to be served or by an appropriation from the general fund. It is self-supporting, and for that reason it is necessary to determine whether its operations have resulted in a profit or a loss. Its accounting includes provisions for depreciation. The fixed assets of a working-capital fund are usually housed in the working-capital fund itself.

The fund operates as follows: Capital contributions are invested in necessary equipment or are retained in liquid form to finance operations pending periodic service billings to departments in amounts sufficient to recover all costs. Billed departments remit the amount called for to the working-capital fund, thus providing a capital turnover and repeated operations.

A *utility fund* accounts for services rendered by the municipality to the public for compensation; examples are the production or purchase and distribution of electric power, water, and gas, and the furnishing of transportation. Municipally operated enterprises are accounted for in the same manner as privately operated utilities: their assets are both current and fixed and their liabilities consist of current debt and both matured and unmatured bonds; their income expenses pertain to the operation of the enterprise. Depreciation of fixed assets appears among the expenses.

The *general fixed-assets fund* accounts for all of the municipality's fixed assets except those carried in the working-capital and utility funds. They are recorded either at the time the expenditure is incurred or at the end of a fiscal year, by transfer from other funds.

Fixed assets financed from bond funds or special-assessment funds are frequently not reflected in the general fixed-assets fund until the project is completed.

A *general bonded-debt fund* embraces unmatured general bonds payable from taxes yet to be levied, as distinguished from special-assessment and utility bonds, which are payable from special assessments already levied, or from utility revenues. The liability continues to appear in this fund until the bonds mature. At maturity, the bonds are taken out of this fund and set up as a liability of the general fund, a special-revenue fund, or a sinking fund, depending on when the taxes or other revenues pertaining to these funds are levied or collected.

Other funds. The above discussion has been concerned with types of funds. With the exception of the general fund, the general fixed-assets fund, and the general bonded-debt fund, a municipality may have many funds of the same type. Thus, a city may issue bonds of differing types and serving numerous purposes, each issue being accounted for in a separate fund. Similarly, a municipality may operate a number of utilities, each of them separately accounted for. For practical purposes, each fund is an *accounting unit* or *entity.* A balance sheet combining a group of related funds should indicate the amount of assets, liabilities, reserves, and surplus applicable to each fund within the group. The revenues and expenditures of each fund must likewise be kept independent, and the revenues of one fund should not be used to meet the expenditures of another without legal authority or opinion behind the action.

Combined statements for unrelated funds. A balance sheet in which the assets, liabilities, reserves, and surplus of unrelated funds are combined should contain or be supported by a schedule showing the amounts applicable to each fund. Or a worksheet form with a separate column may be provided for each fund, except that, if there are many funds in a related group, such as trust funds, the total assets, liabilities, reserves, and surplus for the entire group may be shown together. In that case, however, the following additional steps are required.

A subsidiary schedule is prepared to show the amounts of assets, liabilities, reserves, and surplus applicable to each of the related funds in the group. If any of the funds in the group have bank overdrafts, the overdrafts are included among the liabilities. Finally, if some of the funds in the group have deficits, the deficits must not be combined with the surpluses of other related funds, but must instead be shown separately in the top statement. Interfund receivables and payables should not be offset against each other, because legal or other requirements may make it mandatory for one fund to pay over to another the amount owed without being able to collect the amount which it has coming from that fund.

While it is possible to prepare a combined balance sheet for unrelated funds, no statement combining the revenues and expenditures, respectively, of unrelated funds is usually provided: the revenues of one fund cannot be used to finance the expenditures of another fund or funds; and, in the case of the general fund, for example, it is important to compare the revenues of a particular year with the expenditures for the same year.

In short, the accounts of each fund must be designed in such a way as to make possible a complete separation of the assets, liabilities, reserves, surplus, revenues, expenditures, receipts, and disbursements.

Governmental accounting. In Federal-government accounting, a fund is created for each Congressional appropriation, of which there are many hundreds each year. If the program of the organization to which the administration of the fund is assigned is continued from one year to the next, the fund accounts are continued without interruption, although the expenditures of each fund are carefully segregated by fiscal years. See *activity accounting.*

fund account Any account reflecting transactions of a *fund* (*3*).

fund asset An asset belonging to a particular *fund* (*3*) or a group of funds.

fund balance sheet A balance sheet divided

into self-balancing sections, each of which shows the assets and liabilities of a single fund or group of related funds. This form of balance sheet is more or less standard for various types of governmental bodies and for educational, religious, charitable, social, and other institutions.

funded debt Debt evidenced by outstanding bonds or long-term notes. Floating and funded debt constitute total liabilities to outsiders.

funded reserve A reserve offset by segregated cash, securities, or other assets, available only for a stated purpose.

fund group A group of *funds* (*3*) of similar character which are brought together for administrative and reporting purposes. Examples: current funds; loan funds; endowment funds; plant funds; agency funds.

funding bonds Bonds issued to retire current or long-term indebtedness or to finance current expenditures.

fund liability A *liability* of a fund which is to be met out of its existing resources.

fund obligation A *liability* or *encumbrance* of a particular fund.

fund pool The grouping of funds for common investment; consolidated investments.

funds-flow statement A statement of *funds* (*4*) received and expended; a *statement of sources and applications of funds* in which elements of *net income* and *working capital* contributing to an understanding of the whole of financial operations during the reporting period replace totals of these items. Since in the typical business enterprise *fixed capital* and *working capital* are interrelated, interdependent, intertransferable, under common control, and financed from the same sources, this expansion supplies summary fund-management information concerning both noncurrent assets and liabilities and operating income and expense and their joint effects on the components of current assets and liabilities. In the first illustration on page 209, the major source of funds is displayed: *sales;* in the second illustration the increase in bank loans is regarded as being of sufficient importance to add to the period's "receipts" grouping. In this illustration, the "payment" of capital stock to an officer as a bonus or in lieu of cash compensation for current services also appears as a "receipt," the argument being that equivalents of salary-paid and stock-sold transactions were consummated; however, most accountants would probably prefer the "in-short" information as it appears in the first version, or a footnote, and reject the alternative treatment as "unreal". In the first version, cost of sales has been broken down into labor, materials, and overhead, regardless of the year of expenditure; in the second version, the same elements appear but in terms of amounts expended during the current year, thus giving rise to the added showing of the year's combined-inventory variation.

funds statement = *flow statement*.

fund surplus The excess of the resources of a specified fund over its obligations.

fungible Of the same class or quality; interchangeable, referring originally to such raw materials as grain in a public elevator. Fungible materials or other assets are those that lose their physical identity in the process of being mixed or stored with items of like kind, notwithstanding the existence of claims or rights which are regarded as attaching to the originally separate assets. Title may pass under some conditions as in the case of stored grains.

furniture and fixtures Office, store, showroom, and hotel equipment, and the like.

futures price See *contract price*.

[1st version]

BELFORD MANUFACTURING COMPANY

Funds-flow Statement
Calendar year 19-7

Funds were derived from			
Sales to customers		$9 763 400	
Dividends on investments		32 700	$9 796 100
Funds were applied to			
Cost of sales—			
Materials & parts	$4 472 100		
Direct labor	1 234 400		
Factory overhead	1 439 000	$7 145 500	
Other expense		1 664 800	
Income tax		210 000	
Total applied to current expense		$9 020 300	
New equipment, net		443 000	
Stock bonus to officer	$170 000		
Dividends to stockholders		180 000	
Working-capital increase—			
In current assets	$371 700		
In current liabilities	218 900	152 800	$9 796 100

[2nd version]

BELFORD MANUFACTURING COMPANY

Funds-flow Statement
Calendar year 19-7

Funds were derived from			
Operations			
Sales to customers		$9 763 400	
Dividends on investments		32 700	
Sales of retired equipment		40 000	$9 836 100
Other sources			
Increase in bank debt		$1 200 000	
Capital stock paid to officer		170 000	1 370 000
Total funds available			$11 206 100
Funds were applied to			
Processing operations			
Raw material		$4 505 800	
Direct labor		1 255 800	
Factory overhead			
Materials	$ 240 700		
Labor	113 200		
Outside services	1 107 000	1 460 900	
Processing costs		$7 222 500	
Less increases in inventories of work in process and finished stock		77 000	
Cost of current sales			$7 145 500
Other expense			
Selling & general			
Salaries	$ 882 600		
Outside services	568 800		
Supplies	112 400	$1 563 800	
Value of stock issued to officer		170 000	
Loss on sale of investment		101 000	
Income tax		208 700	2 043 500
Dividends to stockholders			180 000
Increases in assets			
Plant equipment		$ 483 000	
Working capital, omitting bank debt and deferred taxes		1 354 100	1 837 100
Total funds applied			$11 206 100

gain 1. Any *pecuniary benefit,* profit, or advantage, as opposed to a *loss; revenue* or *income;* as in the phrase "gain or loss." 2. The excess of revenues over related costs: applicable to a transaction, a group of transactions, or the transactions of an operating period.

gain or loss 1. The net result of a concluded transaction or group of transactions or the transactions of an operating period, following the application of usual accounting rules or rules appearing in income-tax regulations. A *gain,* or credit, increases the capital or wealth of the transactor; a *loss,* or debit, decreases it. 2. = *profit and loss.*

general accountant An accountant who deals with any type of accounting problem within an organization.

general audit *obs.* = *audit (1).*

general average (marine insurance) A loss arising from a sacrifice purposely made for the preservation from common danger of a ship, its cargo, or the persons on board; the loss, incurred for the benefit of all, is made good by a contribution from all; distinguished from *particular average.*

general balance sheet The balance sheet of a governmental body or an educational, religious, charitable, social, or other institution, prepared in the usual commercial form rather than by self-balancing funds.

general bonded-debt fund See *fund.*

general cash Cash available for ordinary operating and asset-replacement purposes. See *cash.*

general contingency reserve A *reserve for contingencies* unrelated to any possible future expense or loss; contrasts with *special contingency reserve.*

general expense (or **burden**) = *administrative expense.*

general fixed-assets fund See *fund.*

general fund (governmental and institutional accounting) The assets and liabilities available for general purposes, as distinct from funds established for specific purposes. See *fund.*

general journal The journal in which are recorded transactions not provided for in specialized journals. See *journal.*

general ledger A ledger containing accounts in which all the transactions of a business enterprise or other accounting unit are classified either in detail or in summary form. See *double-entry bookkeeping.*

generally accepted Given authoritative recognition: said of *accounting principles* or *audit standards,* and the pronouncements concerning them, particularly, in recent years, those of the American Institute of Certified Public Accountants and the American Accounting Association.

general-obligation bonds 1. Bonds for the payment of which the *full faith and credit* of the issuer are pledged. 2. (municipal accounting) Bonds payable from ad-valorem taxes upon all the property assessable by the issuing municipality and from other general revenues.

general operating expense A term often applied to selling and administrative expense and occasionally to production and other costs, such as depreciation, property taxes, rents, royalties, maintenance, repairs, service-contract charges, and other items usually classified elsewhere but which appear separately on an income statement.

general overhead = *general expense.*

general partner A partner who alone or

with others is liable for the debts of the partnership.

general records The general ledger and the journals, registers, files, and papers normally supporting general-ledger items.

geometric mean The number which, when substituted for each of the factors of a product, will give the same product as the factors; the *m*th root of a product of *m* factors; the number whose logarithm is equal to the arithmetic mean of the logarithms of *m* quantities. Thus, $2 \times 2 \times 4 \times 16 = 256$; hence, the geometric mean of the four factors is $\sqrt[4]{256}$, or 4.

Like the arithmetic mean, the geometric mean may be computed in simple or weighted form. The unweighted geometric mean g of a group of m numbers, $N_1, N_2, \ldots, N_m$, is, by definition,

$$g = \sqrt[m]{N_1 \times N_2 \times \cdots N_m} = (N_1 \times N_2 \times \cdots N_m)^{1/m}.$$

In logarithmic terms, this becomes

$$\log g = \frac{\log N_1 + \log N_2 + \cdots \log N_m}{m},$$

and the *antilogarithm* is, of course, the original expression. Assume, for example, that the group of numbers consists of

$$N_1 = 2$$
$$N_2 = 3$$
$$N_3 = 13.5.$$

Substitution in logarithmic terms yields (see illustrative *logarithms*, pp. 268–269):

$$\log g = \frac{\log 2 + \log 3 + \log 13.5}{3} = \frac{0.301030 + 0.477121 + 1.130334}{3} = \frac{1.908485}{3} = 0.6361617.$$

Upon finding the antilogarithm, the result becomes

$$g = \sqrt[3]{2 \times 3 \times 13.5} = 4.3267.$$

To compute the weighted geometric mean, the weights w are introduced as exponents in the product, and the root to be extracted is equal to the sum of the weights:

$$g = \sqrt[\Sigma w]{(N_1)^{w_1}(N_2)^{w_2} \cdots (N_m)^{w_m}},$$

or

$$\log g = \frac{w_1 \log N_1 + w_2 \log N_2 + \cdots w_m \log N_m}{\Sigma w}.$$

The usual basis of weighting is the frequency with which the values occur. To illustrate the process of computation, it may be assumed that, in the previous example, the values 2 and 3 occurred with frequencies 4 and 5, respectively, and the value 13.5 occurred only once. Using the frequencies as weights,

$$g = \sqrt[10]{2^4 \times 3^5 \times 13.5^1},$$

or,

$$\log g = \frac{4 \log 2 + 5 \log 3 + 1 \log 13.5}{10} = \frac{4(0.301030) + 5(0.477121) + 1.130334}{10} = 0.4720059.$$

Reference to the illustrative logarithms shows that antilog $0.4720059 = 2.9649$. The final result, then, is

$$g = \sqrt[10]{2^4 \times 3^5 \times 13.5} = 2.9649.$$

In this example, the weighted geometric mean is lower than the unweighted mean because the small values, 2 and 3, occur more frequently than the larger value, 13.5. In fact, the larger value, 13.5, occurred only once and thus received a weight of only 1. This should make clear that the unweighted geometric mean is only a special case of weighting; it is a weighted geometric mean in which all values receive *equal weights*.

If any group of positive numbers is averaged by using the harmonic, geometric, and arithmetic means, the following relation will be found:

$$h \leqq g \leqq a.$$

The geometric mean is never greater than the arithmetic mean or less than the harmonic mean; it occupies a position intermediate to the harmonic and arithmetic means. This property is sometimes denoted by saying that the arithmetic mean has an upward bias relative to the geometric mean, while the harmonic mean has a downward bias. In other words, relative to the geometric mean, the arithmetic mean overstates and the harmonic mean understates the value of the average.

Which particular mean, *arithmetic*, *geometric*, or *harmonic* (or other type of *average*, such as the *median* or *mode*) should be used depends upon the character of the problem. The arithmetic mean may be used when the arithmetic values or absolute changes in magnitudes are of interest, such as, for example, the average change in value of inventory position over a period of years. The harmonic mean is useful when reciprocals are of interest; an average price per unit when commodities are priced at so many units per dollar would be a case in point. The geometric mean is of interest when an average of ratios or of rates of change is required.

The geometric mean is often used in compound-interest calculations. For example, it may be desired to find the rate of interest implicit in the investment of a certain sum of money in return for a promise to receive a greater sum at a later date. This is a problem in determining the rate of increase of a sum of money (see *compound; compound amount of 1*). What occurs, under compounding, is the multiplication of an initial sum p_o by a given rate $(1 + r)$ over n periods to result in a sum p_n. In other words,

$$p_n = p_o(1 + r)^n,$$

or

$$r = \sqrt[n]{\frac{p_n}{p_o}} - 1.$$

Thus, a U. S. Savings Bond yields \$1,000 ten years hence for a present investment of \$750. Applying the above formula,

$$r = \sqrt[10]{\frac{1{,}000}{750}} - 1$$

and

$$\log(1 + r) = \frac{\log 1{,}000 - \log 750}{10}$$
$$= \frac{3.000000 - 2.875061}{10} = 0.012494.$$

Finding the antilogarithm shows that the rate of increase of the \$750, i.e., the rate of return, over this period of time is $r = 2.92\%$, not $3\frac{1}{3}\%$, the answer secured by use of the arithmetic mean.

In many cases, the arithmetic mean, even though not strictly applicable, serves as an approximation. The geometric mean is more difficult to compute and often not so readily understood. Moreover, if any of the numbers to be averaged is zero, the geometric mean will be zero, since all of the numbers entering into the geometric mean are multiplied together. It is not advisable to use the geometric mean when any of the factors entering into its calculation are negative.

geometric progression A numerical series the values of which increase at a constant ratio. A formula for the value of the sum S of such a series may be derived as follows: Let

$$S = a + ax + ax^2 + \cdots + ax^{n-1}$$
$$= a(1 + x + x^2 + \cdots + x^{n-1}).$$

Then, multiplying through by x,

$$Sx = a(x + x^2 + x^3 + \cdots + x^{n-1} + x^n).$$

Subtracting the first equation from the second,

$$Sx - S = a(x^n - 1),$$

or,

$$S = a\left(\frac{x^n - 1}{x - 1}\right).$$

If $x = 1 + r$, and $a = 1$, the formula gives the *compound amount of 1 per period* for n years:

$$= \frac{(1 + r)^n - 1}{r}.$$

gift (Federal taxation) The conveyance of property from one individual to another without consideration. A gift is neither a deductible expense to the giver nor taxable income to the recipient, and is to be distinguished from a *contribution (1)*. Generally the *basis* of property received as a gift is the same as the donor's. But if the value at the time of the gift was lower than the basis, *and* the gift property is sold by the donee at a loss, the donee's basis for computing loss is the value at the time of the gift. In either case, as to gifts received on or after September 2, 1958, or gift property received before then and held by the donee on that date, the basis is increased by any gift tax paid; but this adjustment may not increase the basis above value at the time of the gift. Under current law, the donor is subject to a gift tax beyond a total $30,000 lifetime exemption, plus annual gifts to each donee in excess of $3,000, provided, however, that the $3,000 annual exclusion for each donee does not apply to gifts of "future interests." However, a gift to a minor, in trust or otherwise, is not a gift of a future interest if the property and income may be spent for his benefit, and any balance will become his at 21 or his estate's if he dies earlier.

giveup A splitting of a stockbroker's commission with participating brokers: a one-time practice following a large trade; now generally forbidden by the stock exchanges.

giving-effect statement A *proforma statement (2)*.

go-and-not-go gauge (statistical quality control) A type of limit gauge designed to determine whether a part is within allowable limits without attempting to measure how far a product is inside or outside tolerance. This type of gauge is used merely to sort between defective and nondefective product. Most gauges conform to American Standard. See *basic dimension*. A go-and-not-go gauge is an *attribute* as distinct from a *variable gauge*.

going concern A business enterprise in operation, with the prospect of continuing operation in the future; its assets, liabilities, revenues, operating costs, personnel, policies, and prospects: a concept basic to accounting, of importance in the valuation of intangible assets and the depreciation of tangible and intangible assets. See *axiom*.

going(-concern) value The value of a single asset or of the net assets of a business, based on assumptions as to the continued usefulness of the asset or the continuation of business operations. If it be assumed that future operations will be generally comparable with those of the past, going value, under standard accounting procedures, is original cost less any applicable portion of any depreciation accumulated against it, or other valuation account, and is synonymous with *book value (1)*.

good Any item of merchandise, raw materials, or finished goods; a single element of wealth; a commodity.

pl. Loosely, inventoriable items or assets of any kind, including cash, fixed assets, supplies, and items in process of production; as in the expression *goods and services*. See *economic good; service, n.*

goods and services The endproducts of *expenditures;* the initial *distribution (2)* of incurred costs. See *good; service.*

goods in process 1. Partly finished product; work in process; raw material and parts on which some labor has been expended in the course of converting or assembling the output of a factory. Under practical operating conditions, the classification may also include raw material and parts removed from stock and waiting the first processing operation. 2. An account in which appear (a) charges for materials, labor, and overhead expended in a manufacturing operation, and (b) credits for product completed or otherwise disposed of, the balance of the account representing partly finished product on hand; an inventory asset valued at cost or less. See *inventory valuation.*

goodwill 1. The present value of expected future income in excess of a normal return on the investment in tangible assets; not a recorded amount unless paid for. 2. The excess of the price paid for a business as a whole over the book value, or over the computed or agreed value of all tangible net assets purchased. Normally, goodwill thus acquired is the only type appearing on books of account and in financial statements.

Various methods exist for computing goodwill on the basis of earning power. Since its value cannot be verified by reference to objective evidence, and since it is, moreover, subject to constant change because of economic conditions generally and other uncontrollable factors, it has been the general practice in recent years to eliminate goodwill from the accounts.

3. On a consolidated balance sheet, the premium, or amount paid by the parent or holding company for the shares of its consolidated subsidiaries in excess of their book values at the dates of acquisition, reduced by the discount, if any, at which shares of other subsidiaries were acquired; *consolidation excess.*

governmental accounting The principles, customs, and procedures associated with the accounting for municipal, state, and national governmental units. Characteristics of such accounting have in the past included the entry on bookkeeping records and financial statements of budgetary accounts and other legal or administratively imposed limitations on costs, and the recording of obligations, both of which are now regarded as optional features. In recent years, ordinary accrual accounting has been gradually replacing the older forms.

graduated life table The tabular counterpart of a survivor-life or *mortality curve.*

grant = *appropriation* (*1*).

grant in aid A donation or contribution, usually by a superior governmental unit, for a specified purpose, such as the support of an institution in which the public as a whole has some interest, or the construction of plant by a publicly owned utility. See *subsidy.*

graph Any connected series of points intended to reflect relations believed to exist between them.

gray market The buying and selling of scarce commodities by employing business methods generally disapproved; thus, after World War II, certain war contractors, given high priorities from governmental authority during the war, continued as regular customers to purchase the output of steel from steel mills and resell it at high prices, thus effectively preventing many manufacturers of products in which steel was an essential part from making direct purchases; the operation continued until this form of merchandising had been exposed, steel output had increased, and demands for steel had decreased. See *black market.*

green sheet (governmental accounting) A term at one time employed in Federal-government agencies to identify a standard form employed in budget presentations and containing comparative operating data, actual for the preceding year, actual and estimated for the current year, and proposed for the next succeeding year. A feature of the form was the breakdown of personal services showing job titles and grades, rates of pay, and other details.

gross *adj.* Undiminished by related deductions, except corrections; applied to sales, revenues, income, expense, and the like.

gross bonded debt (municipal accounting) The amount of debt owing before deducting "self-supporting" debt and sinking funds. See *net bonded debt.*

gross book value The dollar amount at which an asset appears on the books, before deducting any applicable accumulated depreciation or other valuation account.

gross cost of merchandise sold (retail accounting) *Invoice cost* (*2*) of merchandise disposed of by sale, less any return or allowance, plus duty, insurance, and transportation.

gross earnings = *gross income.*

gross income 1. Revenues before deducting any expenses: an expression employed in the accounting for individuals, financial institutions, and the like.
2. = *gross revenue.*
3. Incidental revenue of a manufacturing or trading enterprise. See *income.*

gross loss The excess of the cost of goods sold over the amount of sales; "negative" gross profit.

gross margin (1) the excess of sales over *direct costs* of products sold.
(2) = *gross profit.*

gross (merchandise) margin (retail accounting) *Net sales,* less *merchandise costs.*

gross national product (social accounting) The market value of production within the nation during any given calendar year, "production" meaning domestic sales of goods and services to natural persons, and to government, plus the excess of exports over imports. See *social accounting; national income.*

gross operating spread (retail accounting) *Gross merchandise margin,* less *merchandise procurement cost.*

gross profit Net sales, less cost of goods sold but before considering selling and general expenses, incidental income, and *income deductions.* In a manufacturing concern, gross profit is the excess of net sales over direct costs and factory overhead, and is therefore to be distinguished from *marginal income,* which is the excess of net sales over *direct costs* only.

gross-profit analysis 1. A quantitative expression of proximate causes of change from one year to another in the elements of the gross profits of a business enterprise, the earlier year being the *standard of comparison;* use is made of percentage relationships between the elements, or of unit costs and profits.
2. A similar determination of causes derived from a study of budgeted or standard sales and cost of sales with actual results.

Examples of methods of gross-profit analysis (sense 1):

Example 1: Following is a two-year comparison of the sales, cost of sales, and gross profits of the *AB* Company:

(1)

Particulars	First Year	Second Year	Increase or *Decrease
Sales	$650,000	$700,000	$50,000
Cost of sales	430,000	496,000	66,000
% to sales	66.154	70.857	4.703
Gross profit	$220,000	$204,000	$16,000*
% to sales	33.846	29.143	4.703*

If the same conditions obtaining in the earlier year had existed in the current year,

The increase in sales would have yielded a gross profit of 33.846% of $50,000 or	$16,920
But the increase in purchasing costs reduced the gross profit by 4.703% of $700,000, or	32,920
Thus causing a net decline in gross profit of	$16,000

Example 2: The *FG* Company manufactured and sold products *A*, *B*, and *C* during a two-year period, with a decline in gross profit of $212,943 in the second year as compared with the first, as shown in table (2) on page 216.

Again using the first year as the *standard of comparison,* the quantitative effects on gross profit are shown in the summary in table (3) on page 216.

From this summary, a number of preliminary conclusions may be drawn:

1. Product *A:* Sales volume and price were both reduced by approximately 20 percent; but both component material and labor costs were reduced by 40 percent—enough to produce a small increase in gross profit.

2. Product *B:* Sales quantities increased 5 percent, price and material and labor costs remaining unchanged. A slight increase in gross profit was the result.

3. Product *C:* Although quantities sold increased 11 percent and the average

(2)

	Product A			Product B			Product C		
	Units	Total	Per Units	Units	Total	Per Unit	Units	Total	Per Unit
Sales:									
First year	6,500	$325,000	$50.00	600	$60,000	$100.00	18,000	$450,000	$25.00
Second year	5,000	200,000	40.00	630	63,000	100.00	20,000	560,000	28.00
Materials:									
First year	6,500	130,000	20.00	600	18.000	30.00	18,000	90,000	5.00
Second year	5,000	60,000	12.00	630	18,900	30.00	20,000	224,000	11.20
Labor:									
First year	6,500	65,000	10.00	600	10,200	17.00	18,000	45,000	2.50
Second year	5,000	30,000	6.00	630	10,710	17.00	20,000	168,000	8.40
Overhead:									
First year	6,500	53,300	8.20	600	8,364	13.94	18,000	36,900	2.05
Second year	5,000	21,000	4.20	630	7,497	11.90	20,000	117,600	5.88
Gross profit:									
First year	6,500	76,700	11.80	600	23,436	39.06	18,000	278,100	15.45
Second year	5,000	89,000	17.80	630	25,893	41.10	20,000	50,400	2.52

(3)

Particulars	Product A	Product B	Product C	Net
Units sold	−17,700	+1,172	+30,900	+14,372
Price changes	−50,000	—	+60,000	+10,000
Cost changes—				
Materials	+40,000	—	−124,000	−84,000
Labor	+20,000	—	−118,000	−98,000
Overhead	+20,000	+1,285	−76,600	−55,315
Totals	+12,300	+2,457	−227,700	−212,943

sale price 12 percent, material and labor unit costs advanced 124 percent and 236 percent, respectively, these large increases wiping out the net gains shown elsewhere and accounting for all of the overall loss of gross profit.

Preliminary conclusions such as these, however, are only the commencement for a study of underlying causes; they nevertheless constitute a first step. The significance in terms of physical events and conditions is necessary for each item in the above summary. In addition, a full analysis would require a knowledge of the qualitative changes in the three products manufactured, particularly Product *C*, where, without details of such changes, the large increase in material and labor costs simply remains spectacular.

gross-profit method (of inventory) The method of estimating an inventory by subtracting, from the sum of the cost of the beginning inventory and the cost of purchases (or finished goods produced) during the period immediately preceding, an amount equal to the product of the average gross-profit percentage, known or estimated, and the net sales for the same period; in a highly refined form, known as the *retail method*. Because of its dependence on estimates, it must be corrected from time to time by a physical inventory. It is used principally in the preparation of monthly income statements within a fiscal year.

gross profit on sales = *gross profit*.

gross-profit ratio *Gross profit* divided by *net sales*. See *gross profit; gross-profit analysis; marginal profit*.

gross revenue *sing.* or *pl.* = *gross sales*.

gross sales Total sales, before deducting returns and allowances but after deducting corrections and trade discounts, sales taxes, excise taxes based on sales, and sometimes cash discounts. See *sales; net sales*.

group depreciation See *composite-life method* under *depreciation method*.

group financial statement A combined financial statement of a number of companies having the same ownership and also having, as a rule, similar structures or types of operation. The usual reason given for a group (rather than consolidated) statement is that the operations of the subsidiaries are of a different order than those of the controlling company, and that more and better information would be the consequence if consolidated statements were avoided; or that the activities of certain subsidiaries involve peculiarities that warrant a separate showing. The possibilities of group statements in annual reports to stockholders have as a rule been greatly underestimated. If, for example, an investment company owns controlling interests in a group of manufacturing companies and in a group of hotels, financial statements of the controlling company, unconsolidated, together with combined financial statements for each of the two groups, would be almost essential in a report of the controlling company to its stockholders. Group statements should be as few as possible; the greater the number, the more difficult the interpretation will be. See *consolidated balance sheet; consolidation policy; conglomerate corporation*.

grouping financial statement A summary worksheet having as its purpose the bringing together of recorded underlying data. Statements of individual subsidiaries or groups of subsidiaries may be published in a condensed form with explanations of intercompany eliminations. Groupings may be made by classes of items ordinarily appearing in detail in other statements, especially where the eliminations applicable to such groupings are minor or wanting entirely. Intragroup profit is always eliminated. It is often desirable to display some detail of the interests of outside stockholders. See *consolidating financial statement; consolidation policy*.

growth curve A time-series *graph* in which the ordinate values at any time depend on their predecessors.

growth formula (Federal income taxes) Formerly, the use, as an *excess-profits credit*, of an amount equal to a stated fraction of (a) the net income of the last year of the base period, (b) the average net income of the last two years, or (c) a weighted average taxable period extending beyond the end of the base period, whichever was the highest, provided that the total assets on the first day of the base period did not exceed $20,000,000 and that base-period growth was indicated by an increase in the payroll, or by an increase in gross receipts in the second half of the base period, or as otherwise determined. The privilege was also available, regardless of size, to corporations that had experienced a large increase in net sales of new products during the base period.

guarantee *n.* 1. One to whom a guaranty is given.

2. The obligation involved in a guaranty.

v. = *guaranty*.

guaranteed bond A bond guaranteed by a *person* other than the issuer, the guaranty being in the form of an endorsement on each bond, a contract with the issuing corporation, or a contract with the latter's creditors—the last-named device being often employed where the issuing company holds title for (and has leased its property to) a controlling corporation.

guaranteed dividend A periodic dividend on the capital stock of one company, the payment of which has been guaranteed by another. Examples: Guaranteed dividends may arise out of a lease whereby the guarantor corporation operates the lessor's property and, in terms of the lease or as a collateral condition, guarantees the dividends on the lessor's capital stock; or, a parent company may guarantee to minority stockholders dividends on the capital stock of a subsidiary.

guarantor One who promises to make good if another fails to pay or otherwise perform an assigned or contractual task.

guaranty *n.* A promise by one person to make good on the failure of another who is liable on a debt or in the performance of a duty. See *warranty; surety.*
v. To execute such a promise.

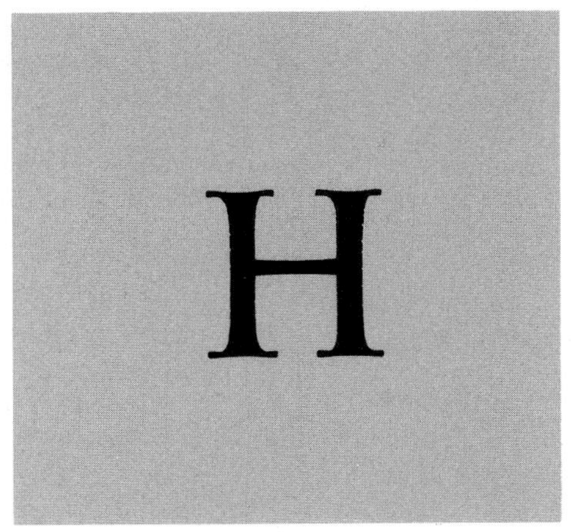

hand tool A hammer, ax, or other implement requiring the hand for its operation; a *tool.* It may or may not be distinguished from portable power tools.

harmonic mean The reciprocal of the arithmetic mean of the reciprocals of a group of numbers; denoted by the symbol *h*. See *arithmetic mean; geometric mean.* If numbers to be averaged are represented by $N_1, N_2, \ldots, N_m$, and the harmonic mean by *h*, then,

$$\frac{1}{h} = \frac{\frac{1}{N_1} + \frac{1}{N_2} + \cdots + \frac{1}{N_m}}{m},$$

or

$$h = \frac{m}{\frac{1}{N_1} + \frac{1}{N_2} + \cdots + \frac{1}{N_m}}.$$

The above formula encompasses the simple or unweighted harmonic mean. The formula for the weighted harmonic mean is

$$\frac{1}{h} = \frac{w_1\left(\frac{1}{N_1}\right) + w_2\left(\frac{1}{N_2}\right) w_m + \cdots + \left(\frac{1}{N_m}\right)}{w_1 + w_2 + \cdots + w_m}.$$

As in the case of the *geometric* and *arithmetic means,* the most common weights (w) are the frequency of occurrence of each value to be weighted, such as units, tons, or feet.

The harmonic mean is useful for arriving at average unit prices for commodities to be priced in terms of standard units, such as commodity units per dollar. For example, if over a period of time a certain commodity has been observed to sell at 4, 5, and 20 units per dollar, and it is desired to compute the average price per unit, the arithmetic mean $\frac{4 + 5 + 20}{3} = 9\frac{2}{3}$, which suggests that, on the average, the commodity has sold at a rate of $9\frac{2}{3}$ units per dollar, or an average price per unit of approximately 10.34 cents. The harmonic mean, however, shows that, on the average, the commodity has sold at a rate of 6 units per dollar, since,

$$\frac{1}{h} = \frac{\frac{1}{4} + \frac{1}{5} + \frac{1}{20}}{3} = \frac{1}{6},$$

and $h = 6$. Thus, use of the harmonic mean results in an average price of approximately $16\frac{2}{3}$ cents. Which of the two averages is correct depends on what is meant by "average unit price"; the result secured by use of the harmonic mean is closer to the ordinary commercial meaning of "quoted unit price." Both the arithmetic and harmonic means used above, however, were "unweighted" (i.e., they were equally weighted). As such, they contain certain assumptions about market behavior. Use of an unweighted arithmetic mean assumes that equal amounts of money were spent at each price, while use of an unweighted harmonic mean assumes that an equal number of units of the commodity were sold at each price. These assumptions may, of course, be modified by introducing different weights.

harmonic progression A numerical series the *reciprocals* of which form an *arithmetic progression.*

head-end business Property transportation in the form of mail, express, baggage, milk, etc., carried directly behind the locomotive of a passenger train.

hedge Any purchase or sale transaction having as its purpose the elimination of profit or loss arising from price fluctuations; specifically, a purchase or sale entered into for the purpose of balancing, respectively, a sale or purchase already made or under contract, in order to offset the effect of price fluctuation. Hedges are made in the marketing of numerous commodities, and in a variety of ways, but all are attempts to transfer risk of price fluctuations from one person or group to others. A firm-price contract represents a type of hedge under which the purchaser transfers risks of gain or loss from price fluctuations to the seller; a cost-plus-fixed-fee contract, on the other hand, is a hedge in which the seller transfers such risks to the purchaser.

In a restricted sense, the term refers to simultaneous purchase-and-sale transactions having the purpose of offsetting one risk by another more or less equal and opposite. To illustrate this process, assume that it requires three weeks from the purchase of wheat to the sale of flour, that spot prices of wheat are $2 per bushel, that it takes 2.3 bushels of wheat and $1 of other costs to mill 100 pounds of flour, and that flour is selling currently for $6 per hundredweight. With this relation between price and cost, a miller may be willing to engage in purchasing wheat and milling flour; but, in the three weeks intervening between the purchase of the wheat and the sale of the flour, fluctuations may occur in the price of the latter. The miller may hedge against the risk of price fluctuations if a futures market exists in flour or if a firm-price contract for flour delivery three weeks hence can be negotiated. If neither of these conditions exist, it may still be possible for the miller to hedge through the medium of a constituent commodity, such as wheat, the price of which fluctuates in a known manner with the price of flour. Assume that flour prices fall $3 for every $1 decline in the price of wheat, and vice versa. The miller may, therefore, hedge fully by selling short three bushels of wheat for every hundredweight of flour he expects to mill. If, when the flour is ready for sale, its price has decreased $1, the price of wheat will also have fallen by 33⅓¢ per bushel. The $1 reduction in flour price will be exactly offset by the $1 gain arising from the short sale of wheat. By selling the flour and simultaneously covering the short sale of wheat, the miller makes 40¢ per unit of flour, assuming that he was able to keep his other milling costs at $1. He loses 60¢ on the barrel of flour but gains $1 on the short sale of three bushels of wheat. The difference of 40¢ is equal to the gain that he expected to make on milling operations when he purchased wheat at $2 per bushel for conversion into flour to be sold at $6 per 100 pounds.

If the price of flour should rise from $6 to $7 per barrel during the process of milling, the miller would realize not only the 40¢ per cwt. he had expected to make, but an additional $1 per cwt. Wheat, because of its assumed relation with flour prices, would, however, have risen 33⅓¢ per bushel, so that the miller would have suffered a loss of $1 on his short sale of three bushels. The $1 of windfall gain on the barrel of flour is exactly canceled by the $1 loss on wheat. Thus, whether the price of flour rises or falls, the miller realizes 40¢ per barrel on flour, provided that he is able to maintain his processing costs at a stable level.

A direct price relationship, such as that existing between wheat and flour, is not necessary to hedging. Other items with prices bearing known relations to flour prices offer the same opportunity for hedging; hedging by means of short sales also requires access to organized futures markets. Should foreign-currency rates, for example, fluctuate directly with flour prices, they would provide the same protection to the miller. It is only essential that there be some correlation between the prices of the items. It is immaterial whether the prices move in the same direction; if wheat prices were to move in a direction opposite to flour prices, the miller could hedge by buying additional wheat long rather than selling it short, for if flour prices should fall and wheat prices rise in response to opposite movements in price, the loss in flour would be offset by the gain in wheat; if flour prices rose, the fall in wheat prices would then eliminate the windfall gain in flour.

Prices of different commodities, or even of the same commodity at different times (such as the relation between spot and futures prices), are usually subject to individual eccentricities in their movements. It is, therefore, impossible to hedge fully by simultaneous purchases and sales. Other devices, such as price contracts, may, however, be available within the industry for accomplishing this objective.

Hedging generally is restricted to the elimination of price risks. Hedging against risks such as delayed delivery or physical damage is known as *insurance*. Hedging by locating assets at many different points, or buying them in many different amounts or qualities, is known as *diversification*.

hedge clause A protective statement attached to circulars, advertisements, and letters by brokers, dealers, investment advisers, and others who supply data on securities to customers or clients; its typical postscript form is: "The information furnished herein has been obtained from sources believed to be reliable but its accuracy is not guaranteed." The U. S. Securities and Exchange Commission has held that such a statement should not be represented to investors as relieving the broker, dealer, or adviser from liability under the law or the Commission's regulations.

heuristic Not proved or provable, but supplying a basis for inquiry or argument.

hidden reserve = *secret reserve*.

histogram A particular form of a *bar chart* of a *frequency distribution* in which the altitudes of the frequency rectangles are equal or proportional to the respective *class-interval* frequencies and the frequency rectangles are contiguous, the common boundary between two adjacent rectangles being erected at the common boundary of the two associated class intervals. A "step-function" graphical representation of a frequency distribution is used widely in *statistical quality control* to suggest the outline of the *frequency curve* which represents the underlying probability law governing the variation pattern for a process operating in statistical control.

historical cost 1. Cost to the present owner at the time of acquisition.

2. (public-utility accounting) Cost to the first consumer–owner; = *original cost* (*2*).

hold-harmless agreement A contract under the terms of which the liability of one person for damages is assumed by another.

holding company A *controlling company* having subsidiaries and confining its activities primarily to their management.

holding period (Federal income taxes) The period during which an asset is owned: a period of importance in the determination of whether sales of securities are *wash*(-sale) *transactions* and whether profits from the sale of *capital assets* (*2*) are to be taxed as long-term or short-term *capital gains*. Generally, in a tax-free transaction, such as a gift or a tax-free reorganization, where the transferee of assets has a substituted basis, the holding period of the transferor is added to the holding period of the transferee.

horizontal audit A method of observing accounting procedures by a public accountant designed to *test* the practical operation of internal controls. Example: tracing a purchase transaction from requisition to order, delivery, inspection, inventory, sales, and collection: included in the auditor's area of inquiry would be the method of procurement; the meaning and sufficiency of inspection and approval; adequacy of documentation; safeguards against inaccuracies, including entry in the bookkeeping records; speed of recording and disposing of discovered errors; smoothness of interdepartmental relationships; and so on.

hotchpot A combining of (to put in hotchpot) property of two or more persons in order to effect an equal distribution between them.

hybrid reserve A reserve serving two or more purposes; usually applied to *appropriations* of *retained earnings* against which costs or losses have been erroneously charged; see *appropriated surplus*.

hypothecated asset = *pledged asset*.

hypothecation The pledging of property to secure the payment of a debt: a term sometimes used where a note, acceptance, warehouse receipt, or bill of lading remains in the hands of the debtor, the ledger account or other record being stamped with a reminder that the proceeds therefrom are to be applied to the account of a designated creditor.

hypothesis 1. (logic) A proposition having the status of a *sufficient condition* for a set of other propositions, anteceding the "if" clause in a conditional proposition. In examining a system of internal control, an auditor relies on a hypothesis of adequacy in terms of certain criteria or *rules* of adequacy. He then proceeds to *test* the hypothesis by collecting and sifting *evidence* in accordance with such rules. On this basis, the hypothesis is accepted or rejected. Either eventuality results in the statement of a second hypothesis that provides a *sufficient condition* for a set of propositions concerning the general scope and method to be followed in the remainder of the audit engagement. Other hypotheses will need to be stated, of course, in order to determine in detail what ought to be done in succeeding steps. See *sufficient condition; necessary condition*.

2. (science) A proposition provisionally accepted for the purpose of determining logical consistency between the proposition and an established set or a *primitive* set of propositions; loosely, any conjecture as to the nature or probable causes of events or conditions; a "working hypothesis" is a conjecture which, although not completely verified, is regarded as sufficiently probable to serve as a basis for investigation or other action.

3. (statistics) A proposition involving relations between sets of events, which is to be rejected or tentatively accepted on the basis of *sample evidence* in accordance with stipulated *rules* of *statistical inference*.

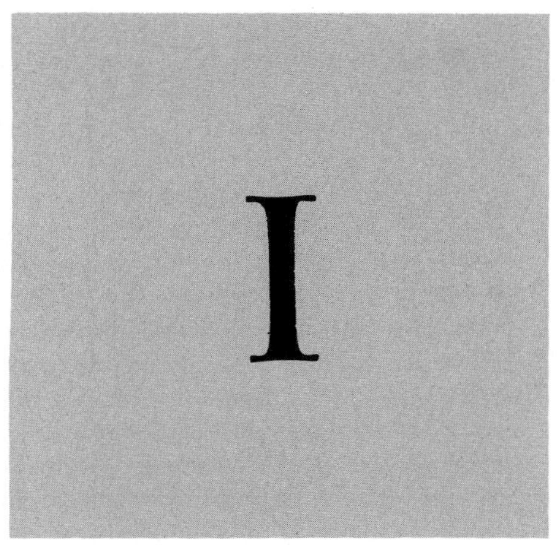

ideal standard cost 1. = *perfection standard cost.*
2. = *current standard cost.*

identity 1. A relation between two mathematical functions or logical expressions, specifying that they always assume the same values in a defined domain of all possible values. To distinguish an identity from an equation (the latter specifying a relation that need not hold for any and all values of the variables it contains), and to indicate the greater force of an identity, an additional horizontal stroke is, by mathematical *convention,* added to the equality symbol ($\equiv$). The so-called balance-sheet "equation" is actually an identity, since, by the *rules* of double entry, the relation: assets $\equiv$ equities $\equiv$ liabilities + net worth, must necessarily obtain. When this expression fails to hold, it implies that a mistake is present in the accounting process; but the converse proposition is not necessarily true. Accounting correctness is a *sufficient condition* for satisfying the relation expressed by the balance-sheet identity; it is not a *necessary condition.* In short, if the accounting process is carried out correctly, the balance-sheet identity will be satisfied; but satisfaction of the balance-sheet identity does not imply that the results of following the accounting process are without error. See *necessary condition; sufficient condition; trial balance; equation.*
2. Sufficient continuity to warrant attribution of the same predicates throughout a specified period of time; this may be a legal fiction, as in the case of a machine that retains its identity for purposes of determining legal ownership although all of its parts may have been replaced.

idle capacity Unused productive potential: said of a machine, operation, or plant not in use or only partially in use; it may be variously measured, as in tons of possible additional output, or in hours available for use.

idle-capacity cost The *variance* attributable to the failure to utilize facilities at projected rates.

idle time Lost time of men or machines arising from lack of business or of material, a breakdown of equipment, faulty supervision, or other cause whether or not avoidable. In the distribution of labor and production-center costs, it may be accounted for in a separate operating-expense account and regarded as an item of overhead.

imaginary number A number of which $\sqrt{-1}$ is a factor.

impairment (of capital) 1. The amount by which *stated capital* has been reduced by dividends or other distributions, and by losses.
2. The amount by which liabilities exceed assets by reason of losses.

implication The relation of a set of *propositions* such that the truth or falsity of one depends upon the truth or falsity of others.

implied contract A *contract* inferred from the actions of the parties, there being no express agreement between them.

implied trust A *trust* where the intent of the parties to create a trust is inferred from the transaction between them. See *trust.*

impound To seize and hold in protective custody by means of some legal process, such as a court order: said of cash and other assets.

imprest cash = *imprest fund (1)*.

imprest fund 1. A fixed *cash fund* or *petty-cash fund* in the form of currency, a bank checking account, or both, maintained for expenditures that must be made in cash, and from time to time restored to its original amount by a transfer from general cash of a sum equal to the aggregate of disbursements: a form of *working fund*.
2. A fund established for a single payroll, dividend, and other periodic class of payments.

imprest system The system under which *imprest cash* is disbursed and from time to time restored to its original amount through reimbursements equal to sums expended. Implicit in the concept is the review by a higher authority of the propriety of the expended amounts before reimbursement is approved.

improvement 1. = *betterment*.
2. The clearing, draining, grading, or other addition to the worth of a tract of land; any cost of developing real estate, whether paid for directly or through special-assessment taxes. See *land improvements*.

impute To apportion causality between variables which combine to produce a common effect, as in *marginal analysis*. Imputations are often made by *convention*, even when no specific causal connection can be established between the effect and the variables which have contributed to the end result. An example frequently encountered is the assignment of portions of fixed or common costs to individual items of production. Another example may be found in the distribution of aliquot portions of material and labor costs between items jointly produced. See *joint cost*. Averaging of total costs over a variety of factors is not a satisfactory method of imputation when it is desired to isolate causes of variation in the total cost of joint products. Recourse to *marginal analysis* may be required. See *marginal cost; marginal productivity*.

imputed cost 1. = *Alternative cost;* a term often used to indicate the presence of arbitrary or subjective elements of product cost having more than usual significance.
2. A fraction of joint or common costs, including overhead, attributed to any item of goods or services acquired in a *lot* or jointly produced; also, the worth of a *factor of production* joined with and inseparable from one or more other factors. Examples: (a) the interest a bank would presumably allow on its accounts with commercial customers if it were not offset by the "value" of services rendered customers; (b) the portion of interest paid by the United States on its bonds and other indebtedness which some would attribute to government agencies having income-producing facilities but no interest-bearing obligations of their own; (c) the cost of a group of services acquired as a unit assignable to a part of the group, such as the depreciated portion (or services-consumed fraction) of a fixed asset; (d) the "value" to a proprietorship of the proprietor's contribution of capital and services, sometimes determined in the light of what he or his investment might earn elsewhere, especially where any realistic separation of such aggregates is usually impossible. In the case of (d), for example, not only are management compensation and investment return subject to wide variations, but situations offering parallels would involve the same difficulty if attempts were made to untangle the merged elements. Except where the spread of a joint cost over items serviced or produced is commonly accomplished by simple averaging, the determination of averages, or the substitution of individual judgment for such objectively determinable facts as those that constitute the subject matter of *transactions*, imputed costs, save for like services, are but rarely expressed in accounting. See *impute; joint cost*.

imputed interest 1. The return on *capital* (*2*) assumed to be a part of the *net income* of an enterprise; normally not separated and usually regarded as inseparable from the balance of net income as *pure profit*

because of (a) the absence of any contractual obligation therefor, and (b) the impossibility of selecting any realistic amount that represents such return.
2. Interest on investment placed on the records as a financial expense, although no contractual liability exists therefor. The expense becomes a part of total expense, but, since the corresponding credit is regarded as revenue, the net effect on net income is nil.

inadequacy The expense or loss of cost caused by insufficiency of capacity or use, necessitating early replacement or abandonment. See *depreciation*. Inadequacy is a factor, with wear and tear and obsolescence, in the determination of depreciation rates.

inadmissible asset (Federal income-taxes) In general, corporate stock and wholly or partially tax-exempt government bonds: an obsolete term. See *admissible asset*.

inadmitted asset (insurance accounting) Any asset having or assumed to have little or no value in liquidation, under regulations prescribed in various jurisdictions; in reporting the financial position of an insurance company, such assets are segregated and deducted as a group, usually on the face of the report.

in-charge accountant (public accounting) The *manager or senior* who assigns and supervises the work of a field staff.

incidence The incurring or sustaining of an expense or loss over which the person affected has little or no control, and for which he may be reimbursed by others; example: an *excise tax* paid by a manufacturer on the production of a commodity and added to the selling price paid by the buyer of the commodity.

income 1. Money or money equivalent *earned* or *accrued* during an accounting period, increasing the total of previously existing net assets, and arising from sales and rentals of any type of goods or services and from the receipt of gifts and windfalls from any outside source: a generic term. See *revenue; gross income; net income; income realization; profit.*
2. Sales of goods or services; in this sense, the term is less used than formerly, *revenue* now being preferred.
3. An addition; a receipt: often in contrast with *outgo;* as, the income and outgo of stores.
4. Now in restricted senses: (a) the revenues of natural persons, such as salaries, interest, or rents [= *earnings* (3)]; (b) the remainder of revenue after deducting costs of sales and operating and other expenses (= *net income*); (c) revenues derived from investments and from incidental sources.
5. (economics) The flow of economic goods and services during a period of time: a term frequently contrasted with "wealth"—i.e., a stock of economic goods at a point of time; sometimes synonymous with (a) "net income"—the residual revenue after contractual payments or accruals for land, labor, management, borrowed capital, and risk have been made or allowed for; (b) "money income" —money or money's worth received during a period for services or for the use of property; (c) "real income"—the purchasing power of money income; (d) "psychic" or "subjective" income—the satisfaction of individual human wants.

In most accounting usage, "income" customarily refers to any factor, other than additional investment, that increases the owner's recorded equity in an enterprise: a concept in harmony with the definition appearing in *Eisner* v. *Macomber*, 252 U.S. 189: ". . . the gain derived from capital, from labor, or from both combined, provided it be understood to include profit gained through a sale or conversion of capital assets."

income account 1. Any account maintained for a particular item of revenue or income.
2. A general term meaning the current year's revenue and expense, as in the expression, "a charge to income account"; *profit and loss* (*2*).
3. *pl.* Revenue and expense accounts, collectively.

income and expense = *revenue and expense.*

income bond An obligation on which interest is paid only if earned; it is like other types of bonds with respect to underlying security, maturity, and other features. Interest may be cumulative or noncumulative; if cumulative, the cumulation may cease after a term of years (often 3). The determination of whether interest has been earned is frequently made dependent on a professional accountant's interpretation of the provisions of the *indenture,* together with what he deems to be "good accounting practice." Some income bonds resemble preferred stock so closely that denial of interest thereon as an allowable deduction for tax purposes has been affirmed by the courts. Income bonds issued by a government utility may be secured as to both principal and interest only by the expectancy of a surplus of the net operating income of future periods.

income deduction One of a class of items making up the final section of the income statement of a business organization, representing expenses (including losses) commonly excluded from operating costs; like other expenses, they are costs necessarily incurred in the conduct of the particular business and are thus customarily regarded as necessary charges before arriving at net income, but as being more in the nature of costs imposed from without rather than costs subject to the controls exercised through everyday operating procedures. They are made up of interest; amortized discount and expense on bonds; income taxes (property taxes being as a rule nominal in character and absorbed as an ordinary operating expense); losses from sales of plants and branches and from other major property disposals; carrying charges on inactive property; prior-year adjustments, as for additional income taxes; charges to contingency reserves; bonuses and other periodic profit distributions to officers and employees; writeoffs of intangibles; adjustments arising from major changes in accounting methods, as in the basis of inventory valuation; flood, fire, and other extraordinary losses; losses on foreign exchange; and the like. For other than interest and income taxes, the usual tests for items in this classification are that they be material in amount and nonrecurrent. Although certain of these expenses are occasionally treated as "surplus charges," it is now considered better practice to include them, with full explanations, in the income statement. See *net income; appropriation of net income; income statement; operating-performance income statement.*

income earned 1. *Realized* income.
2. Income realized from services rendered.

income realization The *recognition* of income, the usual test being the passage of title to or delivery of goods, or the performance of services. See *realize.*

income sheet = *income statement.*

income statement A summary of the *revenues* and *expenses* of an accounting unit, or group of such units, for a specified period. The generally recognized minimum income-statement content may be summarized thus:

Operating (or *gross*) *revenue.* Gross sales less returns, allowances, cash discounts, and sometimes bad debts, plus gross amounts from other regular sources; net sales and miscellaneous revenues; in an organization rendering services: fees earned, or the equivalent. Frequently the gross amount is shown, along with the amount of each of the indicated principal classes of deductions and the amount of any other class of deduction running, for example, to 1 percent or more of the total gross. Many business organizations reflect only net sales in their published statements, but comparisons of returns, allowances, and discounts with the equivalent items in prior years and for other similarly situated organizations may yield information of value to readers of financial statements. Trade discounts have little or no statistical value, and gross sales are always stated with trade discounts excluded.

Cost of sales. Of a retail enterprise: the

cost of goods or services sold; usually a single figure appears representing the composite of invoice cost, freight in, and storage costs, less trade and cash discounts and inventory losses. Of a manufacturing enterprise: raw material *consumed* in production [see *consumed cost* (*2*)], direct labor, and production overhead; usually a single figure but increasingly broken down in published financial statements in terms of the three indicated elements, each element including its share of the *inventory variation*.

Gross profit. Operating revenue less cost of goods or services sold, "cost" meaning the factory cost of manufactured product or the merchandise cost of a trading concern. There has been some tendency in published statements to merge all operating expense into a single item, thus establishing a "one-step" transition from net sales to net operating income. For retail establishments and for many manufacturing concerns as well, comparisons of sales and gross profits are major elements in operating analyses, particularly where the distinction between manufacturing or trading costs and selling and administrative expense marks an important division of internal management controls.

General operating expense. A class of expense (excluding cost of sales and income deductions) reported on income statements, and as a rule broken down by selling (or distribution) expense and administrative (and general) expense. Depreciation, property taxes, rents, royalties, maintenance, and repairs, which under the influence of SEC requirements are sometimes included at this point, are usually left in their original classification and disclosed in footnotes where their importance warrants.

Other income. Interest received, rentals, and incidental income. These items may follow gross profit; or if nominal in character and amount they may be added to the sales figure to produce "total" revenues or even merged with sales where they are, say, less than 1% of sales.

Income deductions. A class of expense reported on an income statement, consisting of any of such items, separately stated, as interest; amortized debt discount; income taxes; capital losses (and gains), as from the disposition of investments or fixed assets; depreciation and other carrying charges on inactive assets; prior-year adjustments; charges to appropriated-surplus (such as contingency) reserves; bonuses and profit distributions to executives; amortization or writeoff of intangibles; major inventory-valuation adjustment; loss from flood and fire; foreign-exchange losses; an additional income-tax assessment for a prior year; and adjustments arising from changes in the basis of accounting. See *income deduction; net income*.

Net income (or *net loss*). The concluding figure on an income statement. Some difference of opinion exists among accountants as to the location of this sidehead on an income statement. Some contend that not all the items appearing in the preceding paragraph should be deducted before arriving at net income, those not so deducted appearing as appropriations of net income or as surplus charges. The prevailing trend is to classify all such items as current-year expense, so that "net income" may signify the final operating result, consistently arrived at, from year to year.

Net income per common share. The amount attributable to each common share outstanding *at the end* of the reporting period, a statistic often following the net-income figure. Where outstanding shares have increased or decreased during the reporting period, a complex arithmetic method of *averaging* the earnings per share may be found in APBO 9; but the simpler method remains as the standard.

See *all-inclusive income statement; operating-performance income statement; net income*.

An income statement, following the outline described above, is sometimes said to be in *report* or *multiple-step* form.

Illustration of report form of income statement
United Steel Works, Inc.
Comparative Consolidated Income Statements

[*a. Abbreviated statement form, with subtotals for gross profit, income before taxes, and net income after taxes.*]

	Years ended December 31 19-2	19-1
Net sales	$59 483 000	$50 347 000
Less cost of sales	38 722 000	34 899 000
Gross Profit	$20 761 000	$15 448 000
Selling, administrative, and general expense	−13 381 000	−12 659 000
Fire loss	−872 000	—
Net income before income tax	$ 6 508 000	$ 2 789 000
Less provision for Federal income tax	3 414 000	1 245 000
Net income, including fire loss in 19–2	$ 3 094 000	$ 1 544 000

[*b. Possible expansion of first two items above, in terms of product (output) class.*]

	19-2	19-1
Net sales-		
Blahhas	$52 647 000	$45 112 000
Other products	6 836 000	5 235 000
Total	$59 483 000	$50 347 000
Cost of sales-		
Blahhas	$36 156 000	$30 922 000
Other products	2 566 000	3 977 000
Total	$38 722 000	$34 899 000
Gross profit	$20 761 000	$15 448 000

[*c. Possible expansion of cost of sales in terms of input costs.*]

	19-2	19-1
Cost of sales-		
Inventory January 1	$ 8 848 000	$ 7 235 000
Import costs added during year-		
Purchased materials services	19 473 000	16 454 000
Compensation of persons	18 285 000	17 691 000
Depreciation	2 421 000	2 367 000
Inventory December 31	−10 305 000	−8 848 000
Total	$38 722 000	$34 899 000

Another form that has gained limited popularity in recent years is the *single-step* form, its purpose being to display factor costs of objects of expenditure that have been assigned to expense during the reporting period. The two forms appear on this page and the next—see above.

income tax A tax on annual earnings and profits of any natural person, corporation, or other defined unit. Expressed as a percentage, the rate of tax often varies with the character and amount of the income on which it is based. It may take the form of a *normal tax, surtax,* or *excess-profits tax,* or a combination of any such taxes.

incomplete transaction A *transaction* that in the normal course of events will lead to another; as, a credit sale followed at a later date by a settlement in cash, or a contract in process against which a part of the cost has been incurred and a portion of the prospective profit has been recognized as earned.

increment Any increase in value from any one point of time to another, without

Illustration of single-step income statement
United Steel Works, Inc.
Comparative Consolidated Income Statements

[*Expense in terms of input costs; dividends per common share; net income employed in business*]

	Years ended December 31 19-2	19-1
Sales	$59 483 525	$50 347 359
Costs:		
Inventories, January 1	$ 8 848 078	$ 7 235 114
Costs incurred during year—		
Purchased materials & services	$28 693 701	$26 103 404
Compensation to persons	22 319 950	20 610 427
Depreciation	2 545 763	2 456 433
Federal income tax	4 287 000	1 246 312
Total costs	$57 846 414	$50 416 576
Inventories, December 31	$10 304 618	$ 8 848 078
Total costs allocated to sales	$56 389 874	$48 803 612
Net income for year	$ 3 093 651	$ 1 543 747
Per common share	$2.70	$1.24
Dividends ($4.50 preferred, $1 common)	1 285 000	1 285 000
Balance of net income	$ 1 808 651	$ 258 747
Balance at beginning of year	607 656	348 909
Net income employed in business at end of year	$ 2 416 307	$ 607 656

reference to cost or book value. *Unearned* increment has reference to an increase in the value of land from causes to which the owner has made no contribution, as from growth of population. See *accretion*.

incremental cost The change in aggregate cost that accompanies the addition or subtraction of a unit of output, or a change in factors affecting cost, such as style, size, or area of distribution; *marginal cost*. The incremental cost of an independent variable constituting a part of the cost of production or marketing reflects the effect of the choice of an alternative.

incur To sustain, become liable for: said of a cost, expense, loss, or debt. See *recognize*.—*incurrence, n.*

in-cycle work Work performed by an operator while a machine is performing its *cycle* of operations; contrasts with *out-cycle work*.

indebtedness A debt *owing;* any liability; an aggregate of liabilities.

indenture An agreement between two or more persons involving reciprocal rights and duties; as, a lease, or a contract between bondholders and the issuer.

independence 1. (logic) The relation between two propositions such that the truth of one does not bear on the truth or falsity of the other.

2. (statistics) The property of two or more chance or random events, the probability of whose joint occurrence is equal to the product of their individual probabilities of occurrence.

3. The property of a relation between the accountant and his client (or superior) such that the accountant's findings and reports will be influenced only by the *evidence* discovered and assembled in accord with the rules and principles of his professional discipline.

independent accountant = *public accountant:* a term used by the U. S. Securities and Exchange Commission and others with reference to a public accountant having no financial stake or other interest in the person on whose statements he has expressed his professional opinion, that, if present, might cause the loss of his objectivity or impartiality or otherwise interfere with the free exercise of his professional judgment. The SEC has said that "an accountant will not be considered [by the SEC] independent with respect to any person, or any affiliate thereof, in whom he has any financial interest, direct or indirect, or with whom he is, or was during the period of report, connected as a promoter, underwriter, voting trustee, director, officer, or employee" [Rule 2.01(b) of Regulation S-X, as amended]. A similar definition of independence may be found in the AICPA Code of Professional Ethics, article 1.01.

independent audit = *audit (4)*.

independent variable A variable the value of which, within its defined range, may be assigned without reference to values assumed by other structural elements (variables or constants) in an equation or other mathematical expression. See *variable; function.*

index number A measure, generally a statistical average, employed to indicate common qualities imputed to a group of items. A single number is often used as an index of the properties of the entire group, notwithstanding that statistical considerations indicate that the usage may lead to misinterpretation and misuse. Care must be exercised when index numbers are employed as group surrogates, particularly when the phenomena to which application is sought have complex interrelations which are not thoroughly understood. The application of a general (e.g., wholesale) price index as a measure of capital value or money purchasing power for an individual business organization is an example of one such application. It is not always appreciated that index numbers are often restricted to ordinal measures and that attempts to use them *cardinally* may lead to serious distortions. See *measurement; inequation.* Another common misuse of index numbers that accountants have had occasion to warn against is the use of particular financial relationships such as the working-capital ratio or the sales-net-worth ratio. The use of such ratios out of context with other ratios as a summary index of a complex of business affairs may be inadvisable. In particular, use of a single "critical" ratio should nearly always be avoided.

index of correlation The coefficient of correlation for a nonlinear equation, such as $Y = a + bX + cX^2$; usually written ρ (rho) or I; see *coefficient of correlation.*

indirect cost Costs not readily identifiable with or incurred as the result of the production of specific goods or services, but applicable to a productive activity generally. It is made up of costs incurred in manufacturing operations and regarded as chargeable to the product, other than the (direct) material that enters into and becomes a part of the finished product and the (direct) labor expended upon such material to change its form, shape, or nature. Examples: wages of foremen; machinery upkeep; prorated charges, such as power, heat, light, taxes, depreciation; and other items of factory overhead. See *overhead.*

indirect expense = *indirect cost; manufacturing cost; overhead.*

indirect labor Labor not applicable directly to a product; the cost of such labor. Examples are found in the compensation of janitors, watchmen, maintenance crews and repairmen, superintendents, cost accountants. See *indirect cost; direct labor.*

indirect liability 1. An obligation not yet *incurred* but for which responsibility may have to be assumed in the future; as, the possible liability from the premature settlement of a long-term contract.
2. A debt of another, as the result of which an obligation to pay may develop; a *contingent liability.*

indirect material Material not entering directly into a product; the cost of such material. Examples are found in supplies *consumed* in cleaning, oiling, and maintenance generally; replacement of small parts. See *indirect cost; direct material.*

individual (statistics) A unit or element of a *population* or *universe*, or *sample;* an *event;* as, a natural person, a corporation, the toss of a coin, a voucher. The aggregate of individuals making up a population or universe is conceived as possessing a trait or characteristic common to each individual and capable of being measured and expressed in the form of a number.

industrial-accident reserve A reserve set aside by an employer, usually on the basis of a percentage of the industrial payroll, to which payments to injured employees for personal injuries may be charged; it may or may not be accompanied by the setting aside or earmarking of a corresponding amount of assets.

inequality A relation between two mathematical expressions stating that one is not less than the other. The relation "greater than" is conventionally denoted by the symbol ($>$), the open side indicating the greater part. Thus $y > x$ or $4 > 3$ states that the expression on the left is larger than the one on the right; the expression $y < x$ denotes the converse relation. The expression $y > x$ (or $y \geq x$) denotes that y is greater than or not less than x. Obviously, the expression $y \geq x$ is less restrictive than the statement $y > x$.

inequation A generalized *inequality* stating a relation between more than two variables. The expression $ay + bx \geq c$ is a simple inequation. Inequations (or *inequalities*) represent a more general form of mathematical relation than equations, just as *ordinal* measures are a more general class than *cardinal* measures. See *measurement*. The relation of inequality may be used to define the notion of equation. Thus, the relations $a \geq b$ and $b \leq a$ can be simultaneously true only if $a = b$. In the usual axiom formulation of mathematics, the notion of equation is defined in this manner. Stated somewhat differently, the notion of ordering or ranking by size (or measure) logically precedes the notion of equality; but the concept of equation or equality cannot be used to define the notion of inequation or inequality. Accounting experience confirms the greater generality of ordinal measures. As is well known in cost accounting, for example, it is frequently possible to determine whether the cost of producing a certain item or performing a certain service is increasing or decreasing without being able to determine the precise amount of increase or decrease. Measurements which give expression to such findings are ordinal rather than cardinal in nature. They imply relations of "greater" or "less" without necessarily implying relations of equality. Similar concepts apply to other fields, such as *index-number* construction. It may be possible to ascertain whether prices are increasing or decreasing without being able to tell the exact amount of change. If a price index shows a certain value—say, 160—at two different points of time, this does not in itself imply that prices were the same in the two periods; except in unusual circumstances, no meaning can be applied to the notion of equality in interpreting such index numbers. There is little question, however, that ordinal indexes are frequently used (or misused) in just this fashion. See *index number; measurement.*

inference A judgment or logical conclusion drawn from given assumptions, facts, or other data. By a wise choice of words, a public accountant gives careful consideration to the possible inferences that may be drawn by others from his reports.

informal record A record that is not a part of the regular bookkeeping system but from which essential or useful information may be derived. Example: a commitment listing by a purchasing officer from which may be derived the total of purchase orders issued during a given period, or purchase orders outstanding on a given date.

information at source (Federal income

taxes) Information required under the Internal Revenue Code and regulations to be furnished by persons who pay income to others. The principal types relate to wages of $600 or more if any are not shown on Form W-2; dividends and interest in excess of $10; and payments to noncorporate recipients of business rents, and royalties of $600 or more. Information returns must also be filed by partnerships, estates, and trusts, the data supplied including details of revenues and expense, and distributable shares of net income, if any.

inheritance tax The term usually applied to a graduated tax assessed by any U.S. state on estates of deceased persons. See *estate tax*.

in kind See *kind*.

in-lieu *adj*. Alternative: as in the expression "in-lieu depreciation" (= *policy* depreciation; see under *depreciation method*) and "in-lieu taxes" (payments to a governmental unit taking the place of taxes).

input-output statement 1. Any statement (often in chart form) showing movements of quantities from one or more positions to other positions. Examples: Leontief's structural representation of the American economy.

2. A *cost-flow statement;* a *funds-flow statement*.

in short In an adjacent and subordinate column, usually at the left: said of supporting details for which a total appears in any accounting or statistical schedule or table.

insolvency 1. Inability or failure to pay debts as they become due.

2. The condition of an individual or organization where liabilities exceed the fair and realizable value of the assets available for their settlement (Federal Bankruptcy Law).

installment 1. Any part payment on a debt.

2. One of an agreed series of partial payments on a debt, each of which is specified as to amount and date due, interest often being included.

installment method of accounting A method of recording revenue from an installment sale whereby the gross profit from the sale is *recognized* in any fiscal year in proportion to the portion of the total selling price collected in cash during that year. Example: A piano that cost a dealer $1,600 is sold for $2,400: one-quarter down, the balance to be paid thereafter in equal installments of $30 each. The gross profit is $800 or $33\frac{1}{3}\%$, and if $780, including the down payment, is collected during the fiscal year in which the sale is made, the gross profit to be included in that year's revenues will be $800 \times \frac{780}{2,400}$, or $260. The same result is, of course, obtained by applying the gross-profit percentage to the year's collections ($33\frac{1}{3}\%$ of $780 = $260).

The installment basis contrasts with the *accrual* and *cost-recovery* bases. The accrual basis *recognizes* the full amount of gross profit at the time the sale is recorded. Many retail dealers having installment sales keep their records on the *accrual basis,* especially where the period of payment extends over a period of a year or two. If the *cost-recovery basis* is followed, cash received from the buyer is credited against the cost of the sale until the cost is completely offset; thereafter, any cash received is credited to revenue. This basis may be favored where the likelihood of full payment by the buyer is regarded, for any reason, as uncertain, or where repossession is expected.

Dealers in real or personal property commonly lump together a year's installment sales and costs of sales in order to obtain an overall average gross-profit percentage for that year; then in subsequent years, the same average percentage is applied to the collections on the earlier year's sales to obtain the revenue to be accounted for from such collections.

Where the property in the seller's hands is subject to a mortgage or other lien that is passed on to the buyer, the selling price (and the cost of the sale) does not include the amount of the mortgage or lien. But where the buyer gives back a mortgage or other obligation to the seller, the amount thereof is properly a part of the selling price, subject to realization, as in the case of a contract or note.

A bad debt from an installment sale may be incurred where the cost of the sale exceeds the sum of (a) the collections made to date less the portion thereof accounted for as realized gross profit, and (b) the value of the property, if repossessed, at the time of the repossession, such value having been adjusted downward for the estimated cost of putting the property into resalable condition.

A repossession may result in a profit or loss depending on the excess of credits over debits, or debits over credits, the debits consisting of the uncollected selling price, the legal and other costs involved in retransferring and physically recovering the property, and the costs of rehabilitation, the credits consisting of the value of property subject to resale (after putting it back in resalable condition) and the unearned gross profit not yet recognized as revenue. The Federal income-tax law and regulations recognize generally the accounting method described above for installment sales of personal property by dealers. As to real property and certain types of casual sales of personal property, the law divides installment sales into two classes: sales on which receipts, during the taxable year in which the sale took place, in cash or property other than evidences of indebtedness of the purchaser, have not exceeded 30 percent of the selling price; and sales on which more than 30 percent was received during such taxable year. In the latter case, the obligations of the buyer are regarded as having been realized to the extent of their fair market value when received: a situation that places such sales on what is virtually an accrual basis.

A relatively simple bookkeeping plan is usually followed for installment sales. Receivables are initially accounted for in the usual way, except that subsidiary accounts may be kept on forms especially suited to the recording of and follow-up on installments. The gross profit pertaining to the uncollected balances of the installment receivables is generally segregated by the fiscal years of the original sales, and the account maintained for each such year is decreased periodically by amounts realized from collections or recognized as uncollectible through repossessions or the charging off of bad debts; the ledger accounts are called "unrealized gross profit" and are classified as valuation accounts deductible on a balance sheet from the receivables to which they pertain, or as deferred-revenue accounts appearing on a balance sheet in a separate classification following current liabilities.

During recent years, control over the down payment and the period over which installments may be collected has been regarded as a device available to the national government for dealing with inflation and for directing the flow of raw materials. By increasing the percentage amount of down payments and shortening the period of installment payments, the demand for certain consumer "luxury" products has been decreased, thus providing an inflationary curb and a more closely controlled application of scarce materials to such special purposes as national defense.

Illustrative entries follow.

During the current year, a dealer in household equipment sold on the installment basis merchandise amounting to $150,796.23, which included a loading charge (for handling the account) of 2 percent. The merchandise cost was $108,573.29, and down payments and collections on these sales amounted to $62,540.82. During the same year, collections of $40,269.77 were made on the previous year's installment sales, on which the gross profit averaged 30 percent, while reposs were masessionde of merchandise sold during the same previous year on which the following data had been collected: original selling price, $15,204.00;

	Debit	Credit
(1)		
Customers' installment accounts (current year)	$150,796.23	
Merchandise inventory		$108,573.29
Unearned gross profit on installment sales		42,222.94
Installment sales for current year on which a gross profit of 28% (42,222.94/150,796.23) is expected; a loading charge of 2% appears in the selling price.		
(2)		
Cash	102,810.59	
Customers' installment accounts (current year)		62,540.82
Customers' installment accounts (previous year)		40,269.77
Cash collections on installment accounts.		
(3)		
Unearned gross profit (current year)	17,511.43	
Unearned gross profit (previous year)	12,080.93	
Gross profit on installment collections		29,592.36
Gross profit of 28% and 30% on current and previous years' collections shown in preceding entry.		
(4)		
Repossessed merchandise	4,225.00	
Unearned gross profit (previous year)	2,308.17	
Loss on repossessions	1,663.03	
Customers' installment accounts (previous year)		7,693.90
Repossession expense (or accounts payable)		502.30
Repossession of merchandise sold in previous year; unearned gross profit is 30% of uncollected balances of $7,693.90; loss of $1,663.03 on repossessions is excess of credits over debits.		

collections in the previous year, $6,275.00, and in the current year, $1,235.10; costs of repossession, $502.30; merchandise value of recovered items, $4,225.00.

The 2 percent loading charge has not been separated out from the selling price, since it covers "handling" costs throughout the collection period. Less commonly, the practice has been to regard a loading charge primarily as a reimbursement of the initial cost of establishing the customer's credit, and hence as having been earned at the time the sale is made. If such a practice had been followed in the illustration, entry (1) could have been modified by decreasing the unearned-gross-profit credit of $42,222.94 to $39,266.15 and adding to the entry a credit of $2,956.79 to "Income from loading charges." Entries (2) and (3) would also require modification because of the reduction of the gross-profit percentage for the current year from 28 to 26.56.

installment sale A sale of real or personal property paid for in a series of equal amounts over a period of weeks or months. The selling price may include a *loading* cost, and a down payment at the time of sale is commonly required. Title may be conveyed with the transfer of the property, subject to a chattel mortgage given to the seller, or subject to lien for the balance of the purchase price; or title may be conveyed to a third person during the payment period. Title may also be passed to the buyer after a certain number of payments have been made, or only following the final payment. See *sale; installment method of accounting.*

institutional buyer Any organization periodically having substantial sums for investment, the principal types being: life-insurance companies; educational, charitable, and religious institutions; foundations; commercial and savings banks and organizations; trust companies that have in their possession the funds of individuals and estates; and investment trusts. Life-insurance companies are the country's largest investors in real-estate mortgages, buy-and-lease financing, corporation bonds, and governmental issues.

insurable interest A person's interest in or legal relationship with the property of another, such that its damage or destruction would cause him pecuniary loss.

insurable value Current replacement cost new, with materials of like kind and quality, less a reasonable deduction for depreciation.

insurance The method whereby those subject to similar hazards contribute to a common fund, out of which any loss sustained by a contributor is paid. The business of assuming the management of such funds is carried on by (a) "stock" companies, i.e., profit corporations; (b) mutual (not-for-profit) companies whose stockholders insure each other; (c) unincorporated reciprocal organizations whose members appoint an "attorney-in-fact" as manager to collect premiums in advance, pay losses and expenses, and refund to members any balance remaining at the end of each fiscal year; (d) Lloyd's, an association of marine underwriters, each underwriter becoming personally liable for the amount of insurance for which he subscribes; (e) self-insurers, whose risks are sufficiently numerous and diversified to permit them economically to assume the risks themselves; and (f) governmental organizations, such as the Federal Deposit Insurance Corporation (FDIC), established for the purpose of assuming banking risks.

insurance fund A fund created for the payment of losses by a person carrying his own risks. The additions thereto may be based on the premiums which would otherwise be payable to insurance companies, or, more correctly, on a loss factor independently determined for the type of risk involved.

insurance premium The cost to a person of a contract to reimburse him for a property or business loss caused by various types of events over which he has little or no control; the period covered may range from a year or less to five years. Premium costs are amortized on a straight-line or benefits-received basis over the period of protection. A premium rate is often expressed as "cents percent"—the cost in cents for each $100 of insurance coverage.

insurance register A record of essential facts concerning insurance carried, often including the amounts of premiums expiring in successive accounting periods.

insurance reserve A reserve created on the books of a self-insurer by an appropriation of net income or retained earnings for the purpose of covering fire or other risks. The reserve is appropriated surplus, the preferred practice being to regard losses as operating costs when they occur.

insure To contract with another to assume the financial loss or obligation contingent upon a risk.

intangible (asset) 1. Any "two-dimensional" or "incorporeal" asset; any asset other than cash or real estate; in this sense used by some tax authorities.
2. A *capital asset* having no physical existence, its value being limited by the rights and anticipative benefits that possession confers upon the owner. See *goodwill; patent; trademark.*

intangible value The value of an enterprise in its entirety, as a going concern, in excess of the value of its *net tangible assets*. Intangible value, arising from a monopoly, secret processes, patents, trademarks, customer goodwill, managerial skill, growth of population, or numerous other possible causes, is often reckoned as the present worth of total earning power in excess of a normal return on the value of net tangible assets. See *goodwill; going-concern value.*

integer Any *digit* or any group of digits expressing a *number;* examples: 1;—24; 63,762. However, a number containing a fraction, such as 54.25 or $6\frac{2}{7}$, although a *rational number*, is not an integer.

interchangeable part (statistical quality control) Mating or matching components in an assembly which insure satisfactory functioning even when each component is selected at *random*. The chief advantages of a manufacturing system using interchangeable parts are that it facilitates mass production by eliminating selective assembly, simplifies operations, reduces costs, and helps solve problems of replacement.

intercompany elimination The subtraction of intercompany investments, receivables, payables, sales, purchases, and other items necessarily omitted in the preparation of consolidated and group balance sheets and income statements. The principal types of eliminations are: investments in stocks and bonds; advances and current accounts; profit or loss in receivables, inventories, fixed and other assets, valuation accounts, and liabilities; purchases and sales; service, interest, and other income and expense; dividends. It is usually held that eliminations of intercompany gains and losses should be complete, notwithstanding the existence of minority stockholders' interests in subsidiaries; thus, if a parent company owns 60 percent of the outstanding capital stock of a subsidiary, 100 percent of the intercompany profit is eliminated from the inventory owned either (a) by the parent or (b) by the subsidiary; in (a), 40 percent of the inventory profit could be eliminated against the book value of the *minority interest*, or 100 percent could be absorbed by the majority interest; in (b), 100 percent would be absorbed by the majority interest.

Where eliminations are numerous and complicated, an *eliminations ledger* may be maintained.

Elimination of intercompany investments in capital stock against the equities shown by the records of the issuing company may give rise to differences that should be distinctively labeled on the balance sheet. The difference between the investment cost and the book equity is in practice variously disposed of. An excess of investment cost has at times been merged in an undisclosed amount with recorded goodwill, added to tangible fixed-asset accounts, shown separately, or subtracted from the combined capital-stock and surplus accounts. An excess of book equity at the date of acquiring control has been merged in an undisclosed amount with "capital surplus" or paid-in surplus, subtracted from tangible fixed-asset accounts, or shown separately. In some instances, both "goodwill from consolidation" and "capital surplus from consolidation" have appeared on the same consolidated balance sheet; in other instances, they have been merged.

Where an excess as to any one subsidiary is substantial (perhaps 20 percent or more of the investment in that subsidiary), and cannot readily be explained, the subsidiary may not be consolidated; instead, the facts peculiar to that subsidiary can best be displayed in separate financial statements. The excess of investment or book value may be ascribable to an earning power disproportionate to teh investment appearing on the subsidiary's books; to the provision of too much or too little depreciation on fixed or intangible assets; or, in general, to asset valuations differing from those on which the controlling company's acquisition has been based. If the cause has been inaccurate bookkeeping procedure, the remedy lies in determining the amount of the excess and correcting it. If the cause has been the earning power of the subsidiary, there can be no objection to adding the subsidiary to the consolidated picture. But if the cause cannot be determined, or if no basis exists for correcting the books of account, the inclusion of the subsidiary with the consolidated group might lead to substantial inaccuracy in interpretation.

If the net excess is one of investment cost, it should not be confused on the consolidated balance sheet with goodwill or another intangible item which bears the label of something acquired in a direct purchase with other assets; it should be designated "Excess from consolidation with subsidiaries" or "Consolidation excess." This treatment avoids a merging with items usually associated with individual companies. The necessity for such a showing on a consolidated balance sheet has been eliminated in many instances during recent years by the amortization of investment cost down to the underlying value reflected in the subsidiary's records.

An excess of book equity at the date of acquisition over investment cost becomes "Consolidation surplus." On the consolidated balance sheet, the consolidation excesses should be separated from the consolidation surpluses, in view of the possibility that the former may become a loss and that the latter may ultimately be surplus of the controlling company available for distribution to its stockholders.

Retained earnings on the consolidated balance sheet arising from subsidiary companies is confined to undistributed profits earned since the date of acquisition, without regard to the period prior to that date during which an interest less than controlling may have been owned. Retained earnings applicable to shares acquired after the controlling-interest date is computed only from the date of acquiring such shares.

Shares of the controlling company's capital stock owned by a subsidiary before the date of acquisition may be treated as the equivalent of treasury stock purchased on that date. Any subsequent acquisition or sale by a subsidiary may be treated in the consolidated statements as though it had been the act of the controlling company.

Elimination in consolidation of intercompany investments in obligations against the accumulated obligations shown by the books of the issuing company gives rise to the adjustment of the consolidation excess or surplus or of current loss and gain as the circumstances may require. Any premium or discount at the date of acquisition arising from the difference between the investment cost and the accumulated obligation on the books of the issuer (i.e., face amount less any unamortized discount, plus any accumulated premium to be paid on retirement) is combined with the consolidation excess arising from the subsidiary affected; any differences from acquisitions thereafter may be regarded as current gains or losses.

See *consolidation policy*.

intercompany profit Book profit representing the excess of charges by one related company to another for services rendered or goods sold over and above their cost to the related group conceived as a unit. Under standard procedures in the preparation of consolidated statements, intercompany profits are eliminated in their entirety regardless of minority holdings, in order that only profits on sales and services to the public may be shown as having been realized.

interdepartmental profit The excess over cost of goods or services charged by one division to another within the same economic unit; under standard procedures, they are eliminated in the final accounting, since no profit is realized except through sales to outsiders.

interest 1. The service charge for the use of money or capital, paid at agreed intervals by the user, and commonly expressed as an annual percentage of outstanding principal.

2. The return on any investment of capital.

3. A portion of the equity in a business enterprise, expressed as a fraction or in terms of dollars invested.

interference (statistical quality control) See *tolerance*.

interfund transfer The transfer of money or other asset or of a liability from one *fund* to another.

interim *adj.* Occurring between major, fixed, or prominent dates: said of a trustee's report during a period of administration, of financial statements covering less than a full fiscal year, or of any statement, as from a bank, for less than the customary reporting period.

interim audit 1. That portion of an

audit (*1*) conducted while the accounting period to be covered by the completed audit is still in progress.
2. An audit of an interim period or partial fiscal year.

interim closing Any *closing* of the books other than at the end of a fiscal year, not involving the elimination of income and expense accounts.

interim dividend Any one or more dividends declared during a fiscal year, often quarterly and before earnings are known, as contrasted with the *year-end dividend* which is declared after the year's net income has been determined.

interim report A report at any date other than the end of a fiscal year; example: a brief report of a corporation in which profits for the quarter or year to date are announced. The report usually contains a warning that a number of contingencies attach to the figures it contains: inventories may be estimated, income-tax rates may be changing, adjustments peculiar to the year-end have not yet been made; book figures shown are unaudited; the business is subject to seasonal variations—e.g., the first half or three-quarters, for which a net income has been reported, may be followed by a second half or final quarter with no net income or even an operating loss. Many quarterly reports of corporations disclose only sales, net income, and a few other items, varying in character.

interim statement A statement prepared as at any date, or for a period ended on any date within a fiscal year or other regular reporting period.

internal audit(-ing) The relatively independent internal appraisal activity having responsibility for the review of the effectiveness of records, controls, and operations generally within an organization and serving as a protective and constructive service to management. Carried out as a staff function by company employees, it constitutes an important element of *internal control* and is not to be confused with line operations such as the preaudit of vouchers that make up normal operating procedures within an organization (see *internal check*) or with the audit work of (outside) public accountants. As a general rule, the scope and responsibilities of internal auditing are conditioned by the scope and responsibilities delegated to the immediate superior of the internal auditor. The most satisfactory application of internal auditing is found where its organizational status is highest and its delegated functions the widest.

Internal auditing in fully developed situations involves:

(a) the verification and appraisal of the reliability of accounting records and statistical data;

(b) the ascertainment that assets of all kinds, both those on hand and those disposed of, are safeguarded and have been accurately and fully accounted for, and that normal accounting processes provide information that discloses losses and wasteful practices;

(c) the determination that management-prescribed plans, policies, and procedures are being complied with by operating units;

(d) the reporting of observations with recommendations for improvement in the various sectors of the business; and

(e) the work of internal audit carried on by an internal auditor having a professional status.

In the majority of business organizations, the internal-audit activity is first concerned with the verification of completed financial transactions and records. Using post-transaction verification procedures as a base, the internal auditor proceeds to examine and appraise related management policies and plans and records and procedures in terms of their adequacy and effectiveness. An important part of the internal auditor's activities is the review and appraisal of accounting-personnel performance under established policies and procedures.

Because of his contact and familiarity with details of operations, the modern internal auditor is often called upon to make special studies for management covering such diverse matters as a review of the methods of accounting for and control over scrap material or the analysis of a plan for the decentralization of accounting and other operating activities. Special studies often have as one purpose the development of information necessary in the formulation of general policy, and may not be concerned with financial matters. The findings of routine internal audits may also indicate areas where changes in policies or procedures ought to be considered.

The internal auditor's responsibility in the development, maintenance, and appraisal of adequate *internal checks* is his principal contribution toward making fraud difficult and toward the early discovery of fraud through the processes of daily operating methods and controls. Some frauds are revealed through normal verification techniques of the internal auditor's program; the prevention of fraud through recommendations of adequate protective devices as a part of operating procedures rather than the detection of committed frauds is likewise considered to be a function of internal auditing. Where fraud is discovered, the internal auditor is concerned not only with the amount involved, but also with a study of the fraudulent mechanism employed and the persons responsible, and with the appraisal of established checks and controls, to the end that the recurrence of the fraud may be prevented or made less likely.

Often the similarity of the mechanics of the work of the internal auditor with those of the public accountant leads to the supposition that there is little distinction between their basic objectives. Actually, the contrast reflected in their different approaches, attitudes, and practices is considerable. The public accountant is primarily concerned with the financial statements of the organization and with a very general review of its operations over a stated period. He is interested in procedures mainly to the extent necessary to satisfy himself that the established internal controls (such as accounting procedure and internal auditing) have provided adequate safeguards against fraud and manipulation.

The internal auditor, entrusted with the responsibility of reporting to management on the continuing activities of the organization, must shape his activities to follow the operating pattern within the specific organization. His examination is directed to what is done, who does it, where it is done, and how well it is done, and to pointing up the significance of the end result after the doing is over.

Concerned with being able to certify to the results of the operation of an entire business or of its major segments, the public accountant necessarily gives comparatively little regard to component functional units. His examination of transactions is likely to cut across organizational lines.

The internal auditor must follow established organizational lines closely; he must be able to report on the performance of a particular department, division, or other operating unit. His examination includes a study of prescribed controls and the routines leading up to the final results. If the controls and routines are well conceived and administered, the results should be correctly stated, as will be evidenced by both his own and the public accountant's examination.

An important element in the success of an internal auditing program is the method of reporting the internal auditor's findings and recommendations. His reports are often gauged to the understanding and interests of operating executives, such as those in charge of production and sales, who may have little interest in accounting terminology and techiques. Some of the essentials of reporting are:

1. The review of findings with personnel of any organizational unit examined before the preparation of the final report;

2. The elimination of minor discrepancies in the final report, particularly

those immediately corrected by the operating personnel and reflecting no weakness in basic procedures;

3. The minimum reporting or omission of routine audit steps;

4. Emphasis on exceptions and recommendations; and

5. A discussion, after submission of the report, with operating executives concerned, leading to agreement on constructive and corrective measures that need consideration.

As one of the elements of managerial control, internal auditing is receiving increasing recognition and management acceptance. In any organization of moderate to large size, it can be an indispensable aid to management limited only by the abilities and background of the internal auditor himself.

internal auditor One responsible for the conduct of *internal auditing*.

internal check The design of transaction flows that provide effective organization and operation and protection against fraud. A principal feature is the allocation of organizational responsibility in such a manner that no single individual or group has exclusive control over any one transaction or group of transactions, each transaction being cross-checked or cross-controlled through the normal functioning of another individual or group. Effective internal check is so devised that a transaction can be consummated only through prescribed operating procedures, of which the mechanism of internal check is invariably an integral part. The term should not be confused with the post-transaction, staff function of *internal auditing* or with overall *internal control*, of which internal check is but an element.

The separation of responsibility for custody and accounting is an essential of internal check which may be best understood by citing several examples taken from practice:

Example 1. The purchasing function in the *W* Company is confined to the responsibility for placing orders and determining prices. Vendor's invoices first go to the voucher-accounting unit to be compared for agreement with the purchase order and with the receiving report from the receiving unit, the latter having neither purchasing nor accounting supervision. Upon finding all in order, the voucher unit prepares a disbursement check. The treasury division, after finding supporting documents in order, indicates final approval by placing a signature on the disbursement check.

Example 2. The receipt, custody, and deposit of the incoming cash of *W* Company are functions of the cashier, whose unit is a part of the treasurer's office and who reports the amount and nature of each item, such as the details of collections from customers, to the accounting unit, where records of total cash in banks and of detailed accounts receivable are maintained.

Example 3. Although the depositing of *W* Company's receipts and the making of disbursements are the responsibility of the cashier, maintenance of the record of cash balance is part of the accounting function. The reconciliation of bank statements, which acts as a check on both the cashier and the accounting functions, is assigned to a unit which has no authority or responsibility for either handling or accounting for cash.

Example 4. In the operation of *W* Company's storeroom, the accounting for items in stock is the responsibility of a unit separate from the unit responsible for the physical maintenance and handling of storeroom receipts, issues, and stock.

These examples illustrate the widely observed principle of internal check: the separation of the responsibility of accounting from that of custody.

Internal check is a deterrent to fraud; a fully developed scheme of internal check makes it impossible for a defaulter to abstract funds or other assets for which he is responsible and at the same time cover up his manipulations by entering corresponding amounts in the accounting records. As long as accounting and custody are separated, fraud can be completely concealed only through collusion between employees responsible for each of these functions. Fraud by an employee in either function is virtually certain to be discovered when quantities on hand (as reported by the custodial function) are verified with what the records show should be on hand (a product of the accounting function).

Carefully designed internal checks often yield definite advantages and economies because of the relative efficiency of a specialized operation. An employee preparing disbursement checks continuously tends to become highly efficient in that single operation. If he is replaced, a new employee may be readily trained because of the limited part of the work which is comprised in the specialized job. In larger accounting and treasury units, specialization results in the delegation of the mechanics of accounting to bookkeeping machines or data-processing or computer devices, and this delegation within the accounting unit acts as an additional internal check by removing the detailed accounting function even further from the custodial function.

There is sometimes a tendency to treat certain elements of internal check as axiomatic, and to claim that they must be invariably followed without regard to the conditions surrounding a particular situation. The full development of this notion easily results in the overelaboration of records and in a too costly operation. Standards of internal check, particularly the separation of custody and accounting, should be considered as standards to be followed within practicable limits.

Various considerations may dictate a deviation from standards, and the resultant exposure to possible fraud should be recognized and compensated for in other ways, as by more frequent or more comprehensive verification through internal audit.

Internal check is so much a part of the organization and the procedures of most businesses that the elements of it may be overlooked. These must always be recognized and given consideration in establishing new procedures and in the appraisal of procedures in use.

internal control The general methodology by which management is carried on within an organization; also, any of the numerous devices for supervising and directing an operation or operations generally.

Internal control, a management function, is a basic factor operating in one form or another in the administration of every organization, business or otherwise. Although sometimes identified with the administrative organism itself, it is often characterized as the nervous system that activates overall operating policies and keeps them within practicable performance ranges. A particular system of internal control, notwithstanding its superficial resemblance to common patterns of organization and management, is usually unique in detail, having developed around individuals with varying authorities and capacities of supervision and with varying abilities to delegate or assume authority. In a corporation, internal control commences with the institution and enforcement of top policies established by the board of directors and continues down through the organizational structure, taking form in the development and operation of management policies, administrative regulations, manuals, directives, and decisions; internal auditing; internal check; reporting; employee training and participation. A suggestions plan, for example, is of importance to the scheme of control existing in many organizations. In general, well-designed and carefully operated internal control is said to exist where an organization runs smoothly, economically, and in conformity with top-policy objectives.

An important element in maintaining internal control is provided in the work of the *internal auditor*. Although his presence may and often does act as a deterrent to departures from required practices, his aim is to neither deter nor enforce, but to investigate and comment. This gives him a quasi-independent, professional status and tends to develop and maintain his capacity as an unbiased observer and reporter on whom management can depend for its information concerning the functioning of internal control. Originally the duties of the internal auditor were confined to examinations of the correctness of accounts; in recent years, his field has extended to the examination of all internal controls, often not involving the accounts; see *internal audit*.

Policies, administrative directives, and business behavior given life and maintained by internal controls, are of three sorts: the formal types, expressed in resolutions of the board of directors, regulations such as an office or accounting manual, or written instructions covering limited activities; the informal type, within the framework of the formal type and given effect by oral directions, such as procedural instructions by a supervisor to his staff; and the implicit type—operating habits and standards, unwritten and unspoken, yet nonetheless common to an industry, community, form of organization, or business generally, or accepted human conduct presumably understood and observed by all as a matter of course. The operating quality of any organization is influenced as much by implicit policies and standards as by the explicit types. See *policy; corporate action; administration; administrative action; decision.*

Internal control does not end with the testing of conformance to policies and operating standards but extends to practical operations involving individuals or group decisions or actions that, intentionally or otherwise, are within the discretion of the individual and are covered neither by rule nor convention; as, a determination based on individual judgment to deny credit to a customer. The general characteristics usually attaching to an operating *decision* are its dependence on individual discretion and its freedom from appraisal, at the time it is made, as to its rightness or wrongness. After being put into effect, decisions may be tested for their propriety in the normal course of operation of the internal controls, but only on a postaction basis.

The principal elements contributing to internal control are usually these:

1. Recognition that within every *organizational unit* there are one or more *functional* or action components known as *activities, cost* or *responsibility centers,* or *management units;*
2. Delegated operating authority in each organizational unit permitting freedom of action within defined limits;
3. The linking of expenditures—their incurrence and disposition—with specified individual authority;
4. *Endproduct* planning (a) by means of a *budget* fitted to the organizational structure and to its functional components, thus maintaining dual forward operating disciplines; and (b) the adoption of *standards of comparison* and other *performance* measurements such as *standard costs, quality controls,* and timing goals;
5. An *accounting process* that provides organizational and functional administrators with prompt, complete, and accurate information on operating performance, and comparisons with predetermined performance standards;
6. Periodic reports, consonant with accounting and related records, by activity heads to supervisory management: reports serving as *feedbacks* of informative pictures of operations, and as displays of favorable and unfavorable factors that have influenced performance;
7. *Internal check,* built into operating procedures, and providing maximum protection against fraud and error;
8. Frequent professional *appraisals,* through *internal audit,* of management and its policies and operations generally, as a protective and constructive management service, its emphasis varying with the quality of operating policies and their

administration; and

9. The construction of the above controls in such a manner as to stimulate and take full advantage of those natural attributes of individual employees the recognition and exercise of which may obviate the need for some internal controls and determine the extent and rigidity of others.

internal reporting The supplying of operating data and other information by one person or unit to another within an organization; as, monthly financial statements prepared by a controller; feasibility reports on proposals for fixed-asset replacements; unit-cost determinations supplied by a cost accountant; purchase orders, expense reports, receiving and shipping notices, collection details, daily cash statements, and other data on recurrent organizational activities that others have an interest in controlling or being guided by. See *accountability; reporting.*

internal transaction A bookkeeping entry reflecting the periodic adjustment of a *prepaid expense,* an *accrual* of a revenue earned or of an expense incurred, the recording of a liability, a *provision* for depreciation, an *allocation* of costs, the correction of an error, and the like; known also as an "accounting" transaction; contrasts with *external transaction* or transaction with an outsider. See *transaction.*

interpolation (statistics) The estimation of intermediate values within a collection of available data; as, an estimate of production for a period the records for which have been lost, based on production data before and after such a period. Compare with *extrapolation.*

An interpolation formula that may be used with interest accumulation tables is

$$s = s_1 + pD_1 + \frac{p(p-1)}{1\times 2}D_2 + \frac{p(p-1)(p-2)}{1\times 2\times 3}D_3, \text{ etc.,}$$

where s is the sum desired; s_1 the next lower related value in the table; p the fractional interval between the two most nearly related values in the table; and D_1, D_2, D_3, etc., the first, second, third, etc., differences between the preceding or following table values. Thus, from the table of compound amounts of 1 (pp. 96–97), values for D_1, D_2, D_3, and D_4 may be developed as in the following table.

Rate	Compound Amount *(10 periods)*	D_1	D_2	D_3	D_4
6.0	1.7908 477				
5.5	1.7081 445	827 032			
5.0	1.6288 946	792 499	34 533		
4.5	1.5529 694	759 252	33 247	1 286	
4.0	1.4802 443	727 251	32 001	1 246	40
3.5	1.4105 988	696 455	30 796	1 205	41
3.0	1.3439 164	666 824	29 631	1 165	40
2.5	1.2800 845	638 319	28 505	1 126	39
2.0	1.2189 944	610 901	27 418	1 087	39
1.5	1.1605 408	584 536	26 365	1 053	34
1.0	1.1046 221	559 187	25 349	1 016	37
0.5	1.0511 401	534 820	24 367	982	34

If, for example, corresponding compound amounts for the rates $1\frac{1}{4}$ percent, 0.6 percent, and 0.65 percent are desired, they may be derived as follows, correct to the sixth decimal place:

$1\frac{1}{4}$%

Item	Interval Fraction	Amount
s_1	1%	1.1046 221
D_1	+0.5	+ 279 593
D_2	−0.125	− 3 169
D_3	+0.0625	+ 64
D_4	−0.039	− 1
Total		1.1322 708

0.6%

Item	Interval Fraction	Amount
s_1	0.5%	1.0511 401
D_1	+0.2	+ 106 964
D_2	−0.08	− 1 949
D_3	+0.048	+ 47
D_4	−0.0336	− 1
Total		1.0616 462

	0.65%	
Item	*Interval Fraction*	*Amount*
s_1	0.5%	1.0511 401
D_1	+0.3	+ 160 446
D_2	−0.105	− 2 558
D_3	+0.0595	+ 58
D_4	−0.0402	− 1
Total		1.0669 346

The interval fractions are the coefficients of the formula, readily obtained once the value for p is determined. In the first example above, p is 0.5 since $1\frac{1}{4}$ is halfway between 1 and $1\frac{1}{2}$; and

$$\frac{p(p-1)}{1 \times 2} = \frac{0.5(0.5-1)}{2} = -0.125,$$

$$\frac{p(p-1)(p-2)}{1 \times 2 \times 3} = \frac{0.5(-0.5)(-1.5)}{6} = +\,0.0625, \text{ etc.}$$

The fractions are then applied to the differences shown opposite the lower rate; i.e., $0.5 \times 559187 = 279593$; $-\,0.125 \times 25349 = -3169$; etc. In the second illustration, 0.6 is two-tenths of the interval from $\frac{1}{2}$ to 1; hence,

$$\frac{p(p-1)}{1 \times 2} = \frac{.2(0.2-1)}{2} = -0.08, \text{ etc.}$$

Where interpolations employing the above formula must be frequently computed, a schedule of fractions for commonly recurring differences may be prepared as in the following table.

SCHEDULE OF FRACTIONS APPLICABLE TO SUCCESSIVE DIFFERENCES

D_1	D_2	D_3	D_4	D_5	D_6
$\frac{1}{2}$	$\frac{1}{8}$	$\frac{1}{16}$	$\frac{5}{128}$	$\frac{7}{256}$	$\frac{21}{1024}$
$\frac{1}{4}$	$\frac{3}{32}$	$\frac{7}{128}$	$\frac{77}{2048}$	$\frac{231}{8192}$	$\frac{1463}{65536}$
$\frac{3}{4}$	$\frac{3}{32}$	$\frac{5}{128}$	$\frac{45}{2048}$	$\frac{117}{8192}$	$\frac{663}{65536}$
$\frac{1}{3}$	$\frac{1}{9}$	$\frac{5}{81}$	$\frac{10}{243}$	$\frac{22}{729}$	$\frac{154}{6561}$
$\frac{2}{3}$	$\frac{1}{9}$	$\frac{4}{81}$	$\frac{7}{243}$	$\frac{14}{729}$	$\frac{91}{6561}$
$\frac{1}{5}$	$\frac{2}{25}$	$\frac{6}{125}$	$\frac{21}{625}$	$\frac{399}{15625}$	$\frac{1596}{78125}$
$\frac{2}{5}$	$\frac{3}{25}$	$\frac{8}{125}$	$\frac{26}{625}$	$\frac{468}{15625}$	$\frac{1794}{78125}$
$\frac{3}{5}$	$\frac{3}{25}$	$\frac{7}{125}$	$\frac{21}{625}$	$\frac{357}{15625}$	$\frac{1309}{78125}$
$\frac{4}{5}$	$\frac{2}{25}$	$\frac{4}{125}$	$\frac{11}{625}$	$\frac{176}{15625}$	$\frac{616}{78125}$

The formula may also be applied in the computation of *extrapolations* or extensions of the intervals of a given table. Where the extension is to be made to the next higher interval, the formula becomes

$$s = s_1 + D_1 + D_2 + D_3, \text{ etc.,}$$

D_1, D_2, D_3, etc., being the differences obtaining from the highest table value; and where the extension is to be made to the next lower interval,

$$s = s_1 - D_1 + D_2 - D_3, \text{ etc.,}$$

D_1, D_2, D_3, etc., being the differences obtaining from the lowest table value. The following will illustrate: In the first example it is assumed that the intervals from 2 to 4% as shown in the table on pp. 96–97 are known; in the second, that the intervals from 6 to 4% are known; in the third, that the intervals from $2\frac{1}{2}$ to $\frac{1}{2}$% are known.

Item	4 TO $4\frac{1}{2}$%	4 TO $3\frac{1}{2}$%	$\frac{1}{2}$ TO 0%
s_1	1.4802 443	1.4802 443	1.0511 401
D_1	+ 696 455	− 727 251	− 534 820
D_2	+ 29 631	+ 32 001	+ 24 367
D_3	+ 1 126	− 1 246	− 982
D_4	+ 39	+ 40	+ 34
Totals	1.5529 694	1.4105 987	1.0000 000

interpretation An explanation, often involving the supplying of information concerning the purpose, context, or implications of a statement or action. "Reasonable" interpretations are those consistent with the fund of factual information regarded as the most adequate. Because interpretation often involves surmise, individuals differ in the reasonableness of their interpretations because of differences in the character and extent of past experiences with which the instant cases may be compared and because of differences in *bias*.

inter-vivos trust A trust created between living persons, as contrasted with a *testamentary trust*. See *trust*.

intestate One who dies without making a will.

inventory *n.* 1. Raw materials and supplies, goods finished and in process of manufacture, and merchandise on hand, in transit and owned, in storage, or consigned to others at the end of an accounting period: (a) their aggregate value, usually at cost or some portion of cost; (b) the process of counting, listing, and pricing them; (c) the listing in which they are itemized, showing description, quantities, unit prices, extensions, and totals; (d) a physical inventory.

2. In general, any class or group of materials or supplies, not yet expensed or capitalized; as, maintenance supplies or construction materials.

3. (sometimes *pl.*) The title of a balance-sheet item representing the sum total of finished goods, materials, supplies, and merchandise on hand. Its valuation is cost; cost or market, whichever is lower; or other stated basis. See *inventory valuation; balance sheet.*

4. In the accounts of executors, administrators, trustees, and receivers: (a) the property, tangible and intangible, of an estate or trust, as it existed on a certain date; (b) its estimated or realizable value; (c) the process of taking an inventory of the property of an estate or trust; (d) the list required by law to accompany the accounts or statements filed with the courts.

5. The detailed list of property that often accompanies a bill of sale or a lease of furnished premises.

inventory certificate A representation pertaining to inventories of stock on hand obtained by an auditor from the management of an enterprise under examination. It usually sets forth the method used in determining quantities, the basis on which the items were priced, and other matters relating to ownership, condition, and the like. See *representation.*

inventory control The control of merchandise, materials, goods in process, finished goods, and supplies on hand by accounting and physical methods. An accounting control is effected by means of a stock or stores ledger, mechanical storage records, or a ledger account in which the quantities or amounts (or both) of goods received during an accounting period are added to corresponding balances at the beginning of the period and amounts of goods sold or otherwise disposed of are deducted at a calculated cost based on individual identification or any of various methods of averaging. Physical controls consist of various plans of buying, storing, handling, issuing, supervising, and stocktaking. Stock-ledger control is made more effective by physical control in the nature of a continuous check of the goods on hand. See *continuous inventory; perpetual inventory.*

inventory pricing See *inventory valuation.*

inventory profit The excess during a period of rising prices of the cost, on a *fifo* or average basis, of an inventory of materials or merchandise over its cost on a *lifo* basis: a term employed by those who advocate lifo as the basis of costing sales; see *inventory valuation*. Thus, if a certain inventory item at the beginning of a year's operations consists of 500 units at $2 each on a lifo basis and $3 on a fifo basis, and purchases in lots of 1,000 each were made successively during the year at $3, $3.50, and $4, an inventory of 700 units remaining at the end of the year on a fifo basis would contain an "inventory profit" of $1,200, arrived at as follows:

Cost of inventory on first-in-first-out basis (700 units at $4)	$2,800
Less—cost of inventory on a last-in-first-out basis (500 units at $2 and 200 units at $3)	1,600
"Inventory profit" (the excess of the one valuation basis over the other)	$1,200

The difference of $500 at the beginning of the year (500 units at $1) is a part of the valuation excess of $1,200; hence it is said that, of the "inventory profit" of $1,200, only $700 pertains to the current year, the difference being a carryover from one or more preceding periods.

Accountants who favor fifo as the basis of costing sales have called the difference of $1,200 an "anticipated cost," contending that, since older goods are ordinarily disposed of first, whether in manufacturing or trading operations, the application of the cost of such goods to recent purchases during a period of inflation has the effect of writing off the cost of goods not yet sold, thus anticipating the costs of the period following and undervaluing inventory.

inventory reserve 1. A valuation account covering the reduction of inventory cost to market or other less-than-cost basis due to the use of a lifo method of inventory valuation or to price declines, obsolescence, shortages, and other causes. The amount of the reserve is customarily supported by details from inventory sheets or records relating to specific items. When any such item is sold, the reserve may be relieved of the amount pertaining to it; or, what is more common, the reserve is carried forward intact until the end of the next year and increased or decreased by the requirements of the inventory at that time, the other half of the adjustment being debited or credited to cost of goods sold or its equivalent. If the size of the reserve warrants, its amount at the beginning and end of the reporting period may be a necessary disclosure on the income statement.
2. A contingency reserve created for the purpose of absorbing future inventory declines, i.e., declines below market at the latest balance-sheet date. Such a reserve is similar in nature to other contingency reserves: a provision therefor is not an expense, but rather an appropriation of retained earnings, and any charge thereto representing the realization of an inventory decline as described belongs in the income statement for the period in which the decline occurred. Reserves of this type, formerly created as a protection against war-production hazards, tended to disappear (i.e., were returned to earned surplus) within a few years following World War II. See *postwar reserve*.

inventory turnover The number of times that the investment in merchandise or stocks on hand is replaced during a stated period, usually 12 months. Merchandise turnover is commonly computed by dividing the cost of sales for the period by the cost of the average inventory carried during the period; or, less correctly, by dividing the amount of sales by the average inventory at estimated sales price. Raw-materials and supplies turnover is computed by dividing the cost of the average inventory into the cost of goods issued.

inventory valuation 1. The determination of the cost or the portion of cost assignable to on-hand raw materials, goods in process, finished stock, merchandise held for resale, and supplies.
2. The determination of the market price of securities in the case of a dealer in securities or an investment fund or of the pricing of other goods or commodities on hand, where cost or a fraction of cost is not employed as the valuation basis.

Like other assets, inventories of goods are normally priced at their original cost, or such part of original cost as may be equal to "market" value (see below) or other amount that may "reasonably" be carried forward to the following year. "At the lower of cost or market" is a standard balance-sheet term attaching to an inventory sidehead. Because of the fungible character of many inventory items, variations in cost-accounting methods and the individual judgments that enter into determinations of what costs ought to be carried forward create many different patterns of valuation.

The cost of purchased materials, parts, and merchandise is invoice cost, plus transportation, duty, and other direct purchase costs, less discounts and allowances, the former including trade discounts and now usually cash discounts. Most accountants prefer to see prices net of *all* discounts, but the idea persists that cash discounts of 2 percent or less are in the nature of interest and should, therefore, be regarded as belonging to the same category as interest received. Since discounts received are credits, any resemblance to interest must arise from the notion of *prepayment*—that is, payment before the "net" date. Terms of "2% 10 days, net 30" mean that if the interest concept is adhered to, the 2 percent discount relates to the period lying between the 10th and 30th days, which is $\frac{1}{18}$ of a year—an implied "interest" rate of 36 percent a year. The current rate of interest is too small a portion of this amount to separate.

The cost price to be applied to the units of materials remaining at the end of a fiscal year may not be their individual costs, even though the units may be identified beyond a doubt with particular purchase transactions. The fungible or interchangeable nature of most purchased items, particularly those of the average manufacturing enterprise, gives rise to six distinct types of cost; the use of any or all of them is recognized by many accountants as valid in inventory valuations:

Basis	*Principal Supporting Argument*
Actual	Cost relates to specific items.
First-in-first-out (fifo)	Oldest acquisitions are disposed of first: an assumption usually in agreement with fact.
Last-in-first-out (lifo) and base-stock	Recent acquisition costs are most nearly related to the prices at which sales are made; saves taxes on a rising market.
Average	Easily determined; many people think in terms of averages; more consistency between inventory and cost-of-sales bases; often regarded as the most practicable method of imputing costs in a mixed inventory, since in most cases the method results in but minor variation from *actual.*
Standard	More often applied to work in process and finished stock; resembles average cost, except that unusual costs are excluded.
Retail	Also resembles average cost, but results in less than average cost because of markdowns; easily computed; provides for normal margins on future sales.

The recent widespread use of the last-in-first-out (lifo) method has arisen from the claim that it more nearly reflects the operating point of view, whether or not selling prices have been affected, since operating people are inclined to think in terms of margins between current market prices—wholesale and retail, or raw material and intermediate or finished product. The effect during a period of rising prices is to keep the cost of the inventory at a "safer" lower level than current replacement cost, thus reducing margins and making it possible to decrease selling prices, when the market swings in the other direction, without having to provide for inventory losses. If inventory quantities tend to be constant and inventory costs are kept at the lowest point in a long-range price cycle, the "lifo" method of costing inventories becomes the "base-stock" method.

The "lifo" method was first advocated principally within the metal industries and others where the ratio of inventory to sales is relatively large. It is not suited to enterprises where inventory stocks are small or variable, turnover is rapid, or hedging operations protect future sales. It has the effect of creating a secret reserve, often having the effect of grossly understating both assets and retained earnings. It does not obviate the need in some instances of reducing cost to an amount not exceeding market. Its wider use has resulted from savings in income tax that it makes possible.

In most situations involving fabricated and semifabricated products, the inventory at the end of the year is much less than, perhaps only a fraction of, the year's production, and the costing of sales and inventory is a joint problem. Where, however, the ratio of the cost, assigned to the inventory, to the year's gross margin is significant, which is usually the case, a good deal of importance attaches to the distinctions between normal and exceptional production costs, the natural tendency being to exclude the latter from the inventory and load it, sometimes as an extraordinary item, on operations.

By "market," as the term is employed in inventory-valuation processes, is meant that portion of inventory cost that can justifiably be carried forward to future periods as the result of giving weight to prices and other conditions likely to accompany disposal, particularly in the local market. It may be equal in amount to a price quotation on an active market at the balance-sheet date, the offering price of a competitor in an inactive market, a "junk" price on a "dead" market, or some other cost fraction that experience and good judgment by management have indicated as a realistic base for application against currently available estimates of possible realization.

As a rule, there should be no reduction of cost to a market figure for that portion of the inventory that will remain in the business as a minimum quantity to be kept on hand, or where the selling price has not yet reacted to a reduction in raw-material cost. Raw material that has been purchased in connection with the manufacture of a product for which a firm price exists and on which a normal profit is expected should never be marked down despite a lower market.

Market price in the case of work in process and finished stock is usually conceived to be the lower of (a) the cost of replacement or (b) the anticipated selling price less the cost to complete, selling expense, and the customary gross margin.

A market quotation should reflect the price on the balance-sheet date of a similar item, which would have to be paid in the area in which the purchase would ordinarily be made for the same quantity usually acquired at one time. Market prices are ordinarily applied to individual items rather than groups or classes, and when once a market price has been adopted in an inventory valuation as a basis for the amount of cost to be carried forward, it remains as cost for future reckoning.

Reductions of costs to amounts equal to market are sometimes collected together in an *inventory reserve.* To justify the reserve as a *valuation account* rather than as a subdivision of retained earnings, (a) details of reductions to market by individual items or groups should be available, and (b) in the succeeding period, the reserve is best adjusted as these items are disposed of.

Markdowns of cost because of age or surplus or slowmoving items may be regarded as equivalent to market reductions, since the common purpose is to carry forward only those costs that may fairly be applied against future realizations. These markdowns are often accomplished by adopting a percentage scale whereby the cost of an item is progressively decreased, as it is continued in stock, until scrap value is reached. In the retail method of determining inventory cost, the same purpose is served by reducing the expected selling price by an average markon percentage.

In all these situations, cost reductions made in accordance with the principles indicated should be justified by past experience or present facts, and should be fairly applied to all inventory items. If the methods adopted differ from those in use at the end of the previous fiscal period, unless the effect is unimportant, the change calls for a balance-sheet footnote, giving some indication of the approximate effect in dollars. An inventory on the lifo basis is preferably accompanied by a balance-sheet disclosure of the cost that would have been reflected had a fifo basis been followed.

An allowance for possible future inventory losses, over and above the write-down to current market, is best regarded as a reservation of retained earnings. See *inventory reserve* (*2*).

inventory variation The difference between inventories at the beginning and end of a period covered by an income statement, where *perpetual inventories* are not maintained. An increase has the effect of decreasing cost of sales, and vice versa. See *income statement.*

invested capital 1. The amount of *capital* contributed to a business by its owners; = *capital (1).*
2. The amount so contributed, plus retained earnings (or less accumulated losses) and appropriated surplus. See *capital (2); net assets; net worth.*
3. A similar concept, subject to numerous adjustments, used as a factor in determining excess profits under wartime tax and profit-limitation laws.

investigate (auditing) To search for and relate underlying causes.

investigation An examination of books and records preliminary to financing or for any other specified purpose, sometimes differing in scope from the ordinary *audit (1).*

investment 1. An expenditure to acquire property—real or personal, tangible or intangible—yielding income or services.
2. The property so acquired.
3. = *savings.*
4. A security owned.
5. = *net worth.* "Economic" investment is sometimes described as including long-term debt.
6. *pl.* A balance-sheet title, generally qualified by *permanent* or *temporary,* according to the expected holding periods, and often by phrases indicating the existence of *control (3).*

investment adviser (or **counsel**) One who on a professional or service basis gives advice to another on investment problems. Investment advisers are required by the Investment Advisers Act of 1940 to register with and report to the U. S. Securities and Exchange Commission.

investment banker An organization that buys bond or stock issues in their entirety from the issuing corporation, or participates with others in such a purchase; it distributes the issues to dealers, in which case it is referred to as a "wholesaler"; or, as a "retailer," it sells them direct to investors. Sometimes it does both.

The investment banker acts as a middleman for corporations needing original or additional financing and investors willing to risk their savings. In boom times, with investors eager to put their money into speculative enterprises, the investment banker is under considerable pressure to approve undertakings involving new products and untested managements. In depression periods, new issues are confined for the most part to modest offerings of seasoned enterprises, or to refunding issues, where risk is at a minimum. Maintaining "conservative" relationships both with seekers after new funds and with investors calls for an objective attitude comparable in some ways with that of the public accountant who, too, must do justice to those standing on opposite sides of the market. Although compensated by and hence ostensibly serving those obtaining the capital, the investment banker must give equal consideration to the protection and interests of investors.

investment company (or **trust**) An organization serving to bring together the savings of individuals for joint investment.

investment credit The allowance permitted under the Federal income-tax law reducing the tax payable by a limited percentage of capital additions during the taxable period. Although intended by the Congress to be an encouragement to expand or replace capital facilities, and thus simply to be treated as a reduction of the current year's tax, the investment credit has sometimes been regarded as a *deferred credit,* allocable as a reduction of depreciation expense over the years of useful life.

investment in default A security owned on which there exists a default in the payment of principal or interest.

invoice A document showing the character, quantity, price, terms, nature of delivery, and other particulars of goods sold or of services rendered.

invoice cost 1. Cost incurred by a buyer and reflected on an invoice which, unless otherwise specified, is net after deducting both trade and cash discounts.

2. (retail accounting) Billed cost less trade discount, but not less cash discount.

invoice register A book of original entry, often columnar in form, for the consecutive record and summarization of invoices received from creditors; sometimes, another name for a *voucher register*.

involuntary conversion The substitution of one item of property for another as the result of a casualty, condemnation, or other cause over which the owner has no control. In general, under the Internal Revenue Code (section 1033), a loss from such a transaction is recognized, but not a gain, to the extent that an amount equal to the proceeds is reinvested in similar property by the end of the tax year after the year of the conversion. See *replacement fund*.

IOU An informal document evidencing a cash debt. Under usual standards of internal control, an advance by a cashier to an employee is forbidden; in the few instances in which it is permitted, approval in writing by a higher official is customarily required.

irrational number A number whose terminus has an infinite extension without *repetends;* examples: π (= 3.1415926536 . . . ∞); e (= 2.7182818285 . . . ∞); $\sqrt{2}$ (= 1.41421356237 . . . ∞). See *rational number*.

irregularity Any error in a bookkeeping record. It may be one of principle, a clerical inaccuracy, or a deliberate falsification.

irrevocable trust A trust that cannot be set aside by its creator. See *trust*.

issued capital (stock) That part of a corporation's authorized capital stock represented by certificates legally issued for cash or other consideration, whether or not such certificates are in the hands of the public or have been reacquired by the issuer. The term thus includes treasury stock, or stock otherwise reacquired, as well as outstanding stock.

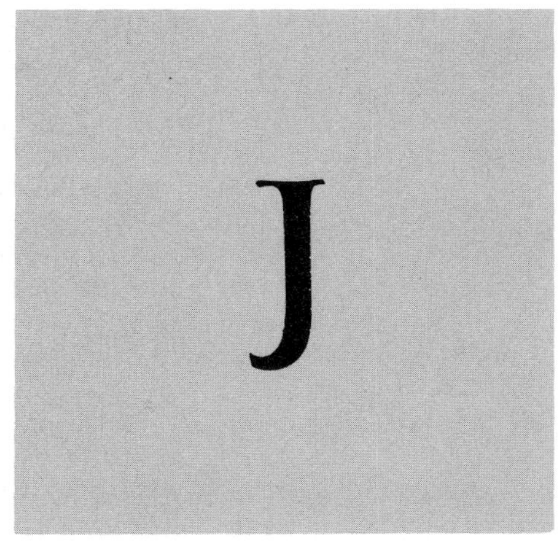

job costing = *job-order costing.*

job lot 1. A contract for 1,000 or 2,000 bushels of grain, as compared with the "regular" contract unit of 5,000 bushels: a term employed on grain exchanges; compare with *odd lot.*

2. A miscellaneous collection of goods acquired or salable at a lump-sum price.

job order An order authorizing and directing the production of a specified number of units of product, the construction or repair of specified equipment, or the rendition of specified services; known also as a production, construction, repair, or service order, it may serve as the basis for the accounts or subaccounts in which costs are recorded, grouped, and accumulated.

job-order costing A method of *cost accounting* whereby costs are compiled for a specific quantity of products, equipment, repairs, or other services that move through the production process as a continuously identifiable unit; applicable material; direct labor; direct expense; and usually a calculated portion of overhead being charged to a *job order;* distinguished from *process costing.*

joint account 1. A record of transactions in which two or more persons or business units have a financial interest.

2. A bank account which may be drawn upon by two or more persons, their rights being similar to those of joint tenants.

joint adventure = *joint venture.*

joint-and-several liability A liability for the settlement of which one or all of a group of named persons may be held accountable.

joint cost The *common cost* of facilities or services employed in the output of two or more simultaneously produced or otherwise closely related operations, commodities, or services. The production of one item, as in a single plant or process, may be possible only if another or several others are produced at the same time; these joint products, called *complementary,* are illustrated in the varied output of a meat-packing plant, the costs of individual items, whatever the basis of cost distribution, being less for each new joint product added; an increase in the production of one complementary product leads to an increase in the others, although not necessarily in the same proportion. In some cases, the production of one joint product impedes or makes impossible the production of another joint product; thus, the drawing off of more of a certain chemical from a mother liquor may reduce the amount of another chemical which could otherwise have been obtained. Such joint products are called *substitutes;* they constitute that class of products in which the production of both tends to raise the cost of producing each. Costs that are not joint are said to be *independent.* Dividing and averaging joint costs is always arbitrary, because the level of costs of one product depends in a variety of ways on the level of production of the joint commodity, so that averages tend to lose meaning, except where direct, additional, and independent costs for each commodity are involved. In fact, jointness, to the extent it exists, implies that any decision affecting one commodity cannot be made without affecting those jointly related to it. See *impute.*

joint-facilities income A term used in public-utility accounting to designate revenues derived from facilities operated jointly to produce two or more types of services; as, rental from a power-company pole carrying both power and telephone lines.

joint liability A liability for the settlement of which others have equal responsibility. Persons jointly liable must be proceeded against together.

joint ownership The ownership of real or personal property by two or more persons as either joint tenants or tenants in common. See *joint tenant; tenant in common.*

joint product One of two or more products derived from the same raw material; a related product: a product whose production impedes or facilitates the production of another product. See *joint cost.*

joint services Related services: services derived from labor, capital, or materials that affect the efficiency with which other services are performed. When the efficiency of a related service is increased, the two are said to be cooperant; when the efficiency of a related service is decreased, the two are said to be rival; when employment of one has no effect on another service, the two are said to be independent. See *joint cost.*

joint-stock association (or **company**) 1. A group of individuals, acting jointly to establish and operate a business enterprise under an artificial name, and having an invested capital divided into transferable shares, an elected board of directors, and other corporate characteristics, but in most states operating without formal governmental authority; a common-law corporation. Its shareholders have unlimited liability for corporate debts and obligations, and it is taxed generally as a corporation. Because of the comparative ease with which a corporation can be created under state laws, joint-stock associations are now rare. 2. (British usage) = *corporation.*

joint tenant Any one of two or more persons who together own real or personal property, whereby upon the death of any one of them his interest passes to the other joint tenant(s) without becoming a part of his estate. Where, for example, a certificate of capital stock is jointly owned by husband and wife, the owner's name is likely to appear on the certificate thus: "James Smith and Alice Smith as joint tenants with right of survivorship and not as tenants in common." See *tenant in common.*

joint venture A commercial undertaking by two or more persons, differing from a partnership in that it relates to the disposition of a single lot of goods or the completion of a single project. Its duration is limited to the period in which the goods are sold or the project is carried on.

journal 1. Any book of *original entry;* see *double-entry bookkeeping.*
2. The book of original entry in which are recorded transactions not provided for in specialized journals; a *general journal.* See *journal entry.*
3. A journal entry, as in the expression, "to prepare a journal for a given transaction."

journal entry An item in or prepared for a book of original entry, interpreting a business transaction in bookkeeping terms and showing the accounts to be debited and credited, together with an explanatory description of the transaction. Frequently transactions are analyzed in journal-entry form in order to demonstrate their effect on the accounts.

The conventional journal-entry form is as follows:

(Date or number, or both)		
Returned goods	$165.43	
Accounts receivable (J. Holder)		$165.43
Defective merchandise returned by J. Holder, originally sold to him on June 21, invoice F3582; credit memo GC182.		

The standardized elements of this form

are: (a) the date or number of the entry, placed in the center; (b) the titles of the accounts to be charged at the extreme left, followed by the amounts applicable to each, offset by the width of a money column from the right; (c) the titles of the accounts to be credited, offset from the left, followed by the amounts applicable to each at the extreme right; (d) the explanation and justification of the entry, in the form of a narrative, appended at the end, its beginning offset halfway between the debit and credit account titles and extending as far to the right as the debit dollar column. A journal entry in this form often appears outside formal books of original entry, as in the preparation of cases or problems (e.g., see illustration under *installment method of accounting*), the listing of adjusting journal entries in audit reports, demonstrations of the consequence of taking some proposed action affecting the accounts, and explanations of adjustments that have been incorporated into a working trial balance.

In formal bookkeeping practice, this form of entry may often be observed on "general-journal" vouchers, and even in the form of the general journal itself. Journals or journal vouchers that may be purchased in bookstores are usually in this form:

Professional accountants often find general journals of this type containing entries not sufficiently explained. Emphasis is frequently laid on the necessity of including in the explanation reference to document numbers and dates, as well as a clear statement of the reason for the entry. Occasionally explanations are omitted by design from periodic adjusting journal entries, as at month-ends, but the entries instead bear numbers clearly identifying them with some routine pattern governing such entries to which an outside auditor or income-tax examiner may refer, when necessary. A *journal voucher*, with authorizations and supporting papers attached, often supplements journal entries.

See *adjusting entry; compound journal entry; entry; posting; journal; cash journal; book of original entry; double-entry bookkeeping.*

journalize To interpret a transaction in terms of required debits and credits and to give it expression as a *journal entry.—journalization, n.*

journal voucher A voucher supporting a noncash transaction. A file of journal vouchers may take the place of a general journal, or journal vouchers may be summarized periodically in the general journal or in a journal-voucher summary.

judgment 1. An amount due to be paid

MONTH July — PAGE NO. 54 — YEAR 19X1

DAY	ACCOUNT AND EXPLANATION	REF.	DEBIT	CREDIT
15	Returned goods	261	165 43	
	Accounts receivable (J. Holder)	5/V		165 43
	Defective mdse. returned, originally			
	sold 6-21; inv. F3582; C/M GC 182.			

GENERAL (OR SIMPLE) JOURNAL FORM

or collected as the result of a court order. In the case of governmental units, judgments include condemnation awards in payment for private property taken for public use.
2. The assertion, implied or explicit, of a proposition concerning the meaning, significance, or structure of a set of concepts, evidence, or actions. By *convention*, the accountant's *judgment* expressed on the basis of his audit findings is referred to as an *opinion* appearing as one section of his short-form report accompanying audited financial statements. See *opinion; fact; valuation; value judgment.*

judgment sample A sample whose size and the items composing it have been determined by someone who is familiar with the universe undergoing the test and capable of exercising informed and unbiased discretion in making the selection. Such samples are sometimes necessary when data are needed quickly or when interest is confined to only a part of the universe. A judgment sample is usually less reliable for estimation and prediction purposes than a random sample.

junior accountant An employee of a public accountant, who engages in field work and whose activities are closely supervised by a *senior* accountant.

junior security A bond or mortgage secured by a property on which there is one or more senior or prior issues, and subject to the prior claims of such issues in case of foreclosure or liquidation.

justification (governmental accounting) A narrative analysis of the need of funds for any of the programs of an administrative or other agency.

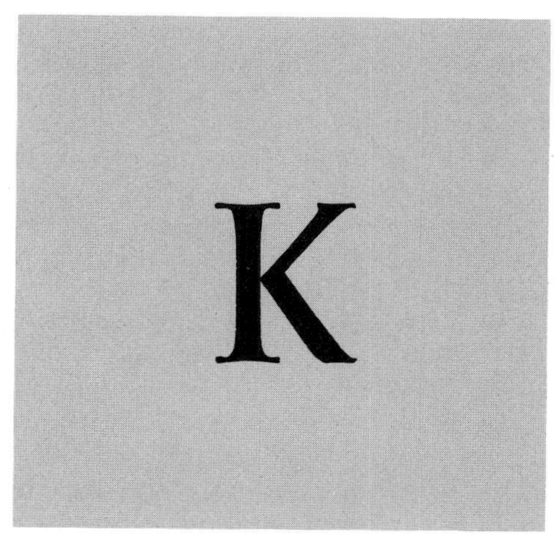

KD Knocked Down; applied to sales or shipments of machines and the like, that are to be assembled by the recipient.

kind An *asset*, or assets, other than cash and receivables; the use of the word is confined to the expression *in kind*.

kiting 1. The act of drawing and cashing an unrecorded check on one bank, followed shortly by a covering deposit in the form of an unrecorded check on another bank that will in turn be covered by a check drawn on a third bank; the process may go on indefinitely among several banks. The time taken for checks to clear through the banking system is thus taken advantage of in order to cover an unauthorized "borrowing" or theft of money.
2. Hence, the inclusion in a bank deposit of any item for which no concurrent credit appears on the books of account, the purpose being to cover a concurrent or previous cash theft or shortage.
3. Also, the withdrawal (check or cash) from uncollected bank deposits. Thus, two persons residing in different cities may exchange checks with each other, deposit them in local banks, draw against the balances thus created, and make covering deposits on or before the collection date of the deposited checks. This can occur only where banks do not prohibit the customer's use of uncollected deposits.

kurtosis (statistics) The degree of peakedness or concentration about the central value exhibited by a statistical distribution.

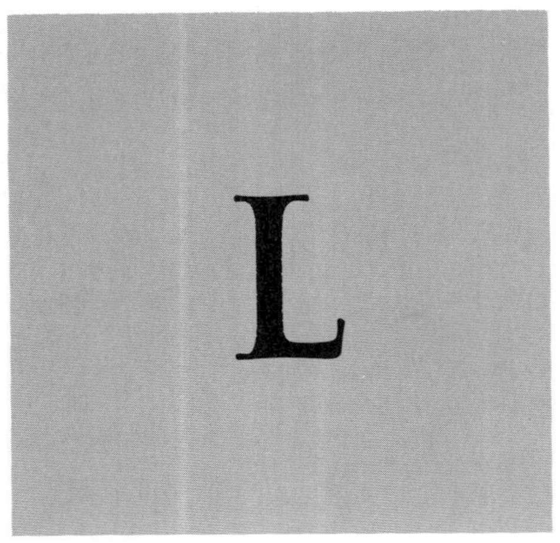

lag The time interval between successive, often related, events such as the receipt and deposit of cash.

laity The body of persons outside a *profession;* in accounting, those unskilled in the art, particularly those for whom auditors' reports are intended.

land The investment in real estate, usually including *land improvements* completed before the purchase of the real estate but not including buildings or other *limited-life* structures.

landed price The quoted or invoiced price of a commodity, including costs of loading, shipping, and unloading at destination.

land improvements Paving and sidewalks; sewer, water, and gas lines; clearing; grading; fencing; spur-railway tracks; and other items customarily paid for by the owner of a tract of land and installed by him or by local government. The term may also include buildings, but generally "building" or "land and building(s)" is the standard of description where a man-made structure has been added to the land. A separate account is maintained where the improvements are being depreciated. The usual practice, however, is to regard improvements as being as durable as the land itself and not subject to depreciation; replacements of paving and other improvement items are then expensed, although if the replacement cost has been greater than the first cost, the excess may be capitalized. See *fixed asset; capitalize.*

language sheet (governmental accounting) A term employed in Federal-government agencies to designate the administrative draft of the narrative of an appropriation bill accompanying the submission of an agency's budget to the Congress.

lapping The theft, as by a defaulting cashier, of cash received from a customer, made good and credited to the customer's account at a later date by the theft of cash received from another customer, the process continuing indefinitely until the fraud is discovered, or until restitution is made or a fictitious covering entry, as to an expense account, can be made.

lapse 1. To expire or be forfeited: said of an insurance policy and the rights and benefits under it upon expiration of the policy or upon cancellation for nonpayment of premium.

2. (governmental accounting) To become unavailable for future spending: said of the unexpended balance of an ordinary appropriation at the end of the fiscal year or years to which it applies. See *continuing appropriation.*

lapsing schedule A worksheet on which are entered the costs of individual fixed assets, or, more commonly, the total annual additions to a class of fixed assets, together with the detail of the distribution of their costs over accounting periods succeeding their purchase. The purpose of the schedule is to supply the detail of an annual or other periodic (a) provision for depreciation, (b) write-off of costs fully depreciated or of amortized and unamortized costs of items disposed of, and (c) verification of the balance of accumulated depreciation at any time and its identification with individual fixed assets. See *depreciation.*

A lapsing schedule may also be prepared by a Federal internal-revenue agent for comparison with a taxpayer's computation of depreciation. Where the taxpayer's records indicate no clear and defensible method of accruing depreciation, the agent's lapsing schedule may serve as the basis for a depreciation allowance and for the computation of gains and losses on the retirement of items within the related category of fixed assets.

The depreciation computation resulting from the use of a lapsing schedule is essentially straight-line. The rates employed would normally be lower than those necessary to the application of formula (5) under *depreciation* because of the recognition, where a lapsing schedule is found, of gain or loss from the disposal of individual assets.

Numerous varieties of lapsing schedules are found in practice, including the following alternatives:

1. The depreciation base is (a) the balance of the capital-asset account at the beginning of the year, (b) the balance at the beginning of the month, or (c) either of such balances plus one-half of the additions from the beginning of the year or month to the accrual date.

2. The cost of a fixed asset or group of fixed assets is removed from the accounts when (a) it has been fully covered by depreciation, (b) the asset is formally recognized as having been retired from service, or (c) the asset is scrapped or sold. At the same time, the amount of depreciation accrued on the asset is also removed from the depreciation reserve.

3. Depreciation expense on retirements is computed (a) to the beginning of the year of retirement, (b) to the beginning of the month of retirement, (c) to the end of the month of retirement, or (d) at half rate for the fractional year or for the month.

4. The net debit or credit, if any, resulting from combining the cost of the fixed asset or group of fixed assets, upon its removal from the accounts, with the accrued depreciation thereon and the proceeds from its sale or other disposition, is treated in the current income statement as (a) a loss or gain, or (b) an addition to or deduction from current depreciation expense.

There is little preference for any one combination of these variations, provided it is followed with consistency, and provided the depreciation rate is corrected from time to time as the result of engineering studies of accrued depreciation and remaining life. See *depreciation*.

Example: The furniture-and-fixtures account of a company contains the details shown in the table below.

Date		Particulars	Debits	Credits
Jan. 10	19–2	Purchases	$ 568.98	
Mar. 26	19–2	〃	2,640.34	
Aug. 1	19–2	〃	3,250.00	
Jan. 4	19–3	〃	1,500.00	
Feb. 10	19–7	Sale for $23.00 of items purchased 1-10--2 at a cost of		$ 261.04
Apr. 12	19–7	Purchases	634.33	
Sep. 14	19–0	〃	156.10	
Dec. 18	19–3	Sale for $1,000 of items purchased 8-1--2 at a cost of		1,634.40
Jul. 9	19–5	Purchases	387.20	
Sep. 3	19–6	Sale for $64.25 of items purchased 4-12--7 at a cost of		335.58
Jan. 26	19–7	Purchases	2,384.18	
Nov. 8	19–7	Sale for $82.80 of items purchased 1-10--2 at a cost of		120.00
Dec. 31	19–7	Balance		9,170.11
Totals			$11,521.13	$11,521.13

Lapsing Schedule Showing
Depreciation Expense and Accumulation Details

Year	*Months of Use*	*Base*	*Expense*	*Accrued at Retirement*	*Balance of Accumulated Depreciation*
19–2	11	$ 568.98	$ 52.16		
	9	2,640.34	198.03		
	4	3,250.00	108.33		$ 358.52
19–3	12	6,459.32	645.93		
	11	1,500.00	137.50		1,141.95
19–4	12	7,959.32	795.93		1,937.88
19–5	12	7,959.32	795.93		2,733.81
19–6	12	7,959.32	795.94		3,529.75
19–7	2	7,959.32	132.66		
	10	7,698.28	641.52		
	8	634.33	42.29		
	61	261.04		$ 132.70	4,213.52
19–8	12	8,332.61	833.26		5,046.78
19–9	12	8,332.61	833.26		5,880.04
19–0	12	8,332.61	833.26		
	3	156.10	3.90		6,717.20
19–1	12	8,488.71	848.87		7,566.07
19–2	1	307.94	2.57		
	3	2,640.34	66.01		
	8	3,250.00	216.67		
	12	2,290.43	229.04		8,080.36
19–3	1	1,500.00	12.50		
	12	790.43	79.05		
	120	1,634.40		1,634.40	6,537.51
19–4	12	790.43	79.04		6,616.55
19–5	12	790.43	79.04		
	5	387.20	16.13		6,711.72
19–6	9	1,177.63	88.33		
	3	842.05	21.05		
	113	335.58		316.00	6,505.10
19–7	4	298.75	9.94		
	12	543.30	54.33		
	11	2,384.18	218.55		
	120	120.00		120.00	6,667.92

Shown above is one form of a lapsing schedule in which details of the depreciation computations appear; another form is on page 259. Expressed in terms of the varying methods listed above, the computations have been made in accordance with these rules:

depreciation base	1b
adjustment of accounts	2c
end of depreciation	3c
reporting method	4a.

In the financial statements, a net loss from the disposal of capital assets would have been reported for 19–7 in the amount of $105.34; for 19–3, 19–6, and 19–7, net gains from that source would have been $1,000.00, $44.67, and $82.80, respectively.

The following summary proves the arithmetic accuracy of the accumulated-depreciation balance of $6,667.92 and demonstrates the connection of each remaining asset with a specific portion of the reserve. Thus, an asset item of $96.80, constituting a quarter of the group of assets purchased on July 9, 19–5, is regarded as having been depreciated in the amount of one-fourth of

Illustration of Lapsing Schedule (Rate: 10%)

Conditions:

(1) Depreciation base: balance at beginning of month
(2) Recognition of retirement: when asset is scrapped or sold
(3) End of depreciation period: end of month of retirement
(4) Reporting method: loss or gain recognized on removal

Date of Item	*Amount*	*19-2*	*19-3*	*19-4*	*19-5*	*19-6*	*19-7*	*19-8*	*19-9*
1-10--2	568.98	52.16	56.90	56.90	56.90	56.90	56.90	30.80	30.79
3-26--2	2,640.34	198.03	264.03	264.03	264.03	264.04	264.03	264.03	264.04
8- 1--2	3,250.00	108.33	325.00	325.00	325.00	325.00	325.00	325.00	325.00
1- 4--3	1,500.00		137.50	150.00	150.00	150.00	150.00	150.00	150.00
2-10--7	261.04						21.75		63.43
4-12--7	634.33						42.29	63.43	
9-14--0	156.10								
12-18--3	1,634.40								
7- 9--5	387.20								
9- 3--6	335.58								
1-26--7	2,384.18								
11- 8--7	120.00								
Yearly total		358.52	783.43	795.93	795.93	795.94	816.47	833.26	833.26
Accrued at retirement							132.70		
Balance in reserve		358.52	1,141.95	1,937.88	2,733.81	3,529.75	4,213.52	5,046.78	5,880.04

Date of Item	*Amount*	*19–0*	*19–1*	*19–2*	*19–3*	*19–4*	*19–5*	*19–6*	*19–7*
1-10--2	568.98	30.79	30.80	2.57					
3-26--2	2,640.34	264.03	264.03	66.01					
8- 1—2	3,250.00	325.00	325.00	216.67					
1- 4—3	1,500.00	150.00	150.00	150.00	12.50				
2-10--7	261.04	63.44	63.43	63.43	63.44	63.43	63.43	63.44	9.94
4-12--7	634.33	3.90	15.61	15.61	15.61	15.61	15.61	15.61	15.61
9-14--0	156.10				—				
12-18--3	1,634.40								
7- 9--5	387.20						16.13	38.72	38.72
9- 3--6	335.58							8.39	
1-26--7	2,384.18								218.55
11- 8--7	120.00								—
Yearly total		837.16	848.87	514.29	91.55	79.04	95.17	109.38	282.82
Accrued at retirement					1,634.40			316.00	120.00
Balance in reserve		6,717.20	7,566.07	8,080.36	6,537.51	6,616.55	6,711.72	6,505.10	6,667.92

the accumulation of $93.57 applicable to the asset group purchased on that date, or $23.39.

Date of Purchase	Balance in Asset Account	Months Depreciated	Balance of Accrued Depreciation
1-10--2	$ 187.94	120	$ 187.94*
3-26--2	2,640.34	120	2,640.34*
8- 1--2	1,615.60	120	1,615.60
1- 4--3	1,500.00	120	1,500.00
4-12--7	298.75	120	298.75*
9-14--0	156.10	87	113.17
7- 9--5	387.20	29	93.57
1-26--7	2,384.18	11	218.55
Totals	$9,170.11	87+	$6,667.92

*Differs from accruals by offsetting fractional cents.

last in, first out (lifo) A method of *inventory valuation* (*q.v.*).

lay days The agreed number of days that a chartered ship may remain in port for loading and unloading without penalty. See *charter party*.

lead time The time required after placing an order or adopting a plan of operation or production before materials and facilities can be acquired and made ready and actual production initiated. Thus, in addition to setup time, the term generally is understood to include the period preceding machine preparation.

lease A conveyance of land or of the use of a building or a part of a building from one person (lessor) to another (lessee) for a specified period of time, in return for *rent* or other compensation.

leasehold An interest in land under the terms of a *lease*, normally classified as a (tangible) *fixed asset*.

least-squares method (statistics) The mathematical process for determining the relationship between two or more variables, so that, when expressed as a curve, the sum of the distances (deviations) of the plotted available data (observations) from the curve is zero. This condition is met when the curve is so constructed that the sum of the squares of the deviations is less than that obtainable from any other curve of the same type. For most accounting and business purposes, the curve usually employed is a straight line, and the method is applied principally in studies of trends in revenues, costs, production, and other related data, covering past or projected periods and real or assumed operating conditions. The method rests on a statistical *model* in which it is assumed that the data to be treated are subject to two sets of forces: (a) an underlying relation, the general form of which is assumed to be determinable, and (b) *random variations;* it is used to find the best values of the constants in the assumed relation, but the result secured depends to a large extent on assumptions regarding the underlying form of the relation. Even in the case of a straight line, it should be noted that the minimization of the sums of the squares of vertical deviations will not, in general, yield the same values for the constants as the minimization of the sums of the squares of horizontal deviations, since each minimization implies a different direction of application of the random forces.

For curves of the same type, such as a straight-line equation of the form $Y = a + bX$, many cases are possible, depending on the values assigned to the constants a and b. The method of least squares seeks to choose values assigned to these constants in a manner that will make the sum of the squares of the deviations of the observations from the curve less than from any other assigned value. The process of minimizing the sum of the squares of these deviations gives the method of least squares its name. While this method will not always point to the underlying relation, it can be shown that, in an extensive class of cases, the curve thus determined is more likely to represent this relation than a curve determined by any other method.

For a straight-line equation of the form $Y = a + bX$, the choice of values for two constants, a and b, is necessary. These constants are chosen by solving the two so-called normal equations

$$\Sigma Y = Na + b\Sigma X$$

and

$$\Sigma XY = a\Sigma X + b\Sigma X^2,$$

where ΣY is the sum of the observed Y values, ΣX is the sum of the observed X values, and ΣX^2 is the sum of the cross-products—i.e., each value of X is multiplied by the value of Y observed as occurring with that value of X and the results of all such multiplications are then added. N is the number of pairs of observations. Solution of the normal equations is the equivalent of the least-squares method for determining the constants a and b.

In each case, the first normal equation is the result of simply writing down the form of the equation whose constants are to be determined, and then adding the terms. For example, in the case of the straight line, the form of the equation is $Y = a + bX$. Adding the terms in this equation yields $\Sigma Y = \Sigma a + \Sigma bX = Na + b\Sigma X$. ($\Sigma a = Na$, since a constant added N times is equal to N times the constant, and $\Sigma bX = b\Sigma X$, since the constant b appears in each term added and, hence, may be taken out as a common factor.) This can be recognized as the first normal equation for the straight line. The second normal equation results from multiplying each term by X before adding, thus yielding $\Sigma XY = a\Sigma X + b\Sigma X^2$.

Fitting a straight line to the following data will serve to illustrate the process. In the summary as given, A Company's sales Y over a period of ten years X (in units of $100,000), the problem is to determine the trend in a *time-series analysis*. The application of the least-squares method, however, is not restricted to a time series. X and Y might be any other pair of variables, such as rate of production and cost.

Y	X	XY	X^2
3.0	1	3.0	1
5.0	2	10.0	4
3.5	3	10.5	9
5.0	4	20.0	16
6.0	5	30.0	25
5.5	6	33.0	36
5.0	7	35.0	49
8.0	8	64.0	64
7.5	9	67.5	81
8.5	10	85.0	100
57.0	55	358.0	385
$\Sigma(Y)$	$\Sigma(X)$	$\Sigma(XY)$	$\Sigma(X^2)$

From this table the following values obtain:

$$N = 10$$
$$\Sigma(Y) = 57$$
$$\Sigma(X) = 55$$
$$\Sigma(XY) = 358$$
$$\Sigma(X^2) = 385,$$

which can be substituted in the two normal equations

$$\Sigma(Y) = Na + b\Sigma(X)$$
$$\Sigma(XY) = a\Sigma(X) + b\Sigma(X^2)$$

to obtain

$$57 = 10a + 55b$$
$$358 = 55a + 385b.$$

Upon solving the last two equations, the values of the constants are found to be $a = 2.73$ and $b = 0.54$, and the straight-line equation $Y = a + bX$ then becomes

$$Y = 2.73 + 0.54X.$$

This means that, when analyzed by the method of least squares, sales during the past 10 years have gone up from a base amount of $273,000 at an average rate of 0.54, or $54,000 per year.

For more complex problems where classified data are used, a shorter method of computing straight-line equations may be found under *correlation table*.

ledger A book of *accounts(1)*; any *book of final entry*. See *general ledger; subsidiary ledger; private ledger; double-entry bookkeeping*.

ledger asset (insurance accounting) A term used in reports to denote any asset appearing on a ledger, whether or not stated at its realizable value; both ledger assets and nonledger assets appear on the balance sheet.

ledger clerk One employed in the posting and balancing of a ledger.

ledger control The control of a subsidiary record or ledger by the use of a *control account.* Ledger control is limited to a proof that all items were recorded in the subsidiary record or that they were accurately made, as required, to the debit and credit sides of that record. It does not furnish proof that every item was recorded in its proper account in the subsidiary record.

ledger journal A multicolumnar record that functions as both journal and ledger. As usually devised, the record contains debit or credit columns or both for the minimum number of accounts, thus providing an all-inclusive record, practicable, however, only when a small number of accounts are required and transactions are relatively few and simple. See *cash journal.*

ledger transfer The now obsolete method of transferring items or balances from one ledger account to another without the medium of a journal; a blind entry.

legacy A gift of personal property by will. A general legacy is one to be paid from the general assets of the testator; a *specific* legacy is one involving an indicated sum of money or personal property; a *residuary* legacy is the gift of the balance of a testator's estate after payment of debts and costs and other legacies.

legal capital That part of the paid-in capital of a corporation which by law, agreement, or resolution of directors becomes the par or stated value of the capital stock; the portion of net assets restricted as to withdrawal under corporation law; *stated capital.*

legal debt margin (municipal accounting) The excess of authorized debt over outstanding debt applicable to such limitation. See *debt limit.*

legal entity An individual, partnership, trust, corporation, association, or other form of organization empowered by law or custom to own property or transact business. See *business enterprise; economic unit.*

legal liability 1. A responsibility for some obligation, enforceable at law, as distinguished from a moral responsibility.
2. (of a public accountant) The contract of employment between an accountant and his client creates a relationship out of which an obligation arises to perform services with the honesty and due care consonant with his profession of special skills and knowledge of the auditing process. The scope of his duties may be either broadened or limited by the terms of the employment contract. It has been asserted that an auditor is liable to third persons whom he intends to inform through the medium of his report—or, according to another view, who he might reasonably anticipate would rely upon the report—provided he knows that the report is false or provided he has certified to the truth of the report when he had no knowledge of its truth or falsity or when it has been prepared with such gross negligence as to amount to constructive fraud. The accountant's liability to his client or to third persons has been modified and in many respects clarified by such statutes as the Securities Exchange Act of 1933 and the Securities Exchange Act of 1934.

Claims against an accountant or firm of accountants by persons who allegedly and to their detriment have relied on financial statements bearing the accountant's certificate have involved extreme carelessness or at best doubtful issues from which general conclusions cannot be drawn.

Legal liability contrasts with *accountant's responsibility.* See also *ethics; opinion.*

legal reserve 1. That part of a bank's cash assets that must be kept as a protection for depositors.
2. Any reserve required by law. Examples: the reserves of a life-insurance company; the portion of profits that must be set aside under foreign corporation laws for various purposes.

legal value See *legal capital.*

legend A voucher number or other source reference often supplemented by a descriptive word or phrase that accompanies a journal *entry* or ledger *posting.*

less-than-carload lot A term referring to the goods the shipment of which requires less space than that available in a single freight car, or to the freight rate applicable to such a shipment.

letter of credit 1. An authorization by a bank to an exporter to draw on it for funds, within a stated amount and time, in payment for specified goods to be shipped abroad. The authorization proceeds from an order of a correspondent bank abroad in which an importer has deposited or will ultimately deposit an equivalent amount in his local currency. When the goods have been delivered by the exporter or his agent to the inland carrier (FOB) or to the port of exit (FAS) in accordance with the terms of the letter of credit, the documents evidencing the type and quantity of goods delivered and the fact of their delivery are presented to the bank, which thereupon makes payment to the exporter. See *foreign trade financing; bank acceptance.*

2. An instrument purchased from a domestic bank by one going abroad, calling for a total amount not in excess of that appearing on the face of the instrument. The traveler is then entitled to receive from designated correspondent banks the local-currency equivalent of his letter of credit either in a lump sum or in whatever smaller amounts he may choose, these amounts being endorsed on the instrument. The bank paying the remaining amount retains the instrument and returns it to the bank of issue; or the traveler is refunded any undrawn amount upon his return.

leverage 1. The tendency of net income to vary disproportionately with sales (operating leverage), or of *residual net income* to vary disproportionately with net income (capital leverage). Operating leverage increases as the ratio of fixed costs to total costs increases, since variations in sales then produce much larger variations in net income. Capital leverage, referring to the distribution of income among the equities, is large when most of the capital is in the form of fixed commitments, such as bonded debt and preferred stock, and only a small proportion is in the form of common stock, which receives all income after costs and fixed commitments, such as bond interest, are met; under such conditions, small fluctuations in net income tend to produce large variations in earnings per share of common stock.

2. (social accounting) The chain effect produced on *gross national product* by the addition of an expenditure within the economy, often expressed as a multiple of the expenditure. Lord Keynes estimated that, in the American economy, the recipient of the added expenditure spends two-thirds and saves one-third, thus leading to the formula $l = 1 + \frac{2}{3} + (\frac{2}{3})^2 + (\frac{2}{3})^3 \ldots$, where l is the leverage multiple or factor; since the increments are less than 1, $l = 1/(1 - \frac{2}{3}) = 3$. See *social accounting.*

levy *n.* 1. An assessment of taxes.

2. A demand on the members of an organization for a contribution of additional working capital or to make good a loss. See *assessment(5).*

v.t. & *i.* To assess for purposes of taxation.

liability 1. An amount owing by one *person* (a debtor) to another (a creditor), payable in money, or in *goods or services:* the consequence of an *asset* or *service* received or a *loss incurred* or *accrued;* particularly, any debt (a) *due* or past due (current liability), (b) due at a specified time in the future (e.g., funded debt, accrued liability), or (c) due only on failure to perform a future act (deferred income, contingent liability).

2. *pl.* The title of the credit half of a balance sheet, often including *net worth* as well as obligations to outsiders; when thus used, the inference is that the

organization reflected in the balance sheet has a status independent of both its creditors and its owners—to whom it must account in the amounts shown.

liability certificate A term applied to a representation or a portion thereof, obtained by an auditor from the management of an enterprise under examination, and containing expressions of opinion or fact relating to recorded, unrecorded, and contingent liabilities. See *representation.*

liability dividend A dividend paid through the issue of evidences of indebtedness. Example: a dividend paid in bonds or scrip. See *scrip dividend.*

liability for endorsement A contingent or secondary liability usually arising from the endorsement of an obligation owing by another, and continuing until it is ascertained that the original debtor has paid or has failed to meet the obligation; in the latter event, the obligation becomes a direct one of the endorser. See *note receivable discounted; contingent liability.*

liability reserve = *accrued liability;* so called because of the often uncertain amount of accruals for such items as income taxes: a term no longer sanctioned by good usage.

liability to an outsider 1. A liability other than to an owner, except that a nominal amount owing to an owner or stockholder for services, supplies, or any other usual day-to-day transaction is commonly accounted for and reported as an ordinary liability.

2. In the case of an affiliated group, a liability remaining as a consolidated-balance-sheet item after intercompany eliminations have been made.

licensed public accountant One who has registered under state law to practice as a public accountant. Approximately one-half of the states have licensing requirements, and in all but one or two the licensee must be a certified public accountant.

lien The right of one person to satisfy a claim against another by holding the other's property as security or by seizing and converting the property under procedures provided by law.

life annuity An annuity the payment of which ceases on the death of the beneficiary.

life table A table showing additions, retirements, and other mortality and survivor characteristics of a group of assets.

life tenant One entitled to the use or income of property during his life.

lifo = *last in, first out.* See *inventory valuation; cost absorption(2c).*

limited audit 1. An audit limited to definite transactions or accounts, excluding all others.

2. An *audit(1)* of all accounts for a short period.

3. An audit in which, usually by agreement, certain customary features have been omitted.

limited company A business corporation; a British term, the abbreviation "Ltd." appended to the corporate name signifying registration under the Companies Act, thus establishing the limited liability of stockholders, as in the case of stockholders of most U. S. corporations.

limited liability A liability restricted by law or contract. Examples: the liability of a special partner in a firm; the liability of a stockholder in a corporation.

limited-life asset Any *capital asset,* as a building, machine, or patent, the usefulness of which to its owner is restricted by its physical life or by the period during which it contributes to operations. See *capital asset; fixed asset.*

limited partnership A partnership in which one or more partners, but not all, have a limited liability to partnership creditors.

linear Having the mathematical properties of a straight line or a plane surface. For example, the algebraic expression

$$Y = a + bX$$

plots as a straight line in a *Cartesian*

coordinate system, the constants *a* and *b* relating each *abscissa* to its corresponding *ordinate*, so that all pairs of *coordinates* lie on the same straight line. See *coordinate system* and the illustration thereunder.

The constant *a* is called the *intercept*. It locates the ordinate $Y = a$ at the abscissa $X = O$. The constant *b* is called the *slope*. It shows the rate of change of the ordinate values per unit change in the abscissa.

linear programming A mathematical method of planning an operation; involved is the construction of a *model* of a real situation containing the following elements: (a) *variables* representing the available choices, and (b) mathematical expressions (i) relating the variables to the controlling conditions, (ii) reflecting the criteria to be used in measuring the benefits derivable from each of several possible plans, and (iii) establishing the objective. The method may be so devised as to insure the selection of the best of a large number of alternatives.

For example, a plan may be sought for the most profitable loading of the available time of 12 hours for machine *A* and 10 hours for machine *B* in the processing of two products. These products must be sold together, the condition being that the quantity of the first, which yields a profit of $1 per unit, must be equal to or less than the quantity of the second, which yields a profit of 50¢ per unit. The first product requires 3 hours' time on machine *A* and 5 hours' time on machine *B*. The second product requires 2 hours' time on machine *A* only. To establish the model, these relations are expressed in the form of the following limiting conditions ("constraints"):

$$\begin{aligned} 3x_1 + 2x_2 &\leq 12 \\ 5x_1 \phantom{{}+ 2x_2} &\leq 10 \\ x_1 - x_2 &\leq 0. \end{aligned}$$

The first two constraints refer to the machines and the last to the quantity relations ($x_1 \leq x_2$) between the two products. The numbers (*constants*) on the left-hand side of each *inequality* are known as "technological" or "structural" *coefficients;* x_1 and x_2, the quantities of the two products, respectively, are the *variables*, and the numbers on the right-hand side are the "stipulations."

Once the objective is prescribed, the methods of linear programming can be used to discover the best of the possible plans. Thus, if the objective is to maximize the profit, the solution of $x_1 = x_2 = 2$ is indicated. This program, which returns $3, is said to be an "optimum." Other equally good programs can be determined, such as $x_1 = 0$ and $x_2 = 6$. When this occurs, the model is said to yield "alternate" optima. Lacking such alternatives, the optimum is "unique."

Linear programming can also be availed of for such secondary objectives as disclosing less profitable programs that are less sensitive to possible errors in the basic data. Linear programming methods may also be applied to such diverse problems as determining a product mix that will maximize sales volume or minimize purchase costs, utilizing storage, shipment, or distribution facilities more fully, cutting down on the setup time in a machine shop, or otherwise making the most economical use of available manpower and physical facilities.

linear trend A trend portrayed in a graph by a straight line. See *trend analysis*.

line of credit = *credit line*.

liquid asset Cash in banks and on hand, and other cash assets not set aside for specific purposes other than the payment of a current liability, or a readily marketable investment. The term is somewhat less restrictive than *cash asset* and much more restrictive than *quick asset*.

liquidating dividend 1. A prorata distribution to stockholders or owners by an organization in liquidation, consisting of cash or other assets becoming available from the winding up of its business. 2. A prorata distribution to the stockholders of a company having wasting assets (as, mines, oil wells, timber), representing a return of paid-in capital.

3. A prorata distribution of assets to stockholders which has the effect of reducing paid-in capital or appreciation surplus; a return of capital.

liquidation 1. Payment of debt.

2. Conversion into cash; examples: the liquidation of accounts receivable, investments, or inventory.

3. The sale of assets and the settlement of debts in the winding up of a business, estate, or other economic unit.

liquidation value 1. The price that can be obtained from the sale of assets in liquidation proceedings; forced-sale value.

2. The agreed amount per share to be paid to preferred shareholders upon the voluntary or involuntary liquidation of a corporation.

listed Admitted to trading privileges: said of a security with reference to an established stock exchange.

list price A printed price, as one appearing in a catalog, subject to trade and cash discounts; hence, any quoted price in excess of that obtaining in an actual sale.

load-factor pricing Differential price-making at different periods of time for the purpose of maximizing the utilization of production facilities: a principle applied in an effort to overcome seasonal or time-of-day depression in demand, or to attract lower-income groups. In the former situation, a wider distribution of fixed costs over sales may be achieved by price concessions to attract off-season or off-hour consumers. It is often regarded as practical to reduce prices to the point whereby all current costs are met along with some part of fixed costs.

Where a load-factor pricing policy is applied as a stimulant to sales, and plant capacity is limited, prudent merchandising may dictate the establishment of a high price until the high-income-consumer market is saturated. When this point is reached, plant capacity may be increased and prices lowered to tap the mass-purchasing, lower-income market. This method finds practical justification as long as the rate of return supporting the expanded operation or the action has the effect of forestalling competitors.

loading 1. The amount often added to an installment contract to cover selling and administrative expenses, interest, risk, and sometimes other factors.

2. In an investment trust or mutual fund, the amount added to the prorated market price of underlying securities, representing administrative and selling costs, trustee's fees, and brokerage.

3. Arbitrary additions used in preparing statistics or indexes in order to adjust the subject matter to a basis suitable for comparison or presentation.

4. The addition of *overhead* to *prime cost*.

loan fund (institutional accounting) A fund from which loans are to be made. The term has particular significance in colleges and universities. When both principal and interest of a fund are available for loans, the entire amount is placed in the loan-funds group; when only the income of the fund may be loaned, the principal is included in endowment funds, only the income constituting the loan fund.

loan value (life insurance) The maximum amount that may be borrowed from the insurer on a life-insurance contract.

local-improvement fund = *special assessment fund*.

log = *logarithm*.

logarithm The power, known also as the *index* or *exponent*, to which one number, called the *base*, is raised in order to make it equal to another number. Thus, the logarithm of 100 to the base 10 is 2, since $10^2 = 100$, and the logarithm of 1,000 to the base 10 is 3, since $10^3 = 1{,}000$. The *antilogarithm* is the number obtained when the base is raised to the power specified by a given logarithm; it is frequently called the original number and is signified by N. Thus, the antilogarithm of 2, using the base 10, is 100, and the antilogarithm of 3 is 1,000. The base is generally restricted to a number greater than 1.

Tables making possible the use of logarithms are available in two forms: (a) the *common* logarithms, with the base 10, and (b) the *natural* logarithms, with a base of 2.71828+ (an irrational number designated as e). Common logarithms are generally designated by the symbol "log," and natural logarithms by "ln"; any base ("b") may be mathematically designated as $\log_b$. Since the common and natural logarithm systems are related, for any number N, by the formula $\log N/\log e = \ln N$ ($\log e = 0.43429448$), it is always possible to convert from one base to the other.

Logarithms facilitate calculations in many problems involving multiplication, division, extraction of roots, and raising to powers, but they cannot be used for subtraction or addition. Before proceeding to examples, the nature of the illustrative six-place common logarithms appearing on pp. 268–269 will be explained.

Any positive number may be expressed as a power of 10. The examples cited below indicate this general law:

N (Antilog)		Power of 10	Log
1	=	10^0	0
10	=	10^1	1
100	=	10^2	2
1000	=	10^3	3

and so on, where N, the number to be expressed as a logarithm, or "log," is also the antilogarithm, or "antilog." (Note that any number raised to "zero power" is 1, and that $\log 1 = 0$.)

The logarithms of numbers standing between any two of the above numbers are expressed in decimal fractions; thus the logarithm of 5 is found to be 0.698970, while that of 55, the number halfway between 10 and 100, is 1.740363; both of these values are found in the illustrative table on page 269.

Positive fractions of 1 may be similarly expressed:

N (Antilog) (Fraction of 1)		Power of 10	Log
$0.1 = \frac{1}{10}$	=	10^{-1}	-1
$0.01 = \frac{1}{100}$	=	10^{-2}	-2
$0.001 = \frac{1}{1000}$	=	10^{-3}	-3

These results may thus be extended to any positive number:

N (Antilog)	Power of 10	Log
6	$10^{0.778151}$	0.778151
60	$10^{1.778151}$	1.778151
600	$10^{2.778151}$	2.778151
660	$10^{2.819544}$	2.819544
6600	$10^{3.819544}$	3.819544

It will be noted that the portion of the logarithm at the right of the decimal, known as the *mantissa,* remains unchanged regardless of the position of the decimal point of the antilog. The portion of the logarithm at the left of the decimal, the *characteristic,* shows the number of times 10 multiplied against itself is present in the number. The number 6 has 0 for the characteristic component of its logarithm, since 10 is present zero times in 6. The number 60 has 1 as its characteristic, since 10 is present once in 60. Again, in 600 the base 10 is present twice. The law governing the formation of the characteristic is not expressed in logarithm tables. To find the characteristic for the logarithm of 660, it is necessary to note only that $10^2 = 100$, giving the characteristic 2, which is writtten down immediately; the mantissa of 660 is found in the table to be 0.819544. Hence, the log of 660 is 2.819544; and, because the characteristic of 66 is 1, the logarithm of 66 must be 1.819544. As the sequence of digits in 66.0 and 660 is the same, only the characteristic is affected; the mantissa remains unchanged. The logarithms of the numbers 0.66, 6.6, 66, 660, etc., differ only in their characteristics; each has the same mantissa.

n	0	1	2	3	4	5	6	7	8	9	d
100	000000	000434	000868	001301	001734	002166	002598	003029	003461	003891	432
1	4321	4751	5181	5609	6038	6466	6894	7321	7748	8174	428
2	8600	9026	9451	9876	010300	010724	011147	011570	011993	012415	424
3	012837	013259	013680	014100	4521	4940	5360	5779	6197	6616	420
4	7033	7451	7868	8284	8700	9116	9532	9947	020361	020775	416
125	096910	097257	097604	097951	098298	098644	098990	099335	099681	100026	346
6	100371	100715	101059	101403	101747	102091	102434	102777	103119	3462	343
7	3804	4146	4487	4828	5169	5510	5851	6191	6531	6871	341
8	7210	7549	7888	8227	8565	8903	9241	9579	9916	110253	338
9	110590	110926	111263	111599	111934	112270	112605	112940	113275	3609	335
135	130334	130655	130977	131298	131619	131939	132260	132580	132900	3219	321
6	3539	3858	4177	4496	4814	5133	5451	5769	6086	6403	318
7	6721	7037	7354	7671	7987	8303	8618	8934	9249	9564	316
150	176091	176381	176670	176959	177248	177536	177825	178113	178401	178689	289
1	8977	9264	9552	9839	180126	180413	180699	180986	181272	181558	287
2	181844	182129	182415	182700	2985	3270	3555	3839	4123	4407	285
175	243038	243286	243534	243782	244030	244277	244525	244772	245019	245266	248
6	5513	5759	6006	6252	6499	6745	6991	7237	7482	7728	246
7	7973	8219	8464	8709	8954	9198	9443	9687	9932	250176	245
8	250420	250664	250908	251151	251395	251638	251882	252125	252368	2610	243
9	2853	3096	3338	3580	3822	4065	4306	4548	4790	5031	242
200	301030	301247	301464	301681	301898	302114	302331	302547	302764	302980	217
1	3196	3412	3628	3844	4059	4275	4491	4706	4921	5136	216
2	5351	5566	5781	5996	6211	6425	6639	6854	7068	7282	215
295	469822	469969	470116	470263	470410	470557	470704	470851	470998	471145	147
6	471292	471438	1585	1732	1878	2025	2171	2318	2464	2610	146
7	2756	2903	3049	3195	3341	3487	3633	3779	3925	4071	146
8	4216	4362	4508	4653	4799	4944	5090	5235	5381	5526	146
9	5671	5816	5962	6107	6252	6397	6542	6687	6832	6976	145
300	477121	477266	477411	477555	477700	477844	477989	478133	478278	478422	145
1	8566	8711	8855	8999	9143	9287	9431	9575	9719	9863	144
2	480007	480151	480294	480438	480582	480725	480869	481012	481156	481299	144
315	498311	498448	498586	498724	498862	498999	499137	499275	499412	499550	138
6	9687	9824	9962	500099	500236	500374	500511	500648	500785	500922	137
7	501059	501196	501333	1470	1607	1744	1880	2017	2154	2291	137
400	602060	602169	602277	602386	602494	602603	602711	602819	602928	603036	108
1	3144	3253	3361	3469	3577	3686	3794	3902	4010	4118	108
2	4226	4334	4442	4550	4658	4766	4874	4982	5090	5197	108
3	5305	5413	5521	5628	5736	5844	5951	6059	6166	6274	108
420	623249	623353	623456	623559	623663	623766	623869	623973	624076	624179	103
1	4282	4385	4488	4591	4695	4798	4901	5004	5107	5210	103
2	5312	5415	5518	5621	5724	5827	5929	6032	6135	6238	103
n	0	1	2	3	4	5	6	7	8	9	d

n	0	1	2	3	4	5	6	7	8	9	*d*
430	633468	633569	633670	633771	633872	633973	634074	634175	634276	634376	101
1	4477	4578	4679	4779	4880	4981	5081	5182	5283	5383	101
2	5484	5584	5685	5785	5886	5986	6087	6187	6287	6388	100
3	6488	6588	6688	6789	6889	6989	7089	7189	7290	7390	100
4	7490	7590	7690	7790	7890	7990	8090	8190	8290	8389	100
435	8489	8589	8689	8789	8888	8988	9088	9188	9287	9387	100
6	9486	9586	9686	9785	9885	9984	640084	640183	640283	640382	99
7	640481	640581	640680	640779	640879	640978	1077	1177	1276	1375	99
500	698970	699057	699144	699231	699317	699404	699491	699578	699664	699751	87
1	9838	9924	700011	700098	700184	700271	700358	700444	700531	700617	87
2	700704	700790	0877	0963	1050	1136	1222	1309	1395	1482	86
550	740363	740442	740521	740600	740678	740757	740836	740915	740994	741073	79
1	1152	1230	1309	1388	1467	1546	1624	1703	1782	1860	79
2	1939	2018	2096	2175	2254	2332	2411	2489	2568	2647	79
600	778151	778224	778296	778368	778441	778513	778585	778658	778730	778802	72
1	8874	8947	9019	9091	9163	9236	9308	9380	9452	9524	72
2	9596	9669	9741	9813	9885	9957	780029	780101	780173	780245	72
660	819544	819610	819676	819741	819807	819873	819939	820004	820070	820136	66
1	820201	820267	820333	820399	820464	820530	820595	0661	0727	0792	66
2	0858	0924	0989	1055	1120	1186	1251	1317	1382	1448	66
700	845098	845160	845222	845284	845346	845408	845470	845532	845594	845656	62
1	5718	5780	5842	5904	5966	6028	6090	6151	6213	6275	62
2	6337	6399	6461	6523	6585	6646	6708	6770	6832	6894	62
750	875061	875119	875177	875235	875293	875351	875409	875466	875524	875582	58
1	5640	5698	5756	5813	5871	5929	5987	6045	6102	6160	58
2	6218	6276	6333	6391	6449	6507	6564	6622	6680	6737	58
790	897627	897682	897737	897792	897847	897902	897957	898012	898067	898122	55
1	8177	8231	8286	8341	8396	8451	8506	8561	8616	8670	55
2	8725	8780	8835	8890	8945	8999	9054	9109	9164	9218	55
3	9273	9328	9383	9438	9492	9547	9602	9656	9711	9766	55
4	9821	9875	9930	9985	900039	900094	900149	900203	900258	900313	55
800	903090	903144	903199	903253	903307	903361	903416	903470	903524	903578	54
1	3633	3687	3741	3795	3849	3904	3958	4012	4066	4120	54
2	4174	4229	4283	4337	4391	4445	4499	4553	4607	4662	54
900	954243	954291	954339	954387	954436	954484	954532	954580	954628	954677	48
1	4725	4773	4821	4869	4918	4966	5014	5062	5110	5158	48
2	5207	5255	5303	5351	5399	5447	5495	5543	5592	5640	48
995	997823	997867	997910	997954	997998	998041	998085	998129	998172	998216	44
6	8259	8303	8347	8390	8434	8477	8521	8564	8608	8652	44
7	8695	8739	8782	8826	8869	8913	8956	9000	9043	9087	44
8	9131	9174	9218	9261	9305	9348	9392	9435	9479	9522	44
9	9565	9609	9652	9696	9739	9783	9826	9870	9913	9957	44
n	0	1	2	3	4	5	6	7	8	9	*d*

An easily remembered rule for obtaining characteristics is as follows: For numbers other than fractions of 1, the characteristic is equal to the number of places to the left of the decimal point minus 1. A simple extension of the rule covers positive fractions of 1, since

$$6 \times 10^{-1} = \tfrac{6}{10} = 0.6$$
$$6 \times 10^{-2} = \tfrac{6}{100} = 0.06$$
$$6 \times 10^{-3} = \tfrac{6}{1000} = 0.006.$$

The characteristics of these last numbers are −1, −2, and −3. For decimals or fractions less than 1, the rule for determining the characteristic, therefore, becomes: (a) add one to the number of zeros to the right of the decimal point, and (b) attach a minus sign to this number. These rules are illustrated in the following table:

N	*Characteristic*	*Log*	
0.006	−3	−3.778151	(or 7.778151 − 10)
0.06	−2	−2.778151	(or 8.778151 − 10)
0.6	−1	−1.778151	(or 9.778151 − 10)
6.0	0	0.778151	
60	1	1.778151	
600	2	2.778151	

A logarithm with a negative characteristic may be written alternatively by adding +10 to the characteristic, a fact indicated by following the mantissa by −10, as shown in parentheses above.

The basis of most practical computations in common logarithms, base 10, turns on the following rules:

1. Log 1 = 0 and log 10 = 1.
2. The logarithm of a product is the sum of the separate logarithms [$\log (N_1 \cdot N_2 \cdot N_3) = \log N_1 + \log N_2 + \log N_3$]. But, $\log (N_1 + N_2 + N_3)$ is unrelated to $\log N_1 + \log N_2 + \log N_3$.
3. The logarithm of a quotient is equal to the logarithm of the dividend less the logarithm of the divisor:

$$\log \left(\frac{N_1}{N_2}\right) = \log N_1 - \log N_2.$$

But,

$$\log (N_1 - N_2) \neq \log N_1 - \log N_2.$$

4. The logarithm of a power is the exponent times the logarithm of the number: $\log (N^p) = p \log N$. It should be noted that this rule also includes fractional powers:

$$\log \sqrt{N^p} = \log N^{p/2} = \frac{p}{2} \times \log N.$$

These rules may be used in combination or separately. For example, extracting the ninth root of

$$\left(\frac{6 \times 15^3 \times 0.7}{3^4}\right)^2$$

requires the use of all four rules. Since

$$\log \sqrt[9]{\left(\frac{6 \times 15^3 \times 0.7}{3^4}\right)^2}$$
$$= \log \left(\frac{6 \times 15^3 \times 0.7}{3^4}\right)^{2/9}$$
$$= \frac{2}{9} (\log 6 + 3 \log 15 + \log 0.7 - 4 \log 3),$$

the work may be systematically arranged by adding

log 6	= 0.778151		= 0.778151
3 log 15	= 3(1.176091)		= 3.528273
log 0.7	= 9.845098	− 10	= 9.845098 − 10
giving a total of			14.151522 − 10

and, subtracting,

$$4 \log 3 = 4(0.477121) = \frac{1.908484}{12.243038 - 10}.$$

Thus,

$$\log \left(\frac{6 \times 15^3 \times 0.7}{3^4}\right) = 2.243038.$$

What was required, however, was

$$\log \left(\frac{6 \times 15^3 \times 0.7}{3^4}\right)^{2/9}.$$

Application of rule 4 yields

$$\log \left(\frac{6 \times 15^3 \times 0.7}{3^4}\right)^{2/9} = \frac{2}{9} \log \frac{6 \times 15^3 \times 0.7}{3^4}$$
$$= \frac{2}{9} (2.243038) = 0.498451.$$

This result is the logarithm of the answer, or $10^{0.498451}$. Next the antilogarithm of 0.498451 must be determined by reversing the usual process: the body of the table is searched for the value of logarithm 498451.

The logarithm 498451 lies between the logarithms 498448 and 498586. The antilogarithms corresponding to these logarithms are 3151 and 3152, respectively. For most purposes, it will be sufficient to take the number corresponding to the closest logarithm; since 498448 is closer to 498451 than 498586, the number 3151 might be chosen in this case. If more exact results are required, *interpolation* may be used. Interpolation may be accomplished by noting that the difference between 498451 and 498448 is 000003. In other words, only $\frac{3}{138}$ or 02 of the necessary increase in the logarithm to raise the number by 1 is present. The number of zeros to the right of the decimal point indicate how the addition is to be made. The resulting number becomes 315102.

All that remains is to insert the decimal point in its correct position. Since the logarithm is 0.498451, the decimal rule indicates that the number which corresponds to this logarithm will have only one place to the left of the decimal point. The correct result then becomes 3.151, or 3.15102, depending on whether interpolation is undertaken. Hence,

$$\left(\frac{6 \times 15^3 \times 0.7}{3^4}\right)^{2/9} = 3.15102.$$

If the final logarithm had been 1.498451 instead of 0.498451, the answer would have been 31.5102. This follows the rule on characteristics and location of the decimal point.

Negative numbers have no logarithms. Log 1 = 0.00000—which means that if the base 10 is raised to the power 0, it will be equal to 1. This is as far as the logarithm system goes. Thus, the logarithm −1.498451 should be read: characteristic, minus 1; mantissa, plus 498451. The notation is meant to instruct the reader to obtain the number 315102 corresponding to the mantissa and then enter the decimal at such a point that the first figure will appear to its right; the result beocmes $N = 0.315102$. Similarly, for −2.498451, N becomes 0.0315102.

As pointed out above, the results obtained from the illustrative six-place table on pp. 268–269 may be made slightly more accurate by *interpolation.* The process is also, obviously, applicable to the location of logarithms within the table. For example, it might be desired to obtain log 420.55. The table gives values only to 420.5. But, since 420.55 lies halfway between 420.5 and 420.6, the logarithm of 420.55 is found by adding to log 420.5 one-half the difference between the two given logarithms, as follows:

$$\begin{array}{ll} \log 420.6 = & 2.623869 \\ \log 420.5 = & \underline{2.623766} \\ \text{difference} & 0.000103 \end{array}$$

The result, thus, becomes

$$\log 420.55 = 2.623766 + \frac{0.000103}{2} = 2.6238175.$$

The process of interpolation could also have been accomplished by subtraction from the larger of the two logarithms.

To facilitate interpolation, the average of all such differences in any row is provided in the column marked d in the table. Where extensive interpolations or accurate results are required, a more extensive table of logarithms may be employed, such as Vega's *Logarithmic Tables,* or Bruhns' *New Manual of Logarithms,* both carried to seven places. For particular purposes, such as interest calculations, special tables such as Kent's *Ten Place Interest and Annuity Tables* are available.

long *n.* A buyer or owner of stocks or commodities, often on margin.

adj. Owning more of a stock or commodity than is owed under contracts to deliver.

long account (brokerage accounting) The account on a broker's books in which the securities or commodities carried for a customer are recorded.

long-form report = *audit report(2)*.

long-term compensation (Federal income taxes) A concept of a form of *taxable income* now replaced by *average income*.

long-term contract Any contract for goods or services the completion of which extends into one or more succeeding fiscal years. The term is often applied to agreements covering the production of heavy equipment, such as electric generators, construction projects, and ships. The propriety of the accrual of revenue by the producer, as sections of the work are completed, has long been recognized in accounting. See *revenue realization*. The relative size of the amount yet to be paid may require disclosure in the balance sheet or in a balance-sheet footnote.

long-term debt (on balance sheet) Debt due after one year. The term applies generally to all forms of corporate obligations, secured and unsecured: mortgage bonds; sinking-fund bonds; income bonds; bank loans; debentures (whether or not convertible); loans from insurance companies; and so on. The principle features of each such obligation are disclosed in the *sidehead* or in an appended note; these will include nature of underlying security, if any; rate of interest; redemption rates; convertible privileges. Its position on the *balance sheet* is between current liabilities and stockholders' equity (net worth); any portion maturing during the following 12 months usually appears as a *current liability*.

long-term lease An obligation for rent of real or personal property over an extended period of years. Present usage of the term applies not only to ordinary or *executory leases* but also to *sell-and-leaseback agreements* and to contracts resembling leases but which are in effect *installment purchases*. Because of the importance and often involved character of this modern type of financing, financial statements containing these items are supplemented by detailed notes the content of which is outlined in APB 10.

long-term liability An obligation which will not become due within a relatively short period, usually a year. Examples: *mortgages;* mortgage bonds; *debentures;* secured-note issues; *funded debt* generally.

loss 1. Any item of expense, as in the term *profit and loss*.

2. Any sudden, unexpected, involuntary expense or unrecoverable cost, often referred to as a form of *nonrecurring charge;* an expenditure from which no present or future benefit may be expected. Examples: the undepreciated cost of a building destroyed by fire and not covered by insurance; damages paid in an accident suit; an amount of money stolen.

3. The excess of the cost or depreciated cost of an asset over its selling price.

4. = *net loss*.

loss and gain = *profit and loss*.

loss ratio (insurance) The ratio of the losses paid or accrued by an insurer to premiums earned, usually for a period of a year.

lost discount See *discount lost*.

lost usefulness The gradual dissipation from any cause of the service potential, or worth in exchange, of anything owned; *depreciation*.

lot Any group of goods or services making up a single transaction; if the group consists of a known number of similar items, the price or cost of each is obtained by simple division; if the items are dissimilar and the total price is independent of the prices, if any, of individual items, the cost of each item is usually indeterminable, except by any of several possible methods of imputation. See *imputed price; cost-recovery basis; job lot*.

lot-acceptance sampling (statistical quality control) = *acceptance sampling.*

lot tolerance percent defective (statistical quality control) A degree of quality, generally in terms of number or percentage of defective items in a lot or batch of goods, which is generally regarded as just satisfactory or tolerable, the implication being that any quality of lower degree is unsatisfactory; often referred to as *LTPD.* See *rejectable quality level.*

lump-sum appropriation (or **allotment**) An *appropriation* (or *allotment*) for a stated purpose, or for a named department or departmental subdivision, authorizing an aggregate of expenditures, but not specifying beyond general purposes the amounts that may be applied to individual objects or activities thereunder.

lump-sum purchase The acquisition of a group of assets for an indicated figure, without breakdown by individual assets or classes of assets: a type of transaction often accompanying the purchase of a going concern. For example, the amount paid may have been determined by determining the present worth of future earning ability, by bargaining between individuals whose sense of "values" has little to do with formal records or with reports of earnings, or by other considerations not reflected in the accounts. An appraisal of the acquired assets by engineers may then establish the basis (replacement cost or book value) for recording the assets, with due allowance for depreciation, any excess of the purchase price over such depreciated basis being regarded as *goodwill.* Where the depreciated basis exceeds the purchase price, the items of which the basis is composed are usually reduced prorata; or the accrued depreciation, as estimated, is increased. In numerous cases, the book values reflected on the records of the seller are continued on the books of the buyer, particularly where the purchase price has been based on the seller's financial statements, the balancing amount, if any, being designated as an intangible. This is the procedure prescribed by regulatory bodies for recording lump-sum purchases of a utility enterprise; the valuation basis thus established is referred to as *original cost,* and the purchase excess as *acquisition adjustment.*

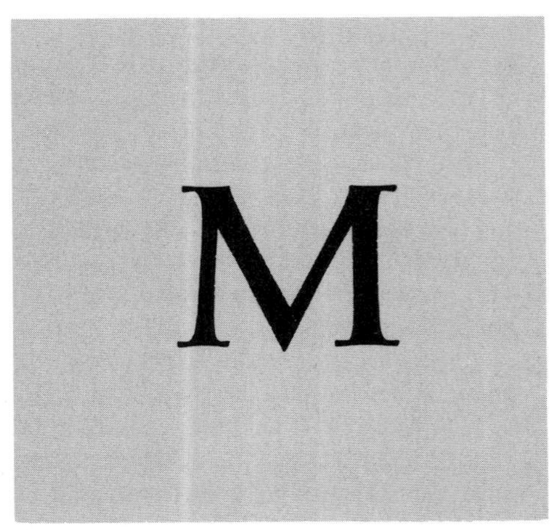

machine-hour rate A rate of cost per hour of work performed by a machine, applied to goods in process. Cost consists of direct and indirect expense—labor, depreciation, power, maintenance, supplies, and often an allocated portion of factory overhead—and may be estimated (a standard rate) or actual. Machine hours, the divisor of cost employed to determine the hourly rate, may likewise be estimated or actual. If the rate is estimated, the difference between estimated and actual, attributable to variations in both costs and hours, and periodically determined, is often spread over the preceding period's production by a supplementary rate or carried into the following (monthly) period for inclusion in that period's estimates. A single, accurate rate is subject to the criticism that its determination delays the postings to cost sheets or other production records for too protracted an interval after the close of the period. See *cost; standard cost; job-order costing.*

machine tool 1. Any device, usually stationary, composed of a number of moving parts, at least partially automatic in action, and operated by power, used for shaping, turning, planing, assembling, or otherwise performing useful work on materials.

2. A replaceable part such as a cutting or shaping attachment of such a device.

maintenance 1. The keeping of property at a standard of operating condition; also, the expense involved. Example: recurring operations of cleaning, oiling, repairing, and adjusting. Maintenance costs include outlays for (a) labor and supplies; (b) the replacement of any part that constitutes less than a *retirement unit;* and (c) major overhauls the items of which may involve elements of the first two classes. Items falling under (a) and (b) are always regarded as operating costs, chargeable to current expense directly or through the medium of a *maintenance reserve* (see *equalization reserve*). Costs under (c) are similarly treated unless they include the replacement of a retirement unit the outlay for which is normally capitalized. See *deferred maintenance.*

2. = any *operating cost.*

maintenance reserve An *equalization reserve* for maintenance costs. See *deferred maintenance.*

majority-owned subsidiary A subsidiary more than 50 percent of whose outstanding voting capital stock is owned by its parent or by another of the parent's majority-owned subsidiaries.

makeready time The time spent on the preparation of machines and other facilities before starting production; the cost of labor and other factors applied to such preparation. See *lead time; setup time.* The term is used principally in the printing trade.

malfeasance The wrongful doing of an act that the doer has no right to do or has contractually obligated himself not to do.

management 1. Executive authority: the combined fields of policy and administration.

2. As applied to individuals:

(a) the head of an organization, or

(b) collectively, the head and his immediate staff and any or all persons possessing supervisory persons' delegated authority.

It is often said that management *delegates* (or assigns or grants) authority to subsidiary levels of activity, but cannot delegate *responsibility*. The latter can only be *assumed* (i.e., when the delegation has been accepted and agreed to) by the activity (suborganizational-subfunctional) head who operates within the defined limits of the delegation and is *accountable* to (i.e., reports to or has a *feedback* relationship with) the delegator.

management accounting Accounting designed for or adapted to the needs of information and control at the various administrative levels. The term has no precise coverage but is used generally to refer to the extensions of internal reporting for the design and submission of which a corporation controller is responsible. Repetitive reports on performance involving both product quantities and dollars, special reports covering operational areas undergoing change or proposed for reorganization, and reports of investigations of malfunctioning or suspected inefficiencies are illustrative of the manifold activities in which the present-day controller, frequently with the assistance of the public accountant, is expected to engage. Emphasis is often given to prompt, authoritative, and complete reports that can lead to and even induce management decision-making. An illustration of management accounting is *actitivity accounting* (*q.v.*).

management by exception A phrase used in connection with the presumed action required where reports on performance differ from original projections (actual costs versus standard costs or budgeting prescriptions). Characteristically these reports bring out "favorable" and "unfavorable" variances, the latter being the basis for "management by exception"; see, however, *favorable difference.*

management-investment company An investment company the management of which is permitted a large discretion in buying and selling securities. There are two principal types: closed-end and open-end companies. The former, also known as *leverage* companies, often have several types of bonds and stocks outstanding, some of which may be listed on exchanges and the prices of which bear no necessary relationship to book values; the latter usually have only a single type of outstanding stock, in which only licensed dealers are permitted to trade and the value of which is based on the market value of securities owned.

management performance See *operating performance.*

management review An *appraisal(2)* by a public accountant or other professional person of management *performance:* a testing of adherence to governing policy; profit capability; adequacy of operating controls and of operating procedures; relations with employees, customers, the trade, and the public generally; adaptability to and conformity with the current concept of the *public interest.* See *efficiency.*

management science 1. The field of management problems and their solutions, particularly those of a complex nature, an understanding of which is susceptible to testing, verification, and generalization.

2. The study of new and improved management techniques having general application.

The complexity and subtlety of problems investigated by management often lead to mathematical or statistical *models;* the employment of such models has sometimes supplied a ready means of distinguishing management-science research from other types of investigation in the same area. Thus, the design of an accounting system might take the form of a series of flow charts, manuals, and accompanying codes and account descriptions when executed by an accountant. An *operations-research* specialist might reformulate the design in terms of a mathematical model and, by establishing algebraic relationships, study the possible variations in accounting structure required to adapt the system to an electronic computer.

manager (public accounting) In the office of a public accountant, a supervisor of audit engagements to whom the field staff reports and to whom varying degrees of authority may be given in the processes of initiating, supervising, closing, and reporting of such engagements.

mantissa The decimal portion of the common logarithm; see *logarithm.*

manual of accounting = *accounting manual.*

manual rate (insurance) An established standard premium rate, usually expressed in dollars per thousand dollars of risk.

manufacturing cost = *factory cost.*

manufacturing expense The cost of manufacturing other than the cost of raw materials consumed and direct labor; *factory expense; indirect expense;* (factory) *overhead.*

manufacturing statement A statement showing particulars of the cost of goods manufactured.

March 1, 1913 (Federal income taxes) The effective date of the 16th amendment to the U. S. Constitution, as recognized by the Congress. Gain on property sold after but acquired before that date is based on the excess of the selling price over the fair value on that date if greater than cost. A loss on such property is based on the March 1, 1913, value only if such value is less than original cost.

margin 1. = *gross profit.*
2. The excess of the market price of collateral over the loan it secures.
3. A deposit or advance by an investor with or to a broker, representing a part payment on the purchase price of a security or commodity.
4. The remaining equity of a broker's customer when a security or commodity so purchased is sold.
5. = *marginal income.*

marginal analysis A method for imputing the source of a variation to the factors that have contributed to a common effect. The term derives from economics, where it is assumed that it is possible to study variations from one cause while fixing all others at preselected values. See *marginal productivity; marginal cost.* In practical affairs, the conditions for realizing the requirements of this approach are usually absent. It has been necessary for accountants to develop their own methods. The concept of marginal costs is frequently replaced in accounting practice by the concept of *incremental costs.* Such costs are regarded as approximations of the theoretical ideal. The methods used to obtain the estimates making up incremental costs necessarily depend on the nature and object of the study and also on the types of *controls* that can be established when practical application is given to these estimates. The necessity for such controls, and their relevance to the way estimates can be formed or modified, feature the accounting approach.

marginal balance The excess of revenue over variable cost; see *marginal income.*

marginal cost 1. The increase or decrease in total cost which occurs with a small variation in (such as a unit of) output.
2. Hence, *incremental, differential,* or *direct cost,* excluding any element of *fixed cost.* Ascertaining marginal cost is of importance in determining whether to vary a rate of production. Fixed costs of facilities will continue whether or not the facilities are put to use; it may therefore be profitable to solicit new business at lower prices even if fixed costs are not completely covered, the test being whether revenues from new business are sufficient to cover the added (marginal) costs of production. At less than *optimum output,* an increase in the rate of production will result in a marginal unit cost lower than average total unit cost; production in excess of the optimum point will result in a marginal unit cost greater than average total unit cost; at optimum output, the two costs coincide. Also, marginal unit cost is the lowest amount at which a sale may

be made without adding to the producer's loss or subtracting from his profits; a sale at a price in excess of marginal unit cost will increase the net income of the producer even though the sales price does not cover average total unit cost.

marginal costing The assignment of marginal or variable costs to an activity, department, or product, as contrasted with *absorption costing* and *direct costing.*

marginal income The excess of sales over related *direct costs:* the *contribution(5)* of revenues to other costs and profit; see *gross profit; gross margin; contribution theory.*

marginal-income ratio The percentage of the sales dollar available to cover fixed costs and profits after deducting the percentage required for variable costs: the complement of the *variable-cost ratio.*

marginal productivity An increment in total dollar value (or physical quantity) which results from a one-unit increase in the amount of a *factor of production* employed in any program or process. The successful measurement of the marginal productivity of any factor of production can be attained only when it is possible to isolate its variations from other causes of yield variation. In particular, all other factors of production must be approximately constant at known levels before yield variations can be *imputed,* with any validity, to the factor in question. Such ideal conditions are seldom met with, and it may be necessary to resort to rather complex means for obtaining *approximations* to the desired measures. See *productivity; variance.*

marginal unit cost See *marginal cost.*

marginal utility The added *utility* supplied by one additional unit of production.

margin of safety The excess of sales over the breakeven sales volume, expressed as dollars or in other quantity units or as a ratio. See breakeven chart, page 66.

markdown 1. In retail stores, the reduction of an originally established selling price or *markon.*
2. In banks and brokerage houses, a revaluation of securities based upon a decline in their market quotations.
3. = *writedown.*

markdown cancellation The portion of original markon restored after a markdown has been made.

market 1. A place or geographical area where products and their competitive substitutes are bought and sold by buyers and sellers who thus have ready access to each other; hence, any established medium for supplier–consumer communication, such as advertisements in newspapers, catalogs, or door-to-door salesmen.
2. = *market price.*

marketing cost The cost of locating customers, persuading them to buy, delivering the goods, and collecting sales proceeds; *selling cost.*

market price (or **value**) 1. Recent invoice or quoted price at the close of an accounting period, less customary adjustments, including cash discount; the price at which a seller willing to sell at a fair price and a buyer willing to buy at a fair price will trade, assuming that both have a reasonable knowledge of the facts, that similar quantities, qualities, and delivery periods are involved, and that the market has been canvassed by both buyers and sellers. In the absence of present or prospective buyers, a market price is conceived (as in the phrase, "the lower of cost or market") to be the lowest price quoted by a prospective seller.
2. The lower of (a) *replacement* or *reproduction cost* and (b) estimated net selling price less estimated costs of carrying, selling, and delivering, and, in the case of unfinished product, less the estimated cost of bringing the product to a completed state, provided that (a) is not applied so as to reduce residual cost to a point below that at which it is anticipated a normal profit can be earned, this being the meaning generally ascribed to the term when used in the

inventory-valuation method known as *cost or market, whichever is lower.* See *price; inventory valuation.*

3. The price (usually representative) at which bona-fide sales have been consummated for products of like type, quality, and quantity in a particular market at any moment of time; it reflects, in addition to economic forces, the contemporary resolution of market vagaries, rumors, even misinformation, and personal, often arbitrary decisions of buyers and sellers. See *normal price.*

markon The amount added to cost, in setting selling prices, to cover operating expenses and profit margin; the ratio to the selling price thus established of the amount added to cost, expressed as a percentage; formerly known as *markup.*

markup 1. The amount added to an established selling price for the purpose of determining a new and higher selling price; the percentage of markup is based on the previously established selling price.

2. The total amount by which established selling prices are increased during a given period in setting new selling prices.

3. = *markon.*

4. In banks and brokerage houses, a revaluation of securities based upon a rise in their market quotations.

markup cancellation The elimination of a markup or such portion thereof as pertains to referent unsold merchandise. See *markup.*

marshal 1. (applied to assets) To establish the order and classes of assets with respect to their application to the liquidation of liabilities.

2. (applied to liabilities) To establish the classes and priority of liabilities to be liquidated; to arrange priorities so that creditors are equitably treated.

Massachusetts trust = *business trust.*

master budget A budget that provides an overall plan for a forthcoming fiscal period, including the profit objective and the coordinated program for meeting it.

master control account A control account maintained in the general ledger supported by a subsidiary ledger or other record containing control accounts each relating to a limited number of accounts receivable or other *detail accounts.*

matching 1. The principle of identifying related revenues and expense with the same accounting period. The principle is in most cases observed as a matter of course, since the outgo for the great bulk of operating costs coincides with the inflow of revenue. In recognizing accruals and deferrals, the principle of matching is often invoked. Less common transactions involving income and expense often cannot be "matched." See *income realization; cost absorption; income deduction.*

2. The determination or recognition of items that are to compose an *income statement.*

material *n.* = *raw material.*

adj. Of relative importance; see *materiality(1).*

material control The supplying of commodities required in manufacturing at the lowest cost per unit consistent with required quality and with the least investment in inventory.

material in process = *goods in process.*

materiality 1. The relative importance or relevance of any item included in or omitted from books of account or financial statements, or of any procedure or change in procedure that conceivably might affect such statements. Certain items become material through law, administrative regulation, directors' resolution, or other fiat. Other items are regarded as material because of convention or custom and may differ in importance even among similar organizations. *Value judgments* are the usual and often the only means of determining relative importance; they are based on such factors as the relative size and general characteristic of the item and the assumed responsibilities of management to stockholders, employees, and the public. Moreover, the factors of importance today may be of greater or less importance tomorrow. Financial statements, as representations of corporate management, can be prepared intelligently only where value judgments on questions of materiality have been well developed. Unimportant items are merged with other items or may perhaps be omitted altogether (e.g., minor accruals or prepayments); important items may require any of varying degrees of disclosure: a separate listing, a footnote, or parenthetical mention. Some accountants have endeavored to establish standards of materiality by rules of thumb; as, for example, by requiring that any item or item class the money amount of which is 5 percent or more of total assets or 10 percent or more of net income appear as an integral detail of a financial statement. Such a rule, however, leaves unsolved the problem of smaller items whose disclosure may be essential, regardless of their size, as where matters of importance are disclosed or where items, now of minor importance, may develop into major items upon the passage of time or the happening of events now contingent.

2. The characteristic attaching to a statement, fact, or item whereby its disclosure or the method of giving it expression would be likely to influence the judgment of a reasonable person. See *significant.*

3. (auditing) The relative importance of any audit coverage, such as the testing of accounts receivable by correspondence where circumstances seem to warrant its omission or some departure therefrom, such as the fact that at the time of the audit the accounts have been collected in full; or the relative importance of any impropriety or series of improprieties encountered in the amounts or financial statements, such as a missing document, a wrong classification, an unauthorized transaction, a restriction on information furnished by management, a weak link in internal controls, or a violation of an accounting principle. Here an opinion of materiality, like that attaching to items in financial statements, can be reached only by a value judgment on the part of the auditor provided accepted minimum requirements have been met. The factors of size and recurrability are the more common determinants. Some improprieties, even though minor, may be of such importance as to warrant the auditor's refusal to approve the financial statements; others, of less importance, may justify a qualification in his report and a disclosure of their quantitative effect; others call for discussions with management, looking to the elimination of the impropriety, at least for the future; still others, not being significant amounts, may be ignored altogether.

materials and services A term employed in business generally as an inclusive designation of the immediate objects of expenditure; what is received in, or the debit portions of, *external transactions.* See *object classification; goods and services.*

mathematical programming = *linear programming.*

matrix A rectangular array of mathematical symbols.

matured liability An obligation due or past due. The term is applied chiefly to the principal amount of a bond or note issue.

maturing liability An obligation that will shortly fall due.

maturity The date on which an obligation becomes due.

maturity basis The basis for calculating bond values and rates of return, on the supposition that the bonds will be held until maturity. See *bond valuation.*

maximize profit To develop volume to the point where the cost of one additional unit equals the net receipts that can be obtained for it.

mean A midpoint in an array of numbers. See *arithmetic mean; geometric mean.*

meaning The referent of a term, statement, concept, or symbol: the object, condition, event, relation, or characteristic intended by a person employing language. An emotional or emotive attitude or feeling of the user may be implicit in the intended notion in addition to an objective reference.

measurement The assignment of a system of *ordinal* or *cardinal* numbers to the results of a scheme of inquiry or apparatus of observation in accord with logical or mathematical rules. In the case of ordinal measurement, the following two properties are exhibited with respect to an ordering or ranking relation, expressed by the sign "$\geq$" (read "ranks"), among three arbitrary measures 0_L, 0_M, and 0_N, an example of which is found in the notion of preference or of valuation:

1. One and only one of the three possibilities obtains in the case of two measures 0_L and 0_M: either $0_L \geq 0_M$ or $0_M \geq 0_L$, or $0_M = 0_L$.

2. If $0_L \geq 0_M$ and $0_M \geq 0_N$, then $0_L \geq 0_N$.

In the case of cardinal measurement, which presupposes the existence of a zero or origin measure as well as that of a unit measure, the following properties hold in addition to those which apply to ordinal measurement:

3. $0_L + 0_M = 0_M + 0_L$ (commutative rule of addition).

4. $k(0_L) = k0_L$, where k is some real number (distributive rule of multiplication).

5. $(0_L + 0_M) + 0_N = 0_L + (0_M + 0_N) = 0_L + 0_M + 0_N$ (associative rule of addition).

6. If $0_L \geq 0_M$, then there exist some 0_N such that $0_L = 0_M + 0_N$.

measurement concept (of accounting) The identification of *economic activity(1)* with time periods whereby for each period the activity can be measured and reported; see *continuity concept; accounting period.*

median The central item in a collection of numbers arrayed according to size; often represented by the symbol *Md.*

The median is also called an average of position, because of the like number of items on either side of it, notwithstanding the numerical values taken on by the group. It is therefore more stable and less likely to be influenced by extreme values than is the arithmetic mean. Thus, the median remains unaffected at 50 when the three values 49, 50, and 54 are changed to 49, 50, and 57; the arithmetic mean, however, changes from 51 to 52. The *mode* (the number appearing with the greatest frequency) is even more stable than the median. Introduction of extreme values which tend to produce *skewness* in a *frequency distribution* thus have their greatest effect on the arithmetic mean and their least effect on the mode, with the median lying between the mean and the mode. This relation between the mean, median, and mode occurs because the mode is not influenced by extreme values; the median depends only on the position of the extreme values, while the arithmetic mean is directly influenced by extremes. Thus, the introduction of extremes on the high side will tend to move the median above the mode, and the mean above the median; introduction of extremely low values will tend to reverse this relation, with the mean tending to move below the median while the median tends to move below the mode.

It has been empirically established (i.e., by observation) that in a moderately skewed, but continuous, distribution, the median falls about two-thirds of the distance from the mode toward the mean. Mathematically, where $\bar{X}$ is the arithmetic mean, *Md* the median, and *Mo* the mode,

$$(\bar{X} - Md) = {}^1\!/_3(\bar{X} - Mo).$$

This relation can be substituted in the formula given under skewness,

$$Sk = \frac{\bar{X} - Mo}{\sigma},$$

to produce the more easily computed value

$$Sk = \frac{3(\bar{X} - Md)}{\sigma},$$

where the denominator, σ, is the *deviation,* and *Sk,* the skewness.

In a symmetric distribution, the mean, median, and mode all coincide, and the value of the above relation is zero. As skewness occurs, the mean moves increasingly farther away from the median, the direction of skew being determined by whether the mean exceeds or is less than the median.

The value of the median may or may not coincide with the value of any number in the array, depending on whether the number of items is even or odd. If the number of items in the array is odd, the central item is chosen as the median; if the number of items is even, the average of the two central items is chosen as the median. Thus, if an additional value, say, 60, were added to the numbers 49, 50, and 54 given above, the array would have become 49, 50, 54, and 60, and the median $(50 + 54)/2 = 52$. Whereas 50 can be recognized as one of the items existing in the series, 52 cannot be so recognized. (*Note:* the same value would obtain for the median if 100 had been added instead of 60; the arithmetic mean, on the other hand, would have been markedly affected.)

For grouped data, the process of locating the median value proceeds on the assumption that the distribution of items is uniform within each class. The total frequency is then divided by 2 in order to locate the number of items which lie on each side of the median. Beginning at either end of the distribution, the frequencies are then summed, class by class, until the total indicates that the next succeeding class will contain the median. The remaining number of items necessary to reach 50 percent of the total frequency is then divided by the frequency in the median class to form a ratio; this ratio is applied to the class interval and the result added to the lower limit of the class to yield the median value. The process of calculation is illustrated by the following data on merchandise purchases. The purchases at various prices have been grouped into a frequency distribution of class interval 2. That is, all 5 items purchased at prices ranging from $1.00 to $2.99 have been placed in a single class. The 10 items which were purchased at prices ranging from $3.00 to $4.99 are also placed in one class, and so on, as shown in the table which follows.

Class Interval	f	Cumulative	
1.00– 2.99	5	5	
3.00– 4.99	10	15	
5.00– 6.99	35	50	← Median Class
7.00– 8.99	33	83	
9.00–10.99	4	87	
	87		

Since the median is located at the point of equal frequency, it occurs where $N/2 = \frac{87}{2} = 43.5$. That is, 43.5 purchases occurred at prices below, and 43.5 purchases occurred at prices above the median price. The price which was simultaneously higher than the prices paid for 43.5 purchases and lower than the prices paid for the remaining 43.5 purchases is the median price. Cumulating the frequencies, from the lowest value ($1.00) upward, it is seen that this value occurs somewhere in the class interval 5.00–6.99. In accordance with the preceding instructions, the median value is

$$5.00 + \frac{43.5 - 15}{35} \times 2 = 6.63.$$

Medians rather than arithmetic means may be used in valuing an inventory on the basis of average cost where it is desired to avoid having a few large or small items unduly influence the result.

merchandise Purchased articles of commerce held for sale; the inventory of a merchant.

merchandise account A ledger account used for recording purchases and sales, inward and outward freight, returned sales and purchases, and often many kinds of expenses, the balance of which, after making adjustments for goods on hand at the beginning and end of an accounting period, represents gross profit for the period; such an account was formerly in common use, particularly in small retail stores. It has now been displaced by separate accounts for the principal elements indicated.

merchandise cost. (retail accounting) Invoice cost, less *discount earned.*

merchandise inventory See *inventory.*

merchandise procurement cost Cost accompanying a purchase; particularly (*retail accounting*) buying, receiving, transferring, warehousing, and marketing costs pertaining to merchandise acquired for resale. Merchandise procurement cost is deducted from *gross merchandise margin* to obtain *gross operating spread.*

merchant One who buys and sells articles of commerce without change in their form.

merchant's rule See *United States rule.*

merger 1. The fusion of two or more enterprises through the direct acquisition by one of the net assets of the other or others. A merger differs from a *consolidation* in that in the former no new concern is created, where as in a consolidation a new corporation or entity acquires the net assets of all of the combining units.

2. Loosely, any *business combination.*

millnet price See *administered price.*

minority interest The portion of the net worth of a subsidiary relating to shares not owned by the controlling company or other members of the consolidated group.

The amount of outside-ownership equities, consisting of prorata amounts of capital stock, capital surplus, and retained earnings as they are reflected on the records of subsidiaries, and adjusted by the elimination of intercompany gains or losses, may be desirable details on the face of the consolidated balance sheet. A full elimination of intercompany profits and losses (see *intercompany elimination*) necessitates an adjustment of the equities of the outside stockholders of the subsidiary that has taken the profit or loss. This is justifiable, since the purpose of a consolidated balance sheet is to display both assets and equities in the amounts at which they would be stated if the several legal entities composing the consolidated group were reduced to one. Outside stockholders are entitled to know what portion of their book equity is represented by a "controlled" profit: that is, a profit that has not yet been realized through a sale to the public.

Minority stockholders' equities, including their shares of the surplus account, are preferably regarded as liabilities on the consolidated balance sheet rather than as a portion of net worth. Although not legal obligations, these equities possess some of the attributes of obligations in that their interests do not parallel those of the controlling equities. This is recognized in the frequent absorption by the controlling company of the entire operating loss or deficit of a subsidiary not fully owned, or in the assumption by the controlling company of all the writedown of an unrealized profit.

The absorption of a loss or deficit is a policy the adoption of which is a matter that warrants the approval of the boards of directors of both the controlling company and its subsidiary. This policy, often followed where the intercompany transactions of a subsidiary have not been maintained at arm's length, should be recorded on the books of the controlling company and the subsidiary by entries covering the entire amount of the subsidiary's loss or deficit, or, better, the entire amount of the differences attributable to the failure to preserve an arm's-length relationship.

Where there are two or more subsidiaries, the balance-sheet summary of outside-ownership equities may be supported by a supplementary schedule if their importance warrants it. See *consolidation policy.*

miscellaneous asset An asset, usually of

minor significance, that cannot be classified under any of the other headings or subheadings of the balance sheet.

miscellaneous expense Incidental expense, not classifiable as manufacturing, selling, administrative, or general expense, and appearing on an income statement below operating income or as a subdivision of *income deductions.*

miscellaneous revenue Minor and incidental revenues. Examples: sales of waste paper; occasional rent of unused facilities; interest on bank balances.

misfeasance The doing wrongfully of a legal act or an act the doer has a right to do.

misleading With respect to a financial statement, containing an obscure, *distorted,* or untrue statement, or omitting a material fact. See *material.* A financial statement may be judged misleading without regard to the intent of the one who prepared it. The experience, skill, imagination, and independence of the public accountant, together with his reliance on accepted standards of auditing practice and statement presentation, are his professional safeguards for the prevention of misleading characteristics in financial statements on which he reports.

missed discount See *lost discount.*

mixed account 1. An account which includes both *real* and *nominal* elements. Examples: a *merchandise account;* an account containing unadjusted prepaid expenses.

2. (brokerage accounting) A customer's account containing both long and short security or commodity positions.

mixed inventory An inventory of a class of goods the items of which are not or cannot be identified with a particular lot.

mixed reserve An account with a credit balance representing a combination of a *liability,* a *valuation account,* and *appropriated surplus,* or any two of them. Examples: a reserve for plant rehabilitation; an insurance reserve.

mixed surplus A net-worth account containing not only retained earnings, but also elements of paid-in capital or appreciation credits, or both. See *surplus.*

mix variance A *variance* resulting from changes in the proportions of goods produced or activities carried on.

mnemonic system An indexing of accounts or groups of accounts by means of letters or combinations of letters that suggest their name or nature.

mode The item of most frequent occurrence in a group of numbers; often represented by the symbol *Mo;* the class of greatest frequency in a frequency distribution. See *median; arithmetic mean; average.*

model A pattern, system, or postulational set of functional relations, including definitions, between variables and parameters, the purpose of which is to conceptualize empirical findings and to plan, design, and analyze the results of systematic investigations. Sometimes models may take physical form (e.g., scale models of ships or buildings) as an aid to planning or analysis, but more frequently they retain the form of abstract constructs. Often thought of as being confined to investigations in mathematical and developed sciences, models are essential to systematic work in any field dealing with complex problems involving relations between facts and objectives. Business or governmental budgets, systems of accounts, audit working papers, and student practice sets, more or less suitably adapted to particular situations, provide models for grouping *facts* and guiding thought in a manner indispensable to the orderly presentation and solution of complex problems. See *decision.*

money 1. *Currency* and *specie,* collectively.

2. = *cash;* used in referring to any payment other than *in kind.*

money equivalent The objective value of property or services acquired as the result of a business transaction or a portion of such a transaction not involving the receipt of money or a promise to pay; the stated money amount attaching to a business transaction or a portion of such a transaction involving a barter; it may be equal to the face amount or market value of what is received, or, in certain instances, to the *book value* of the thing given in exchange. See *barter; price.*

money's worth = *money equivalent.*

money wages Compensation for services in terms of money received, as contrasted with *real wages*, or the purchasing power of the money over the necessities of life and other things desired by the recipient of the money; also known as *nominal wages.*

mortality The tendency of an asset or class of assets to expire or depreciate through use or the passage of time.

mortality chart (life insurance) An assemblage of data on life expectancy; what is known as Commissioners' 1958 Standard Ordinary Mortality Table, reproduced on page 285, is commonly employed in life-insurance calculations in the United States.

mortality curve A curve showing the actual or estimated life spans of a large number of persons or things. It differs from the survivor-life curve only in method of presentation. While the mortality curve shows the number of persons dying or number of items of property retired over a period of years, the survivor-life curve shows the number of items remaining over a period of years. Both curves are usually computed on a cumulative basis, generally appearing as a less-than (survivor-life) or more-than (mortality) ogive. See the illustration below.

mortgage A lien on land, buildings, machinery, equipment, and other property, fixed or movable, given by a borrower to the lender as security for his loan; sometimes called a *deed of trust* or a *defeasible conveyance.* When a mortgage constitutes the security against which bonds are issued, the lien is conveyed by what is ordinarily known as a *deed of trust.* A mortgage bond or note may be designated as "senior," "underlying," "first," "prior," "overlying," "second," "third," and so forth, depending upon the priority of the lien. The first three designations do not always imply a first lien, for such mortgages may be anteceded by a prior purchase obliga-

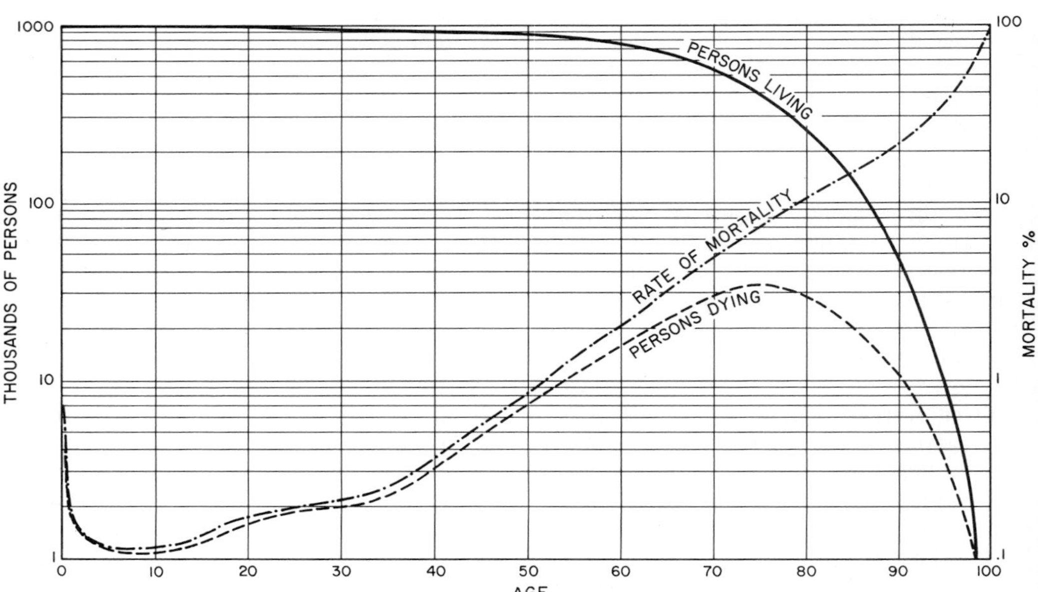

STANDARD ORDINARY MORTALITY TABLE*

Age	Persons Living	Persons Dying Number	Persons Dying Rate
0	1,000,000	7,080	00708
1	992,920	1,748	00176
2	991,173	1,507	00152
3	989,666	1,445	00146
4	988,221	1,384	00140
5	986,838	1,332	00135
6	985,505	1,281	00130
7	984,224	1,240	00126
8	982,984	1,209	00123
9	981,775	1,188	00121
10	980,587	1,187	00123
11	979,401	1,205	00123
12	978,196	1,233	00126
13	976,963	1,290	00132
14	975,674	1,356	00139
15	974,318	1,423	00146
16	972,895	1,498	00154
17	971,397	1,574	00162
18	969,832	1,639	00169
19	968,184	1,685	00174
20	966,499	1,730	00179
21	964,769	1,766	00183
22	963,004	1,791	00186
23	961,213	1,817	00189
24	959,400	1,832	00191
25	957,564	1,848	00193
26	955,716	1,873	00196
27	953,842	1,898	00199
28	951,944	1,932	00203
29	950,012	1,976	00208
30	948,036	2,019	00213
31	946,017	2,072	00219
32	943,945	2,124	00225
33	941,821	2,185	00232
34	939,636	2,255	00240
35	937,381	2,353	00251
36	935,028	2,469	00264
37	932,559	2,611	00280
38	929,948	2,799	00301
39	927,149	3,013	00325
40	924,136	3,262	00353
41	920,874	3,536	00384
42	917,338	3,825	00417
43	913,512	4,138	00453
44	909,374	4,474	00492
45	904,900	4,841	00535
46	900,059	5,247	00583
47	894,811	5,691	00636
48	889,120	6,180	00695
49	882,941	6,710	00760
50	876,231	7,290	00832
51	868,940	7,916	00911
52	861,024	8,576	00996
53	852,449	9,283	01089
54	843,165	10,034	01190
55	833,132	10,831	01300
56	822,301	11,685	01421
57	810,616	12,597	01554
58	798,019	13,566	01700
59	784,453	14,583	01859
60	769,970	15,659	02034
61	754,211	16,774	02224
62	737,437	17,927	02431
63	719,510	19,117	02657
64	700,393	20,339	02904
65	680,053	21,592	03175
66	658,461	22,875	03474
67	635,587	24,178	03804
68	611,409	25,484	04168
69	585,925	26,724	04561
70	559,201	27,843	04979
71	531,359	28,773	05415
72	502,586	29,477	05865
73	473,109	29,929	06326
74	443,180	30,189	06812
75	412,991	30,301	06812
76	382,690	30,301	07918
77	352,388	30,200	08570
78	322,188	28,983	09306
79	292,206	29,568	10119
80	262,637	28,885	10998
81	233,752	27,898	11935
82	205,854	26,590	12917
83	179,264	24,986	13938
84	154,278	23,143	15001
85	131,135	21,131	16114
86	110,004	19,011	17282
87	90,993	16,846	18513
88	74,147	14,700	19825
89	59,448	12,630	21246
90	46,817	10,681	22814
91	36,137	8,881	24577
92	27,255	7,248	26593
93	20,007	5,788	28930
94	14,219	4,503	31666
95	9,717	3,413	35124
96	6,304	2,525	40056
97	3,779	1,846	48842
98	1,933	1,292	66815
99	642	642	1.00000

* Source: Actuarial Society of America; *Transactions*, 1964

tion. A mortgage may be "closed," which means that its amount may not be altered during its life; or open, which means that the amount borrowed has not reached the sum authorized by the indenture. A mortgage may be a "blanket" or "general" mortgage, covering all the fixed and movable property of an enterprise; a "chattel" mortgage, covering specific movable property only; or a "development" mortgage, where funds are raised for the construction or development of property which becomes or remains the underlying security. It may be a "consolidated" or "unified" mortgage, meaning that it takes the place of several previously existing mortgages. Mortgage obligations may become due and payable on a specified date, in definite installments, or by amortization. They are placed on the balance sheet among the long-term liabilities, except that any amount due within the next succeeding year, as well as any accrued interest, is often classified among current liabilities.

See *bond.*

mortgage bond One of an issue of bonds secured by a mortgage against specific properties of the issuer.

mortgagee One to whom a mortgage is given as security for funds loaned by him.

mortgagor One who gives a mortgage as security for funds borrowed.

moving average One of a succession of simple averages of groups made up of a fixed number of terms within a series, each group, except the first, being equal to the next preceding group less the first term of that group plus the next following term.

Example 1: The output in tons of a certain plant during the working days of one week were 590, 625, 580, 640, 630, and 450; the following week's output was 550, 601, 592, 584, 630, and 507. The simple average of the first week's production, Monday through Saturday, was 586. The average from Tuesday through the following Monday was 579, a figure obtained from the simple average of the six items involved or from adjusting the previous average by the increased or decreased production of the second Monday as compared with the Monday of the previous week. The latter method is often employed; thus $586 - (590 - 550)/6 = 579$, the moving average for Monday. On Tuesday the moving average declines to 575 $[579 - (625 - 601)/6]$.

Example 2: The following summary of transactions, see table (1) at the top of the next page, is abstracted from a perpetual-inventory card and illustrates the derivation and application of moving-average prices to the valuation of stores issues and balance on hand.

Here the moving unit-price averages are 1.22, 1.17, 1.13, and 1.09, obtained after each purchase by dividing the quantity then on hand into the money balance of the account. The balance shown compares with lifo and fifo valuations as shown in table (2) on page 287.

In this instance, the moving average falls between fifo and lifo versions of cost, as it generally does; lifo cost here is the highest of the three because purchase costs declined during the month.

In the case of banks, for Federal income-tax purposes, a 20-year moving average ratio is applied to year-end loans outstanding to determine or test the reasonableness of bad-debt provisions.

moving budget = *continuous budget.*

moving projection The forward view revealed by a *continuous budget;* the phrase suggests a budgeting procedure frequently modified (e.g., monthly), always looking ahead the same number of weeks, months, or other periods, without regard to fiscal years.

multiphase sampling (statistics) A sample design or set of sampling procedures wherein certain items of information are collected for all the units of a sample and other items of information on only some of these units, the latter so selected as to constitute a subsample of the units

(1)

Date	Quantities Detail	Quantities On Hand	Prices Detail	Prices Average	Amounts Detail	Amounts Balance
Inventory Jan. 1		534		1.22		651.48
Jan. 3–10	−203	331	1.22		−247.66	403.82
Jan. 11	+488	819	1.14	1.17	+556.32	960.14
Jan. 11–21	−531	288	1.17		−621.27	338.87
Jan. 22	+360	648	1.10	1.13	+396.00	734.87
Jan. 23–30	−215	433	1.13		−242.95	491.92
Jan. 31	+422	855	1.05	1.09	+443.10	935.02

(2)

Purchase Date	Quantity	Fifo price	Amount	Quantity	Lifo Price	Amount
Prior to January	—	—	—	288	1.22	341.36
Jan. 11	73	1.14	83.22	—	—	—
Jan. 22	360	1.10	396.00	145	1.10	159.50
Jan. 30	422	1.05	443.10	422	1.05	443.10
Totals	855	1.08	922.32	855	1.10	943.96

of the original sample; in this case, the sampling would be of two-phase character. This species of design is often adopted on grounds of convenience or economy. Information collected at a second or subsampling phase may be collected at a later time, and in this case information obtained on all the units of the first-phase sample may be utilized, where advantageous, in the selection of the second-phase sample. This type of design may be amplified to permit the addition of further phases.

multiple-product pricing A method of determining the prices of a seller of two or more products. Producers and distributors of multiple products are the general rule; rare is the single-product firm. The problem of establishing a price for each of several products is a complex one involving the computation of direct costs and the allocation of overhead or of fixed-cost burden. In price-competitive industries, multiple-product pricing is employed to ascertain the range of prices for each product within which the firm may profitably react to meet competitors' prices or initiate a price reduction. In non-price-competitive industries, the method will suggest the most profitable product based on a rational distribution of costs and permit the concentration of effort on the most profitable items. The extent to which prices can be freely adjusted depends upon the physical limitations imposed by byproduct characteristics of the production and the elasticity of demand for each product.

multiple sampling See *acceptance sampling.*

multistage sampling (statistics) A sample design or set of sampling procedures wherein the material to be sampled is regarded as being made up of a number of first-stage units, each composed of second-stage units, and so on, the units at the several stages being selected at preassigned and frequently differing sampling rates. See *sample; random sampling; unit of sampling.*

municipal corporation The form provided by law under which a county, city, town, village, school district, or other territorial division of a state transacts its business.

mutual corporation A form of corporation permitted under state laws, limited mostly to savings banks and insurance companies.

mutual fund A corporation that provides an investment service for its stockholders. Organized under state laws and subject to SEC as well as state regulation wherever its shares are sold, its operations are carried on through an affiliated management company whose officers are usually officers of the fund. Known also as an open-end company, its shares are continuously marketed by the management company, through salesmen or through securities dealers, at prices based on the current market value of the fund's portfolio plus fees often ranging from 0 to 10 percent or more. Capital gains are generally distributed annually, and net income from dividends and interest, quarterly; either type may be paid out in cash or be reinvested. Redemptions may be made at any time.

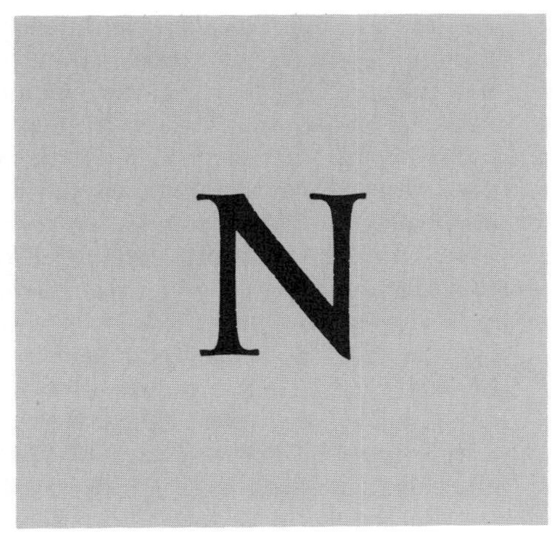

narrative form = *report form.*

national income (social accounting) 1. The estimate, on an annual basis, of a nation's purchasing performance with respect to consumer and capital goods; it consists of *personal income* (*2*), and corporate *net income* before income taxes. Increased by indirect business taxes, business pensions and contributions to pension funds, and the excess of the net income of governmental business enterprises over governmental subsidies paid to business, national income is converted into *net national product.* See *social accounting.*

2. = *gross national product.*

natural business year A *fiscal year* ending with the annual low point of business activity or at the conclusion of a season.

natural grouping = *object classification.*

natural person An individual human being. See *person.*

natural tolerance (statistical quality control) A term used in connection with a *control chart* for *variables* to describe process capability. When the charts for averages and ranges (or *standard deviations*) exhibit a state of *statistical control,* an estimate of the standard deviation σ' in the process is available from $\sigma' = R/d_2$ (see *control chart*). Then, assuming the variation in the process to follow the *normal curve* variation model, natural tolerance is estimated to be $6\sigma'$. If the value of $6\sigma'$ is greater than *total tolerance,* some predictable proportion of product from the process will fail to conform to specification requirements no matter where the process is centered. If the value of $6\sigma'$ is equal to or less than total tolerance, and the process is properly centered, all or a negligible proportion of product can be expected to conform to specification requirements.

necessary condition A property of a proposition so related to another that the latter cannot be true unless the first is also true. Compare with *sufficient condition.*

necessity certificate = *certificate of necessity.*

negative asset A *liability(1);* also, a credit *valuation account.*

negative assurance A communication from a public accountant to an investment dealer stating that during his examination of the issuer's records or in a stated period immediately following, nothing was disclosed of an adverse character relating to certain named schedules (e.g., supplementing audited financial statements) or relating to the events of the period succeeding the date of his audit report. See CAP 35 (1965).

negative confirmation See *confirmation.*

negative goodwill = *surplus from consolidation.*

negligence Failure to exercise due care.

Ordinary negligence arises from errors of judgment attributable, for example, to a lack of seasoned experience, and from oversights and mistakes that might be committed by anyone, but never from willful deceit.

Gross negligence adds the element of recklessness and an extreme disregard of common standards—for example, of auditing and reporting. The deliberate concealment or intentional misrepresentation of a material fact, event, or condition constitutes *fraud* (*q.v.*).

negotiable Transferable by endorsement and delivery or by delivery in the ordinary course of business, a holder in due course being free of the equitable defenses available to prior parties.

net *adj.* Diminished by all relevant and commonly associated deductions. Examples: net sales (sales less returns and allowances, discounts, sometimes provisions for bad debts); net income (revenue less expenses recognized during the period covered by the revenue); net assets or *net worth* (assets less liabilities to outsiders); net *current assets* (current assets less current liabilities—i.e., *working capital*); net *fixed assets* (fixed assets at cost less accumulated depreciation); net salvage (selling price or value as scrap less costs of selling and removal); net price (a price from which all discounts have been deducted).

v.t. To subtract a related smaller amount from a larger; as, to net current liabilities against current assets.

net assets The excess of the book value of the assets of an accounting unit over its liabilities to outsiders; = *net worth.*

net avails The net proceeds of a discounted note.

netback price See *administered price.*

net bonded debt (municipal accounting) *Gross bonded debt* less debt self-supporting as to principal and interest requirements, and less the amount of sinking funds available for the payment of other than self-supporting debt.

net book value The difference between the gross amount of an asset or asset group as shown in the books of account and any reserve or other applicable offset, such as *accumulated depreciation.* See *book value.*

net current assets = *working capital.*

net cycle time *In-cycle time* plus *out-cycle time.*

net earnings See *earnings.*

net income Revenues less operating costs: the balance remaining to the stockholders of a business enterprise after deducting from the gross revenue for a given period all operating expense and income deductions during the same period. See *revenue; income; income deduction; income statement; cost absorption.*

There is some disagreement among accountants as to the items making up "net income," aside from the common desire to have it mark the termination of the income statement. The divergence arises from the attempt on the part of some to give to the income statement an "all-inclusive" concept, while others would have it cover only "current operating performance." The former was sponsored in AAA statements of principles, the latter by AICPA pronouncements; see *accounting principles.* The main points of difference lie in the treatment of the following items, most of which are *income deductions:* if "material" in amount and "nonrecurrent" in nature, and hence having a "distorting" effect, the "operating-performance" adherents would expunge them from the income statement (if not material or if recurrent, the "all-inclusive" concept would be agreed to by all):

1. Eliminations or reductions of accumulated provisions for valuation accounts created in previous periods by charges to expense;
2. Charges made directly to surplus reserves where the provisions creating the reserve have not been included in this year's or prior years' operating expenses;
3. Adjustments of the amount of past years' income taxes;
4. Provisions for pension plans applicable to services rendered in past years;
5. Other prior-year adjustments;
6. Gain or loss from sales of other than regular product;
7. Losses from risks not normally insured;
8. Writeoffs of intangibles;
9. Elimination of unamortized discount where a bond issue is retired or refunded; and
10. Foreign-exchange adjustments.

The principal reasons supporting the "operating-performance" statement, as advanced by its proponents, are these:

1. The income statement should reflect usual or typical business operations

under the conditions existing during the year, and hence items of the type appearing above should be excluded.

2. Business managements, aided by professional accountants, "are in a stronger position than outsiders to determine whether there are unusual and extraordinary items which, if included in the determination of net income, may give rise to misleading references with respect to current operating performance."

3. The "net income for the year should show as clearly as possible what happened in that year under that year's conditions, in order that sound comparisons can be made with prior years and with the performance of other companies."

Those who argue for the all-inclusive statement reason thus:

1. The viewpoint of accounting is primarily historical, and the accountant is bound to report all the gain-or-loss events of a period without discriminating between usual and unusual items.

2. An income statement is a report of events and of decisions by management that have led to an increase or decrease in corporate net worth. A partial report of such events and decisions, omitting unusual items, could readily lead to the presentation of grossly distorted results and would actually invite manipulation, since it is most unlikely that standards of materiality or what is "customary" can ever be put on a wholly objective basis. The public accountant, in particular, should not give recognition to standards that are likely at times to expose his profession to pressure from management.

3. The supposition that the management or the auditors of a business enterprise, or both working together, are in a "stronger position than outsiders" in deciding what items should be omitted from an income statement carries with it the assumption that the investor or other "outsider" reading the statement cannot be relied on to observe the unusual elements of operating results or to decide for himself what items to leave in or omit should he wish to determine what the "usual" operating results have been. Such an assumption, it is argued, is hardly fair to the intelligence of the investor; moreover, it suggests an esoteric quality in accounting, a high priesthood of determination at the management and audit level that the facts themselves as noted in individual cases fail to justify. The items sought to be excluded from the income statement are invariably uncomplex in structure and can be explained briefly and simply.

4. Whether any of the ten items enumerated above are sufficiently "material" or "unusual" to be omitted from an income statement is almost always a matter of debate that will be decided differently by persons of varied training and experience, whether they be corporate officers, professional accountants, investors, or the lay public. A decision of management to exclude an expense might not be in agreement with the interest of the public; and the question of what is the public interest is not one that can always be interpreted fairly by the auditor. Even if the auditor is an astute observer of current phases of the public interest, it would be unfortunate if he were burdened with the necessity of determining what is the *best*, safest, or even the least misleading information to give the public, as well as investors, whether of the present or the immediate future. He would be in a much safer and much more defensible area of responsibility if he reported all the facts, events, and decisions in "one package" and left the interpretation of the income statement to its readers.

5. Certain items among the ten listed that might be deemed "unusual" for the current year may turn out to be not so unusual in succeeding years. Rarely is the accountant able to determine what the future conditions surrounding the business will be; he may be putting himself in a defenseless position for the future by assenting now to call any item unusual or nonrecurring, regardless of its character.

6. Material and, at the same time,

unusual and nonrecurring items, habitually included in "regular-product" sales and operating costs, may often point to future changes of more importance to future operating performance than any or all of the ten items proposed for omission from the statement; examples may be found in shifting sales and costs of sales of individual products; discontinued product lines; drops in product prices; changes in wage rates; and compensation of executives. Yet proponents of the operating-performance statement have not suggested that such items be disclosed.

7. By omitting items of gain or loss from the income statement, the accountant fails to produce a series of statements which together over a period of years present the real operating results of the business; he succeeds only in presenting a statement that will be interpreted as displaying "earning power": an untenable assumption, since the net income the accountant shows no longer exists at the end of the year if concurrent material expenditures or losses suffered during the year have been excluded. Again, what has been "earned" during the past year does not establish a criterion of earnings that will hold for the future.

8. Comparisons of one year with another can be made more readily by means of all-inclusive statements than by employing statements from which certain items have been omitted each year. The latter statements will always be suspect, especially in future years, where different standards for the character of excludable items have been followed.

9. Giving a full account of all gains and losses in a single statement is the only objective basis of reporting annual operating results. The ten items of exceptions can be segregated in the all-inclusive statement in a final section following operating income, thus giving the reader his choice of the items, if any, that he wishes to exclude from "net results."

net loss The reverse of net income or profit, determined in a similar manner: the excess of the sum of expenses and losses over revenues and income.

net national product (social accounting) *National income* plus indirect taxes paid by business, pensions and contributions to pension funds by business, and the excess of net income from governmental enterprises over governmental subsidies. See *social accounting. Gross national product* is net national product plus business and institutional depreciation or other currently measured capital-asset consumption.

net operating profit = *operating income.*

net proceeds *Proceeds* from the sale or other disposition of property or the marketing of an issue of securities, less costs directly connected therewith.

net profit 1. *Profit* remaining from revenue after deducting related costs. Although it usually designates the final figure on an income statement (= *net income*), some tendency has been noted to confine its application to (a) the excess of *revenues* over *operating costs:* an amount identical with "net income before income deductions"; or (b) the excess of revenues over both operating costs and income deductions, excluding from the latter "distributions" such as income taxes, bonuses to officers, and other items based or otherwise dependent on the existence of such excess. Ordinarily, however, net profit is synonymous with net income, and, unless clearly indicated to be otherwise, the computation of a bonus, for example, designated as a percentage of "net profit," is based on the net-profit amount after deducting the bonus and even an income tax in the computation of which the bonus figures as an allowable expense.

2. *pl.* The profits over a specified period of a corporation or other business after deducting *operating costs* and *income deductions;* = *net income.*

net profit on sales The balance remaining after deducting from gross profit on sales selling and other expense varying directly with sales; also known as *net trading profit.*

net purchases The cost of purchases plus freight-in, less returns and allowances and usually cash discounts taken.

net sales Gross sales less returns and allowances, freight-out, and often cash discounts allowed. In recent years the trend has been to report as net sales the net amount finally received from the customer.

net working capital = *working capital.*

net worth The aggregate appearing on the accounting records of the equities representing *proprietary interests;* the excess of the *going-concern* value of assets over liabilities to outsiders; in the case of a corporation, the total of paid-in capital, retained earnings, and appropriated surplus; in a sole proprietorship, the proprietor's account; in a partnership, the sum of the partners' accounts. A British equivalent sometimes employed is *total equity.*

nominal account 1. Any of the *accounts (1)* the balances of which are transferred to retained earnings at the close of each fiscal year: so called because such accounts reflect *completed transactions* or *expired costs;* a revenue or expense account: contrasts with *real account.*
2. Any account representing a subclassification of a *real account;* e.g., revenue and expense accounts subsidiary to a retained-earnings account; an account containing disbursements only, subsidiary to a cash account. See *split ledger account;* illustration accompanying *cash-flow statement.*

nominal capital The amount of capital represented by the *par* or *stated value* of a corporation's issued stock. See *capital stock.*

nominal element The portion of an asset or liability account reflecting expired cost or realized income, transferable to profit and loss.

nominal wage 1. =*money wage.*
2. A token wage.

nomograph A graphic representation, in a *coordinate system,* of an equation of *variables* so ranged, scaled, and positioned that, given the values of *independent variables,* a *dependent variable* can be determined with a straightedge. In its simpler forms, a nomograph is essentially an additive device. In the first diagram above, a line joining any point on scale *A* with any point on scale *B* will intersect their total in scale *C*. In the second diagram, scale *C*, placed at one-fourth of the distance between scales *A* and *B*, yields a weighted average of any point on *A* (here assigned a weight of $\frac{3}{4}$) and any point on *B* (with a weight of $\frac{1}{4}$).

(1)

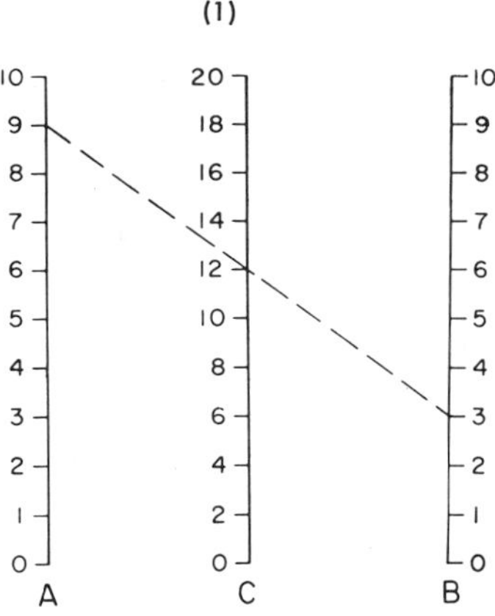

(2)

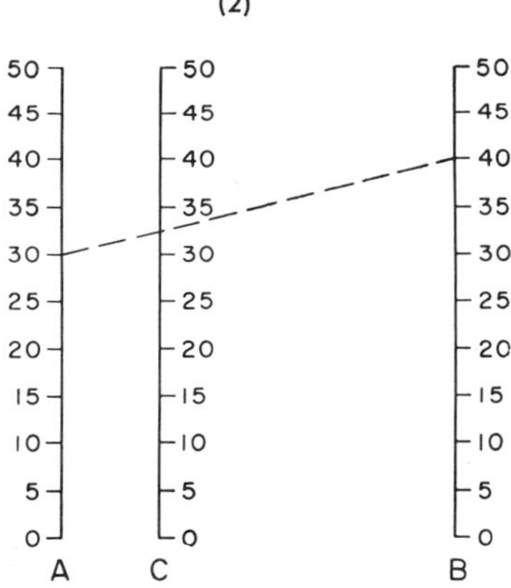

By employing logarithmic scales, a product (*C*) may be obtained from a multiplicand (*A*) and a multiplier (*B*), as in diagram (3), page 294. where area in acres may be obtained from lot dimensions in feet; here the values sought lie on a line

(3)

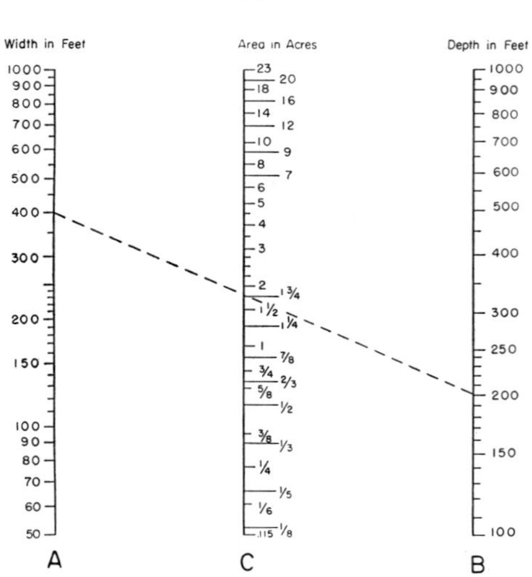

approximately .435 (= 1 ÷ [1.301] + 1) of the distance between lines *A* and *B*. Thus, a plot of land 400 × 200 feet contains approximately $1\frac{3}{4}$ acres.

A more involved nomograph (adapted from Kulmann, *Nomographic Charts*, New York: McGraw-Hill Book Company) is shown in diagram (4), below. From this diagram, an approximation of the compound amount of 1 (*C*) at any of the indicated rates of compound interest (*B*) may be obtained for any of 100 periods (*A*); this amount may then be restated (*E*) in terms of an original investment (*D*). From this nomograph it is also possible to obtain (a) the investment required to accumulate to a given amount at a given rate of interest, or (b) the rate of compound interest required to raise one sum to another over a given period of years. Example: Three thousand dollars is invested at 6%, compounded semiannually; what will be the accumulated amount 10 years hence? Since there are 20 periods of compounding at 3 % per period, the straightedge is placed on the "20" point of the "periods" scale and on the "3" point of the interest-rate scale;

(4)

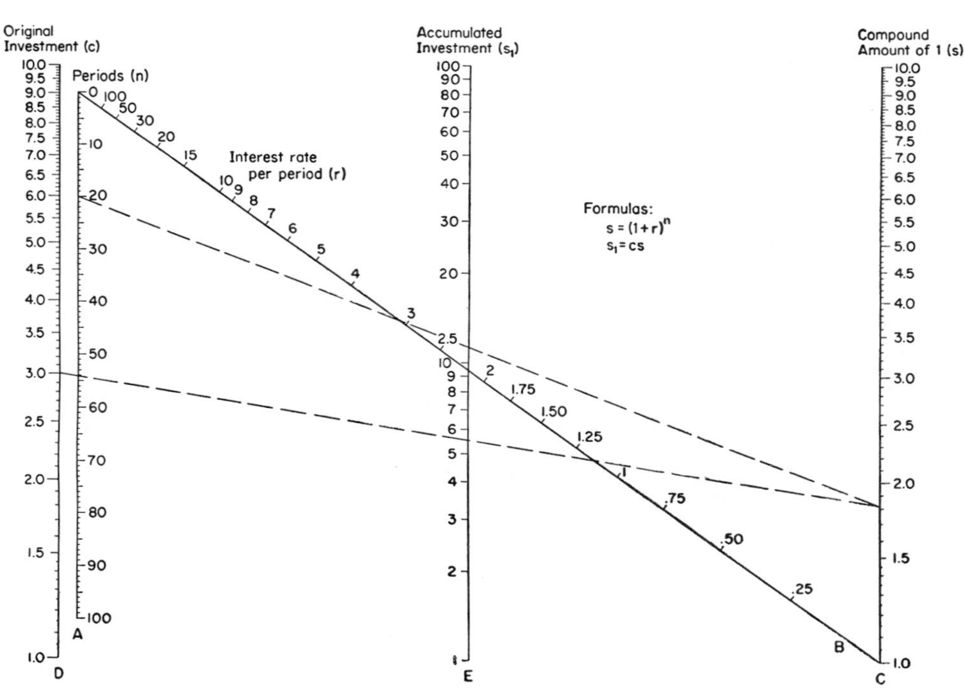

this gives a reading of approximately 1.81 on the "amount of 1" scale, which is what one dollar of the investment will be worth at the end of the 10-year period. With this point as a pivot, the straightedge is moved down to the "3" mark on the "original investment" scale, and a reading of roughly 5.4 ($5,400) is obtained on the "accumulated investment" scale. An interest table will show $5,418. Many nomographs serve the purpose, as here, of providing approximations that may be accurate enough for indicating the effect produced by a selection from a series of alternatives.

nonadmitted asset (insurance accounting) = *inadmitted asset.*

nonassessable capital stock Fully paid capital stock not subject to double or other liability of stockholders: the type of stock ordinarily issued by American corporations.

noncontrollable cost Cost assigned to an *organizational unit* but incurred and controlled from without.

noncumulative dividend A dividend on preferred stock, which, if passed, does not have to be made up at a later date; in some states, the courts have held that such a dividend is in effect cumulative, if earned (e.g., *Day* v. *Cast Iron Pipe Co.*, 96 N. J. Eq. 736).

nonexpendable fund (institutional accounting) A fund the principal of which must be kept intact; examples: a loan fund, only the income from which is available for loans; an endowment fund; a fund which is subject to an annuity agreement.

nonfeasance Failure to perform a required duty; compare *misfeasance.*

nonledger assets Assets or increments therein that by custom, as in financial enterprises, are not carried on the books of account; as, accruing revenues not yet due; asset appreciation; existing property written off; the amount by which property has been written down below unexpired cost.

nonoperating *adj.* Resulting from a minor, incidental activity: said of revenue or expense.

nonoperating company 1. A corporation whose properties, if any, are idle, and whose activities result in wholly incidental (or no) profits or losses.
2. A corporation, its properties leased to and operated by others, which merely distributes its net revenues to its shareholders.

nonoperating expense = *income deductions.*

nonoperating revenue The revenue of an enterprise derived from sources other than its regular activities; = *other revenue.*

nonprice competition Competition between rival sellers who charge identical or comparable prices, often mutually agreed to, and who appeal to consumers by claiming superiority in such merits as quality and service. In recent years, competition of this character between business concerns has been growing, and business standards are often evolved to discourage unilateral price action by an individual seller. Price changes now tend to be made on the basis of industry-wide action in recognition of modified economic conditions, such as increased wage rates or raw-material costs, the impact of new demand created by government procurement, and other "market conditions" not always specified. In industries where price competition does exist, the same practices identified in nonprice competition may also be present.

nonproductive labor A term formerly used for *indirect labor.*

nonprofit corporation An incorporated charity, or any corporation operated under a policy by which no stockholder or trustee shares in the profits or losses, if any, of the enterprise.

nonrecurring charge Any expense or involuntary *loss(2)* regarded by management to be of a type not likely to be encountered again; on an income statement it may be classified, if material, as an *income deduction.*

nonrevenue receipts (governmental accounting) Collections, other than revenue, during a given period; applied to receipts from loans and recoverable expenditures.

nonstandard material Raw material or a subassembly of a standard above or below that appearing in a standard engineering specification.

nonstandard method See *standard method.*

nonstock corporation A corporation having no issued shares; examples: a mutual savings bank; a savings-and-loan association; a religious or charitable association; a credit union.

no-par-value capital stock Capital stock having no specified par or nominal value, but to which there may attach, under articles of incorporation or by virtue of determinations by stockholders or directors, a specified amount as *legal* or *stated value*. No-par-value preferred stock usually has a definite liquidation value which must be deducted from total paid-in capital to determine the book value of no-par-value common stock.

norm An authoritative *standard;* a *rule.*

normal curve (statistics) A curve, also referred to as a *normal function, normal curve of error*, or Gaussian curve, used in statistical analysis to describe the behavior of magnitudes subject only to chance or random forces.

The curve is defined, in so-called standardized form, by

$$y = \frac{e^{-\frac{1}{2}\left(\frac{x}{\sigma}\right)^2}}{\sigma\sqrt{2\pi}}$$

where e (2.718+) is the base of the natural-*logarithm* system, $x = X - \mu$—that is, the deviation of any value X from the arithmetic mean μ—and σ is the *standard deviation*. The curve is symmetric about the mean μ and has a bell-like shape, with y reaching its maximum value at μ and falling off toward zero rapidly on either side. The curve is, however, of unlimited range, so that y never actually reaches zero. There are only two points of inflection, or bend points, where the slope, or shape, of the curve changes sharply; these points gives the curve its bell-like shape, and are located at $\pm\sigma$. The quartiles are located at 0.67+ units from $\mu = 0$, which forms the basis of the usual probable-error formula 0.67σ, the range of error in which 50 percent of the cases may be found, if the normal curve applies.

The curve has many uses, the most important of which comes from calculating exact probabilities for the occurrence of events which are subject only to chance causes. Whether the normal curve can be used depends on such factors as the number of occurrences examined, size of sample, etc. Other curves may have to be used, but it is a remarkable property of the normal curve that many other curves themselves tend to become normal under general conditions. Even where *universe variables* are not distributed in the form of a normal curve, the arithmetic means of samples become distributed approximately in the form of a normal curve. Hence, the standard *normal table* can be used to derive *probability* estimates for such sample values, or to design samples for desired levels of *precision* and *reliability*.

normal distribution = *normal curve.*

normal hours *Standard machine* and *labor time* for a specified operation.

normal price The value of a commodity resulting from the interaction of economic forces over a period of time, as distinguished from those prevailing at a moment of time (i.e., *market price*). A short-run normal price is the dollar amount for which a commodity would sell in the market if only short-run adjustments were effective. Although there may be numerous short-run periods which, as they increase in length, permit a more extensive adjustment to new conditions, the basic distinction which divides the short-run from the long-run is that (a) the former does not allow sufficient time for the adaptation of plant or other individual large-scale assets, and (b) it does not allow for changes in the productivity of the industry as a whole. A long-run normal price is the amount of money for which a commodity would sell in the market if (a) no new disturbances occurred during the market- (or short-run-) price periods, and (b) sufficient time were allowed for all adjustments, including alteration of plant and expansion or contraction of the industry. A secular price is a long-run price the determinants of which run over a still greater length of time and, in the words of Alfred Marshall, are "caused by the gradual growth of knowledge, of population, and of capital, and the changing condition of demand and supply from one generation to another." Because of the imponderables involved, secular prices have received but little formal attention in economics, although they have been the subject of institutional and empirical studies.

normal return Income on investment at a standard interest rate. The choice of interest rate in computing normal return is usually arbitrary. Often an average rate of return, or an average return from "like investments," is used, but both of these averages may include compensation for risk as well as return for productivity of capital. The rate of interest on government bonds is sometimes used as a measure free from elements of risk. Standard rates, such as 6 percent, may also be used as a company policy in determining the feasibility of new undertakings.

normal standard cost A standard cost based on the average cost of a number of past periods and on expected future changes in prices, efficiency, or volume. See *standard cost*.

normal table (statistics) A tabular presentation of selected values calculated from the *normal curve*. An example follows.

Normal Table of Areas Under the Normal Curve

x/σ	P
0	0.50
1	0.16
1.64	0.05
1.96	0.025
2.33	0.01
3.09	0.001

The normal table is calculated in terms of standard units $x/\sigma = (X - \mu)/\sigma$ (where X represents an individual variable, μ the *universe* mean, and σ the universe *standard deviation*) and shows the proportion of cases which will fall beyond certain limits. Also, taking advantage of the symmetry of the curve, only one-half of the values are reproduced; the other half, or the probability (proportion of cases) falling beyond this limit on either side of the mean, may be found by multiplying the decimal appearing in the body of the table by 2. Thus, values of X in an amount exceeding 1σ more than the universe mean ($X - \mu = 1\sigma$, or $X = \mu + 1\sigma$) will occur only 16+ % of the times in the positive direction—read opposite the value 1 in the first column; similarly, such a deviation will occur only 16+ % of the times in a negative direction as a result of *random* factors alone. Deviations of such magnitude in either direction will thus occur only 33 times in 100, or 0.33. Alternatively, about two-thirds of the time, the deviations in either direction will be smaller than 1σ.

Under *coefficient of variation*, a problem in determining sample size is illustrated in which it is desired to secure the specified *precision* with a reliability of 0.95. That is, only 0.05 proportion of the times is the designer willing to fail in securing the desired precision. Since both positive and negative deviations are equally of interest, the two 0.025 tails of the distribution are relevant—i.e., only 0.025 proportion of the times is he willing to fail in the positive direction and 0.025 proportion of the times in a negative direction. This value, 0.025, is, therefore, located in the body of the table, and opposite it is read the value 1.96. Thus, $\pm$ deviations from μ as high as (or higher than) 1.96σ will occur in only 5% of the cases (see *replication*). If deviations in only a single direction were of interest, the appropriate value, 1.64, would be read opposite the probability $P = 0.05$.

The abbreviated table contains most of the values which are of interest in applied work. The left-hand column contains selected possible deviations of X from μ in standard units (x/σ); the right-hand column, or body of the table, states the probability of occurrence (in decimal proportions) of deviations this large or larger. Only one-half the distribution is included in the table; the maximum probability is thus 0.5—the probability of getting a deviation of zero or greater. To obtain the probability of deviations in both directions, the fraction appearing in the body of the table should be multiplied by 2. It should be noted that a deviation as high as 3σ will almost never occur; for this as well as other reasons, such as convenience, tradition, and caution, this level is used extensively in applied work such as *statistical quality control.*

normal tax In Federal income taxation, the initial tax of 30 percent on corporate incomes for the tax years beginning before July 1, 1962; and 25 percent for tax years beginning after June 30, 1962. See *income tax; surtax; excess-profits tax.*

normal value The price that economic forces tend to establish and toward which many market prices gravitate.

note A *promissory note.*

note payable 1. A term applied to a promissory note with reference to its maker.
2. *pl.* The name of a ledger account or balance-sheet item showing separately or in one amount the liabilities to banks, trade, and other creditors evidenced by promissory notes.

note receivable 1. A promissory note in the possession of the payee or a holder in due course.
2. *pl.* The name of a ledger account or balance-sheet item showing the amounts owing on promissory notes from customers and other debtors.

note receivable discounted A note receivable not due which has been sold or transferred by endorsement, or otherwise, to a bank or other third party, at face or maturity value, sometimes less a discount representing interest for the unexpired term. The amount of notes receivable discounted is a contingent liability of the endorser and a contingent asset to the one who sells the note with recourse; on a balance sheet, it appears as a reduction of notes receivable, being shown parenthetically or in short, or in a footnote; if there is likelihood of nonpayment by the maker at maturity, it is classed as a current liability.

note register A book in which notes receivable or notes payable are recorded chronologically as received or issued; the details may include date drawn and date due, number, maker, endorser if any, reason for acquiring or giving, amount, and dates and amounts of interest collected or paid.

notional Imaginary or unreal: said, for example, of the value of a service not yet rendered, or a liability not yet incurred, but in either case merely in prospect, and hence not to be recorded in the accounts. A long-term lease has been cited as an example of a notional liability.

nuisance value The premium in excess of fair value that must be paid for a claim, an asset, or an equity in a business or other organization because its existing ownership is damaging to the prospective buyer or to the interest of equity holders, or because of the cost of instituting an alternative legal action.

number One or a series of digits expressing quantity; thus, 0; 1; -4; $486\frac{7}{11}$; $\sqrt{-1}$. See *digit; integer; rational number; irrational number; imaginary number.*

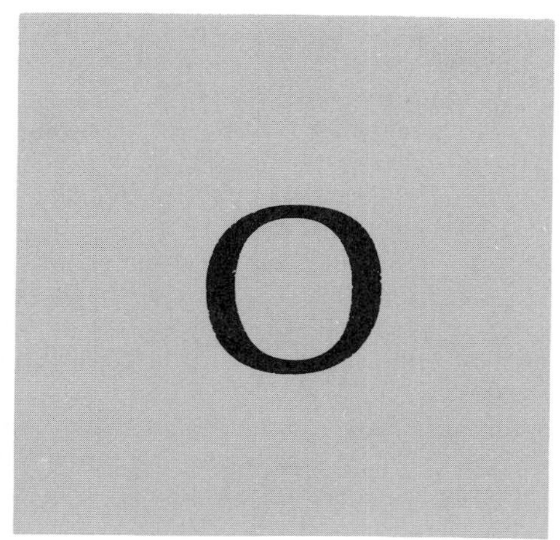

object The initial designation of an expenditure such as raw material which, after its initial classification as raw-material inventory, may, with other costs, be transferred in successive stages to work in process, finished goods, and cost of sales, often, but not necessarily, losing its identity in such transfers. See *cost flow*.

object cost Cost of a good or service in terms of *object*, or what is received in an exchange. Examples: personal service; raw material; equipment. In a subsequent transfer an object cost may lose its identity when merged with other costs; e.g., *raw material* transferred to *work in process*. Costs appearing in *primary accounts* are object costs. See *materials and services; objective statement; cost flow.*

objective *adj.* 1. Having a meaning or application apart from the individual, or the peculiarities of his experience or of the environment; and substantiated or capable of being substantiated by an independent investigator: said of a fact, judgment, or inference; as, objective evidence: often to be interpreted as possessing a doctrinaire, propagandistic, or *ad-hominem* tinge. By comparison, one fact may be said to be more objective than another because it is observable by more persons, experimentally repeatable, more promptly recorded after observation, recorded by more competent or more disinterested observers, more precisely determinable, more coherent or interrelated with other generally accepted facts, or observed under less confusing circumstances.

2. Pertaining to a classification of transactions or accounts by *object;* see *object classification.*

n. A target or goal.

objective statement A statement of expenses in terms of the original objects of expenditure; contrasts with a *functional statement,* in which expenses have been reclassified in accordance with their contribution to the ultimate product or final operating function. Most income statements reflect a mixture of the two; in recent years there has been some trend in reports to stockholders to put the income statement on an objective basis.

objective value Value established by competent independent appraisal, or by market quotation for a similar quantity, quality, condition, utility, and place.

obligated balance (governmental accounting) 1. *Obligations outstanding:* that portion of an appropriation unexpended but committed for expenditure.

2. *Obligations* and *liabilities outstanding:* that portion of an appropriation undisbursed but expended or committed for expenditure.

obligation 1. Any kind of indebtedness; a *liability.*

2. (governmental accounting) An *encumbrance* or *commitment,* but sometimes including, as under practices of the Federal Bureau of the Budget, *liabilities.* The "obligations basis" of accounting for the operating expense of a given period is understood to be the *accrual basis* adjusted by *obligations outstanding* at the beginning and end of the period.

obligations incurred (governmental accounting) The whole of the *obligations* entered into during a particular period, expressed as a total of the liabilities expected to arise therefrom. It is equal to the total of recorded expenditures for the period modified by the opening and closing balances of *obligations outstanding.*

obligations outstanding (governmental accounting) The amount of purchase orders or contracts on which goods or services have not yet been received, but sometimes including current and other liabilities. See *obligation(2)*.

observed depreciation 1. Accrued depreciation determined not by annual provisions based on expectancy of service life, but by physical inspection or appraisal of operating condition, and ordinarily expressed as a percentage of original cost or replacement cost. The numerator of the fraction represented by the percentage is the quantity of services already given off by the referent asset; the denominator, the total quantity, past and future, of the expected service yield of the asset.
2. Estimated deterioration: an engineering or appraisal term bearing no necessary relation to the accountant's concept of depreciation and sometimes described as the outlay required to restore an asset or asset group to full operating efficiency.

observed life table = *life table.*

obsolesce To become or cause to become *obsolete.*

obsolescence The loss in usefulness of an asset, occasioned by the approach to the stage of economic uselessness through progress of the arts; economic inutility arising from external causes; disappearing usefulness resulting from invention, change of style, legislation, or other causes having no physical relation to the object affected. It is distinguished from exhaustion, wear and tear, and deterioration in that these terms refer to a functional loss arising out of a change in physical condition. Obsolescence may be classified as ordinary obsolescence, or loss due to normal progress or development of industry; and extraordinary obsolescence, or loss due to sudden, unforeseen causes, such as an unheralded new invention, unexpected style change, or unanticipated cessation of demand for an article produced. Ordinary obsolescence is customarily included as a factor in determining depreciation rates to allow for the gradual lessening of service life through factors other than physical wear and tear. See *depreciation.*

occupancy expense Expense relating to the use of property. Examples: rent, heat, light, depreciation, upkeep, and general care of premises occupied.

odd lot A smaller than customary unit of trade; in stock exchanges, a transaction of less than 100 shares, or, in the case of an inactive stock, less than ten shares; see *round lot.—odd-lot, adj.*

office equipment Major items of movable property used in furnishing an office. Examples: office furniture; movable partitions; typewriters; calculating and bookkeeping machines; filing cabinets; duplicating equipment.

officer Any principal executive of a corporation to whom authority has been delegated by the board of directors or the bylaws; often, any member of the top staff of an organization.

offset 1. An amount equaling or counterbalancing another amount on the opposite side of the same or another account or statement. See *absorption account.*
2. An amount having the effect of canceling or reducing a claim of any kind.

offset account An account acting as an *offset(1)*, in whole or in part, to another account; an *absorption account.*

offsetting error An error that eliminates or reduces the effect of another error; thus, a debit of $10.00 posted to an account as a debit of $1.00, and a credit of $65.48 posted to another account in the same ledger as a credit of $56.48: both postings are understated $9.00 and are exactly offsetting, and a trial balance would not reveal either error; but if the credit had been posted as $55.48, the resulting deficiency of $10.00 in credits would have been partially offset by the $9.00 deficiency in debits, causing the trial-balance credit total to be $1.00 larger than the trial-balance debit total. It is always necessary, therefore, to run down and correct a trial-balance difference, no matter how trivial it may appear to be, since an offsetting error may be involved.

ogive (statistics) A cumulative *frequency curve* or *chart*, generally *S*-shaped. When frequencies are accumulated by addition from lowest to highest values, a less-than ogive is obtained; when accumulated values are subtracted from the total *frequency*, a more-than ogive is obtained. A *mortality curve* or *retirement curve* is generally presented as a less-than ogive, while a survivor-life curve is generally drawn on a more-than basis. The *ordinate* of a mortality curve for a fixed-asset group shows the total number of units which have been or are expected to be retired over the entire range of years up to the corresponding *abscissa*. If the abscissa reads 3 years, and the ordinate yields a value of 20 percent, 20 percent of the assets will be (or have been) retired in three years or less. The ordinate of a survivor-life curve shows the number of units which have survived or are expected to survive at least this long. Abscissa and ordinate readings of 3 years and 20 percent for a survivor-life curve mean that 20 percent of the assets will survive (or have survived) three years or more.

oil-and-gas payment (petroleum industry) The interest, as of a driller, in the production of crude oil and gas from a particular well or tract of land; it is paid out of production allocable to the *working interest*.

oligopoly and oligopsony prices An oligopoly price is the price that prevails in a market of few sellers and many buyers, a price reflecting the power a few large sellers may exert over the market. An oligopsony price is the price that prevails in a market where buyers are few and sellers numerous, a price reflecting the power a few large buyers may exert over the market. Oligopoly prices tend to be greater (and oligopsony prices less) than prices that would prevail in perfectly competitive markets. Where a few sellers (oligopoly) confront a few buyers (oligopsony), price is determined by relative bargaining power. See *cartel*.

on account 1. On credit terms: said of a sale or purchase, delivery of which is followed by payment at a later dapt.

2. In part payment: a term applied to the settlement of a portion of a debt.

on consignment Consigned to another for the purpose of sale, display, or other use.

oncost = *indirect cost;* a British term.

on hand In possession, whether or not owned. In a balance-sheet presentation, however, the term connotes *owned*, unless explained or qualified by the item title or in a footnote. Thus, *inventory* on hand, without further description, means only items owned and in possession. The term does not include owned items in the custody of others, such as goods in warehouse or on consignment.

open *adj.* In a condition permitting additional entries or postings: said of books of account at the end of a reporting period.

open account 1. Any account not closed out.

2. An unsecured amount owing by a debtor or to a creditor arising through credit sales or purchases, payable in cash, subject to usual trade customs or to specified terms as to discount and payment period; an unsecured loan.

open credit An unsecured receivable or payable not evidenced by a note, subject to settlement in accordance with usual trade or other specified terms.

open-end company = *mutual fund.*

opening balance 1. The balance of an account at the beginning of a specified period, such as a month or a year.

2. *pl.* General-ledger accounts constituting the balance sheet at the end of one year carried into the next.

opening entry 1. An entry or one of several entries by means of which the assets, liabilities, and proprietary interests of a new enterprise are recorded on its books.

2. An entry or one of a series of entries beginning a new system of accounts for an enterprise already established.

3. An entry to reopen the asset and liability accounts at the beginning of an accounting period where they have been closed by journal entry at the end of the preceding period: a practice now largely obsolete.

open(-end) mortgage (or **bond**) A mortgage (or bond) the terms of which provide no limit on the amount that may be borrowed on the pledged security.

open the books 1. To record in a ledger, usually by means of one or more journal entries, the assets, liabilities, and proprietary accounts of an enterprise at its inception or reorganization, or when a new accounting system is installed.
2. To reopen the asset, liability, and proprietary accounts at the beginning of an accounting period, either by means of a journal entry or by carrying down the balances at the close of the immediately preceding period, after the accounts have been ruled off.

open to buy A term used in retailing, particularly department stores, to designate a stated amount of money or merchandise to which a buyer is limited in his purchases.

open-to-buy report A statement of existing or expected relations between inventory and sales, used to calculate open-to-buy amounts.

operating *adj.* Pertaining to any usual type of activity in which an organization engages. See *operation; operations.*

operating accounts *Revenue and expense accounts.*

operating budget A budget covering operating revenue and expense: contrasts with *capital budget.* See *budget.*

operating-characteristic curve (statistical quality control) A curve that portrays graphically the probability of acceptance as a function of submitted quality; generally referred to as an *OC* curve and most widely known in connection with *acceptance sampling.* Every sampling plan has a unique *OC* curve which thus makes clear what protection can be expected from the plan as lots of varying quality are submitted to it for judgment. Valid comparison between various sampling plans as to cost, amount of inspection required, etc., cannot be made unless the plans being compared have approximately "matching" (congruent) *OC* curves.

Although *OC* curves originated in the field of acceptance sampling, the concept is of general interest, being applicable to any statistical test based on the use of *random samples.* In fact, the discriminatory power of standard statistical tests cannot be fully understood or utilized efficiently until the associated *OC* curves have been constructed. Batteries of *OC* curves for these standard tests appear in statistical texts.

operating company A corporation actively engaged in business with outsiders.

operating cost (or **expense**) An expense incurred in conducting the ordinary major activities of an enterprise, usually excluding "nonoperating" expense or *income deductions.*

operating cycle The elapsed time between the purchase of inventory items (raw materials or merchandise) and their conversion into cash. The typical succession of transactions involved is (a) the purchase, offset by accounts payable; (b) the liquidation of the payables; (c) the manufacturing operation with its added costs, or the warehousing in the case of merchandise; (d) the sale of the finished product or merchandise; and (e) the liquidation of the amount receivable from the customer. A normal operating cycle—greater than one year, for example, in the business of an installment dealer—is generally regarded as one of the determinants of the character of items classified as *current assets.* It is also of importance in establishing working-capital requirements.

operating income (or **profit**) The excess of the revenues of a business enterprise over the expenses pertaining thereto, excluding income derived from sources other than its regular activities and before *income deductions.*

operating ledger A ledger containing only *nominal* accounts; i.e., transactions relating to operating revenues and expenses.

operating leverage See *leverage.*

operating performance The degree of skill and success attained in any activity the qualitative measure of which is a distinctive function of *internal auditing.* The scope of this function has been extended in recent years from verifications of transaction accuracy to testing applications and effects of management policies and other factors the operations of which are expected to conform to various standards of *efficiency.*

operating-performance income statement An income statement limited to items reflecting revenue and costs of normal operating factors. It differs from the *all-inclusive income statement* mostly in the exclusion from *income deductions* of material amounts of such items as nonrecurring prior-year adjustments, sales of assets not acquired for the purpose of resale, nonrecurrent losses against which insurance would not normally be carried, the elimination of an intangible, and the writeoff of the balance of discount (or premium) and expense following a retirement or refunding of a bond issue before maturity. See *income statement; income deductions; net income.*

operating ratio See *ratio.*

operating report An internal report revealing budgeted costs, standard costs, actual costs, and the like.

operating reserve 1. A reserve created by a charge or charges to operations and deducted on the balance sheet from its related asset; a *valuation account.*

2. = *equalization reserve.*

operating results 1. = *net income* or *net loss.*

2. = *operating income.*

operating revenue 1. Gross sales or gross revenue, less returns, allowances, and cash discounts, together with gross amounts received from any other regular income source.

2. Net revenue from sales of services.

operating statement An *income statement,* especially one showing considerable detail.

operation 1. Any planned action.

2. An act or a method of acting, conforming to rules.

3. The performance of any planned work; as, a step or limited series of steps in production or other activity associated with an individual, machine, department, or process.

operational 1. Pertaining to the property of an interpretation placed upon a set of postulates, theorems, or individual propositions, such that procedures or transactions are specified in correspondence with designated abstract constructs which appear in the propositions. In scientific work, auditing, and certain phases of accounting, such procedures generally refer to the assembly of evidence for the purpose of testing or validating a *hypothesis* or set of hypotheses (see *test*); in administration or business practice, to methods of planning, guiding, adjusting conduct, or internal control. A policy or program stated in such form that procedures cannot be, or are not, specified in a manner that will give effect to the propositions it implies is said to be nonoperational.

2. Pertaining to an *operation (3);* as, an operational cost.

3. Capable of execution; operable.

operational game The *simulation* of *operations* planning and *decision (1)* making within the limits provided by a representative *model.*

operational research A British term; = *operations research.*

operations 1. The activities of an enterprise exclusive of financial transactions and those of an extraordinary character; as, *production,* or the rendering of service, distribution, or administration.

2. Hence, the activities generally of an enterprise resulting in charges or credits to revenue or expense.

3. Revenue and expense accounts generally. Example: a charge (or credit) to operations.

operations research Any examination of the problems of an organization having as its aims the identification, definition, and interrelation of individual problems, the study of the underlying human and mechanical variants that delimit their solution, the selection of possible goals, the development of one or more practicable solutions, the staff training required to give effect to them, and management reports capable of leading to decision and action; more narrowly, the application of *management science* to the solution of particular problems. Operations research (OR) is ultimately concerned with the welfare of the organization as a whole; intermediate purposes include the best uses of men and machines, the stabilization of production, and the maximization of profit. Typical operations-research studies proceed by means of *models*, especially mathematical models, which are suited to the use of such tools as *linear programming;* the skills of engineers, psychologists, mathematicians, economists, and accountants are often combined in such examinations.

opinion *n.* (auditing) The written finding of an auditor, following an audit, as to the "fairness" of the representations of financial position and operating results reflected in financial statements, and as to the following of "generally accepted" accounting principles in the recording of the underlying transactions and in the preparation of the statements; and the consistency of these principles with those followed in the previous year. These are to be found in the "opinion" or second paragraph of the uniform short-form audit report, the purpose being to inform the reader of the report whether what he is looking at is subject to the usual interpretations given financial statements. See *judgment*.

A qualified opinion contains the auditor's exception to one or more specified items in the financial statements, and sometimes his reasons therefor. Where no reason for the exception is stated, the statement of opinion in the short-form audit report may commence with "Subject to . . . ," or "Except for." Qualified opinions cover such cases as

1. The presence of a large lawsuit which, if lost, would have a materially adverse effect on the scope of future operations as well as on financial position.

2. The indeterminate amount of income-tax liability attaching to the realization of profit from a transaction the character of which differs from those heretofore covered by the income-tax law and regulations.

3. A possible major loss, for which there has been no provision as yet, arising from performance, now in process, under a contract for services.

4. Failure to provide for depreciation at a rate comparable to that generally found in the industry.

5. Provision for depreciation at rates greatly in excess of normal rates, because of the belief that costs of new construction have exceeded average costs of similar assets over a preceding period of years.

6. Refusal of the client to separate the elements of paid-in surplus and retained earnings, both being contained in a single surplus account.

7. Inability to inspect or confirm a portion of the inventory because of its location in various parts of the world.

See *judgment*.

opportunity cost Prospective change in cost following the adoption of an alternative machine, process, raw material, specification, or operation; see *alternative cost*.

optimum output Production at a rate that results in the lowest marginal unit cost and average unit cost; see *marginal cost*.

option A legal right to buy or sell something at a specified price, usually within an agreed period of time. See *stock option*.

optional dividend A *dividend* authorized to be paid in more than one form, according to the election of the individual stockholder—e.g., in cash or capital stock.

ordinal number The designation of one of a particular order or series of units; as, first, second, third, etc.

ordinary annuity An annuity payable at the end of each period; contrasts with *annuity due;* = *annuity*.

ordinary depreciation The loss of utility of a fixed asset through normal wear and tear, aging, action of the elements, and the like. See *depreciation*.

ordinary interest Simple interest based on a year of 360 days, contrasting with *exact interest* having a base year of 365 days. The ratio of ordinary interest to exact interest is $1.013\dot{8}$, its reciprocal being $0.\dot{9}863013\dot{6}$.

ordinate The vertical or y axis in a two-dimensional Cartesian coordinate system. See *abscissa.*

organic act A law giving authority to a government agency to engage in specified activities, laying down the policies and general method to be followed in its operations, and authorizing subsequent appropriations to support it; distinguished from *appropriation act.*

organization 1. A developed process of administration.
2. Any existing association of people and functions.

organizational unit 1. Any administrative subdivision of an enterprise, especially one charged with carrying on one or more functions or activities; see *activity; activity accounting.*
2. (governmental accounting) The smallest administratively recognized subdivision of an agency.

organization cost (or **expense**) Any cost incurred in establishing a corporation or other form of organization; as, incorporation, legal and accounting fees, promotional costs incident to the sale of securities, security-qualification expense, and printing of stock certificates. These and similar costs constitute, theoretically, an intangible asset of value which continues throughout the life of the corporation and hence, strictly, do not constitute a deferred charge. However, because the total usually is not large, it has become customary arbitrarily to write off such costs either at once or over the first few years of corporate existence.

Under section 248 of the Internal Revenue Code, organization expenditures of a corporation (such as those for legal and similar services to obtain a charter, fees paid to the state, and expenses of temporary directors) may be amortized over a 60-month period; expenses of issuing stock or of corporate reorganization are regarded as capital expenditures.

original capital The amount of enterprise capital paid in at the time of incorporation or organization.

original cost 1. Outlay for an asset by its owner, not including any adjustments of cost arising from postacquisition alterations, improvements, or depreciation.
2. = *primary cost.*
3. (public-utility accounting) Cost of an operating unit or system to the person first devoting it to public use: said of assets coming under the surveillance of governmental utility-control bodies. *Net* original cost results from the deductions of acquired liabilities.

As used in public-utility accounting, the term dates from the early 1930's. In 1933 the public-service commissions of 21 states, led by New York, petitioned the Interstate Commerce Commission to prescribe the original-cost basis of plant accounting in the system of accounts for interstate telephone companies over which the ICC then had jurisdiction. Shortly thereafter, the Federal Communications Commission was given jurisdiction over such companies and prescribed the original-cost principle in a system of accounts made effective on January 1, 1936. The system was attacked in the courts by the American Telephone and Telegraph Company but was upheld by the Supreme Court (299 U. S. 232). The original-cost basis is prescribed in other utility-accounting systems, notably the electric (1936) and gas (1939) systems prescribed by the Federal Power Commission and numerous state commissions and the system for steam railroads prescribed by the ICC. Interstate-telephone, electric, and gas utilities have been required to state their utility plant in its entirety on an original-cost basis, whereas steam railroads have been required thus to record acquisitions commencing January 1, 1938. It is estimated that the original-cost principle is now in effect for more than 90 percent of the plant of telephone, carrier, and electric utilities.

Under the original-cost principle, detailed plant accounts are stated at cost to the person first devoting utility property to public service. As to plant which the present owner was the first to devote to public service, such as constructed facilities, original cost and cost are synonymous. The principle in reality relates to acquisitions of operating utility plant units or systems usually as going concerns. The original cost of such acquired plant is reflected in the detailed plant accounts, and the difference between cost to the acquiring utility owner and net original cost (i.e., original cost less accrued depreciation) is recorded in a special plant account known as *acquisition adjustment*. Amounts in the latter account may be either debits or credits. In this manner, both original cost and cost to the present owner are expressed on the records.

Amounts in an acquisition-adjustment account are subject to depreciation or writedowns as commissions may approve or direct. It is the practice of the numerous state commissions to require amortization of debit amounts over a period not in excess of 15 years. Amortization charges are generally required to be "below the line of return" by the state commissions; other state commissions have sanctioned charges to the operating section "above the line of return" of the income statement. There has been little experience with credit acquisition adjustments, but it appears that most of them have been transferred to the depreciation reserve.

original entry An entry, in proper form for *posting* to a *ledger*, recording a *transaction* in a *book of original entry*. It either includes full information concerning the transaction or refers to supporting vouchers or memorandum books, which contain data, previously recorded, upon which the entry is based.

origin period (statistics) The period of time within a time series selected as the base period. See *least-squares method*.

other assets A balance-sheet term for minor assets not classifiable under other usual headings; its amount is generally a small fraction (e.g., less than 5 percent) of total assets.

other deductions 1. A collection of minor costs in various types of operating statements shown as a single total in order to avoid unimportant detail.
2. = *income deductions*.

other liabilities A balance-sheet figure for minor liabilities not classifiable under other usual headings; its amount is generally a small fraction (e.g., less than 5 percent) of total liabilities.

other revenue (or **income**) Revenue from minor sources or from other than the regular activities of a business; nonoperating revenue; examples: interest on customers' notes, installment accounts, and overdue accounts; dividends and interest from minor investments; incidental profit from the disposal of assets other than inventory.

out-cycle work Work performed by an operator while a machine is at rest; contrasts with *in-cycle work*.

outgo 1. = *expenditure*.
2. A subtraction; a disbursement; often contrasted with *income(2)*.

outlay 1. The paying out of cash, the incurring of a liability to pay cash, or the issue of a corporate equity or the transfer of property, in exchange for goods or services received.
2. The purchase price of property or service, measured in terms of the cash or the book value of property given in exchange; *cost*.

outlay cost Cost represented by an expenditure of cash or transfer of property; generally, any recorded cost, contrasting with *imputed cost* and *opportunity cost*.

outlay expiration The reduction of outlay that would normally be recognized by the owner of an asset as the consequence of any related event or condition—e.g., lapse of time, wear and tear, outright destruction, or decline in demand—that diminishes likely future utility or recoverable price as applied to *fixed assets; depreciation*. See *loss; amortization*.

out-of-pocket expense (or **cost**) 1. An expense incurred by an individual, as on a business trip, paid for in cash, for which reimbursement may be sought; contrasts with *allowance(2)*.
2. Any cost, other than a *fixed* or *sunk cost* chargeable directly to any product, order, or operation; hence, a cost that may be saved; *direct cost;* a *variable cost.*

output The quantity, or cost of goods or services, produced in any *operation(3)*.

output cost See *cost of production.*

outsider A person not affiliated or otherwise related. A corporation's outsiders may or may not include stockholders, depending on the context.

outstanding 1. Uncollected or unpaid: said of an account or note receivable or payable, or of a check sent to the payee but not yet cleared against the drawee bank.
2. In the hands of others: said of the units of funded debt of a corporation or of the certificates representing issued shares of capital stock in the hands of the public; treasury stock is defined in terms of shares *issued* but not outstanding.

outstanding capital stock Issued capital stock, less treasury stock; capital stock in the hands of the public.

overabsorption The result produced where the credits in an absorption account exceed the total of the account—e.g., a factory-expense account to which it is related; because the corresponding debits may have become intermingled with other expense or inventory accounts, the amount of an overabsorption usually appears on an operating statement. See *variance.*

over-and-short The name of an account in which appear daily or other periodic and often unavoidable and minor differences between actual cash receipts and payments and the covering documents therefor. At the end of an accounting period it is customarily closed out as miscellaneous expense or income: a procedure usually judged as justifiable in the administration of, for example, *change funds.*

overdraft 1. The amount by which a check, draft, or other demand for payment exceeds the amount of the credit against which it is drawn.
2. = *bank overdraft.*

overhead A generic name for costs of materials and services not directly adding to or readily identifiable with the product or service constituting the main object of an operation. Other terms covering the same concept are burden, manufacturing and commercial expense, *indirect cost,* supplementary expense, and *oncost.* The distinctions sometimes drawn between these terms are not consistently observed.

In speaking of overhead, the unit of operation or production needs to be specified, for a cost chargeable directly to a department or work center (e.g., salary of the department supervisor), although a direct cost of the department, constitutes overhead which may be allocated to product units worked on in the department. Thus there may be product, departmental, and factory overheads. Accountants sometimes speak of "direct departmental overhead," an expression which refers to costs charged directly to the department that are indirect costs of products to which the services performed by the department are applied. The overhead concept often extends beyond the factory and on occasion may be identified with manufacturing, selling, or administrative costs.

The present-day importance of overhead cost reflects the employment of expensive equipment and elaborate organizations in which many employees do not work directly on the product sold to customers. Where handicraft methods of production prevail, the costs which can be traced directly to the product may be only material and labor.

Overhead costs were at one time viewed as the result of "nonproductive" factors, particularly when they arose from the presence of personnel not working on the product (supervisors, clerks, accountants, engineers, maintenance men, and so on). However, much of the progress made in reducing costs of goods and services can be attributed to the use of staff specialists who devise improved methods and organize the information that management uses to direct operations more economically. Similarly, lower product costs often result from the employment of more specialized machinery and less labor, although the proportion of overhead cost may at the same time be increased.

Ratios of overhead to portions of or all direct costs are seldom useful as measures of efficiency between companies or even between plants within a company, because differences exist in the amount and type of machinery relative to labor. Differences in organization and in the classification of costs also affect such comparisons.

Distinctions between overhead costs and direct costs rest upon the methods of measuring unit costs. Direct costs can be identified with units to be costed (i.e., with departments, activities, orders, products) at the time the cost is incurred. This is accomplished by measuring quantities of materials and hours of labor used for each costing unit. Source records are then coded to permit subsequent assembly of the costs for each costing unit. For example, direct-labor tickets may bear both department and job numbers.

Overhead costs cannot, as a practical matter, be traced directly to individual costing units, either because the process of making direct measurements is judged wasteful or because there is no acceptable method of direct measurement available. As an example of a too costly measurement, electric power used by each department in a factory can be measured, but this is not always done because management does not wish to incur the expense for meters and records. Examples of the lack of a method of distribution may be observed in any endeavor to determine how much of the cost incurred for plant protection, accounting, or the president's office applies to each unit of production.

Since overhead costs cannot be charged to individual costing units at the time the costs are incurred, they may be collected as totals and subsequently spread over the various units by allocation. In allocating overhead costs, the accountant proceeds by searching for some index of production that fluctuates with indirect costs and possesses the characteristic of being capable of direct measurement. For example, some indirect costs may vary with the hours of direct labor spent on the various orders. Hence direct labor hours can be and often are used as an index for distributing overhead costs to orders. Correlation between an item of overhead cost and the factor used to allocate it does not necessarily hold for short-period fluctuations in its amount. For example, building-occupancy cost may be causally related to the total amount of space provided, although changes in the latter occur infrequently. This method is similar in principle to methods widely used in other fields where exactness and accuracy are required, although it often falls somewhat short in the application.

The distinction between direct and overhead costs, most marked in job-order manufacturing, becomes comparatively unimportant in continuous-process manufacturing operations. In accounting for the latter, it is common to include all labor with overhead in costing production.

Accounting for overhead costs has three possible objectives:

1. To provide information useful to management in exercising control over such costs;

2. To determine product costs for inventory-cost purposes by allocating manufacturing-overhead costs to products; and

3. To provide information with respect to variation in overhead costs with changes in volume and other factors for use in profit planning, pricing, and similar problems.

With a carefully designed plan, all

three of these objectives can be attained.

Any classification of overhead costs begins with the determination of responsibilities for cost incurrence. For this purpose a responsibility constitutes an organizational unit such as a department having a single head accountable for costs incurred by the activities of the unit. The classification of overhead costs by responsibilities or departments fixes responsibility for control, and at the same time facilitates allocation of the costs to products.

Costs incurred by each responsibility are classified by nature of expenditure or object for which the expenditure was made. This subclassification indicates the costs for which the department head is held responsible. The classification by nature of expenditure is usually uniform throughout an individual company, in order that costs incurred in different departments may be combined whenever desired (for example, management may wish to know the total cost of supervision for all departments) and to facilitate interpretation of costs on departmental statements. Following is an illustration showing classification of overhead costs in the manner described:

Classification of Overhead Costs

Factory Departments	*Overhead Expense Accounts*
Heavy machine	Supervision
Turret lathe	Clerical
Small machine	Indirect labor
Heat treating	Supplementary labor costs
Forge & welding	Personnel
Paint shop	Factory supplies
General machine	Maintenance and repairs
Power	Insurance
Repair and maintenance	Taxes
Shipping	Depreciation
	Other factory expenses

Reports prepared to assist management in controlling overhead costs provide comparisons between actual costs of the most recent period and costs of a prior period or budgeted costs. When the costs in such reports are limited to those controllable by a single supervisor, it is relatively easy to determine how successful each department head has been in his efforts to minimize costs. By study of the details, it is possible to trace variances to individual items of cost.

Accumulation of overhead costs by departments facilitates costing of products by bringing together costs allocable on the same basis. However, for this purpose it may be desirable to subdivide a responsibility or department into cost centers or activities. Where different types of equipment or different operations exist, in a single department, individual cost-center rates may yield more accurate product costs. Multiplication of cost centers increases clerical expense, and hence a practical compromise between accuracy of costs and the amount spent to obtain them must be made.

Departments are divided into two classes: production and service (sometimes called direct and indirect). Service departments are those that provide benefits (e.g., power, maintenance, purchasing, accounting) to other departments but do not work directly on products for sale to customers. Costs of service departments are distributed to producing departments and thus become part of the producing department overhead applied to products.

Another basis used in the classification of overhead costs is variability of costs with volume of production. Separation of fixed and variable components of overhead and determination of rates at which variable elements of each cost should vary with volume assists in controlling overhead costs under conditions of rapidly fluctuating volume. This classification also has a wide field of usefulness for such purposes as profit planning and pricing. In some companies, fixed and variable costs of service departments are distributed to producing departments on different bases.

The classification of overhead costs by

variability with volume cuts across classifications by responsibility and nature of expenditure. For this reason, in each overhead account fixed and variable components must be separated. Some accountants incorporate this basis of classification into charts of accounts. Where this is done, there are two accounts for each class of costs containing both fixed and variable components. For example, indirect labor for a given department appears as indirect labor, variable, and as indirect labor, fixed. More commonly the classification is made apart from the accounts.

Predetermined overhead rates are widely used for applying manufacturing overhead to products, because—

1. Overhead rates developed from actual volume make it necessary to delay completion of product costs until the close of the period, because neither the full amount of the overhead cost nor the total quantity of production is known until that time.

2. Wide fluctuations in unit product cost often result from fluctuations in volume of production and as between short periods of time. Irregularly occurring costs have a similar but usually less marked effect on unit cost.

Cost allowances in the standard-volume budget are suitable only for the standard volume of production. When actual volume deviates from the standard, expense components that vary with volume should be controlled with departmental activity. For this purpose, flexible budgeting techniques are often employed to adjust the overhead-cost control budget to the actual volume experienced.

Predetermined rates at which costs should vary with changes in volume is the essential characteristic of flexible-budget methods. This proceeds from either of the following approaches:

1. A flexible standard is established for each overhead cost, expressing the cost as a fixed sum plus a rate per unit of volume; the formula sometimes quoted is $y = a + bx$, where y is the amount of overhead sought, a the fixed sum, b the units of volume, and x the rate per unit. From this straight-line formula the amount of expense allowed at any given volume can be computed and is usually accurate enough for the purpose.

2. Expense budgets are prepared in advance for a series of volumes covering the expected range of activity. For example, budgets may be prepared at intervals of 10 percent between 50 percent and 120 percent of standard capacity. Expense allowances for any volume within this range are then set by reference to the pre-established budget and may be derived by the formula above quoted. This approach allows recognition of a step variation in costs.

Where volume fluctuates considerably from month to month, a flexible budget provides department supervisors with expense goals reflecting the current rate of production and at the same time makes possible the separation of overhead-expense variances into the portion due to over- or underspending and that due to the deviation of actual volume from standard volume.

A careful study of conditions existing in each situation is needed before bases for allocating costs are chosen. Bases suitable elsewhere are not applicable if equipment, methods of operation, and other conditions differ. For this reason, generalizations with respect to the advantages or disadvantages of specific bases lack significance.

Under some forms of direct costing, fixed-overhead costs are treated when incurred as general production expense, and are not allocated to units of production (see *direct costing*) or to inventories; on an income statement they are deducted as a cost-of-sales element or as general expense.

Under other forms of direct costing, fixed-overhead common costs in an a multiproduct operation are management-allocated to the several lines of product, not necessarily in proportion to labor or machine-hours or other direct-cost factors, but in proportion to price yields, *price margins*, or relative importance assigned to different product lines. Judgments concerning the relative importance of product lines are necessarily those of top-level management: a principal product, accounting for 60 percent of direct-labor costs, may be assigned 90 percent of the common costs, an assignment that will carry through to residual inventories; a byproduct, none. On the other hand, profitable byproducts supporting a highly competitive major product may be assigned the burden of *absorbing(3)* common costs. As used here, *common* costs are costs of of goods and services contributing to two or more product classes, whether or not simultaneously processed; they include *joint* costs serving simultaneously processed or otherwise closely related classes of product. See *direct* cost.

overhead rate A *standard rate* at which overhead is allocated; see *overhead.*

overlapping debt (municipal accounting) The proportionate share of the debts of the political subdivisions or special districts lying wholly or partly within the boundaries of a municipality, excluding only the debt of the state government. The municipality's share of the debt other than special-assessment debt is usually determined on the basis of the ratio of the assessed valuation of taxable property lying within the corporate limits of the municipality to the assessed valuation of each overlapping district. Assessed values are used as a basis of allocation because they represent the tax base which will furnish the revenues to be used in paying off the bonds and meeting the interest charges.

To determine the real debt burden carried by taxable real estate within a municipality, it is essential to take into account not only the municipal debt but the overlapping debt as well. Overlapping debt is often greater than direct debt.

In the case of debt payable from special assessments, the total amount of special assessments levied, rather than the assessed values, is used as the basis of allocation because special assessments are based on the relative worth of benefits received rather than on assessed values, and because special assessments will be used to pay the special-assessment bonds and interest. The allocation ratio, computed by dividing the special assessments levied on property located within the corporate limits of the municipality by the total special assessments levied, is applied to the special-assessment debt outstanding.

overriding royalty interest (petroleum industry) The interest, usually of a third party, such as a sublessor of a tract of land, in the production of crude oil and gas from the tract; it is usually a fraction of the original *working interest.*

over-the-counter *adj.* Pertaining to transactions not consummated through an established stock exchange; applied to transactions of brokers and dealers in unlisted securities, including government bonds and notes. Over-the-counter markets exist in all large cities.

over-the-counter sale The sale of an unlisted security.

owe To be under obligation to pay or render something to another in return for something received; to be indebted to another.

owners' equity = *net worth.*

ownership The right to and enjoyment of services or benefits flowing from an asset, usually evidenced by the possession of legal title or by a beneficial interest in the title. See *asset; sale; title; liability; equity ownership; proprietorship.*

paid-in capital The total amount of cash, property, and services contributed to a corporation by its stockholders and constituting a major balance-sheet item. It may be reflected in a single account, now generally preferred, or divided between *capital-stock* and *paid-in-surplus* accounts; see these terms.

paid-in surplus 1. Capital contributed by stockholders credited to accounts other than capital stock. The principal sources are the excess over par or *stated value* received from the sale or exchange of capital stock, the excess of par or stated value of capital stock reacquired over the amount paid therefor, and surplus from recapitalization. Paid-in surplus is often displayed on the balance sheet as a separate item or combined with par or stated value and designated *paid-in-capital;* on the books a separate account may be maintained for paid-in surplus from each principal source.
2. The name of the account maintained for such contributions.

paid-up capital The aggregate of the par or stated value of capital stock for which full consideration has been received.

paper Bills of exchange and other short-term evidences of indebtedness.

paper profit A profit not realized; anticipatory profit; a profit based on premature, uncertain, or conjectural estimates of operating or trade results. Example: appreciation of unsold marketable securities.

par The nominal or face value of a security.

parameter (statistics) Any measure or set of measures, such as an arithmetic mean or standard deviation, calculated directly from or defined for a universe rather than samples; sometimes referred to as the "true" value a sample is designed to estimate or test.

parent company A *controlling company* having *subsidiaries.* Without a trade or business of its own, a parent company may also be termed a *holding company.*

parity price A price level for a particular commodity or service which bears a predetermined relationship to another price or composite average of prices, established on the basis of a historical period, and expressed as an index number of 100. As these two sets of prices change, they are reflected in the index number. This measuring device is widely employed in the Federal farm-price-support program, and has also been incorporated in industrial wage contracts. The index is intended to reflect, during any period, the real wages of labor, or the real income of farmers, and the purchasing power of that income for the principal commodities which such groups consume. Social-control programs are largely governed by some parity-price device. Farm prices are supported or pegged by the Federal government at parity levels through open market purchases and loans (and rates of interest) to producers.

The major significance of the parity-price concept is not in its mechanics, but in the social-control purpose for which it is employed. Underlying its application is the assumption of the need of replacing the free-price system by government regulation to achieve an optimum distribution of national income among farmers, laborers, and industry. The parity-price device is but one of several means employed by the Federal government in an effort to achieve a balanced economy, and falls in the same category as import duties, tax-reducing depletion allowances to petroleum producers, and social-security benefits.

par of exchange The ratio of one country's unit of currency to that of another country, as defined by the official exchange rates between the two countries.

participating capital stock Preferred stock which, in addition to having a fixed dividend rate, shares under varying conditions with the common stock in further distributions of profits. See *participating dividend.*

participating dividend A dividend paid to preferred stockholders over and above that paid at a stipulated minimum rate, where preferred stockholders share, to a predetermined extent, in profits that otherwise would be distributable only to common stockholders. In the absence of provisions to the contrary, it is held in some jurisdictions that preferred stockholders are entitled to share prorata with common stockholders in all dividend distributions after both preferred and common stocks have received dividends at a stipulated rate.

particular average (marine insurance) An unavoidable loss suffered (and borne) by one of the several interests in a ship and its cargo, arising from damage caused by perils at sea. See *general average.*

partnership A contractual relationship, based upon a written, oral, or implied agreement, between two or more persons who combine their resources and activities in a joint enterprise and share in varying degrees and by specific agreement in the management and in the profits or losses; a co-partnership; a *firm.* A partnership may be *general,* in which case the acts of each partner are binding upon the others and each is liable for all its debts; or it may be *limited,* in which case the liability of certain but not all partners is restricted to the amount of their individual contributions to or interest in the firm's capital.

par value The *face amount* of capital stock or other security.

par-value capital stock Capital stock each share of which has been assigned a fixed nominal or face value by the terms of the corporation's charter. The par value of each share of capital stock is ordinarily expressed in round amounts, such as $5 or $10 or multiples thereof, but usually not exceeding $100 per share. The corporation laws of a number of states limit minimum and maximum par values.

passed dividend A dividend not declared on any class of stock at or about a customary dividend date; if relating to preferred stock, a *dividend in arrears.*

past due Delayed beyond an agreed time for payment.

patent A grant by the Federal government to an inventor, giving him for a period of 17 years the exclusive right to produce and sell his invention. The cost of obtaining a patent is nominal and is often not capitalized; however, the experimental and developmental work preceding the discovery on which the patent is based may be very large and is occasionally capitalized and amortized over the life of the patent. More often the costs of such work, included in operating budgets, are expensed as incurred.

patronage dividend A distribution by a *cooperative* to members and customers; ordinarily it is a rebate on purchases or an increase in profits on sales which have been made on their behalf. Such distributions are deductible by the cooperative on its Federal income-tax return, and, in the hands of the member or customer, they are a reduction of the cost of his purchases or an addition to the gross profit he has realized from sales.

payable *adj.* Unpaid, whether or not *due.* *n.* A liability; a debt owing to another; an account or note payable.

payment The discharge of a pecuniary obligation by a disbursement of money or by property or services accepted as the equivalent of money; the satisfaction, by or in the name of the debtor, to the creditor, of an amount owing, putting an end to the obligation between them. Where payment is made by check, it is recorded with the issue of the check, although legally such an act constitutes only conditional payment.

payroll 1. A record showing the wage or salary earned by employees for a certain period, and the various deductions for *withholding* tax, health benefits, and so on.
2. Total wages and salaries accrued or payable for a given period.

payroll distribution 1. An analysis of the total amount of salaries and wages paid or accrued for a period, showing the component amounts to be charged to the various departments, operations, activities, or products affected.
2. The entry by which the amount of salaries and wages paid or accrued for a period is charged in the required detail to the accounts or records.

payroll records The records relating to the authorization, computation, distribution, and payment of wages and salaries. They include payrolls, time slips, time-clock cards, withholding authorizations, canceled payroll checks or receipts for wages paid, wage and salary authorizations, and individual-earnings records.

pecuniary benefit That portion of cash or money equivalent remaining from a transaction or group of transactions after deducting applicable costs; see *transaction; profit; cost.*

pegging 1. The act of fixing a price by a dealer or other person or group, during the initial distribution of a security, or for other purposes; it is accomplished by a series of buying or wash transactions and is permitted in certain cases as a stabilizing device under the regulations of the U. S. Securities and Exchange Commission. See *stabilization; seasoning.*
2. The fixing of the rate of exchange of one currency with another, usually by a government or an agency authorized by the government.

pension fund A fund for the payment of annuities or pensions, consisting of actual cash set aside or specific investments in securities the income from which accrues to the fund. Where title to fund assets rests in a separate organization, such as a trust to which periodic contributions are made under contract with the creator and in accordance with an agreement with employees, the question of whether the creator should report fund assets in its balance sheet has not yet been satisfactorily settled; in general, if the plan is irrevocable, if fund assets cannot be utilized except for pension payments, and if the payment of pensions is not a business obligation but rather an obligation only of the fund, the omission of the fund from the balance sheet of the creator has been regarded as a preferred practice. Where fund assets may legally be utilized for other purposes, and contributions to the fund are voluntary or revocable, they are merely earmarked items and remain as business assets until disbursed. An offsetting *pension reserve,* if any, may be equal to, or greater or less than, the fund. See also *pension plan; reserve for contingencies.*

pension plan The method adopted by a business or other organization for the payment of *annuities* or *pensions* to retired or disabled employees. There are numerous varieties, many of them the result of agreements with employee unions. In a few instances a "pay-as-you-go" plan has been instituted; more common are plans involving funding or insurance. If the plan meets the requirements of sections 401 and 404 of the Internal Revenue Code, contributions by the employer organization are deductible in its Federal income-tax return, and the employee is taxed only as the pension is received by him.

pension reserve An obligation recognized in full or in part by an employer as representing a future liability to pay *annuities* or *pensions* to employees. If created by a charge to expense, such a reserve ordinarily represents a liability. If the plan is a revocable one, the reserve is likely to be regarded simply as a reservation of retained earnings, whether or not it offsets earmarked assets. See *pension fund.*

percent Any decimal fraction, times 100. See *ratio.*

percentage depletion (Federal income taxes) Depletion expense computed as a percentage of gross income notwithstanding that the accumulative aggregate of provisions for tax purposes, whether based on income or cost or both, may exceed the cost of the property. Rates currently prevailing, listed in section 613 of the Internal Revenue Code, include the following: $27\frac{1}{2}$ percent for oil and gas wells, 23 percent for sulfur, uranium, and certain other listed minerals (if produced from U. S. deposits), 15 percent for metal mines and various other mineral mines and deposits, and 10 percent for coal mines; but the amount thus computed must not exceed 50 percent of the net income (before the depletion deduction) from the property. See *depletion.*

percentage statement An operating statement containing not only monetary amounts but also the ratio of each item to any of several bases. In an income statement, the base is ordinarily the total of net revenues; in a manufacturing statement, the cost of goods manufactured or total manufacturing cost; in a balance sheet, total assets.

percentile Any of the values that divide a frequency distribution into 100 parts each containing 1 percent of the total number of items.

perfection standard cost A *standard cost* based on the best possible performance obtainable under the most favorable conditions.

performance A general term applied to a part or all of the conduct of activities of an organization over a period of time; often with reference to past or projected costs, *efficiency(5)*, management *responsibility* or *accountability*, or the like.

performance budget (governmental accounting) = *program budget.*

perils of the sea (marine insurance) Fortuitous marine perils or risks such as sinking, collision, and unusually heavy weather, excluding those attributable to the ordinary action of wind and weather.

period See *accounting period.*

period cost (or **charge** or **expense**) 1. Any expenditure assigned to expense on a time basis rather than on a basis of service yield, although in most instances the two bases coincide; rent, interest, real-estate taxes, and income taxes are examples; contrasts with *product cost.* Straight-line depreciation is often looked upon as a period cost. See *straight-line method; cost absorption; direct costing.* 2. Any cost applicable to the operations of period without allocation to inventory.

periodic audit An audit covering an intermediate accounting period such as a month.

periodic income Income accounted for proportionately with elapsed periods of time and under varied conditions; as, a part or all of (a) an amount not previously recorded and receivable in the future, as bond interest; (b) an amount already received and recorded, as rent paid in advance; or (c) an amount already recorded (as deferred income) but not yet received, as profit from an installment sale.

periodicity concept (of accounting) The identification of *economic activity(1)* with time periods whereby for each period the activity can be measured and reported; see *continuity concept; accounting period.*

periodic payment accumulating to 1 The amount required, as for a sinking fund, to be deposited periodically at compound interest in order to reach the desired total of 1 at a specified time.

Both the *compound amount of 1 per period* and a *periodic payment accumulating to 1* involve fixed periodic payments drawing compound interest and resulting in a single endproduct; in the former, the fixed payments are a known element but the endproduct unknown; in the latter, the fixed payments are unknown and the endproduct known. If the compound amount of 1 per period be represented by s and the periodic payment accumulating to 1 by p, then $1 : s :: p : 1$; hence, $p = 1/s$. Since the formula for s is $[(1 + i)^n - 1]/i$ (see page 95), p is its reciprocal, or

$$\frac{i}{(1+i)^n - 1}.$$

Illustrative values for this formula will be found on pp. 318–319.

periodic payment with present value of 1 Any of a series of equal periodic payments required to liquidate a present debt of 1 where the unpaid balance draws interest.

Both the *present value of 1 per period* and a *periodic payment with present value of 1* involve a present sum of money or charge that will be liquidated by fixed periodic payments drawing interest; in the former, the endproduct is a known element but the fixed payments unknown; in the latter, the endproduct is unknown and the fixed payments known. If the present value of 1 per period be represented by p and the periodic payment with present value of 1 by p_1 then $p : 1 :: 1 : p_1$, and $p_1 = 1/p$. Since the formula for p_1 is $[(1 + i)^n - 1]/i(1 + i)^n$ (see page 000), p is its reciprocal, or

$$\frac{i(1+i)^n}{(1+i)^n - 1}.$$

Illustrative values for this formula will be found on pp. 000–000. These values are greater by the rate of interest per period than those appearing in the table for the *periodic payment accumulating to 1* (see preceding definition) because of the relationship between the two formulas:

$$\frac{i(1+i)^n}{(1+i)^n - 1} - \frac{i}{(1+i)^n - 1} = \frac{i[(1+i)^n - 1]}{(1+i)^n - 1} = i.$$

permanent asset 1. = *capital asset.* 2. *Land.*

permanent file (auditing) Papers and schedules kept in a separate file for use in succeeding audits. It usually contains copies, extracts, or summaries of such documents as the charter or articles of incorporation; bylaws; trust or partnership agreements; minutes of the board of directors; long-term contracts; progressive schedules of capital stock, surplus, and capital assets; descriptions of and comments on accounting policies, methods, and internal controls; and other matters of similar import.

permanent investments Investments in securities and other property or rights to property, not held for sale, and hence excluded from the classification of current assets; long-term investments.

permutation Any *arrangement* or ordering of all or a part of a collection of numbers, symbols, or other units. The five letters *a b c d e*, in alphabetical sequence, constitute a permutation, as do also *b a c d e* and *b c e a d*; altogether there are 120 different arrangements of these letters. The varieties of four-letter arrangements of the five letters (e.g., *a b c d*, *b c d a*, *a b d e*) are also 120; of three-letter and two-letter combinations, there are 60 and 20, respectively. Or, some of the units may be alike, and indistinguishable from each other; thus, *a b b a b* is one of ten possible permutations of five units consisting of two *a*'s and three *b*'s. The number of permutations under these different conditions may be determined by formulas derived as follows:

1. *No like symbols; each ordered.* Continuing the five-letter illustration, with *a* in any one of five possible positions, *b* can occupy any one of the remaining four, *c* any one of the remaining three, and *d* any one of the remaining two, leaving only one position for *e*. The possible number of arrangements of the five letters is thus $5 \times 4 \times 3 \times 2 \times 1$, or 120, a result that may be referred to as "*factorial 5*" or "*5* factorial" and written as 5!, the exclamation point serving as the factorial symbol; or it may be expressed as $P_5{}^5$, "the number of permutations of 5 things taken 5 at a time," meaning, in the illustration, the total number of sequential arrangements of the five letters when all

five are employed in each arrangement.

2. *No like symbols; not all ordered.* Should it be desired to determine the possible permutations of any four of the five letters mentioned above, with the fifth letter occupying the remaining position, it will be found that the number is again 120, since $5 \times 4 \times 3 \times 2$ equals that figure. The mathematical expression is P_4^5. Hence, $P_4^5 = P_5^5$. The possible number of permutations involved in placing three letters in any three of the five positions, without regard to the identity of the two letters occupying the remaining positions, is represented as P_3^5, and the number of different sequences becomes $5 \times 4 \times 3$, or 60. The ordered sequence of any two of the five letters without regard to the positioning of the remaining three (P_2^5) may be made in 5×4 ways, as may be readily demonstrated by experiment; and, finally, if the number of positions of only one of the letters (P_1^5) is to be reckoned with, only five different permutations are possible. The generalization to be deduced from these considerations is the following formula, where n is the total number of units or items of which the number of permutations (P) of r units is sought:

$$P_r^n = \frac{n!}{(n-r)!}$$

Thus,

$$P_2^5 = \frac{5!}{(5-2)!} = \frac{5 \times 4 \times 3 \times 2 \times 1}{3 \times 2 \times 1} = 20.$$

The reason for stating permutation formulas in terms of factorials is that, in dealing with large quantities, as in sampling procedures, factorial solutions are readily obtained by using logarithm tables especially devised for factorials.

3. *Some like symbols; each ordered.* The number of permutations discussed in formula 1 would have been a fraction of the amount shown if two or more of the letters had been the same. Last would have been the permutations equal in number to the permutations among similar letters. Thus, if the letters had been *a a b b c*, the posssible permutations would have been

$$\frac{5 \times 4 \times 3 \times 2 \times 1}{(2 \times 1)(2 \times 1)} = 30.$$

or, if the letters had been *a a a b b*, and the number of *a*'s is represented by j and the number of *b*'s by k, the possible permutations would have been

$$P_n^n = \frac{n!}{j!k!} = \frac{5!}{3!2!} = \frac{5 \times 4 \times 3 \times 2 \times 1}{(3 \times 2 \times 1)(2 \times 1)} = 10.$$

4. *Different symbols; group ordered.* Where permutations are to be considered without regard for the sequence or position in which the desired items appear, they are referred to as *combinations.* Thus, in the selection of any three (r) of the five first letters of the alphabet, *a b c*, *a c b*, *c a b*, etc., would be permutations, their number being $r! = 3 \times 2 \times 1$, or 6, but they would constitute only one combination. Hence, the number of permutations, obtained in the usual way, would have to be divided by 6, or $r!$. The formula for combinations is thus expressed as

$$C_r^n = \frac{n!}{r!(n-r)!},$$

and the solution of the illustration would be

$$C_3^5 = \frac{5!}{3!2!} = \frac{120}{12} = 10,$$

a total readily proven by experiment. A working knowledge of combinations is basic in the study of probability and in the devising of sampling methods. See *probability; sample.*

perpetual budget = *continuous budget.*

perpetual inventory A *book inventory* kept in continuous agreement with stock on hand by means of a detailed record that may also serve as a subsidiary ledger where dollar amounts as well as physical quantities are maintained. Sections of

n	$\frac{1}{2}\%$	1%	$1\frac{1}{2}\%$	2%	$2\frac{1}{2}\%$	3%
1	1.0000 000	1.0000 000	1.0000 000	1.0000 000	1.0000 000	1.0000 000
2	.4987 531	.4975 124	.4962 779	.4950 495	.4938 272	.4926 108
3	.3316 722	.3300 221	.3283 830	.3267 547	.3251 372	.3235 304
4	.2481 328	.2462 811	.2444 448	.2426 238	.2408 179	.2390 270
5	.1980 100	.1960 398	.1940 893	.1921 584	.1902 469	.1883 546
6	.1645 955	.1625 484	.1605 252	.1585 258	.1565 500	.1545 975
7	.1407 285	.1386 283	.1365 562	.1345 120	.1324 954	.1305 064
8	.1228 289	.1206 903	.1185 840	.1165 098	.1144 673	.1124 564
9	.1089 074	.1067 404	.1046 098	.1025 154	.1004 569	.0984 339
10	.0977 706	.0955 821	.0934 342	.0913 265	.0892 588	.0872 305
11	.0886 590	.0864 541	.0842 938	.0821 779	.0801 060	.0780 774
12	.0810 664	.0788 488	.0766 800	.0745 596	.0724 871	.0704 621
13	.0746 422	.0724 148	.0702 404	.0681 184	.0660 483	.0640 295
14	.0691 361	.0669 012	.0647 233	.0626 020	.0605 365	.0585 263
15	.0643 644	.0621 238	.0599 444	.0578 255	.0557 665	.0537 666
16	.0601 894	.0579 446	.0557 651	.0536 501	.0515 990	.0496 108
17	.0565 058	.0542 581	.0520 797	.0499 698	.0479 278	.0459 525
18	.0532 317	.0509 820	.0488 058	.0467 021	.0446 701	.0427 087
19	.0503 025	.0480 518	.0458 785	.0437 818	.0417 606	.0398 139
20	.0476 665	.0454 153	.0432 457	.0411 567	.0391 471	.0372 157
21	.0452 816	.0430 308	.0408 655	.0387 848	.0367 873	.0348 718
22	.0431 138	.0408 637	.0387 033	.0366 314	.0346 466	.0327 474
23	.0411 347	.0388 858	.0367 308	.0346 681	.0326 964	.0308 139
24	.0393 206	.0370 735	.0349 241	.0328 711	.0309 128	.0290 474
25	.0376 519	.0354 068	.0332 635	.0312 204	.0292 759	.0274 279
26	.0361 116	.0338 689	.0317 320	.0296 992	.0277 687	.0259 383
27	.0346 856	.0324 455	.0303 153	.0282 931	.0263 769	.0245 642
28	.0333 617	.0311 244	.0290 011	.0269 897	.0250 879	.0232 932
29	.0321 291	.0298 950	.0277 788	.0257 784	.0238 913	.0221 147
30	.0309 789	.0387 481	.0266 392	.0246 499	.0227 776	.0210 193
35	.0262 155	.0240 037	.0219 336	.0200 022	.0182 056	.0165 393
40	.0226 455	.0204 556	.0184 271	.0165 557	.0148 362	.0132 624
45	.0198 712	.0177 050	.0157 198	.0139 096	.0122 675	.0107 852
50	.0176 538	.0155 127	.0135 717	.0118 232	.0102 581	.0088 655
55	.0158 414	.0137 264	.0118 302	.0101 434	.0086 542	.0073 491
60	.0143 328	.0122 444	.0103 934	.0087 680	.0073 534	.0061 330
65	.0130 579	.0109 967	.0091 909	.0076 262	.0062 846	.0051 458
70	.0119 666	.0099 328	.0081 724	.0066 676	.0053 971	.0043 366
75	.0110 221	.0090 161	.0073 007	.0058 551	.0046 536	.0036 680
80	.0101 970	.0082 189	.0065 483	.0051 607	.0040 260	.0031 117
85	.0094 702	.0075 200	.0058 940	.0045 632	.0034 931	.0026 465
90	.0088 253	.0069 031	.0053 211	.0040 460	.0030 381	.0022 556
95	.0082 493	.0063 551	.0048 168	.0035 960	.0026 479	.0019 258
100	.0077 319	.0058 657	.0043 706	.0032 027	.0023 119	.0016 467

PERIODIC PAYMENT ACCUMULATING TO 1

$3\frac{1}{2}\%$	4%	$4\frac{1}{2}\%$	5%	$5\frac{1}{2}\%$	6%
1.0000 000	1.0000 000	1.0000 000	1.0000 000	1.0000 000	1.0000 000
.4914 005	.4901 961	.4889 976	.4878 049	.4866 180	.4854 369
.3219 342	.3203 485	.3187 734	.3172 086	.3156 541	.3141 098
.2372 511	.2354 900	.2337 436	.2320 118	.2302 945	.2285 915
.1864 814	.1846 271	.1827 916	.1809 748	.1791 764	.1773 964
.1526 682	.1507 619	.1488 784	.1470 175	.1451 789	.1433 626
.1285 445	.1266 096	.1247 015	.1228 198	.1209 644	.1191 350
.1104 766	.1085 278	.1066 097	.1047 218	.1028 640	.1010 359
.0964 460	.0944 930	.0925 745	.0906 901	.0888 395	.0870 222
.0852 414	.0832 909	.0813 788	.0795 046	.0776 678	.0758 680
.0760 920	.0741 490	.0722 482	.0703 889	.0685 707	.0667 929
.0684 839	.0665 522	.0646 662	.0628 254	.0610 292	.0592 770
.0620 616	.0601 437	.0582 754	.0564 558	.0546 843	.0529 601
.0565 707	.0546 690	.0528 203	.0510 240	.0492 791	.0475 849
.0518 251	.0499 411	.0481 138	.0463 423	.0446 256	.0429 628
.0476 848	.0458 200	.0440 154	.0422 699	.0405 825	.0389 521
.0440 431	.0421 985	.0404 176	.0386 991	.0370 420	.0354 448
.0408 168	.0389 933	.0372 369	.0355 462	.0339 199	.0323 565
.0379 403	.0361 386	.0344 073	.0327 450	.0311 501	.0296 209
.0353 611	.0335 818	.0318 761	.0302 426	.0286 793	.0271 846
.0330 366	.0312 801	.0296 006	.0279 961	.0264 648	.0250 045
.0309 321	.0291 988	.0275 456	.0259 705	.0244 712	.0230 456
.0290 188	.0273 091	.0256 825	.0241 368	.0226 696	.0212 785
.0272 728	.0255 868	.0239 870	.0224 709	.0210 358	.0196 790
.0256 740	.0240 120	.0224 390	.0209 525	.0195 494	.0182 267
.0242 054	.0225 674	.0210 214	.0195 643	.0181 931	.0169 043
.0228 524	.0212 385	.0197 195	.0182 919	.0169 523	.0156 972
.0216 026	.0200 130	.0185 208	.0171 225	.0158 144	.0145 926
.0204 454	.0188 799	.0174 146	.0160 455	.0147 686	.0135 796
.0193 713	.0178 301	.0163 915	.0150 514	.0138 054	.0126 489
.0149 983	.0135 773	.0122 704	.0110 717	.0099 749	.0089 739
.0118 273	.0105 235	.0093 431	.0073 203	.0064 615	.0056 937
.0094 534	.0082 625	.0072 020	.0062 617	.0054 313	.0047 005
.0076 337	.0065 502	.0056 021	.0047 767	.0040 615	.0034 443
.0062 132	.0052 312	.0043 875	.0036 669	.0030 546	.0025 370
.0050 886	.0042 018	.0034 543	.0028 282	.0023 071	.0018 757
.0041 883	.0033 902	.0027 305	.0021 892	.0017 480	.0013 907
.0034 610	.0027 451	.0021 651	.0016 992	.0013 275	.0010 331
.0028 692	.0022 290	.0017 210	.0013 216	.0010 100	.0007 687
.0023 849	.0018 141	.0013 707	.0010 296	.0007 695	.0005 725
.0019 866	.0014 791	.0010 933	.0008 032	.0005 868	.0004 268
.0016 578	.0012 078	.0008 732	.0006 271	.0004 479	.0003 184
.0013 855	.0009 874	.0006 980	.0004 900	.0003 420	.0002 376
.0011 593	.0008 080	.0005 584	.0003 831	.0002 613	.0001 774

n	$\frac{1}{2}\%$	1%	$1\frac{1}{2}\%$	2%	$2\frac{1}{2}\%$	3%
1	1.0050 000	1.0100 000	1.0150 000	1.0200 000	1.0250 000	1.0300 000
2	.5037 531	.5075 124	.5112 779	.5150 495	.5188 272	.5226 108
3	.3366 722	.3400 221	.3433 830	.3467 547	.3501 372	.3535 304
4	.2531 328	.2562 811	.2594 448	.2626 238	.2658 179	.2690 270
5	.2030 100	.2060 398	.2090 893	.2121 584	.2152 469	.2183 546
6	.1695 955	.1725 484	.1755 252	.1785 258	.1815 500	.1845 975
7	.1457 285	.1486 283	.1515 562	.1545 120	.1574 954	.1605 064
8	.1278 289	.1306 903	.1335 840	.1365 098	.1394 673	.1424 564
9	.1139 074	.1167 404	.1196 098	.1225 154	.1254 569	.1284 339
10	.1027 706	.1055 821	.1084 342	.1113 265	.1142 588	.1172 305
11	.0936 590	.0964 541	.0992 938	.1021 779	.1051 060	.1080 774
12	.0860 664	.0888 488	.0916 800	.0945 596	.0974 871	.1004 621
13	.0796 422	.0824 148	.0852 404	.0881 184	.0910 483	.0940 295
14	.0741 361	.0769 012	.0797 233	.0826 020	.0855 365	.0885 263
15	.0693 644	.0721 238	.0749 444	.0778 255	.0807 665	.0837 666
16	.0651 894	.0679 446	.0707 651	.0736 501	.0765 990	.0796 108
17	.0615 058	.0642 581	.0670 797	.0699 698	.0729 278	.0759 525
18	.0582 317	.0609 820	.0638 058	.0667 021	.0696 701	.0727 087
19	.0553 025	.0580 518	.0608 785	.0637 818	.0667 606	.0698 139
20	.0526 665	.0554 153	.0582 457	.0611 567	.0641 471	.0672 157
21	.0502 816	.0530 308	.0558 655	.0587 847	.0617 873	.0648 718
22	.0481 138	.0508 637	.0537 033	.0566 314	.0596 466	.0627 474
23	.0461 347	.0488 858	.0517 308	.0546 681	.0576 964	.0608 139
24	.0443 206	.0470 735	.0499 241	.0528 711	.0559 128	.0590 474
25	.0426 519	.0454 068	.0482 635	.0512 204	.0542 759	.0574 279
26	.0411 116	.0438 689	.0467 320	.0496 992	.0527 687	.0559 383
27	.0396 856	.0424 455	.0453 153	.0482 931	.0513 769	.0545 642
28	.0383 617	.0411 244	.0440 011	.0469 897	.0500 879	.0532 932
29	.0371 291	.0398 950	.0427 788	.0457 784	.0488 913	.0521 147
30	.0359 789	.0387 481	.0416 392	.0446 499	.0477 776	.0510 193
35	.0312 155	.0340 037	.0369 336	.0400 022	.0432 056	.0465 393
40	.0276 455	.0304 556	.0334 271	.0365 557	.0398 362	.0432 624
45	.0248 712	.0277 050	.0307 198	.0339 096	.0372 675	.0407 852
50	.0226 538	.0255 127	.0285 717	.0318 232	.0352 581	.0388 655
55	.0208 414	.0237 264	.0268 302	.0301 434	.0336 542	.0373 491
60	.0193 328	.0222 444	.0253 934	.0287 680	.0323 534	.0361 330
65	.0180 579	.0209 967	.0241 909	.0276 262	.0312 846	.0351 458
70	.0169 666	.0199 328	.0231 724	.0266 676	.0303 971	.0343 366
75	.0160 221	.0190 161	.0223 007	.0258 551	.0296 536	.0336 680
80	.0151 970	.0182 189	.0215 483	.0251 607	.0290 260	.0331 117
85	.0144 702	.0175 200	.0208 940	.0245 632	.0284 931	.0326 465
90	.0138 253	.0169 031	.0203 211	.0240 460	.0280 381	.0322 556
95	.0132 493	.0163 551	.0198 168	.0235 960	.0276 479	.0319 258
100	.0127 319	.0158 657	.0193 706	.0232 027	.0273 119	.0316 467

PERIODIC PAYMENT WITH PRESENT VALUE OF 1

$3\frac{1}{2}\%$	4%	$4\frac{1}{2}\%$	5%	$5\frac{1}{2}\%$	6%
1.0350 000	1.0400 000	1.0450 000	1.0500 000	1.0550 000	1.0600 000
.5264 005	.5301 961	.5339 976	.5378 049	.5416 180	.5454 369
.3569 342	.3603 485	.3637 734	.3672 086	.3706 541	.3741 098
.2722 511	.2754 900	.2787 436	.2820 118	.2852 945	.2885 915
.2214 814	.2246 271	.2277 916	.2309 748	.2341 764	.2373 964
.1876 682	.1907 619	.1938 784	.1970 175	.2001 789	.2033 626
.1635 445	.1666 096	.1697 015	.1728 198	.1759 644	.1791 350
.1454 766	.1485 278	.1516 097	.1547 218	.1578 640	.1610 359
.1314 460	.1344 930	.1375 745	.1406 901	.1438 395	.1470 222
.1202 414	.1232 909	.1263 788	.1295 046	.1326 678	.1358 680
.1110 920	.1141 490	.1172 482	.1203 889	.1235 707	.1267 929
.1034 839	.1065 522	.1096 662	.1128 254	.1160 292	.1192 770
.0970 616	.1001 437	.1032 754	.1064 558	.1096 843	.1129 601
.0915 707	.0946 690	.0978 203	.1010 240	.1042 791	.1075 849
.0868 251	.0899 411	.0931 138	.0963 423	.0996 256	.1029 628
.0826 848	.0858 200	.0890 154	.0922 699	.0955 825	.0989 521
.0790 431	.0821 985	.0854 176	.0886 991	.0920 402	.0954 448
.0758 168	.0789 933	.0822 369	.0855 462	.0889 199	.0923 565
.0729 403	.0761 386	.0794 073	.0827 450	.0861 501	.0896 209
.0703 611	.0735 818	.0768 761	.0802 426	.0836 793	.0871 846
.0680 366	.0712 801	.0746 006	.0779 961	.0814 648	.0850 045
.0659 321	.0691 988	.0725 456	.0759 705	.0794 712	.0830 456
.0640 188	.0673 091	.0706 825	.0741 368	.0776 696	.0812 785
.0622 728	.0655 868	.0689 870	.0724 709	.0760 358	.0796 790
.0606 740	.0640 120	.0674 390	.0709 525	.0745 494	.0782 267
.0592 054	.0625 674	.0660 214	.0695 643	.0731 931	.0769 043
.0578 524	.0612 385	.0647 195	.0682 919	.0719 523	.0756 972
.0566 026	.0600 130	.0635 208	.0671 225	.0708 144	.0745 926
.0554 454	.0588 799	.0624 146	.0660 455	.0697 686	.0735 796
.0543 713	.0578 301	.0613 915	.0650 514	.0688 054	.0726 489
.0499 983	.0535 773	.0572 704	.0610 717	.0649 749	.0689 739
.0468 273	.0505 235	.0543 431	.0582 782	.0623 203	.0664 615
.0444 534	.0482 625	.0522 020	.0562 617	.0604 313	.0647 005
.0426 337	.0465 502	.0506 021	.0547 767	.0590 615	.0634 443
.0412 132	.0452 312	.0493 875	.0536 669	.0580 546	.0625 370
.0400 886	.0442 018	.0484 543	.0528 282	.0573 071	.0618 757
.0391 883	.0433 902	.0477 305	.0521 892	.0567 480	.0613 907
.0384 610	.0427 451	.0471 651	.0516 992	.0563 275	.0610 331
.0378 692	.0422 290	.0467 210	.0513 216	.0560 100	.0607 687
.0373 849	.0418 141	.0463 707	.0510 296	.0557 695	.0605 725
.0369 866	.0414 791	.0460 933	.0508 032	.0555 868	.0604 268
.0366 578	.0412 078	.0458 732	.0506 271	.0554 479	.0603 184
.0363 855	.0409 874	.0456 980	.0504 900	.0553 420	.0602 376
.0361 593	.0408 080	.0455 584	.0503 831	.0552 613	.0601 774

the stockroom are inventoried at short intervals and the quantities or amounts or both are adjusted, where necesary, to the physical count. See *continuous inventory*.

person Any individual, corporation, or other entity given recognition as the possessor of rights, privileges, and responsibilities for which an accounting unit has been or can be established. The accounting use of the word corresponds very generally to its legal use. See *natural person*.

personal account An amount receivable from or payable to any *person*.

personal holding company (Federal income taxes) A corporation, popularly known as an "incorporated pocketbook," a majority of the outstanding capital stock of which is owned by a small group of natural persons. Current features of the law or regulations provide that (a) stock owned includes stock constructively owned; (b) the number of stockholders collectively owning, directly or indirectly, over 50 percent of the value of the outstanding shares does not exceed five at any time during the last half of the taxable year; (c) at least 60 percent of the gross income consists of such items as dividends, interest, royalties, annuities, rents (unless such rents constitute 50 percent or more of the gross income); (d) regular corporate normal tax and surtax are imposed and a special surtax of 70% on undistributed net income (section 1,541–1).

personal income 1. The income of an individual, of the type commonly found in an income-tax return.

2. (social accounting) The income, usually for a year, of the individuals and unincorporated and nonprofit enterprises resident within a country. Under current concepts, it consists principally of wages and salaries from all sources including government, less employees' contributions to social-insurance funds; net income before depreciation of the enterprises indicated; pensions and contributions to pension funds from government and business; net rentals, including the imputed rental of owned homes; dividends; interest; and uncollectible accounts of private business. See *social accounting*.

personal liability An amount owing by a natural person.

personal property Property or assets of a temporary and movable character, as contrasted with *real property;* also known as *personalty*.

pert Program evaluation review technique: a system under which an activity such as factory production is organized and controlled on the basis of the sequented time periods required for each operating step.

petty cash (fund) A relatively small amount of cash on hand or on deposit, available for minor disbursements, and usually maintained under the *imprest system*.

phenomenon An appearance; any *event*, *condition*, thing, or characteristic that is observed or observable; sometimes contrasted with "reality" (i.e., the object independent of possible errors of observation), although the contrast between appearance and reality suggests merely the possibility of correcting observation, since correction must proceed from observation.

physical asset = *tangible asset*.

physical budget A budget expressed in units of materials, number of employees, or number of man hours or service units, rather than in dollars.

physical depreciation Loss of usefulness in a fixed asset attributable to purely physical causes; wear and tear. Example: the master plates from which a book is printed may suffer little physical depreciation from wear but a much larger obsolescence from the exhaustion of their earning power as the book's sales decrease with the lapse of time.

physical inventory An inventory determined by observation and evidenced by a listing of the actual count, weight, or measure. Physical inventories are of three types: the *continuous inventory*, supplementing perpetual-inventory records; periodic counts of selected items; and the annual inventory, or overall count and pricing, taken at the end of the fiscal year. The methods followed in each case differ in scope and in the number of protective devices surrounding the operation. The first of these is normally a feature of a perpetual-inventory system, the counting process covering the entire stock being spread over a year or less. The second may be carried on as a part of the internal-audit program. The third is common even where perpetual records are maintained and may be completed during a period of temporary shutdown at the end of the fiscal year; or it may be instituted before the end of the year and adjusted to the balance at the close of the period through the use of temporary and often informal perpetual records.

Chief among the requirements of the third type, or annual physical inventory, is a well-designed plan through the operation of which the counting, listing, verification, pricing, extensions, footings, recapitulation, and approval may proceed with accuracy and dispatch. If more than three or four persons are to be involved in the process, the plan may be in writing, and will include such points as the following:

1. General responsibility for inventory: one individual is named who will carry out the plan and who is given commensurate authority.

2. Dates, including close-down dates, on which the inventory or sections of the inventory are to be taken: these may often be arranged to coincide with the time the external auditor will be available—possibly a month or more before the end of the year.

3. Locations of inventory: floor plans may be prepared showing the location of the various classes of items to be inventoried; subsequently, the numbers of tags and sheets assigned to each location may appear on such plans.

4. Training of employees: the organization and instruction of crews so that there will be no loss of time when the counting and listing process begins; they must be told precisely what to put on paper, and it is usually necessary to familiarize them with the stock they are to count. It is often desirable to assign counters and checkers to stocks with which they are already familiar but as to which they have had no interest or control.

5. Forms: the forms and precise function and use of inventory tags and sheets are described in detail so that their printing, numbering, distribution, filling in, collection, and summarization may be clearly understood by all inventory workers. Once printed and numbered, they are kept under strict control, carefully allotted to locations and individuals, and each accounted for when the inventory taking has been completed.

6. Revisions: defects in the preceding year's physical-inventory procedures should be borne in mind in preparing the current year's procedures in order that mistakes may not be repeated.

7. Quantity controls, if not already in existence: temporary cards or other devices are employed to keep the physical count up-to-date between the inventory date and the year-end.

8. Sorting of stock: the plan for the sorting and rearrangement, in piles or other orderly form, of materials and supplies, especially those items not in the storeroom, wherever the count will thereby be facilitated.

9. Work in process: where possible, the plan provides for cleaning up work in process, particularly delayed or abandoned work; and, for active in-process items, for developing temporary cost collection sheets for individual items or lots if job or work orders cannot be readily identified with physical work.

10. Items of same type: if the possibility of double counting exists with respect to items of the same type, arrangements are made for a simultaneous count.

11. Two independent counts: where no stockroom quantity records are main-

tained, a preferred procedure is to provide for two separate and unrelated counts. One method is to have tags made in two sections, each bearing the tag number. The tag is attached to the item, pile, or bin by the first counter, who fills in a lower, detachable section. Subsequently, the lower section is removed by another person who at the same time makes sure that a tag has been attached to every item. The top section of the tag is filled in by a second counter, and collected by another employee who also notes the completeness of the attachments. Other employees match the two sections and trace differences. A *single* count is usually adequate where stockroom records have been kept.

12. Duplicates: where counts are transcribed directly during the calling operation to inventory sheets, the same degree of control is exercised over the issue of these sheets as that surrounding tags. In addition, the inventory sheets may be prepared in duplicate, the duplicate to be held by the external auditor until the originals have been priced, extended, footed, and summarized, perhaps several weeks later. By this device the auditor is assured that inventory items and quantities are not modified except as changes are revealed by comparing the duplicates with the completed originals. With respect to quantities, the external auditor's main job will then be to test the propriety of additions, reductions, or changes made since the joint preparation of both copies.

13. Condition: observations of defects, age, and other comments on the condition of inventory items are noted on the tag or sheet as the count is made. A coding is provided to show condition.

14. Cutoff on receipts: a part of the physical inventories may be items found on the balance-sheet date in the receiving room and in trucks or freight cars yet to be unloaded. The inventory procedure provides that these items are to be included in the count on that date, one procedure being to give them distinctive labels. When the date of count precedes the balance-sheet date and additions and subtractions are to be expressed only in dollar amounts rather than in item quantities, it may be necessary to follow the same procedure on the date of count also. To facilitate the count in the receiving room, the instructions may call for closing the receiving room for several hours.

15. Accounts payable: a search for and listing of receiving reports, for the period under audit, that are not yet matched with recorded invoices, is called for, and also a search for and identification of items received on which no receiving report has as yet been issued.

16. In-transit purchases: a figure is to be built up for purchases in transit and, to avoid duplication, a comparison is to be made of supporting details with items recorded as being on hand. In some cases a satisfactory solution to this problem is found by comparing the dates appearing on receiving tickets for the first few weeks of the next following fiscal period with the shipment dates appearing on suppliers' invoices. It is considered better practice to include in-transit items in the inventory, although some accountants take the position that this is unnecessary where in-transit items (a) are normal in volume, year after year, and (b) relate to normal amounts of recurrent purchases.

17. Cutoff on sales: of no less importance is the cutoff procedure to be established for sales. This may involve the closing down of the shipping room for the final hours of the last day of the year, everything in the shipping room at that time being regarded as inventory. The date of shipment appearing on the retained copy of the invoice, as well as the date of the invoice itself, will ordinarily give a satisfactory clue, provided an adequate internal control exists safeguarding the accuracy of these dates.

18. Inventory belonging to others: provision is made for an internal procedure that will develop an accurate list

of materials and finished goods in the hands of others but not sold to them; and, in contrast, a list of items on hand belonging to others that are on consignment or on approval. It may be that sales to others have been made for which shipment has not yet taken place; agreements with customers will provide for storing them at the convenience of the customer. The first of these three classes of items should be included in the inventory, with due allowance for possible loss on recovery (which may be substantial if samples or display goods are involved); the second class should be excluded from the inventory, and the third class also, provided the customer has been billed.

physical life Total potential operating life, as of a machine, as contrasted with useful or *economic life*, which may be much less because of the presence of obsolescence or inadequacy, or both. See *service life.*

physical variance = *efficiency variance.*

pi The ratio of the circumference of a circle to its diameter. Its value is 3.1415-9265 3589+.

planning-programming-budgeting (PPB) (government accounting) A term applied to a system of administration for Federal agencies. Its features, sharing those embodied in modern concepts of management, are mainly these: (a) long- and short-range planning of clearly identified objectives and endproducts, programming its expression in timing and required outlays of manpower and materials, and budgeting its practical adaptation to available resources and to fiscal years; (b) the uninterrupted association of realistic costs with all three stages from their beginnings; (c) an intensive, ever-in-process search for improved, alternative courses of operation, particularly those promising cost savings; (d) budgetary projections of outputs in terms of authorized inputs of goods and services; (e) reports on current and prospective outlays, so designed as to service management controls and to supply throughout each fiscal year timely information on budgetary administration to the Government's fiscal agencies, the President, and the Congress.

plant 1. Land, buildings, machinery, furniture, and other equipment permanently employed; fixed assets generally.
2. In a restricted sense, buildings only; or land and buildings, as in the term "plant and equipment."

plant capacity The maximum potential of production within a given plant; expressed in units of product, labor hours, or other measure of full-time employment of the plant's facilities. Deductions made necessary by a single shift, a 5-day week, seasonal or other usual periods of idleness, and other factors, yield *practical capacity* or projected output.

plant fund (institutional accounting) A fund established for the acquisition of land, buildings, improvements, and equipment.

plant ledger A supporting record of fixed assets owned, often consisting of one or more subsidiary ledgers and sometimes containing details of accumulated depreciation. See *fixed asset; depreciation.*

The relative importance of the investment in land, buildings, and equipment requires an adequate plan for the orderly maintenance of supporting detail. The justification for such records may be said to be these: (a) at all times the total of the investment in fixed assets is supported by verifiable detail, (b) adjustments can be made readily upon the disposal of additions and retirements, (c) property accountabilities may be more easily assigned and maintained, (d) an insurance basis is provided, (e) an acceptable foundation is assured for reports to tax and regulatory authorities, and (f) more accurate depreciation provisions and accumulations can be supplied for any purpose.

The scope of plant records is determined by circumstances. The simplest plan is to provide two or more general-ledger fixed-asset accounts without attempting currently to maintain details for individual items of property. A somewhat more detailed plan would provide a catalog of individual items of plant without tying in their cost with general-ledger accounts. Such an arrangement would be useful but would not be as accurate or in the long run as satisfactory as the institution of controlling and subsidiary accounts. A fully adequate plan would involve the following:

1. A classification and numbering plan based on the location or characteristics of the items involved;
2. A scheme for maintaining controlling accounts governing detailed property records for asset costs and depreciation reserves;
3. A subsidiary-ledger card for each significant item or class of plant and equipment; and
4. An established procedure for recording transactions relating to fixed assets, such as original purchases, additions, renewals (replacements), maintenance, retirements, and gains or losses, if any, from retirement.

Information appearing in a plant ledger is of importance in connection with income taxation. Treasury Department Mimeograph 4170 (CB 1934-1, p. 59; rev. CB 1936-2, p. 1936), often serving as a guide in determining minimum requirements, specifies the following information as necessary in support of depreciation deductions or adjustments:

Account
Original estimated useful life
Depreciation rate
Year acquired
Original cost and subsequent additions by years, including current year
Deductions for sales and other dispositions in prior years
Adjusted cost at beginning of year
Credits to depreciation reserve, prior years (depreciation allowed or allowable)
Charges to depreciation reserve, prior years (other than retirements or sales)
Depreciation reserve, beginning of year
Balance remaining, beginning of year
Estimated remaining life
Deductions for sales and other dispositions, current year
Adjusted cost, end of current year
Depreciation claimed for current year
Charges to depreciation reserve, current year
Net depreciation reserve, end of current year

The form of plant ledger of Pumphrey Manufacturing Company shown on page 327 provides this information satisfactorily. In this instance, the record of depreciation is maintained for each asset, but the Treasury requirements are equally well served by group methods. See *depreciation*. Included in the illustration is the purchase of a machine, an addition to the machine in a later year, periodic depreciation, a change in the applicable rate of depreciation, and finally the disposal of the machine by sale. Depreciation is initiated at the beginning of the month succeeding installation, no scrap value is assumed, the addition is spread over the remaining life of the machine, the change in rate is made effective back to the beginning of the calendar year, and depreciation is computed through the month of retirement.

pledge *n.* 1. = *collateral.*

2. A promise in writing to contribute a stated money amount to a nonprofit organization on or before a given date. Although a pledge may be a legal claim on the donor, enforcement is rarely undertaken, and it is commonly regarded as a contingent asset only.

v.t. To transfer personal property to a creditor or trustee for the purpose of partly or fully securing a debt; to *collateralize.*

pledged asset An asset placed in trust or mortgaged to secure an obligation or contract; a collateralized or hypothecated asset. It is carried on the balance sheet under its regular heading and, if a current asset, is generally so captioned as to show the extent to and purpose of the pledge.

policy In the field of management, that branch dealing with *decisions* and their planning, formulation, and assessment, establishing the objectives and general methods of administration by which the operations of any organization are con-

PUMPHREY MANUFACTURING CO.-- PLANT-RECORD CARD

DESCRIPTION *Metal-turning lathe model 58CA* SERIAL NUMBER *BW808954*

MANUFACTURER *Bryan-Wicks Tool Co.*

PURCHASED FROM *Mfr.* ☒ NEW ☐ SECOND HAND DATE INSTALLED *7/22/1* DATE FIRST OPERATED *8/12/1*

LOCATION *Main building* FLOOR *3* DEPARTMENT *Finishing* CENTER NO. *402*

REMOVED TO (LOCATION AND DATE)

CONTROL ACCOUNT *Machinery*

DEPRECIATION	DATE	RATE %	DATE	RATE %	DATE	RATE %
	8/1/1	*8⅓*	*6/2/6*	*10 on balance*		

APPRAISAL RECORD

DATE	REFERENCE	PAGE	AMOUNT

NATURE OF RETIREMENT

DATE RETIRED *8 8 7*

HOW DISPOSED OF *Improved model 60CA will take the place of this item. Sold to Farnham Brothers Inc. of Detroit, through BW T Co.*

ACCOUNTING RECORD

DETAIL	DATE			REF.	AMOUNT DR.	AMOUNT CR.	BALANCE
INVESTMENT INVOICE COST	*7*	*8*	*1*	*8329*	*2,897.40*		*2,897.40*
FREIGHT	*7*	*14*	*1*	*8526*	*180.54*		
CARTAGE	*7*	*22*	*1*	*8943*	*28.10*		
INSTALLATION	*7*	*22*	*1*	*8944*	*50.12*		*3,156.16*
added safety rails	*3*	*4*	*3*	*2387*	*250.00*		*3,406.16*
RETIREMENT							
PROCEEDS	*8*	*16*	*7*			*1,500.00*	*1,906.16*
DEPRECIATION *Before Jan. 1, 7*	*8*	*22*	*7*	*J 4010*		*1,445.36*	*460.80*
Jan. 1 – Aug. 31		*—*		*—*		*144.80*	*316.00*
LOSS OR GAIN *(loss)*	*12*	*10*	*7*	*J 6364*		*316.00*	*0*

PLANT-RECORD-UNIT FORM (front)

DETAILS OF DEPRECIATION

PARTICULARS	DATE			REF.	DR. OR CR.	DETAILS	BALANCE
Provision 19X1 (5 months)	*12*	*31*	*X1*	*J 381*	*Cr.*	*109.59*	*109.59*
— 2	*—*	*—*	*X2*	*J 5840*	*—*	*263.01*	*372.60*
— 3	*—*	*—*	*X3*	*J 47a*	*—*	*281.16*	*653.76*
— 4	*—*	*—*	*X4*	*J 562*	*—*	*287.20*	*940.96*
— 5	*—*	*—*	*X5*	*J 87AJ*	*—*	*287.20*	*1,228.16*
— 6	*—*	*—*	*X6*	*J 4250*	*—*	*217.20*	*1,445.36*
— 7 (8 months)	*—*	*—*	*X7*	*J 6365*	*—*	*144.80*	*1,590.16*
Carried to P & L	*—*	*—*	*—*	*J 4010*	*Dr.*	*1,590.16*	*0*

PLANT-RECORD-UNIT FORM (reverse)

ducted; a *rule* or set of rules that guide and govern action; a collection of stated or implied intentions of an organization. "Top" policy in a business enterprise refers to decisions originating as directives from the board of directors, the executive committee of the board, or the president and other principal officers; or it may refer to general principles of conducting business on the basis of which lesser policies, sometimes decisions of subordinate management, and administrative practices are devised and put into channels of control over day-to-day operations. The testing and comparison of an intention or decision with actual performance and the determination of the degree of consistency between the two are functions of both *internal* and *external auditors*. The distinction between policy and *administration(1)*, or policy and *operation(1)*, is never entirely clear, although elaborate attempts have been made in a number of large business corporations to draw a rigorous line between them so that the fields of activity of the board of directors, top administrators, and other executives within the organization are cleanly separated and overlap as little as possible. See *public interest; administration; corporate action; administrative action; decision.*

policy depreciation See *depreciation method.*

pooling of interests A consolidation or merger in which each beneficial interest continues in a new or modified organization with its book value and relative interest in paid-in capital and earned surplus substantially unchanged. See *merger; consolidation; acquired surplus.* Since the elements of a purchase and sale are absent, no new costs are established, as is often the case when a *business combination* is brought about by a purchase of the net assets of one company by another.

population (statistics) = *universe.*

position = *financial condition.*

position bookkeeping The procedure involved in keeping a self-balancing section within a double-entry system that indicates the position, long or short, in foreign currency, or in a commodity or security market. It shows, on the one hand, the purchases and sales, usually "futures," in each currency, commodity, or security, and, on the other hand, the obligations to pay to—or the rights to receive from—individual creditors or debtors corresponding amounts of domestic currency.

positive confirmation See *confirmation.*

post To transfer to a ledger the account changes indicated by the record of transactions appearing in journals or other posting mediums. See *enter.*

postaudit An *audit* at some point after the occurrence of a *transaction* or group of transactions. Audits by public accountants are sometimes so called. The term may also be applied to an examination made by an *internal auditor,* in contrast to *preaudit* or *voucher audit.*

postclosing balance sheet A balance sheet the details of which are supported by the open balances of the general-ledger accounts at the end of a fiscal year, after year-end and audit adjustments have been recorded and revenue and expense (nominal) accounts have been closed out.

postclosing trial balance The trial balance of a general ledger at the end of a fiscal period after eliminating the period's revenue and expense or *nominal* accounts. See *balance-sheet account; trial balance.*

postdate To affix a date following the date a document is written or executed: a postdated check cannot be cashed or deposited until the date appearing on its face. See *antedate.*

posting 1. The bookkeeping process of transferring dollar amounts and their accompanying *legends* from a document or book of original entry to a ledger. See *entry.*

2. An item in a ledger; an amount posted.

posting medium 1. A *book of original entry;* a *journal.*

2. A voucher, invoice, or other document, or an intermediate summary from which a posting may be made.

postulate Any of a series of *axioms* or *assumptions* constituting the supposed basis of a system of thought or an organized field of endeavor. The truth of a postulate, like that of other assumptions, is taken for granted as something generally admitted as self-evident, or as being common to other fields, and thus serving as a point of departure in a specialized field. Postulates are chosen for their convenience and fruitfulness in organizing and promoting inquiry or useful action; within the same field, the postulates of one school may differ from those of another, and they may be expected to change as activities within the field are modified, and as the *public interest* in the field alters its views concerning the value of the field to society. Postulates may also have their origins at one or more of the several stages of a process; thus, some may be concerned with moral values, while others may be chosen from among the alternatives present in established customs. See *axiom; principle.*

postwar reserve A reserve created during the period of World War II by many corporations out of retained profits, provisions for which were often deducted on income statements as quasi "costs." In some instances, the provisions were based on estimates of costs to convert buildings, machinery, and production lines back to peacetime uses; in other cases, the provisions were round sums unsupported by specific plans for their ultimate use. Much confusion was caused by the resulting indeterminate character of net income. After several years of indecision by accountants, first condoning such provisions as expense provided they had been based on "reasonable" estimates of reconversion costs and finally ending with a general condemnation of such reserves because of the universal failure of postwar rehabilitation to match the estimated costs of earlier years, the practice was discontinued and the reserve balances were returned to earned surplus, in most cases without a full or even any matching of costs against them. Among the reasons contributing to the creation of these reserves were (a) the conviction that under the theory of revenue-and-expense "matching," war earnings should pay for both conversion and reconversion costs, peacetime prices presumably containing no allowance for plant reconditioning; (b) the belief that there would be substantial operating losses during a period of postwar adjustment and that there was a need for a store of profits against any such eventuality; (c) the desire to make a prima-facie showing to price and renegotiation boards that the hazards of the road ahead warranted the retention of what otherwise might appear to be unjustifiable profits; (d) the fear of the taxation of "unemployed" retained profits; (e) the fear of demands from stockholders for distributions that it might be more prudent to retain; and (f) the fear that unearmarked windfalls remaining from war business might be used as an argument or spur in a demand for higher wages. The purpose and effect were largely transparent and the device failed to accomplish any of these purposes. See *reserve for contingencies.*

power of attorney An instrument authorizing one person to act as agent for another, either generally or for some specified purpose.

practical capacity Utilized *plant capacity*: the ratio obtained by dividing anticipated (e.g., budgeted) or actual (after-the-fact) production units by the maximum (theoretical) production units that the plant would be capable of yielding under a 24-hour, 365-day schedule. When applied to *fixed production* (*overhead*) *costs* the ratio yields the portion ascribable to production. Reduced by allowances for nonutilization arising from a single-shift operation and for customary shutdowns or decreased-production periods due to vacations, holidays, inventory-taking, cleanup, setup time, and seasonal preparations for new models, the theoretical production is reduced to an attainable level.

practice set A comprehensive problem designed to familiarize students of bookkeeping and accounting with realistic details of transactions, journals, ledgers, adjustments, and financial statements.

preacquisition profits Retained earnings of a corporation prior to the existence of *control* by another corporation. See *consolidated surplus.*

preaudit The examination of (a) creditors' invoices, payrolls, claims, and proposed reimbursements before payment (voucher audit), or (b) sales transactions at or before delivery; also known as *administrative audit.* Responsibility for preaudit rests on the controller of an enterprise; the frequent testing of the adequacy of preaudit procedures and the effectiveness of their application is a feature of the work of the internal auditor. Among activities normally regarded as preaudit functions are: (for costs) the review of contracts before their approval; comparisons of details of invoices or other claims with such contracts, or with purchase orders and other original authorizations; the determination that goods or services of the kind and amount ordered have been received, adequately inspected for quality and quantity, and placed in stock; the verification of price, extensions, additions, returns, and discounts; an inquiry into the authenticity of signatures indicating receipt and approval; (for revenues) review and confirmation of customer's order; independent inspection and delivery; tie-in with shipping documents; delivery receipts from customers; (on cash sales) comparison of sales tickets with cash received.

precision 1. Degree of refinement; relative absence of error: the smaller the error, the greater the degree of precision.
2. The closeness with which a measurement agrees with a related set of measurements of the same kind. Thus, the precision of a set of measurements may be said to be inversely related to their *standard error*. See *accuracy; replication.*
3. (statistics) The magnitude of the deviation of any sample value or function of sample values from the population parameter which is being estimated. See *standard deviation.*

preclosing trial balance A *trial balance* prepared before giving effect to final *adjusting* and *closing* entries.

predate = *antedate.*

predecessor company A business entity the net assets and operations of which have been taken over by one or several other entities. The successor or successors may be one or more newly formed companies or the party or parties to a business combination.

predetermined cost A cost ascertained in advance of the operation for which it is incurred.

predicted cost = *standard cost.*

pre-emptive right The privilege accorded an existing stockholder under the common law to subscribe for his prorata share of any new capital stock the corporation is about to issue. See *right.* Under the laws of many states, the privilege has been limited and may be eliminated by provision in the articles of incorporation or bylaws, or waived by an agreement with stockholders and reflected in each stock certificate.

preferred capital stock The class of stock which has a claim prior to common stockholders upon the earnings of a corporation, and often also upon the assets in the event of liquidation.

preferred creditor A person whose claim against another, particularly an insolvent or bankrupt, takes precedence over the claims of other creditors. Mechanics' liens, compensation of employees, and state and Federal taxes are examples.
pl. The class of creditors ranking highest among claims of creditors generally. See *statement of affairs.*

preferred(-stock) dividend A dividend to holders of preferred stock, usually at a fixed rate per quarter expressed in a percentage or in dollars per share.

preferred value (statistical quality control) See *basic dimension.*

preliminary audit (auditing) 1. Field work undertaken by an auditor before the close of a period under review, often consisting of a review or testing of internal controls, records, and individual transactions, the purpose being to expedite the completion of his report after the period has ended. A preliminary audit differs from a periodic audit in that it usually involves no report and is a part of a regular annual audit.
2. In an initial engagement, the investigation of the business and its accounting system and operating methods preceding the determination of the scope of the audit procedures to be employed.

preliminary balance sheet = *tentative balance sheet.*

premium 1. The amount by which the price of a security or other asset exceeds its nominal, face, par, quoted, or market value.
2. The amount paid periodically to an insurer or his agent by one insured. See *insurance premium.*
3. The price paid for an option or contract.
4. An amount paid over and above the usual wage, for superior workmanship, loyal service, and so forth.

premium on capital stock The amount in excess of par or stated value received by an issuing corporation for its capital stock; *paid-in surplus.*

prepaid asset = *prepaid expense.*

prepaid expense 1. An expenditure, often

recurrent, for future benefits: a type of *deferred charge*. Examples: prepaid rent, taxes, royalties, commissions; unexpired insurance premiums; stationery and office supplies. Such items are classifiable as current assets and constitute a part of working capital; they are charged to future operations on the basis of measurable benefits or on a time or *period-charge* basis. Other types of deferred charges are concluded transactions that are to be applied more or less arbitrarily to the operations of one or more succeeding periods; in contrast, *accrued expense*, a liability, is made up of items charged to past operations because of benefits already received.
2. sometimes *pl.* The title of a balance-sheet item representing the portion of such outlays for benefits carried into the next accounting period or periods. See *balance sheet*.

prepaid income = *deferred revenue*.

prepaid interest The excess of the face value of a loan over the proceeds of the loan, often classified as a *prepaid expense*. The name is misleading since the amount is to be a future payment. A more logical but seldom followed practice would be to deduct it from the face value of the liability.

prepay To pay for a service *before* its receipt or enjoyment; such prepayment, as for insurance or rent, reflecting long-established commercial practices, contrasts with *accrue* (or the *recognition* of the receipt or enjoyment of other types of services paid for *after* their receipt or enjoyment). See *deferred charge*.

preproduction costs *Makeready time* and expense required to initiate production on particular orders.

present value (or **worth**) The price a buyer is willing to pay for one or a series of future benefits, the term generally being associated with a formal computation of the estimated worth in the future of such benefits from which a *discount(1)* or compensation for waiting is deducted.

present value of 1 The present sum which, if compounded at a given rate of interest over a given period of time, will yield 1; the discounted value of 1; the reciprocal of the compound amount of 1.

Thus, the sum of $78.85, compounded at 2 percent per period, will amount to $100.00 at the end of 12 periods. The present value of 1 may be formulated by expressing it in terms of the *compound amount of 1*. In both cases the process of compounding is the same; their difference lies in the fact that the endproduct of the compound amount of 1 is unknown and the initial amount known, whereas the endproduct of the other is known and its initial amount or the present value of 1 unknown. Hence, if the compound amount of 1 is s and the present value of 1 is p, then $1 : s :: p : 1$, and $p = 1/s$ or $1/(1 + i)^n$.

Illustrative values for p appear on pp. 334–335.

present value of 1 per period The deposit necessary to yield 1 at the end of each of a stated number of succeeding periods, the declining balance remaining on deposit being compounded at an agreed rate of interest per period.

Each payment of 1 may be regarded as a compounded portion of the original deposit, and the latter as the sum total of a series of present values of 1. Thus, if a deposit is made now to cover a series of six annual payments of $1,000 commencing one year hence, and if interest is allowed at 3 percent, compounded annually, the present value of each of the six payments may be determined from tables giving the *present value of 1* as follows:

Number of Payment	Interest Periods	Formula ($i = 0.03$)	Present Value (see p.)
1	1	$1/(1 + i)$	$ 970.87
2	2	$1/(1 + i)^2$	942.60
3	3	$1/(1 + i)^3$	915.14
4	4	$1/(1 + i)^4$	888.49
5	5	$1/(1 + i)^5$	862.61
6	6	$1/(1 + i)^6$	837.48
Present deposit required			$5,417.19

If n be the number of periods, i the rate of interest, and p_1 the sought-for present value of 1 per period, the table on page 331 may be formulated as follows (see formula for present value of 1):

$$p_1 = \frac{1}{(1+i)^{n-5}} + \frac{1}{(1+i)^{n-4}} + \frac{1}{(1+i)^{n-3}} + \frac{1}{(1+i)^{n-2}} + \frac{1}{(1+i)^{n-1}} + \frac{1}{(1+i)^{n}}; \quad (1)$$

multiplying by $(1 + i)$,

$$p_1(1+i) = 1 + \frac{1}{(1+i)^{n-5}} + \frac{1}{(1+i)^{n-4}} + \frac{1}{(1+i)^{n-3}} + \frac{1}{(1+i)^{n-2}} + \frac{1}{(1+i)^{n-1}}; \quad (2)$$

subtracting (1) from (2),

$$p_1(1+i) - p_1 = 1 - \frac{1}{(1+i)^{n}}; \quad (3)$$

simplifying, and dividing by i,

$$p_1 = \frac{(1+i)^n - 1}{i(1+i)^n}. \quad (4)$$

The relation between the *amount of 1 per period* and the *present value of 1 per period* lies in the fact that both involve the fixed periodic sum of 1, but that in the first the amount sought is the accumulation resulting from a series of deposits of 1, while in the second the amount sought is the present sum that will make possible a series of payments of 1. The second is thus the present value of the endproduct of the first, and the formula for p_1 may be derived by applying the present-value formula to that of the amount of 1 per period:

$$p_1 = \frac{(1+i)^n - 1}{i} \times \frac{1}{(1+i)^n} = \frac{(1+i)^n - 1}{i(1+i)^n}.$$

Illustrative values will be found on pp. 336–337.

pretax accounting income Income reported for accounting purposes before deduction for income tax. See APBO 11, p. 159 (1967).

price 1. The money consideration asked for or offered in exchange for a specified unit of a good or service; in a barter transaction, the ratio at which a unit of any good or service exchanges for a unit of another good or service is determined by the relation of their prices. Prices are classified in a variety of ways: (a) by their trend over a period of time; see *normal price;* (b) by type of market; see *competitive price; oligopoly and oligopsony prices;* (c) by the freedom of individual business concerns to react to economic forces; see *free price; administered price;* (d) by commercial practices in various industries; see *list price; trade price; cash price; spot price; fixed resale price; FOB price; FAS price; C&F price; CIF price; upset price; contract price; transfer price;* and (e) by their relation to the value of money in exchange for the same goods during different periods of time, independent of the relation to the demand and supply of the commodity. See *current price; real price.*

2. As frequently employed in accounting: (a) the amount received or receivable from a sale; (b) the amount paid or payable for a good or service, in either case less discounts (now often excluding cash discounts); or (c) the amount received in exchange for the issuer's securities (stocks, bonds, and the like).

price contract 1. A contract between buyer and seller in which a seller agrees to supply a specified item to a buyer at a stated price or under a price formula, with no minimum quantity specified, but usually with a proviso that the buyer will purchase from the seller all his required needs up to a specified maximum quantity.

2. Hence, any contract between buyer and seller, customarily not enforced by the seller should the buyer fail to call for delivery during the contract period. The purpose of such a contract is to protect the buyer by assuring him of a source of supply at a price he is likely to be willing to pay; it can be the product of either a buyers' or a sellers' market.

price discrimination The charge by a seller of varying prices under similar conditions of sale. If the effect is to lessen competition or to tend to create a monopoly, Federal law may have been violated. When a commodity is sold at a competitive delivered price to customers located nearer competing sellers, it is often necessary that the seller absorb the excess freight. This freight absorption results in a lower price (netback or mill-net) than that received on sales made to nearby customers on which less or no freight is incurred. If this geographical price discrimination by an individual seller results from the effort to meet competition in good faith, it is not generally held to be illegal; but if identical prices are charged by several or all sellers, the presumption of illegality may be raised, notwithstanding the absence of any explicit agreement among sellers. Some latitude is recognized in the exercise of discretion by sellers in charging different prices in consideration of volume sales, terms of payment, and class of customer. Such price differentials can be justified on grounds of lower costs of sales and economic necessity.

price index See *index number*.

price leader An item of merchandise priced abnormally low for the purpose of attracting customers—a device employed by retail stores to increase sales of other products, and by manufacturers and distributors to attract attention to their brand and increase sales of other items. The practice runs some risk of violating Federal law. Less diversified competitors are particularly vulnerable to such competition, their survival being dependent on a normal margin on the price-leader item.

price leadership The practice followed by rival sellers of recognizing and adopting the price established by one or more other members of the industry. Price leadership is usually provided by the largest or dominant firm. A firm may elect to accept the price of a competitor as its own selling price rather than determine its selling price on the basis of other considerations. If the acceptance of a competitor's price is an independently exercised judgment, the risk of violating antitrust acts is probably minimized, since the prerequisites of a conspiracy—a meeting of the minds for the achievement of a uniform price—are lacking. Although adherence to price-leadership practices may be independently decided by individual firms, it may well be dictated by fear of consequences resulting from unilateral price action as well as by anticipated benefits. Industries having only a few large sellers are likely to engage in this practice. As long as the major firms comply, marginal small firms who do not comply are tolerated.

The effect of this practice is the establishment of industry-wide prices high enough to permit the high-cost firms of the industry to survive. If the dominant firm is the high-cost producer, its prices automatically establish a profitable price for the passive firms. If the dominant firm is a low-cost producer, the price established must be high enough to provide a comfortable margin for the high-cost firms.

Price leadership relegates competition to nonprice elements (see *nonprice competition*), may well distort the distribution of national income, dislocates capital formation, and discourages the expansion of efficient firms.

price level A term indicating the money amount of commodities and services purchased in a given period, usually in comparison with some preceding period; also, a term descriptive of the general or average price of a firm's sales, as compared with the prices of its trade or industry. The price at which a product is sold ordinarily varies by class of customer, terms of payment, and volume of purchases. The price level of the firm is, therefore, a computed or composite price which can usually be predicted on the basis of past experience. A distinction should be drawn between net and gross or list prices. The difference is substantial in the case of manufacturers who quote retail list prices that include dis-

n	½%	1%	1½%	2%	2½%	3%
1	.9950 249	.9900 990	.9852 217	.9803 922	.9756 098	.9708 738
2	.9900 745	.9802 960	.9706 617	.9611 688	.9518 144	.9425 959
3	.9851 488	.9705 901	.9563 170	.9423 223	.9285 994	.9151 417
4	.9802 475	.9609 803	.9421 842	.9238 454	.9059 506	.8884 870
5	.9753 707	.9514 657	.9282 603	.9057 308	.8838 543	.8626 088
6	.9705 181	.9420 452	.9145 422	.8879 714	.8622 969	.8374 843
7	.9656 896	.9327 181	.9010 268	.8705 602	.8412 652	.8130 915
8	.9608 852	.9234 832	.8877 111	.8534 904	.8207 466	.7894 092
9	.9561 047	.9143 398	.8745 922	.8367 553	.8007 284	.7664 167
10	.9513 479	.9052 870	.8616 672	.8203 483	.7811 984	.7440 939
11	.9466 149	.8963 237	.8489 332	.8042 630	.7621 448	.7224 213
12	.9419 053	.8874 492	.8363 874	.7884 932	.7435 559	.7013 799
13	.9372 192	.8786 626	.8240 270	.7730 325	.7254 204	.6809 513
14	.9325 565	.8699 630	.8118 493	.7578 750	.7077 272	.6611 178
15	.9279 169	.8613 495	.7998 515	.7430 147	.6904 656	.6418 619
16	.9233 004	.8528 213	.7880 310	.7284 458	.6736 249	.6231 669
17	.9187 068	.8443 775	.7763 853	.7141 626	.6571 951	.6050 164
18	.9141 362	.8360 173	.7649 116	.7001 594	.6411 659	.5873 946
19	.9095 882	.8277 399	.7536 075	.6864 308	.6255 277	.5702 860
20	.9050 629	.8195 445	.7424 704	.6729 713	.6102 709	.5536 758
21	.9005 601	.8114 302	.7314 979	.6597 758	.5953 863	.5375 493
22	.8960 797	.8033 962	.7206 876	.6468 390	.5808 647	.5218 925
23	.8916 216	.7954 418	.7100 371	.6341 559	.5666 972	.5066 917
24	.8871 857	.7875 661	.6995 439	.6217 215	.5528 754	.4919 337
25	.8827 718	.7797 684	.6892 058	.6095 309	.5393 906	.4776 056
26	.8783 799	.7720 480	.6790 205	.5975 793	.5262 347	.4636 947
27	.8740 099	.7644 039	.6689 857	.5858 620	.5133 997	.4501 891
28	.8696 616	.7568 356	.6590 992	.5743 746	.5008 778	.4370 768
29	.8653 349	.7493 421	.6493 589	.5631 123	.4886 613	.4243 464
30	.8610 297	.7419 229	.6397 624	.5520 709	.4767 427	.4119 868
35	.8398 231	.7059 142	.5938 661	.5000 276	.4213 711	.3553 834
40	.8191 389	.6716 531	.5512 623	.4528 904	.3724 306	.3065 568
45	.7989 640	.6390 549	.5117 149	.4101 968	.3291 744	.2644 386
50	.7792 861	.6080 388	.4750 047	.3715 279	.2909 422	.2281 071
55	.7600 928	.5785 281	.4409 280	.3365 042	.2571 505	.1967 672
60	.7413 722	.5504 496	.4092 960	.3047 823	.2272 836	.1697 331
65	.7231 127	.5237 339	.3799 332	.2760 507	.2008 856	.1464 133
70	.7053 029	.4983 149	.3526 769	.2500 276	.1775 536	.1262 974
75	.6879 318	.4741 295	.3273 760	.2264 577	.1569 315	.1089 452
80	.6709 885	.4511 179	.3038 901	.2051 097	.1387 046	.0939 771
85	.6544 625	.4292 232	.2820 892	.1857 742	.1225 946	.0810 655
90	.6383 435	.4083 912	.2618 522	.1682 614	.1083 558	.0699 278
95	.6226 215	.3885 702	.2430 670	.1523 995	.0957 707	.0603 203
100	.6072 868	.3697 112	.2256 294	.1380 330	.0846 474	.0520 328

$3\frac{1}{2}\%$	4%	$4\frac{1}{2}\%$	5%	$5\frac{1}{2}\%$	6%
.9661 836	.9615 385	.9569 378	.9523 810	.9478 673	.9433 962
.9335 107	.9245 562	.9157 300	.9070 295	.8984 524	.8899 964
.9019 427	.8889 964	.8762 966	.8638 376	.8516 137	.8396 193
.8714 422	.8548 042	.8385 613	.8227 025	.8072 167	.7920 937
.8419 732	.8219 271	.8024 510	.7835 262	.7651 344	.7472 582
.8135 006	.7903 145	.7678 957	.7462 154	.7252 458	.7049 605
.7859 910	.7599 178	.7348 285	.7106 813	.6874 368	.6650 571
.7594 116	.7306 902	.7031 851	.6768 394	.6515 989	.6274 124
.7337 310	.7025 867	.6729 044	.6446 089	.6176 293	.5918 985
.7089 188	.6755 642	.6439 277	.6139 133	.5854 306	.5583 948
.6849 457	.6495 809	.6161 987	.5846 793	.5549 105	.5267 875
.6617 833	.6245 970	.5896 639	.5568 374	.5259 815	.4969 694
.6394 042	.6005 741	.5642 716	.5303 214	.4985 607	.4688 390
.6177 818	.5774 751	.5399 729	.5050 680	.4725 694	.4423 010
.5968 906	.5552 645	.5167 204	.4810 171	.4479 330	.4172 651
.5767 059	.5339 082	.4944 693	.4581 115	.4245 811	.3936 463
.5572 038	.5133 732	.4731 764	.4362 967	.4024 465	.3713 644
.5383 611	.4936 281	.4528 004	.4155 207	.3814 659	.3503 438
.5201 557	.4746 424	.4333 018	.3957 340	.3615 791	.3305 130
.5025 659	.4563 869	.4146 429	.3768 895	.3427 290	.3118 047
.4855 709	.4388 336	.3967 874	.3589 424	.3248 616	.2941 554
.4691 506	.4219 554	.3797 009	.3418 499	.3079 257	.2775 051
.4532 856	.4057 263	.3633 501	.3255 713	.2918 727	.2617 973
.4379 571	.3901 215	.3477 035	.3100 679	.2766 566	.2469 785
.4231 470	.3751 168	.3327 306	.2953 028	.2622 337	.2329 986
.4088 377	.3606 892	.3184 025	.2812 407	.2485 628	.2198 100
.3950 122	.3468 166	.3046 914	.2678 483	.2356 045	.2073 680
.3816 543	.3334 775	.2915 707	.2550 936	.2233 218	.1956 301
.3687 482	.3206 514	.2790 150	.2429 463	.2116 794	.1845 567
.3562 784	.3083 187	.2670 000	.2313 774	.2006 440	.1741 101
.2999 769	.2534 155	.2142 544	.1812 903	.1535 196	.1301 052
.2525 725	.2082 890	.1719 287	.1420 457	.1174 631	.0972 222
.2126 592	.1711 984	.1379 644	.1112 965	.0898 751	.0726 501
.1790 534	.1407 126	.1107 097	.0872 037	.0687 665	.0542 884
.1507 581	.1156 555	.0888 391	.0683 264	.0526 156	.0405 674
.1269 343	.0950 604	.0712 890	.0535 355	.0402 580	.0303 143
.1068 753	.0781 327	.0572 059	.0419 465	.0308 028	.0226 526
.0899 861	.0642 194	.0459 050	.0328 662	.0235 683	.0169 274
.0757 659	.0527 837	.0368 365	.0257 515	.0180 329	.0126 491
.0637 929	.0433 843	.0295 595	.0201 770	.0137 976	.0094 522
.0537 119	.0356 588	.0237 200	.0158 092	.0105 570	.0070 632
.0452 240	.0293 089	.0190 342	.0123 869	.0080 775	.0052 780
.0380 774	.0240 898	.0152 740	.0097 055	.0061 804	.0039 441
.0320 601	.0198 000	.0122 566	.0076 045	.0047 288	.0029 472

n	$\frac{1}{2}\%$	1%	$1\frac{1}{2}\%$	2%	$2\frac{1}{2}\%$	3%
1	.9950 249	.9900 990	.9852 217	.9803 922	.9756 098	.9708 738
2	1.9850 994	1.9703 951	1.9558 834	1.9415 609	1.9274 242	1.9134 697
3	2.9702 481	2.9409 852	2.9122.004	2.8838 833	2.8560 236	2.8286 114
4	3.9504 957	3.9019 656	3.8543 846	3.8077 287	3.7619 742	3.7170 984
5	4.9258 663	4.8534 312	4.7826 450	4.7134 595	4.6458 285	4.5797 072
6	5.8963 844	5.7954 765	5.6971 872	5.6014 309	5.5081 254	5.4171 914
7	6.8620 740	6.7281 945	6.5982 140	6.4719 911	6.3493 906	6.2302 830
8	7.8229 592	7.6516 778	7.4859 251	7.3254 814	7.1701 372	7.0196 922
9	8.7790 639	8.5660 176	8.3605 173	8.1622 367	7.9708 655	7.7861 089
10	9.7304 119	9.4713 045	9.2221 846	8.9825 850	8.7520 639	8.5302 028
11	10.6770 267	10.3676 282	10.0711 178	9.7868 480	9.5142 087	9.2526 241
12	11.6189 321	11.2550 775	10.9075 052	10.5753 412	10.2577 646	9.9540 040
13	12.5561 513	12.1337 401	11.7315 322	11.3483 737	10.9831 850	10.6349 553
14	13.4887 078	13.0037 030	12.5433 815	12.1062 488	11.6909 122	11.2960 731
15	14.4166 246	13.8650 525	13.3432 330	12.8492 635	12.3813 777	11.9379 351
16	15.3399 250	14.7178 738	14.1312 640	13.5777 093	13.0550 027	12.5611 020
17	16.2586 311	15.5622 513	14.9076 493	14.2918 719	13.7121 977	13.1661 185
18	17.1727 680	16.3982 686	15.6725 609	14.9920 313	14.3533 636	13.7535 131
19	18.0823 562	17.2260 085	16.4261 684	15.6784 620	14.9788 913	14.3237 991
20	18.9874 191	18.0455 530	17.1686 388	16.3514 333	15.5891 623	14.8774 749
21	19.8879 793	18.8569 831	17.9001 367	17.0112 092	16.1845 486	15.4150 241
22	20.7840 590	19.6603 793	18.6208 244	17.6580 482	16.7654 132	15.9369 166
23	21.6756 806	20.4558 211	19.3308 614	18.2922 041	17.3321 105	16.4436 084
24	22.5628 662	21.2433 873	20.0304 054	18.9139 256	17.8849 858	16.9355 421
25	23.4456 380	22.0231 557	20.7196 112	19.5234 565	18.4243 764	17.4131 477
26	24.3240 179	22.7952 037	21.3986 317	20.1210 358	18.9506 111	17.8768 424
27	25.1980 278	23.5596 076	22.0676 175	20.7068 978	19.4640 109	18.3270 315
28	26.0676 894	24.3164 432	22.7267 167	21.2812 724	19.9648 887	18.7641 082
29	26.9330 242	25.0657 853	23.3760 756	21.8443 847	20.4535 499	19.1884 546
30	27.7940 540	25.8077 082	24.0158 380	22.3964 556	20.9302 926	19.6004 413
35	32.0353 713	29.4085 801	27.0755 946	24.9986 193	23.1451 573	21.4872 201
40	36.1722 279	32.8346 861	29.9158 452	27.3554 792	25.1027 751	23.1147 720
45	40.2071 964	36.0945 084	32.5523 372	29.4901 599	26.8330 239	24.5187 125
50	44.1427 863	39.1961 175	34.9996 881	31.4236 059	28.3623 117	25.7297 640
55	47.9814 454	42.1471 922	37.2714 668	33.1747 875	29.7139 793	26.7744 276
60	51.7255 608	44.9550 384	39.3802 689	34.7608 867	30.9086 565	27.6755 637
65	55.3774 611	47.6266 078	41.3377 862	36.1974 655	31.9645 771	28.4528 915
70	58.9394 176	50.1685 143	43.1548 718	37.4986 193	32.8978 570	29.1234 214
75	62.4136 454	52.5870 512	44.8416 003	38.6771 143	33.7227 404	29.7018 263
80	65.8023 054	54.8882 061	46.4073 235	39.7445 136	34.4518 172	30.2007 634
85	69.1075 049	57.0776 760	47.8607 222	40.7112 900	35.0962 149	30.6311 510
90	72.3312 996	59.1608 815	49.2098 545	41.5869 292	35.6657 685	31.0024 071
95	75.4756 943	61.1429 800	50.4622 005	42.3800 225	36.1691 709	31.3226 559
100	78.5426 448	63.0288 788	51.6247 037	43.0983 516	36.6141 053	31.5989 053

PRESENT VALUE OF 1 PER PERIOD

3½%	4%	4½%	5%	5½%	6%
.9661 836	.9615 385	.9569 378	.9523 810	.9478 673	.9433 962
1.8996 943	1.8860 947	1.8726 678	1.8594 104	1.8463 197	1.8333 927
2.8016 370	2.7750 910	2.7489 644	2.7232 480	2.6979 334	2.6730 119
3.6730 792	3.6298 952	3.5875 257	3.5459 505	3.5051 501	3.4651 056
4.5150 524	4.4518 223	4.3899 767	4.3294 767	4.2702 845	4.2123 638
5.3285 530	5.2421 369	5.1578 725	5.0756 921	4.9955 303	4.9173 243
6.1145 440	6.0020 547	5.8927 009	5.7863 734	5.6829 671	5.5823 814
6.8739 555	6.7327 449	6.5958 861	6.4632 128	6.3345 660	6.2097 938
7.6076 865	7.4353 316	7.2687 905	7.1078 217	6.9521 952	6.8016 923
8.3166 053	8.1108 958	7.9127 182	7.7217 349	7.5376 258	7.3600 871
9.0015 510	8.7604 767	8.5289 169	8.3064 142	8.0925 363	7.8868 746
9.6633 343	9.3850 738	9.1185 808	8.8632 516	8.6185 178	8.3838 439
10.3027 385	9.9856 478	9.6828 524	9.3935 730	9.1170 785	8.8526 830
10.9205 203	10.5631 229	10.2228 253	9.8986 409	9.5896 479	9.2949 839
11.5174 109	11.1183 874	10.7395 457	10.3796 580	10.0375 809	9.7122 490
12.0941 168	11.6522 956	11.2340 150	10.8377 696	10.4621 620	10.1058 953
12 6513 206	12 1656 689	11.7071 914	11.2740 662	10.8646 086	10.4772 597
13.1896 817	12.6592 970	12.1599 918	11.6895 869	11.2460 745	10.8276 035
13.7098 374	13.1339 394	12.5932 936	12.0853 209	11.6076 535	11.1581 165
14.2124 033	13.5903 263	13.0079 365	12.4622 103	11.9503 825	11.4699 212
14.6979 742	14.0291 599	13.4047 239	12.8211 527	12.2752 441	11.7640 766
15.1671 248	14.4511 153	13.7844 248	13.1630 026	12.5831 697	12.0415 817
15.6204 105	14.8568 417	14.1477 749	13.4885 739	12.8750 424	12.3033 790
16.0583 676	15.2469 631	14.4954 784	13.7986 418	13.1516 990	12.5503 575
16.4815 146	15.6220 799	14.8282 090	14.0939 446	13.4139 327	12.7833 562
16.8903 523	15.9827 692	15.1466 114	14.3751 853	13.6624 954	13.0031 662
17.2853 645	16.3295 857	15.4513 028	14.6430 336	13.8980 999	13.2105 341
17.6670 188	16.6630 632	15.7428 735	14.8981 273	14.1214 217	13.4061 643
18.0357 670	16.9837 146	16.0218 885	15.1410 736	14.3331 012	13.5907 210
18.3920 454	17.2920 333	16.2888 885	15.3724 510	14.5337 452	13.7648 312
20.0006 611	18.6646 132	17.4610 124	16.3741 943	15.3905 522	14.4982 464
21.3550 723	19.7927 739	18.4015 844	17.1590 864	16.0461 247	15.0462 969
22.4954 503	20.7200 397	19.1563 474	17.7740 698	16.5477 257	15.4558 321
23.4556 179	21.4821 846	19.7620 078	18.2559 255	16.9315 179	15.7618 606
24.2640 532	22.1086 122	20.2480 206	18.6334 720	17.2251 705	15.9905 430
24.9447 341	22.6234 900	20.6380 220	18.9292 895	17.4498 542	16.1614 277
25.5178 492	23.0466 820	20.9509 791	19.1610 703	17.6217 674	16.2891 227
26.0003 966	23.3945 150	21.2021 119	19.3426 766	17.7533 041	16.3845 439
26.4066 887	23.6804 083	21.4036 336	19.4849 700	17.8539 473	16.4558 481
26.7487 757	23.9153 918	21.5653 449	19.5964 605	17.9309 529	16.5091 308
27.0368 037	24.1085 312	21.6951 103	19.6838 162	17.9898 725	16.5489 467
27.2793 156	24.2672 776	21.7992 407	19.7522 617	18.0349 540	16.5786 994
27.4835 042	24.3977 556	21.8828 003	19.8058 906	18.0694 473	16.6009 324
27.6554 254	24.5049 990	21.9498 527	19.8479 102	18.0958 394	16.6175 462

counts to distributors and retailers, a practice commonly employed by producers of branded products for the purpose of inducing consumers, for example, to associate a published price level with the product.

The phrase "price-level changes" usually has reference to prospective replacement costs of fixed assets at a level higher than that prevailing at some previous point of time. It has been urged by some accountants that financial statements should embody present or future rather than past fixed-asset costs.

price maintenance The prescription by a manufacturer or wholesaler of the minimum resale price of his product.

As applied to the sale of securities to the public, prices are maintained by underwriters and dealers during the initial distribution period by purchasing the security when offered by sellers below the fixed price. See *stabilization*.

In the commodity field, price maintenance is a common practice of manufacturers of branded products. Under the Miller–Tydings Fair Trade Act (1937), not only did the manufacturer maintain a fixed sales price level to his distributors, but he also fixed the price at which distributors and retailers could sell to consumers. This result was achieved by contractual agreement between the manufacturer or distributor and the reseller. Following rejection by the courts of the Miller–Tydings Act and the fair-trade acts of nearly all the states—which had also permitted agreements between the manufacturer or distributor and the reseller prescribing minimum resale prices of a commodity bearing the label, trademark, brand, or name of the manufacturer or distributor—many such agreements have been replaced by the adoption of an almost equally effective producer's "suggested" consumer price.

Protected by the Miller–Tydings Act, manufacturers and distributors of all but bulk or fungible commodities had prevented price competition among resellers of their products. This legal protection had shifted the price-making function from the market place to the manufacturer, where it may still be found.

price margin = *gross margin* (*1*).

price system Any comprehensive scheme of determining selling price to the trade, particularly that to which the leaders within an industry subscribe. See *price; competitive price*.

During the 19th century, rapidly expanding American industry, in an attempt to strengthen the security of investments in corporate enterprise and to escape the rigors of competition, frequently entered into agreements having both the object and effect of maintaining or increasing prices. Before American antitrust policy had crystallized, pooling arrangements, openly concluded price-fixing agreements, market sharing, and the like were common business practices. In more recent years, business rivals, while trying to avoid arrangements in conflict with antitrust statutes, have sometimes sought the security of concerted behavior by the employment of newer devices, such as *zone* and *basing-point* pricing systems.

Although the existence of these systems can be demonstrated, the methods by which they evolve are not as easily ascertained. The antitrust division of the U. S. Department of Justice and the Federal Trade Commission are constantly combing industry practices for evidence of implied or explicit agreements to fix uniform prices. Economists search for fundamental reasons: the institutional school tends to favor the explanation that whenever two or several large firms in an industry control a major share of total production and have their production facilities dispersed but capable of supplying common markets, the prerequisites exist to support one or the other type of price-fixing system. The classical school of economic thought would add a further explanation that such systems are likely to develop where (a) the industry's product is standardized, (b) fixed costs represent a large part of total costs, (c) average out-of-pocket costs tend to remain constant over a wide range of output, (d) freight charges represent a substantial part of delivered prices, (e) demand is relatively unresponsive to price changes, or (f) surplus capacity exists. In such industries, unrestrained competition tends to drive prices below average costs, and if long continued would force readjustments which, however desirable from the consumer's point of view, would be costly to those upon whom the impact immediately falls. Zone and basing-point pricing systems offer to business rivals a relatively simple means of avoiding such consequences.

Under zone systems, all sellers quote a uniform delivered price for all buyers within a zone, regardless of where the shipment originates. There may be one or several zones. As a general rule, for products of high value that may be transported at a relatively low cost, the number of zones is likely to be fewer than when freight costs make up a relatively high percentage of the product price.

Under the basing-point system, each firm quotes identical delivered prices for each customer at a given delivery point, regardless of the origin of shipments. A basing-point system differs from a zone system in that the delivered price to each customer depends upon his distance from the basing point. A basing-point price is determined by formula: the sum of the FOB basing-point price plus freight to destination. The single basing-point, such as the famous "Pittsburgh-plus" system, has largely given way to so-called multiple systems where numerous points or price bases have been established. This extension from single to multiple basing points finds its furthest development in so-called "plenary" systems in which base points are established at every mill. Although the essential character of a basing system does not depend upon the number of price bases, it does affect the degree of price discrimination in practice. The fewer the basing points relative to the number of mills, the greater the possible degree of price discrimination or distortion; given levels of prices at the basing points result in higher delivered prices to those customers located near the mills that are not basing points. Different FOB prices may be used at various points in a multiple basing-point system. When this is done, each seller nevertheless quotes identical delivered prices to any particular point, the delivered price being equal to the lowest combined base price and freight to the point of delivery. Under economic conditions in which a seller's market prevails, sellers are not likely to absorb freight and tend either to charge the full freight or to forego sales to more distant markets.

Both zone and basing-point systems result in geographical price discrimination as measured by the difference in *millnet* prices realized by sellers. Since a zone system results in uniform prices for each zone, the millnet amount will vary depending on the amount of freight. On sales to customers located near a plant, the seller will realize a higher millnet price than on sales to more distant customers.

A basing-point system illustrates even more vividly geographical price discrimination, particularly when a buyers' market prevails. Customarily, all supplies will quote the same delivered price: the sum of the governing FOB basing-point price plus rail freight to destination, regardless of the location of the shipping point or the mode of transportation. Where the shipping point is closer to the destination than the basing point, or where cheaper methods of transportation are used than rail freight, "phantom freight" is added to maintain the uniform delivered price. Conversely, the added costs of longer hauls or costlier methods of transportation are absorbed by the supplier. As a result, millnet prices range widely. Customers located near a nonbase mill, who could otherwise benefit from lower-cost transportation, are not permitted the benefit of these advantages.

If such systems are held to be undesirable, the objections should rest as heavily upon the initial fixing of basing-point and zone prices as upon the discrimination resulting from its mechanical operation. This point has not always been emphasized, more critical attention having been focused on the relative position of buyers who are subject to the same basing-point system.

Industry pricing systems often have the effect of maintaining higher price levels than would prevail if each supplier arrived at prices independently, based on considerations of maximizing returns by full utilization of capacity, and by expanding sales—if necessary, by price competition. The general effect of such industry pricing systems is to restrict or eliminate price competition, replacing it by so-called quality competition, sales-expansion techniques, concentrated advertising campaigns, featuring attempts to "drive home" names and slogans, decorative packaging, and other methods of overcoming customer price resistance. Critics argue that these price systems protect high-cost inefficient operation and stifle the expansion of low-cost operation. They contend that serious social consequences flow from the regularization and systematization of prices by industry; not only may society be saddled with the necessity of carrying high-cost or inefficient producers and be denied the full benefits of technical progress, but also repercussions may be felt in industries that utilize goods so priced and passed on with still further distorted prices to other industrial tiers—and so on in greatly compounded form to the final consumer. See *administered price.*

price variance A *variance* resulting from a change in the price of materials or labor.

pricing policy The body of principles followed over a period of time by the management of a business enterprise in fixing the selling price of its product or service; contrasts with *ad-hoc* price-making, characteristic of traders, which is likely to lack continuity with past or future price actions. The management of manufacturing, processing, distributing, and service firms must deal with complex factors relating to price decisions, such as the maintenance of a general cost-price relationship; the continuance of the firm's position in the industry; the desire for expansion; the percentage of plant capacity utilized; the consequences of meeting, beating, or changing, at higher or lower levels, competitors' prices; consumers' ability or willingness to employ substitutes or to forgo purchases; compliance with fair-trade laws, FTC regulations, and antitrust laws; the development of better labor relations; and the creation of public goodwill. Although many of these factors are closely related, they may be arrayed in the order of importance and given such varying weights as are warranted by the position and structure of the firm. Once established, a pricing policy makes possible the fixing of firm prices, either in specific amounts or by formula. Basing-point pricing, price leadership, and zone pricing are familiar examples.

From the viewpoint of internal controls, the fixing of a pricing mechanism eliminates most of the judgment factor in determining individual sales prices. In large organizations engaged in far-flung operations, it is regarded as being of paramount importance to centralize the discretion involved in price-making by adopting a well-rounded, defensible, consistent price policy.

In integrated systems of two or more separate but affiliated corporate entities with one entity buying from or selling to another, the parent company is likely to determine the pricing policy governing intercompany sales or transfers. Sales to outside consumers may consist of semi-finished products as well as the finished product of the company. Intercompany transactions usually lack arm's-length bargaining and the influence of market forces. Under these conditions, the parent company performs the price-making function, and makes the optimum distribution of the gross income (from outside sales) among the component corporate entities, in accordance with the open-market price, the minimizing of the total tax burden, the most favorable division of retained earnings, or other factors.

primary account Any account to which *external transactions* are first carried. Some or all of the contents of certain primary accounts, upon clearer identification or determination of activities benefited, are transferred to *secondary accounts.* Examples: an account with a depositary (not transferable); a sales account (ultimately carried to profit and loss); a dividend account (transferred to retained earnings); a *clearing* account (closed out as items are identified); see *terminal account.*

primary classification The initial classification given to an *external transaction;* a component element of a *primary account;* see *secondary classification; basic expenditure.*

primary liability (negotiable instruments) The liability of the person on whom rests the absolute requirement to pay a negotiable instrument. The maker of a promissory note or the drawer of an unaccepted check or draft who assigns it, and the acceptor of an accepted draft, are primarily liable for the obligations upon which their signatures appear. All other parties to such obligations have a *secondary* liability.

prime cost The cost of direct materials and direct labor entering into the manufacture of a product; direct cost, excluding direct (and indirect) overhead.

primitive An undefined term or concept used in the construction of *axioms, postulates,* and *definitions,* serving as a starting point in an effort to avoid circular reasoning. Thus, the primitive, undefined terms in the axiom system of mathematics constructed by Peano are: zero, number, and successor. Primitive terms in the axiom system of Newton are force, mass, and acceleration; in Woodger's formulation of the axioms of biology, they are cell, part of, and precedence in time. In accounting, the notion of *transaction* constitutes one such primitive, as also does the notion of *claim, property, ownership,* and *continuity.* A term undefined in one system may be defined in another. See *axiom.*

principal 1. A sum on which interest accrues; capital, as distinguished from income.

2. The original amount of an estate or fund together with accretions which may, but usually do not, include income; capital sum.

3. A natural or legal person who authorizes another to represent him in some business transaction.

4. A partner or other person in a professional accounting firm authorized to deal with clients on major problems and having the responsibility of supervising audit engagements.

5. One primarily liable on an obligation, as distinguished from an endorser or surety.

principle A proposition asserted to be controlling in a given system or activity and having acceptance among members of a professional group deemed to be competent in a society; growing out of observation, reason, or experiment, a principle purports to be the best possible guide in the choice of alternatives leading to the qualities desired in an endproduct. Some principles are descriptive or classificational and have either the form "All, some, or no *A*'s are *B*'s" (a general proposition) or the form "*Y* is a function of *X*" (a propositional *function*). Other principles are normative and are not concerned with the existence of anything, but rather state what is preferred or prescribed. Among normative principles are definitions—the meanings assigned to words—and professional, legal, and moral *norms* or *standards.* Principles are not equally self-evident to all persons. The assertion of a descriptive principle establishes neither the truth nor the wisdom of a normative principle. If a principle is accepted without evidence or proof, it may be called an *axiom, assumption*, or *postulate*.

private acccountant An accountant whose technical skills and employment are confined to a single organization. See *controller*.

private corporation 1. Any corporation other than one created for the purpose of local government or the administration of a governmental program.

2. A corporation created to promote private interests—business, financial, social, religious—of its members or stockholders. When used in this sense, the term contrasts with *public corporation* in that it does not offer its products or services to the public and has a relatively small number of stockholders. It is synonymous with *close corporation*, where all stockholders are engaged in the company's affairs. When the shares are held by persons related to each other, it is sometimes called a "family" corporation.

private ledger A ledger in which confidential accounts are kept; now seldom employed. It is linked with the general ledger through a control account.

private offering The sale of an issue of securities by the issuer, rather than through an investment banker. The buyers may be existing stockholders, officers, employees, dealers, creditors, customers, friends of the management, or an insurance company or other institution. The distinction usually drawn between private and public offerings is that the former ordinarily involve but few subscribers who are in a position to be well acquainted with the affairs of the business. Many private offerings are exempt from registration under the Federal Securities Act and state blue-sky laws.

probability 1. Likelihood; belief that a future condition or event will develop or occur.

2. (statistics) A measurement of the likelihood of occurrence of a chance event. The range of probability is between 0 and 1, denoted $0 \leq p \leq 1$. The classical definition, attributed to Bernoulli, may be stated as follows: If an event can occur N mutually exclusive and equally likely ways, and if n of these outcomes have an *attribute* A, then the probability of A is the fraction n/N. There has been much difficulty concerning a satisfactory definition of the term, some persons wishing to devise an all-inclusive definition covering such items as credibility or subjective probability, others wishing to restrict it to objectively measurable events. Kendall, in *The Advanced Theory of Statistics*, presents the following summary: All probability statements involve states of mind and "(a) they concern propositions . . . (b) there are degrees of probability . . . (c) the degree of probability attributed to a proposition varies according to the amount of relevant evidence available to the particular mind considering the proposition . . . (d) certainty can be regarded as a limiting form of probability. . . ." To give these notions definiteness, two approaches have been advocated: "The first [axiomatic] approach takes the notion of event or class of events to be an undefined idea [primitive], like the straight line of Euclidean geometry, and builds up the theory from certain *axioms*. The second [relative-frequency] approach seeks to define probability in terms of the relative frequency of events. . . ." Both the relative-frequency approach and Bernoulli's classical or *a priori* approach themselves rest on axioms and seem to be slowly giving way to axiomatic formulation.

The axioms of probability, stated in many different ways, have been subjected to a variety of interpretations. The following formulation is that of the mathematician A. Kolmogoroff: The probability of the occurrence of an event A is the relative frequency or proportion of times the event A is found to occur under a stipulated set of conditions. More exactly, if in n trials it is found that the event A occurs in m of these trials, the ratio or relative frequency m/n is presumed to approach the probability of the event A, written $P(A)$, as the number of trials n

increases without bound. Restated formally, four axioms may be cited:

1. *The axiom of construction or specification.* There is assumed a *universe* of instances or events, termed *elementary* events, which may be classified into sets. Any class or set is termed a *random* event if it is comprised of elementary events belonging to the universe. The random events are taken to constitute a system having the property that all possible combinations of them in terms of their joint occurrence or nonoccurrence belong to the given system.

2. *The axiom of classification.* The classification system is taken to be complete in the sense that each elementary event belongs to one or more random events.

3. *The axiom of measurement.* Given the system of random events, to each random event, which is in effect a class, there is assigned a nonnegative *real number*, written $P(A)$. The event which constitutes the contradiction of A, written not-A, therefore is assigned the probability P (not-A).

4. *The axiom of total probability.* Since the universe may always be classified into two mutually exclusive and exhaustive sets, A and not-A, in respect to any random event, it is postulated that the probability of the universe is equal to the number 1, written $P(\text{universe}) = 1$.

Given the above system of axioms and their interpretation, it follows that the probability of a certain event is equal to 1, while the probability of an impossible event is 0. Since the interpretation placed on the axioms rests on the notion of relative frequency, it follows that if the probability of an event is 0, this does not imply that the event is impossible. In such a case, it may be validly claimed that the probability of occurrence of the event on a single trial is exceedingly small—i.e., that the event will almost never occur on a single trial.

probability sample A *random sample* with a computable sampling error. The computed error indicates the degree of representativeness (or lack thereof) which should be taken into consideration in interpreting the sample results.

probable life *Age* already attained plus *expected life.*

probable-life curve A curve, deduced from a study of *frequency distributions*, of the use of equipment and its accompanying *mortality.*

procedural audit (or **review**) The critical examination by an external auditor of internal controls and other procedures employed within an organization, (a) looking to recommendations for their improvement whether by simplification, elaboration, or readaptation, or (b) as a regular feature of a periodic examination. The review may be a general one or may be applied to a segment of the business, often on a rotating basis, as in successive annual examinations; frequently the review involves procedures other than accounting. See *internal control; voucher audit; postaudit; internal check; horizontal audit.*

proceeds 1. The amount of cash, other assets, and services received from the sale or other disposition of property, from a loan, or from a sale or issue of securities.

2. = *net proceeds.*

process 1. Any unbroken series of acts, steps, or *events* or any unchanging, persisting *condition.*

2. Hence, the sequence of *operations(3)* making up a plan of production, as on an assembly line; any continuous system involving an unbroken chain of *activities(1)* and a more or less continuous operation or constant output, as distinguished from a job-order system of production.

process control See *statistical quality control.*

process costing A method of cost accounting whereby costs are charged to processes or operations and averaged over units produced; it is employed principally where a finished product is the result of a more or less continuous operation, as in paper mills, refineries, canneries, and chemical plants; distinguished from *job costing*, where costs are assigned to specific orders, lots, or units.

producer(s') capital (or **goods**) (economics) *Capital goods* (fixed assets) and other goods (e.g., raw materials) that are the basis for or aid in the production of other goods rather than being used directly to satisfy human wants. See *consumers' goods*.

producer's risk (statistical quality control) A calculated *probability*, under a given sampling plan, that a lot of any given quality will be rejected by the plan. It is generally stated only for lots at the acceptable quality level.

product A good or service to the utility or value of which an operation or series of operations has contributed. An intermediate product is one on which further operations are to be performed; a final product is any good on which all contributory operations have been completed, or any service that has been fully rendered.

product cost 1. The material, labor, and overhead outlay making up the output of any operation.
2. Material and labor cost of output; in this sense, the term is employed in contrast with *period cost;* see *direct costing*.

production 1. The making available of *goods* or *services* for the satisfaction of *demands(1)*.
2. The function of making or fabricating, as distinguished from distributing or financing; hence, the addition of value by an operation or process, reflected in accounting by the recording of the costs of the contributory factors.
3. Output, usually for a specified period.

production control The planning, routing, scheduling, dispatching, and inspection of the operations of a department producing goods or services, the purpose being to so coordinate men and machines that established standards of quality, quantity, time, place, and lowest possible cost are fulfilled.

production cost 1. A cost contributing to any *factor of production*.
2. The total of all such costs relating to the same time and place; factory cost.
3. (petroleum accounting) The cost, including depletion, of raising crude petroleum to the mouth of a well.

production function A listing of the possible relations, under assumed technological conditions, between quantities of factors or inputs employed, and quantities of products, or outputs of salable goods resulting from that employment. Thus, $3L + 4C = P$ is a production function specifying that one unit of product results from every three units of labor and four units of capital employed; the total product increases at a rate three times as fast as the increase in the rate at which the factor labor is added to a given stock of capital; that total product increases at four times the rate of the increase in capital when labor is held fixed; and so on for all possible quantitative relations satisfied by the above equation. It should be understood, of course, that only a simple example of a production function is used here for purposes of illustration, and that more complicated expressions of the production, or input–output functions expressing relations between multiple products and factors, will generally be needed for analysis in any actual situation. Standard costs, particularly so-called efficiency standards, are, however, often set on the basis of such highly simplified *models* of production functions. Little confidence can be placed in efficiency standards when variations in production occur beyond the narrow range covered by the assumptions underlying the standards.

production method (of depreciation) See *depreciation method*.

production statement A summary for a specified period of the elements that comprise production quantities and costs of an entire enterprise or of a division, plant, department, or product.

productive labor (or **wages**) Compensation

of labor engaged in the physical production of marketable goods or in the physical performance of salable services; = *direct labor*.

productivity The yield obtained from any process or product by employing one or more *factors of production*. Productivity is usually calculated as an *index number:* the ratio of output to input. These measures may take a variety of forms. Measures of value relate dollar costs to dollar receipts or profits; measures of physical productivity may be constructed by direct reference to physical units or by adjusting value indexes for variations in purchasing power. Different systems of weighting the items entering into indexes of productivity will often produce different results. Like any index number, such measures need to be interpreted with caution and with reference to a restricted context. Particular care is required where it is desired to isolate and measure the productivity of separate factors of production that jointly contribute to the same endproduct. Thus, if labor and capital are two factors of production which contribute to one or more endproducts, it may be logically indefensible to isolate average yields which can be separately *imputed* to each factor. Separate indexes calculated under such circumstances are characterized as "indexes of output per man hour" or "indexes of output per dollar of capital investment," in order to avoid the implication that either factor is capable of completing any portion of the output without assistance from the other factor of production. It is sometimes possible to construct indexes of *marginal productivity*, these relating to increments in yield attributable to increments in one factor of production when all other factors are fixed at constant amounts.

profession A vocation (a) generally recognized by universities and colleges as requiring special training leading to a degree distinct from the usual degrees in arts and sciences, (b) requiring principally mental rather than manual or artistic labor and skill for its successful prosecution, (c) recognizing the obligations of public service and of the public interest, and (d) having a code of ethics generally accepted as binding upon its members.

professional accountant 1. One engaged in public accounting.

2. A certified public accountant so engaged.

profit 1. A general term for the excess of revenue, proceeds, or selling price over related costs; any pecuniary benefit arising from a commercial operation, from the practice of a profession, or from one or more individual transactions of any person; usually preceded by a qualifying word or phrase signifying the inclusiveness of the offsetting expense or cost, as "gross" or "net," according to and followed by an indication of the source and time covered, as "from operations for the year." Either the singular or the plural of the word may be used where two or more related transactions are considered together. *Net income* is now preferred as a designation of the ending figure of an *income statement*. See *net profit; gain; income*.

2. (economics) A payment or commitment to a person (entrepreneur) undertaking the hazards of enterprise; remuneration or reward for uncertainty-bearing. "Pure" profit is a residual and cannot ordinarily be predetermined. By way of contrast, *risk*, being calculable in advance, like rent, and frequently insurable, is a cost rather than a profit. In any *objective probability* sense, profit can be accurately measured only in retrospect; hence, any preliminary imputation of profit is wholly subjective in character and is labeled accordingly.

profit and loss 1. The ledger account to which the balances of accounts reflecting revenues, income, profits, expenses, and losses are periodically transferred. Its balance, the net income or net loss for the period, is transferred to *retained*

earnings (earned surplus) or other suitable proprietary account.
2. A general term indicating the eventual repository of any gain or loss. Example: a chargeoff to profit and loss.
3. (railroad accounting) = *retained earnings;* also a British usage, particularly when appearing in the adjectival form and followed by *account.*

profit-and-loss statement (or **statement of profit and loss**) = *income statement.*

profitgraph = *breakeven chart.*

profit planning The process of so conducting operations as to realize a given profit goal: an aspect of an overall budget in which the more important factors affecting profits (e.g., selling prices, volume, prices of cost elements, operating efficiency, etc.) are related to profits, and a plan is prepared which sets forth a desired, presumably attainable, balance between these factors.

profit prior to consolidation *Net income* of any enterprise prior to its acquisition by another through capital-stock control. Such profit does not form part of the consolidated income or *retained earnings* of the group.

profit prior to incorporation A profit made in a business prior to its incorporation. Since a corporation cannot make a profit before it comes into being, such profit is, in effect, represented in the net assets of the business which are transferred to the corporation. See, however, *pooling of interests.*

proforma *adj.* A term applied to a balance sheet or other statement, or an account (a) which contains in whole or in part assumed figures or other facts, some indication of the character and purpose of the contents of the statement or account and the assumptions on which it is based ordinarily accompanying the use of the phrase; or (b) which contains no figures and is intended to indicate form, range, descriptions, or other characteristics of a proposed presentation.

proforma balance sheet 1. A balance sheet showing hypothetical or tentative amounts, or no amounts, prepared for the purpose of displaying a proposed form or possible future financial condition.
2. A *tentative* balance sheet.
3. A balance sheet in which effect is given to transactions not yet consummated. Example: a balance sheet giving effect to a proposed financing or refinancing whether or not covered by a firm contract.

proforma statement 1. A financial statement containing at least in part hypothetical amounts, or no amounts, prepared to exhibit the form in which data of a particular kind is to be presented.
2. A financial statement modified to show the effect of proposed transactions which have not yet been consummated; an "as-if" statement.

program (governmental accounting) 1. Any (or a number) of the major activities of an agency or of a group of agencies, expressed as a primary *function,* and covering a fiscal year or larger period.
2. Hence, any major expense within an agency, as contrasted with a *project;* often repetitive from period to period.

program budget (governmental accounting) A *budget* of a government agency which is essentially a projection of the agency's accounts—on the accrual basis—for the budget period. It consists largely of planned-transaction totals and a narrative support or *justification.* The transaction totals reflect (a) operating expenses classified by function and activity and set forth wherever practicable in terms of work-loads and unit costs; (b) goods and services produced and sold or otherwise disposed of; (c) acquisitions of inventories and fixed assets, and changes generally in financial structure; and (d) other assemblies and explanations of prospective costs the realized counterparts of which will eventually be lodged in the agency's accounts. Revenues are classified by source and collection agency. As compared with earlier budget forms, its objectives are to provide a closer linkage between planning and action and to establish a more consistent common basis for review by higher authority, including legislative bodies, for management controls, and for intermediate and final reporting. It is known also as *performance budget*, and is so designated by the first and second Hoover Commissions, and by numerous publications of the U.S. General Accounting Office and the U. S. Bureau of the Budget.

A program budget may be contrasted with one arranged by organizational units without regard to the activities carried on by such units, or by *object*. For example, in a municipality, a budget of current expenses for a city department of health by object costs set up as indicated immediately below is of little help to the department head in planning its work or to the chief executive or to the legislative body that must review the estimates.

Department of Health— Current Expenses:	
Salaries	$200,000
Materials and supplies	50,000
Contractual services	20,000
Total	$270,000

On the other hand, in a program budget these same budgetary estimates, broken down and rearranged by principal activities, might appear as shown below.

In large municipalities where the character of the work justifies, some of these activities would be given the more general designation "function" and would be broken down into component activities. Thus, "regulation and inspection" might consist of such separate operations as regulation and inspection of milk and dairy products, regulation and inspection of other food, regulation and inspection of drugs, and sanitary inspection. Again, "control of communicable diseases" might be subdivided into activities concerned with tuberculosis, venereal diseases, polio inoculations, and other communicable diseases.

The more extensive the breakdown by actual activities, the more readily detail and total expenditures can be estimated, reviewed, and compared with similar activities in other communities. The ideal situation exists where the activity can be broken down into sufficient detail to permit its measurement in terms of cost per unit of performance. To illustrate, if sanitary inspection is set up as a separate activity, and if a determination is made on a realistic basis of the average time required by a sanitary engineer for an inspection and the number of inspections he is likely to make each working day, then the number of inspectors required and the estimated annual cost become largely a matter of arithmetic. In the review of prospective costs the proposed units of performance can be compared with those of past years and

Department of Health—Current Expenses:			
General supervision—			
Salaries		$25,000	
Materials and supplies		500	
Contractual services		1,000	$ 26,500
Vital statistics—			
Salaries		$ 8,000	
Materials and supplies		600	
Contractual services		300	8,900
Regulation and inspection—			
Salaries		$40,000	
Materials and supplies		1,500	
Contractual services		800	42,300
Control of communicable diseases	Under each of these heads are similar breakdowns		
Child-health service			
Adult-health service			
Laboratories			192,300
Total Department of Health—Current Expenses			$270,000

with the corresponding performance standards (both time and cost) maintained in other cities.

Again, the smaller the recognized activity the more accurate and comprehensible the resulting unit costs are likely to be. Thus the average cost per inspection by the Sanitary division will not be as significant as the average cost for each kind of inspection it makes.

progression Orderly arrangement in a sequence; examples: a schedule of tax rates varying with income; *arithmetic*, *geometric*, and *harmonic progressions;* the first n squares, $1^2 + 2^2 + 3^2 + \cdots + n^2$, the total being $n(n+1)(2n+1)/6$; the first n cubes, $1^3 + 2^3 + 3^3 + \cdots + n^3$, having the total of $(n[n+1]/2)^2$.

progressive average One of a series of simple averages, each of which is the arithmetic mean of a group of items consisting of all the items in the next preceding group, plus a new one. Example:

Series	*Items*	*Progressive Average*
A	5, 9, 3, 7, 4	5.60
B	5, 9, 3, 7, 4, 8	6.00
C	5, 9, 3, 7, 4, 8, 5	5.85
D	5, 9, 3, 7, 4, 8, 5, 6	5.87

In this table, a new average can be derived from its predecessor by the formula

$$a_2 = \frac{a_1 n + b}{n + 1},$$

where a_2 is the new average to be determined, a_1 the old average, n the number of items in the series not including the new item, and b the quantity being added to the series. Progressive averages may be used, for example, in statements of earnings, costs, expenses, and the like, that cover the accounting periods since the beginning of the current fiscal year and that show the cumulative averages of a steadily increasing number of periods, usually in comparison with the corresponding amounts of the previous fiscal year or years. See *moving average.*

progressive ledger = *Boston ledger.*

progressive schedule A comparative schedule of financial or operating data to which new data are added as they become available.

progressive tax A tax the rate of which increases with the size of the property or income on which it is levied; contrasts with *regressive tax.*

project *n.* A unit of construction work, or other capital acquisition, such as one undertaken by a governmental unit, the cost of which is accounted for separately from other work and is ordinarily financed by the employment of special funds or by a bond issue. See *program.*

projected financial statement A financial statement of a future date or period, based on estimates of transactions not yet consummated: a statement frequently accompanying a budget; a *pro-forma statement* (2).

promise to pay An agreement, between buyer and seller or debtor and creditor, that cash will be delivered by the former to the latter on a certain future date or within a certain future period. The agreement may be explicit and hence contained in a contract or promissory note; or implicit, in accordance with usual trade custom or terms appearing in the seller's advertisement or on his invoice.

promissory note An unconditional written promise, signed by the maker, to pay a certain sum in money, on demand or at a fixed or determinable future date, either to the bearer or to the order of a designated person. A promissory note is a note payable to the maker and a note receivable to a holder in due course.

promotion expense An expense incurred in the formation or furtherance of a new enterprise or activity. See *organization expense; deferred charge.* Thus, advertising expense publicizing a new product, or introducing a product into a new market, constitutes a deferred charge amortizable against the revenues of the years to be benefited. Although promotion expenses frequently develop a prospectively continuous benefit, practical considerations and their repetitive character suggest their amortization over a short period and, except where the promotion is out of the ordinary course of business, or where their amounts are sufficient to distort the income of a single year, it is preferable to absorb them against the income of the year in which they have been incurred.

proof of loss (insurance) A formal submission by an insured to his insurer containing sufficient data in support of a claim to enable the latter to determine its liability.

proper In line with common practice; meeting specifications deemed fitting in the circumstances; ethical as well as legal.

property Any asset, including cash, title to which is ordinarily transferable between persons. See *asset.*

property account 1. An account maintained for a *fixed asset.*
2. *pl.* = *fixed assets.*

property accountability The responsibility for observing and reporting on the existence, location, use, and condition of assets, particularly mobile fixed assets, and also small tools and other items which for any of various reasons have not been capitalized. See *fixed asset; internal control.*

property dividend A dividend paid in property other than cash, as distinct from a distribution in cash, scrip, or the company's own bonds or stock; a dividend in *kind.*

property ledger = *plant ledger.*

property reserved = *accumulated depreciation;* a British term.

proportion 1. Any ratio; as a/b.
2. A ratio representing the relation to a whole of one of its parts; as, $a/(a + b)$.
3. A ratio, as in sense (*2*), its source often inferred, applied to an independent quantity; as, $ac/(a + b)$. It is in this sense that the derived adjective, *proportionate,* is often used; as, a proportionate part of an annual prepaid insurance premium being charged off monthly—meaning that the quantity thus disposed of during each of 12 months has been one-twelfth of the total premium cost. A further example: proportionate credits of deferred gross profits from installment sales are made to income as the installments are collected. Here either of two ratios may be inferred: g/s or c/s, where g is the anticipated total gross profit, c the installment collected, and s the selling price; the final result is, however, the same, since $(g/s)c$ and $(c/s)g$ both equal cg/s.

proposed dividend The liability for a dividend recognized in the accounts, but not yet made certain by a formal *declaration:* a British usage.

proposition Any declarative statement that may be believed, doubted, or denied, and, hence, characterized as either true or false: not synonymous with "sentence," since a number of sentences may be required in expressing the statement.

proprietary accounts 1. The accounts, including *nominal* accounts, containing the *equities* of *owners.*
2. (governmental accounting) The accounts reflecting the assets and liabilities, and displaying the results of operations in terms of revenue, expense, surplus, or deficit. See *budgetary accounts.*

proprietary interest Net worth or a part thereof; the excess of assets over liabilities; net assets classified as to capital paid in, retained income, and other sources.

proprietor 1. The possessor of a proprietorship.
2. The owner of property such as a stock or bond.

proprietorship 1. = *net worth; net assets.*
2. = *sole proprietorship.*
3. Ownership of an unincorporated business by an individual; the business so owned.

proprietorship account The account maintained for the net worth of the business of an individual proprietor.

propriety That which meets the tests of

the *public interest*, commonly accepted customs and standards of conduct, and, particularly as applied to professional performance, requirements of law, government regulations, and professional codes.

prorata *adj.* Proportional. The term relates to the distribution of an expense, fund, dividend, or other item, the inference being that the distribution is made upon some equitable basis.

prorate *v.* To assign or redistribute a portion of a cost, such as a joint cost, to a department, operation, activity, or product according to some formula or other agreed-to, often arbitrary, procedure.—*proration, n.*

prospectus Any written offer to sell a security in which representations, often implied, as to the qualities of the security are made by the seller; specifically, a formal informational document, prepared for prospective investors by the issuer of a security in conformity with regulations under state blue-sky laws or the U. S. Securities and Exchange Commission. A preliminary prospectus, permitted under SEC rules, is known as a *"red-herring" prospectus.*

Section 2(9) of the Securities Act of 1933 defines *prospectus* as any "... notice, circular, advertisement, letter, or communication, written or by radio, which offers any security for sale ..."; the SEC requires the prospectus to contain a fairly extensive disclosure of essential facts pertinent to the security, such as (a) a description of the registrant's business and its development, (b) a description of the principal provisions of the security and its relationship to the registrant's other capital securities, (c) information as to management, how much it is paid and what dealings it has with the registrant, (d) certified financial statements, (e) the conditions under which the security is to be sold, and (f) the offering price.

prove To *verify* or subject to a satisfactory *test*.

provision 1. A charge for an estimated expense or loss or for a shrinkage in the cost of an asset offsetting an addition to a valuation account such as a reserve or accumulation of depreciation or the accrual of a liability such as an income tax.
2. (British usage) (a) An amount entered on the books of account covering an estimated or accrued liability. (b) The amount of a reserve for depreciation, bad debts, or inventory decline; a *valuation account.*

proxy Written authority to act for another, as in a meeting of stockholders of a corporation.

proxy statement An informational statement accompanying the solicitation of a proxy, particularly one prepared in conformity with Regulation X-14 of the U. S. Securities and Exchange Commission. This regulation, relating primarily to solicitations from stockholders on behalf of the management of a corporation the securities of which are listed on a national securities exchange, specifies the minimum content, timing, and other features that attach to such a statement.

prudent investment 1. An investment, as by a trustee, made with the care and judgment reasonably expected of an ordinary businessman.
2. A term employed by the courts and by public-utility regulatory boards to denote the minimum outlay for an operating unit or system that a utility management, putting the public interest ahead of interests of stockholders and management, would incur for the same items. Such a theoretical cost, devoid of profits to promoters, "insiders," or affiliates, based on reconstructed need at the time of acquisition, and not infrequently lower than recorded or even original cost, may become a part of the rate base against which a "fair return" to investors is computed. See *original cost (2).*

public accountant An accountant who offers his services professionally to the public. See *certified public accountant;* a registered accountant. The term may also refer to a firm of public accountants.

public accounting The profession of the

public accountant; specifically, the offering to the public of independent professional accounting skills consisting principally of the design and installation of financial and cost systems of accounting, audits, investigations, reports (certificates) based on audits, advice on management structure and financial policies, and income-tax service. The services of the public accountant are offered to the public generally, as contrasted with the employment of a private accountant on a full-time basis by a single business enterprise. The services offered may be general, or restricted to a particular type of accounting service. The public accountant is not required to perform services for all who request them. In every state, practice as a certified public accountant is regulated by statute and is confined to those who meet certain qualifying conditions. See *certified public accountant.*

public corporation 1. A corporation that offers its goods or services to the public and the bulk of whose stock is held by persons other than officers or employees. 2. = *municipal corporation.*

public interest The basic concern of a people as a body in establishing, defending, and from time to time widening its domain by its tolerance of or by its regulatory and moral prescriptions for private affairs. In the United States, the public interest is conceived by many as a policing operation having as its aim the preservation of the *status quo;* by others as a dynamic force for welfare progress. In either case, it is generally conceded that a profession such as that of the public accountant must conduct itself in harmony with what appears to be the trend of the public interest and that its moral qualities must be of the highest order if it is to continue freely to lay down the standards to which its practitioners ought to conform.

public offering A sale of securities to the general public, usually through the medium of an investment banker; contrasts with *private offering.*

public-service (or **-utility**) **company** A corporation supplying to the consuming public services commonly regarded as necessities of life. It operates under a Federal, state, or municipal franchise or monopoly and is subject to regulation and control through a commission or other body representing the public. Examples: railroads and other common carriers; electric light, gas, power, telegraph, telephone, and water companies.

purchase An outlay for property or service; the property or service acquired.

purchase contract (securities) See *underwriting contract.*

purchase group (or **syndicate**) = *underwriting syndicate.*

purchase-money obligation A mortgage or other form of debt secured by a lien existing or created at the time property is acquired, and having priority over any lien subsequently created.

purchase order A document authorizing a vendor to deliver described merchandise or materials at a specified price. Upon acceptance by a vendor, a purchase order becomes a contract. Several copies of a purchase order are customarily prepared. In a typical case, the copies are distributed as follows: one (the original) to the vendor; three to the receiving department, of which, following the receipt of the goods, one is returned to the purchasing department and another is sent to the accounting department; one to the accounting department, serving as a basis for a commitment record; two remain in the purchasing department, one serving as the basis of a purchase record, the other being placed in a follow-up file.

purchase records Records relating to the purchase of merchandise, materials, supplies, and similar items. Examples: vouchers and invoices; voucher or purchase register; creditors ledger; purchase contracts, orders, and requisitions; the files of a purchasing department.

purchasing power The ability to buy; hence, (a) the quantity of a particular class of goods or services that may be purchased for a given sum of money, such as one dollar, or (b) the percentage relationship of such a quantity to that so purchasable at some preceding point of time.

pure profit Net income in excess of returns, including *imputed interest(1)*, on the several *factors of production*. Some economists ascribe such an excess to the existence of any of a variety of conditions such as imperfect competition.

put A transferable option or offer to deliver a given number of shares of stock at a stated price somewhat below current market at any time during a stated period, usually not exceeding three months. Such an option is purchased by a speculator who looks forward to a price decline during the period to a point below that appearing in the option; should that event occur, he will purchase the shares on the market and deliver them to the maker or issuer of the agreement, thus gaining a profit; should the price remain unchanged or rise, the holder of the option will allow it to expire, with a loss equal to his cost. See *call*.

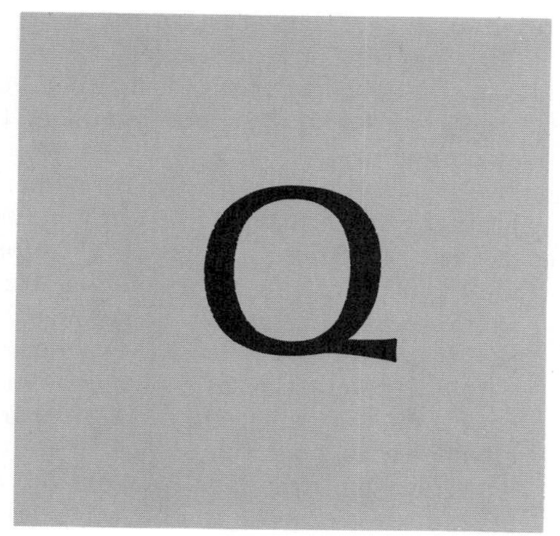

qualification A statement in an auditor's *report* or certificate directing attention to any important limitation attending his examination or to his doubt or disagreement as to any item reported; distinguished from *disclosure*, the latter relating to facts of interest to readers revealed on financial statements, in accompanying footnotes, or, less frequently, in the report or certificate. See *exception(1)*.

qualified report (or **certificate**) An audit report containing one or more *qualifications* or *exceptions*.

qualified stock option (Federal income taxes) A privilege granted an employee of a corporation to purchase at a specified price a limited number of shares of its capital stock, under conditions laid down in the Internal Revenue Code (section 1,422–2); among these conditions are that the option plan, its proposed beneficiaries (individuals or classes), the option price, and the option period (not to exceed five years) must be approved by the stockholders. The option is not transferable; the price at which it may be exercised may not be less than the market price at the time the option is issued, and the grantee may not be the owner of more than 5% of the grantor's voting power or 5% of the value of all classes of its outstanding stock. These ratios are increased to 10% where the equity capital of the corporations is less than a million dollars. When these and certain minor conditions are satisfied, no income tax is incurred by the employee at the time of the grant or when the option is exercised; if he sells the stock he has acquired within three years, ordinary income (i.e., compensation for services) is realized on the difference between his cost and the market price of the stock when the option is exercised, the balance realized being treated as a *capital gain;* if held more than three years, the entire profit is classed as a capital gain.

On the books of the corporation the amount received from the stockholder when the option is exercised, plus the amount recognized as compensation to the employee, is treated as paid-in capital, the offsetting items being cash and compensation expense, respectively.

qualifying reserve = *valuation account.* The term has sometimes been applied to "less-than-full-depreciation" reserves, as in the case of power companies before January 1, 1937, the date established by the Federal Power Commission after which power companies were required to begin building up their depreciation accumulations to a full straight-line basis.

quality control Any of the policies and procedures, especially those relating to plant and product design and operating and output inspection, used to determine and maintain a desired level of satisfactoriness of operations or products. See *control; statistical quality control.*

quantification Any statement expressed in numbers; particularly, a *proposition* expressed or restated in numerical terms.

quantile (statistics) Any of the values that divide an array or frequency distribution into equal numbers of individual units. See *quartile; decile; percentile.*

quantity discount An allowance given by a seller to a purchaser because of the size of an individual purchase transaction. This practice is not in violation of

Federal laws dealing with price discrimination provided the allowance granted represents a saving in selling costs. It is sometimes justified on the ground that the seller, in good faith, must meet a competitor's price. Legal restriction on dual pricing serves the purpose of preventing large buyers from taking advantage of their bargaining power to reduce acquisition costs and to reflect these savings in lower resale prices: competition that smaller firms could not meet. While it is argued that this restriction is detrimental to consumers, there is no certainty that, if small firms are eliminated by price competition, large firms would continue to pass on such savings to consumers.

quartile (statistics) The value of any of three points (upper quartile, *median*, and lower quartile) setting off four divisions of a frequency distribution each containing the same number of individuals.

quasi contract An obligation imposed by law for the purpose of preventing an injustice or an unjust enrichment; its imposition is independent of any agreement or any indications of the parties' intent.

quasi-public company A corporation operated privately but for purposes in which the public has some general interest. Examples: charitable and religious corporations.

quasi rent 1. That portion of a producer's gross revenue attributable to some unique operating efficiency or other low-cost factor not available to a competitor.
2. Consideration for the use of another's property other than real estate; = *rent*.

quasi reorganization A recapitalization, a principal feature of which has been the absorption of a deficit; specifically, the procedure whereby a corporation, without the creation of a new corporate entity or the intervention of a court, eliminates an operating deficit or a deficit resulting from the recognition of other losses, or both, and establishes a new *retained earnings* (earned-surplus) account for the accumulation of net income subsequent to the effective date of such action. See *dated earned surplus*.

queuing problem The situation arising from the impact of demands on production facilities in excess of their capacity, or within limited periods of time where the volume of *demand* is of a *random* character or is not otherwise readily determinable.

quick asset A current asset normally convertible into cash within a relatively short period, such as a month. Examples: cash, call loan, marketable security, customer's account, a commodity immediately salable at quoted prices on the open market.

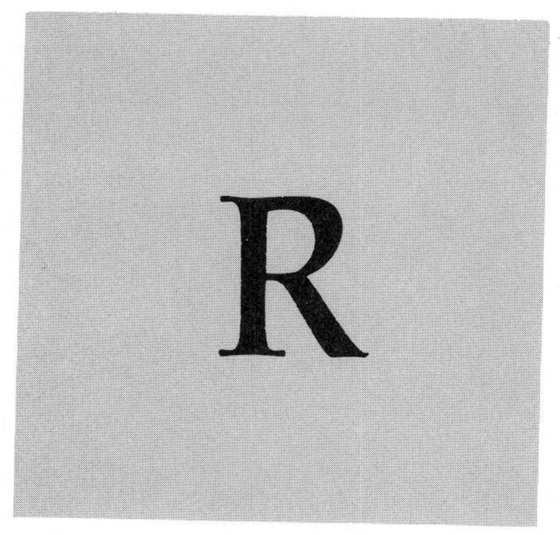

random Arising from chance alone, in contrast with haphazard or systematic; as, a random defect in the output of a machine. When a process is random, it obeys known laws of chance behavior; when haphazard, the mixture of chance and other elements is so compounded that it is impossible to take advantage of any laws of behavior. Systematic error, or *bias,* if known and measurable, may be allowed for, thereby improving estimates, predictions, or tests. Where the amount of bias is unknown, its practical effect is the same as that of haphazardness. Randomization requires careful planning to make certain that only chance elements are present, or that bias, if present or introduced, is known and measurable.

random numbers A set of numbers formed at random, generally arrayed in tabular form to assist in sample selection. Several such tables are available. The numbers on pp. 356–357, extracted from *Random Decimal Digits* (U. S. Interstate Commerce Commission), will be found sufficient for most audit uses; where large surveys are undertaken, however, recourse may be had to the entire table. The ICC tables contain 105,000 random numbers, of which 700 are reproduced here. Fisher and Yates, *Statistical Tables for Biological, Agricultural and Medical Research* (Oliver & Boyd, 1938), contains 100,000 numbers, and M. G. Kendall and B. B. Smith, *Tracts for Computers No. 24* (Cambridge, 1939), also contains 100,000 numbers.

To illustrate the use of the table, imagine that a random sample of 100 serially numbered vouchers is selected for audit. The vouchers from which the selection is made are numbered, say, 453,650, 453,651, and so on, up to and including 454,108. Subtraction indicates that 459 items constitute the *universe* or *frame* out of which the sample is to be drawn. Only three-digit numbers are, therefore, needed. Turning to column 12 of the table (any horizontal or vertical column or line would have done equally well), the first three digits of the first number are 378. Hence, voucher number 454,028 is included in the sample. The next three-digit combination below is 727. Since this number exceeds the total universe number, it may be discarded and the next number within the limit of 459, or 129, may be employed instead. This, however, constitutes a wasteful use of the table. One of numerous alternative procedures would consist of deducting the highest number in the universe from the random number specified in the table, the difference being used for sample selection: under these conditions, voucher number 453,918 could be the second voucher included in the sample. The process may thus be continued until the entire sample is drawn.

Any systematic method of selection from the table will result in a set of random numbers. Thus, column 1 may be read up or down and then column 2, and so on. The table may also be read across or diagonally. Moreover, in reading down the columns, the movement need not be from one to the next. Thus, when the first column is exhausted by three-digit readings, the same column may be used again by reading the last three digits of each item in the column. Through devices such as these, the table included here may be made to generate many more random numbers.

Col. / Line	(1)	(2)	(3)	(4)	(5)	(6)	(7)
01	88188	99345	94118	40373	50387	24802	81352
02	05200	50533	59428	02797	16833	10038	18901
03	82828	41316	92617	31346	89263	06589	07121
04	71006	99318	19269	35233	79183	78538	06326
05	05937	00875	32264	82808	00229	03868	71072
06	06021	04370	93070	90737	05354	68427	25554
07	54789	10960	44023	57857	56556	83993	70787
08	90400	05707	29128	14859	84117	72206	53740
09	51424	01651	99970	73521	82356	03297	36288
10	79743	88757	43370	86536	07166	06401	14413
11	77418	00322	98854	51507	00565	33066	65791
12	17580	49302	16408	05678	75532	46218	74359
13	15489	45559	28548	64330	42126	43145	81287
14	56342	66773	18536	32600	73958	75993	84250
15	20202	19216	23762	47856	04623	70728	86657
16	84877	51708	69357	67914	55372	97225	52837
17	01647	00311	44989	21900	96079	15793	13148
18	45652	89311	45302	14539	32045	86727	40595
19	79975	06153	08932	59185	71386	19070	87098
20	49744	54713	37053	77467	15348	03383	96086
21	40922	94903	29638	46870	14108	84391	87313
22	53319	48020	77444	51447	07916	99506	83504
23	76682	10559	85446	56236	85919	76388	59850
24	48869	97229	69581	84581	71728	45150	16901
25	95961	19279	38078	17473	43945	21562	90937
26	16521	25945	94076	91281	92272	41233	58614
27	78282	26332	44072	55104	16895	98311	56005
28	43473	39179	53174	43498	72674	13087	54261
29	06513	31352	09177	21367	64725	23784	18125
30	48734	39737	03448	99009	98136	34562	30339
31	54832	70111	48339	75270	11652	41697	43277
32	55844	69515	22658	75438	83086	41325	04694
33	42829	54398	93338	90705	00626	97752	93482
34	81128	63461	10925	44382	73365	98875	77605
35	62885	26354	10368	78026	00186	46783	02059
36	19525	10375	27010	42791	49471	90607	98103
37	26570	99202	73924	59888	01827	93314	63949
38	04772	17749	01537	96036	02102	02622	06007
39	49129	12491	62552	64323	44856	29045	76871
40	19937	75104	57780	95871	94547	53541	77723
41	52571	67962	72775	28480	87411	12075	45177
42	54943	80723	81195	84069	28144	48106	04169
43	16375	88048	29625	08111	92924	53335	09525
44	38745	91458	30363	95005	55854	38628	13599
45	09937	17776	86425	88916	80594	28347	08092
46	30097	47192	27960	15937	42080	61048	14358
47	02410	60124	62825	42947	74590	89730	16073
48	44804	80165	19442	72194	76910	40274	93861
49	37352	79142	51032	58844	03167	57351	51850
50	60640	14199	48263	71533	94235	42431	4411

(page 11 of *Table of 105,000 Random*
Interstate Commerce Commission, 1949)

(8)	(9)	(10)	(11)	(12)	(13)	(14)
61640	56614	71506	75541	37818	88047	94144
40743	99449	49825	44637	72724	42649	67052
07151	23905	98435	50453	12983	04738	76421
62715	28701	52809	56581	05925	85210	17745
11519	44876	34508	07859	62424	54319	32842
11165	00123	80338	03876	85648	24978	01687
28193	65872	33723	00125	99818	85571	69509
00464	51853	78852	83593	82926	48985	64355
93531	69269	84798	78962	06336	95618	89718
23643	21527	91902	91384	31444	54783	38760
47857	32483	38493	52606	91078	13631	67863
77556	82242	00134	70154	09027	79459	18730
73884	69312	03395	06879	49662	40000	61598
19254	06677	54192	53422	58200	74464	73949
70801	53719	25214	65635	07565	49977	45525
46723	00256	96221	26641	00309	36009	48392
01433	78721	02647	25454	53913	97554	41578
55953	93448	07805	53622	27330	18749	57867
19392	13899	56096	83645	45871	35950	52272
93295	12413	55774	97318	66402	11209	52495
65969	43349	85142	25650	01896	48680	51236
22290	63835	45589	04884	92760	70462	00538
03262	60347	31077	07165	26588	31296	56112
88717	62688	24828	89469	35483	76532	30256
52140	73771	56084	08775	94820	78139	25987
18912	58454	34011	85969	83621	92099	19131
23331	21939	03463	53828	78930	30987	40988
01844	45738	93150	13240	16694	59155	67589
74873	83971	92678	96950	69821	41119	43312
93143	07350	94289	76144	47238	08110	00037
58089	70520	96997	71007	87803	52458	06637
40359	28351	53492	73134	02370	72313	53039
27726	51835	23966	50279	26329	25754	43530
27351	49177	36914	50258	62361	38229	89608
98892	98061	15330	31705	71923	29266	72716
31752	04842	13693	84292	48485	76178	41716
35394	12989	05867	11568	45056	16609	20470
52239	61201	57415	35609	38761	19589	24238
80449	81351	73642	48643	23848	48390	56829
54114	90290	62627	65151	15687	81062	06729
08796	99297	48807	88310	75454	45456	85394
16575	62665	97861	71650	56981	61794	94285
88290	17679	08945	25816	11848	95106	22031
73065	40870	82576	37089	86738	16284	44725
64255	55604	78635	13197	72213	95102	36723
44508	72683	51088	55368	85587	27046	11198
28184	30078	92578	83789	08044	76238	47599
06568	92482	70037	66779	63312	00619	94053
92810	35331	78995	44221	41532	51606	26430
90993	41149	06159	39242	11163	14764	19246

If the universe had consisted of 100 items, all but one of the numbers needed (1 to 99) would require only two places. To avoid wasting the extra place, the numbers may be redefined by setting 1 = 01 and 100 = 00, and restricting the readings to two digits only. Numerous devices may, with a little thought, be developed to economize in the use of the table.

The method of random selection may result in choosing duplicate items. Thus, the item 001 occurs in both the 5th, 9th, and 10th columns. Two choices then exist: (a) the item may be retained both times and given a double weight in estimates prepared from the sample, or (b) the instruction for selection may be ignored if the item is already in the sample, and the process of reading may be continued by selecting another item. The procedure to be followed will depend on the *model* used—i.e., whether sampling is assumed to be conducted with or without replacement of the items drawn before proceeding to the drawing of the next item, or whether the universe is infinite or finite in character. In most practical situations, the accountant deals with finite universes or sampling without replacement, and it is satisfactory to use the second alternative—ignoring duplicate drawing instructions. Indeed, the formulas suggested elsewhere, as in the definitions of *variance*, *coefficient of variation*, and similar items, are specifically designed to allow for sampling without replacement.

Because of the difficulty of clerical training and the necessity of avoiding the disordering of files, the device of a "random start" rather than random selection may be used. Thus, if a 10 percent sampling of a file of 1,000 items is to be made utilizing the accompanying table of 700 random numbers, a sampling interval of 7 could be chosen, commencing, say, with the first three digits of column 1 opposite line 4, which are 710; the next number could then be 774, the first three digits of column 1, line 11; and so on. This method of drawing is referred to as *systematic-random sampling*. Not only is it administratively more convenient, but, depending on the type of correlation present in the file, it may, under certain circumstances, be statistically more efficient than an unrestricted random drawing. Correlation in the files may introduce inefficiency and *bias* as well. To guard against this, or to form some estimate of the bias, it is desirable to use multiple-random starts, widening the sampling interval accordingly. Thus, if two random starts were desired, the sampling interval might be increased to 14. Reading down the fourth column in the table, the first random start could be at line 2, and then every 14th item thereafter would be included in the sample; the second random start could be at line 5 (= 828 in the table) and then every 14th item, as on lines 19, 33, 47, and so forth, would be included. The sample selected under each random start could then be analyzed separately and compared for significant differences. Generally, it is advisable to conduct small preliminary analyses in the form of pilot studies to determine the character of the files and the suitability of systematic samples before beginning the main drawing. The results of such pilot studies may be made not only to provide such tests but also to furnish useful estimates of *parameters* for sample redesign, thus taking full advantage of the information gained. Moreover, pilot results may also be combined by appropriate techniques with the results of the main study, so that no information is lost in the process. This technique is referred to as two-phase or multiphase sampling, depending on the number of separate studies involved.

random sample (statistics) A sample in which all the elements have been drawn at random, or according to the laws of chance. The procedure by which the sample is constructed characterizes a random sample, rather than its specific content. See *stratified sampling; systematic sampling; multiphase sampling; multistage sampling; replication.*

random sampling (statistics) A procedure for selecting a sample of arbitrary size n with preassigned probability from a given *universe;* exemplified by the use of random numbers. The universe may be finite or infinite. See *unit of sampling.*

random variation (statistics) 1. A fluctuation resulting from chance alone. In statistical quality control, a random variation is defined as a fluctuation in quality or quantity not attributable to an assignable, nonchance cause disclosed by systematic investigation.

2. In time-series analysis, the term is often used to denote a variation in data which is (a) explainable, and (b) the result of more or less unique, nonrecurring events. A marked fluctuation in the price level caused by a war may be classified as random to distinguish it from movements or variations caused by trend, seasonal, and cyclical factors.

range The difference between the largest and smallest items in a group of numerical data. See *dispersion.*

rate 1. The price of a unit of service over a unit of time; as, a labor rate of $2 per hour.

2. The measure of movement over a unit of time; as, a monthly rate of production.

rate of exchange The price at which one currency may be purchased with another currency; sometimes used as an equivalent of *price.* See *foreign exchange.*

rate-of-return pricing A method of determining prices by adding a markup on costs which will produce a predetermined return on investment. This method is comparable to target pricing in price-competitive industries. A dominant firm that establishes price in a price-leadership industry may employ this method to determine a price level not only for its own products but also for those of competitors. In fixing the rate of return on investment, consideration is given both to the opportunity created for new investment and to the possibility of forcing high-cost firms out of business. See *price.*

rate of turnover = *turnover.*

rating 1. The financial or credit standing of a person as determined by a mercantile agency.

2. The relative worth of a security as determined by any of several investment advisory services.

3. A projected *rate(2)* of working.

ratio The relation of one amount, a, to another, b, expressed as "the ratio of a to b"; $a{:}b$ ("a is to b"); or as a simple fraction, integer, decimal fraction, or percentage; thus, the ratio 6:5 may also be written as $\frac{6}{5}$ or 1.2 (or "1.2 to 1") or 120 percent. Financial ratios are those derived from comparisons of balance-sheet items, or of balance-sheet items with profit-and-loss items; operating ratios are those derived from comparisons of items of income and expense. The purpose of ratios is to epitomize and facilitate comparisons with periods, another organization, or an industry average.

Among ratios employed by accountants, credit men, and investment analysts are the ones shown in the table at the top of page 360, where a is the numerator of the ratio expressed as a fraction and b the denominator.

The current ratio is regarded as an index of liquidity, a ratio of $2\frac{1}{2}$ (i.e., current assets two-and-a-half times current liabilities, described also as a "two-and-a-half-to-one" ratio) being commonly regarded as reflecting a "safe" financial condition. In most situations, however, it is only one of a number of factors the effects of which must be weighed before any conclusion as to financial strength or weakness is warranted. Among these factors are the possible demand of next year's business for larger working capital because of expanded volume or increased prices, the possible insufficiency of working capital

Usual Designation	a	b
Current ratio	Current assets	Current liabilities
Turnover (or inventory turnover)	Cost of sales	Average inventory at cost
Or	Net sales	Average inventory at retail
Or	Units sold	Average units on hand
Or, less accurately,	Net sales	Average inventory at cost
Collection ratio (or receivables turnover)	Net credit sales	Average receivables
Liabilities-to-worth ratio	All liabilities	Net worth
Or	Long-term debt	Net worth
Or	Current liabilities	Net worth
Equity ratio	Total assets	Net worth
Equity turnover	Net sales	Net worth
Working-capital turnover	Net sales	Working capital
Operating ratios	Income-statement items	Net sales

during future peak production periods as compared with those of past years, an increase in length of the production period, an increased stocking of scarce raw materials, expanded credit terms to customers, the approaching maturity of long-term obligations, and an expected replacement of depreciating assets at higher prices; the presence of any or a combination of such factors may point to a prospective working-capital deficiency, although the present working capital and working-capital ratio may be high. Among bank credit men, the determination of the working-capital ratio is only one of a series of tests that must be applied before the propriety of either a short-term loan or a term loan may be determined.

A variation of the current ratio is known as the *acid test:* the ratio of current assets, omitting inventories and prepaid expense, to current liabilities. Its asserted value lies in the indication of relative ability to pay current obligations from existing liquid or nearly liquid assets of the business.

Turnover, the ratio of goods sold to inventory, is in practice computed in a variety of ways but usually in terms of cost. Its object is to determine the number of times during a given period that a stock of goods has been replaced. In retail establishments, the turnover figure is watched closely, a decline in turnover usually signalizing not only a falling off of business and reduced net income, but also the possibility of poor management, failure to meet competition, or overbuying; on the other hand, an increase in turnover can be accompanied by decreased retail prices without disturbing the rate of profit. In retail enterprises, the management may set both turnover and gross-profit-ratio standards for each department; periodic results from operations are compared with these standards and with those of similar departments in other establishments. Such standards, and trends in such standards, are given wide publicity in many retail trades.

A change in a collection ratio in a particular enterprise, in comparison with similar ratios of preceding periods, may denote a trend in business conditions, a shift in the character of customers, a modification of credit terms, or an increase or decrease in the number of customers anticipating adjustments, as from defective products sold to them. A collection ratio is converted into an average carrying period for customers' accounts by dividing it into 360. Thus, a ratio of 6 indicates that a period of 60 days is required for the collection of the average credit sale.

Comparison of liabilities or various

groups of liabilities with net worth gives some clue to the relative safety of the debt and also gives a comparison of the relative contributions of classes of investors. Over a period of time, a series of these ratios is likely to be interpreted as indicating a trend varying all the way from a larger "trading on the equity" to the building up of a greater safety factor or buffer for creditors. The same trends can also be discerned from a comparison of a series of equity ratios: total assets (often excluding intangibles) divided by net worth.

The turnover of net worth (i.e., annual sales divided by average net worth during the sales period) reflects roughly what is regarded as the effectiveness of stockholders' investment. In recent years, sales have increased at a greater rate than invested capital, and in nearly all industry the ratio has increased materially. Before World War II, a ratio of approximately 1 was not uncommon in many enterprises, but at present, thanks to spiraling prices (which have included proportionately higher profits) and a substantially larger current indebtedness, a ratio of much more than 2 is often encountered.

A substantial working-capital turnover (sales divided by net current assets), amounting, for example, to 4 or 5, may denote some degree of management effectiveness, particularly where a stable increase is noted. Like other ratios, it bears comparison with those of preceding periods and of similar organizations.

Commonly found operating ratios are (a) comparisons of income-statement items with net sales, (b) comparisons of details of production cost with total production cost, (c) the times-interest factor, (d) earnings (= net income) per share, and (e) return on investment. See, for example, *gross-profit analysis.* Income statements often feature percentage relationships of both expense items and income balances with net sales. The *times-interest* factor, the ratio of net income before deducting interest usually on long-term debt to such interest, is often cited by security analysts as a measure of the safety margin available to a prospective bondholder. Similarly employed are "earnings per share" coupled with and in contrast to "dividends per share"; this may relate (a) to preferred shares, obtained by dividing net income by the number of preferred shares outstanding, or (b) to common shares, obtained by dividing net income pertaining to common shares (= net income less preferred-dividend requirements, if any) by the number of common shares outstanding. An indicated percentage "return on investment" is in most instances one of the earnings-per-share figures just described, divided by any of several amounts: the related par value, the related paid-in value, or, in the case of common stock, the related paid-in value plus a proportionate share of earned surplus. For the business as a whole, "return on investment" may likewise be variously computed: net income divided by the par value or paid-in amount of capital stock, by net worth at the beginning or end of the year, or by net worth averaged over the year. The basis, clearly described, of any quoted operating ratio must be set forth if the ratio is to be accurately interpreted.

In obtaining an annual average, as of net worth, the commonest averaging method is to divide by 2 the sum of the amounts at the beginning and end of the year. Or, for greater precision, the quarterly or monthly average may be computed, although it will be found in most cases that the resulting ratio is not materially affected, if at all, by the added effort.

rational number An integer or the quotient of two integers; as, 1; -173; $\frac{3}{4}$ (= $0.75\dot{0}$); $0.\dot{1}4285\dot{7}+$ (= the *repetend* of $\frac{1}{7}$). Every rational number employed as a single number or as a fraction can be expressed in terms of a distinctive *repetend* (e.g., $\frac{5}{1} = 5.\dot{0}$). An *irrational number* has no repetend. See *integer; number; imaginary number.*

raw material Goods purchased for use as an ingredient or component part of a finished product. They range from goods in their natural state requiring further treatment or fabrication, to finished parts that may be assembled without further processing. They do not include *supplies* used in the manufacturing process that do not become a part of the product.

reacquired stock Capital stock title to which has reverted to the issuing corporation, following repurchase, donation, or settlement of a debt to the corporation. If the reacquired shares are kept alive, i.e., the certificates are not canceled, they are known as *treasury stock* or *treasury shares.* If the certificates are reacquired in accordance with a plan of redemption, as in the case of certain types of preferred stock, cancellation is usually deemed to have occurred simultaneously with the act of repurchase, the "treasury" status thus being bypassed, and the shares are said to be retired. See *redemption.*

real account A ledger account, the balance of which is carried forward into a succeeding fiscal period; hence, any balance-sheet item; distinguished from *nominal account.*

real cost 1. Cost expressed in terms of physical units of measurement; as, tons, bushels, miles, man hours; or in terms of some measure of prices obtaining on a base or comparison date.

2. Money cost reduced to a common measure of sacrifice attendant on an economic activity.

real estate (or **property**) *Land* and *land improvements,* including buildings and appurtenances; also, standing timber and orchard trees.

realize To convert into cash or a receivable (through sale) or services (through use); to exchange for property which at the time of its receipt may be classified as, or immediately converted into, a current asset. See *revenue realization; depreciation.—realizable, adj.; realization, n.*

realized appreciation Appreciation that has found its way into current assets through production or sale. The term appeared during World War I as the result of the imposition of a tax on profits exceeding a certain return on invested capital, and the consequent attempt to include in the latter all elements of retained income. The amount was determined in most cases by applying to accumulated depreciation provisions, based on appreciated values, a ratio obtained by dividing the original amount of appreciation surplus by the total appreciated value. Thus, assume that the appraised and recorded value of a building was $150,000, its cost $100,000, accrued depreciation $27,000 at the beginning of the year, based on appraised value, and the current year's provision for depreciation an additional $3,000; the appreciation of $50,000 indicates a ratio of $\frac{1}{3}$ to the appraised value, and the realized appreciation is one-third of $27,000, or $9,000, plus one-third of $3,000: a total of $10,000 at the year's end. In the past, the effect on the books of account was often that reflected in the entry below covering the one year.

Plant expense	$3,000.00	
Appraisal surplus	1,000.00	
Reserve for depreciation		$3,000.00
Earned surplus		1,000.00
Provision for depreciation at 2% of $150,000; realized appreciation at 2% of $50,000.		

The reasoning behind this type of entry was that appreciation as well as historical cost was being charged to operating costs each year, and by passing from the status of fixed asset to inventory and from inventory to accounts receivable and from accounts receivable to cash, the appreciation was converted into a liquid asset.

realized depreciation = *recapture of depreciation.*

realized revenue (or **profit**) Profit; a profit in the form of cash or some asset which at the time the transaction was consummated could have been converted immediately into cash or another current asset.

real price (or **value**) 1. The price of record during different periods subject to index-number adjustment to include a change in money value. See *price*.
2. The value of a product of land in terms of its purchasing power over the necessities and luxuries of living desired by the producer.

real wages The purchasing power of money wages; the ability of money wages to purchase satisfactions.

reasoning 1. Inference; mental activity involving the consideration of data for the purpose of reaching a conclusion concerning them.
2. The use of any or all of the processes, or the processes themselves, by which arguments are conducted or conclusions are reached.

rebate 1. An allowance; a deduction; a refund of a part of the price paid for a good or service.
2. In banking practice, discount deducted when a loan is paid before maturity.

recap = recapitulation; also, a résumé of mixed data by principal classes.

recapitalization Any major change in the character and amount of the outstanding capital stock or paid-in surplus of a corporation, including the absorption therein of a deficit. See *reorganization; quasi reorganization.*

recapture of depreciation (Federal income taxes) Realized depreciation: that portion of a gain (selling price less *book value*) from the disposition of depreciable property attributable to deductions accounted for as depreciation expense during the period of ownership; taxable as ordinary income (Section 1.1245–1).

receipt 1. The acquisition of cash or any other asset.
2. A written acknowledgment of something acquired; hence, an accounting document recording the physical receipt of goods; a receiving ticket or slip.
3. *pl.* Cash or other assets acquired, from any source.

receivable *adj. Collectible,* whether or not *due.*
n. 1. An account or note receivable.
2. *pl.* The title of a balance-sheet item representing the sum total of accounts and notes receivable (i.e., amounts due from customers); classified as a current asset. A split in the item is made if amounts owing from persons other than customers—e.g., officers—has been included, unless such amounts are nominal, arise from ordinary sale transactions, and are to be collected within the usual credit period accorded customers. Amounts owing from officers and employees are given a separate classification beneath current assets if they are not currently collectible. Sometimes notes receivable are distinguished from customers' accounts and displayed separately, where they are of an unusual character; in the case of a material amount of installment notes or accounts, the separation is accompanied by some indication of the range or mean of due dates. Installment accounts not to be collected within a year are sometimes excluded from the current-asset classification; however, trade practice in that type of business permits their retention. If an allowance for bad debts is required, the amount of the allowance (reserve) is deducted and only the net amount appears on the balance sheet. See *balance sheet.*

receive To acquire cash, any other asset, or a service.

receiver 1. A person appointed by a court to take charge of property pending its disposition or the attainment of an imposed objective.
2. One appointed to receive money or goods; a cashier or receiving clerk.

receiver's certificate An evidence of indebtedness issued by a receiver from the proceeds of which he has secured funds or other assets necessary for the preservation or operation of the property in his charge; it constitutes a lien on the property, ranking ahead of other secured liabilities.

reciprocal (of a number) The quotient obtained by dividing any number into 1. Thus, the reciprocals of 2, 3, 0.07, and $\frac{12}{17}$ are 0.5, $0.\dot{3}$, $14.\dot{2}8571\dot{4}$, and $\frac{17}{12}$, respectively. See *repetend.*

reclassify To break down a transaction or transaction group into *secondary classifications,* usually accompanied by transfers to *secondary accounts.*

recognize 1. To determine the amount, *timing, classification,* and other conditions precedent to the entry of a *transaction.*
2. Hence, to give expression on books of account: said of transactions. See *transaction; accrue; revenue realization; cost absorption.*
—*recognition, n.*

reconciliation 1. The determination of the items necessary to bring the balances of two or more related accounts or statements into agreement. Example: In the reconciliation of a depositor's bank balance, outstanding checks which have not been presented to the bank for payment, deposits not credited by the bank, collection fees, protest fees, and the like, charged by the bank but not entered on the customer's books, drafts collected, rebates of interest, and so forth, credited by the bank but also not entered on the customer's books, are factors the net amount of which will bring the balances between the depositor and the bank into agreement when added to the smaller or subtracted from the larger of the two balances.
2. A statement of the details of the difference between any two or more accounts. Thus, a reconciliation of an account on home-office books containing transactions with a branch would involve a showing of the balance of that account and of the corresponding account (with the home office) on the branch-office books, and a listing of the details making up the difference.
—*reconcile, v.t.*

reconciliation of surplus 1. A statement of changes in surplus accounts during an accounting period.
2. A statement, at one time often appended to accountants' reports, explaining the difference between book and reported surplus amounts; under current standard practice, the public accountant no longer certifies a financial statement not in agreement with the books.

reconciliation statement = *reconciliation (2).*

record *n.* 1. A book or document containing or evidencing some or all of the activities of an enterprise or containing or supporting a transaction, entry, or account. Examples: a book of account; subsidiary ledger; invoice; voucher; contract; correspondence; internal report; minute book.
2. *pl* = *books of account.* The expression "books and records," though redundant, is in common use.
v.t. To give expression to a transaction on (or in) the *books of account;* to *enter.*

record date See *stockholder of record.*

recording medium The cash voucher, journal, journal voucher, or other document, summary, or book employed as the means of giving initial expression to a transaction and serving as a basis for transferring the amount of the transaction to a ledger; a *posting medium.* Examples: a journal entry; a voucher evidencing a payment, from which a ledger posting is made in detail, or, joined with other similar items, in total.

recoup To recover an outlay through sale, use, or charge to profit and loss; to *realize.*—*recoupment, n.*

recover To convert into cash or other current asset: said of all or part of the cost of a good or service, or operation, upon its sale or upon the recognition of its contribution to production; to *realize.* See *recognize; transaction.*

recovery The absorption of cost as the result of sale, use, or depreciation or other process of allocation; realization. See *cost absorption.*

recovery cost (or **expenditure**) 1. = *residual cost.*

2. (governmental accounting) An expenditure for or on behalf of another governmental unit, fund, or department, or for a private individual, firm, or corporation, ultimately to be recovered in cash or its equivalent.

recovery value 1. Estimated revenue from the resale or scrapping of a fixed asset; *salvage(2).*

2. = *residual cost.*

redemption The retirement of stocks or bonds by the issuer by means of repurchase, usually at a preagreed rate.—*redeem, v.t.*

redemption fund = *sinking fund.*

redemption premium The premium paid on the retirement of a security, in accordance with the terms of the contract between the issuer and the original security purchasers. It is a financial expense in the case of bonds, and is recorded when paid or accrued as is *bond discount.* A premium paid in the retirement of capital stock is accounted for as a charge to paid-in surplus or earned surplus, or both, following the rule applying to the acquisition of *treasury stock.*

red-herring prospectus An announcement and description of an anticipated issue of securities, given restricted circulation during the "waiting" period of 20 days or other specified period between the filing of a registration statement with the U. S. Securities and Exchange Commission and the effective date of the statement. It generally takes the form of the final prospectus, except that the offering price, commissions to dealers, and other data dependent on price are omitted; also emblazoned across each page is an inscription printed in red, stating that the document is not an offer to sell or the solicitation of an offer to buy and that neither kind of offer may be made until the registration statement has become effective. See *prospectus.*

red-ink entry 1. An entry made in red to indicate its subtractive effect upon the aggregate. Example: a credit in a column or book where ordinarily only debits are entered. The use of symbols such as a minus sign or parentheses obviates the use of red ink.

2. Any item in an account having such an effect; as, an encircled posting or one preceded by a minus sign.

3. = *loss.*

rediscount *n.* A negotiable instrument, previously acquired by a bank at a discount, sold to a Federal Reserve Bank; to be eligible for rediscount, the note, bill, or acceptance must (a) be the product of an agricultural, commercial, or industrial transaction, (b) have a maturity of 90 days or less, (c) bear the endorsement of a member bank, and (d) if in excess of $15,000, be accompanied by a financial report of the first endorser. —*rediscount, v.t.*

redistributed cost See *circulation of costs.*

reducing-balance form = *report form.*

reducing-balance method See *depreciation method.*

reference *v.* To determine the accuracy of the facts and figures in a draft report or letter by comparison with working papers or other source data and by recomputing totals, extensions, and other derived amounts.

refund *n.* An amount paid back or a credit allowed on account of an overcollection; a *rebate.*

v.t. 1. To pay back or allow credit for an overcollection.

2. To provide for the payment of a loan by means of cash or credit secured by a new loan.

refunding bond One of an issue of bonds having as its purpose the retirement of a bond already outstanding. The new issue may be sold for cash and the proceeds applied to the redemption of the outstanding bonds, or the new bonds may be exchanged for the outstanding bonds.

register A record for the consecutive entry of any class of transactions, with notations of such essential particulars as may be needed for subsequent reference. Its form varies from a one-column sheet to one of many columns on which entries are distributed, summarized, and aggregated as a means of determining periodic adjustments or totals. It may serve as a journal, a subsidiary ledger, or both. See *journal.*

registered bond A bond the principal of which, and usually the interest, are payable only to the person whose name is recorded on the books of the obligor or trustee.

registered warrant (municipal accounting) A warrant registered by the paying officer for future settlement because of present lack of funds, and payable in the order of registration. In some cases a warrant is registered when issued and in other cases it is registered when presented to the paying officer by the holder. See *warrant.*

registrar An agent, usually a bank or trust company, officially appointed by a corporation to account for the original and subsequent issues of its capital stock, the cancellation of certificates presented for transfer, and their reissue. He maintains the corporation's stock register, by means of which an overissue is prevented. His signature validates each outstanding certificate, and his statement of the number of shares outstanding is accepted by the public accountant as a confirmation of his client's book record. The office of registrar is often combined with that of *transfer agent.*

registration (of securities) The process of qualifying a security for sale to the public, accomplished by filing documents in acceptable form with state blue-sky commissions or with the U. S. Securities and Exchange Commission; frequently public hearings are required, especially where deficiencies are found in the information filed, and these may be sufficient cause for the postponement or suspension of the normal effective date of the registration, which, under SEC regulations, is normally 20 days after the filing date. See *stop order.*

registration statement 1. A formal statement by a corporation filed with the U.S. Securities and Exchange Commission or other government body, containing financial and other data for the information of buyers in a proposed sale of securities.

2. A similar statement required by a state or local authority.

3. The statement required to be filed with the U. S. Securities and Exchange Commission by a national security exchange.

regression equation An equation expressing average relationships between two or more variables. This term and equivalent terms, such as lines of regression, derive their names from Francis Galton, who, in a study of relationships between heights of children and parents, believed he detected a tendency for the former to regress toward average heights. For example, regardless of whether the height of fathers was above or below the average, sons, Galton believed, tended to go back or regress toward the mean. See *least-squares method.*

regressive tax A tax the amount of which, remaining unchanged or decreasing, varies inversely with the size or value of the property or the amount of the income on which it is levied; contrasts with *progressive tax.*

reinsurance An agreement between two insurers whereby one assumes all or part of the risk of loss on a policy issued by the other: a practice followed, for example, where large single risks are underwritten.

rejectable quality level (statistical quality control) A term synonymous with, and often preferred to *lot tolerance percent defective* (*LTPD*): commonly designated by *RQL*, in contrast with *AQL* (*acceptable quality level*).

related company = *affiliated company.*

related cost 1. A *cost* incurred in securing a sale or other revenue; any *variable* or *semivariable* cost.

2. A *cost* consequent upon or leading to another cost.

3. = *common cost.*

release (of a mortgage) A formal document, recorded in the same manner as a mortgage, stating that the obligation under the mortgage has been discharged.

reliability 1. (auditing) The measure of confidence that may be placed in a set of records or reports. The test of reliability is whether a reconstruction, following accepted accounting practices, would yield approximately the results actually obtained. The closeness with which the records or reports conform to the results thus theoretically obtainable constitutes the degree of reliability. See *replication.*

2. The confidence generated in a reader of financial statements by their appearance, fullness of information presented, and general capacity to communicate both favorable and unfavorable information.

3. (management) The condition of operating effectiveness in which continuity of function, adherence to present standards, capacity for avoiding failure, and other desirable factors are believed to be present.

4. (statistics) Relative ability to repeat results in a given set of trials or experiments. See *accuracy; trend analysis.* —*reliable, adj.*

relief (governmental accounting) The allowance of credit to an *accountable officer* or employee for an amount *disallowed* or a charge made by the Comptroller General, in compliance with a specific direction of the Congress or as the result of the exercise of the Comptroller General's statutory authority.

remainderman One entitled to the corpus of an estate upon the expiration of a prior estate, such as a life tenancy.

remittance slip A printed form accompanying a remittance, indicating what debt it is meant to cover and detailing any adjustments, corrections, or deductions. A check or voucher check may also supply this information.

renegotiation The procedure, followed by governmental agencies, often leading to the adjustment of a contract price or contract amount after delivery has been made and the profit derived from the contract has been determined.

renegotiation reserve A current liability estimated to be the amount refundable under government contracts.

renewal 1. The replacement of a part, having more than a nominal value or having a life generally of more than a year; of a machine; or of any unit of plant and equipment: an addition to fixed assets accompanied by the removal therefrom of the item replaced. See *cost absorption.*

2. The cost of replacing a part, having a small value or having a life ordinarily not exceeding a year, of a machine or other unit of plant and equipment: usually classified as a repair and constituting a charge to operations.

3. *pl.* The cumulative costs of the replacements in sense 2 over a period of time, as a year, the ledger account consisting of such costs, often combined with repair costs and commonly entitled Repairs & Renewals. See *replacement.*

renewal (or **replacement**) **fund** Cash or securities set aside to provide for the replacement or renewal of plant and equipment: a procedure occasionally followed by a public utility, less often by a commercial enterprise.

rent 1. Compensation for the use of land or buildings, or of equipment or other personal property. The amount paid constitutes income to the owner of the property and an expense to the tenant or user of the property.

2. One of a series of annuity payments.

3. (economics) Payments or commitments to factors of production, the terms of which, if modified, will *not* alter the supply. Like *costs,* rents are known, with certainty, in advance. But, unlike costs, they represent a surplus over and above necessary payments to secure a particular volume of product.

A tax which affects costs will thus generally affect supply and price. A tax whose impact or incidence is entirely on rents will not affect either supply or price. See *quasi rent*.

rent of an annuity The periodic payment or payments to or from an *annuity fund*.

rent of ordinary annuity See *compound interest*.

rent roll A landlord's or agent's record of rentals periodically receivable from each property or subdivision thereof owned or managed, and showing also vacancies, arrears, recoveries of arrears, and other information concerning deviations from the regular terms of the lease. It may have characteristics of a journal and subsidiary ledger.

reorganization 1. A major change in the financial structure of a corporation or a group of associated corporations resulting in alterations in the rights and interests of security-holders; a *recapitalization*, *merger*, or *consolidation*.

2. A realignment of or change in management.

3. A major change in business policy or in production or trading methods.

repair 1. The restoration of a capital asset to its full productive capacity after damage, accident, or prolonged use, without increase in the previously estimated service life or capacity.

2. The charge to operations representing the cost of such restoration.

3. *pl.* The cumulative costs of such outlays over a period of time, as a year. See *renewal(3)*.

repayment with penalty A phrase used to indicate that section of certain loan agreements imposing a charge (usually stated as a percentage) against a borrower should he pay off his indebtedness (or any installment or other fraction) before its due date. Presumably the charge represents compensation for a break in the lender's investment program, for the waiting period preceding the reinvestment of the funds, and for the risk of a possible decline in interest rates at the prepayment date (a frequent cause for prepayments followed by refinancing elsewhere). Forestalling possible prepayments, lenders (e.g. insurance companies) have been known voluntarily to lower interest rates and to extend due dates when faced by competition from other lenders.

repeating audit = *periodic audit*.

repetend The repeating or circulating series of digits, including zeros, appearing in the quotient, when sufficiently extended, of any integer divided by a prime number or by a multiple of a prime number; thus, $\frac{1}{3} = .\dot{3}\dot{3}\ldots$; $\frac{2}{37} = .\dot{0}5\dot{4}\ldots$; $\frac{5}{21} = .\dot{2}3809\dot{5}\ldots$ The dot (·) above the number 3 indicates that 3 is the repetend; the dots above the numbers 0, 4, 2, and 5 indicate that these decimal fractions may be carried out to further places by repeating the included series of digits; thus $\frac{2}{37} = .\dot{0}5\dot{4}\dot{0}5\dot{4}\dot{0}5\dot{4}\ldots\ \infty$. See *rational number*.

replacement 1. The substitution of one fixed asset for another, particularly of a new asset for an old, or of a new part for an old part. On the books of account, the recognition of the cost of the new asset requires the elimination of the cost of the asset it replaces. See *fixed asset; renewal(1)*.

2. = *renewal(2)*; in this sense, the often-encountered phrase "renewals and replacements" is a redundant one.

replacement cost (or **value**) The cost at current prices, in a particular locality or market area, of replacing an item of property or a group of assets. See *current cost*.

replacement method (of depreciation) See *depreciation method*.

replacement unit An asset or asset part taking the place of a *retirement unit*, and hence capitalized; a *capitalization unit* or part thereof. See *retirement unit*.

replication The repetition of methods by which evidence is gathered. Thus, if under similar conditions of selection and verification, two *independent* testchecks are made of a group of vouchers, each is a replication of the other, although the particular vouchers examined may not be the same.

In statistics, replication and randomization together constitute the basis of modern experimental and survey design. What these terms mean may be clarified by an example:

Assume that it is desired to test the relative speed of two computing machines for a certain kind of calculation. An operator might be assigned to each machine by a random choice, as by tossing a coin, each operator being assigned the complete set of calculations to be run. Where one operator is more skilled than the other, as on one type of calculation, the results of the test will necessarily reflect a mixture of operator and machine efficiencies. A more refined test could be instituted by replicating the experiment in a variety of ways, and with varying efficiencies, thus yielding different types and degrees of information. If it is desired to determine merely which machine is faster, a very simple replication design may suffice. If it is desired to determine *how much* faster, or how much faster on certain operations, a more complicated set of replications may be necessary.

Having one operator assigned to each machine, as noted above, may introduce an operator bias. Another method might be to exchange operators and machines after the first calculations. But even this may prove unsatisfactory, since the switch might tend only to confirm the operator bias. Moreover, it might not be sufficient to compare the results of the same operator on each of the two machines, because both operators might show an improvement on the second machine, once having learned the routine. An enlarged replication might consist of having a series of operators each of whom is assigned by a random process to one of the machines for a run of computations—the amount and character of the runs also being chosen at random. Similarly, the two operators may be assigned to each machine for short runs, and several complete runs essayed in this manner until the desired information is secured.

Every process of auditing carries with it the notion of replication, the assumption being that the repetition of the same auditing procedures by others having equal skills would produce the same general conclusions. The replication of audit methods may be regarded as a test of the *precision* with which the procedures were carried out. The standard form of audit certificate implies not only a high degree of *precision*, but *accuracy* and *reliability* as well. See *accuracy; validity*.

report 1. = *financial statement*.
2. = *audit report*.

report form The style usually followed in presenting an income statement whereby the subject matter is read from top to bottom, beginning with sales and ending with net income, with subtotals at various points between. See *income statement*. The report form of balance sheet is sometimes encountered. See *balance sheet*, and illustrations thereunder.

reporting The giving, often periodically, of information to others; particularly (a) *internal* reporting as by an *internal auditor*, and (b) *external* reporting: the supplying of financial data by the management of a corporation to stockholders, government agencies, and the public; or the furnishing by a public accountant of his *opinion*, information, or comments at the conclusion of an *audit*. Among commonly recognized essentials of reporting are: brevity; the simplest language permitted by the complexity of the subject matter; intelligibility to the widest possible audience; inclusion of all essential items; and consistency and continuity with the next preceding report of the same type. See *audit; audit report; accountability; internal reporting; feedback*.

representation 1. (auditing) A written statement of fact or opinion requested of and obtained from the management of an enterprise under audit. The representations customarily obtained by the auditor from management at the close of an audit serve a threefold objective: a confirmation of business practices already observed by the auditor; an acknowledgment from management of its responsibility for the institution and operation of overall financial policies; and an opportunity to review with executives basic procedures with which they may not be wholly familiar, thereby more firmly fixing future top controls over such procedures. Among the items constituting a representation are: the nature, collectibility, and anticipated period of collection of receivables; the character and condition of and title to inventories; the nature of fixed assets and the liens thereon; the adequacy of depreciation-reserve provisions and balances; the inclusiveness of stated liabilities and the existence and character of contingent liabilities; the meaning of any extraordinary items appearing separately or merged with other items in the income statement; the consistency with which last year's accounting principles were applied during the current year; and the nature of any event or condition following the balance-sheet date that might affect the significance and interpretation of the financial statements.

2. The statement in the public accountant's short-form report that his client's financial statements "present fairly" *financial position* and *operating results*. See *audit report*; *fairness*.

3. Any statement of fact or opinion, such as one of those attributed to the management of a corporation and appearing in its published financial statements or in a prospectus. Management's representations as to published financial statements aside from those given to the auditor (see above) are, with respect to others, usually implicit but are generally understood to cover not only the auditor's representation of *fairness* but also the broader aspects implied in the continuation of the *going concern*. When an auditor certifies to financial statements only on condition that they are in agreement with the books of account, management's representation is made to cover the whole field of the auditor's examination.

representative sample Any *random sample* selected for observation, whether or not containing a determinable error. See *probability sample*.

reproduction cost Estimated cost to reproduce in *kind:* a term used in the appraisal of fixed assets.

repurchased stock Reacquired capital stock that has been bought from stockholders. See *reacquired stock; treasury stock*.

requisition A formal written demand or request, usually from one department to another within an organization, for specified articles or services.

reserve 1. A segregation or earmarking of retained earnings (earned surplus) evidenced by the creation of a subordinate account; *appropriated surplus:* a *true* reserve. The earmarking may be temporary or permanent, the purpose being to indicate to stockholders and creditors that a portion of surplus is recognized as unavailable for dividends. Examples: reserve for contingencies; reserve for improvements; sinking-fund reserve.

2. The total amount of recognized shrinkage in the cost of any fixed asset or class of fixed assets, credited to a separate account; a *valuation* or *allowance* account. Examples: *reserve for bad debts; reserve for (accumulated) depreciation* (of fixed assets); *reserve for amortization* (of intangibles); see these terms.

3. = *accrued liability;* as, reserve for Federal income tax.

4. The understatement of financial condition as employed in the phrase *secret* (or *hidden*) *reserve.*

5. In the Federal government, an appropriation or a part thereof not *apportioned* but set aside for possible future use or for return to the Treasury.

Uses of the term other than in senses 1 and 5 are declining, the substitution of *allowance* having gained considerable support in recent years.

reserve account = *retained earnings:* British usage.

reserve adequacy The sufficiency of the amount of an existing *reserve,* or of a reserve being accumulated at a planned rate, to offset a given cost or loss; as, the ability of a *depreciation reserve,* by the time the retirement of a fixed asset takes place, to absorb its *depreciable cost;* or the ability of a *pension reserve* to cover prospective payments to retired employees over a specified period of time. Under standard accounting procedures, a material inadequacy in a reserve must be disclosed in a financial statement.

reserved surplus = *appropriated surplus.*

reserve for accidents Retained earnings appropriated for possible future accidents. Amounts estimated to be payable for accidents that have already occurred are ordinary liabilities, provision for which is made through profit and loss.

reserve for amortization A valuation account set up to reduce the investment in an asset, in recognition of a plan for the extinction of such investment within a specified time, regardless of its physical condition. The term is applied principally to the accelerated writedown of assets having a legal or physical life greater than their economic life, such as patents, copyrights, franchises, and other intangibles, and of tangible assets such as leaseholds, leasehold improvements, mine equipment, and timber roads. See *amortization.*

reserve (allowance) for bad debts A valuation account set up to reduce the recorded amount of notes and accounts receivable to the amount anticipated as collectible; it is credited periodically with amounts offsetting provisions for estimated losses from receivables, and debited with the losses from the accounts against which the reserve was originally created. See *bad debt.*

reserve for contingencies *Earned surplus* (retained earnings) earmarked for expenses or losses that may or may not occur: a form of *appropriated surplus.* Its purpose is to store up earned surplus against the possibility of such expenses or losses, thus causing a lesser amount to be available for the absorption of dividends to stockholders. Among the items of uncertainty which have often given rise to a reserve for contingencies —and which may be reported under descriptive titles—are: damages to persons and property arising from past transactions; costs of repairs arising from long-term guaranties of product; guaranties of performance by others; losses from future operations; possible future decline in market price of inventory on hand; losses from purchase contracts that may prove to be unfavorable as to price or quantity. Like other appropriated-surplus reserves, a reserve for contingencies is a subdivision of earned surplus and so remains. Under standard practice, losses, if any, against which the reserve has been provided are losses of the year in which they are recognized and they are so reported on that year's income statement; when the period of contingency has passed, whether or not attended by losses, the full amount of the reserve is returned to its source: earned surplus. Formerly, such losses were often charged against the reserve, thus causing a larger *net income* to be reported for the period of the charge. See *postwar reserve; contingent liability; appropriated surplus;* see also AICPA Bulletin No. 43.

reserve for depletion The credit offsetting depletion provisions, less retirements; the account in which these items appear. See *depreciation.*

reserve for depreciation The credit offsetting depreciation provisions, less retirements; the account in which these items appear. See *accumulated depreciation.*

reserve for discounts A valuation account reflecting the estimated shrinkage in receivables that may result from the granting of *cash discounts* to customers in the settlement of their outstanding accounts. A *provision(1)* for such a reserve is not a standard requirement, usually because the amount involved is not *material.*

reserve for encumbrances (governmental accounting) A reserve set up within an appropriation to provide for *unliquidated encumbrances.*

reserve for overhead See *equalization reserve.*

reserve for renewals and replacements See *equalization reserve.*

reserve for repairs See *equalization reserve.*

reserve for retirement of preferred stock Earned surplus appropriated as a feature of a plan for the gradual reacquisition and cancellation of an outstanding issue of preferred stock.

Often required by the original agreement with preferred stockholders, the reserve may also be created voluntarily by board resolution; in either case, it serves to earmark earned surplus, thus forestalling demands for additional dividends by common stockholders. The total amount of the reserve may include the premium, if any, and the anticipated expense of retirement, the latter consisting primarily of advertising and fees of banks, brokers, or other appointed agents of the issuer; or the expense, if small, as is usual, may not be provided for in advance where the preferred stock was sold at a premium or where the issuer has been gradually acquiring it on the open market and has been able to repurchase it at less than par, the paid-in surplus account or accounts thus created serving as a part of the retirement-reserve requirement. When the retirement has been completed, the account maintained for the preferred stock will have disappeared; the paid-in-surplus accounts will have been absorbed (or diminished) by a portion (or all) of the retirement premium; a charge will have been made to retained earnings (earned surplus) for any portion of the retirement premium not absorbed by the paid-in-surplus accounts arising out of transactions in preferred stock; remaining will be the retirement reserve, intact, the amount of which is the sum total of the successive provisions therefor, and the balances, if any, of the paid-in capital; the former, being a subdivision of retained earnings (earned surplus) as are all appropriated-surplus items, is restored intact to its source.

Interim retirements of preferred stock should have no effect on succeeding provisions for the retirement reserve, since roughly the same total quantity of liquid assets will have to be expended on the repurchasing operation regardless of the time of its occurrence. A retirement reserve, whether pertaining to bonds or stock, serves no really useful purpose and is actually unnecessary in a well-operated corporation unless required by contract with security-holders. The board of directors could as easily permit the earned-surplus account to grow, explaining the need for its continued growth in a balance-sheet footnote, and contracts with stockholders have sometimes thus provided. The reserve serves only as an assurance to the security-holders that the board will be barred from dissipating as dividends the presumably liquid assets acquired through earnings—the normal source of funds for retirement.

reserve for wear, tear, obsolescence, or inadequacy = *reserve for depreciation.*

reserve fund Cash or securities segregated from working capital for some specific purpose, often accompanied by a corresponding liability or appropriation of surplus.

residual cost (or **value**) Cost (of an asset) less any part of cost amortized or treated as an expense or loss; *book value; residuary outlay; recoverable cost;* distinguished from *salvage,* which implies that the usefulness or recoverability (other than from the sale of scrap) has been reduced to zero.

residual net income (or **profit**) Net income remaining for common stock after satisfying fixed obligations to prior income claimants (operating costs, preferred stockholders). See *leverage.*

residuary legatee One entitled to receive the balance of an estate after specific bequests, taxes, and other liabilities have been satisfied.

residuary outlay *Outlay* less any outlay expiration; *residual cost.*

resolution 1. An action or proposal for action by the board of directors of a corporation ranging from a directive to management (e.g., the declaration of a *dividend*) to expressions of opinion, thanks, censure, and the like.

2. Any expression of a desire or intent.

resource 1. = *asset.*

2. *pl.* An inclusive term often applied to the assets of a bank or other financial institution; as commonly used it may also include unrecorded sources of assumed organizational strength such as management, repeat customers, and so on.

responsibility The obligation prudently to exercise assigned or imputed *authority* attaching to the assigned or imputed role of an individual or group participating in organizational *activities* or *decisions.* See *authority.*

responsibility costing A method of accounting in which costs are identified with persons assigned to their control rather than with products or functions. It differs from *activity accounting* in that it does not in itself (a) require an organizational grouping by activities and subactivities or (b) provide a systematic criterion of system design.

restricted cash Cash deposits that can be withdrawn in whole or in part only under special conditions or for specified purposes. A separate bank account is usually required.

restricted fund A fund the control of the principal or income of which is restricted by agreement with or direction by the donor or other outside person, in contrast to a fund over which the owner has complete control. Example: in a university, a scholarship fund.

restricted random sampling See *systematic, stratified, multiphase,* and *multistage sampling.*

restricted receipts Receipts earmarked for specific purposes.

restricted stock option (Federal income taxes) A privilege granted by a corporation to an employee to purchase its stock. See *qualified stock option.*

restricted surplus (or **retained earnings)** That portion of *retained earnings* not legally available for dividends, as where preferred-stock dividends are in arrears, working capital or the working-capital ratio falls short of the minimum specified in a loan agreement, and so on; also retained earnings made unavailable for dividends by voluntary action of the board of directors. On a financial statement containing such an item, the nature of the restriction is disclosed in the accompanying sidehead or in a footnote.

results from operation *Net income,* sometimes before adding *other income* and before subtracting *income deductions.*

retail accounting The accounting methods of retail stores, particularly the methods advocated by the National Retail Dry Goods Association.

retail cost A term indicating that the *retail method* has been used in determining cost of sales or inventory.

retail method (of inventory) A method of maintaining a *book inventory* by which the cost of sales and inventories of department and other retail stores are determined at the close of intermediate accounting periods without a physical stocktaking. Generally, the method involves ascertaining the ratios between costs and selling prices of purchases, including the beginning inventory, and applying this percentage to net sales to obtain cost of sales. *Markons, markdowns,* and revisions of both also enter into the computation. As in the case of any book inventory, a periodic physical verification is an invariable accompaniment. Under the retail method, physical inventories are valued at selling prices and reduced to cost by application of the computed percentage.

retained earnings (or **income)** Accumulated *net income,* less distributions to stockholders and transfers to paid-in capital accounts. It may be appropriated, but an *appropriation(5)* remains as a subdivision of retained earnings, ultimately to be returned without diminution. Also known by the older title *earned surplus.*

retirement 1. The removal of a fixed asset from service, following its sale or the end of its productive life, accompanied by the necessary adjustment of fixed asset and depreciation-reserve accounts.
2. The asset so removed.
3. The cost of such an asset, particularly (*pl.*) the cumulative amount of such costs over a period of time, as a year.
4. The cancellation of reacquired shares of capital stock by a corporation. Retired shares are generally held not to be reissuable. See *treasury stock; outstanding capital stock.*
—*retire, v.t.*

retirement accounting (or **method**) See *depreciation method.*

retirement allowance A sum paid or payable to an employee retired from active service; an annuity or *pension.*

retirement curve = *mortality curve.*

retirement plan A plan providing for *retirement allowances.*

retirement table = *mortality table.*

retirement unit An asset or asset part the replacement of which is accompanied by the removal of its cost from the asset account. It is the credit counterpart of a replacement unit and may be the same or more or less than a *capitalization unit.* If less than a capitalization unit, its minimum dollar amount is often specified, in order that the capitalization of small items may be avoided. See *fixed asset; depeciation.*

retrospective rating (insurance) A method of adjusting the amount of a premium to the actual loss experience during the period of protection, subject to maximum and minimum limits.

return 1. A statement of information required by governmental bodies from individuals and business enterprises. Example: an income-tax return.
2. (with *on*) Earnings on investment, i.e., *income;* also, gross revenues or sales.
3. *pl.* Goods sent back to the seller, the amount being deducted by the seller from his gross sales and by the purchaser from his gross purchases.

revaluation reserve (or **excess** or **surplus**) The valuation account created when the book value of capital assets is adjusted to a higher level in accordance with an appraisal of such assets. See *realized appreciation.*

revenue 1. Sales of products, merchandise, and services, and earnings from interest, dividends, rents, and wages.
2. (governmental accounting) The gross receipts and receivables of a governmental unit derived from taxes, customs, and other sources, but excluding appropriations and allotments.
3. *pl.* The principal classes of gross operating income of common carriers and other public-utility companies; corresponds to *sales.*

revenue bond (municipal accounting) One of an issue of bonds by a governmental unit for the purpose of financing the construction or purchase of or additions to income-producing enterprises, where repayment of the bonds and periodic payments of interest are made dependent on earnings. Construction or purchases thus financed include bridges, airports, housing projects, school dormitories, electric plants, water plants, transportation terminals, markets, street-railway and bus systems, and public garages.

Revenue bonds are issued by three types of governmental organizations: states, local governments such as cities, and agencies established for the sole purpose of operating a revenue-bond-financed enterprise (e.g., a toll-bridge authority). From the standpoint of security, the type of issuing agency is ordinarily of little importance, since neither a state nor a local government can use its general credit to support such bonds. The safety of the investment is dependent on the profitability and good management of an income-producing venture.

One of the reasons for the emergence of revenue bonds has been the exhaustion of the legal *debt limit* of many governmental units. Revenue bonds are not as a rule held to constitute a part of a governmental unit's indebtedness for the purpose of computing such a limit. Even if a governmental unit has an ample margin, it may nevertheless decide to issue revenue bonds instead of *full-faith-and-credit bonds* in order to avoid the possibility of having to pay bonds and interest from other sources if the earnings of the enterprise should be insufficient. If the operations of an enterprise involve more than one governmental unit, revenue bonds may be the only source of construction funds.

The disadvantages of revenue bonds are twofold. Because they are payable solely from the revenue of the enterprise, they may represent a (1) high risk and thus carry a (2) higher interest rate than full-faith-and-credit bonds.

From the standpoint of the investor, revenue bonds offer a better yield and at the same time retain many of the advantages that full-faith-and-credit bonds possess. For example, the interest on revenue bonds is exempt from Federal income taxes. Revenue bonds are usually considered to be legal investments for banks, insurance companies, and trustees. While they do not have the backing of the governmental unit's taxing power, considerable protection is provided for the bondholder. The bond indenture usually provides that the governmental unit must charge sufficiently high rates for the service it renders in order that periodic costs, including depreciation, interest, and principal, may be met. Sometimes depreciation charges are not included among the operating expenses in computing required earnings on the theory that it is unfair to expect the users of the service to pay for the old plant (in the form of debt-service charges) and also for its eventual replacement (in the form of funds built up from depreciation charges). The indenture usually contains a pledge of the revenues of the enterprise for the payment of debt-service charges, thereby preventing their pledging for any other purpose. Another protection is the usual requirement of an annual audit by public accountants. Another customary remedy is the possibility of a mandamus to force the management to take whatever action is necessary to protect bondholders' interests, or an injunction prohibiting officials from incurring certain expenses or performing any acts contrary to the provisions of the bond indenture or likely to injure the bondholders' investment.

Moreover, the bondholders may also have a mortgage on the property, and are thus in a position to foreclose in the event of default. Foreclosure may, however, do more harm than good, since a public enterprise frequently receives open or hidden subsidies from the governmental unit in whose territory it operates. These subsidies may consist of (a) the payment of higher charges for services than are paid by other customers of the enterprise, (b) free engineering, legal, and accounting services, or (c) the exemption of the enterprise from state and local taxes. Should the bondholders take over the enterprise, these benefits would likely be lost. A better solution, although not a complete one, is for the bondholders to appoint a receiver and work out a plan of reorganization for getting the enterprise back on its feet.

The degree of risk involved is often dependent on several other factors. Revenue bonds issued for the purpose of acquiring a going concern present a smaller risk than those issued for the purpose of constructing a new project; the former have a known purchase price and the gross and net earnings are established; the latter, on the other hand, run the risks that actual construction costs may be greater than expected (a common fault in governmental operations) and that net earnings may not come up to expectations. Another factor is the relative need of the service. If the service rendered by the enterprise is highly essential, the governmental unit in whose territory the enterprise operates will not stand by idly and watch the enterprise fail, but will, in most situations, work out some plan of relief.

revenue deduction (municipal accounting) An expense, tax, or uncollectible account receivable of a municipal utility or other self-supporting enterprise.

revenue expenditure An expenditure charged against operations: a term used to contrast with *capital expenditure;* = *expense.*

revenue realization The recognition of revenue by a seller of goods or services. The amount involved, or price, is the agreed amount of money or money equivalent the buyer pays or promises to pay to the seller, net of allowances and discounts. The time of recording by the seller is often described as being at the point of performance: in the case of goods, when title passes; of services, when rendered. See *sale.*

revenue receipts Revenue collected in cash during a given period.

revenue reserves That portion, or any detail thereof, of the *net worth* or *total equity* of an enterprise representing *retained earnings* available for withdrawal by proprietors: a British term, contrasting with *capital reserves.*

reverse splitup The calling in of shares by the issuer, followed by the issuance of fewer shares in exchange; also known as *splitback* or *splitdown.* See *splitup.*

reversing entry An entry in which all the debits are identical as to account and amount with all the credits in a previous entry, and all the credits are identical as to account and amount with all the debits in the same previous entry. It is frequently employed at the beginning or end of an accounting period when, in the preceding *closing,* record was made of revenues not yet received, of liabilities for which no bills had been rendered, or of other transactions the exact amounts of which were unknown. The use of reversing entries makes possible a record of actual receipts and disbursements in the regular manner as if no adjustments had been recorded in the preceding period. See *adjusting (journal) entry; journal entry.*

review To examine critically any operation, procedure, condition, event, or series of transactions: a general term the application of which remains obscure unless accompanied by a statement of procedures or objectives.

revocable trust A trust terminable at the pleasure of or under certain conditions by its creator. See *trust.*

revolving fund 1. A fund from which moneys are continuously expended, replenished, and again expended. Examples: *imprest cash; working fund;* assets available for loans the repayments of which are available for other loans. 2. (governmental and institutional accounting) A fund created by an appropriation or issue of securities for the purpose of providing working capital that is to be replenished through revenues or transfers from users of the fund's facilities.

right 1. A claim having a natural, moral, or legal justification.

2. The privilege of a stockholder to subscribe to his proportionate share of any new issue of capital stock by a corporation, usually at a price somewhat less than market, unless, under the articles of incorporation or by agreement, the privilege has been waived; the existence of this privilege makes it possible for him to preserve his relative equity (*pre-emptive right*) in the business and at the same time maintain undiminished his interest in the retained earnings. It generally takes the form of a transferable subscription warrant issued by the corporation which must be exercised within a specified period of time. A single right is the privilege attaching to each old share of capital stock to buy a designated number of shares (or a fractional

share) of the new capital stock. The relation of the market value of a right to the market value of the old stock is sometimes expressed by the formula

$$m_1 = \frac{m - s}{n + 1},$$

where m_1 is the market value of one right, m the market price of an old share, s the subscription price of one new share, and n the number of old shares required to obtain the right or rights to purchase one new share. Thus, if m is 22, s is 20, and n is 4, the market price of a right to purchase $\frac{1}{4}$ share may be expected to be 40 cents.

right-of-way A *leasehold* or *easement*, temporary or permanent, permitting the construction and operation of a railway, road, power line, or pipeline over another's land. The cost of right-of-way is a *fixed asset*, and is subject to depreciation only following a decision ultimately to abandon.

risk Chance of loss: the subject matter, person or thing, of insurance; degree of probability of loss; the amount of insurance underwritten. See *probability*.

Robinson–Patman Act A Federal law (49 Stat. 1526), passed in 1936 as an amendment of the *Clayton Act*, its primary purpose being to specify additional competitive practices designated as "unfair." Ingredients, nature of manufacture, and origin of product were required to be disclosed; price differentials were permissible only where differences in cost could be demonstrated.

Rochdale principles See *cooperative*.

round lot A trading unit of 100 shares or multiples of 100 shares of an active stock: a stock-exchange term which may also be applied to units and multiples of 10 shares of an inactive stock.

round off To simplify the presentation of a quantity by omitting its terminal digits, with the express purpose of displaying only *significant* figures. Thus, in the preparation of an income statement, if the annual sales of a business concern are $2,648,465.23, this precise amount, although of importance for bookkeeping purposes, could be shortened to $2,648,-465, or to $2,648.5 thousands, or perhaps to $2.65 millions. Much will depend on the size of other amounts in the same schedule or the amounts with which it is to be compared or into which it is divided. For most purposes, a "significant" amount, particularly one that is not to be subdivided, rarely extends beyond a number of three or four digits. A decimal is often used to denote a fraction of a hundred, thousand, or million, as in the above example. An indication of the nature of abbreviated figures is given in the heading of the statement; examples: "000's omitted"; "in millions of dollars"; that is, $2,648.5 thousands or 2.65 millions for $2,648,465.23.

round sum A number the last digit or digits of which have been *rounded off*.

routine *adj.* Regular; customary; ordinary; repetitive; everyday; performed at the point of operations. Routine transactions are those consummated by operating employees with minimum supervision.

n. Repetitive operating work.

routinize To reduce to *routine:* said of methods of operation, particularly those surrounding *transactions* that recur in volume, the objective being speedy and accurate processing with a minimum of supervision and cost. Many *internal checks* and *controls*, including *internal-audit* programs, are concerned with the constant testing of these methods and with the institution and maintenance of shortcuts and other improvements of routinized procedures.

royalty Compensation for the use of property based on an agreed portion of the income arising from such use; as, the periodic payment to the owner of land for oil, coal, or minerals extracted; to an author for sales of his book; to a manufacturer for use of his processing equipment in the production operations of another person.

royalty interest (petroleum industry) The fractional interest of the owner or lessor of a tract of land in the production of crude oil and gas from the tract; the fraction most often encountered is $\frac{1}{8}$. See *working interest; overriding royalty interest; oil-and-gas payment.*

rule 1. An order, directive, or instruction, usually detailing something to be done or a prescribed operation; contrasted with *principle*, a rule covers a narrower field of activity and allows less discretion in its application. Rules of professional conduct may be self-imposed prescribed standards, such as those provided by an agreed-to code; see *ethics; principle; standard.* 2. A statement, explicit or implied, governing meanings, procedures, interpretations, or inferences belonging to subordinate languages, systems of analysis, or sets of operations and decisions. Since a rule governs the subordinate system, its validity cannot be logically proved or disproved within the same system; the logical demonstration of the validity of a rule is demonstrated by reference to a more *primitive* set of rules. The validity of the "realization rule" for measuring operating income, for example, cannot be tested by reference to whether it conforms to the policies of a particular company. A challenge to the validity of such a rule requires reference to more primitive rules concerned with more basic objectives of accounting *per se.* Policies and procedures of particular companies are judged in the light of rules thus derived, rather than the reverse.

rule off To underscore the last entry in a journal or the last posting in a ledger account for the purpose of indicating a total and preventing any further entry or posting thereabove; a process often followed by bookkeepers at the end of accounting periods when the books are closed, or when an account balances.

running form = *report form.* See also *account form.*

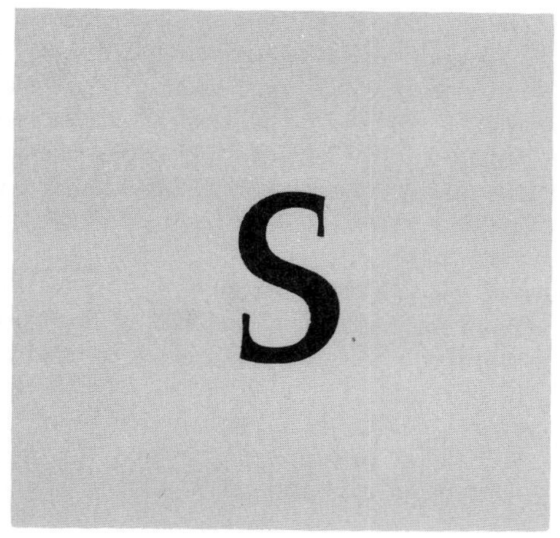

salary The compensation paid periodically for managerial, administrative, professional, and similar services; contrasts with *wages;* from salary amounts are deducted withholding tax and benefit provisions, leaving "take-home" pay.

salary roll The payroll for salaried employees.

sale 1. A *business transaction* involving the *delivery* (i.e., the giving) of a *commodity*, an item of *merchandise* or *property*, a *right*, or a *service*, in exchange for (the receipt of) *cash*, a *promise to pay*, or *money equivalent*, or for any combination of these items; it is recorded and reported in terms of the amount of such cash, promise to pay, or money equivalent. A sale is sometimes distinguished from an *exchange* (*1*), particularly in the phrase "sale or exchange," where the latter is confined to transactions involving no cash or an incidental amount of cash, thus being used in the sense of *barter;* but except for such use or where specifically qualified, the term extends to any transaction where something is parted with and as compensation therefor something is received. A sale differs from a *gift*, for which there is no consideration; from a *bailment*, which involves no transfer of title; and from a *chattel mortgage*, under which a transfer can occur only in case of default on the obligation it secures.

2. *pl.* The aggregate of such recorded and reported amounts during any given accounting period, appearing on books of account as a credit. On an *income* statement, unless otherwise qualified, sales are *net*, i.e., gross less returns, allowances, discounts, and (rarely) provisions for uncollectible accounts.

sales allowance See *allowance*(*2*).

sales discount See *discount*.

sales journal The book of original entry in which sales are recorded individually or in groups; it may also contain columns classifying sales by departments, products, and the like.

sales records Books and documents that serve as the evidence or record of cash and credit sales, including sales orders, tickets, slips, invoices, journals and summaries, and customers ledgers.

sales return See *return*.

sales revenue Total sales, usually with reference to a given period.

sale value The price at which an asset of any kind can be sold, less whatever cost is yet to be incurred.

salvage 1. Value remaining from a fire, wreck, or other accident or from the retirement or scrapping of an asset.

2. Actual or prospective selling price as second-hand material or as junk or scrap, of fixed assets retired, or of product or merchandise unsalable through usual channels, less any cost, actual or estimated, of disposition; *scrap value*. See *residual cost*.

3. (marine insurance) The award to those who have voluntarily given aid to the saving of marine property in peril.

salvage value = *salvage*(*2*).

sample *n.* 1. (statistics) A portion of a group of related *transactions*, *financial statements*, or other *universe* of data chosen to reflect or assist in determining the accuracy, propriety, or other characteristics of the whole. Sampling is an important element in the process of auditing and in the determination of national income. See *testcheck*.

2. A physical specimen used for selling or testing a quantity of goods; many articles of commerce are sold on the rep-

resentation by the seller that the quality (e.g., size, color, weight, strength, BTU's) of the entire lot conforms, within standard or agreed deviations, with the specimen.

v.t. & *i.* To select a sample.

sample size See *statistical quality control; expected value.*

sampling distribution (statistics) The graphical or mathematical form of the distribution taken by the value of any *statistic* or set of statistics calculated from samples of a given size. For example, the means of sufficiently large samples drawn at random from any *universe* tend to array themselves in a normal distribution. See *expected value.*

sampling error (statistics) *Standard error* of a sampling distribution.

sampling inspection (statistical quality control) See *acceptance sampling.*

satisfactory control (statistical quality control) See *statistical control.*

savings 1. The excess of income over consumption (sometimes stated in the form of purchases of consumers' goods and services) during a given period; often referred to as *current savings.*

2. Accumulated holdings of liquid assets and investments, including hoarded money, bank accounts, securities, real estate, machines; for the national economy as a whole, often referred to as the *stock of savings.* Total savings are stated on a gross or net basis, depending upon whether liabilities to third parties have been deducted.

savings-and-loan association A type of cooperative having as its purposes the promotion of thrift and home ownership. It exists in the form of state-incorporated building-and-loan associations, and Federally incorporated savings-and-loan associations.

scan (auditing) To look at the entries in an account, accounting record, or group of accounts or records, for the purpose of testing general conformity to pattern, noting apparent irregularities, unusual items, or other circumstances appearing to require further study. The term indicates a general and rapid review as opposed to a detailed examination or substantiation of each item, and often a review requiring the skill of an experienced auditor and having as its purpose the discovery of the qualitative aspects of a procedure, classification, or collection of transactions. See *analyze.*

scarce 1. In short supply.

2. (economics) Not *free;* said of any commodity or service which must be paid for if acquired.

scarcity (economics) A condition of insufficiency to supply all levels of demand: said of any economic good, or a good which requires economizing.

scatter diagram (statistics) A diagram consisting of coordinate axes and points designed to show relations between two or more variables; generally restricted to statistical data. Its purpose is to portray, simultaneously, central tendencies, such as regressions, and tendencies toward scatter or dispersion.

The analysis, on page 381, of sugar-refining-process costs plotted against output per week, is an illustration of a scatter diagram. On the coordinate axes (X and Y) are sales of output and cost; zero and certain intervening points are omitted, as indicated by the break or tear symbols "≀≀" on the chart. In the body of the diagram, all pairs of observations revealed by the data are noted by the symbol "x"; for example, the first "x," labeled ① in the lower left-hand corner, denotes that one week's record showed production of 38 tons at a total cost of $1,180; the Y axis reads $118, since it is stated in units of $10. In plotting the "$x$'s," it is well to denote them by a number code such as the ① used for the first "x." This not only facilitates plotting and checking large masses of data, but may serve to point toward other regularities, such as *time series,* deserving investigation.

Scatter diagrams are useful tools of analysis because they condense to visible form large masses of data whose meaning might otherwise be overlooked. As a tool, the scatter diagram is, moreover, flexible,

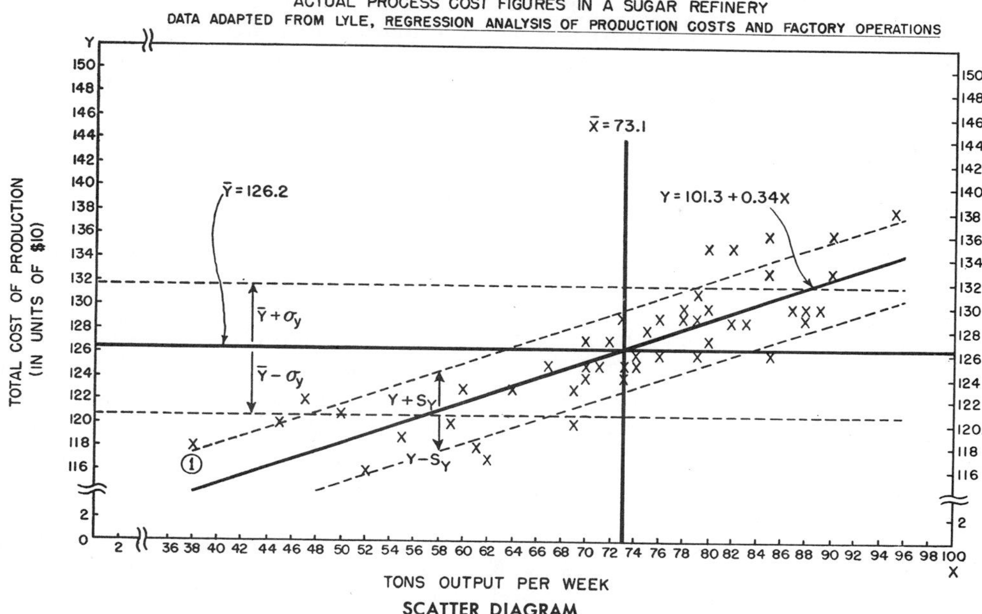

SCATTER DIAGRAM

permitting condensation without committing the investigator to more rigid limits, as an assumption of linearity may do in the *least-squares method*. The diagram may be used to indicate the mode of analysis. Inspection of the points shows that the relation between refining costs and volume is generally positive; costs increase, for the most part, with increasing production rates. There is, however, a slight tendency for costs to decrease with increasing production rates near the lower ranges of output. This tendency, plus the tendency of costs at higher levels of output to increase somewhat faster than at intermediate levels, suggests nonlinear relations of the form $Y = a + bX + cX^2$, or even $Y = a + bX + cX^2 + dX^3$.

The diagram also shows a tendency for the data to scatter or disperse. To illustrate this scatter, a straight-line curve of central tendency, $Y = a + bX$, is fitted to the data (see *curve fitting*). In the illustration under *correlation table*, this curve was calculated, by the method of least squares, to have constants $a = 101.3$ and $b = 0.34$, and it is, therefore, plotted on the diagram here as $Y = 101.3 + 0.34X$. Of course, for many purposes less rigorous methods, such as freehand curves, perhaps a piece of string, etc., might have been used; for most purposes the use of least squares at an early stage of investigation is not desirable.

Around the curve $Y = 101.3 + 0.34X$ is drawn a so-called "band of error" at $S_Y = 3.31$ units away (see computation under *correlation table*); the broken lines drawn symmetrically about $Y = 101.3 + 0.34X$, as indicated by the arrows $Y + S_Y$ and $Y - S_Y$, show these limits. Within this "band of error" fall approximately two-thirds of the observation points.

A similar, but wider, "band of error" is drawn about the arithmetic mean of the total costs, $Y = 126.2$. Here, the measure to use in determining the width of the band is $\sigma_y = 5.43$ (see computation under *correlation table*). Again, approximately two-thirds of the observations lie within the "band of error."

The computation of the arithmetic mean $\bar{Y}$ (= 126.2) is equivalent to fitting a least-squares equation of the form $Y =$

a. In other words, $\bar{Y}$ represents the next lower-order least-squares equation after $Y = a + bX$, just as the latter represents the order lower than $Y = a + bX + cX^2$. The curve for $\bar{Y}$ assumes that there is no *trend* in the data. This assumption is, however, contradicted not only by the wider error band of $Y \pm \sigma_y$ compared to $Y \pm S_y$, but also by the fact that, toward the left-hand portion of the diagram, all the observations lie below $\bar{Y}$, while on the right they lie above it. The crossover point seems to lie in the vicinity of $\bar{X}$, the average output.

It will be noted that the least-squares regression equation crosses $\bar{Y}$ at $\bar{X}$. This is true of all regression equations fitted by the method of least squares: $Y - \bar{Y} = b(X - \bar{X})$. It is true not only for the regression of Y on X which yields $Y = a + bX$, but also for the regression of X on Y which yields $X = a' + b'Y$ and for higher-order equations as well.

Inspection of the patterns revealed by the scatter diagram shows that not only does the curve $Y = 101.3 + 0.34X$ fit the data and lend itself to analysis much better than $\bar{Y} = 126.2$, but also that the latter, the average total cost, had best not be used at all. It is a meaningless average of the relations between total cost and output. The tendency of the data to drift above the curve $Y = 101.3 + 0.34X$ suggests that the use of a higher-order curve such as $Y = a + bX + cX^2 + \cdots$ might well be examined—a suggestion reinforced by findings of accountants and economists in other areas of cost-production analysis—or that other classifications, such as analyses of product, labor, and material mixes, should be studied.

schedule 1. A supporting, explanatory, or supplementary analysis accompanying a balance sheet, income statement, or other statement prepared from the books of account.
2. An accountant's or auditor's working paper covering his examination of an account or group of accounts.
3. Any written enumeration or detailed list in orderly form.

scheduled cost = *standard cost.*

science Knowledge systematized by general principles, and by methods leading to its correction and expansion.

scope (auditing) The character of an audit, primarily with reference to the procedures utilized in a particular case, or the extent to which the transactions, records, or accounts examined serve as a basis of adequate testing and substantiation. The "scope" covered by the first paragraph of the uniform short-form audit report sets forth (a) the nature of the audit (usually an examination of the financial statements of a specified company), (b) the period covered, (c) that "generally accepted" audit standards were followed, and (d) that other tests or procedures were instituted as the auditor deemed necessary. See *opinion; audit report.*

scrap value = *salvage* (2).

screening (statistical quality control) A sorting operation involving the complete inspection of all items in some designated segment of production, such as a submitted lot of goods, a day's production, etc., the purpose of the operation being to find and remove from this segment of production all defective items present in it; often referred to as "100% inspection."

scrip 1. A fractional or temporary share of stock or other security, issued in connection with a recapitalization or reorganization, and ultimately convertible into regular certificates.
2. The obligation issued by a corporation in connection with a *scrip dividend.*
3. Paper "money" issued by corporations to pay wages and accepted by company stores.

scrip dividend 1. A dividend paid in promissory notes called *scrip.* The notes may be negotiable, bear interest, mature at different dates, and call for payment in cash, stock, bonds, or property. Scrip dividends are rare. They are occasioned by lack of cash, as where the business of a corporation is highly seasonal. See *liability dividend.*
2. That portion of a stock dividend rep-

resenting a fractional share, taking the form of a certificate exchangeable for cash or, in combination with other similar certificates, for whole shares.

seasonal variation (statistics) Changes within a year, tending to follow the same pattern from one year to another. An example is the tendency of retail sales to rise before Easter, fall during the summer, and climb to a peak in December. For this reason, comparisons of current figures are often made with those of corresponding periods of preceding years.

seasoning The period of time required for the stabilization or market acceptance of a security, following which only minor fluctuations in its market price are expected to occur. The term "seasoned security" often refers to a listed stock having such a market price, yielding regular quarterly dividends, and backed by net assets and an earning capacity deemed adequate for the protection of the investor.

secondary account An account built up from *internal transactions* involving transfers from *primary accounts* and other secondary accounts; examples: a finished-product account, a bad-debt account, a retained-earnings account. See *terminal account.*

secondary classification The reclassification or any of a series of reclassifications of a transaction or transaction group, following initial entry; thus, the total of a payroll-expense (or -clearing) account eventually distributed to other expense accounts reflecting the nature of work performed or of products on which the labor has been expended.

secondary distribution The sale of a block of securities by an investment dealer as an "off-the-board" offering to other dealers or to the members of the exchange on which the security is listed. The source of the offering is usually an institution, an investment trust, or sometimes an individual whose investment policies compel the sale of the block as a single lot. The plan for the disposal in certain cases must be filed with the U. S. Securities and Exchange Commission. The reason for this method of sale is that, if the block were offered on the floor of the exchange, the price of the security might be unduly depressed. Commissions to dealers who resell to their customers are generally higher than those of regular trading transactions. During the process of disposal, the price of the security may be stabilized.

secondary liability The liability of a party to a negotiable instrument that is contingent upon the failure of the party primarily liable to liquidate the obligation at maturity. It attaches to the endorsers of a check, to the drawer of an assigned acceptance, and to a guarantor or surety on a note.

second mortgage A mortgage on real estate already encumbered with a first mortgage. See *mortgage.*

secret reserve The amount by which net worth has been deliberately understated; a hidden reserve. Such a condition exists where assets are omitted or undervalued or where liabilities are overstated. The term does not represent any actual account bearing that name.

section 306 stock (Federal income taxes) In general, capital stock (other than common stock) received on or after June 22, 1954, as a tax-free dividend on common stock or as a redistribution in a tax-free reorganization. The proceeds are taxed as ordinary income when sold; or, if redeemed, at the time of redemption. Under the 1939 Code, gains from the sale or redemption of such dividends were referred to as *preferred-stock bailouts*, taxable as long-term capital gains, a loophole closed by section 306 of the 1954 Code.

section 531 (formerly section 102) **surtax** (Federal income taxes) The tax assessed on the accumulated taxable income of corporations which exceeds $100,000 plus whatever portion of the balance is judged to have been retained for the reasonable needs of the business.

section 1231 (formerly section 117(j)) **asset** (Federal income taxes) Land, depreciable assets, and certain other property used in business and owned for more than six months; also timber or an unharvested crop, under certain conditions, and livestock held for draft, breeding, or dairy purposes for at least 12 months. In general, any net gain from the sale or conversion of such assets is regarded as long-term *capital gain;* any net loss, as an ordinary loss, deductible in full.

secular Continuing over a long period of time, as in *secular trend.*

secular price A price resulting from the interaction of economic forces over a term of years. See *normal price.*

secular trend (statistics) The growth or decline reflected in time-series data based usually on assumptions as to occurrences of events over extended periods of time; applied to population growth, price levels, interest rates, consumption of electric power, and many other collections of useful data. To evaluate management effectiveness, for example, it may be necessary to eliminate from a time series such secular trends as population growth.

secured account Any account against which collateral or other security is held.

secured creditor A person whose claim against another is protected by *collateral* or by a *mortgage* or other *lien;* if the protection is ample, the claim is designated as "fully secured"; if the protection is not complete, the claim is designated as "partially secured."

secured liability An obligation against which specific assets have been pledged or guarantees given.

security 1. A general term for any kind of transferable certificate of ownership or indebtedness. It is applied primarily to permanent or long-term equities or obligations, such as stocks and bonds, and rarely to notes, acceptances, and other short-term evidences of indebtedness, unless they are of the type traded in on an established exchange.

2. Collateral adequate in amount to protect a debt.

security income and expense Income from dividends and interest, and profit or loss from the acquisition and sale of stocks and bonds held for short-term or long-term investment: an item (or one bearing a similar title) of frequent appearance in income statements. Recognition of security income and expense arises in the following situations:

1. Declaration of dividend or accrual of interest; until converted to cash, the offset to the income item is a receivable.

2. Occasionally a dividend is paid in property or in some form other than cash. The general rule is that a *fair market value* (which thereupon becomes "cost") is assigned to the asset acquired, with a credit of a like amount to income. If the asset received is subsequently liquidated in whole or in part, a corresponding portion of such "cost" is expensed, any gain or loss being independently accounted for.

3. To the recipient, a dividend is income of the year of declaration, notwithstanding that the issuing corporation may have paid it from earnings of some prior year.

4. A dividend in the issuing corporation's own stock is valued as outlined under *stock dividend.*

5. When sold, the selling price of a security, less its cost, is regarded as current income, although the sale may be looked upon as a realization of stored-up increments accumulated over a period of years. In estate accounting, a profit from the sale of a security may have to be accounted for as capital rather than income. See also *capital gain.*

6. Following a reorganization or recapitalization, the exchange of old securities for new, plus, in some cases, the receipt of "boot"—cash or other form of property—will give rise to income or expense, according to the valuation that is put on the new securities. The usual rule is to follow the Federal income-tax regulations in determining gain or loss, most of these rules being equitable and tending to set a standard known to many individuals.

7. An investment in an affiliated company is best treated like any other investment. Occasionally, the practice of tak-

ing up the undistributed earnings of a subsidiary or controlled company is encountered—a practice long followed, for example, by E. I. du Pont de Nemours & Company during the period of its ownership of a 22 percent interest in the common stock of General Motors Corporation. Although General Motors was undoubtedly controlled by du Pont, notwithstanding the minority holding, this practice permitted earnings to be included in surplus (in the du Pont case, its interest in General Motors' undistributed earnings was credited directly to a *mixed-surplus* account): earnings that were reflected neither in the income statement nor in an increment in working capital.

self-balancing Containing equal debits and credits, as in a *general ledger;* but not applicable to a subsidiary ledger unless it contains an account complementary to a general-ledger controlling account.

self-employment income (Federal income taxes) Income of self-employed persons (except physicians) which under the social-security provisions of the Revenue Act are currently subject to a tax of 4.7 percent of the amount in excess of $400 but not in excess of $4,200.

self-insurance The assumption by a person of a risk of loss arising out of the ownership of property or from other cause. See *insurance.*

sell-and-leaseback agreement A term applied to an arrangement whereby a business enterprise owning and occupying improved real estate sells it to an investor, such as an insurance company, and takes back a long-term lease on the property and often, in addition, an option or agreement to buy, effective at the termination of the lease. This arrangement, which may also apply to personal property (machinery and equipment), has certain *tax advantages*, serves the purpose of minimizing the investment in *fixed assets*, and simplifies the financial structure of the lessee; in a footnote to the balance sheet of the lessee, disclosure is made of the number and character of such leases, together with the amount and nature of the minimum and conditional rental obligation thereunder, the years effective, and the obligation of the lessee upon the expiration of the lease. See *long-term lease.*

sellers' market A favorable condition for sellers within an industry characterized by an excess of demand over supply; contrasts with *buyers' market.* Under competitive conditions among buyers, a sellers' market results in higher prices.

selling and administrative expense A composite class of expenses standing on an income statement between cost of sales and income deductions. See *selling cost; administrative cost; general operating expense.*

selling expense (cost) Any expense or class of expense incurred in selling or marketing. Examples: salesmen's salaries, commissions, and traveling expense; advertising; selling-department salaries and expenses; samples; credit and collection costs. Shipping costs are often so classified.

selling syndicate (or **group**) A group of persons, usually security dealers or brokers, each of whom agrees to assume the responsibility for the distribution of a part of an issue of securities. They are usually selected by the manager of the underwriting syndicate for their established ability in disposing of allied issues; if the issue is subject to the Federal Securities Act, their appointment is not confirmed until the effective date of the registration statement filed with the U.S. Securities and Exchange Commission, and then only if they accept the offering price and the number of shares or bonds allotted to them. The term "selling group" often refers to selling arrangements where the participating dealers are given the right to enter into firm commitments up to specified limits, and to "subscribe" for additional shares, the latter subject to the overall allotment by the manager.

semisenior accountant An accountant employed on the staff of a public accountant, acting under the general direction of a senior accountant, ranking midway between junior and senior classifications and capable of assuming responsibility in well-defined areas without close supervision.

semivariable cost An operating expense, as an item of indirect factory expense, that varies, but not necessarily at the same rate, with costs of manufactured quantities.

senior *adj.* A term applied to a class of securities or to a bond, note, or share of that class to indicate its preference, in case of liquidation, over another class; antonym: *junior*. Examples: a first-mortgage bond is a senior security as compared with a second-mortgage bond; preferred stock is senior to common stock.

senior (accountant) 1. An accountant employed on the staff of a public accountant, qualified by training and experience to conduct an audit under the supervision of a principal. His duties usually include the formulation of an audit program subject to review by a manager or partner, the carrying out of the approved program either directly or through assistants, the preparing of financial statements and reports reflecting the results of his examination, and the exercise of professional judgment in making decisions on accounting and auditing matters arising during the course of his examination. As often employed, the term has no precise application but is used generally to describe the relative ranking of a public accountant in terms of ability, experience, and responsibility.
2. = *accountant in charge;* the word is employed in this sense in texbooks and manuals.

senior security See *junior security*.

separable cost A cost that may be identified with a particular product, as distinguished from one common to joint products. See *common cost; joint cost*.

sequential analysis (or **sampling**) (statistical quality control) See *acceptance sampling*.

serial bonds An issue of bonds redeemable in installments.

service *adj.* Capable of being used; useful; contributing to the production or operations of its owner: said of a limited-life asset employed, for example, in a manufacturing plant, its application being confined principally to the expression *service life*.
n. The useful work done by a person or machine for the performance or yielding of which he or it is employed. The object of every expenditure is the acquisition of either an asset or a service, present or past, the difference between them being that an asset is acquired for its convertibility into another asset or into a future service or a series of future services, while a past or present service is an expense the whole benefit yield from which will have been ended during the accounting period in which the expenditure is incurred; = *benefit*.

service capacity The greatest number of service units that a machine, operation, or plant can yield within a specified period of time; productive capacity.

service cost 1. The cost of any *service*.
2. The amortizable cost of a limited-life asset; i.e., the asset cost, less estimated recovery, if any, from resale or scrap. Service cost is the amount to be depreciated over the useful life of a fixed asset; *depreciable cost*. See *depreciation base*.
3. The operating cost of a *service department*.

service department 1. A department rendering a distinct class of service to other operations. Examples: a power plant; a paint shop; a factory-accounting department.
2. A department that repairs and reconditions articles or merchandise returned by customers.

service life 1. The period of usefulness of an asset or asset group to its owner; hence, the period during which depreciation is accrued; useful life. The original estimate of service life when the asset, asset group, or asset class is first acquired is the basis for the initial depreciation rate; subsequent revisions of the estimate, up or down, may be necessary as experience with the asset or asset type grows. Economic service life may be less than physical service life because of such factors as obsolescence and inadequacy. See *depreciation.*

2. Hence, the age of an asset upon retirement.

service unit An item of work done; a single performance or operation, as of a machine. The cost of a machine or other fixed asset may find justification in the reasonableness of the cost of each item, or group of items (such as 100, 1,000, etc.), of useful work, such item cost being determined by dividing depreciable cost by the estimated number of items or groups of items that the asset is expected to yield over its life. The estimated number of service units may also supply a basis for depreciation on a production basis; see formula (1) under *depreciation.*

service-yield basis (of depreciation) The method of computing and recording depreciation whereby cost is spread over useful life in proportion to service units consumed; the *production method* of depreciation. See *depreciation.*

set of accounts The journals, ledgers, forms, classification of accounts, and records and files generally, maintained under a system of accounts; *books of account.*

settlement warrant (governmental accounting) See *warrant(5).*

setup time 1. The time required in changing over a machine or method of production from one product or production plan to another. See *starting-load cost; lead time.*

2. The cost of any such changeover.

share One of the equal parts into which each class of the *capital stock* of a corporation is divided.

share bonus = *splitup;* a British term.

share capital *Capital (3)* represented by shares of capital stock; a British term.

shareholder = *stockholder.*

share-premium account = *paid-in surplus;* a British term.

Sherman Anti-Trust Act A Federal law (26 Stat. 209), passed by the Congress in 1890 and administered by the U. S. Attorney General, its objective being the invalidation of contracts and business combinations that restrain interstate trade or create monopolies. It has been largely ineffective; in 1914 it was supplemented by the *Clayton Act,* and in 1937 by the *Miller–Tydings Act.*

short *adj.* 1. Unable to account for the disposition of cash or other property.

2. (brokerage accounting) Owing securities or commodities.

3. Subordinated in position; see *in short.*

short account (brokerage accounting) An account representing the speculative interest of a customer in securities or commodities not owned but sold, usually with the hope of a later purchase following a decline in the market.

short covering The purchase of a security or commodity for the purpose of making delivery on a short sale.

shortfall Gain from the sale of an *investment(6)* owned for a brief period (e.g., six months).

short-form report See *audit report(1).*

short rate An insurance rate based on a period less than a year; a rate proportionately higher than the annual rate; used in determining the cancellation value of a premium but disregarded in the computation of unexpired premiums in a going concern.

short sale The sale of a security or commodity for future delivery and prior to its purchase, with the expectancy that the market price will be no higher or will decline by the time a covering purchase must be made.

short-term liability Any current liability, including the current maturing portion of a long-term liability. See *term loan.*

sidehead A horizontal title of an item in a financial statement the specifications of which include a) clarity: the title is descriptive of the item content—it communicates to the reader an understanding of the item equivalent to that held by the maker of the statement; b) brevity: where more than a word or two is required, a footnote elaborating on an abbreviated title would be in order; c) the word or phrase making up the title must be commonly used by others in similar situations. Thus, "Cash" is cash in bank, in transit to bank, on hand, and freely available to management for liquidating current indebtedness; "Receivables" listed among current assets would mean (perhaps no less than 95%) the total of amounts currently owing from sales to customers, collectible (and collected if the statement is more than a month or two old) within the regular credit or collection period; and so on. Exceptions would call for splitting the item or for explanatory notes attached to the statement.

sight draft A *draft* payable by the drawee upon demand or presentation; distinguished from *time draft* or *acceptance*. An employee or agent may be given the right to draw sight drafts on his principal for advances to cover purchases being made by him or to cover his travel or other expense. Sight drafts are sometimes used by creditors in attempts to collect overdue accounts.

sight test (auditing) to examine accounts without formal analysis; to *scan*.

significant 1. Of sufficient magnitude, as measured by a departure from some norm or standard, to raise doubt that the deviation is the result of chance, *random*, or compensating factors; hence, indicating behavior calling for a better awareness or understanding of the cause, the removal of the cause, or a modification of the *standard* because of its inadequacy.

2. Of sufficient importance to warrant *disclosure* or the treatment accorded larger or more important items; likely to influence *judgments* or *decisions:* said of individual *transactions*, transaction groups, or other *events* or *conditions* peculiar to a given establishment. See *materiality*.

significant amount A *rounded-off* number, as of dollars, conveying to the observer the same impression as would the fully expressed quantity. Thus the total assets of a certain bank were recently reported as $4,935,468,311.89. To the average stockholder or depositor, the significant figure would probably be a rounded-off $4.9 billions, an amount informative to him and readily recalled. To the bank's *controller*, however, who must test total assets against total liabilities, the significant quantity would be no less than all 12 digits. In many reports to stockholders, larger corporations now omit cents, substitute zeros for hundreds, often thousands of dollars. For most readers, only the first two or three digits of any item in financial statements have significance.

simple average The arithmetic mean obtained by dividing the sum of differing items in a series or group by the number of such items, regardless of the frequency of any one of them. See *arithmetic mean; weighted average*.

simple interest The charge for the loan of money or for a deferment of the collection of an account, computed by applying a rate (of interest) against the amount of the loan or account; contrasts with *compound interest*. On page 389, table (1), is a simple-interest table from which computations of interest on a principal of $1,000 for a fractional 360- or 365-day year may be readily derived by simple addition. This table permits the ascertainment of simple interest on a principal of $1,000 for a fractional year at various rates per annum by employing only addition. The interest in each case, for one, two, four, or seven days, is stated in the form of a decimal fraction of $1. Example: $4\frac{1}{2}$% on $18,000 for 151 days is resolved as illustrated in table (2), page 389.

simple journal A book of original entry containing but two money columns, one for debits, the other for credits. See illustration under *journal*.

simple trust (Federal income taxes) A trust that must distribute its income currently but does not distribute corpus before its termination. See *complex trust*.

simulation A method of studying operational problems that cannot be solved by ordinary techniques, whereby a *model* of the *system* or *process* is subjected to a

(1)

Simple Interest for Partial Year on Principal of $1,000

A = Year of 360 days ("ordinary" interest)
B = Year of 365 days ("exact" interest)

Note: The values shown are decimal fractions of $1; the dot or dots above numerals denote repetends or circulating decimals: 0034/72̇ = $0.003472222 . . . ; 003̇4/2465/75̇ = $0.00342465753424657534 . . . ; etc.

Days	1/8%		1/4%		3/8%	
	A	*B*	*A*	*B*	*A*	*B*
1	0034 72̇	003̇4 2465 75̇	0069 4̇	00̇68 4931 5̇	0104 16̇	010̇2 7397 26̇
2	0069 4̇	00̇68 4931 5̇	0138̇	0̇136 9863̇	0208 3̇	02̇05 4794 5̇
4	0138̇	0̇136 986̇3	027̇	0̇273 9726̇	0416̇	0̇410 9589̇
7	0243 05̇	023̇9 7260 27̇	0486 1̇	04̇79 4520 5̇	0729 16̇	071̇9 1780 82

Days	1/2%		1%		1 1/2%		2%	
	A	*B*	*A*	*B*	*A*	*B*	*A*	*B*
1	0138̇	0̇136 9863̇	027̇	0̇273 9726̇	0416̇	0̇410 9589̇	05̇	0̇547 9452̇
2	027̇	0̇273 9726̇	05̇	0̇547 9452̇	083̇	0̇821 9178̇	1̇	1̇095 8904̇
4	05̇	0̇547 9452̇	1̇	1̇095 8904̇	16̇	1̇643 8356̇	2̇	2̇191 7808̇
7	0972̇	0̇958 9041̇	194̇	1̇917 8082̇	2916̇	2̇876 7123̇	38̇	3̇835 6164̇

Days	2 1/2%		3%		3 1/2%		4%	
	A	*B*	*A*	*B*	*A*	*B*	*A*	*B*
1	0694̇	0̇684 9315̇	083̇	0̇821 9178̇	0972̇	0̇958 9041̇	1̇	1̇095 8904̇
2	138̇	1̇369 8630̇	16̇	1̇643 8356̇	194̇	1̇917 8082̇	2̇	2̇191 7808̇
4	27̇	2̇739 7260̇	3̇	3̇287 6712̇	38̇	3̇835 6164̇	4̇	4̇383 5616̇
7	4861̇	4̇794 5205̇	583̇	5̇753 4246̇	6805̇	6̇712 3287̇	7̇	7̇671 2328̇

Days	4 1/2%		5%		5 1/2%		6%	
	A	*B*	*A*	*B*	*A*	*B*	*A*	*B*
1	125	1̇232 8767̇	133̇	1̇369 8630̇	1527̇	1̇506 8493̇	16̇	1̇643 8356̇
2	25	2̇465 7534̇	27̇	2̇739 7260̇	3055̇	3̇013 6986̇	3̇	3̇287 6712̇
4	5	4̇931 5068̇	5̇	5̇479 4520̇	61̇	6̇027 3972̇	6̇	6̇575 3424̇
7	875	8̇630 1369̇	972̇	9̇589 0410̇	1.0694̇	1.0̇547 9452̇	1.16̇	1.1̇506 8493̇

(2)

	First Method			Second Method		
	Days	*Ordinary Interest (A)*	*Exact Interest (B)*	*M Dollar Days*	*Ordinary Interest (A)*	*Exact Interest (B)*
	100	$12.50	$12.3287 6712	2000	$250.00	$246.575
	40	5.00	4.9315 0685	700	87.50	86.301
	10	1.25	1.2328 7671	20	2.50	2.466
	1	.125	.1232 8767	−2	−.25	−.247
Interest on $1,000	151	$18.875	$18.6164 3835			
Interest on $18,000		$339.75	$335.10	2718	$339.75	$335.10

series of assumptions and manipulations in an effort to find one or more acceptable solutions.

single-entry bookkeeping A system of bookkeeping in which only records of cash and of personal accounts are maintained; it is always incomplete *double-entry*, varying with circumstances. There is usually no detailed record of gains or losses; a statement of financial condition is prepared from whatever data are available from the records or by inspection or count, and the net profit or loss for a period is derived from a comparison of financial condition at the close of the period with that at the beginning, unless adequate profit-and-loss data can be derived from cashbook distribution totals. Where transactions are infrequent and receivables, payables, and assets other than cash are few, single-entry records, carefully maintained, may be adequate.

single-step income statement A form of income statement in which all the elements of expense appear in the same section, thus eliminating such intermediate remainders as gross profit, gross income, and operating profit; contrasts with *multiple-step income statement*. See illustration, page 229.

sinking fund Cash or other assets, and the interest or other income earned thereon, set apart for the retirement of a debt, the redemption of stock, or the protection of an investment in depreciable property; sometimes paralleled by a *sinking-fund reserve*. A sinking fund established for the purpose of extinguishing indebtedness or reacquiring capital stock may also be known as a *redemption fund*. See also *fund*.

sinking-fund bond Any of an issue of bonds where the indenture requires the issuer to set aside periodically a sum which, with interest, will be sufficient to meet the redemption price of the bonds or to equal a specified fraction of the total, the balance unprovided-for being left for refunding.

sinking-fund method (of depreciation) See *depreciation method*.

sinking-fund reserve An appropriation or earmarking of earned surplus, usually in the form of planned periodic transfers, for the purpose of providing an equity counterpart for assets being accumulated, sometimes in a separate *sinking fund*, for the retirement of an outstanding security. See *appropriated surplus*.

site audit (governmental accounting) An audit conducted on the premises of the organization under examination: a term now obsolescent; contrasts with an older form of examination whereby the organization's vouchers were reviewed in the office of the Comptroller General.

skewness (statistics) Lack of symmetry between the two sides of a curve. In a symmetric (bell-shaped) curve, the arithmetic mean, median, and mode coincide. The mean deviates increasingly from the mode as skewness develops; moreover, it deviates in the direction of the skewness. By comparing the difference between mean and mode, it is possible to define a measure of skewness.

To facilitate comparisons between curves, Pearson's measure in standard units is employed:

$$Sk = \frac{\bar{X} - Mo}{\sigma},$$

where $\bar{X}$ is the arithmetic mean, Mo the mode, and σ the standard deviation. Another more easily calculated measure (Bowley's) is

$$Sk = \frac{q_2 - q_1}{q_2 + q_1},$$

where q_1 is the first quartile, and q_2 the second quartile or median. See *median*.

small tools Minor, easily portable, and comparatively simple implements used in any processing operation. Examples: hand tools, such as hammers, saws, drills, and shears, sometimes power-driven.

smoothing Any treatment designed to remove irregularities in data, such as unusual peaks or valleys in a curve that may be the result of nonrecurring operating conditions.

social accounting The application of double-entry bookkeeping to socioeconomic analysis; it is concerned with the construction, estimation, and analysis of national or international income, national or international balance sheets, and the design of the system of component accounts. The Subcommittee on National-Income Statistics of the United Nations describes the process thus:

> Instead of seeking to build up a single total, such as the national income, an investigation is first made of the classification of accounting entities, of the types of accounts that they keep and of the transactions into which they enter. In this way, all the transacting entities of an economic system are classified into broad sectors such as productive enterprises, financial intermediaries, and final consumers, and a series of accounts is set up in which the separate entities represent economically distinct categories of transactions. Economic activity is represented by money flows and related bookkeeping transactions, actual or imputed, between accounts. The national income and other similar aggregates are derived from the system by selecting and combining the constituent entries in the accounts.

See *personal income (2)*; *national income; net national product; gross national product.*

sole proprietorship A business enterprise the net worth of which belongs entirely to one individual.

sound 1. Conforming to tradition; consonant with the views, often of untested objectivity, of the practical man; leading to a profitable end or meeting some other measure of commercial success.

2. Hence, in harmony with accounting or management doctrine of purported general acceptance.

sound value Replacement cost less observed depreciation and deferred maintenance; present value as determined in an appraisal: a term used principally in fixed-asset appraisals.

source-and-disposition (or **sources-and-uses**) **statement** = *statement of sources and applications of funds.*

span of control The extent of a supervisor's jurisdiction, often represented in organization charts by subordinate lines of authority extending to activities or subunits: a term formerly employed in referring to an asserted limitation on the number of persons that could effectively report to another.

special agent See *agent.*

special assessment (municipal accounting) The charge made by a local government against a benefited property or person for the cost of an improvement or service. Examples of services for which *annual* assessments are frequently levied are street cleaning and street lighting. Of particular importance to the accountant, however, are *special* assessments used in the financing of construction projects, such as sewers, pavements, and street widening, because they present accounting problems not involved in the financing of continuous services. Assessments levied for the purpose of financing improvement projects are frequently payable in installments over a number of years. In the meantime, construction expenditures must be financed from other sources, frequently from bonds. Either "general" or "special" special-assessment bonds may be issued. The former are a charge against the *full faith and credit* of the governmental unit if assessment collections are inadequate to meet maturing interest or principal payments. A "special" special-assessment bond is one which is not a charge against the governmental unit as a whole but only against the assessment money collected, or against the properties benefited, the government's responsibility being limited to the enforcement of collections and the proper application of the proceeds.

Usually serial bonds are issued, with maturity dates arranged so that a block of the issue may be retired as each special-assessment installment is collected. Frequently, too, bonds are identified with particular installment collections. In that case, bonds can be paid only from the collections of the installment to which they apply and no other. Bonds sometimes constitute liens against specific pieces of property, each bond being payable solely from the assessments levied against that property.

A first step in accounting for special assessments is the authorization of the project by the legislative body or special-district commissioners after notice and hearings. If construction is to be financed through the sale of bonds, the next step is the authorization of the bonds. An interval of time may elapse between authorization and sale, pending the completion of certain formalities, or during unfavorable market conditions. But if in the interval construction has commenced, contractors must be paid as the work progresses. Delay in the sale of bonds may force the issue of short-term notes, which are sometimes issued even though bonds can be sold immediately because the former may bear a lower interest rate, thus affording a saving in interest expense, and because the construction cost may be indeterminable except within wide limits. After the bonds have been issued, the proceeds are applied to paying off the principal and interest of the notes.

Assessments are levied on the basis of benefit as soon as construction is authorized or as the project is completed. The benefited area is designated as the benefit district. Districts are numbered and are usually referred to by number. The area benefited varies with the size and nature of the project and the methods of assessment. For example, the widening of a long street will involve a wider benefit area than the widening of a short street, since not only are abutting properties then included, but also properties that may be several streets removed from the improvement.

The governmental unit as a whole may receive some benefit from an improvement and may therefore bear part of the cost. The governmental unit's share will vary, for the reason that property owners are not expected to pay more than the increase in the value of their properties. If the total benefits are smaller than the cost of the improvement, the governmental unit makes up the difference, but if benefits are deemed equal to or greater than the estimated cost of the improvement, the governmental unit may assume no part of it. The total benefits and the distribution of cost between the benefited properties and the government at large are both governed by many arbitrary rules.

A police station, a fire station, or other government property may be located within the benefit district. Obviously, it would be unfair to exempt this property from assessment and spread the cost over privately owned property only. The governmental unit pays in the same manner as any property owner. Assessments on properties owned by government other than the governmental unit constructing the project (for example, assessments on state or county property located in a city) cannot be levied unless authorized by statute.

If bonds are issued, the bond interest is usually paid from the interest charges made against those property owners who choose to pay their assessments in installments, rather than from special-assessment collections. The reason why interest is not commingled with the assessments is that the amount of interest to be paid will usually depend on the length of time that installments remain unpaid. In fact, the property owner is usually given the right of paying the entire assessment at one time, thereby avoiding interest charges, in addition to the privilege of paying in installments if he so desires.

Special assessments and interest receivable may be recorded either on a special-assessment roll or on individual special-assessment records. A special-assessment roll is a record showing the assessments levied against each piece of property, payments received thereon, and related information. Some governments find it practicable to use individual special-assessment records, or a single record may serve to reflect both ad-valorem taxes and special assessments receivable.

In spite of the fact that some assessments may prove to be uncollectible, no reserve for uncollectible assessments is set up, since the government is acting in a trust capacity, its duty being to see that the assessments are collected and properly disbursed. The trust character of special-assessment funds is evident where they can only be paid from the particular special assessments against which they were issued. Even if general special-assessment bonds are issued, a reserve for uncollectible assessments is impractical. If such a reserve were set up, assessments against all the benefited properties would have to be increased by a corresponding amount. But these properties are not supposed to be assessed for more than the amount of benefit. If the bonds are of the general special-assessment variety, any deficiencies resulting from uncollectible assessments must be made up by the governmental unit; if they are special special-assessment bonds, the bondholders must stand the loss.

Where the project costs more or less than anticipated, the problem arises of disposing of the resulting surplus or deficit. The disposition of surplus will vary with the assessment procedure. If assessments are levied after the project is completed, there can be no surplus or deficit, since the assessment will be made large enough to recover only the actual cost of construction. If assessments are levied before the project is completed and they are payable in one installment, rebates are granted in the form of cash or a reduction of the unpaid assessments. If they are payable in installments, reductions are made in the installments remaining unpaid and cash refunds are made to those property owners who have paid their assessments in full.

A deficit is made up through the levy of supplemental assessments. If the assessments are payable in installments, the latter are adjusted to reflect the supplemental levy; or a separate supplementary roll may be prepared.

Delinquent special assessments and delinquent interest receivable may necessitate short-term borrowing, and, if ultimately uncollectible, may cause a deficit in the funds used to pay special-assessment bonds or interest. Special assessments by statute are usually a lien against the property against which they are levied, and at the expiration of a certain statutory time, the property may be sold and the proceeds used to satisfy the lien. In fact, the statutes usually permit the use of the proceeds to pay off not only the assessment itself but also interest applicable to the unpaid installments up to the date of the sale as well as the cost of holding the sale. The excess of the amount realized from the sale of the property over the amount of special assessments, interest, and the cost of holding the sale is set up in a *trust-and-agency fund*, where it is held for the benefit of the property owner until claimed by him. If, on the other hand, the proceeds are not sufficient to cover special assessments, interest, and the cost of the sale, the property owner may or may not be called upon to make up the difference, depending on local legal provisions. If the law does not provide for this, the procedure followed depends on whether special special-assessment or general special-assessment bonds were issued; if the former, the bondholder bears the loss. On the other hand, if general special-assessment bonds were issued, the excess of the amount of bonds and interest due over the amount realized from the sale of the property is borne by the governmental unit.

special-assessment bonds (municipal accounting) Bonds of a municipality issued for public improvements, and repaid from assessments levied against benefited properties. If the bonds are issued not only with the understanding that they will be paid from special assessments, but, in addition, with a pledge of the *full faith and credit* of the municipality, they are known as "general-obligation special-assessment bonds."

special-assessment fund (municipal accounting) A fund set up to provide for financing improvements or services out of bond issues or proceeds of assessments levied against the properties benefited. See *fund.*

special audit An audit having a special or general scope: a *limited audit.* See *audit.*

special contingency reserve A *reserve for contingencies* related to one or more specific items of possible future expense or loss. Like other contingent reserves, it is classified as a subdivision of *earned surplus;* but if such a reserve is actually a liability already incurred, it is so classified for balance-sheet purposes.

special fund (municipal accounting) A fund that must be used in accordance with specific legal or administrative restrictions; any fund other than the general fund. See *fund.*

specialist On stock or commodity exchanges, one who represents a single stock, industry, or commodity (known as a "specialty"). He operates at a designated "trading post" on the floor of the exchange, executes brokers' orders, and, in general, endeavors to maintain an orderly market for his specialty.

special order = *job order.*

special-purpose financial statement A financial statement having limited use or application. Professional accountants as a rule report only on *all-purpose financial statements* around which standard practices of presentation, disclosure, and qualification have grown. Some corporate managements follow the practice of accompanying special-purpose statements with certified all-purpose statements, or the latter may be supplied in lieu of the former. Special-purpose statements are encountered primarily in connection with forms used in the compilation of statistics by trade or governmental bodies; examples may be found in corporate reports filed with the Department of Commerce; the Federal Trade Commission; income-tax returns; Dun & Bradstreet's and other credit firms; and trade-association questionnaires. Financial statements for internal use are now often all-purpose statements accompanied by supplemental schedules.

special-revenue fund (municipal accounting) A fund used to finance particular activities and created out of receipts of specific taxes or other revenues. Such a fund is usually authorized by statutory or charter provisions to pay for certain activities with some special form of continuing revenues. See *fund.*

specie Metallic or "hard" money, as compared with paper money; sometimes limited to gold or silver coin.

specification cost = *standard cost.*

specific cost Cost readily identifiable with a particular product or service; *direct cost; historical cost; actual cost;* used principally in contrast with *average cost, fifo, lifo,* and *retail cost.*

specific-order cost system See *job-order costing.*

speculator One who undertakes the purchase or sale of foreign exchange, a security, a commodity, or a service in anticipation of a shortage or surplus at different times or places, hoping to gain thereby; one who deals in risk and uncertainty.

spinoff (Federal income taxes) The transfer by a corporation of a portion of its assets to newly formed corporation in exchange for the latter's capital stock, which is thereupon distributed as a property dividend to the stockholders of the first corporation. Also, distribution by the parent corporation of the stock of an already existing subsidiary. See *splitoff; splitup(2).*

split ledger account (a) An account supported by two or more *nominal accounts* each containing—and limited to—a single class of transactions, the relationship being similar to that of a *retained-earnings* account and income-and-expense accounts; or (b) any such supporting account. Thus, two separate general-ledger accounts, "Receipts" and "Disbursements," may be maintained throughout a fiscal year; at the year-end, like other nominal accounts, they are closed into a "*real account*," in this instance "Cash," this account being burdened with only three items: the balance at the beginning of the year, total receipts and total disbursements for the year, thus yielding the cash balance at the end of the year (i.e., the opening balance for the year following when the process is repeated). In the illustration on pp. 396–397 there are 77 general-ledger accounts: 57 nominal and 20 real accounts, the latter being the opening or balance-sheet accounts carried over from the preceding year. General-ledger accounts expanded in this manner facilitate the preparation of financial statements, particularly a *flow statement*. See *cash-flow statement; funds-flow statement; statement of sources and applications of funds.*

splitoff 1. (Federal income taxes) The transfer to its stockholders by a parent corporation of the capital stock of a subsidiary corporation in exchange for a prorata surrender of their stockholdings in the parent. Compare with *splitup(2); spinoff.*

2. See *splitoff point.*

splitoff point In an operation involving two or more products, the position at which *joint costs* end and costs identifiable with individual products begin.

splitup 1. The issue to present stockholders of additional shares of a corporation's capital stock without changing the amount of paid-in capital applicable to outstanding shares. It may be accomplished by calling in outstanding shares and issuing in their stead a larger number of shares each with a lesser par value; or an additional number of no-par shares may be issued prorata to existing stockholders. Where outstanding shares are called in and fewer shares issued in their place, the transaction is known as a *reverse splitup*. A transfer of paid-in surplus to capital-stock account, accompanying the issue of additional shares, does not alter the character of a splitup, but a transfer out of *retained earnings* (earned surplus) causes the issue to take on the appearance of a *stock dividend*, unless the amount so transferred is small in relation to the fair value per share of the stock outstanding.

2. (Federal income taxes) A corporate reorganization whereby two or more new corporations replace a previously existing corporation with the stockholders of the old owning the stock of the new, and the assets of the old being divided among the new; also, a distribution in liquidation by a parent corporation of its stock in two or more already existing subsidiaries. See *spinoff; splitoff.*

spot cash Cash immediately available, as for a purchase.

spot price The price of a commodity available for immediate sale and delivery, the commodity being referred to as a *spot* commodity. See *price.*

spot sale (or **purchase**) The sale (or purchase) of a commodity for immediate delivery, often on a cash basis.

spread *v.* To *enter* or *post,* usually in detail, the word being limited to such expressions as: "to spread on the records."

n. 1. The act of journalizing or posting the detail of one or a group of transactions.

2. The excess of selling price over direct cost; gross profit; hence, a percentage of gross profit.

3. Underwriters' commission. See *underwriting contract.*

4. The range between the bid and asked prices of a stock or commodity.

5. A gambling device representing a combination *put* and *call:* a transferable option entitling the holder to either buy or sell within a stated period a given number of shares of stock at stated prices.

spread sheet 1. A worksheet providing a two-way analysis or recapitulation of costs or other accounting data. If used as a basis for postings, it may be regarded as a journal, necessitating its preservation like any other book of original entry.

2. Specifically, a worksheet containing an analysis of a group of related accounts or classes of accounts, e.g., horizontal lines

BELFORD MANUFACTUR

General-ledger Trial Balance
Year ended Dec

(thousands

Name of Account	A/c No.	General ledger: Account totals: Debits	Credits	B/S & I/S	Flow statements: Cash	Funds	S/A/F
Cash	1	Z 75 4					
	2–3	c 11 936 5	d 11 940 9	71 0	4 4	4 4	
Investments	4–5	Z 528 7	c 312 0		312 0		
	6–7	d 296 5	f 101 0	412 2	−296 5	116 5	
Customers	8–9	Z 1 218 9	c 9 351 8		9 351 8		
	10–11	a 9 832 1	f 64 6				
Bad-debt allowance	12–13	f 64 6	Z 7 3				
	14		f 68 7	1 623 2		−411 6	
Processed inventory							
Materials & parts	15	Z 128 2					
	16–17	e 4 505 8	e 4 472 1				
Direct labor	18	Z 31 5					
	19–20	d 1 255 8	e 1 234 4		−1 255 8		
Overhead-materials	21	Z 2 4					
	22–23	b 240 7	e 235 6		−240 7		
-labor	24	Z 5 2					
	25–26	d 113 2	e 108 1		−113 2		
-services	27	Z 18 5			k −30 3		
	28–29	b 1 107 0	e 1 095 3	262 8	−1 107 0	−77 0	
Materials & parts	30	Z 881 6			k−298 4		
	31–32	b 4 509 0	e 4 505 8	884 8	−4 509 0	−3 2	
Prepaid services	33	Z 5 4					
	34–35	d 68 0	f 67 2	6 2	−68 0	−8	
Bank loan	36		Z 1 000 0		−1 000 0		
	37–38	d 1 000 0	c 2 200 0		2 200 0	1 200 0	
Accounts payable	39		Z 1 420 3				
	40–41	d 7 661 8	b 6 679 4			−982 4	
Deferred income tax	42		Z 123 6				
	43		g 1 3	−2 762 8		1 3	
Working capital (Z = 344.6)				497 4		−152 8	−153

In the above illustration are the ingredients common to . . .

In the above illustration are the ingredients common to contemporary forms of *financial statements* one may observe in annual reports of business corporations to stockholders. Called by accountants a *trial balance*, this display of the financial affairs of a prototypic manufacturing corporation (Belford) begins with *opening balances* of 20 items (labeled *Z*) belonging to one year (19-6) and carried over to the succeeding year (19–7). Added are 57 items reflecting the totals of business transactions during 19–7. Various combinations of these figures yield the components of the *balance sheet* and *income statement* appearing on page 398–399, and a *flow statement*, the last-named being any one of the indicated variations: a *cash-flow statement* (see page 80), a *funds-flow statement* (page 209), or a *statement of sources and applications of funds* (page 413).

Known as *accounts*, the 77 items in the illustration are totals abstracted from the corporation's *general ledger*: a summary record maintained by every organization, whether business, nonprofit, or governmental. The 20 *Z* items are *real* accounts, the "debit" portion being *assets*; the "credit" items, here with two exceptions (13 and 47), are *equities* or claims on assets. The other 57, in contrast, are *nominal* accounts: subdivisions of parent real accounts; thus, accounts *5, 6,* and *7* are subdivisions of account *4*; and accounts *58* to *77* are subdivisions of account *57*. At each year-end the nominal accounts are merged with their parent accounts, only to be reopened immediately thereafter for the following year's transactions. The *58–77* group of nominal accounts supply the details of the income statement; the remaining nominal accounts furnish useful running analyses of the real or balance-sheet accounts.

Each year, in a business of the size indicated here, there will be thousands, even hundreds of thousands, of transactions, each requiring immediate identification and classification in two quite different

ING COMPANY

and Derived Financial Statements
ember 31, 19-7

of dollars)

Name of Account	A/c No.		Debits		Credits	B/S & I/S	Cash	Funds	S/A/F
	General ledger (cont.)						Flow statements		
		Account totals							
Fixed assets	44	Z	2 176 8						
	45–46	d	483 0	f	255 9	2 403 9	−483 0	−483 0	−483
Accrued depreciation	47			Z	968 6				
	48			c	40 0		40 0	40 0	40
	49–50	f	255 9	f	224 8	−977 5			
Goodwill	51–52	Z	220 0	f	120 0	100 0			
Capital stock	53			Z	1 000 0				
	54			h	100 0	−1 100 0		100 0	100
Paid-in surplus	55			Z	400 0				
	56			h	70 0	−470 0		70 0	70
Retained earnings	57			Z	372 8	−372 8			
Net income for year					261 0	−261 0			261
Dividend paid	58	d	180 0			180 0	−180 0	−180 0	−180
Sales	59–60	f	68 7	a	9 832 1	−9 763 4		9 763 4	
Other income	61			c	32 7	−32 7	32 7	32 7	
Cost of sales-materials	62	e	4 472 1						
-labor	63	e	1 234 4						
Overhead-materials	64	e	235 6						
-labor	65	e	108 1						
-services	66	e	1 095 3			7 145 5		−7 145 5	
S & A-salaries	67	d	882 6				−882 6	−882 6	
	68	h	170 0				k 3 0	−170 0	
-services	69	b	501 6				−501 6		
	70	f	67 2					−568 8	
-supplies	71	b	112 4			1 733 8	−112 4	−112 4	
Investment loss	72	f	101 0			101 0		−101 0	
Depreciation expense	73	f	224 8			224 8			225
Goodwill amortized	74	f	120 0			120 0	k −656 7		120
Income tax	75	b	208 7				−208 7	−208 7	
	76	g	1 3			210 0		−1 3	
Net income for year	77		261 0			261 0			

. . . features associated with the accounting process that this illustration makes possible.

ways. For most enterprises, the transaction classes are few in number; here, six classes make up as much as 99% of the year's financial transactions: (a) sales to customers, (b) purchases from suppliers, (c) cash from customers and other receipts, and (d) cash paid to suppliers, to the corporation's labor force, and to others in pursuit of business operations—these four classes constituting *external* transactions; (e) the shifting (or reclassification) of certain costs in order to continue their identification with items passing in and out of the stream of production (*cost flows*), and (f) parts of assets that have been wasting away during the year (*depreciation* and *losses*)—two classes of *internal transactions*. Occasionally, other classes, such as (g) and (h), not being run-of-the-mill items, may be either internal or external, and require individual consideration and treatment; in the course of a year, the total of such items normally falls well within the remaining one percent. The items labeled *k* have the effect of offsetting the changes during the year in account 39, thereby facilitating the preparation of a statement of *cash flow, q.v.*

By noting the appearance of the letters "a" to "h" alongside the account numbers, it will be noted that for any one letter, the amount or amounts shown in the "debit" column equal the amount or amounts in the "credit" column. Thus, for the item "a," $9,832,100 appears under "Customers" (10) as a "debit" and under "Sales" (60) as a "credit"; item "b," $6,679,400 appears under "Accounts Payable" (41) as a "credit" and is divided among six other accounts in the forms of "debits"; and so on. The general-ledger accounts thus contain debits equal to credits, and the total of the items in the debit column must therefore equal the total of the items making up the credit column. The remaining four money columns, all derived as extensions of the debit-and-credit columns, are self-balancing: their totals are zero.

The mathematics of accounting is extremely simple: addition and subtraction. But the amount of

BELFORD MANUFACTURING COMPANY

Comparative Balance Sheets

	December 31 19-7	19-6
Assets		
Current assets		
Cash	$ 71 000	$ 75 400
Investments, at cost	412 200	528 700
Receivables, net	1 623 200	1 211 600
Inventories-		
Finished goods and work in process	262 800	185 800
Materials and parts	884 800	881 600
Prepaid services	6 200	5 400
Current assets	$3 260 200	$2 888 500
Fixed assets		
Land, buildings, and machinery, at cost, less accumulated depreciation of $977 500 & $968 600	$1 426 400	$1 208 200
Goodwill unamortized	$ 100 000	$ 220 000
Total assets	$4 786 600	$4 316 700
Liabilities		
Current liabilities		
Bank loan	$1 200 000	$1 000 000
Accounts payable	1 437 900	1 420 300
Deferred income tax	124 900	123 600
Current liabilities	$2 762 800	$2 543 900
Net worth		
Capital stock: 11 000 and 10 000 shares	$1 100 000	$1 000 000
Paid-in surplus	470 000	400 000
Retained earnings-		
Balance 12–31–46	372 800	334 300
Net income, 19–7	261 000	188 500
Dividend paid, 19–7	−180 000	−150 000
Total net worth	$2 023 800	$1 772 800
Total liabilities	$4 786 600	$4 316 700

Comparative Income Statements

	Years ended December 31 19-7	19-6
Sales and other income	$9 796 100	$9 032 400
Cost of sales-Materials	$4 707 700	$4 218 100
Labor	1 342 500	1 202 000
Services	1 095 300	1 131 200
Total cost of sales	$7 145 500	$6 551 300
Selling and administrative	1 733 800	1 720 200
Depreciation	224 800	230 500
Goodwill amortized	120 000	120 000
Investment loss	101 000	
Income taxes	210 000	221 900
Total costs	$9 535 100	$8 843 900
Net income	$ 261 000	$ 188 500

each transaction is, as noted above, twice entered: once as a credit (−) and once as a debit (+). Not only does this process of double entry serve to keep the record in balance, but it also serves the purpose of indicating, respectively, the "source" of each transaction and its "disposition."

Where profits have been earned and "reinvested," a recurrent question asked of accountants is "where did the money go?" By studying the illustration, the reader will note that the profits of $81,000 retained in the business after paying the dividend of $180,000 will be found to have been intermingled with the increase of $153,000 in "working capital" and the other items appearing in the "S/A/F" column, or as presented in greater detail in the cash-flow and funds-flow columns.

Having followed the details of the illustration thus far, the reader, if a nonaccountant, may wish to develop a further understanding of the accounting process that a list of accounts similar to the above makes possible. He will find additional information, much of it referring back to this illustration, under *balance sheet*, *income statement*, *working capital*, *general ledger*, and other terms that have been employed here. A professional accountant could also point out numerous other features associated with the accounting process that this illustration makes possible.

representing debits and vertical lines credits; the amount, if any, appearing at one of their intersections, often obtained by analysis, represents the total of the transactions debited to the account or account class named by the sidehead and at the same time credited to the account or account class named by the column head; when prepared as an exhibit, sometimes referred to as an *articulation statement;* see *cash flow; cost flow.*

Thus, the transaction classes of the *M* Company have been traced back to their sources by a study and summarization of its accounts which appear on page 399 (data from illustration under *double-entry bookkeeping,* page 168).

A system of *split ledger accounts* would have yielded the same information in vertical rather than horizontal form, and without the need for analyzing each general-ledger account.

A further example will be found under *trial balance.*

stability Property of a *time series* relative to a specified time sequence construed as the criterion series or path, such that the given time series deviates from the criterion path from a given time onward by no more than a designated quantity. The property is typically of interest for time series generated through some systematic or regular process, where the process is subject to occasional erratic disturbances. The stability of the time series is determined through comparison of the criterion path generated by the undisturbed process and the time series containing the results of the disturbances. In *statistical quality control,* the term "constant-cause-system" is often used to describe a time series which displays such stable properties. The device of "hidden reserves" is closely associated with attempts to produce the appearance of stability, or of greater stability than actually exists, as in profits or liquid position.

stabilization A term applied to the pegging or fixing of the price of a security on the market by the issuer or dealer to prevent or retard a decline during the period beginning with the original offering and usually ending with the absorption of the issue by the public. See *pegging; seasoning.—stabilize, v.t.*

staff auditor 1. An accountant in the employ of a public accountant.

2. A member of the bookkeeping or ac-

M COMPANY

Account Analysis Year 19-1
(In Dollars; 00.00's Omitted)

Account Debit ↓	Credit →	Cash	Investments	Receivables	Inventory	Payables	Capital Stock	Sales	Purchases	Expenses	Totals (Debits)
Cash	(a)		1.0	21.5			20.0			0.3	42.8
Investments	(b)	5.1									5.1
Receivables	(c)							32.4			32.4
Inventory	(d)								5.6		5.6
Payables	(e)	28.8									28.8
Capital stock											—
Sales	(f)			0.8							0.8
Purchases	(g)					28.7					28.7
Expenses	(h)			0.2		6.3					6.5
Totals (credits)		33.9	1.0	22.5	—	35.0	20.0	32.4	5.6	0.3	150.7

Key to transactions, reading across:

(a) Sale of investment
Collections of accounts
Sale of capital stock
Refund of overcharge

(b) Purchase of investments
(c) Sales of merchandise
(d) Purchases unsold
(e) Payment of liabilities

(f) Return of sale
(g) Purchases of merchandise
(h) Bad debt written off
Operating expense

counting division of an economic unit whose time is devoted to the inspection of its accounts as a part of the procedure of internal control; an *internal auditor*.

standard 1. A desired attainable objective; a performance goal; a *model*. Established by custom, common consent, scientific, professional, or government bodies, administrative action, or law, after extensive observation, experimentation, research, testing, or planning, and often compromise, a standard normally falls short of an ideal and its duration may be limited; its purpose is to serve as a working basis for the institution of procedures that will assure conformity on the part of a group or groups of persons, within the ranges of technological, institutional, or other limiting conditions under which they operate, and to provide a criterion for and a medium of control over future activity when accompanied by inspection, reporting, publicity, or other device at the level at which enforcement can be best applied. Because standards, man-made, grow out of efforts to meet immediate needs and sometimes to justify or freeze attainable practices, they may originate in different fields of interest and thus conflict. To keep pace with a changing world, old standards must often give way to new.

2. A quality or measure agreed to as between persons or as specified in purchase contracts.

3. A cost yardstick. See *standard cost; standard of comparison*.

standard cost A forecast or predetermination of what actual costs should be under projected conditions, serving as a basis of cost control and as a measure of productive efficiency (or standard of comparison) when ultimately aligned against actual cost. It furnishes a medium by which the effectiveness of current results can be measured and the responsibility for deviations can be placed. A standard-cost system lays stress upon important exceptions and permits concentration upon inefficiencies and other conditions that call for correction; it is usually less expensive to maintain than a job-order of cost-finding system, for the work of repeatedly calculating the cost of normal production activities is eliminated. To give maximum utility, standard costs must be relatively stable and subject to change only when important increases or decreases occur in the cost of materials or labor or in operating conditions. Variances between actual and estimated expense arise in every accounting period; because of seasonal fluctuations and other causes, they are usually accumulated to the close of the fiscal year and written off as a general processing expense. A standard-cost system preferably ties in with the financial records.

A standard cost is a form of *estimated cost;* the latter, however, may refer to any prediction of cost, without the discipline in its computation that customarily attaches to standard cost, and in practice it may be subject to numerous revisions as operations progress. Standard costs remain relatively fixed over a period of time except, as already stated, major changes necessitated by new and severe economic conditions or drastic alterations of production methods. In most systems of estimated costs, the chief emphasis is on actual costs, whereas with standard costs a more nearly ideal cost is predetermined as a measuring standard for actual performance. See *basic standard cost; current standard cost; ideal standard cost; normal standard cost; perfection standard cost*.

A standard cost is thus a carefully formulated advance estimate of what a future cost should be under conditions expected to prevail. While predetermined costs in the form of estimates have long been used by business management, the present-day concept of a standard cost is a product of the scientific-management movement. The leaders in this movement have stressed improvements in manufacturing methods, the increased ability of management in exercising *controls*, and the embodiment of approved methods in standards which serve both as goals toward which to work and as measures of performance.

Such standards were a great improvement in the basic data used by management for two reasons: they were based upon systematic observation, measurement, and controlled experiment—all factors which mean a marked increase in reliability; and they were recorded and made generally available within the company. These standards are engineering or quantitative standards expressed in methods of operation, units of material, and hours of labor. They are basic standards.

Since the ultimate objective of improved manufacturing methods is a better product at a lower cost, it was soon seen that basic standards could be translated into cost standards.

In most modern applications, standard costs serve primarily as attainable goals to be striven for in management's attempt to control production. From comparisons with actual costs variances are computed. These constitute loss or gain occasioned by failure or success in observing the pre-established standards.

Although standard costs may be employed for purposes of cost control without incorporating them into the accounts, experience has shown that their usefulness is strengthened by doing so. Predetermined overhead rates which were essentially standard costs were employed for some years before predetermined costs for direct labor and direct material came into use. The bookkeeping techniques generally used are similar to those of the so-called estimating-cost systems. However, instead of adjusting the predetermined costs when the actual costs are found to differ, the standard-cost approach has viewed standard costs as "command" costs through managerial action.

A variety of terms for what are now generally called standard costs are found in the early literature on the subject: "scheduled costs," "predicted costs," and "specification costs." Supposed differences between these terms no longer exist.

In cost systems where the primary objective is to provide data to be used by management in exercising controls over costs, the following features are evident:

1. The primary classification of accounts is by responsibility for cost incurrence, with a secondary classification by nature of expenditure. This plan of classification tells, first, who is responsible for the cost and, second, for what the money has been spent. (See *activity accounting*.)
2. Costs are predetermined.
3. Actual costs are compared with the standard costs. By comparison, it is possible to measure the success management has had in achieving planned costs, i.e., controlling costs.
4. Variances, differences between actual and predetermined costs, are analyzed to determine why they arose.
5. Managerial action is taken to prevent unfavorable differences from recurring in the future.
6. Standard rates are reviewed at least once annually but are modified only where a consensus of management, engineering, and accounting reviews point to the necessity for change.

Reports to management follow the principle of exceptions and emphasize variances. The point of view is that management needs to concern itself with costs only when they deviate materially from those established beforehand as valid costs. Supervisors are thereby freed from the necessity for having to examine large masses of figures to keep themselves informed as to current performance. However, see *favorable difference; management by exception*.

Quantitative standards are usually developed by engineers or others qualified by technical knowledge and experience with production processes. Standards are established for:

1. *Materials*

(a) Specifications covering kind, quality, and other characteristics affecting production costs.

(b) Quantity that should be used to make the desired product after allowing for scrap, shrinkages, and other losses considered impossible or impractical to eliminate.

2. *Labor*

(a) Methods and equipment to be used, and other factors which influence the effectiveness with which the employee performs his task.

(b) Qualifications of the operators, including both training and experience.

(c) Operation time, using time and motion-study techniques to determine how long it should take to perform each operation when working under standard conditions.

3. *Overhead*

Types and quantities of individual supplies and services which should be consumed are established where these are important enough to be controlled closely. However, the fact that overhead cost represents a variety of different items, many of which are either difficult or impractical to measure closely, commonly leads to the expression of overhead standards in terms of dollar cost without underlying quantitative standards. In some cases, quantitative standards are set for important components of overhead cost (e.g., indirect labor) while dollar allowances are used for the remainder.

Standards for nonmanufacturing activities are set in a similar manner when standards are applied to such operations. For example, standard quantities are set for materials used in packing products for shipment, and operation time standards are determined for shipping-department labor. Time standards may also be set for typing, posting entries, and other repetitive clerical operations. Activities of field salesmen, technical staff employees, and executives are usually so varied that aside from hoped-for quotas reliable standards cannot be set.

Problems of coordinating standard costs with the accounts arise when the standard costs are used as a basis of reporting.

Cost systems with standard costs incorporated into the accounts follow the general procedure outlined below:

1. Actual costs of cost factors used in manufacturing are charged to variance or clearing accounts.

2. Work-in-process accounts are debited and the variance accounts credited with standard cost of production. Variance balances accumulate for the fiscal period.

3. Transfers from work-in-process to finished-goods accounts are made at standard cost, leaving the work-in-process inventory at standard cost.

4. Transfers from finished goods inventory to cost-of-goods-sold accounts are made at standard cost, leaving the finished-goods inventory at standard cost.

5. Balances in the variance accounts are closed to cost of goods sold or prorated between inventories and cost of goods sold.

Process methods are generally followed where standard costs are in use. Standard costs suffice for costs of individual products or orders. Actual costs are accumulated only as totals by elements and departments. However, where desired, actual costs can be accumulated by job orders and comparisons of actual and standard cost can be for each order.

Raw materials are frequently costed at standard prices on receipt of the materials. Hence, the raw-materials inventory is stated at standard cost and the material-price variance is developed in the period in which the materials are purchased.

Under a different bookkeeping routine sometimes used, charges to work in process for direct materials and direct labor are made at actual cost. Credits to work-in-process account are entered for the standard cost of production completed and transferred, and for the closing inventory of work in process. The remaining balance in the work-in-process account then represents the variances from standard cost.

For bookkeeping purposes, variances need be determined only at the close of the period. The number and classification can be limited to those considered necessary for purposes of variance disposal. For this reason, variance accounts are usually few in number, although numerous variances may be calculated and reported statistically. For purposes of cost control, variances should be known as soon as possible after the event which caused them to arise. It is also desirable to report them at their source. Therefore, variance reports are generally prepared to inform operating management of variances on a current basis. Examples are reports of labor variances (often reported daily), of scrap and spoilage, and of departmental-overhead-expense variances. Periodic summaries of these reports may later serve as a basis for accounting entries.

The method of determining actual cost through the use of ratios to base is a form of averaging, and the resulting actual costs are average costs. In setting up the inventory accounts, care is taken to avoid grouping together materials or products exhibiting diverse cost fluctuations, for otherwise the ratios made may be distorted.

Variances are unabsorbed cost balances which may be viewed either as *period costs*, to be charged in their entirety against income of the period in which they arise, or as product costs, to be divided at the end of the period between inventories and cost of goods sold. Under the first of these views, inventories are costed at standard cost of the products contained therein.

Opponents of standard costs for inventories may, however, accept standard costs for measuring efficiency, facilitating bookkeeping, and disclosing variances due to idle-plant capacity. Variances arising from other causes are excluded from the general accounts or proportionately divided between inventories and cost of goods sold.

Inventories priced at standard cost are subject to the usual end-of-period adjustments for obsolescence, physical condition, and realizable value (see *inventory valuation*). A reduction in book costs to a lower market figure is often accomplished by adjusting inventories to revised standard costs. Thus, a decrease in material price is reflected in a new standard cost at which the costing inventory is stated. In general, the use of standard costs for pricing inventories offers no special problems, for the comparison with market prices can be applied to standard costs in the same manner in which it is applied to actual costs.

standard-cost system A method of accounting whereby *standard costs* are the basis for credits to work-in-process accounts; standard costs may also be applied to charges of materials, labor, and other costs to work in process, and to physical as well as book inventories; differences between actual costs and standard costs are carried to *variance* accounts. See *standard cost.*

standard deduction (Federal income taxes) A deduction which an individual taxpayer may elect in lieu of itemized deductions. Generally the amount of the standard deduction is the lesser of $1,000 or 10% of adjusted gross income; for a married person who files a separate return the deduction is $500. If adjusted gross income is less than $5,000, the only way to take the standard deduction is to use the "Tax Table" instead of the rate schedule.

standard deviation (statistics) A measure of dispersion: the square root of the average of the squares of the differences between a group of numbers and their arithmetic mean; also called *root-mean-square deviation;* usually denoted by σ (sigma).

The ability of an arithmetic mean or other measure of central tendency to represent a group of numbers is determined by the amount of dispersion or variation in the numbers. Thus, it is much more meaningful to say that the average variable cost is \$50 per unit when this cost is identical for every unit or ranges from \$45 to \$55, than when the costs range from negligible to very large amounts, as from \$1 to \$1,000.

Although other measures of dispersion, such as *range* and *average deviation*, are available, the preferred measure of dispersion in statistics is the standard deviation, σ. This measure takes into account not only the spread between lowest and highest, but also the intermediate values; it logically relates the amount of dispersion to the arithmetic mean, and leads directly and easily to the type of statistical relations used in the *least-squares method* and *correlation table*.

The mathematical expression of the standard deviation is

$$\sigma = +\sqrt{\frac{\Sigma f(Y - \bar{Y})^2}{N}},$$

where σ is the standard deviation, which is always positive, Σ is the "sum of," f is the frequency (the number of times each Y occurs), N is Σf or the number of Y's, Y is any value, and $\bar{Y}$ is the arithmetic mean of Y's.

A tabular representation developed from the discussion of sugar-refining costs under *arithmetic mean*, where it was found that $\bar{Y} = 126.4$, appears below. The last two columns in the table are added as a check, since

$$\sqrt{\frac{\Sigma f(Y - \bar{Y})^2}{N}} = \sqrt{\frac{\Sigma f Y^2}{N} - (\bar{Y})^2}.$$

Substituting in the preceding equation,

$$\sqrt{\frac{1{,}472}{50}} = \sqrt{\frac{800{,}320}{50} - 15{,}976.96} = \sqrt{29.44}$$

or

$$\sigma = 5.43,$$

which is equal to the value σ_y calculated under *correlation table*.

As can be seen by the check calculation introduced in the table, σ can be arrived at in either of two ways. Either method is, however, tedious and involves a prior calculation of the mean $\bar{Y}$. Simplification is possible, however, through the same device used for a shortcut method of calculating the *arithmetic mean*. In grouped data, an arbitrary value A can be chosen as the starting point of calculations, letting $A = 0$ and measuring Y values from this starting point. The differences $Y - A$ may also be stated in units of 1 instead of the class interval 5 used in the

Y	$Y - \bar{Y}$	$(Y - \bar{Y})^2$	f	$f(Y - \bar{Y})^2$	Y^2	fY^2
Cost of Refining	Cost of Refining Minus Average of Costs	Column 2 Squared	Frequencies	Frequencies Times Column 3	Column 1 Squared	Frequencies Times Column 6
118	−8.4	70.56	8	564.48	13,924	111,392
123	−3.4	11.56	13	150.28	15,129	196,677
128	1.6	2.56	19	48.64	16,384	311,296
133	6.6	43.56	7	304.92	17,689	123,823
138	11.6	134.56	3	403.68	19,044	57,132
143	16.6	275.56	0		20,499	
Totals			50 Σf, or N	1,472.00 $\Sigma f(Y - \bar{Y})^2$		800,320 ΣfY^2

table. These "class-interval units" need only be reintroduced, at the end of the calculation, since the substitution of $d = Y - A$, or $Y = d + A$, in the above equations, yields

$$\sigma = \sqrt{\frac{\Sigma f d^2}{N} - \left(\frac{\Sigma f d}{N}\right)^2} \times c,$$

where c (= 5) represents the class-interval adjustment. In other words, the value of σ can be determined directly in terms of unit deviations d, which will not only reduce calculations to much smaller figures but also eliminate the necessity of calculating the mean, $\bar{Y}$.

The following table illustrates the process of calculation when an arbitrary value, here 128, is chosen as A.

Y	d	d^2	f	fd	fd^2
Original Values	Deviations in Class Interval Units	Column 2 Squared	Frequencies	Frequency Times Column 2	Frequency Times Column 3
118	−2	4	8	−16	32
123	−1	1	13	−13	13
128	0	0	19	0	0
133	1	1	7	7	7
138	2	4	3	6	12
143	3	9	0	0	0
			50 Σf, or N	−16 Σfd	64 Σfd^2

Substituting,

$$\frac{\sigma}{c} = \sqrt{\frac{\Sigma fd^2}{N} - \left(\frac{\Sigma fd}{N}\right)^2}$$

$$= \sqrt{\frac{64}{50} - \left(\frac{-16}{50}\right)^2} = 1.085.$$

Multiplying through by c (= 5) to effect the class-interval adjustment, the same result, $\sigma = 5.43$, is secured as under the longer methods.

The definition of σ as given above provides a sample estimate of the standard deviation of the universe from which the sample came. This estimate, however, is biased. If an unbiased estimate is required, this can be obtained by dividing σ by the correction-for-bias factor c_2, which depends on sample size and which approaches unity in value as sample size increases. Values of c_2 for small samples are available in Table B2 of the *ASTM Manual* (see *control charts*) and elsewhere in textbooks on statistics.

A common practice in statistics is to use the divisor $N - 1$ rather than N in the formula for σ. Although this practice does not make σ an unbiased estimate in the strict sense, it does give an approximate compensation for the bias resulting from the use of N as a divisor. For practical purposes, this approximation may be regarded as satisfactory for sample sizes greater than $N = 5$. See also *variance*.

standard error (statistics) The standard deviation of a sampling distribution. See *expected value*.

standard error of estimate (statistics) The standard deviation about a regression line, usually denoted as S_y or S_x. See *correlation table*.

standard labor rate Base pay plus incentives and premiums estimated attainable under efficient working conditions.

standard labor time Man hours of specified quality, determined by an engineering study and required for the production of a given quantity of goods or services or for the performance of a specified operation.

standard machine time The time normally required for a machine or group of machines to produce a specified quantity of goods; such data may include setup and teardown as well as operating time.

standard material Raw material or a subassembly conforming to predetermined engineering specifications which may cover both quantity and quality.

standard method A prescribed set of operations determined by engineering study to be desirable in executing an assignment, work order, or other operation.

standard of comparison 1. Any model serving as a basis for judgment.
2. As applied to the reading of financial

statements: any basis (see *standard*) against which *performance* revenues and costs and *financial position* may be measured; e.g., a budget or other forward estimate devised by management; a level of operations or position recommended by professional advisers; financial statements of preceding periods, or of another organization similarly circumstanced; averages, expressed as *ratios* (*q.v.*) derived from collective experiences of others. Typical of published standards of comparison are those to be found in the FTC-SEC *Quarterly Financial Report for Manufacturing Corporations*, *Annual Financial Statements* of the Robert Morris Associates, and Dun & Bradstreet's *Key Business Ratios*. Meanings ascribed to particular statements by investors and investment analysts derive largely from observed variations from such standards. Thus, the 1–1/2 *working-capital ratio* of a certain manufacturer differs substantially from the average 2–1/2 ratio maintained for the past two decades by American manufacturing corporations. The difference may suggest any of a number of possible causes: a persistent or newly developed shortage of working capital, expanded credits to customers or from creditors or both, inventory overstock, major acquisitions of fixed assets, removal or neglect of cash-discount opportunities, and so on. The choice from among such possible causes may be narrowed by studies of variations in other ratios; or by a knowledge of industry trends, market conditions, familiarity with the peculiarities within a particular business, and other factors not reflected in ratios.

3. Hence, deviations from standards, even those painstakingly determined by management for application to special situations, do not in themselves warrant ready conclusions, *favorable* or *unfavorable*. The chief function of the continued employment of standards of comparison is to keep management aware of the peculiar and often variant conditions and procedures that reside within its domain of operations. With the passage of time, even increases in departures from standards do not lend themselves to immediate inferences, for the same unprojected events and conditions that have given rise to the variances may have altered the standards themselves. See *favorable difference*.

Both *internal-* and *external-auditing* procedures call for the use of a variety of standards of comparison as a prelude to *judgments* concerning the accuracy, meaning, and general propriety of financial-statement components; these often lead to reductions or extensions of audit *scope*.

standard of performance A projection of operations under known or estimated controlling and attainable operating goals, evidenced by a *budget*, programmed output quality or quantity, *standard costs*, manpower limitations, and other imposed conditions.

standard preparation hours A standard value or other measure for *setup* or *make-ready time* determined from an engineering study.

standard price The price of raw materials estimated to be obtainable by the exercise of prudent procurement practices.

standard profit The net amount that should be earned per unit when a job is executed or a service is performed under a *standard method* employing *standard material* and *labor time*.

standard purchase price = *standard price*.

standard-run quantity = *economic lot size*.

standard values (statistical quality control) Used in connection with *control charts* (*q.v.*). When the central line and control limits are computed from the data plotted on the chart, the chart is said to be constructed with "no standards given": a procedure followed when the chart is being used as a guide for attaining a state of *statistical control* for the process. In this case, the data are obtained and plotted first: the central and limit lines are then calculated and placed on the chart. After a satisfactory state of statistical control has been attained, or, in the case of a *chart for attributes,* when it is desired to set a goal for future attainment, the chart is made up by drawing in central lines and control limits first and then plotting the data as they arise against these assigned *standard values.* The chart then becomes an instrument for helping to maintain control of the process within the framework set by the standard values selected rather than an instrument for investigating process capabilities. Discretion is exercised in the choice of standard values to make sure that they are realistically related to process capabilities. Charts based on standard values serve more effectively as control instruments if their use is deferred until experience under charting with no standards given has developed to a point that warrants a shift to standard-values operation.

standby cost = *fixed cost.*

standby equipment One or more machines or other fixed assets considered necessary to production but remaining idle during periods of offpeak or otherwise limited operations. Where carefully maintained, a standby asset may be subject to a separate depreciation policy—i.e., to a lesser rate of depreciation than that applicable to similar equipment employed full time. The presence of a substantial investment in standby equipment may in some instances result in higher costs of production.

standby underwriting An agreement to purchase the balance of an issue of securities remaining after a portion of the stockholders have exercised their preemptive rights or have absorbed, under an optional arrangement, new securities in exchange for old, as in reorganization or recapitalization following bankruptcy proceedings. See *underwriting contract; underwriting syndicate.*

standing cost (charge, or expense) = *fixed cost.*

standing order 1. An order authorizing broad classes of work that must be performed regularly in the operation of a plant or a division of a plant. Examples: an order for the general repair, upkeep, and maintenance of property and often the standards therefor that are to be maintained; an order for the generation of power, heat, and light.
2. A continuing *work order* directing the production of an item to meet specified inventory requirements, or to fill gaps in a productive period or process.

staple 1. The chief commodity traded in a market.
2. Raw material on hand.
3. A linen, wool, cotton, or artificial fiber; the relative length or other commonly expressed fiber quality.

starting-load cost The cost of preparing to operate: cost of designing, tooling, recruiting, and training the labor force before production starts: a term having reference to the opening of a new plant or department, the reopening of a plant or department after a shutdown, or the beginning of work on a new or altered method of production or product. See *lead time; setup time.*

stated capital 1. The amount contributed to a corporation by the purchasers of its capital stock; or, under varying state laws, the portion of the amount contributed by purchasers of no-par-value stock that is credited to the capital-stock account, the balance, if any, being credited to *paid-in surplus:* a distinction, comparable to that accorded *par value* and paid-in surplus. Often the state law or the regulations thereunder require that the articles of incorporation or bylaws disclose the division between the two accounts; in some instances, the decision may be made by the stockholders or board of directors as an issue or a block of no-par-value stock is sold. See *paid-in capital; paid-in surplus.*
2. *Legal capital.*

stated liabilities Liabilities as they appear in the books of account or in a financial statement. The term is used when no proof of accuracy exists, as in the case of an unaudited statement prepared from books and records which may be incomplete and may or may not give evidence of errors after an examination has been made; or when the amount of liabilities taken over from participants in a merger or purchase of net assets is subject to subsequent adjustment.

stated value Stated capital per share; stated value of new stock issued is determined by dividing the stated capital resulting from the new issue by the number of shares issued; this will change if an additional block of shares of the same class is assigned a disproportionate amount of stated capital, the stated value of each old and new share then becoming an average.

statement 1. A formal presentation of account names and amounts, usually in conventional order, or groups of such accounts, prepared for the purpose of displaying financial condition, operating results, and the like.
2. A summary of transactions between a debtor and his creditor for an accounting period, presented by the creditor to the debtor to show the amount due or owing; a statement of account.

statement analysis The analytical study of a balance sheet, income, and any other statement of a business enterprise, by themselves or in comparison with those of other dates or other enterprises, regarded as an aid to management or as a basis for measuring credit and investment risks; often prepared by employing accepted financial and operating *ratios* ostensibly showing conditions and trends.

statement form = *report form.*

statement heading The title of a balance sheet or other financial statement; three elements are commonly regarded as a minimum requirement: name of organization, name of statement (or descriptive phrase indicating content, if there is no common name), and date or period. Other title content sometimes found in accounting exhibits include: (a) name of state of incorporation, an addition common a generation ago when the effect on financial statements of a series of new state business-corporation acts then being adopted was uncertain, but now considered unnecessary; (b) the name of a principal subsidiary or names of principal subsidiaries forming a part of consolidated figures.

statement of account A report of transactions between debtor and creditor, usually prepared by the creditor, and concluding with the open or unpaid balance, if any. Examples: a monthly bill from a retail store to a customer; a bank statement (here prepared by the debtor).

statement of affairs 1. Any statement showing the assets, liabilities, and net worth of an enterprise.
2. A tabular summary of the estimated effects of immediate liquidation on a person, a recent balance sheet serving as the starting point. Although prepared principally in cases of actual or pending bankruptcy, it is occasionally employed where a creditor or prospective creditor wishes to observe the results that would follow the enforcement of his or another's claim. Four classes of creditors are commonly recognized: preferred, fully secured, partially secured, and unsecured, the form of the statement centering about them.

A statement of affairs may assume any of several forms; one is shown on page 409. Payson & Fromes, Inc., is a corporation for whom a trustee was appointed by a Federal District Court. Unable to pay its maturing obligations, the company had applied for permission to reorganize under the Bankruptcy Act, and the trustee, as an officer of the Court, had immediately called in a public accountant for assistance, the statement of affairs being the product of the latter's initial survey. The trustee, at the instance of the public accountant, corresponded with customers who claimed substantial credits for defective products shipped to them and for overcharges. No net loss was anticipated from the disposition of inventory items, since much of the inventory was in the form of warehoused raw material, receipts for most of which had been pledged as security for the bank loan; the small amount in the company's possession, although valued at cost, was deemed to be

PAYSON & FROMES, INC.
JAMES B. JACKSON, TRUSTEE

Statement of Affairs—April 22, 19-1

Assets	Book Value	Estimated Shrinkage	Transfers to Secured Creditors	Available for Unsecured Creditors
Cash	$ 5,213	$ —		
Notes receivable—			$ 17,023	$ 4,024
Good	15,834	—		
Doubtful	17,276	8,638	—	8,638
Discounted	2,550	1,000	1,550	—
Bad	5,235	5,235	—	—
Accounts receivable—				
Pledged	7,588	2,319	5,269	—
Good	58,003	—	—	58,003
Doubtful	6,674	3,337	—	3,337
Bad	34,751	34,751	—	—
Inventory—				
Warehouse receipts	50,507	—	42,500	8,007
Other	3,160	—	—	3,160
Prepaid expenses	1,525	1,525	—	—
Land	30,000	−8,000		
Buildings less depreciation	138,275	−17,500	129,600	64,175
Equipment less depreciation	176,843	111,922	—	64,921
Totals	$553,434	$143,227	$195,942	$214,265

Liabilities		Book Value	Application of Assets	Unsecured Claims
Preferred creditors—				
Accrued taxes	$ 5,235			
Accrued salaries & wages	11,788	$ 17,023	$ 17,023	$ —
Fully secured creditors—				
4% first mortgage bonds	$120,000			
Accrued interest, 2 years	9,600	129,600	129,600	—
Partially secured creditors—				
Bank loan	$ 65,000		42,500	22,500
Accounts payable	21,942	86,942	5,269	16,673
Unsecured creditors—				
Accounts payable		223,854	—	223,854
Contingent liability—				
Notes receivable discounted		2,550	1,550	1,000
Equity of stockholders—				
Paid-in capital:				
2,000 shares, $100 par value	$200,000			
Deficit	−106,535	93,465	—	—
Totals		$553,434	$195,942	$264,027

Deficiency Account—April 22, 19-1

Estimated deficiency from realization of assets—		
Deficiency to unsecured creditors—		
Amount of claims, as above	$264,027	
Assets available, as above	214,265	$ 49,762
Possible dividend to unsecured creditors		81%
Deficiency to owners—		
Paid-in capital	$200,000	
Less accumulated operating deficit	106,535	93,465
Total estimated deficiency		$143,227

Causes of deficiency—		
Receivables—		
Doubtful items	$ 11,975	
Uncollectible items	43,305	
Prepaid expenses	1,525	
Equipment: excess of book over resale value	111,922	
Appreciation of land & buildings, based on offer to purchase	—25,500	$143,227

safely covered by the worth as scrap of defective products returnable by customers. The large loss anticipated from the disposal of the equipment was determined by consultation with the manufacturers of the equipment, second-hand dealers in similar equipment, and independent engineers; much of the equipment had been specially designed for the company's operation. Some gain, however, was in prospect from the forced sale of the company's plant, for which an offer had been received. (The language in this paragraph illustrates the type of information one would expect to find in a public accountant's no-opinion report in such a situation, thus limited, one would expect, because of the hypothetical nature of many of the items in the statement.)

The structure of the statement, in the light of the preceding explanations, is probably sufficiently obvious. The liquidation value of the assets is matched against the ranked liabilities in such a way as to display finally the array of the unpledged assets of the business and the unsecured claims of its creditors. A summarization is then assembled in a "deficiency account" showing, in whatever detail desired, the causes and amounts of individual losses resulting from a full liquidation—the proposed liquidation in this instance.

As the result of the study, by the Court and his advisers, of the statement of affairs and a collateral report prepared for the trustee, management changes were made, improved operating and customer policies were introduced, and two-year non-interest-bearing notes covering past unpaid purchases were issued to principal suppliers who, in accepting them, looked forward to a continued outlet for their products; the outstanding shares of capital stock were changed from a par value of $100 to no par value, the deficit thus being absorbed, and the company was off to a fresh start. Had liquidation taken place, a *statement of realization and liquidation* would have been in order.

statement of assets and liabilities (or **of condition, financial condition,** or **financial position**) 1. = *balance sheet;* these alternative names are occasionally encountered.
2. A statement prepared for an organization that does not maintain double-entry records, or that keeps no records.

statement of loss and gain (or **profit and loss**) = *income statement.*

statement of realization and liquidation A statement showing in summary form the results of winding up the affairs of an enterprise going out of business: the amounts received from the sale of the various classes of assets (realization), the amounts paid toward the settlement of various classes of liabilities (liquidation), and a statement of the operating revenue, expense, and losses for which the liquidator has been responsible. The statement follows whatever form is suited to the circumstances, one type being illustrated in the example that follows.

Report of John P. Stevens, Receiver in Equity for Conrad Mercantile Company, not inc.

Immediately after taking over the going concern on June 1, 19–2, the receiver surveyed the business and its prospects, and, with the approval of the Court and the consent of the owner, continued operations on a limited scale with the object of winding up its affairs and paying off its creditors who had asked the Court for such a proceeding.

Attached is a statement of realization and liquidation to which the auditors have affixed their report and which presents a keyed summary of the transactions to which the receiver has been a party. These transactions are briefly explained in paragraphs a to n following:

a. During the three-and-one-half-month period ended September 15, sales (in thousands of dollars) were made as follows: in fulfillment of contractual obligations, $222.6; resale to suppliers, at average discount of 11% as compared with prices invoiced by them, $248.1; auction sales, $111.2.

b. Accounts of 28 customers amounting to $32.4 have been charged off as worthless, and a list of these accounts has been supplied to the Court for possible action.

c. Receivables arising from receiver's sales of merchandise have been collected in full. Of the $106.1 uncollected on June 1, a total of $45.0 has been collected; and the balance of $28.7, represented by nine accounts, after de-

CONRAD MERCANTILE COMPANY, NOT INC.

John P. Stevens, Receiver
Statement of Realization and Liquidation
June 1, 19–2 to September 15, 19–2
(Thousands of Dollars)

Item	*Items Taken Over*	*Transactions Debit*	*Transactions Credit*	*Items Remaining*
Assets:				
Cash	7.3	c 626.9	i 50.0	
		g .5	k 58.0	
		h 31.0	l 550.2	7.5
Receivables	106.1	a 581.9	b 32.4	
			c 626.9	28.7
Inventory	321.5	d 268.8	e 557.2	33.1
Investment	185.3		h 185.3	—
Land & building	87.4	f 2.5 }	g 61.7	—
Depreciation reserve	−28.2			
Total assets	679.4			69.3
Liabilities:				
Bank loan	50.0	i 50.0		—
Payables	285.4	l 550.2	d 268.8	
			f 2.5	6.5
Accrued wages & interest	14.3	k 58.0	j 46.8	3.1
Mortgage	51.5	g 51.5		—
Proprietor's account	278.2	m 218.5		59.7
Total liabilities	679.4			69.3
Revenue, expense, & losses:				
Merchandise sales			a 581.9	
Cost of sales		e 557.2		
Wages & interest		j 46.8		
Loss from disposal of—				
Investment		h 154.3		
Land & building		g 9.7		
Receivables		b 32.4		
Net loss			m 218.5	

ducting the worthless accounts described in the preceding paragraph, is believed by Mr. Conrad to be collectible.

d. During the same period merchandise purchases consisted of the following classes: items necessary to meet commitment obligations, $204.5; items in transit on June 1, $28.9; items required to fill balance of firm-sales contracts, $35.4. With the approval of the Court, the balance of the inventory on hand, $33.1, will be turned over to the proprietor for whatever disposition he may see fit.

e. The cost of sales, $557.2, represented the actual cost of item lots completely closed out, and the average cost of items the counterparts of which are also on hand.

f. A balance of $2.5 remained to be paid on a new drainage installation at the rear of the building, the original obligation having been the result of the completion of a contract by the Rex Construction Company entered into in October, 19–1; payment was made on August 15.

g. The building, purchased by Mr. Conrad in 19–8, was advertised in June and sold in July to the highest bidder, J. Makon & Sons, for the nominal sum of $.5. This disposal price, approved by the Court, was deemed fair in view of the appraisal value determined by the real-estate board of $60,000.

h. An investment in the Golden State Supply Company had been made by Mr. Conrad in 19–0, a venture in which he was joined by one J. L. McCloud, each contributing $100.0 in cash. Since then net cash advances of $85.3 had been made by Mr. Conrad. The company was declared a bankrupt in the early part of the current year and a final liquidating dividend was declared on July 2, 19–2, bringing the amount realized from the liquidation to a total of but $31.0.

i. The bank loan was paid off on June 25. It was a discount loan, due on that date.

j. Mortgage interest accrued during the period, at 4 percent, was $1.0; the only other out-of-pocket operating cost was for compensation of 26 employees, 22 of whom were terminated as at September 15.

k. Accruals of wages and interest were paid in full, except for accrued wages of the four employees who are to continue with Mr. Conrad. These four individuals have furnished the receiver with statements indicating their willingness to look for reimbursement from funds arising out of the future business to be carried on by Mr. Conrad.

l. All obligations for merchandise and supplies were paid off except for an amount of $6.5, dating from 19–0, owing to Reese Valve Company, and involving a shipment of defective supplies. No reply has been received to receiver's requests for a claim from this creditor and the latter has been notified of the closing of the receivership and of the transfer of the obligation to the continuing organization.

m. A net loss of $218.5 resulted from the receiver's operations, attributable mainly to the asset disposals above mentioned. A gross profit of $24.7 arose from the merchandise transactions: an indicated margin of 4.2 percent. Omitting the resales to suppliers, the margin was 16.5 percent; omitting also the sales at auction, which were virtually at cost, the margin was very nearly 25 percent, a margin common in this type of retailing.

n. Based on the final accounting as reported in the above statement, the remaining assets and liabilities, with the approval of the Court, have been taken over and assumed, respectively, by Mr. Conrad.

John P. Stevens

Report of Accountants

In our opinion, the above statement of realization and liquidation and accompanying explanations, a to n, inclusive, present fairly the position of the Conrad Mercantile Company, not inc., a proprietorship, at June 1, 19–2 and September 15, 19–2, and the classes and totals of transactions between these two dates.

Hyatt, Paterson & Company
Certified Public Accountants

September 23, 19–2

statement of receipts and disbursements A list of incoming and outgoing cash during any specified period of time; usually classified on an *object* basis; see *cash-flow statement*.

statement of resources and their application = *statement of sources and applications of funds*.

statement of revenues and expenditures 1. A statement identical with an income statement, or with an income statement to which the cost of assets acquired during the same period has been added. 2. (municipal accounting) A statement prepared for a municipal fund or department, except utilities and other self-supporting enterprises, setting forth the revenues earned, the expenditures incurred, and the excess or deficiency of revenues compared with expenditures.

statement of sources and applications of funds A report summarizing the flow of *funds (4)* (= *working capital*) within an organization during a designated period of time, the purpose being to depict, on an accrual basis, the leading events and conditions, and trends and other changes during the period; the source: differences between *comparative balance-sheet* items, supplemented by breakdowns of certain items. From the comparative balance sheets on page 396 the illustration on page 413 was drawn. In this illustration, "net income" is the "profit for year" shown on page 397, less the four surplus charges amounting to $291,000. To obtain the gross intake of operating funds, three of these must be added back; the fourth item, a loss of $101,000 from the sale of investments, is a real loss of current assets and hence of working capital. The depreciation provision of $224,800 included in factory overhead, being a "loss" (i.e., *consumption*) of *fixed* assets, does not alter working capital and must also be added back. Because working capital has advanced during the period from $344,600 to $497,400, the increase may be set forth as a reinvestment of funds, or as here, as the excess of funds provided over funds disposed of.

Many variants of this statement, developed over the half-century or more of its use, are found in published reports to stockholders and in accountants' long-form reports. Where net income is broken down between sales, cost of sales, and other expenses, the title is generally *funds-flow statement;* an illustration,

BELFORD MANUFACTURING COMPANY

Statement of Sources and Applications of Funds
[or of Changes in Working Capital]
Year ended December 21, 19-7

Sources of funds		
Profit for year		$261 000
Add back costs and losses not involving current expenditures		
Depreciation, machinery & equipment	$224 800	
Goodwill amortization	120 000	
Stock bonus to officer	170 000	514 800
Funds derived from operations		$775 800
Sale of old equipment		40 000
Total funds provided		$815 800
Disposition of funds		
Purchase of new equipment	$483 000	
Dividends to stockholders	180 000	663 000
Increase in working capital		$152 800

based on the same figures, appears under that head on page 209.

Further breakdowns of balance-sheet and income-statement variances yield the *cash-flow statement* shown on page 80. Of these three statements, the cash-flow statement, essentially a statement of cash receipts and disbursements, appears to be best suited as a budgetary vehicle. The statement illustrated here will probably yield to the funds-flow form when it is realized that the movement of funds in operations is of equal importance to and is always closely interrelated with the management of working capital.

statement of stockholders' equity (or **investment** or **net worth**) A financial statement often appearing in auditors' reports and in annual reports to stockholders; it shows the amount of paid-in capital and *retained earnings* and the changes therein since the preceding report.

statistic Any value, such as an arithmetic mean, median, or standard deviation, calculated from a sample rather than a universe; more generally, any numerical measure of a physical or economic condition or activity, as a wage, a national-income total, or a summation of assets. It may, when suitably modified, be used to estimate a universe value or parameter. See *expected value.*

statistical control (statistical quality control) A system of appraisal and action pertaining to the nature of the variation present in a set of observed data; usually associated with variation patterns found on *control charts.* When all the variations in a set of data can be judged to have been generated by random factors consistent with some underlying *statistical distribution* model, the data are said to exhibit a state of statistical control.

It should be emphasized that *statistical control* is not synonymous with *satisfactory control:* the latter term includes the former, but not conversely. A process may exhibit strong evidence of statistical control but at a wrong level or with too wide a *natural tolerance* to be satisfactory relative to specification requirements. A process is in satisfactory control with *variables data* when it exhibits statistical control centered on or near the *basic dimension* with a natural tolerance that matches the total tolerance allowed by specifications in the sense that the natural tolerance may be less than, equal to, or greater than the total tolerance.

The last of these three conditions is associated with satisfactory control only when it would cost more to reduce the natural tolerance than to accept (or sort out) some predictable proportion of out-of-tolerance product. A process is in satisfactory control with *attribute* data when it exhibits statistical control at a level that strikes a profitable balance between the cost of quality and the value of quality—i.e., when any further improvement in quality would cost more than can be recovered through such improvement.

statistical distribution A mathematical function specifying the *probability* of occurrence of any *random* event in a designated system of random events, where the random events are characterized by the relation $P[x_1 \leq x \leq x_2] = k$. This relation specifies the probability of a chance or random variable greater than or equal to some real number x_1 and less than or equal to x_2 is equal to k, where k is a number such that $0 \leq k \leq 1$.

statistical inference The use of a limited quantity of observed data as a basis for generalizing on the characteristics of a larger, unknown universe or population; the study, methodology, or use of relations between statistics and parameters. See *statistic; descriptive statistics.*

statistical quality control The application of statistical science, in conjunction with other disciplines, to the field of *quality control.* The American Society for Quality Control, a professional engineering society, was founded in 1946 "to create, promote, and stimulate interest in the advancement and diffusion of knowledge of the science of quality control and of its application to industrial processes." Like other professional societies, ASQC publishes a journal, *Industrial Quality Control,* and sponsors other publications that serve the objectives of the Society. Among these, the *ASQC Standard A1–1951* defines basic terms and symbols for control charts as formulated by the Society's Standards Committee. A projected standard will define basic terms and symbols for acceptance sampling.

Pioneering work in statistical quality control was undertaken by Dr. W. A. Shewhart of the Bell Telephone Laboratories in the early 1920's as the "... outgrowth of an investigation...to develop a scientific basis for attaining economic control of quality of manufactured product through the establishment of control limits to indicate at every stage in the production process from raw materials to finished product when the quality of product is varying more than is economically desirable." Since that time, and particularly since the outbreak of World War II, the field of statistical quality control has undergone rapid development and extension. In the field of accounting, its principles may be applied to budgeting, cost and inventory control, and other fields such as ratio forecasting and analyses.

Statistical quality control is divided into two major but closely related parts: process control and *sampling inspection* or *acceptance sampling.*

Process control is primarily concerned with infinite *universes* of repetitive operations, such as continuing manufacture of similar parts; it attempts to analyze production operations both as a means of anticipating and forestalling trouble and as a means of eliminating useless investigations, slowing or shutting down of operations, or resetting of machines caused by variations which may appear significant but are actually only *random* in character.

Acceptance sampling is generally concerned with sampling from finite universes, such as a "lot" of completed product, for the purpose of reaching a decision, based on the evidence available in the sample, concerning what disposition to make of the lot.

The principal tool of process control is a control chart which serves as a guide for decisions on the process. The principal tool of acceptance sampling is a battery of standard sampling plans providing enough flexibility in lot sizes, sample sizes, and risk control features to make possible the selection of a plan (or plans) to be used on submitted lots for the purpose of reaching a decision regarding disposition of these lots. Choosing a plan is a matter of seeking to strike an economic balance between the risks of making wrong decisions on the lots and the cost of minimizing these risks by more inspection. The protection features possessed by a proposed sampling plan are graphically portrayed by its associated *operating-characteristic* (*OC*) curve; its corresponding inspection cost features are graphically portrayed by its associated average-sample-number (*ASN*) curve. See *operating-characteristic curve* and *average sample number*.

Both process control and acceptance sampling recognize and seek to deal with the inherent variability of all phenomena by systematic statistical means. In a group of "identical" parts there is present not only variation resulting from differences in materials and the machines and quality of labor applied in the preparation of the parts, but variation in the quality of inspection and reporting itself.

The use of *tolerances* and *allowances* in manufacturing and design constitutes evidence of widespread recognition of this inherent variability. It remained for statistical quality control to recognize that all variability could be systematically grouped into two classes: (a) those variations resulting from *random* or chance causes which cannot be eliminated and which make detailed investigation of individual variations useless, and (b) those variations which are the result of assignable or nonrandom causes and which it is possible and profitable to discover and eliminate. Recognition of these two broad groups of causes made it possible to specify limits of variation of product within which a state of statistical control may be said to exist and beyond which statistical control does not exist. These limits, known as *control limits,* are constructed so that variations of product within this range should represent only random variations, while variations beyond this range, or other evidence of lack of control (such as trends) imply either lack of control or the fact that the process is moving out of control.

Control limits are not, generally, the same as tolerance limits. It has been one of the contributions of statistical quality control to test the feasibility of design specifications against actual production capabilities, forcing, where necessary, alterations in either design or production methods. But tolerance limits and control limits may, under certain circumstances, be combined or coordinated by the use of "modified control limits."

With systematic recognition of the presence of random variation, it has often been possible to substitute sample inspection for 100 percent inspection, or *screening.* This has resulted not only in reduction of inspection costs but in substantial improvement of inspection results as well. A reduced burden of inspection makes possible the use of a more carefully selected and trained staff and allows this staff to devote more careful attention to the items which are actually inspected.

Process control and acceptance sampling constitute what have been called the routine "bread-and-butter" areas of statistical quality control. A third area, now recognized to be of fundamental importance in this field, is that of planned investigation in research and development, pilot runs, laboratory work, and direct manufacturing operations. This area of application involves modern concepts and techniques of experimental design and calls for a fairly high degree of statistical maturity on the part of personnel responsible for its initiation and administration in industrial operations.

Not the least of the accomplishments of statistical quality control has been the development of orderly and systematic "feedback" reporting, with concomitant beneficial effects on production and supervisory personnel. From the need for carefully devised records and reports has arisen also the articulation of standards which worker, supervisor, and all others concerned with quality of product can accept and respect. For opinion and "judgment" backed by authority and the mysteries of managerial "know-how" are substituted the careful marshaling and analysis of evidence in a form which is readily comprehended and appraised by all concerned. The result is often not only improvement in quality and quantity of product at reduced cost but improved employee morale as well. See *control(2); control chart.*

Statistical quality control and the methodology associated with it are closely allied to *standard costing;* in practice they complement each other: the one the engineer's concept of product control, the other the accountant's concept of cost control over that product. Both feature important elements in the art of management.

statistical series (statistics) A group of numerical data arranged according to magnitude, time, position, class, or other systematic order; examples: a frequency distribution; a time series.

statistics 1. The discipline that deals with the study of *universes* (*populations*) through the medium of samples and their interrelationships; it is often described as having two branches: statistical description, involving the condensation of large masses of material to a few significant features; and statistical inference, or the study of the relations between populations and samples. The major problems of statistical inference may be divided into three categories: estimation, the testing of hypotheses, and prediction. See *expected value.*

2. A number, such as an arithmetic mean, or an array of numbers, such as the set from which the arithmetic mean is calculated; usually represented by $\bar{X}$.

3. In accounting practice, "statistics" are sometimes distinguished from accounting data by the fact that the former may not tie in directly with the books of account and thus be subjected to the discipline of double-entry bookkeeping.

statute of limitations The limitation set by law on actions that may be taken on matters involving the title of property, contracts, crimes, and torts. Particularly, the period of time set by statutory law within which recovery may be had for a right to which the litigant might otherwise be entitled; for example, section 6511(a) of the Internal Revenue Code provides that a taxpayer may not recover an overpayment of tax unless he submits a refund claim within three years from the time the return was due or within two years from the time the tax was paid. Again, section 6501 of the Code provides generally that no income tax may be assessed more than three years after the return was filed. These limitations do not apply where fraud exists, no return has been filed, or waivers have been signed by the taxpayer and the Treasury Department has extended the period.

stepped cost A cost that advances by steps with increased volumes of activity, as foremen's compensation upon the expansion of an operation or the addition of a new shift.

stochastic As applied to a *system* or *process:* developed by chance; operated on the basis of probabilities rather than a controlled planning.

stock 1. The legal capital of a corporation divided into shares. See *capital stock.*

2. A stock certificate.

3. = *inventory.*

stock company A corporation whose capital is divided into shares evidenced by transferable certificates.

stock discount The excess of *par value* over *paid-in capital;* once treated as a deferred charge, it is now generally regarded as a debit valuation account to be combined with the capital-stock account to which it is related before the appearance of the latter on a balance sheet, or subtracted on the face of the balance sheet from that account. Under the laws of most states, the discount is in effect an unpaid subscription and, in case of insolvency, collection from original subscribers can be enforced. Ultimate absorption of the discount by charging it to earned surplus does not relieve the stockholder of the contingent liability. The liability does not attach to a subsequent purchaser of the stock from the original stockholder unless he had notice or should have known of the existence of the discount.

stock dividend A dividend in the form of shares of any class of the distributing company's own stock. It may be charged to retained earnings, or to any other surplus account legally available for such use. The distribution of a stock dividend charged to retained earnings has the effect of capitalizing past earnings. A distribution of shares of another company's capital stock held by the distributing company is not a stock dividend but a property dividend. A stock dividend charged to retained earnings should not be confused with a *splitup*.

In CAP Bulletin 11 (1941), a number of principles intended to govern common-stock dividends to common stockholders were laid down; two years later, they were endorsed in an official letter of the New York Stock Exchange. They follow:

1. The resolution of the board of directors or stockholders of a corporation authorizing a stock dividend should specify (a) the number of shares to be issued and (b) the amount of earned surplus to be capitalized.

2. The amount of earned surplus to be capitalized should be the higher of (a) the existing average paid-in capital (par or stated value of capital stock plus paid-in surplus), or (b) an amount bearing "a reasonable relationship" to the "fair market value" of the dividend shares about to be issued. In the case of recurrent stock dividends (e.g., of certain investment trusts) the amount capitalized should not exceed the net income of (a) the period in which the dividend is issued, or (b) "a comparatively small number of fiscal periods immediately preceding."

3. Earned surplus capitalized should be credited to the capital-stock account in the amount of par or stated value, any balance being credited to paid-in surplus.

4. Stockholders, in receiving such a dividend, should be told (a) the amount of earned surplus capitalized, per share and in total, (b) the corporate accounts charged and credited, and (c) the percentage reduction in their equity ownership should they dispose of the dividend shares.

5. No income should be recorded by the recipient of such a dividend; he should spread the cost of his old shares prorata over the old and the new.

The above rules may be applied to any stock dividend received by a common stockholder—wherever the stockholder's equity remains unchanged. The cost of the old shares is divided equally between the old and the new shares, the same cost per share thus applying in case any old or new shares are sold. If a dividend to common stockholders is in the form of another class of stock, the cost of the old shares is divided between the old and the new shares on the basis of their market value at the time the dividend is received. Any type of stock dividend distributed to a preferred stockholder would as a rule reflect an increase in the stockholder's equity—a new and separable form of property. For income-tax purposes a distribution of stock in discharge of preference dividends is taxable. The same valuation basis has also been generally followed in accounting records and reports, the valuation reflected on the books being regarded as the "cost" of the new shares.

stockholder The legal owner of one or more shares of the *capital stock* of a corporation. Stockholders attend annual and special meetings or give their voting proxies for such meetings to others, usually a management group. They are expected to authorize or ratify, usually at the instance of management: charter amendments; amendments of bylaws, unless control over bylaws has been passed to the board of directors; a merger or consolidation with another company; sale of a major portion of the corporate assets or business; dissolution of the corporation; assessments on stock; election or removal of directors; approval of acts of directors and management during the fiscal period immediately preceding.

Stockholders, as owners, have the power to establish basic corporate policies, but in the case of publicly owned companies, stockholders only rarely take concerted action except to adopt or approve policies fixed by and originating with management. It is sometimes said that such independent action is exercised infrequently because its possibility imposes restraints on those who would not adequately safeguard stockholders' interests; but the primary cause lies elsewhere: stockholders of public companies have no readily available means for acting as a unit. Management, on the other hand, has devices in its favor that are supported by law and custom and that tend to perpetuate it: an annual meeting with stockholders that management usually dominates with ease; stock control secured by direct ownership, voting trusts, or proxies; and bylaws that give management technical advantages in meetings and elections. Individual stockholders representing only a minority interest are given the right, by most states, to examine the books of account and to procure other information, and the courts have often aided them in preventing undesirable management actions. But for the most part, stockholders who are not numbered among the management play no role in policy-making or in administration; in the average case, stockholders undoubtedly regard their everyday interests as being too far removed from management affairs to justify any active participation on their part. Thus, left to its own devices, management perpetuates itself and the policies it devises.

Individual nonmanagement stockholders, however, occasionally have more influence on corporate affairs than stockholders acting as a unit. A single stockholder or a group of minority stockholders, in possession of factual material and a strong popular or public-service point of view, for example, can be and often has been instrumental in instituting and modifying management policies, sometimes through court action, but more often by publicity.

stockholder of record A stockholder whose name is registered in the corporate transfer books. The term often appears in dividend resolutions, acccompanied by a date, the purpose being to provide a point midway between the date of the resolution and the date of payment that will permit a verification of the records and the preparation of dividend checks so that payment can be made at the appointed time. See *dividend*.

stockholders' equity = *net worth*.

stock in trade Merchandise held for sale in the regular course of business.

stock on hand The inventory of raw materials, supplies, finished and partly finished product, merchandise, and like items; see *inventory*. A British term.

stock option The right, under fixed conditions of time, price, and amount, to purchase shares of a corporation's capital stock. Often such rights are given to corporate officers or to underwriters or promoters as compensation for services. The transaction may be one of simple sale and purchase, in which case the recording of the transaction follows ordinary procedures. But where the option is given in part compensation of an officer or employee, the price paid for the stock may be and usually is less than its market price, thus making it possible for the individual exercising the option to have at least a potential profit at the moment of acquisition. Most option agreements provide that the purchaser must retain his stock for a minimum period, thus eliminating to some extent the possibility of speculation. The amount of compensation is measured by the excess of the market price of the stock over the amount to be paid in by the individual. The time of the accrual on the books of the corporation has on some occasions been the time at which the option becomes the property of the individual—whether thereafter exercised or not. The entry required is a debit to current (compensation) expense for the excess of the market price over the option price and a credit to "Option rights outstanding"—the latter account being a separate balance-sheet item appearing as paid-in capital; should the option not be exercised or exercised only in part, a reversal of the entry is not made, but the credit becomes a part of paid-in surplus because of its character as contributed capital. If exercised, the full credit is made to capital stock. Because the exercise of the option will in most cases be dependent on the existence or emergence of a market price greater than the option price, a more realistic date for the initial entry would be that on which the option is exercised: the date on which the possibility of the stock purchase becomes for the first time anything more than a mere contingency. The date of exercise will usually be the date on which a similarly measured amount becomes taxable income to the individual and deductible expense for the corporation for Federal-income-tax purposes. In all cases, a full disclosure of the details of the option agreement is requred in a balance-sheet footnote.

Since 1963, most stock options have been conformed to the specifications of *qualified stock options*, q.v.

stock-purchase warrant A privilege (in the form of a coupon or certificate) sometimes attached to preferred stock or to a debenture or other type of bond, giving the owner the right to purchase an indicated number of shares of stock at a specified price within a specified time. See *warrant; right.*

stock register A corporate record, usually kept by a registrar, containing the details of the issuance of stock certificates and of the disposition of those returned for transfer or cancellation.

stock right See *right.*

stock-transfer book A record in the nature of a journal wherein transfers of capital stock are entered, usually for posting to the individual shareholders' accounts in a capital-stock ledger. It is kept by the company or by its transfer agent.

stop order (securities) An order issued by a regulatory body or court suspending the sale of a security until specified remedial action has been taken by the seller. Under Federal law and the regulations of the U. S. Securities and Exchange Commission, a stop order may be issued by that body suspending the effectiveness of a registration statement. Such an order is usually the consequence of the finding, after a hearing, that the registration statement contains an untrue or misleading statement of fact; the order ceases to be operative and the registration becomes effective when the registration statement has been amended to meet the Commission's objections. See *registration.*

stores *Raw materials* and *supplies(3)* used in the manufacture and distribution of goods or in the upkeep of plant and equipment. The term is rarely applied to finished goods or materials in process of manufacture.

straight-line method The assignment of equal segments of the *service cost* of any item to the benefits to be yielded by the item: a procedure followed in depreciation computations and in the spread of prepaid expenses and bond discount. In practice, a *period charge* for depreciation is usually substituted for a more exact measurement of benefits yielded because of (a) its relative simplicity, (b) the presence of only minor differences between the two methods, (c) the impossibility of estimating with any degree of realism the total prospective output of services, as in the case of many types of machinery, or (d) the absence of any readily determinable unit of service, as in the case of buildings. See *depreciation; depreciation method; period charge; cost absorption; deferred charge.*

stratified sampling (statistics) Drawing of *random samples* within strata or relatively homogeneous subgroups of the *population*. Generally, the strata are sampled independently so that sample results in one stratum does not affect sampling procedures in other strata. The data may also be classified into strata on the basis of cost, ease, facility of handling materials, and other criteria, as well as statistical homogeneity.

stub-survivor curve (statistics) A survivor-life curve which is not extrapolated to zero survivors, generally because of lack of sufficient information with which to validate the extrapolation.

stumpage 1. Standing timber or the log feet derivable therefrom.
2. The price paid for the privilege of removing timber from land.
3. The portion of the cost of timberland assigned to timber removed.

subjective 1. Having a meaning or application reflecting the characteristics of an individual, the peculiarities of his experience or environment, not independently substantiated: said of an event, fact, judgment, or inference. Reliance on a subjective judgment is conditioned by convenience, cost, or faith. In the projection of future events, dependence on subjective judgments can never be wholly avoided. Agreement of opinion does not of itself signify objectivity; nor does subjectivity imply that an opinion is whimsical, prejudiced, or unwise. In the absence of evidence, the extent, for example, of doctrinaire or hasty prejudgment cannot be measured; hence the widespread effort to reduce areas of subjective thinking. See *objective*.
2. In a pejorative sense, expressing disparagement of another's view.

subjective value 1. Value assigned to an asset, as by a corporate management, without independent verification or relation to market value.
2. Value not independently determinable because of the impossibility of replication, arising from any of numerous causes, such as intractability of materials or lack of adequate records.

subject to A phrase sometimes employed in audit reports to introduce a qualified opinion, indicating that the auditor's endorsement of the financial statements is tempered by an unwillingness to approve specified items, or by the limited scope of the examination.

subordinated debt A debt ranking below amounts owing to general creditors; such an *arrangement* may be agreed to in the case of a financially embarrassed debtor where a creditor has faith in the debtor's business future.

subrogation The substitution of one creditor for another, as where an insurer, following the settlement of a loss, acquires part or all of the insured's right of indemnification from third persons.

subscribed capital stock That part of the capital stock of a corporation against which unpaid subscriptions are outstanding. It is sometimes found in corporate records as a credit account offsetting subscriptions, portions of it being transferred to the capital-stock account (and sometimes paid-in surplus also) as subscriptions become fully paid and stock certificates are issued.

subscription 1. An agreement to buy a security; the contract between a corporation and a purchaser of shares of its capital stock.
2. A written agreement to make a contribution to a fund for a charitable, educational, political, or other purpose.
3. An agreement to pay for a publication or a series of publications to be issued in the future.

subscription right (or **warrant**) A transferable instrument evidencing the right of a corporate stockholder to buy his proportionate amount of new shares about to be issued by the corporation. See *right; pre-emptive right; warrant; stock-purchase warrant*.

subsidiary (company) A corporation owned or controlled by a holding or parent company, most often through the ownership of voting stock. See *control(3)*.

subsidiary accounts A group of similar accounts relating to the same activity or object, maintained in a separate record and controlled by an account in the general ledger. Examples: customers' accounts; factory accounts. See *control account; subsidiary ledger*.

subsidiary-company accounting The method followed by a subsidiary company in recording transactions with its parent or controlling company. It is not uncommon among manufacturing and trading enterprises to find wholly owned branches separately incorporated but with assets and liabilities merged with the parent's. Many practical difficulties arise from such situations, including the confusion which results from attempts to prepare financial statements and tax returns of any one of the corporate entities. Not only is it essential to maintain separate records for each subsidiary, but the transactions of each subsidiary should be, as far as possible, on an arm's-length basis; particularly is that basis desirable where there are outside creditors and stockholders. An exception is necessary for a public-utility subsidiary against which charges are made by the controlling company or other affiliated company for construction or services, notwithstanding the relative importance of minority interests; under such circumstances, the *public interest*, represented by public-utility regulatory boards, generally requires that these less-than-arm's-length acquisitions be valued at their prudent-investment cost or original cost. See *original cost(2)*.

A division of the surplus accounts on the subsidiary's books between the period prior to the date of acquisition and the period thereafter, and the indication by directors of the source of declared dividends, are helpful devices in the preparation of consolidated statements and in the record-keeping of the controlling company.

subsidiary ledger A supporting ledger consisting of a group of accounts the total of which is in agreement with a control account. Examples: a customers' ledger; a creditors' ledger; a factory ledger; an expense ledger; a plant ledger; a branch or departmental ledger.

subsidy 1. A grant of financial aid, usually by a governmental body, to some other person or institution for general purposes. When such grants are restricted to special purposes, they are known as *grants-in-aid*, usually with the restricted purpose added, such as *grants-in-aid* for research, education, or road construction. A "hidden" subsidy is a payment ostensibly for goods delivered or services rendered for some governmental purpose but actually including an excessive charge.

2. = *subvention(1)*.

substantiate To insure the accuracy of, by the weight of evidence; to *verify*.

subvention 1. A grant, as by a foundation to an individual or organization, for some charitable, literary, scientific, or other purpose.

2. = *subsidy(1)*.

sufficient condition Property of a proposition so related to another that the latter follows logically or is deducible therefrom; hence, the truth of the first proposition is denied if the second is not admitted. Compare with *necessary condition*.

sum 1. An amount, as of money.

2. An aggregate or total.

sum-of-the-years-digits method (of depreciation) See *depreciation method*.

sunk cost A past cost arising out of a decision which cannot now be revised, and associated with specialized equipment or other facilities not readily adaptable to present or future purposes. Such cost is often regarded as constituting a minor factor in any decision affecting the future; contrasts with *current-outlay cost*.

supplemental appropriation (governmental accounting) A Congressional grant of spending power having the effect of adding to an *appropriation* previously approved; made necessary by the anticipated insufficiency of an original appropriation or by the imposition of new powers or responsibilities for which no financial provision had previously been made.

supplementary cost The cost of a product other than prime cost.

supply 1. The quantity of an economic good made available for sale by a producer or distributor.

2. The sum total of such quantities made available by all producers or distributors: in economics, a series of levels each representing a price and the quantity of the commodity or service sellers are willing to offer when the price stands at that level or higher.

3. *pl.* A classification often used for minor items of inventory, too small or of too little value to classify as raw material; also, items, sometimes not inventoried, but expensed when purchased, and having use primarily in offices, such as stationery, carbon paper, and cleaning compounds; *stores.*

supply price The price that must be paid to obtain over a specified period of time and at a specified place a given quantity of a commodity.

supporting record A group of cards or ledger sheets that assist in maintaining the accuracy of a ledger account.

support price See *administered price.*

surety One who guarantees the performance or faithfulness of another; he differs from a guarantor in that he is a promissor or debtor under the original agreement and is primarily liable with his principal for every default. The guarantor's obligation is a contingent one, and is a separate undertaking.

surplus 1. = *earned surplus.*
2. Stockholders' equity in a corporation in excess of the par or stated value of capital stock: a generic term covering paid-in, earned, and appraisal surplus. Its use in a balance sheet requires a qualifying adjective disclosing its nature.

surplus analysis 1. A worksheet or exhibit displaying the sources and disposition of the various forms of surplus or of changes therein during a given period.
2. The process of determining the sources and disposition of a corporation's *surplus(2).*

surplus at date of acquisition = *acquired surplus.*

surplus charge Any expense, loss, or other cost charged to (earned) surplus directly rather than through the medium of the income statement. For the principal classes of such charges, see *net income.*

surplus from consolidation The excess of book value at the date of acquisition over cost at which a parent or holding company has acquired shares of certain subsidiaries, less premiums on the purchase of other shares acquired. On the balance sheet, it appears usually as paid-in surplus; but circumstances may warrant its deduction along with a reserve for depreciation from the amount of fixed assets. See *consolidation policy.*

surplus-fund warrant See *warrant(5).*

surplus reserve *Appropriated surplus.*

surrender value The portion of premiums paid or other amount recoverable on an insurance policy or other contract if immediately canceled.

surrogate 1. A person vested with authority to act for another under defined circumstances; as, a corporate vice-president, acting, by virtue of custom, law, regulation, or delegation, as president in the latter's absence or inability to serve.
2. Hence, anything that serves as a full replacement, substitute, or replication of any other thing.
3. = probate judge.

surtax (Federal income taxes) An added tax: a term now confined to the present 22% rate applicable to the taxable income of a corporation in excess of $25,000; a *normal-tax* rate of 26% also applies to all corporate net income.

surviving company An entity which, as the result of a business combination, has acquired the net assets and carries on the operations of one or more predecessor companies, and which may be newly organized at the time of the combination or may be one of the predecessor companies.

survivor-life curve See *mortality curve.*

suspense account An account in which receipts or disbursements are temporarily carried pending their identification. It does not appear in financial statements.

suspension (of the sale of securities) See *stop order.*

sustain = *incur.*

symbolic logic Any process of *deduction* commencing with and dependent on *postulates*, *definitions*, and other *assumptions* through the use of *symbols* representing *classes*, *systems*, or *propositions.*

symbolization 1. The assignment of a letter, number, or other mark or character as a title or as a supplement to the title of a ledger account. Each symbol is intended to have the same meaning wherever used and to suggest immediately and accurately the thing to which it relates as well as its place in the classification of accounts. The careful devising of symbols can result in the saving of much time and space in compiling records and in adding to their precision and accuracy. 2. The assignment of a word, typographical mark, sign, name, or linguistic shorthand term to an object that forms the subject matter of an inquiry, as a convenient aid to reference, discussion, or formal manipulation. A symbol is sometimes contrasted with a sign in the sense that a symbol is a conventional sign which has the same meaning or referent for all parties to a discussion. The degree of abstractness in symbolization is determined by training and convenience. Persons untrained in highly abstract symbolization may contrast "symbolic expressions" with expression in ordinary language: e.g., the instruction in common words for calculating a compounded amount as contrasted with the formula $s = (1 + i)^n$. But the instruction in ordinary language is only a less abstract symbolization which quickly loses its initial advantage of familiarity when the calculation is complicated. In accounting, as in other disciplines such as mathematics and logic, progress is facilitated in dealing with increasingly complex phenomena by developing symbolization. The "symbolization of place" denoted by "Dr" and "Cr" in double-entry bookkeeping, for example, has made it possible conveniently and efficiently to deal with a much wider range of problems than was possible under the more limited symbolization of single-entry bookkeeping. By this device more elaborate explanations accompanying many entries under the older and "simpler" system have been dispensed with.

syndicate A term for a joint venture or short-term partnership, applied principally to a security-distribution operation and to other joint undertakings in the financial field. Its existence is often evidenced by an informal exchange of letters among participants, appointment of a manager with specified powers, transacting business and keeping an independent set of books under the manager's direction, and concluding with a windup of the business at hand and with a final distribution of the assets.

system A collection of objects or events conforming to a plan; the plan itself.

systematic sampling (statistics) A *sample* design or set of sampling procedures, frequently employed, wherein sampling units are selected at some fixed and designated interval, e.g., every fifth file card in a file system. A systematic sample qualifies as a *random sample* if the starting element is selected at random and every kth element (k, an integer) of the *frame* is selected thereafter. If a population is of size N, then this population may, where possible, be viewed as decomposable into k samples (k, an integer) of size n; i.e., $N = kn$. In a systematic sample with random start, a number between 1 and k is selected at random, the element in the frame with this number constituting the starting element in the sample; every kth element thereafter is then included in the sample. A systematic sample design with random start is far easier to execute than a completely random sample design—the former having a probability of selection of the sample of $1/C_n^N$ and the latter a probability of $1/k$. See *combination; permutation*. The sampling errors underlying a systematic sample are, typically, more difficult to calculate. See *random numbers*.

system design The specification for a particular organization of a classification of accounts, the form and use of bookkeeping records, methods of internal check and control, and the character and frequency of internal reporting: a management service offered by many public accountants. Recent emphasis has been not on a "uniform" system but on a system that will meet the needs of a particular management and at the same time will conform with general standards of recordkeeping and reporting.

system of accounts The classification of accounts, and the books of account, forms, procedures, and controls by which assets, liabilities, revenues, expenses, and the results of transactions generally are recorded and controlled.

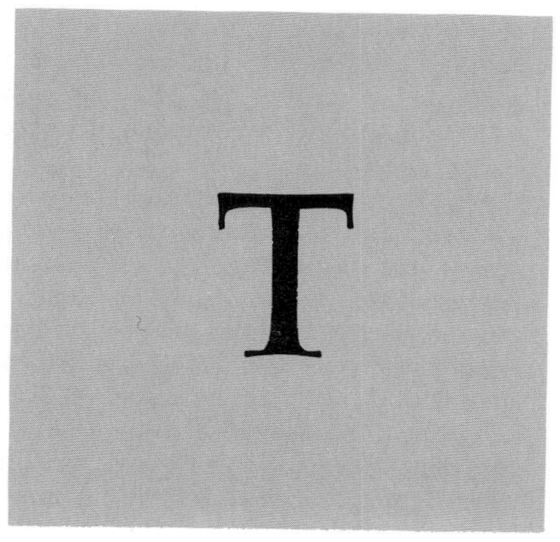

t-account A form of account often used for demonstrating the effect of a transaction or series of transactions, or for solving short accounting problems. It takes the general form of the letter *T*, the space above the horizontal line being used for the name of the account, the space thereunder serving for debits (on the left of the vertical line) and credits (on the right of the vertical line). Thus, if the four entries on page 234 were given expression in t-account form, the following would be the result:

takeover The acquisition of a going business by another through outright purchase, exchange of capital stock, or other device; see *business combination.*

tangible asset = *fixed asset;* a capital asset having physical existence; any capital asset other than an *intangible.*

tangible value 1. The worth of tangible assets, such as plant and equipment, and of current assets: going-concern value of assets other than intangible.
2. That part of the value of a business enterprise which can be imputed to its tangible assets.

tare An amount included in the gross weight of an article such as the weight of a truck, barrel, package, crate, or other carrier or container. Net weight is the gross weight less the tare.

target cost = *standard cost.*

target price See *contract price.*

tariff A *tax* levied on goods imported or exported. Under the U. S. Constitution, a tax on exports is forbidden.

tax A charge levied by a governmental unit against the income or wealth of a person, natural or corporate, for the common benefit of all. The term does not include specific charges made against particular persons or property for cur-

Customers Installment Accounts (previous year)

Debit	Credit
	(2) 40,269.77
	(4) 7,693.90

Merchandise Inventory

Debit	Credit
	(1) 108,573.29

Cash

Debit	Credit
(2) 102,810.59	

Gross Profit on Installment Collections

Debit	Credit
	(3) 29,592.36

Loss on Repossessions

Debit	Credit
(4) 1,663.03	

Customers Installment Account (current year)

Debit	Credit
(1) 150,796.23	(2) 62,540.82

Unearned Gross Profit (current year)

Debit	Credit
(3) 17,511.43	(1) 42,222.94

Unearned Gross Profit (previous year)

Debit	Credit
(3) 12,080.93	
(4) 2,308.17	

Repossessed Merchandise

Debit	Credit
(4) 4,225.00	

Repossession Expense

Debit	Credit
	(4) 502.30

rent or permanent benefits and privileges accruing only to those paying such charges, such as licenses, permits, and special assessments.

taxable income Income subject to tax by any governmental authority.

taxable profit The amount of profit as computed under the provisions of a particular tax law or revenue act upon which an income tax is levied: a term sometimes applied to corporate net income in contrast with *taxable income* (of individuals).

tax advantage A lowering of (income) tax paid or payable resulting from a close reading of provisions of law, legal decisions, or regulations, and attributable to discovered loopholes, alterations in the nature, ownership, and incidence of income and expense, and the like; often the term is employed in a pejorative sense, implying unjustified interpretations, or to a special deduction or rate which the law applies to a limited (pressure) group of taxpayers, such as the $27\frac{1}{2}\%$ depletion allowance.

tax-anticipation note (or **warrant**) (municipal accounting) A note issued in prospect of collection of (property) taxes and repaid from them.

tax-benefit rule (Federal income taxes) The provision in the Internal Revenue Code (section 111) permitting the omission from gross income of items such as a bad-debt recovery if the related deduction in an earlier year did not have the effect of reducing the income tax paid in that year or any year to which a net operating loss of the year of the related deduction is carried.

taxes receivable (municipal accounting) An account, the balance of which represents the portion of current and delinquent taxes levied by a governmental unit remaining uncollected.

tax lien A claim of a governmental unit upon a property pending the payment of taxes levied against it or its owner; a recorded lien.

tax roll The official record of a tax assessed and collected.

temporary investment 1. The amount expended for a security or other asset representing the investment of excess cash.

2. *pl.* The title of a balance-sheet item classified as a current asset. The standard for valuation is cost, or the amount representing current market value, if less, or the value to be received, if liquidation will yield less than cost. Without qualification it may be assumed to be available for conversion into cash that may be applied to any ordinary working-capital purpose, thus excluding investments, notwithstanding their marketability, held for other purposes. The term contrasts with *permanent investments*. See *balance sheet; cash fund.*

tenant in common Any one of two or more persons who together own an item of real or personal property, whereby upon the death of one his share of the property is included in his estate, there being no right of survivorship as in joint tenancy. Tenancy in common of a certificate of corporate capital stock is indicated by an ownership inscription such as "James Smith and Alice Smith." See *joint tenant.*

tentative balance sheet A balance sheet not final as to form or substance, or both, prepared for discussion or other limited purpose and thus remaining open for possible amendment.

term bonds Bonds all of which mature on the same date.

terminal account A general-ledger or expense-ledger account appearing as an item on a balance sheet or income statement, or as one of a group constituting such an item; a terminal account may be a *primary* or *secondary* account; an account in which transactions remain without further *reclassification* or *allocation*.

term loan A form of loan by banks to business enterprise taking the form of five- to ten-year unsecured notes, the proceeds often being used in the purchase of equipment. The agreement with the borrower usually provides for such safeguards as restrictions on additional loans, secured and unsecured, maintenance of a specified working-capital level, management-compensation, and dividend limitations. The term may also be applied to similar loans by insurance companies.

test 1. A specified procedure or set of procedures, including rules for assembling *evidence*, interpretation, and *significance* for accepting or rejecting *hypotheses.* A test may be purely logical, as when a criterion of consistency or independence is applied; or it may refer to empirical (see *fact*) material as well. Where the latter type of test is involved, it becomes necessary to recognize that errors may be made, but that such errors can be limited to a specified magnitude of relative frequency of occurrence (see *probability*). Generally, in experimental design (see *experiment*), two types of error are traditionally recognized: Type I error, rejection of a true hypothesis, and Type II error, acceptance of a false hypothesis; by *probability* methods the risk of occurrence of each type of error may be calculated. It has become increasingly common to recognize that a third outcome, indeterminateness, is possible for given levels of risk of these errors. Where indeterminacy results, the implication is that insufficient evidence has been assembled to arrive at a conclusion under the rules of the test. See *hypothesis; rule; testcheck.*

2. As applied to the quality of a commodity or of a performance, a *sample* or *sampling.* In the testing of complex performances, such as those of a person, an organized group of persons, or a combination of machines and persons, the statistical problems may be the consequence of an unclear determination of performance goals.

testamentary Pertaining to a testator or his estate.

testamentary trust A trust created by will. See *trust.*

testator One who makes a will.

testcheck *v.* To verify selected items in an account or record for the purpose of arriving at an opinion of the correctness of the entire account or record; to *sample.* Provided the selection has been sufficiently representative, absence of error or the limitation of error to a given range is regarded as warranting the assumption that the remaining items are of like accuracy or quality. See *sample; test; detailed audit.—testcheck, n.*

text (of a report) The narrative supplementing and interpreting a presentation of financial statements, as in a report by an auditor to a client, or by management to stockholders.

theory 1. A set of propositions, including axioms and theorems, which, together with definitions and formal or informal rules of inference, is oriented toward the explanation of a body of *facts* or treatment of a class of concrete or abstract operations. In well-defined fields, the support of a theory derives from two considerations: (a) its logical structure with respect to consistency, redundancy of propositions, as well as its deductive potential, (b) the manner in which propositions dependent on the theory (axioms or theorems) may be placed in correspondence with data incorporated in facts relative to rules of measurement, testing of hypotheses, or more generally accepted "rules of evidence."

Choices between theories rest not only on the seeming fitness of their expression but also on (a) their adequacy in explaining bodies of facts, (b) their tendency to lead to the discovery of new problems and facts, and (c) their persuasiveness in formulating or reformulating related theories and hypotheses. Further discrimination between theories may be made on the basis of *judgments* concerning their *operational* or nonoperational character. For example, some persons have adopted the theory that accounting ought to be "completely" truthful, or "as truthful as possible." Such a theory usually is nonoperational, although it may suggest numerous problem areas for investigation as well as other theories which are highly operational; the conditions of consistency and completeness for such a theory are usually impossible to determine, since its *primitives*, *axioms*, and rules of inference are not often stated in a manner that allows logical examination of the relations between the theory and the theorems presumably deduced therefrom. Without rules of measurement and testing it is impossible to invalidate the theory or delimit its applicability. For the most part, therefore, it is probably better to regard such theories as heuristic and more nearly related to *commonsense* rather than to logical or scientific analysis.

On the other hand, certain parts of cost accounting, as understood and practiced by many persons, are governed by theories of system design that are *operational*. Such theories, although satisfying the principles of consistency and completeness, may nevertheless fail with respect to the condition of leading elsewhere. New theories or new-problem areas of accounting have seldom emerged from theories of system design.

2. The body of systematic knowledge concerning a field of inquiry or an art.

3. A proposition advanced to guide investigation.

4. (colloquial) A statement rejected as false, misleading, or irrelevant, especially if emanating from a person lacking in practical experience, or from one who has concerned himself with only one or a few factors in a situation that cannot be understood or controlled without reckoning with many factors. Those who decry "theory," however, may do so in order to secure a hearing for their own theory which they dub "practical experience" and to avoid the need for the critical examination of *evidence*.

third person A person with whom an *arm's-length* relationship is maintained.

throughput accounting An accounting system so devised that original *objects* of expenditure in *primary accounts* may be identified in *secondary accounts* and financial statements, particularly the *income statement;* see *objective statement; activity accounting; spread sheet.* For this purpose, *split ledger* accounts may be maintained—a procedure that lends itself well to mechanical recording and reporting. See *cash flow; cost flow.*

tickler A file or record of maturing obligations or other items of interest maintained in such a manner as to call attention to each item at the proper time. Examples: in a bank, the note tickler; in an insurance office, the policy-expiration tickler and the premiums-due tickler.

time cost = *period cost.*

time deposit A deposit in a banking institution not subject to check and withdrawable only upon notice of not less than 30 days.

time draft A draft payable within a specified time after acceptance by the drawee, usually 30 days; an *acceptance.*

time series A set of quantitative or qualitative measures defined for or related to a number of successive or intermittent time periods. *Trend analyses* are frequently prepared from the numerous time series common to business enterprise.

time-series analysis Classification and study of business, economic, or related movements. The term is usually applied to the breakdown of an economic series (such as prices, production, etc., occurring at different times or over succeeding periods of time) into trends or cyclical, seasonal, and random (or other) movements.

times-interest ratio The ratio to interest on a long-term obligation of net income for a single year or averaged over a period of years before deducting such interest but after deducting income-tax expense. It serves as a rule-of-thumb indication of the relative safety of an obligee's investment.

title The right to property; the means by which such right is established.

title insurance A guaranty, by a title insurer or by a political subdivision of a state, that the title to real estate is vested in a named person on a certain date.

tolerance (statistical quality control) 1. The amount and direction (+ or − or both) of deviation from a *basic dimension* named as acceptable in a specification. Thus, if the specification calls for 4.800 ± .005″, or 1.5 seconds $\left\{\begin{matrix}+.5 \text{ second}\\ -0 \text{ seconds}\end{matrix}\right\}$, or 50 lbs. ±1%, the tolerances are, respectively, ±.005″, +.5 second, and ±1%.

2. A permitted difference in dimension between two mating parts. As distinct from *tolerance*, an *allowance* is designed to provide the degree of tightness or looseness required for assembled parts. Thus, parts within tolerance, e.g., a shaft at maximum tolerance and a hole at minimum tolerance, may fail to provide a required allowance despite the fact that each part is within tolerance. Where an internal part is smaller than an external part, allowance is known as *clearance*. If an internal part is larger than an external part, allowance is known as *interference*. See *basic dimension*. The American Standard series provides a choice of seven different classes of fits: free, medium, snug, tight, medium force, heavy force, and shrink.

tool 1. Any instrument for manual use that aids a mechanical operation; examples: a saw, a hammer, or other *hand tool*.

2. A cutting or shaping part in a machine; a *machine tool (2)*.

3. = *machine tool(1)*.

topical Current (problems, needs, articles, pronouncements); of local or limited application; not related to or assisting in the solving of fundamental problems.

total equity = *equity (2)*; a British usage.

total tolerance (statistical quality control) The difference between the upper specification limit (*USL*) and the lower specification limit (*LSL*) named in connection with a specified *basic dimension*. Thus, total tolerance = *USL* − *LSL;* also referred to as *total print tolerance*.

trace (auditing) To ascertain whether an item has been disposed of in accordance with source indications.

traceable cost = *direct cost.*

trade acceptance A noninterest-bearing bill of exchange or draft covering the sale of goods, drawn by the seller on, and accepted by, the buyer. Its purpose is to put into negotiable form an open account having a short maturity. To be eligible for discount, it must contain the statement that the acceptor's obligation arises out of the purchase of goods from the drawer, and it may be accompanied by a record of the purchase. Attempts to popularize the use of trade acceptances have not been generally successful in the United States. See *draft.*

trade account payable A liability on open account for the purchase of commodities or services used in the regular course of business.

trade account receivable An amount owing from a customer for goods or services sold in the regular course of business, as distinct from a receivable growing out of other transactions or a receivable differing in form from the ordinary unsecured debtor's account.

trade association A nonprofit organization, local or national in character, serving common interests of enterprises engaged in the same kind of business. Specific purposes are to (a) collect and compile industry-wide data on sales, costs, financial structures; (b) devise and sometimes install uniform systems of accounts; (c) provide information concerning the industry to legislative bodies and the public generally; (d) carry on research looking to improvements in technical processes, the elimination of wastes, better marketing facilities, and the promotion of foreign trade; and (e) eliminate undesirable trade practices. A few trade associations have been known to engage in lobbying, price-fixing, lessening competition, and other less desirable activities; on the whole, however, their function has been the improvement of the conditions of trade and the introduction of desirable standards into the relationships of their members with governmental bodies and the public generally. See *community of interest; cartel.*

trade discount The discount allowed to a class of customers on a list price before consideration of credit terms; as a rule, invoice prices are recorded in the books of account net after the deduction of trade and quantity discounts. Trade discounts are sometimes distinguished from cash discounts by being described as any discount exceeding 2 percent; better practice indicates that the term should be applied to any allowance that stands without reference to the date of payment. See *quantity discount; distributor discount; chain discount.*

trade investment (British usage) An investment, often regarded as permanent, by one business corporation in another for the purpose of protecting or enlarging the former's activities; usually represented by a minority interest in capital stock.

trade liability A current account, note, or acceptance payable for goods purchased and services received in the ordinary course of business; ordinarily, any current liability, excluding wages and taxes unpaid.

trademark A distinctive identification of a manufactured product or of a service taking the form of a name, sign, motto, device, or emblem. Under Federal law, a trademark may be registered for 28 years and the registration may be renewed for another 28 years, thus preventing its use by another person.

trade name The name by which a product is known in commercial circles. It may or may not be registered as a trademark.

trade note receivable A promissory note from a customer in payment for goods supplied or for services rendered.

trade price The price charged to regular distributors who generally buy either continuously or in large lots for resale to others: usually, the list price less trade discounts. See *trade discount; price.*

trading on the equity The increase in profit return resulting from borrowing capital at a low rate and employing it in a business yielding a higher rate; thus, if a busines enterprise earns 10 percent on an investment of $100,000, it will net 16 percent for its owners if it is able to borrow half of the investment at 4 percent. The thinner (i.e., the less) the equity of owners, the greater will be the possibilities of higher rates of gain (and also of loss) on their investment.

trading profit 1. = *gross profit;* the first item usually found in a British *income statement.*

2. Profit arising from speculation, as from purchases and sales through stock and commodity exchanges.

transaction An *event* (*1*) or *condition* (*2*) the *recognition* of which gives rise to an entry in *accounting records.* Expressed in money amounts, a transaction as conceived by the accountant is made up of an equality between *credits* and *debits,* the former representing the source, the latter the immediate identification and disposition. The source credit may be a disbursement of cash, credit extended by a supplier, or transfer within the organization, the disposition debit an *asset* or expense. A transaction arising as the result of relations with an outside person is an *external* or *business transaction;* one resulting from the expiration of cost or from the adjustment made necessary by an accrual or transfer or allocation of income or expense, an *internal* or *accounting transaction.*

The moment for recording a transaction is dependent on the occurrence of the *event* or the existence of the *condition,* the customary *timing* of its recognition, ascertainment of the money amounts involved, a determination of the accounts affected, and an *administrative review* of the adequacy of referable supporting data serving as objective evidence of its component elements. For the bulk of transactions, these *decisions*, conforming to general business policy, traditional trade customs, and local conventions, are a vital part of the daily *routine* on which the mechanics of accounting are dependent. See *events and conditions; deal; double-entry bookkeeping.*

transfer The passage of property, usually with title, or of services from one person to another. Transfers in the broadest sense include sales and other revenues.

transfer agent An agent, usually a bank or trust company, officially appointed by a corporation to make legal transfers of the shares of its outstanding capital stock; the agent may, in addition to keeping the current stock-transfer books, keep the shareholders' ledger, in which case he prepares a list of shareholders for the use of the corporation whenever needed for the payment of dividends, the issue of stock warrants, shareholders' meetings, and other corporate purposes. He may also distribute the dividends, warrants, and so forth. The office of transfer agent is sometimes combined with that of registrar.

transfer and counter warrant See *warrant* (5).

transfer ledger A binder for filled ledger sheets or *closed accounts.*

transfer tax (on stocks) The taxes attaching to the sale of stocks. The Federal government levies a tax of 4¢ for each $100 or major fraction in value on stock transfers; maximum, 8¢ per share; minimum, 4¢ each transfer. The State of New York levies a tax of 2¢ a share on transfers other than sales. If the transfer involves a sale, the rate is 1¢ per share for shares selling for less than $5 per share; 2¢ for each share having a selling range of $5–$9.99; 3¢ per share in the $10–$19.99 range; and 4¢ per share selling for $20 or more.

translate (foreign exchange) To determine the equivalent, in local currency, of the amount of any item expressed in foreign money by application to the latter of a *rate of exchange.*

transportation cost The cost of freight, cartage, handling charges, and the like, relating to goods either purchased, in process, or sold.

traveling auditor A staff auditor who examines the accounts at branches and other outlying points as an aid to head-office control. See *internal audit.*

treasury stock (or **shares**) Full-paid capital stock reacquired by the issuing company through gift, purchase, or otherwise, and available for resale or cancellation. Treasury stock is not a part of capital stock outstanding; and the term does not apply to unissued capital stock, or to shares forfeited for nonpayment of subscriptions.

Much attention was paid to treasury stock in the 1930's not only because of the wide prevalence on the part of many corporations (and often their officers) to repurchase and resell their own securities, but also because of the emergence of new business-corporation acts in the early years of that decade. The new acts did not attempt to prohibit such transactions, since it continued to be considered permissible for a corporation to "maintain" the price of a new issue of securities by trading in shares of the new issue for a limited period after the initial marketing (see *stabilization*), and to acquire shares for distribution to employees under various plans of compensation and profit-sharing. But the framers of the new acts endeavored to put a ceiling on the outlay for such shares, as by providing that a repurchase might be made only by employing assets in excess of those required to maintain an equality with capital originally paid in, the argument being that capital paid in ought to be regarded as a trust fund for the protection of creditors: a theory upheld in numerous state courts (e.g., *Clapp* v. *Peterson,* 104 Ill. 26 [1882]); or that the repurchase should not have the effect of reducing the corporation to a state of insolvency (e.g., *Marvin* v. *Anderson,* 111 Wis. 387 [1901]), thereby endangering the equities of both creditors and remaining stockholders. The rule in the English courts had long been that a corporation may not acquire its own capital stock except in satisfaction of a debt not otherwise collectible (*Trevor* v. *Whitworth,* L.R. 12A.C.409 [1887]). Proof of any such excess of assets lies in the existence of an earned-surplus account built up as the result of following usual accounting practices, and lawmakers sought, therefore, by attaching restrictions to the use of earned surplus, to keep treasury-stock purchases within safe limits. They provided in several cases that the cost of the purchases must not impair the sum of the liabilities and paid-in capital (i.e., must not exceed the earned-surplus account); and that the cost must in effect be regarded as a temporary dissipation or "borrowing" of an equal amount of earned surplus until such time as the cost had been recaptured by resale of the stock or by canceling the repurchased stock against capital stock outstanding in accordance with whatever formal action might be required by law.

There had also been a strong public reaction to corporate stock trading. Cases had been publicized in which corporate managements, by issuing alternately reports of poor profits and, perhaps a quarter later, reports of improved profits, had raised and depressed the market price of equity securities, and by buying long or selling short had earned trading profits for themselves as well as for their corporations. These practices had undoubtedly added to the speculative flame of the 1920's. Public opinion, along with the unfavorable attitude of the newly created (1933) U. S. Securities and Exchange Commission, gradually discouraged the practice; today it is rarely encountered and the appearance of treasury stock in published financial statements is relatively infrequent.

Accounting standards for the recording and reporting of treasury stock have gone through several stages. Before 1930, there were no general standards, except possibly the requirement that the existence and quantity of treasury stock be disclosed in annual reports. When the new business-corporation laws came into being, a number of practices developed:

1. The cost of treasury shares was deducted on the face of the balance sheet from the combined total of paid-in capital and earned surplus.
2. The cost was deducted on the balance sheet from the earned-surplus account, thus disclosing free surplus.
3. The cost was distributed on a prorata basis as between the account maintained for that class of stock, paid-in surplus pertaining to that class, and earned surplus.
4. The premium (above par or original paid-in value) was charged to paid-in surplus regardless of its source, and the par or stated value was subtracted from the capital-stock account.
5. The cost of the shares appeared on the asset side of the balance sheet as an investment.

In all cases, the restriction on the use of earned surplus for dividends or for further purchases of capital stock was disclosed.

In instances where treasury stock emerges today on corporate balance sheets, the practice tends in the direction of deducting its cost from combined capital stock, capital surplus, and retained earnings (method 1 above); in addition, the sidehead for contributed capital or retained income recites the facts and restrictions relating to the reacquired shares. Methods 3 and 5 persist notably in the balance sheets of General Motors Corporation and General Electric Company. At one time the accounting profession was well divided on whether it was proper to call treasury stock an asset, measured in terms of cost; today the practice is rare. It is doubtful whether its legal status as an asset was ever sanctioned (e.g., Judge Learned Hand, in *Borg* v. *International Paper Co.* (11 F. [2d] 147 [1925]), referred to treasury stock as an "asset" only in "fiction").

No dividend may be paid or accrued on treasury stock, and no voting rights attach to it.

trend analysis The averaging of time-series data, in order that a smooth curve showing general growth or decline may be developed for some past period of time. Four methods in common use involve the superimposing of a curve on a graph of the data:

1. Freehand method. A trend may be fitted (or averaged) by drawing a freehand line on the face of the graph.

2. Semiaverage method. The data are first divided into two or more equal time subperiods; the simple average for each period is then plotted at the center of each subperiod, and a curve is drawn through the points.

3. Moving-average method. The principle of the moving average is applied, using as a basis a *cycle* of years or less.

4. Least-squares method. The curve is so drawn as to minimize the sum of the squares of the deviations of the data from the curve.

A trend curve is simply an average to which old as well as newly emerging causative factors contribute; it is not a reliable basis for estimating future growth except in those instances where it is known or is assumed that the same factors will influence the future with the same effects as in the past.

trial balance A list or abstract of the balances or of total debits and total credits of the accounts in a ledger, the purpose being to determine the equality of posted debits and credits and to establish a basic summary for financial statements. See *double-entry bookkeeping*. The term is also applied to a list of account balances (and their total) abstracted from a customers ledger or other subsidiary ledger for the purpose of testing their totals with the related control account.

Before abstracting a trial balance, as for a general ledger at the end of a month, the bookkeeper makes sure that all the postings have been made in the ledger that are necessary to assure equal debits and credits. If columnar journals or their equivalent are in use, the bookkeeper satisfies himself that the column totals crossfoot and have been posted to control accounts in the usual manner, and that all the postings of detail items in the latter part of the month have been completed. Where the accounts contain principally summary postings, as is usually the case in the general ledger of a large enterprise, the postings will be relatively few in number and are easily reviewed for completeness.

To reduce the number of general-ledger postings, some bookkeepers are in the habit of making worksheet adjustments at the end of each month rather than going to the trouble of preparing formal journal entries and spreading them on the records. While in some cases this more informal procedure saves time, it is possible to prepare adjustments, as for depreciation, interest, and the like, and even for accrued payroll, well in advance of the end of the month, and to have them posted to the accounts, as are other entries, as part of the routine bookkeeping procedure. When this is done, the trial balance may be subtotaled as it is taken, the subtotals being fitted directly into financial-statement forms without the intermediacy of a worksheet. An advance scheduling and timing of monthly adjustments and end-of-the-month summary entries, the arrangement of general-ledger accounts in the order of their appearance in the financial statements, and a trial-balance form providing for the necessary subtotals are necessary ingredients of rapid and accurate statement preparation.

Three forms of trial balances are illustrated under *double-entry bookkeeping*. The first shows total debits and total credits in each account and is of some value when a spread sheet or articulation statement, illustrated on page 436, is to be prepared in order to summarize the classes of transactions that have been recorded, or, sometimes, to narrow the location of an error disclosed by a trial balance. In another form of spread sheet, the analysis of ledger accounts is made by sources of postings (books of original entry), total debit postings and total credit postings, obtained by the analysis, being compared with the totals on the books of original entry. The second type of trial balance is the more frequent; it, too, proves equally well the equality of debits and credits and furthermore serves as the basis for a worksheet or for financial statements. However, the equality of debits and credits having been established, it does not follow that the individual accounts have been correctly stated. Postings may have been made to wrong acccounts; and certain accounts may not have been sufficiently adjusted to bring them into agreement with "all the facts." Many adjustments may yet be required to make their balances acceptable.

Where postings in a ledger are numerous and no rigorous method has been instituted for proving the correctness of individual postings, trial-balance totals may at the outset be unequal, and the bookkeeper is faced with the necessity of locating and correcting the error. A small error, often the composite of offsetting errors, must be paid the same attention as a large one. Not infrequently offsetting errors of the same magnitude may remain undiscovered for a considerable length of time; when one is disclosed, it is necessary to return to the period between balancing trial balances in which the error occurred and search for the matching item. Thus, an error in addition of $100 may have been made when adding the details of each of two accounts, one on the debit side and the other on the credit side; or the errors may be attributable to different causes: for example, one an error in posting, the other an error in bringing down a balance.

Various devices are employed by bookkeepers in locating the more common types of error; these include:

1. A recheck of the trial-balance items with the account balances appearing in the ledger, and a refooting of the trial-balance columns.

2. A difference equal to a single digit may be caused by errors of addition in the ledger; a recheck of the ledger additions and balances since the last correct trial balance may disclose it.

3. Where the difference is divisible by 2, a posting equal to one-half the difference may have been made on the wrong side of the ledger; thus if the trial-balance debits exceed the trial-balance credits by $267.12, it may be that through a clerical error a credit item of $133.56 has been posted in the ledger as a debit. The bookkeeper would therefore scan for that amount on the debit side of the ledger accounts, covering all postings made since the last correct trial balance.

4. The difference may indicate a posting completely omitted; the excess of $267.12 just described may thus turn out to be an omitted credit posting of that amount, and the bookkeeper would search for such an item among the credit entries in books of original entry. At the same time, he would look for items to which no posting references had been attached, since the difference might have been caused by the failure to post two or more items.

5. A difference made up of two integers (excluding zeros), their sum being a multiple of 9, may point to a transposition or slide. Thus, if a debit

of \$5,396.75 had been posted incorrectly as a debit of \$3,596.75, the trial-balance total of credits would be larger than the debit total by \$1,800.00; or a credit of \$2,459.89 posted incorrectly as \$4,259.89 would have precisely the same effect. Since 18 is twice 9, the difference between the transposed integers is 2, for the reason that the difference between any two digits (e.g., $7 - 3 = 4$) is always the same as one-ninth of the difference between the two digits (when combined as a single number) and their transposition (i.e., $73 - 37 = 36$; $36 \div 9 = 4$). The trial-balance difference divisible by 9 may thus point to its own resolution. Hence, in this case, the bookkeeper would scan books of original entry for debits the thousand digit of which exceeds the hundred digit by 2, or for credits where the hundred digit exceeds the thousand digit by the same number.

6. A slide is the movement of a number right or left one or more decimal points. If the trial-balance difference, particularly one containing several digits, is divisible by 9, a slide may have occurred; to spot the source of the error, the bookkeeper would look (a) for $\frac{1}{9}$ of the excess among the ledger postings on the side *opposite* the excess; if such an item is found, it may be that ten times the item is the figure that should have been posted; or, if not found, (b) for $\frac{10}{9}$ of the excess among the ledger postings on the *same* side as the excess; if found, it may be that $\frac{1}{10}$ of the item found is the figure that should have been posted. Thus, a trial-balance credit excess of \$4.68 might mean that a debit amount of \$5.20 was improperly posted as \$.52, or that a credit amount of \$.52 was improperly posted as \$5.20.

7. A two-point slide may be indicated if the trial-balance difference is divisible by both 11 and 9; in that event, the bookkeeper would look (a) for $\frac{1}{99}$ of the excess among the ledger postings on the side *opposite* the excess; if such an item is found, it may be that 100 times the item is the figure that should have been posted; or, if not found, (b) for $\frac{100}{99}$ of the excess among the ledger postings on the *same* side as the excess; if found, it may be that $\frac{1}{100}$ of the item found is the figure that should have been posted. Thus a trial-balance credit excess of \$51.68 might mean that a debit amount of \$52.00 was wrongfully posted as \$.52 or, on the other hand, that a credit amount of \$.52 was wrongfully posted as \$52.00.

8. A three-point slide may have occurred if the trial balance is divisible by 999. The procedure to be followed for locating a source of error may be inferred from the two preceding paragraphs.

9. A spread sheet or articulation statement for the purpose of establishing the general source of an error in posting is illustrated on page 436.

See *classified trial balance.*

true reserve An appropriation of surplus; a *surplus reserve.*

trust A right, enforceable in courts of equity, to the beneficial enjoyment of property, the legal title to which is in another. The person creating the trust is the creator, settlor, grantor, or donor; the holder of the legal title is the trustee; and the holder of the beneficial interest is the cestui que trust or beneficiary. A trust may be either express or implied. An express trust is created by specific provisions in a deed, will, or other writing. An implied trust is one where the intent of the parties, although not made explicit, may be inferred from the nature of the transaction; it includes a resulting trust, arising from the nature of the transaction or the relationship of the parties, as where in the purchase of property one person pays the purchase price and another takes the deed, and a constructive trust, where one person in a fiduciary capacity is in a position to gain by fraud or otherwise an advantage for himself at the expense of the person to whom he owes a duty. See

A COMPANY—DES MOINES BRANCH

Analysis of General-Ledger Postings
Year Ending December 31, 19-2

Account	Trial Balances December 31, 19–2 Debit	Trial Balances December 31, 19–2 Credit	Trial Balances January 1, 19–2 Debit	Trial Balances January 1, 19–2 Credit	Cash Receipts	Cash Disbursements	Purchases	Sales	General Journal Debit	General Journal Credit
Cash	386,626	355,848	(1) +34,201		(4) +352,425	(5) −355,848				
Receivables	414,158	352,462	(1) +66,587		(4) −352,040			(2) +347,571		(11) −422
Inventory	420,580	234,798	(1) +124,912				(3) +295,668			(10) −1,200
										(13) −2,458
										(6) −231,140
Fixtures	3,152	150	(1) +3,018			(5) +134				(8) −150
Reserve for depreciation	150	2,325		(1) −1,995	(4) −20				(8) +150	(12) −310
Accounts payable	106,734	116,641		(1) −6,377		(5) +105,534 1	(7) −68,106		(10) +1,200	
							(3) −42,158			
Interoffice account	250,000	493,856		(1) −220,346		(5) +250,000	(3) −253,510			(9) −20,000
Sales	422	347,571						(2) −347,571	(11) +422	
Cost of sales	231,140								(6) +231,140	
Selling expense	63,318						(7) +63,318			
Administrative expense	5,098						(7) +4,788		(12) +310	
Home-office supervision	20,000								(9) +20,000	
Obsolete stock	2,458	365			−365				(13) +2,458	
Totals	1,903,836	1,904,016	+228,718	−228,718	—	−180	—	—	+255,680	−255,680

Explanation of transaction groups—

(1) Balances from prior year
(2) Sales
(3) Purchases
(4) Cash receipts
(5) Cash disbursements
(6) Cost of sales
(7) Payment of expense
(8) Cost of retirement
(9) Interoffice service charge
(10) Returns to suppliers
(11) Returns from customers
(12) Provision for depreciation
(13) Loss on obsolete stock

Reference to the cash-disbursements book shows that the item of $134 appearing in the ledger account and in the above analysis of the ledger postings should have been $314; when this error is corrected, the trial-balance postings will be equal.

cestui que trust; business trust.

trust-and-agency fund (municipal accounting) A fund consisting of money and property received and held by a municipality or an institution as trustee or custodian, or in the capacity of an agent for certain individuals or governmental units. See *fund.*

trust deed An indenture conveying title to a mortgaged property from the mortgagor to the trustee, the latter holding it in trust, as mortgagee, for the owners of the obligations secured by the mortgage. It describes the mortgaged property, the duties, obligations, powers, and rights of the trustee, and the terms of the mortgage; it also contains the transfer of title, and the covenants of the mortgagor to pay principal and interest and to maintain and insure the property, and describes the procedure in case of default.

trust fund 1. A fund held by one person (trustee) for the benefit of another, pursuant to the provisions of a formal trust agreement. The investment of the principal of a trust established under the law is restricted by statutory provisions in the various states.

2. Generally, any asset or group of assets owned by or in possession of one person, but in equity belonging to another; sometimes referred to as a quasi trust fund. When such assets have been mingled with other assets, the balance sheet is so drawn as to call attention to the fact.

turnover 1. The number of times that various assets, such as raw material or other items of inventory, personnel, and the like, are replaced during a stated period, usuallly a year; the rate of such replacement. Thus in the table opposite there is shown an opening inventory of $124,912, a closing inventory of $185,782, and a cost of sales of $231,140; the last figure, divided by the average inventory ($155,347), indicates a merchandise turnover of 1.5.

2. The ratio of sales to net worth (equity turnover), it being understood that the comparison is actually between the asset equivalent of net worth and sales. See *ratio.*

3. = *sales.* A British usage.

type A *model;* a range within which a certain characteristic can be predicted. Some theorists have asserted that a typology is the most systematic knowledge possible in much of what is called the social sciences, in contrast to the greater systematization of the physical and biological sciences. See *standard; norm.*

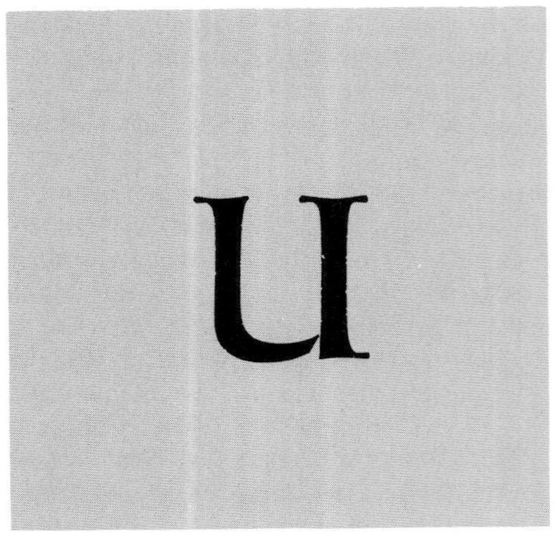

ultra-vires Beyond its powers; exceeding legal authority: applied principally to the acts of a corporation in exercising powers or a degree of power that it does not possess under its charter or under the law. Although technically ultra-vires acts may be void, the corporation and parties dealing with it may nonetheless be bound thereby. Thus, a corporation is liable for a tort committed in the course of an ultra-vires transaction, and a party contracting with a corporation, not knowing that the transaction is beyond the corporation's powers, may hold the corporation if the corporate agent had the apparent authority to enter into the contract. The state may always object to ultra-vires transactions.

unadmitted asset (insurance) = *inadmitted asset.*

unalloted appropriation (governmental accounting) The balance of an appropriation available for allotment for purposes authorized within an appropriation act.

unamortized debt (or **bond**) **discount** The portion of debt discount remaining to be spread over future periods; it is regarded by some accountants as a debit valuation account and on a balance sheet it may be (but rarely is) deducted from the amount of the liability to which it relates. It usually appears as a prepaid expense, if related to a bank loan, or as a deferred charge, if related to a long-term bond issue. See *bond discount.*

unapplied cash (municipal accounting) Cash not reserved for a special purpose, available for any use within the fund of which it is a part.

unappropriated budget surplus (municipal accounting) The excess of the estimated revenues of a fund for a given period over the appropriations made therefrom.

unappropriated earned surplus (or **retained income**) That part of earned surplus which has not been transferred to a subordinate account or otherwise earmarked for any specific purpose, thus remaining available for the absorption of dividends.

unappropriated income (institutional accounting) An account set up for budgetary control to which is credited the excess of the estimated income over estimated expenses as shown by the approved budget.

unavoidable cost Cost that must be continued under a program of business retraction; fixed cost; contrasts with *escapable cost.*

unbalanced addition (national-income accounting) A capital acquisition representing only a portion of a complete producing unit, as a new loading mechanism for charging a cupola in a foundry. A complete new foundry would, in contrast, represent a *balanced addition* to the *capital(6)* of an economy. Since even balanced additions will ordinarily be composed of numerous different types of assets, all such additions made at any single time will ordinarily be averaged or otherwise reduced to a homogeneous, or representative, balanced addition to the total stock of capital.

uncertain 1. Impossible to calculate exact results or to assign probability measures at any point within a range of possible outcomes. Uncertainty may be said to be present when objective calculations of *risk* are impossible or difficult to make. This usually occurs as a result of either (a) a lack of relevant information or (b) the impossibility of *replication.* Thus,

insurers may be unable to calculate premiums required to insure the profits of a speculative venture because (a) they have been unable to acquire or assess relevant information, or (b) the enterprise is too dependent on the personal characteristics of a single individual.
2. Improbable.

unclaimed dividends 1. The amount of dividend checks not cashed by stockholders. Often no record is kept in the accounts of the corporation, and only the reconciliation of bank statements or an examination of the accounts of the paying agent will show the obligation for outstanding dividend checks and the funds available for their payment.
2. Dividends received by stockbrokers or bankers, as stockholders of record for their customers, not claimed by or allocated to the rightful owner.

unclaimed wages Wages earned but not claimed by employees, although cash is available for their payment; the liability to employees or former employees for sums left over from amounts originally drawn for payrolls; wage checks not presented for payment.

underlying company = *subsidiary company;* a term usually limited to a subsidiary that owns franchises or other rights that are not transferable but are essential to the operation of the economic unit, and because of which the legal existence of the subsidiary is continued.

underlying security A *security(1)* issued by a subsidiary company, the return on which is assured by a direct guarantee by the parent company or by a contractual or other relationship.

underwrite To perform the duties of an underwriter.

underwriter 1. A person, usually an investment banker, who (a) has agreed, alone or with others, to buy at stated terms an entire issue of securities or a substantial part thereof for resale to the public, (b) has guaranteed the sale of an issue by agreeing to buy from the issuing party any unsold portion at a stated price, (c) has agreed to use his "best efforts" to market all or part of an issue, or (d) has offered for sale stock he has purchased from a controlling stockholder. The definition appearing in the Federal Securities Act of 1933 (section 2 [11]) is ". . . any person who has purchased from an issuer with a view to, or sells for an issuer in connection with, the distribution of any security, or participates or has a direct or indirect participation in any such undertaking, or participates or has a participation in the direct or indirect underwriting of any such undertaking; but such term shall not include a person whose interest is limited to a commission from an underwriter or dealer not in excess of the usual and customary distributors' or sellers' commission." See *underwriting syndicate.*
2. A person or concern assuming an insurance risk in return for compensation: a profit corporation, or mutual or reciprocal organization; also an agent accepting such business. See *insurance.*
3. The guarantor of the liabilities of any venture.

Underwriters' Laboratories A nonprofit service organization sponsored by the National Board of Fire Underwriters for the examination and testing of devices, systems, and materials as to their relation to life, fire, and casualty hazards, and to crime prevention; if approval is given, a "UL" label is attached to the product.

underwriting contract (securities) An agreement, between the issuer of a security and the underwriter or underwriters or underwriting syndicate that is to market the issue, providing for the outright purchase by the underwriter(s) of the entire issue, or any part of the issue not taken by stockholders in exercising their preemptive rights, or simply for the application of what amounts to the underwriter's "best efforts" to sell the issue to the public. An increase in the last-described type of contract has been brought about as the result of the Federal Securities Act and regulations that attach more responsibility to the investment banker and prescribe a 20-day "waiting period" during which marketing conditions may change materially. At one time an underwriting contract was limited to the taking up at an agreed price of the unsold portion of an issue previously offered to others.

underwriting syndicate A group of persons, usually investment bankers, that agrees, pursuant to the terms and conditions of an underwriting contract, to assume the risks involved in buying and marketing all or a part of an issue of securities; the group consists of the originating person and participating persons, and from their number a manager is chosen to represent them. The agreement between syndicate members or underwriters is in the form of a contract; its duration generally includes the price-support or stabilization period.

undistributed profit The profit of a partnership, trust, syndicate, or joint venture before division among the parties interested; *earned surplus;* retained income.

undivided profit The undistributed amount of a corporation's net income not yet formally transferred to retained earnings: a term in general use on the financial statements of banks, where undivided profits are often combined with earned surplus under the heading "Surplus and undivided profits."

unearned increment An increase in the value of property attributable, not to any expenditure thereon of money or effort by the owner, but to circumstances beyond his direct control. Example: an increase in the value of land caused by the development of nearby areas owned by others.

unearned revenue (or **income**) 1. Revenue (or income) received but not yet earned; = *deferred revenue.*

2. (taxation) Revenue from sources other than personal services.

unencumbered allotment (governmental accounting) That part of an allotment neither expended nor encumbered.

unencumbered appropriation (governmental accounting) That part of an appropriation neither expended nor encumbered.

unencumbered balance (governmental accounting) That portion of an appropriation or allotment neither expended nor encumbered.

unexpended appropriation (governmental accounting) That portion of an appropriation not yet expended, though possibly encumbered in whole or in part.

unexpended balance (governmental accounting) That portion of an appropriation or allotment which has not been expended, though possibly encumbered in whole or in part.

unexpired cost Any expenditure benefiting the future; any asset, including *prepaid expense,* normally appearing on a *balance sheet.*

unfair competition The employment of practices by a seller designed to obtain a larger share of the market by false or misleading advertising, adoption and use of a rival's trademark, discriminatory pricing, selling below costs or dumping, pre-emptive buying of raw materials, establishing exclusive selling contracts with distributors, securing rebates from suppliers, or adopting any other device that unfairly takes advantage of a competing firm. The *Federal Trade Commission* is authorized by law to investigate trade practices and is empowered to issue cease-and-desist orders prohibiting acts in violation of the antitrust acts. Its orders are enforceable in the Federal courts. Damaged competitors may bring a civil action under the *Clayton* and *Sherman Acts* against unfair competitors for treble damages.

Common-law remedies available to business concerns injured by competitors engaging in unfair practices are inadequate protection for the weaker members of the trade. The continuance of such practices may threaten the existence of small firms and thereby assure the establishment of monopolistic industries. The antitrust acts authorize governmental policing of methods of competition employed by business. While the small firm is now protected against vigorous competitive methods, this protection is itself a restraint on the growth of small business.

unfavorable difference See *favorable difference*.

uniform accounting system A system of accounts common to similar organizations, such as those developed or promoted by trade associations, and those promulgated by Federal and state regulatory bodies such as public-utility commissions.

unissued capital stock That part of the authorized capital stock, whether or not subscribed, which has not yet been issued.

unit (of fixed assets) See *fixed-asset unit*.

unit cost The cost of a selected unit of a good or service. Examples: dollar cost per ton, machine hour, labor hour, or department hour. See *cost unit*.

United States rule A method of identifying the amounts of interest and principal included in a partial payment on an interest-bearing debt. The interest element (*ordinary interest* or *exact interest*, depending on agreement) is first computed at the agreed rate from the date of the debt (or of the last repayment) to the date of the current payment; the balance is principal. This method contrasts with one occasionally employed, known as the *merchant's rule*, under which interest is computed to the end of each anniversary of the note (or to an agreed final-settlement date of the obligation, if a lesser period) on both the original amount of the debt (debit interest) and on each payment (credit interest); at any time, the amount of the debt unpaid is the total of the original principal, or the amount unpaid at the beginning of the "note year," plus interest to the end of the note year, less repayments plus interest to the end of such year; during the note year following, the debit interest, based on the unpaid balance at the beginning of the year, thus includes an element of compound interest.

unit-livestock-price method The valuation of the inventoried draft, breeding, or dairy animals, or animals raised for sale, of a farmer or livestock raiser whereby the number of each class and age of animal is multiplied by an average unit cost of raising the animal to that age. For Federal income-tax purposes, each unit cost employed is expected to fall within a given range.

unit of sampling A characteristic element in a defined finite *population* subjected to random sampling. In sampling operations, the sampling unit may be determined by physical conditions, administrative expediency, or cost considerations. From this point of view, the unit of sampling constitutes a classification of the fundamental population under inquiry, where the classification may be broad or may coincide exactly with the units of substantive interest.

In sampling a cabinet file of cards, where the results of specific transactions are recorded, in order to obtain an estimate of the total volume of a set of transactions, a variety of sampling units may be defined. First, the sampling unit may be the individual file card in the cabinet. Second, the sampling unit may be the cards within file partitions. Third, the sampling unit may be, say, three inches of consecutive file cards in the cabinet. In the last two cases, grosser classifications of the file-card population are involved, and the classifications may be considered as *universes* in their own right: viz., the universe of folders or partitions in the cabinet and the universe of three-inch file sections.

In practice, sample designs may incorporate a hierarchy of sampling units, where the fundamental population of substantive interest is subjected to two or more levels of classification. To each classification level there corresponds a stage of sampling and a population of sampling units. There will accordingly be in such a design primary, secondary, tertiary, etc., units of sampling. In each of the sampling stages, *random samples* of the corresponding units of sampling are selected from the defined population of units. An illustration may be given of the sampling of designated economic and demographic characteristics of families in a specified city for a given period. In this case, the city might be classified by enumeration districts according to U. S. Census Bureau criteria; the set of enumeration districts would then constitute the universe of primary sampling units. Second, all primary sampling units might be further classified by individual city blocks or other defined areas; the set of city blocks would comprise the universe of secondary sampling units. All city blocks might then be classified by dwelling units, the tertiary universe. Finally, the set of all dwelling units might be classified by families dwelling in the units. The last or quaternary *universe* coincides with the universe of units on which immediate interest centers.

Given the above four-stage classification scheme, the sample design might specify the following instructions: (a) select a random sample of m out of the M enumeration districts in the city, (b) select randomly from each of the enumeration districts drawn every kth (k, an *integer*) block in the enumeration district, (c) select randomly from each of the blocks drawn every pth (p, an integer) dwelling unit, (d) list the families in all the dwelling units drawn, classified by number of families in the dwelling units. Select randomly every rth (r, an integer) family from the set of one-family dwellings, select randomly every sth (s, an integer) family from the set of two-family dwellings, etc. The numbers m, k, p, r, s, etc., would be determined in the design of certain *population parameters* and specified costs of travel and enumeration. See *random sample; random numbers; probability.*

universe 1. The whole of the subject matter of whatever is under consideration.

2. (statistics) The entire matrix or group of data from which samples may be drawn; sometimes referred to as a *population.* A universe may be either (a) existent, such as the total number of persons in the United States at a given moment of time, or (b) hypothetical, such as the values which may be assumed in successive throws of a pair of dice.

A *frame* is the medium generally employed for actual sample design and execution.

unlimited liability Legal responsibility not restricted by law or contract. Example: the liability of a general partner for the debts of a firm.

unliquidated encumbrance (governmental accounting) An encumbrance not paid or approved for payment.

unpaid dividend 1. A dividend declared but not yet paid.

2. An *unclaimed dividend.*

3. A passed dividend on cumulative preferred stock.

unproductive wages A term sometimes employed for indirect labor.

unrealized revenue Revenue attributable to a completed business transaction but accompanied by the receipt of an asset other than cash or other form of current asset; as, an installment sale (gross revenue) or the prospective profit from such a sale (net revenue). See *realize.* Although expressed on books of account, it does not appear in the income statement, unless minor in amount, until the asset has been realized. The term is sometimes confused with *deferred revenue.*

unrecovered cost The portion of original investment not amortized through the process of *depreciation* or *depletion;* also, uninsured losses from extraordinary obsolescence, fire, theft, or market fluctuations.

unrelated business income (Federal income taxes) That portion of the income of a charitable or other tax-exempt organization which, under sections 511-4 of the Internal Revenue Code, is subject to the corporate income tax because the activity producing the income is unrelated to the exempt purposes of the organization.

unrestricted random sampling See *random sampling.*

unsecured account A personal account supported by the general credit of the debtor against which no collateral or guaranty is held.

unsecured liability A liability for which the creditor holds no security.

upset price The lowest price at which a seller is willing to sell; the initial price asked at an auction before bidding commences; in equity proceedings (bankruptcy), the amount established by the court as the lowest acceptable price for a corporation's assets when sold at public auction.

use-and-occupancy insurance See *business-interruption insurance.*

useful Having some advantage: sometimes said of an accounting concept, principle, or practice favored over another because of its ease or breadth of application, frequency, or other cause not always disclosed.

useful life Normal operating life in terms of utility to the owner: said of a fixed asset or a fixed-asset group; the period may be more or less than physical life or any commonly recognized *economic life;* service life. See *depreciation; economic life.*

usefulness That property of an outlay causing it to have continuing value. Originally applied to expenditures for fixed assets, it is often extended to other types of expenditures the value of which is not exhausted within the current accounting period. See *fixed asset; cost recovery; deferred charge; utility.*

user cost Cost incurred or loss sustained on a fixed asset as the result of (a) continuing it in service rather than disposing of it through sale or as scrap, or (b) giving it restricted use. See *cost; rent; profit.*

utility 1. Capacity for satisfying a specified want or fulfilling a particular purpose, thus having more restricted meaning than *usefulness.* Because there is often more than one purpose or want in a situation where utility is judged, the same object or act may have both utility and disutility. See *service; benefit; marginal utility; depreciation.*

2. = *public-service company.*

utility fund See *fund.*

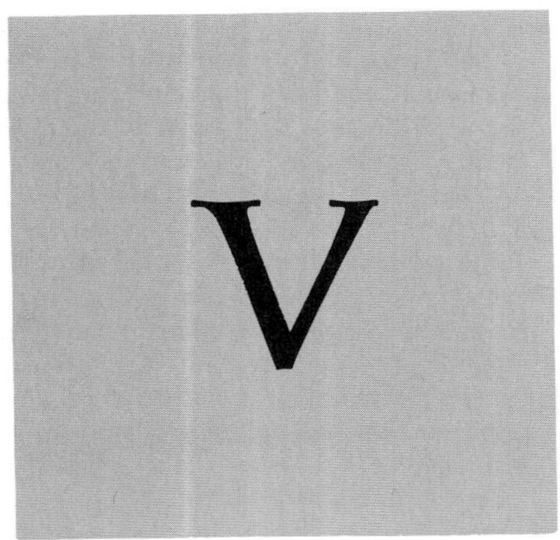

valid 1. Accurate, precise, reliable, authorized, and relevant.
2. Enforceable.

validate 1. To test for or to certify or attest to accuracy, precision, reliability, and relevance.
2. To do what is necessary to make anything effective or legal.

validation (statistics) The determination of whether a test yields desired results with the necessary elements of accuracy, precision, reliability, and relevance. For example, a test of accounting students may be undertaken to determine their aptitude for the profession. At a subsequent date, the test may be validated by undertaking a survey to determine which of the students subjected to the tests had entered upon accounting careers and how their employers had rated them. High positive correlation between the results of the test and the subsequent survey would tend to confirm the validity of the test. But one such test and survey may not be enough. Continued testing and surveying by replication with resulting correlation coefficients of approximately the same magnitude may be required to obtain precision and reliability. Reference to the career situation toward which the test is oriented confirms the relevancy of the test; continuation of the tests with approximately the same results confirms their precision and reliability. Correspondence between test and career is a means of determining accuracy. A combination of all of these measures is encompassed in the term *validity*.

validity See *valid; validation*. As used in deductive logic: propriety established by a strong inference in which no inconsistency appears.

valorize To give a commodity by law, regulation, or other governmental action, a value differing from its economic or market value.

valuation 1. = *accounting valuation*.
2. A judgment expressing or implying preference, or relative approval or disapproval, often expressed in money; when based on a careful weighing of evidence, related experience, training, native shrewdness, and other factors, as is often the case, it may not coincide with a judgment following the formal exercise of logical principles. Valuation methods and bases are numerous and varied. The judgment may be expressed quantitatively and in monetary terms, as in a bid or offer or acceptance, an assessment of real estate, or a balance-sheet or other financial-statement expression. Application may be made to a single asset, a group of assets, or an entire enterprise, as determined by various bases and methods. See *going-concern* or *liquidation values; cost; cost basis; cost of reproduction; present value; market value*.

valuation account (or **reserve**) An account which relates to and partly or wholly offsets one or more other accounts; as, a reserve for depreciation or bad debts; unamortized debt discount. Valuation allowances related to consumed asset costs should always be deducted from receivables, investments, inventories, or fixed assets and not shown on the balance sheet as a liability. See APBO 12 (1967).

value *n*. 1. Any preferred object or interest therein.
2. Attributed worth, expressed in money

and applied to a particular asset, as the value of an automobile; to services rendered, as the value of a man's labor; to a group of assets, as the value of a company's patents; or to an entire business unit, as the value of a plant or business enterprise. Without qualification or more limited definition, including specific, operationally feasible, and generally agreed-to rules for measurement, the term has only subjective significance, and should not be confused with, even though often identified with and measured by, cost. See *accounting valuation; cost basis of accounting.*

When market value is less than cost and the cost of an inventory item is reduced to an amount equal to market in accordance with common inventory-valuation procedures, it is often said that the "value" adopted is market. However, since the practice is not to raise cost to market if market is greater than cost, it is apparent that the value basis is still cost: i.e., original cost has been brought down to a fractional-cost basis justified by—rather than valued at—market. See *inventory valuation.* A similar argument applies to the book value of fixed assets—cost less accumulated depreciation, the last-named being the fraction of cost estimated to have been consumed, absorbed as an operating expense; the net figure is the cost balance carried into—and presumably benefiting—succeeding periods.

3. Hence, loosely, the amount at which an item appears in the books or on a financial statement; cost, or a portion of cost judged to be of benefit to one or more future periods.

4. (economics) The quantity of other goods (or money) required to be given in exchange for a particular good; a *rate of exchange;* the monetary measure of exchangeability of a good; an economic phenomenon based on the process of *exchange* in monetary terms in a market. The term is closely related to the concept of price, the monetary measure of exchangeability of one unit. The value of a quantity of a product is found by multiplying quantity by price.

v. To express individual relative preference for an object or mode of conduct.

value added That part of the cost of a manufactured or semimanufactured product attributable to work performed on constituent raw materials; = *added value,* q.v.

valued policy (insurance) An insurance contract, illegal in many states, under the terms of which the parties have agreed to the value of the property covered and the amount to be paid in case of total loss.

value judgment A choice, preference, or approval based on more than one purpose or policy. It is distinguished from a technical judgment of means to achieve a specified result. Value judgments may be impulsive, habitual, or reflective; they may be derived by various patterns of reasoning and combinations of such patterns: e.g., a ranking of purposes according to ultimate worth or urgency, an analogy to approved precedents, a deduction from an established set of general policies or moral principles, a rejection of undesirable extremes, the limitation of objectives to resources, consideration for the desires of other people, a prediction of advantageous and disadvantageous consequences, and so on. Such reasoning may be difficult to reduce to precise quantitative determinations, and, since it often involves a conflict of purposes, it may be controversial. Acceptance by others of a value judgment having general application is often dependent on its *commonsense* appeal; in a restricted area, acceptance may rest on the esteem in which the author of the judgment is held, or on his position (for example, as a manager). A value judgment is sometimes regarded merely as subjective opinion, sometimes as no more than whimsy: qualities differing in degree rather than in fundamental character.

value variance = *price variance.*

variable (mathematics) A symbol of classification intended to represent a range or a subdivision of a range of values defined in terms of a particular model or set of structural relations, such as an *equation*.

Variables may be *dependent* or *independent*, and are generally defined relative to each other by elements, such as *constants*, appearing in an equation. As usually applied in mathematics, both variables and constants are represented by abstract symbols, the former by the last few letters of the alphabet $(\ldots x,y,z)$, and the latter by the first few letters of the alphabet $(a, b, c, \ldots)$. This device (see *symbolization*) facilitates investigation of general properties of equations by abstracting elements peculiar to a given situation. Thus, in the general equation for a straight line, $y = a + bx$, x is the independent and y the dependent variable, and a and b are constants of intercept and slope, respectively. In terms of the structure specified by this equation, the range of variation may be as great as $-\infty$ to $+\infty$, although interest may attach only to some subdivision of this range, such as $-10 \leqq x \leqq 10$.

By *convention*, independent variables are written on the right and dependent variables on the left side of equations, as above. Within the defined range of variation, x may be assigned any value, and this value will, through the other elements, such as the constants, in an equation, define the value of y, the dependent variable. In the indicated equation of a straight line, the value of y is thus defined uniquely; but this need not be the case: in the equation of a parabola, $y^2 = a + bx$, for example, each value of x, the independent variable, defines two values of y, since $y = \pm \sqrt{a + bx}$; if only real numbers are of interest, values of x which yield imaginary numbers are not admissible in the defined range of variation for x; if a and b are positive, values in $x < -a/b$ are then not admissible.

The general equation, $y = a + bx$, states certain properties of all straight lines. The intercept with the y axis is given by the constant a, and the rate of increase of y relative to x is given by the constant b. Any particular line will have these properties. For example, if $a = 1$ and $b = 2$, a particular straight line $y = 1 + 2x$ is secured, the graph of which is shown immediately following.

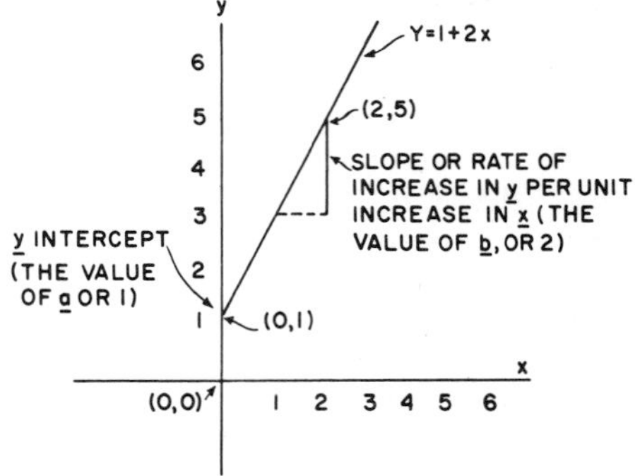

Thus, y increases twice as fast as x (the slope, or b, $= 2$) and the intercept is 1 $(a = 1)$. The presence of two constants shows that only two points, or one point and the value of one constant, a or b, are needed to determine any line (see *least-squares method*), because by substituting the values of the two points, (2,5) and (0,1), respectively, shown on the graph in the general equation $y = a + bx$, we have

$$5 = a + 2b$$
$$1 = a + 0b;$$

by solving these two equations the values of the constants $a = 1$ and $b = 2$ are obtained, thus yielding the particular straight-line equation of interest, $y = 1 + 2x$.

Although the equation of a straight line $y = a + bx$ permits the assignment of any values $-\infty \leq x \leq \infty$, this is not always true. In the equation $\sin y = x$, only values of $-1 \leq x \leq 1$ are admissible, since the maximum and minimum values of the sine of an angle are ± 1. Assignments of values such as $x = 2$ are not admissible; the equation has no meaning for values beyond the range of ± 1. Similarly, the equation $y = \log x$ has no meaning for negative values of x.

More than one *independent variable* may appear in an equation. Thus, in the equation of a plane, $y = a + bx + cz$, the variables x and z are both independent, while y is the dependent variable; x and z may be assigned any values within the range $-\infty \leq x \leq \infty$, $-\infty \leq z \leq \infty$ without reference to each other; but, once these values are selected, the value of y is completely determined. As in the case of the straight line, this general form of equation provides a symbolic device for the study of relations between variables and constants for all planes; the constant of intercept with the y axis is given by a; the constant rates of increase, or slope, of y relative to x and z are given by the constants b and c, respectively; the three points determine a plane; and so on.

Use of variables is by no means restricted to equations. They may be employed, for example, in *inequations*, such as $y \leq a + bx$, or *functions(4)*, such as $f(x, y) = 0$.

variable annuity A contract between an insurance or investment company and an investor under the terms of which periodic distributions differ as changes take place in the value of underlying equity securities.

variable budget = *flexible budget*.

variable cost (or **expense**) 1. An operating expense, or operating expenses as a class, that vary directly, sometimes proportionately, with sales or production volume, facility, utilization, or other measure of activity; examples: materials consumed, direct labor, power, factory supplies, depreciation (on a production basis), sales commissions, etc. See *fixed cost; semivariable cost; direct costing*.

2. That portion of factory or processing expense represented by such costs.

variable-cost ratio The ratio between sales revenue and variable costs.

variable gauge (statistical quality control) A type of gauge used to measure dimensions of manufactured products to some specified unit of accuracy. See *go-and-not-go gauge*.

variance 1. The difference between corresponding items in comparative balance sheets, or in income and other operating statements.

2. The difference for a year or less between the elements (direct material, direct labor, factory overhead) of standard cost and actual cost. See *standard cost*.

3. (statistics) The square of the standard deviation; usually denoted by the symbol σ^2. However, when variance is the *statistic* to be computed, it is the usual practice to employ the divisor $N - 1$—i.e., to define variance as $\sigma^2 = \Sigma(X - \bar{X})^2/(N - 1)$. This convention has the property of making the sample variance an unbiased estimator of the variance in the universe from which the sample came. It is important to note that, contrary to appearances, the square root of the sample variance as defined above is not an unbiased sample estimator of the *standard deviation* in the universe from which the sample came. Variance is a statistic essential in the analysis and interpretation of experiments planned to secure data in accordance with definite objectives.

variate A value assigned to or associated with a *variable*.

venture See *adventure*.

verification 1. The procedure by which *validity* is ascertained. The thoroughness with which evidence is sought and investigated and strictness is observed in applying *rules* of evidence ordinarily varies in accordance with the importance of the item and the cost involved. Thus, the weight of packaged coffee need not be verified to the second decimal, although that may be necessary in the case of fine watch parts. Circumstantial evidence may be regarded as establishing a loss of papers due to rats nesting in a warehouse, but insufficient to verify a theory explaining a net loss shown in an annual report. A foreman's testimony may be sufficient to verify a rumor that a given machine is eccentric in its behavior but not that all machines of the same model are similarly eccentric.

2. (auditing) The process of substantiation involved in proving by customary audit procedures that a statement, account, or item is accurate and properly stated, or is within permissible or reasonable limits.

verify (auditing) To confirm the truth, accuracy, or probability of, by competent examination; to *substantiate*.

viability Power or ability to live or survive, or to operate and develop satisfactorily: said of an economy or nation, less frequently of an industry, a business enterprise, a process, a plan, or an agreement.

virement 1. = allocation; see *allocate(3)*.
2. Any transfer from one account to another.

vis-à-vis Face-to-face: a term used variously by social scientists as a noun, adjective, verb, adverb, conjunction, or preposition, and signifying an opposing or contrasting position or proposition, opposite to, to oppose, to stand opposite to or in contrast with, oppositely, contrastingly, as compared with, in relation to, or with respect to.

volume cost A term of contrast, usually signifying a lower cost or a particular cost otherwise affected by volume.

volume discount An allowance given by a seller to a purchaser because of the aggregate size of the purchases in a series of transactions over a given period of time; distinguished from *quantity discount*.

vote = *fund(3)*; a British term.

voting trust A limited-life trust established for the purpose of concentrating the control of a corporation in the hands of a few persons, known as *voting trustees*. The device is often used in reorganization proceedings. Stockholders consenting to participate in the plan transfer their shares to the voting trustees and receive in exchange transferable certificates of beneficial interest in the trust; the stock is then registered on the books of the corporation in the names of the trustees.

voting-trust certificate A certificate of beneficial interest issued by or in the name of voting trustees following the deposit with them of stock for the purpose of placing the voting control of a corporation in the hands of a limited number of persons for a stated period of time.

vouch 1. To ascertain the nature, propriety, and amount of items of revenues, expenditures, assets, or liabilities by the examination or testing of supporting data; to test by comparison with evidence.

2. To attest the propriety of an expenditure, as by approving it for payment.

voucher 1. A document which serves as evidence of the disbursement of cash. Examples: a receipted bill; a canceled check; a petty-cash receipt; the carbon copy of a check.

2. A document serving as evidence of the authority to disburse cash. Examples: an approved invoice from a supplier; a payroll.

3. A form (used with a *voucher system*) to which bills, receipts, and other evidences of indebtedness are often attached, showing the authority for the payment, the particulars of settlement, and other relevant details; a disbursement voucher.

5. The written evidence of a business or accounting transaction sometimes contained in a single document without attachments. Example: a journal voucher.

voucher audit 1. The examination and approval by administrative authority of a proposed disbursement; = *preaudit*.

2. (governmental accounting) The postaudit of individual disbursements made by the Comptroller General (General

Accounting Office).

voucher check A check showing such particulars of a payment as date, amount, discount, other deductions, and invoice number or other reference to goods or services received or to be received; it may combine the features of a check, a formal receipt, and a detachable remittance slip.

voucher index An alphabetical list of payees' names often used in conjunction with a voucher register. It may be a card index, on which voucher numbers and amounts recorded are listed; or a file of carbon copies of vouchers, arranged by names of payees. As a record of the business done with each payee, it may also serve as a creditors ledger. See *voucher system*.

voucher register (or **journal** or **record**) A record for the entry and registry of vouchers, usually columnar in form, permitting their summarization, distribution, and posting to ledgers, individually or in the aggregate. It may serve as both a *book of original entry* and a *book of final entry*.

voucher system The system by means of which invoices and other evidences of liability are collected, audited, recorded, and settled. It involves the use of vouchers, voucher checks, a voucher register, etc., and is an important feature of any system of internal control.

vouching 1. The preparation under a voucher system of invoices or other statements of liability for entry, distribution, and payment.
2. The process of verification involved in the examination of voucher records.

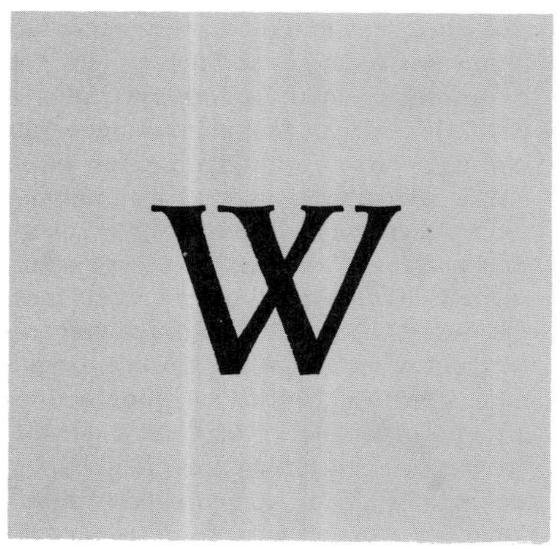

wages 1. The compensation of workers receiving a fixed sum per piece, hour, day, or week for manual labor, skilled or unskilled; or a fixed sum for a certain amount of such labor.

2. Any compensation paid, including salaries.

waiting period Under regulations of the U. S. Securities and Exchange Commission, the 20 days (more where deficiencies are found or less where acceleration is granted) between the filing of a *registration statement* and its effective date.

warehouse receipt The evidence of title given to the owner of goods placed in a public warehouse. Transfer of title is effected by assignment of the receipt. In the event the goods are *fungible*, the warehouseman may make delivery of a commodity of like quality and weight. A negotiable warehouse receipt is made "to bearer" and may be transferred without endorsement, often serving in this form as collateral on bank loans. A non-negotiable warehouse receipt is made to a specified person or to his "order," and must thus be endorsed when transferred or surrendered. Warehouse receipts are governed by the Uniform Warehouse Receipts Act, in effect in most states for many years.

warrant 1. An obligation of a governmental body issued in the settlement of debts and payable immediately by the treasurer of the governmental unit; also known as a *warrant-check*.

2. A short-term, interest-bearing obligation of a governmental body issued in the settlement of debts and payable from taxes or other revenues to be collected for a designated period; a *tax-anticipation warrant*.

3. A certificate, either separate or attached to a bond, short-term note, or certificate of preferred or common stock, that entitles the owner to purchase, usually within a stated period, shares of stock at a specified price per share. See *right*.

4. In municipal accounting, the term "warrant" is used in three senses, the most common of which is to designate a draft on the treasurer by an accounting officer to pay money to a payee designated in the warrant. In this form it resembles a check except that it does not indicate a bank of payment. The payee presents it to the treasurer and receives a check, or cashes it at his local bank, the bank forwarding it to the municipal treasurer for reimbursement.

The procedure followed by the State of Michigan furnishes an excellent illustration of the manner in which the warrant system operates. Both payroll and vendor vouchers are preaudited by the Accounting Division of the Department of Administration and are sent on to the Auditor General, who prepares "warrants" and transmits them to the payees. Payees cash them at their banks, which forward them to either the Federal Reserve Bank of Chicago or the National Bank of Detroit. These banks cumulate the warrants daily and mail them to the state treasurer, who issues a check to each bank in settlement. The checks are usually drawn on the state's checking account in the National Bank of Detroit. The state treasurer settles directly with Lansing banks, but this involves substantially the same procedure as that just outlined.

The warrant system is unsatisfactory

because it involves duplication in that warrants and checks have to be prepared to cover the same set of transactions. Moreover, in actual practice, the banks in effect pay out money without the approval of the treasurer, because they first pay the warrants and then ask the treasurer to reimburse them. The treasurer can, of course, refuse to pay the warrant, but the procedure supplies only a negative control. The treasurer should be in a position to stop improper payments before they are made by the bank. The warrant system inconveniences the paying bank and the payee, because, if the treasurer refuses to pay a warrant, it must be charged back to the depositing bank, which in turn must charge it back to the payee. On the other hand, the use of checks without warrants does not deprive the treasurer of any controls which he possesses under the warrant system.

A second use of the term in municipal accounting is as a general title to a short-term, interest-bearing obligation. There are two types: tax-anticipation warrants and registered warrants. Tax-anticipation warrants (or notes) are issued in anticipation of taxes to be collected and are made payable solely from the collections of the particular tax levy against which they are issued. The warrants are usually issued only against a certain percentage of the tax levy (for example, 75 percent), but the collections therefrom cannot be used for any purpose until all of the related warrants, and any interest thereon, have been paid.

Registered warrants are documents evidencing unpaid obligations "registered," rather than paid when presented to the municipality's paying officer, because of lack of funds. These obligations do not start to bear interest until registered, and they must be called in and paid in the order of registation. In some cases, the warrants are automatically registered when issued; in others, when the claim is presented by the holder.

Least frequently, the term is used in municipal accounting to designate a written order by an accounting officer to the treasurer to accept money. Such warrants are used for the purpose of making sure that the money is credited by the treasurer to the proper funds and accounts, so that there may be no conflict in applied uses. The deposit warrant indicates the accounts and funds to which the money is to be credited and bears the approval of the accounting officer.

5. In Federal-government accounting, a warrant is a document authorizing a transaction or group of transactions, signed by the Secretary of the Treasury and the Comptroller General. Of the following types of warrants, once issued, only the third and fourth are actively employed:

accountable warrant: an authorization to the Treasurer to pay checks drawn by a disbursing officer for a stated amount of money: so called because the disbursing officer must account for the money thus advanced to him; now usually combined with the *appropriation warrant.*

appropriation-transfer warrant: an authorization formerly employed for the transfer of the unexpended balance of one appropriation to the credit of another appropriation, pursuant to authorization by the Congress; its use is now forbidden by law.

appropriation warrant: an authorization for the setting up on the records of a Congressional appropriation for an agency.

covering warrant: a document acknowledging the receipt of money by the Treasury, and designating the accounts affected.

settlement warrant: a document formerly indicating the settlement of a claim by the Comptroller General and authorizing its payment by the Treasurer of the United States: now discontinued.

surplus-fund warrant: a document authorizing the cancellation of the unexpended balance of an *appropriation.*

transfer and counter warrant: a document once serving as the authority for adjustments between appropriation accounts for expenditures previously made: now discontinued.

warrants payable Warrants outstanding and unpaid.

warranty A promise by a seller to defend title and possession of real estate or to make good on a deficiency as to quantity, quality, or performance in a product. The character of the deficiency and the period covered are usually attached to the bill of sale or to the product itself.

wash transaction 1. A transaction reversed or offset shortly after its occurrence. Wash sales between two persons, at one time commonly carried on in listed securities, are now prohibited by stock-exchange rules; their purpose was to make an artificial showing in trading activity and price, and thus induce investors to buy at the price thus established.
2. As defined in the Federal Revenue Act, a wash sale is a sale of a security at a loss, preceded or followed within 30 days by the purchase of, or agreement to purchase, the same security; only dealers are excepted from the rule that such a loss is nondeductible in computing taxable income.

waste Resources of labor or material consumed or produced in a given operation and not returning an economic benefit.

wasting asset 1. A fixed asset having a limited useful life, and subject to depreciation; hence, any fixed asset other than land the outlay for which, less estimated terminal value, is allocable over the period of usefulness; a *limited-life asset.* See *fixed asset; depreciation.*
2. An asset that diminishes in value by reason of and commensurately with the extraction or removal of a natural product such as ores, oil, and timber, which it contains.

watered capital The excess of capital stock issued, at its par or stated value, over the fair value of the assets contributed in exchange.

watered stock Any class of the capital stock of a corporation containing *watered capital.*

wealth Anything having value or utility. In the possession of persons, wealth is often identified with *capital* or *capital goods;* the passage or flow of wealth from one person to another may be designated *revenue* or *income.*

wear and tear That portion of depreciation attributable to ordinary use, disuse, lapse of time, and action of the elements. See *depreciation.*

weighted average A simple average of items reduced to a common basis. Example: purchases of certain raw material are made during a given month as follows:

Units	*Price Each*	*Total Cost*
150	$1.50	$225.00
175	1.40	245.00
50	1.32	66.00
65	1.30	84.50

The simple average of prices paid is $5.52 ÷ 4, or $1.38, but the weighted average would be the total cost divided by the number of units purchased: $620.50 ÷ 440, or $1.41.

will A document prepared by a natural person in contemplation of death and containing instructions for the disposition of his property assets.

windfall profit An unexpected profit arising from causes over which the recipient has little or no control.

window dressing The making of, or attempt to make, a favorable showing of financial position or operating results, sometimes with fraudulent intent, as by (a) not accounting for all expenses, (b) anticipating sales, (c) concealing liabilities, (d) burying unfavorable transactions, (e) delaying writeoffs, (f) underproviding for depreciation, (g) not revealing the mortgaging or pledging of assets, (h) devising transactions designed to produce a more favorable financial showing, and the like.

withdrawal Cash or property paid to an owner or stockholder and accounted for (a) as a *dividend* or other distribution of profit (and charged to the proprietor's account or to *earned surplus* [*retained income*]) or (b) as a reduction of paid-in capital (illustrated by a repurchase of capital stock or a *liquidating dividend*). Unless accompanied by an acquisition of shares of stock, a withdrawal of unrestricted corporate funds by a stockholder is generally presumed to be a distribution of the retained income of the corporation, and only a return of its capital paid in when retained income has been exhausted.

withholding The process of deducting from a salary or wage payment an amount, specified by law or regulation, representing the estimated Federal or state income tax of the individual that the employer must pay to the taxing authority. The term is also applied to deductions from interest, dividends, and other periodic payments to nonresident aliens (section 1441 of the Federal Internal Revenue Code).

working asset Any asset other than a capital asset.

working capital Capital in current use in the operation of a business: the excess of *current assets* over *current liabilities;* net current assets. See *current assets; current liabilities; balance sheet; statement of sources and applications of funds.* The amount of working capital, supplemented by the ratio of current assets to current liabilities (known as *working-capital ratio*), has long served as a credit test and often as the measure of debt-paying ability. One attempting to apply such a test, however, recognizes that other factors, equally and not infrequently more important, remain to be considered before the meaning of working capital in any given situation can be comprehended. The example at the top of the next column will illustrate.

The working capital of a retail store

Current assets—		
Cash	$158,265	
Receivables	287,932	
Inventories, at market which is less than cost	843,679	$1,289,876
Current liabilities—		
Accounts payable	$130,481	
Accruals	177,112	307,593
Working capital (net current assets)		$ 982,283
Working-capital ratio		4.1

at the end of its fiscal year consisted of the items shown listed above. The management, in applying to its bank for a six-month loan of $500,000 at the beginning of the following year, disclosed (a) that obligations arising out of purchase commitments as a hedge against rising prices amounted to $800,000 and would have to be met within the next few months after deliveries had been made; (b) that the rate of merchandise turnover for the coming year would not exceed the rate of 3.5 enjoyed during the past year and might be as low as 2.0 because of larger average inventories (an estimated average of $1,400,000 as compared with $840,000) and possibly a 10 percent decrease in sales attributable to overstocking by customers in recent months. The conclusion of the bank was that, despite a record annual profit of $200,000, a gross margin of 25 percent, working capital of $982,000, and an ostensibly healthy working-capital ratio of 4:1, the risk was a poor one, and the loan was refused on the ground that the situation pointed to a no-profit year and that, other things being equal, in six months' time available cash would be insufficient by several hundred thousand dollars for repaying the loan. Instead, the bank suggested commitment cancellations and retrenchment measures. This illustration serves to indicate that, without a considerable amount of collateral data, particularly information concerning the immediate future, working-capital information alone may be misleading.

working-capital fund (municipal accounting) A fund established to finance activities, usually of a manufacturing or service nature, such as a shop, garage, or asphalt plant, or to control purchases or stores operations; a *revolving fund.* See *fund.*

working-capital ratio The ratio of current assets to current liabilities; see illustration under *working capital.*

working fund Cash advanced for working-capital or expense purposes, and replenished from time to time as needed. It is not on an imprest-cash basis wherever, for various reasons, replenishments are not equal in amount to reported expenditures. See *imprest cash.*

working-hours method (of depreciation) See *depreciation method.*

working interest (petroleum industry) The fractional interest of the lessee of a tract of land in the production of crude oil and gas from the tract; the fraction most often encountered is seven-eighths. The remainder is known as the *royalty interest.* See also *oil-and-gas payment; carried interest.*

working papers (auditing) The schedules, analyses, transcripts, memoranda, and so forth, prepared or collected by an auditor while making an examination, and serving as the basis of and record for his report.

working trial balance (auditing) A *trial balance* to which *adjustments* are appended in supplementary columns; many public accountants make use of the working trial balance as an index to their *working papers.*

work in process (or **in progress**) The partly finished product of a manufacturing concern, also known as *work in progress* or *goods in process.* It is usually included in the inventory at the cost of direct material and labor, plus a portion of factory overhead (or indirect expense) or is valued at the lower of cost or market. If direct-costing methods are in use, overhead may be excluded.

work order The written authority on which the performance and record of substantially all the work in a factory is controlled.

work program (municipal accounting) 1. A plan, including the estimated cost, of work to be done.
2. Hence, the division of a lump-sum appropriation of a department for current operating expenses to activities or departmental units, so that each will get its administratively determined share of the whole. See *allotment.*

work study Any method of investigation designed to provide better job or machine performance within a required operation; objectives may be material conservation, time saving, changes in quality, lower cost, and so on.

work unit A unit of measure, often commonly accepted, for determining *average cost,* time, or efficiency, thus making possible (a) comparisons of one operation with another or with the same operation in a preceding period, and (b) estimates of future operations. Examples of work units in a construction project:

Operation	*Unit*
Land purchases	acre
Acquisitions of land rights	tract or privilege
Family relocation	family
Rented equipment	hours of use
Excavation or backfill	cubic yard
Concrete fill	cubic yard
Concrete framework	square foot
Concrete reinforcement	pound
Brickwork	thousand brick
Glass brickwork	brick
Steel piling	ton
Drainage tile laying	linear foot
Interior tilework	square foot
Sodding	square yard
Oil storage	gallon

worth Value expressed in terms of some standard of equivalence or exchange; *value;* as, *cost; replacement cost; market value.*

write down To transfer a portion of the balance of an asset account to an expense account or to profit and loss.
—*write-down, n.*

write off To transfer the balance of an

account previously regarded as an asset to an expense account or to profit and loss.—*writeoff, n.*

write up To record an increase in the book value of an asset, not represented by an outlay of cash or other property or an inflow of capital.—*writeup, n.*

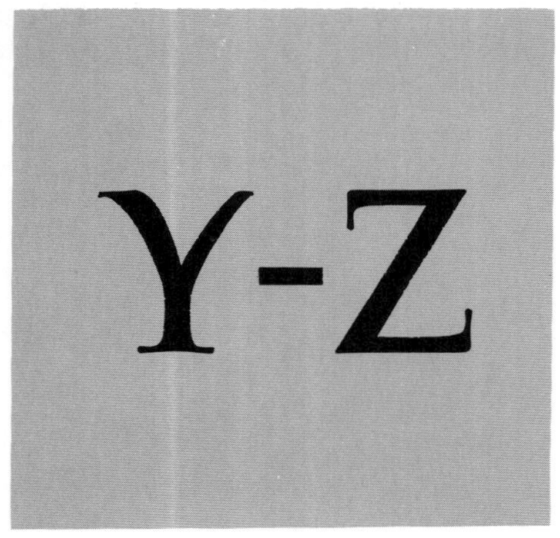

year-end adjustment A modification of a ledger account at the close of a *fiscal period* arising from an accrual, prepayment, physical inventory, reclassification, policy change, audit adjustment, or other unrecorded nonroutine transaction. The term does not ordinarily embrace a correction arising from a clerical error.

year-end dividend A dividend declared after the year's net income has been more or less accurately determined; sometimes employed in contrast with *interim dividend*.

yield *n.* The actual, as distinct from the nominal, rate of return on an investment; the *effective rate*. See *bond valuation*.

v. To give forth; produce: said of interest or other return from an investment or of services or benefits as from a fixed asset.

zone system (of pricing) See *price system*.